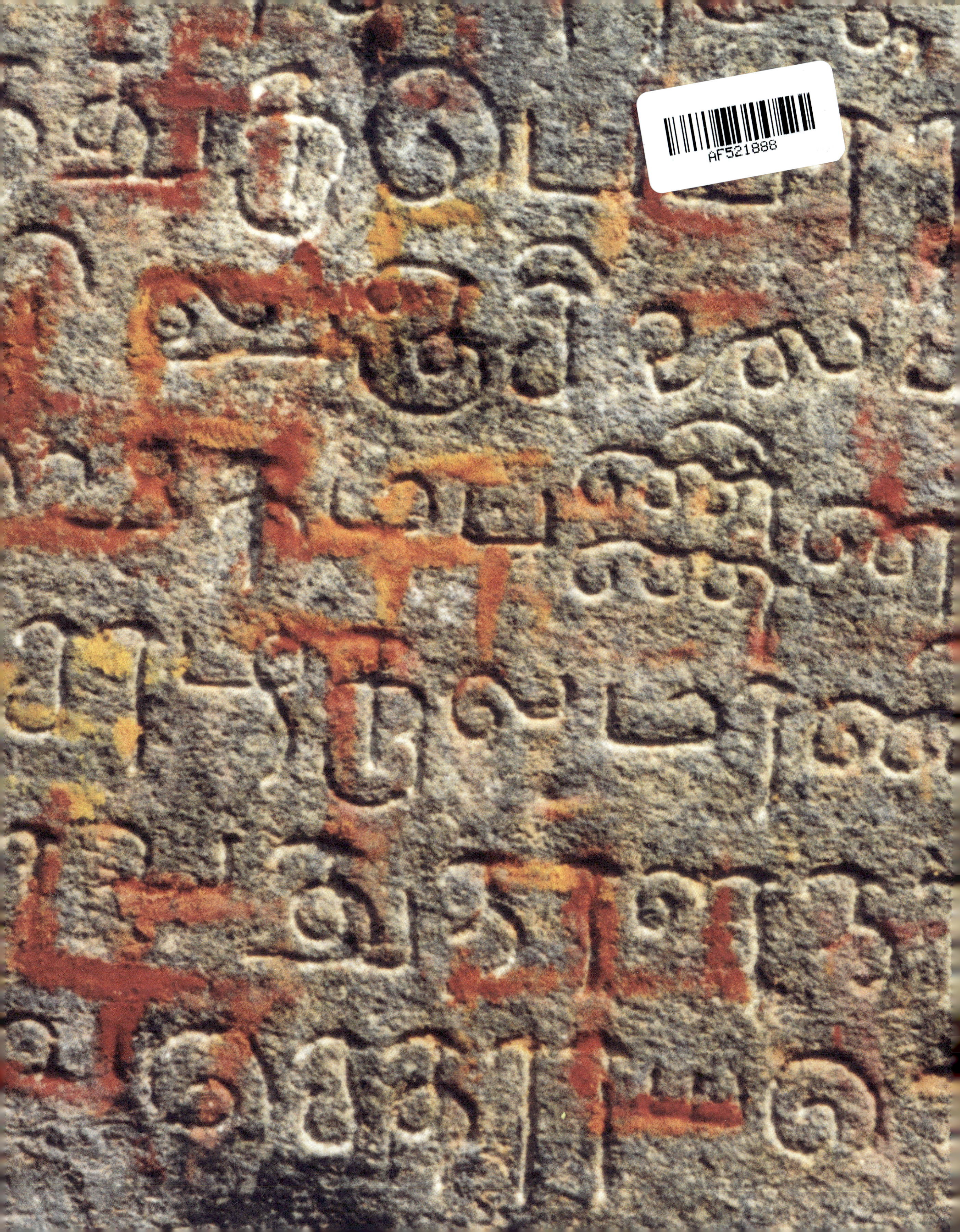

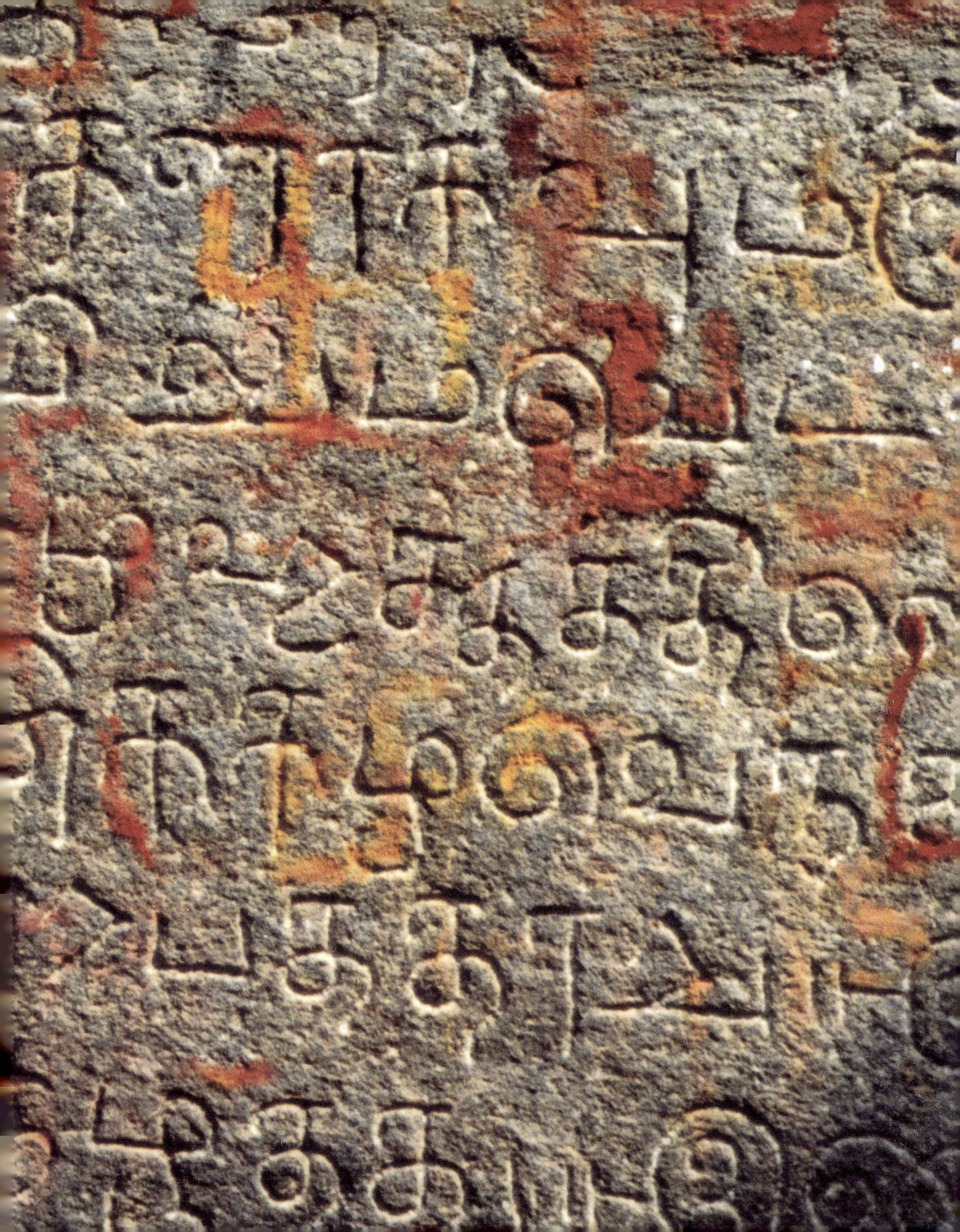

THE SENSUOUS AND THE SACRED

CHOLA BRONZES FROM SOUTH INDIA

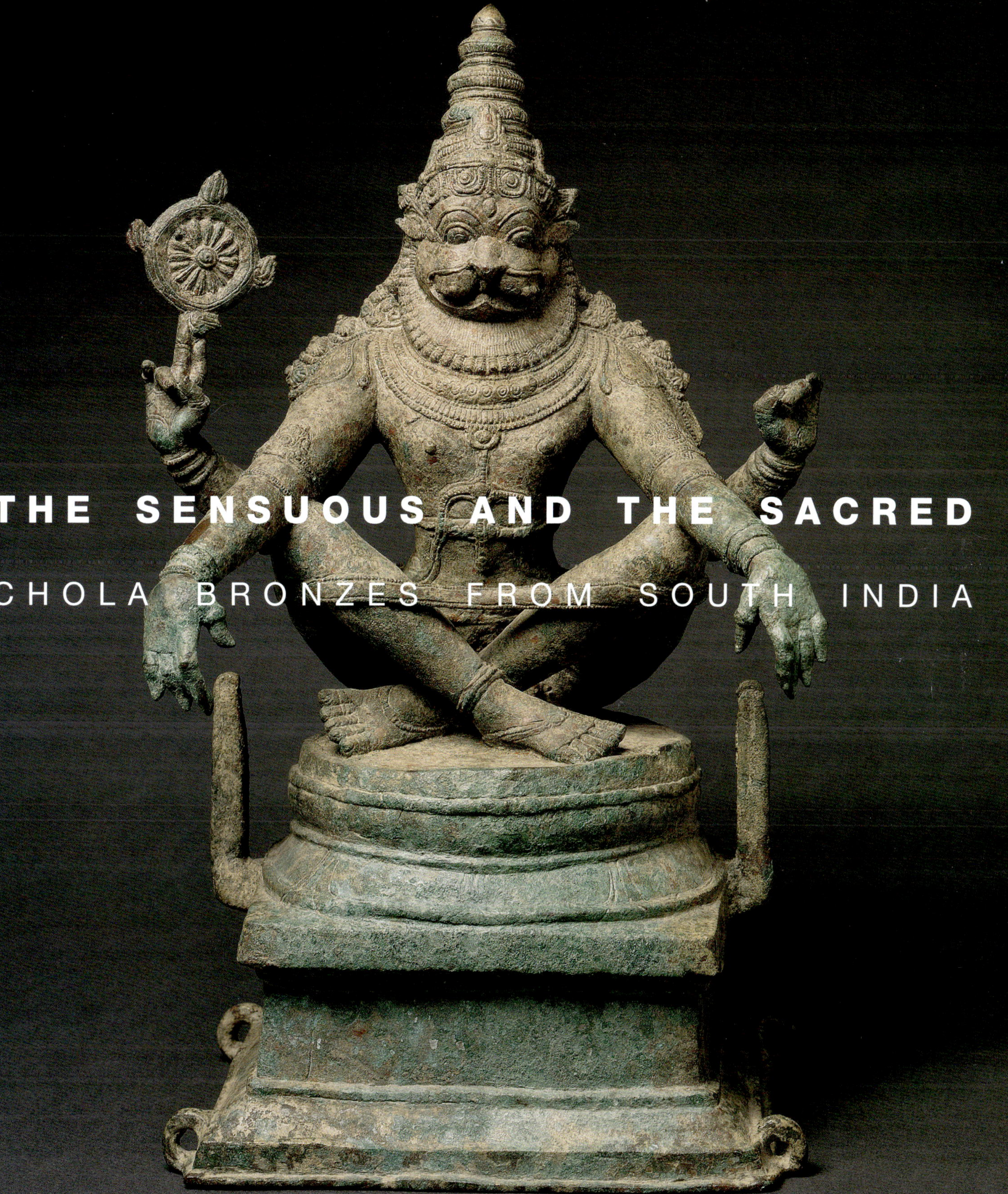

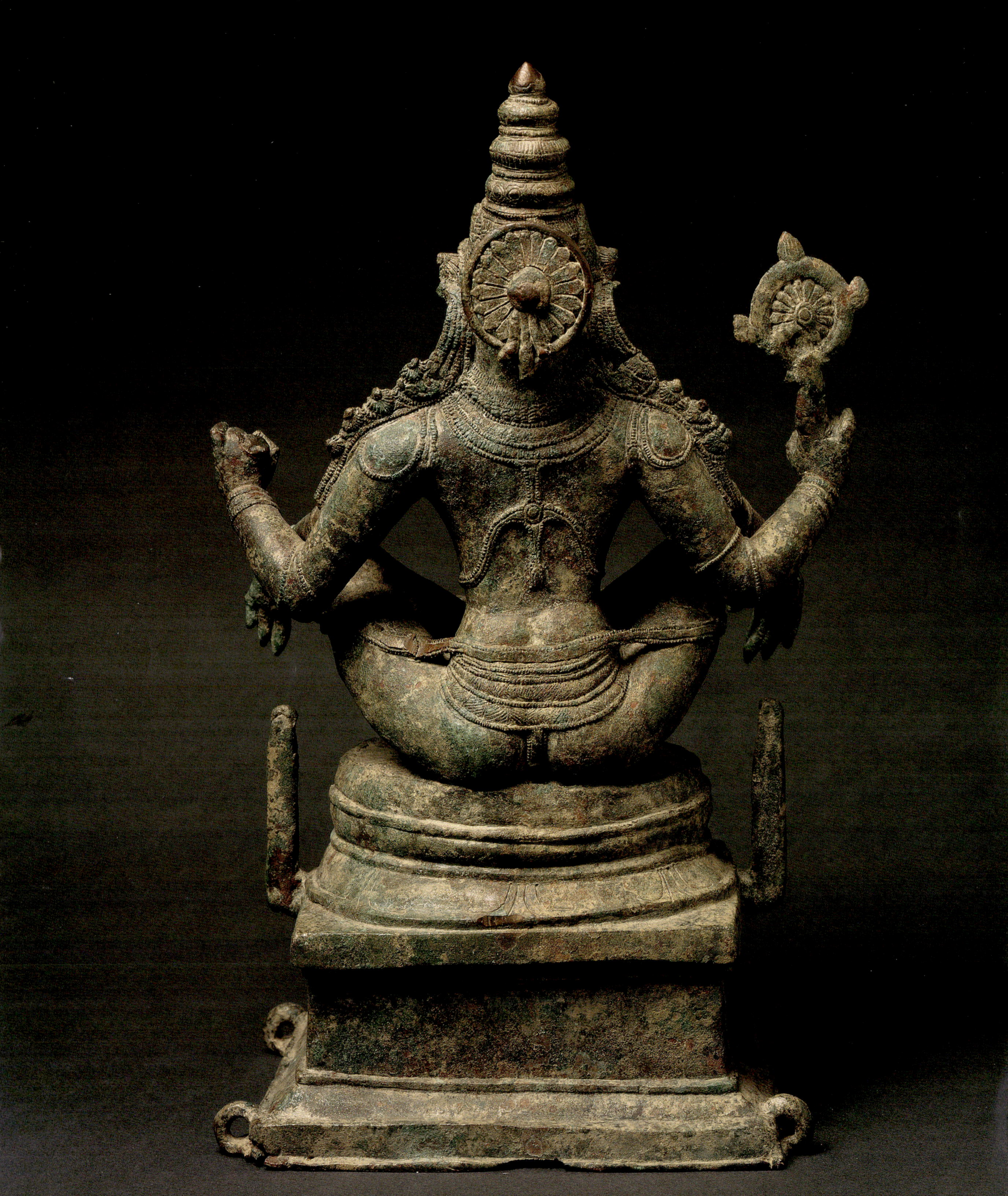

THE SENSUOUS AND THE SACRED CHOLA BRONZES FROM SOUTH INDIA

VIDYA DEHEJIA

WITH ESSAYS BY RICHARD H. DAVIS, R. NAGASWAMY, AND KAREN PECHILIS PRENTISS

AMERICAN FEDERATION OF ARTS, NEW YORK

IN ASSOCIATION WITH

UNIVERSITY OF WASHINGTON PRESS, SEATTLE AND LONDON

This catalogue has been published in conjunction with *The Sensuous and the Sacred: Chola Bronzes from South India*, an exhibition organized by the American Federation of Arts and the Arthur M. Sackler Gallery, Smithsonian Institution. Support is provided by the National Endowment for the Humanities and The Rockefeller Foundation. Additional exhibition support is provided by Gilbert and Ann Kinney, and the Benefactors Circle of the AFA. The catalogue is supported by the E. Rhodes and Leona B. Carpenter Foundation.

Publication Coordinator: Michaelyn Mitchell
Editor: Joseph Newland
Designer: Boxer Design

Library of Congress Cataloging-in-Publication Data
Dehejia, Vidya.
The sensuous and the sacred : Chola bronzes from South India / Vidya Dehejia ; with essays by Richard H. Davis, R. Nagaswamy, and Karen Pechilis Prentiss.
p. cm.
Includes bibliographical references and index.
ISBN 1-885444-25-7 (pbk. : alk. paper)
ISBN 0-295-98284-5 (hc. : alk. paper)
1. Sculpture, Chola--Exhibitions. 2. Bronze sculpture, Indic--India, South--Exhibitions. 3. Sculpture, Hindu--India, South--Exhibitions. 4. Temples, Hindu--India, South--Exhibitions. I. Davis, Richard H. II. Nagaswamy, R., 1930- III. Prentiss, Karen Pechilis. IV. Title.
NB1007.S67 D44 2002
732'.44--dc21
2002008843

Published in 2002 by the American Federation of Arts in association with the University of Washington Press.

Map on page 20 by Daniel Robert Drenger.

Printed in Singapore by CS Graphics

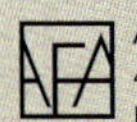

American Federation of Arts
41 East 65th Street
New York, NY 10021
www.afaweb.org

University of Washington Press
P.O. Box 50096
Seattle, Washington 98145-5096
www.washington.edu/uwpress

Front and back covers: *Shiva as Nataraja, Lord of Dance* (cat. no. 1)
Pages 1 and 2: *Yoga Narasimha, Vishnu in His Man-Lion Avatar* (cat. no. 45). Photo John Tsantes

EXHIBITION ITINERARY

Arthur M. Sackler Gallery
Smithsonian Institution
Washington, D.C.
November 10, 2002–March 9, 2003

Dallas Museum of Art
Dallas, Texas
April 4–June 15, 2003

The Cleveland Museum of Art
Cleveland, Ohio
July 6–September 14, 2003

NOTE TO READER

A simplified transliteration system for Indian languages is used throughout. Unless otherwise noted, sculptures are from Tamil Nadu (specific regional designations are stated when possible); and "right" and "left" should be interpreted from the sculpture's perspective.

The objects in the exhibition can be seen at all three venues, with the following exceptions:

cat. no. 3, *Shiva as Nataraja* (Sackler only)
cat. no. 6, *Shiva as Tripuravijaya, Victor of the Three Cities, and Consort* (Sackler and Dallas only)
cat. no. 14, *Uma as Queen Sembiyan Mahadevi* (Sackler only)
cat. no. 15, *Somaskanda, Shiva with Uma and Skanda* (Dallas and Cleveland only)
cat. no. 26, *Trident with Shiva as Ardhanari, Half-Woman* (Cleveland only)
cat. no. 30, *Shaiva Devotee, Perhaps Appar's Sister Tilakavati* (Sackler only)

CONTENTS

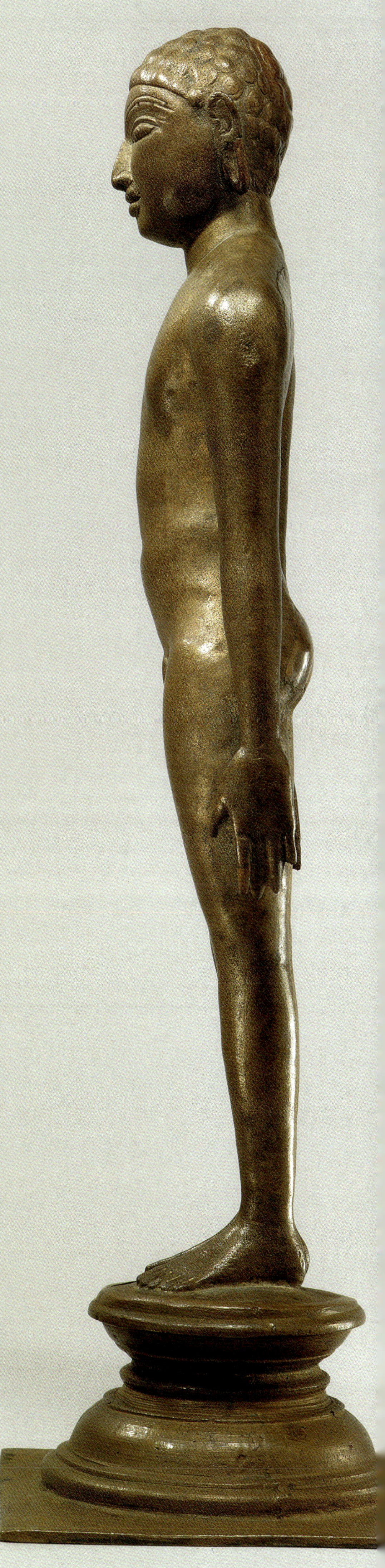

ACKNOWLEDGMENTS

JULIA BROWN
DIRECTOR
AMERICAN FEDERATION OF ARTS

Under the extraordinary patronage of the Chola kings, the Indian subcontinent underwent a period of unparalleled artistic creativity. The temple became the centerpiece of activity for daily life, and the Cholas were responsible for building some of the most impressive temples in south India. Unlike the large and immovable stone sculptures they replaced, the bronzes of the Chola dynasty, worshipped as living entities, were portable and became integral to numerous festivities and rituals both in the temple and in its environs. The first exhibition devoted to these spectacular bronzes, *The Sensuous and the Sacred* exposes a major cultural tradition of India through spectacular works of art rarely seen in the United States—works that represent the apex of bronze-casting in southern Asia, as technically sophisticated as they are beautiful.

Our thanks begin with our guest curator, Vidiya Dehejia, the Barbara Stoler Miller Professor of Indian Art at Columbia University and former Deputy Director and Chief Curator of the Freer Gallery of Art and Arthur M. Sackler Gallery. Ms. Dehejia is to be commended for her astute selection of the works in the exhibition and her discerning texts in this publication, which contribute substantially to the understanding and study of Indian art. We also wish to acknowledge the other eminent contributors to this publication, with whom it has been a delight to work: Richard H. Davis, Associate Professor of Religion at Bard College; R. Nagaswamy, former Director General of Archaeology, State of Tamil Nadu, Madras; and Karen Pechilis Prentiss, Assistant Professor in the Department of Religious Studies at Drew University.

We wish to warmly acknowledge the Arthur M. Sackler Gallery, Smithsonian Institution, with which we have had the great pleasure of organizing this project. In particular, we would like to thank Julian Raby, Director; Milo Beach, former Director; Cheryl Sobas, Exhibitions Coordinator; Debra Diamond, Assistant Curator; Kirstin Mattson, Development Specialist; and Ray Williams, Head of Education. We would also like to thank Tom Lentz, Director of the Smithsonian's International Art Museums Division.

On the AFA staff, numerous individuals have been critical in the organization of *The Sensuous and the Sacred*. Thomas Padon, Deputy Director for Exhibitions and Programs, deserves special thanks for having suggested the idea for the exhibition and for initiating the dialogue with Vidya Dehejia that made it a reality. Tom also provided oversight throughout the organization of the project. Kathryn Haw, Curator of Exhibitions, managed the complexity of the exhibition's organization and negotiation of the loans with intelligence, efficiency, and good humor. Michaelyn Mitchell, Director, Publications and Design, skillfully oversaw the editing, design, and publication of this impressive book. Barbara Elam, Assistant Registrar, coordinated the logistics of traveling the exhibition; Nina Callaway, Media Representative, oversaw the promotion and publicity for the project; Nelly Silagy Benedek, Director of Education, created the educational materials; and Anne Bergeron, Deputy Director for External Afrairs, helped locate funding for the project. Other AFA staff members who should be acknowledged for contributing to the success of this project include Kathleen Flynn, Director of Exhibition Administration; Kathryn Shedrick, Associate Editor; Amy Poll, Curatorial Assistant; and Anne Palermo, Editorial Assistant.

We are delighted to have worked with the University of Washington Press and Mapin Publishing on this publication and wish to particularly thank J. Pat Soden and Bipan Shah, respectively, for their cooperation. We would also like to acknowledge Joseph Newland for his scrupulous editing of the book; Eileen Boxer for her handsome design; and Bob Lorenzson, Maggie Nimkin, and Miki Slingsby for their fine photography.

We wish to acknowledge the many lenders both public and private who generously allowed us to borrow from their collections. To them go our warmest thanks. Our gratitude also goes to those who have given their support to the exhibition: the E. Rhodes and Leona B. Carpenter Foundation, which supported this catalogue; the Rockefeller Foundation; the National Endowment for the Humanities; Gilbert and Ann Kinney, and the Benefactors Circle of the AFA. Without their generosity, this exhibition would not have been possible.

Finally, a special thanks is due the museums participating in the tour of the exhibition. In addition to its presentation at the Sackler Gallery, the exhibition will be shown at the Dallas Museum of Art and the Cleveland Museum of Art. Their cooperation and enthusiasm has played an especially important role in our efforts.

JULIAN RABY
DIRECTOR
FREER GALLERY OF ART AND
ARTHUR M. SACKLER GALLERY

The Chola tradition of figurative sculpture speaks across centuries and cultures, yet it speaks in very different voices to a western audience and to those of the Hindu faith. To the western eye, the naked sculptures combine a lissome grace with corporeal substantiality, marrying, as works of art, a powerful presence with approachability. In the Chola tradition, however, the statues would only have been seen in their naked form by an initiated few, principally by priests whose task was to purify the statues, transmuting them into embodiments of the divine. As naked metal, the statues were "unqualified"; enlivened, dressed, and garlanded, they were the numinous presence of the deities themselves. It is this tension between the western and Hindu appreciations of Chola bronzes that this exhibition seeks to address.

The majority of the exhibition objects date from the tenth, eleventh, and twelfth centuries A.D., the height of the Chola dynasty's power and the acme of this sculptural tradition. The arrangement—by religious theme rather than chronology—has the dual purpose of reflecting the principal groupings found in Chola temples, and introducing the western visitor to the complexities of Hindu iconography and the divine personalities and religious myths. The exhibition evokes a sense of the rituals accorded the statues and of the role the statues played, and still play, in temple devotion and popular processions.

Chola sculptures invoked popular piety, but the sudden efflorescence of this tradition in the tenth century was connected to royal sponsorship for Chola rulers and their courts drew upon the potency of artistic patronage to legitimate dynastic power and increase social prestige.

These themes are explored in detail in the catalogue, the authors opening up new insights into our understanding of the religious, socio-cultural, and even political role of items so long appreciated in the West for their artistic merits alone. Particular thanks are due Vidya Dehejia, who masterminded this project and wrote much of the catalogue. Her background in classical Sanskrit and Tamil, knowledge of a range of modern Indian languages, and extensive explorations of ancient poetry have contributed greatly to these new perspectives.

We are fortunate to have had the American Federation of Arts as our partner in the organization of this project, and we are grateful to Julia Brown, Director, and Serena Rattazzi, former Director. Thomas Padon, Deputy Director for Exhibitions and Programs, is credited with the inspiration for the exhibition and for bringing together the core of the project team, and we are indebted to him for his enthusiasm for the subject matter. On the AFA staff, Kathryn Haw, Curator of Exhibitions, Michaelyn Mitchell, Director, Publications and Design, Kathleen Flynn, Director of Exhibition Administration, and Anne Bergeron, Deputy Director for External Affairs, have made this partnership enjoyable and fruitful.

At the Sackler, the hard work and dedication of our staff contributed to the success of the project. Among them, Debra Diamond, Assistant Curator of South and Southeast Asian Art, coordinated the presentation of the exhibition and provided curatorial expertise. Karen Sasaki, Exhibition Design Specialist, and Nancé Hacskaylo, Graphic Designer, designed the installation and didactics. The thankless burden of all administrative and financial matters fell on the shoulders of Cheryl Sobas, Exhibitions Coordinator. Ray Williams, Head of Education, oversaw the development of the accompanying educational programs, while Kirstin Mattson, Development Specialist, worked with gallery staff and with our AFA colleagues on securing funding for the project.

Special thanks go to the lenders, who often had to part with some of the most important and cherished objects in their collections in order to make the tour of this exhibition possible.

No exhibition of this scale and importance is possible without generous funding, and I would like to thank the Rockefeller Foundation and the National Endowment for the Humanities, in particular program officers David Martz and Sarah Ridley. We also owe a substantial debt to benefactors who supported the Sackler Gallery's presentation of this exhibition. Nunda Ambegaonkar and Sigrid and Vinton Cerf made an invaluable contribution by being early donors to the project; and we deeply appreciate the gifts of several board members and their spouses, Mary and Farhad Ebrahimi, Peg and George Haldeman, and Ann and Gilbert Kinney.

VIDYA DEHEJIA

It has been an undiluted pleasure to return to the subject of Chola bronzes, a topic I first examined at length a decade ago when I delivered the Polsky lectures in New York. Now, as then, I would like to acknowledge the work of the pioneers in the field: S. R. Balasubrahmanyam, who made a painstaking four-volume record of temples and their bronzes; Douglas Barrett, whose art historical analysis laid the foundation for the study of this material; and Dr. R. Nagaswamy, who has made extensive contributions to this field, producing a very important exhibition catalogue, as well as a series of significant articles that have vastly enlarged our knowledge of the subject. Dr. Nagaswamy has effortlessly explored Sanskrit agamic texts, as well as Tamil literature, to produce fresh insights into the sacred significance and iconography of the images. I am much indebted to his scholarship and am enormously grateful to him and to my colleagues Richard H. Davis and Karen Pechilis Prentiss for their thoughtful and thought-provoking essays in this volume. Their contributions provide an important added dimension to my analysis of the art of the Chola bronze image.

M. D. Sampath of the Epigraphical Survey in Mysore very kindly made available to me ink rubbings and copies of two important inscriptions from Tiruvaduturai that form the basis for my discussion of the bronzes necessary to complete the ritual cycle of a temple. Marxia Gandhi, epigraphist with the Tamil Nadu Department of Archaeology, worked with me to translate these inscriptions. She also re-examined the original text of the epigraphs from the great temple at Tanjavur, which revealed information not found in the standard published translation. I also want to acknowledge Jyoti Mohan, who worked with me on several aspects of the project.

I am deeply indebted to Thomas Padon, Deputy Director for Exhibitions and Programs at the AFA, whose appreciation of the artistic quality of Chola bronzes led to this joint AFA/Sackler exhibition. It has since been a pleasure to work with Kathryn Haw, Curator of Exhibitions, who took overall charge of the project.

I am grateful to the individual collectors and museums for generously allowing their bronzes to come together for this exhibition. Movement of bronzes was always part of the temple ritual cycle, although current museum viewing is very different from that of the original ritual viewing.

Joseph Newland's thoughtful, sensitive, and thorough edit of the manuscript has greatly improved the quality of this book; we struggled with the varying orthography of Sanskrit and Tamil terms and must beg the indulgence of the specialist reader on this score. Eileen Boxer's layout has produced pages that are a pleasure to view. Heartfelt thanks are also due Michaelyn Mitchell, Director of Publications and Design at the AFA, whose essential monitoring ensured the quality of the final product.

A number of individuals and museums graciously gave us permission to reproduce their photographs; I would like to make special mention of the Freer and Sackler photographer, Neil Greentree, who made a special trip to south India to produce video and still footage of bronze-casting, processions, temples, and bronzes.

Finally, I must acknowledge the many temple priests of Tamil Nadu who gave me access to bronzes, allowing me to temporarily subject these sacred images to scrutiny as mere works of art! Regretfully, other priests, especially in Vaishnava temples, forbade such access. Only a study of images still standing in their original temples will finally enable us to distinguish stylistically between bronzes produced in the heart of the Chola country and those from the northern region of Tondai, the southern Pandi area, and the western Kongu region.

A postscript to the reader on the complex issue of dating: since very few Chola bronzes carry inscribed dates, it would be wise to treat dates ascribed to bronzes with a plus-minus factor of twenty-five years.

CONTRIBUTORS

Richard H. Davis is Associate Professor of Religion at Bard College, Annandale-On-Hudson, New York.

Vidya Dehejia holds the Barbara Stoler Miller Chair in Indian Art at Columbia University. She is former Deputy Director and Chief Curator of the Freer Gallery of Art and Arthur M. Sackler Gallery, Smithsonian Institution, Washington, D.C.

R. Nagaswamy is former Director General of Archaeology, State of Tamil Nadu, Madras.

Karen Pechilis Prentiss is Assistant Professor in the Department of Religious Studies at Drew University, Madison, New Jersey.

LENDERS TO THE EXHIBITION

The Art Institute of Chicago
Asia Society, New York
Trustees of The British Museum, London
The Brooklyn Museum of Art
Carnegie Museum of Art, Pittsburgh
The Cleveland Museum of Art
Dallas Museum of Art
Erie Art Museum
Freer Gallery of Art, Smithsonian Institution, Washington, D.C.
Linden-Museum, Stuttgart
Los Angeles County Museum of Art
The Metropolitan Museum of Art
Musée national des Arts Asiatiques-Guimet, Paris
Museum of Fine Arts, Boston
The Nelson-Atkins Museum of Art, Kansas City, Missouri
Philadelphia Museum of Art
Rietberg Museum, Zurich
Rijksmuseum, Amsterdam
Arthur M. Sackler Gallery, Smithsonian Institution, Washington, D.C.
Victoria & Albert Museum
Virginia Museum of Fine Arts, Richmond
Worcester Art Museum, Worcester, Massachusetts

Susan L. Beningson
Dr. Siddharth Bhansali, New Orleans
Robert Hatfield Ellesworth
Kapoor Galleries, Inc., New York
Rosemary and George Lois
Zina and Ernest Stern, New York
Doris Wiener, New York
Anonymous

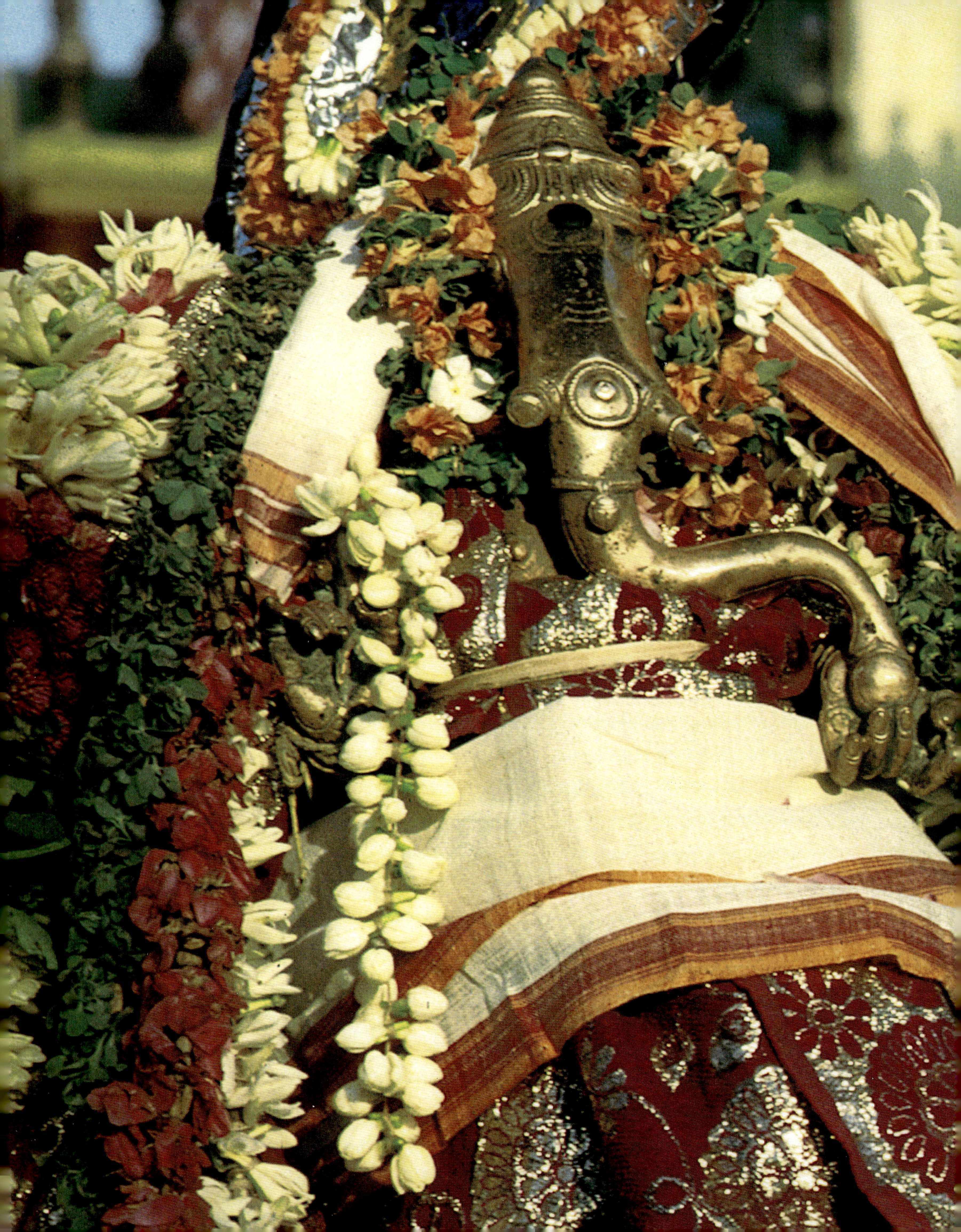

CHOLA BRONZES: HOW, WHEN, AND WHY

VIDYA DEHJIA

Among the most spectacular works of Indian sculptural art are the temple bronzes produced in the Tamil-speaking region of south India during the rule of the Chola dynasty between the ninth and thirteenth centuries of the common era. The numerous ancient copper-alloy images that are still used in worship in the temples of Tamil Nadu (fig. 2), as well as those recovered from buried hoards, testify to the ancient artists' skill in fashioning bronze sculptures. Though the production of bronze images for temple use first began in the days of the later Pallava rulers of the eighth century, bronze sculpture as a specialized art rose into prominence only with the patronage, direct and indirect, of the Chola monarchs.

Intriguing corroboration of this ancient skill in metal-casting in south India comes from an unexpected source in the form of letters written in Arabic during the eleventh and twelfth centuries by Jewish traders in Aden to their counterparts in the Coromandel (correctly "Chola-mandalam") ports of Tamil Nadu. The Coromandel emporia provided them with pearls, areca-nuts, spices, aromatics, silk and cotton products, and also metal-work. A letter from Joseph ibn Abraham, an Aden trader in products of the Indian bronze industry, to Abraham Yiju, who ran a bronze factory in India, for example, carries the date of 1130. Apparently, Coromandel bronze work was sufficiently prized for traders to send used copper items, as well as raw

BRONZE IMAGE OF GANESHA, DECORATED AND ADORNED FOR A TEMPLE PROCESSION, KAPALISHVARA TEMPLE, MYLAPUR, CHENNAI
PHOTO NEIL GREENTREE, 1988
FIG. 1

copper, all the way from Aden to south India for refashioning into new items to be sent back for sale in western markets.[1] Understandably, though regrettably, the letters refer only to products like bowls, ewers, and lamps, marketable in the West, and not to metal images that were clearly irrelevant to the merchants.

South Indian temple bronzes during the Chola period were created through the *cire perdue* or lost-wax technique that remains the standard method to this day. Images are molded from a "prepared wax" consisting of hard beeswax mixed with a small proportion of *dammar,* the resin of the *shal* tree (fig. 3). Sculptors heat the wax, deftly mold it into a torso, hand, leg, or flower, and lower it into a basin of cold water, where it instantly hardens. When pieces are to be joined, they are returned to a malleable state through brief reheating on the flame that stands ready beside the artists. Details, down to the individual beads of a necklace or the patterned fabric of a garment, are worked with a sharp wooden chisel shaped from the core of a tamarind tree, though occasionally a steel chisel is used. Simple tubular struts connect the hands of images to the body, providing a certain degree of stability to the wax model; these will be used later as channels during the final molten metal process. Once the wax image is complete in every detail, it is encased within several layers of clay, of which the first layer, of a fine, smooth texture, is of utmost importance; if the clay is correctly applied, the image that finally emerges will require little or no retouching. The heavily clay-encased image is then baked, and the wax melts and runs out through sprues provided for this purpose, resulting in a hollow clay mold.

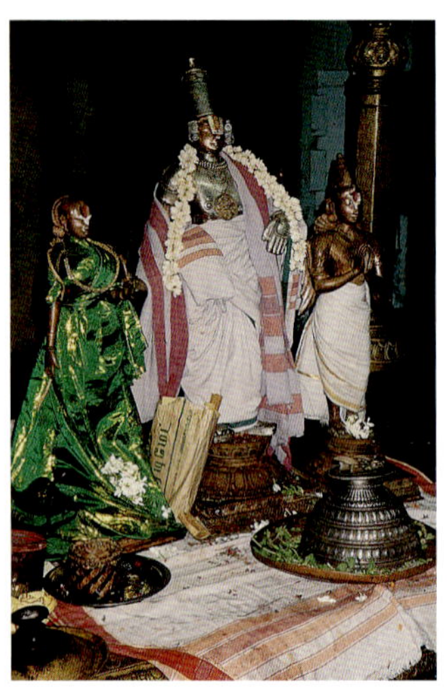

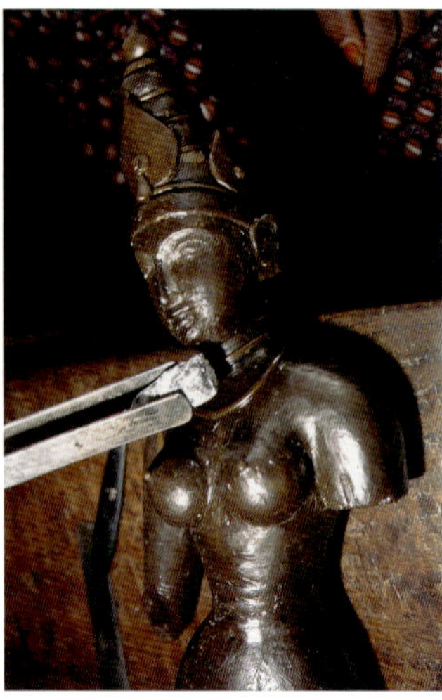

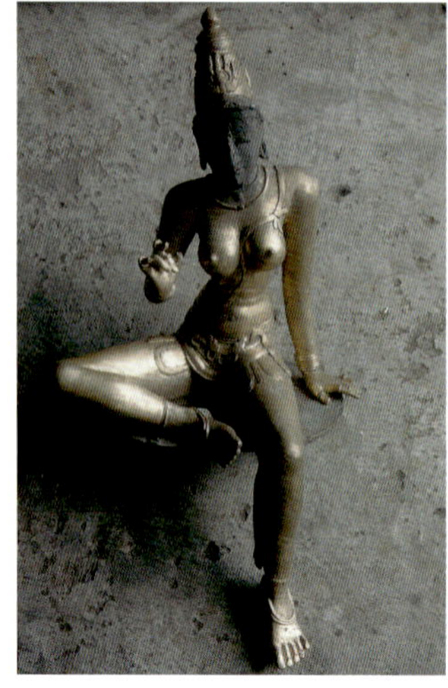

ANCIENT BRONZE IMAGES OF VISHNU, FLANKED BY WOMAN SAINT ANDAL AND DIVINE EAGLE GARUDA, IN WORSHIP IN THE RAJENDRA VINNAGAR TEMPLE, PANDI-NADU
PHOTO VIDYA DEHEJIA
FIG. 2

MODERN WAX IMAGE OF THE GODDESS BEING TREATED WITH COAL TO SMOOTH THE SURFACE, SWAMIMALAI
PHOTO NEIL GREENTREE, 2000
FIG. 3

POLISHED MODERN BRONZE IMAGE OF THE GODDESS, WITH THE FACE LEFT FOR TREATMENT BY THE MASTER, SWAMIMALAI
PHOTO NEIL GREENTREE, 2000
FIG. 4

Specialized metal-workers now take over, heating copper with a small proportion of lead and tin (in ancient times, small amounts of gold and silver too). This is carefully and deftly poured into the clay mold to fill every millimeter, ensuring that the molten metal flows from the torso to the arms and legs and back again. Large castings take into account the cooling process of metal: its expansion, contraction, and the like. Once the metal has completely cooled, the clay mold is broken open to reveal the bronze image; since the mold cannot be reused, every bronze is unique. In Chola times, only the barest minimum of finishing work, like removing the channels of bronze connecting hands to torso (still intact in the bronze image of cat. no. 30), remained to be executed; the product of a well-encased wax model needed only to be polished (fig. 4). Today, however, artists resort to an extensive amount of cold chiseling, which gives a distinct, sharp finish to the details. The professions of the stone sculptor and the wax modeler probably overlapped during the early Chola period, but craft specialization soon arose with the growing demand for temple bronzes. Today, as is clearly evident from current practice in the town of Swamimalai—the main center of bronze-casting that produces images for temples from Chennai (Madras) to Pittsburgh and Malibu—stone sculpting and wax modeling are two very distinct areas of specialization.

The antiquity of the lost-wax process in south India, as well as familiarity with the technique, is reflected in a casual reference in a poem by woman saint Andal (ca. 800), in which she addresses the rain clouds asking them to carry her message of love to the god Vishnu.

O rain clouds
seeming like dark clay outside,
liquid wax within,
rain down upon Venkatam
where the handsome lord dwells...[2]

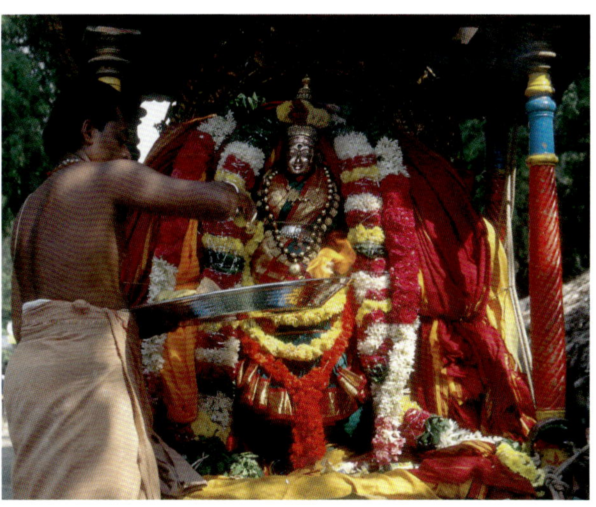

PROCESSIONAL IMAGE OF THE GODDESS, ADORNED WITH SILKS, GOLD, AND FLOWERS, TIRUVANNAMALAI
PHOTO NEIL GREENTREE, 2000
FIG. 5

PROCESSIONAL IMAGES AND THE FESTIVAL CYCLE

From the days when the first Indian temples were built, the image of the deity was enshrined within the darkened mystery of a sanctum sanctorum where he or she received the homage of the devout. The main exchange between deity and worshiper is best typified by the word *darshan* or "seeing." By presenting himself or herself for *darshan*, the deity bestows blessings upon the worshipers who, by their act of "seeing," have made themselves receptive to the transfer of grace. The sanctum image was usually large, heavy, and immovable *(achala).*

From around the sixth century, perhaps even earlier, there was a unique development in south India in which the deity began to be visualized as assuming a public persona not unlike that of a human ruling monarch. In this context, it is noteworthy that the word *koyil* is used in Tamil for both temple and palace *(ko,* "king, lord"; *il,* "place, home"). In such a role, the deity was required to appear in person in public and to preside over a number of festivities that became a part of a temple's ritual cycle. Some of these rituals, like the morning round of the sacred enclosure or the nightly retreat to the sacred bedroom *(tiru-palli-arai)*, were enacted daily; others, like the swing festival, were weekly ceremonies; while yet others, like the marriage of god and goddess, were yearly celebrations. Clearly the large, heavy stone image in the sanctum could not be carried to and fro each time to fulfill all these functions. The production of smaller and lighter processional images of deities began thus as a need to satisfy a ritual requirement (fig. 5).

When the god goes in procession, he becomes accessible to the most lowly of worshipers who in the past were prohibited entry into the sacred premises of a temple. Nandanar, one among the sixty-three saints of Shiva, was one such worshiper. He came from an untouchable *(paraiyan)* community that provided leather for drums and animal gut for stringed musical instruments used in the temples. He made his way to Chidambaram, where he stood outside the high temple walls, dancing in ecstasy because he had reached the holy site but weeping in despair because he was denied entry. Shiva is said to have appeared to the temple priests and commanded them to light a fire through which Nandanar walked unharmed; he entered the sanctum, walked up to the image of dancing Shiva, and disappeared under the raised foot of the lord. (Nandanar's dates are somewhat uncertain, but he may definitely be placed before the year 800.[3]) For the many devotees barred entry into temple premises, or stopped short of the main shrine, the portable image carried in procession through the streets of the town provided an outlet for joyous *darshan*.

The earliest reference to portable processional images appears in the verses of two seventh-century Shaiva saints, Appar and Sambandar. Here are two verses that celebrate the festival of Adirai held in the month of Margali (December–January); today it is often dedicated to dancing Shiva, but Appar's hymn at the Tiruvarur temple speaks of Shiva's form as the Enchanting Mendicant.

He goes on his begging rounds
amid the glitter of a pearl canopy
and gem-encrusted golden fans.
Devoted men and women follow him,
along with Virati ascetics in bizarre garb,
garlanded with white skulls.
Such is the splendor of Atirai day
in Arur, our Father's town!

The ascetic god goes in procession,
led by the immortal gods
whose heads are bowed to him,
while lovely celestial women
with shoulders graceful as the bamboo
follow behind, and ash-smeared devotees
surround him, singing his praise.
Such is the splendor of Atirai day
of the Lord in Arur![4]

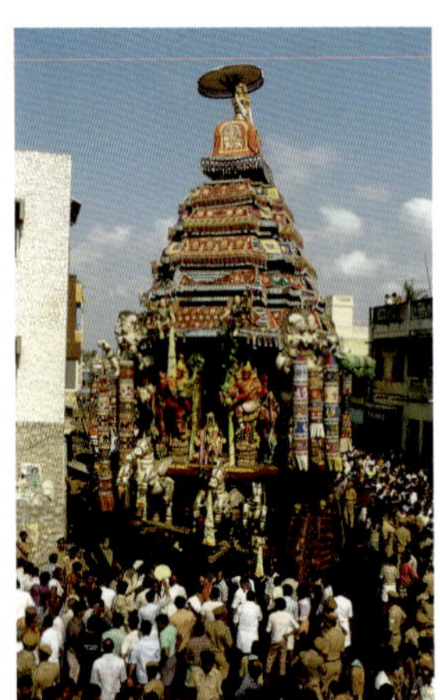

TEMPLE CHARIOT FOR PROCESSIONAL BRONZE IMAGES,
KAPALISHVARA TEMPLE, MYLAPUR, CHENNAI
PHOTO NEIL GREENTREE, 1988
FIG. 6

The Tamil words used for "led by" *(mun chella),* "follow behind" *(pin chella)* and "surround" *(chula)* clearly indicate that Appar is speaking of a procession centered on a portable image.

A hymn of the child-saint Sambandar speaks of an image of Shiva, perhaps in his form as Shrikantha (Blue-Throated Lord Who Drank the Poison), being taken in procession in a temple chariot (fig. 6).

The Lord of Citticcaram shrine in Naraiyur,
who has the river in his hair,
the poison stain on his throat,
and the Veda on his tongue,
goes resplendent in ceremonial dress,
as his devotees and perfected sages
sing, and dance his widespread fame,
and the sound of festival drums
beaten on the streets where the temple-car is pulled
spreads on every side.[5]

Another of Sambandar's hymns is dedicated to the festival cycle at the Kapalishvara (Lord of the Skull-Bowl) temple of Mylapur, once an independent town, but today in the heart of the city of Chennai. It revolves around the legend of a beautiful young girl named Pumpavai who had died of a snakebite, and who was miraculously resuscitated as Sambandar sang the last verse. In each of ten verses,

Sambandar queries Pumpavai as to how she could possibly choose (by dying) not to view the glory of Shiva, lord of Mayilai (Mylapur), at six major monthly festivals, the monthly eight-day rite, the weekly swing ceremony, and the Jain/Buddhist purification ritual. The procession through the streets of Mylapur implied in verses 3 and 7, the procession to the seashore of verse 6, and the swing ceremony of verse 9 would be impossible without portable or processional images. Since this hymn is of considerable significance to our discussion, I append it in its entirety (appendix 1), and here quote only the four above-mentioned verses.

Pumpavai, O beautiful girl! verse 3
Would you go without having seen
on the rich streets of Mayilai,
town of beautiful young women with bracelets,
and town of our Lord in the Kapaliccaram temple,
the flawless celebration of the ancient Karttikai [Nov.-Dec.] feast
at which young girls
with sandal paste on their breasts
light many lamps?

Pumpavai, O beautiful girl! verse 6
Would you go without having seen
in Mayilai,
fringed with coconut palms with broad fronds,
and town of our Lord who dwells in Kapaliccaram shrine,
the festival of bathing in the sea
in the month of Maci [Feb.–Mar.],
at which women dance, singing the praise
of the feet of the Lord
who rides the mighty bull?

Pumpavai, O beautiful girl! verse 7
Would you go without having seen
on the streets of great Mayilai,
always busy with festive crowds,
the festival of Pankuni Uttiram [Mar.–Apr.]
with its great sound of celebration,
at which beautiful women
sing and distribute alms,
at the Lord's Kapaliccaram shrine,
center of many festivals?

Pumpavai, O beautiful girl! verse 9
Would you go without having seen
the ceremony of the golden swing
held for him who dwells in Kapaliccaram shrine,
where devotees praise the feet of the Lord
whom the four-headed god on the lotus seat
and Narayana himself
could not fully comprehend?[6]

The seashore festival of verse 6 is of special interest. Elsewhere I have pointed to the mention of such a festival, at the famed temple of Chidambaram, in the inscriptions of the general Naralokaviran, who served two Chola emperors, Kulottunga (reigned 1070–1125) and Vikrama Chola (r. 1118–35).[7] The devout general made provisions for a road to be built to the seashore for this celebration, a hall on the beach where dancing Shiva could enjoy the sea air, and a fresh water tank for the devotees who accompanied the festival image (fig. 7). In his study on Chidambaram, Paul Younger indicates that the festival reflects a time when it was a coastal town and port of significance.[8] Sambandar's verse suggests that this festival for Shiva (though not necessarily for dancing Shiva) was of importance in all coastal towns from as early as the seventh century. That dancing Shiva was taken in procession at this same early date is evident from a verse by Appar that refers to the monthly festival of Asthami (the eighth day of the bright fortnight) in the temple of Kurukkai Virattam:

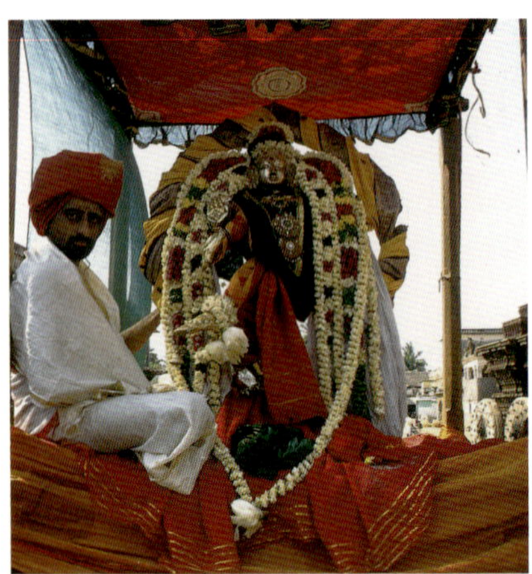

PROCESSIONAL IMAGE OF DANCING SHIVA,
JAMBUKESHVARA TEMPLE, SRIRANGAM
PHOTO NEIL GREENTREE, 1988
FIG. 7

> ***For seven holy days before***
> ***the festival of Attami, the Eighth Day,***
> ***the Lord of Kurukkai Virattam***
> ***goes in procession in his dancing form [kuttar],***
> ***as Ayan [Brahma] and Mal [Vishnu] and all the gods***
> ***bow to him and praise him,***
> ***calling him their Lord.***[9]

The verses of Sambandar and Appar suggest that the change in the visualization of the nature of Tamil divinity belongs to the seventh century or earlier, and not to the start of the Chola period, as I had hitherto suggested.[10] A thorough perusal of the corpus of over one thousand poems of the saints, written in an old form of Tamil and largely untranslated, with this specific issue in mind, will likely reveal further evidence of such festival rites.

The portable images to which reference is made in the seventh-century verses must have been created of perishable material, most likely wood, a material used in India for sacred imagery since early times. For instance, an inscription from the southern Andhra site of Nagarjunakonda, dating from as early as the year 278, speaks of the installation, in the sanctum of a brick temple, of a wooden image of eight-armed Vishnu upon a stone pedestal on which the epigraph is inscribed.[11] It is only in the late eighth century, toward the end of the Pallava period, that processional images first began to be crafted in bronze. However, Pallava bronze images tend to be ten to twelve inches high, and it was Chola craftsmen who produced, for the many stone temples being built in the Tamil country, the superb bronzes that range from two to five feet in height and which are studied in this volume. The practice of lavishly decorating bronze processional images with silks, jewelry of gold and precious stones, and fresh flower garlands—and leaving barely an inch of the bronze visible to the eyes of devotees (fig. 1 on p. 10)—might have arisen from the need to give added richness to an originally stark wooden image, whose simple painted adornment would soon have been lost through the repeated anointments of ritual *puja*.

By the tenth century, when inscriptions speak routinely of the embellishment of the magnificent Chola bronze icons, this custom of adornment was evidently well established. One such inscription of the year 976, in the temple at Konerirajapuram in the heart of the Kaveri Delta, speaks of the disbursement of funds from the Chola queen Sembiyan Mahadevi's endowment to the temple. While providing a fascinating glimpse into the finances of the temple, the inscription is of special interest here for the information it gives us about the ritual worship and decoration of three sets of festival bronzes—Shiva as Victor of the Three Cities (Tripuravijaya) with his consort Uma, Shiva as Rider of the Bull (Vrishabhavana) with his consort Uma, and Ganesha—which, incidentally, are seen in the temple even today (fig. 8; see also fig. 13). We hear of priests who ritually bathed the metal icons in milk, curds, butter, honey, and sugar; carriers of holy water from the river Kaveri for their further bathing; those who prepared sandal paste for anointing the images; the weaver who supplied cloth for draping them; the dyer of such cloth; and those who held a canopy above the bronzes when they were carried in procession.[12]

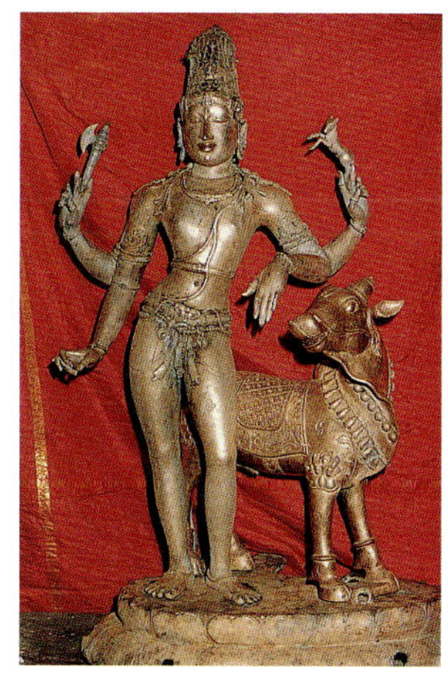

SHIVA AS RIDER OF THE BULL, CA. 969, KONERIRAJAPURAM TEMPLE, KAVERI DELTA
PHOTO VIDYA DEHEJIA
FIG. 8

THE TEMPLE AND TEMPLE-GIFTS IN CHOLA POLITY AND SOCIETY

Since the bronzes that constitute the focus of this study were all sculptures intended for temple ritual, it is instructive to consider the temple in its social, religious, economic, and political milieu. The poems of the Tamil saints reveal that during the sixth and seventh centuries there were two varieties of "temples." One was the simplest of sacred shrines, often consisting of no more than a *linga* of Shiva (his aniconic emblem) beneath a sacred tree in the village square. The other, located in a township known as *uru,* was a more formal structure, probably built of mud and brick. At the beginning of the Chola period, brick was abandoned in favor of stone as the medium for temple construction. During the second half of the tenth century, the Chola queen Sembiyan Mahadevi decided to replace a number of earlier brick temples, translating them into the medium of stone and leaving inscriptions recording her actions. Her inscription of the year 979 in the Shiva temple in Tirukodikaval reveals an extraordinary sense of historical awareness. She collected the twenty-six or so inscribed stones from the earlier brick temple, and ordered that the old inscriptions be reinscribed, specifically marked as "copies," on the walls of the newly rebuilt stone temple.[13]

When her grandson Arulmoli adopted his title of Rajaraja, or King of Kings, he decided to proclaim his power and glory by building a temple several times the size of any previous Chola temple and naming it Rajarajeshvara (Lord of Rajaraja) (fig. 9). This great temple at Tanjavur (Tanjore), completed in the year 1010, rose to a height of 216 feet and was *the* skyscraper of its time, taller than anything built before it anywhere in India. This royal temple was gifted a total of sixty bronze images of deities, of which about one-third (twenty-two) were given by the emperor himself, one-third were gifts from his family (four from his sister and thirteen from his queens), and the remaining third (twenty-one) were given by his officials and nobles. Rajaraja also established several permanent endowments to enable the temple to function in grand style. He decreed, too, that all the villages of his empire, including those in newly conquered Sri Lanka, remit a certain proportion of their income to support the functioning of his temple. While Rajaraja's inscriptions on the great temple provide extraordinarily detailed documentation that enables us to recapture the status of the royal Chola temple in context, almost every temple in Tamil Nadu, large or small, royal or otherwise, provides us with a wealth of epigraphic material engraved on its walls, pillars, and base moldings (fig. 10; see also endpapers). Occasionally these inscriptions record the construction of the temple itself. More often they record endowments for a range of purposes that include the upkeep and maintenance of the temple; the payment of temple priests and other functionaries; the performance of daily, weekly, monthly and annual festivals; or the payment for celebratory music, dance, and drama. They also record the giving of bronze images, of silks and jewelry to adorn images, and of lamps, ritual vessels, and the like. As with Rajaraja's royal temple at Tanjavur, some gifts came from the monarch and his family, others from highly placed officials and temple functionaries, several from wealthy merchants, and an occasional donation came from dancing girls attached to a temple.[14]

Gifting to temples was motivated by a variety of incentives. It might occasionally have been prompted by pure religious fervor, but more often the cause lay, as it does even in the twenty-first century, in the donors' desire to receive *mariyatai* or temple honors.[15] The royal gift to temples and brahmins was in a special category, and was basic to south Indian statecraft; it helped fulfill kingly duties, it earned merit, and it brought prosperity to the kingdom. The royal endowment gave the king

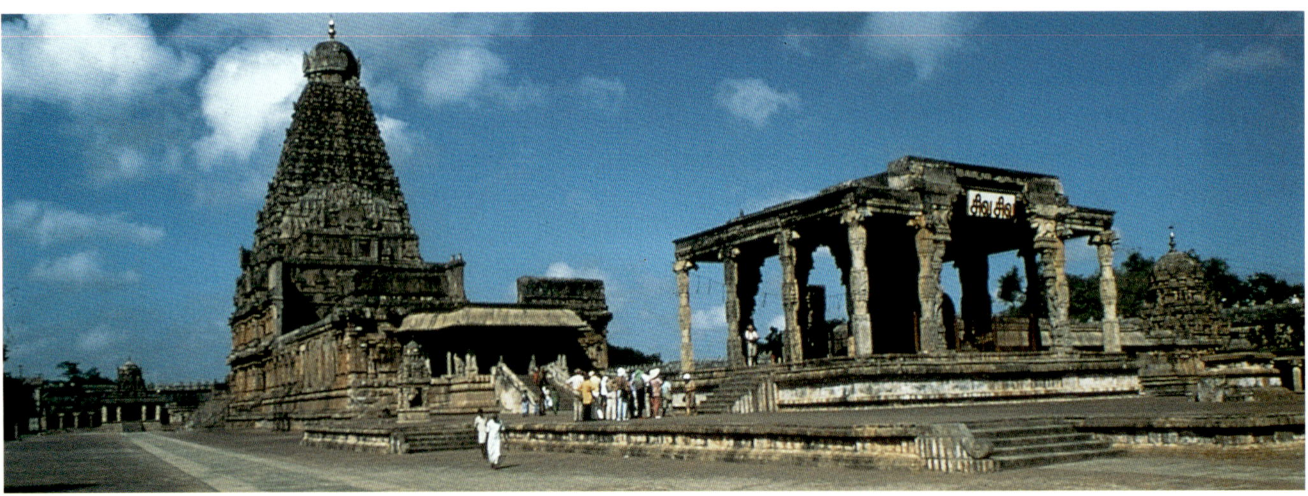

RAJARAJA CHOLA'S TEMPLE AT TANJAVUR
PHOTO VIDYA DEHEJIA
FIG. 9

the ultimate temple honor that brought him into an active and empowering relationship with the deity, and thereby reinforced his authority. Gifts from merchants and officials served to increase their rank and social standing. The greater the donation, the closer one's proximity to the deity. Any gift—whether in the nature of an endowment, or the offering of an individual metal image, or a piece of temple jewelry—guaranteed the donor a share in the honors accorded by a temple. Newly wealthy groups gained special status by sponsoring temple festivals that entitled them to temple honors; it was a conduit that translated wealth into prestige and social status. In elite Tamil circles, prestige is a concomitant of the *mariyatai* to which one is entitled in a temple. To this day, an individual takes greater pride in the temple honors to which he or she is entitled than in personal wealth or landed property, both of which, of course, are tied to the ability to give munificently and thus contribute to status in the temple. While devotion is indeed a factor that induces generous gifts to a temple, the more compelling factor is that many donors see a direct relationship between their temple activities and their business success or enhancement of a family's prestige, and hence lineage. As Nicholas Dirks emphasizes, temples were infinitely more than places of worship; they were fundamental social institutions that decided issues of rank, honor, and authority.[16] The temple honors, or *mariyatai,* given to a family are normally extended by courtesy to their guests. I myself have benefited from such extended honors and have thereby been given the opportunity to view temple jewels, allowed close access to temple bronzes, accorded the privilege of viewing an image without its covering adornment, and, given my art historical interests, granted the occasional permission to photograph such an image.

It was customary for temple gifts to be made on the day of a donor's birth star. All Chola monarchs, for instance, made grants to temples for the celebration of festivals in their honor on the monthly recurrence of the star under which they were born. Thus Rajaraja's monthly celebration was Sadaya tirunal (the star Sadaya's sacred day); Rajendra's was Adirai tirunal; Kulottunga's was Pusha tirunal; and

Vikrama Chola's was Uttirattati tirunal.[17] Nonroyal donors too chose routinely to make gifts on their birth-star-day. For instance, in the year 917, a lady named Chola-perundeviyar made a lavish endowment of gold to the deity of the Shiva temple at Nangavaram on her birthday.[18]

The economic implications of gifting—whether of villages and produce by the monarch, or of permanent endowments for temple ritual by nobles and wealthy merchants—has been the subject of intensive investigation and a number of book-length studies.[19] Donations transformed temples into wealthy institutions whose funds were generally entrusted, for investment, to a *nagaram* or merchant township; the interest was put toward the festivals, lamps, dancing girls, images, and other temple needs. Temples lent money (at 12½ percent interest during the eleventh century) to both institutions and individuals. A statistical survey reveals that just over 95 percent of loans were made to village assemblies while the rest went largely to merchants.[20] Loans were often repaid in kind with goods utilized by temples. For instance, farmers contributed paddy, spices, coconuts, bananas, and other foods for the temple kitchens; merchants gave silks and cottons for temple usage; cowherds produced ghee and oil for temple lamps.

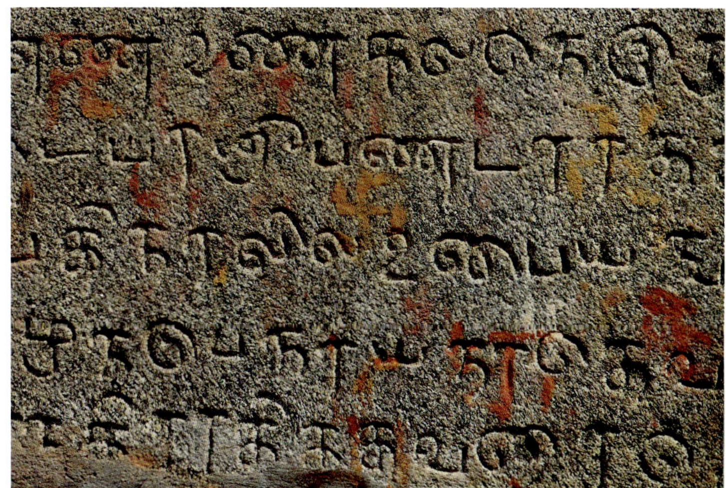

CHOLA-PERIOD INSCRIPTIONS ON WALLS OF TEMPLE AT AVANASHI NEAR COIMBATORE, KONGU-NADU
PHOTO VIDYA DEHEJIA
FIG. 10

CHOLA-MANDALAM

An appreciation of the fluctuating geographical boundaries of the Chola empire, or Chola-mandalam—which at times included territories as far-flung as parts of the island of Sri Lanka and the modern state of Karnataka—is useful in understanding the stylistic differences between individual Chola bronzes. Territorial expansion and contraction was, of course, associated with the political fortunes of the various dynasties of south India, making necessary a brief historical excursus.

Tamil Sangam literature dating from the first and second centuries of the common era speaks of three ruling families in south India—the Cholas, the Pandyas, and the Cheras. Thereafter, the Cholas disappear from the scene, to re-emerge as a significant ruling power only around the year 850, when Vijayalaya Chola captured the town of Tanjavur and established a new line of Chola monarchs. From Sangam literature we know too that the Tamil-speaking region was divided into a number of broad geographical-cum-cultural zones, known as *nadus.* Tondai-nadu, or the Madras region, became the stronghold of the Pallava rulers (sixth to ninth centuries); the basin of the Kaveri River became the Chola heartland and was known as Chola-nadu; Pandi-nadu, with its capital at Madurai, was the center for the Pandya monarchs; while Kongu-nadu, in and around Coimbatore, was an area that was at times in the hand of the Cheras of Kerala along the western Malabar Coast and at times controlled by the rulers of the Tamil region. At the height of Chola power, between 1000 and 1100, Chola-mandalam encompassed all these regions (fig. 11).

Although the early Chola monarchs captured parts of Tondai-nadu, Kongu-nadu, and Pandi-nadu, when the seventh Chola monarch, Rajaraja, born Arulmolivarman, assumed the throne in the year 985, the empire had shrunk to the area around the Kaveri Delta. Rajaraja immediately embarked on an ambitious campaign of territorial expansion. He captured Pallava and Pandya territory, fought successful

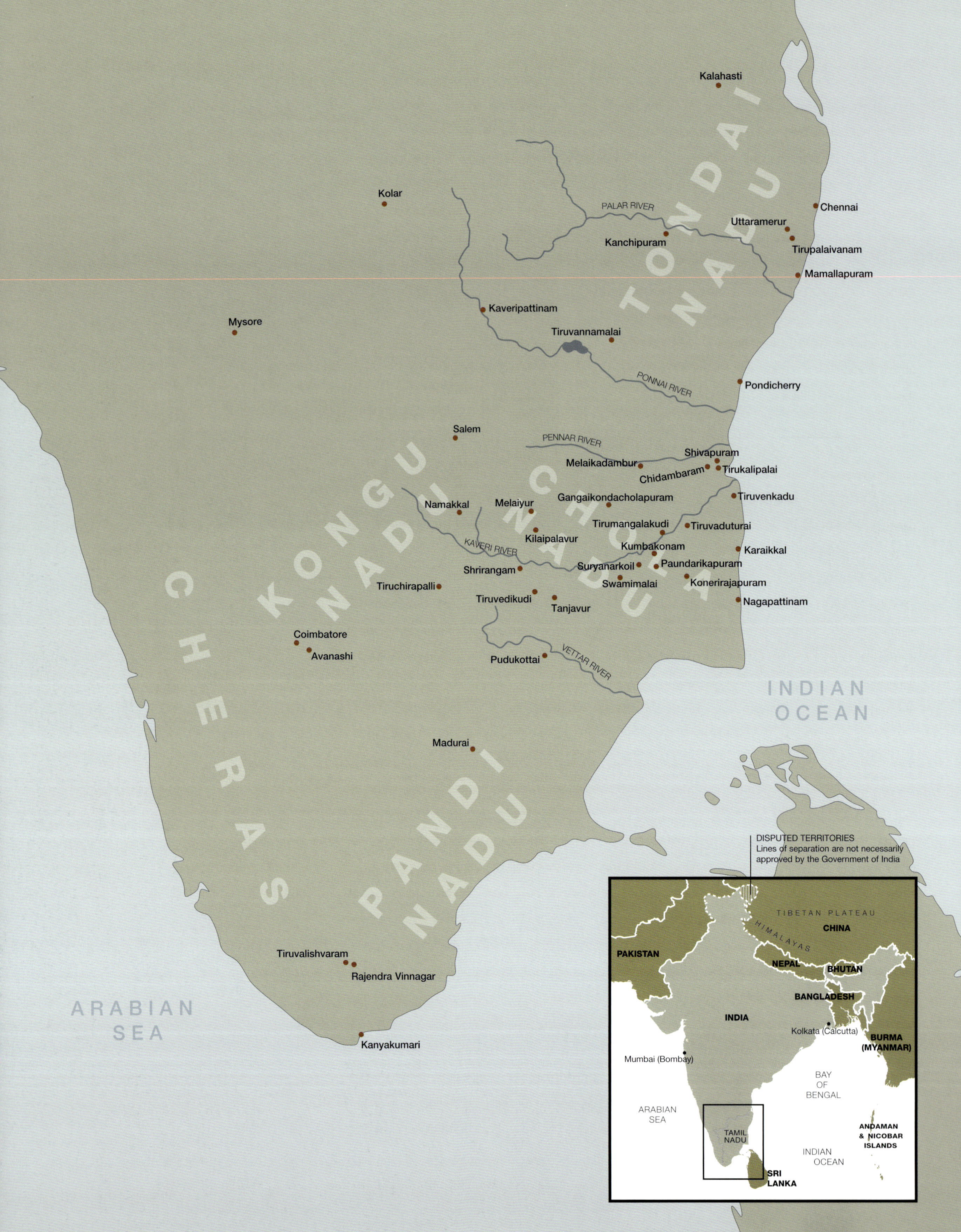

Kalahasti
TONDAI NADU
PALAR RIVER
Chennai
Kolar
Uttaramerur
Kanchipuram
Tirupalaivanam
Mamallapuram
Kaveripattinam
Mysore
Tiruvannamalai
PONNAI RIVER
Pondicherry
Salem
PENNAR RIVER
Shivapuram
Melaikadambur
Chidambaram
Tirukalipalai
KONGU NADU
CHOLA NADU
Tiruvenkadu
Gangaikondacholapuram
Namakkal
Melaiyur
Tirumangalakudi
Tiruvaduturai
Kilaipalavur
KAVERI RIVER
Kumbakonam
Karaikkal
Suryanarkoil
Paundarikapuram
Shrirangam
Swamimalai
Konerirajapuram
Tiruchirapalli
Tiruvedikudi
Tanjavur
Nagapattinam
CHERAS
Coimbatore
Avanashi
Pudukottai
VETTAR RIVER
INDIAN OCEAN
Madurai
PANDI NADU
DISPUTED TERRITORIES
Lines of separation are not necessarily approved by the Government of India
TIBETAN PLATEAU
CHINA
HIMALAYAS
PAKISTAN
NEPAL
BHUTAN
BANGLADESH
INDIA
Kolkata (Calcutta)
BURMA (MYANMAR)
Mumbai (Bombay)
BAY OF BENGAL
ARABIAN SEA
TAMIL NADU
ANDAMAN & NICOBAR ISLANDS
INDIAN OCEAN
SRI LANKA
Tiruvalishvaram
Rajendra Vinnagar
ARABIAN SEA
Kanyakumari

battles against the Chera rulers of Kerala, extended his rule over parts of modern Karnataka, and captured the island of Sri Lanka as a province of the Chola empire. He built temples in his own name in all these areas; for instance, the shrine at Malurpatna near Mysore in Karnataka was named Arulmolishvaram (Lord of Arulmoli), while the temple at Malottam in Sri Lanka, like his Tanjavur temple, was given the name Rajarajeshvara. Sri Lanka was under direct Chola rule for seventy-five years, while Karnataka, specifically the Nolamba region, remained in Chola control for a period of one hundred twenty years. Rajaraja conquered the Maldive Islands in the Indian Ocean and sent missions to the Indonesian Shrivijaya empire. In a magnanimous gesture he encouraged the Shailendra monarch of Java to build a Buddhist monastery at the Chola port of Nagapattinam, gifting the produce of a local village for its maintenance.

CHOLA-MANDALAM AND ITS *NADU* DIVISIONS, CA. 850-1275
FIG. 11

Rajaraja's son Rajendra (r. 1012–44) further consolidated Chola power. He created a Chola viceroyalty in Madurai, appointing his son as the first Chola-Pandya viceregal prince. He next turned his attention northward to the Western Chalukyas and their allies. In a series of campaigns he marched all the way to the river Ganga (Ganges), brought back some of its sacred water in golden pots, emptied these into a tank named Chola-ganga, and assumed the title of Gangai-konda, or Capturer of the Ganges. While it was indeed only Ganges water that Rajendra "captured" and brought back to his new capital—where he built a temple known as Gangai-konda-cholishvaram (Lord of Gangaikonda Chola) (fig. 12)—this was a gesture that clearly held deep significance for the monarch. The Chola relationship with Shrivijaya deteriorated somewhat, and Rajendra sent a naval expedition against the kingdom to enforce acknowledgement of Chola suzerainty. He also sent two diplomatic missions to China.

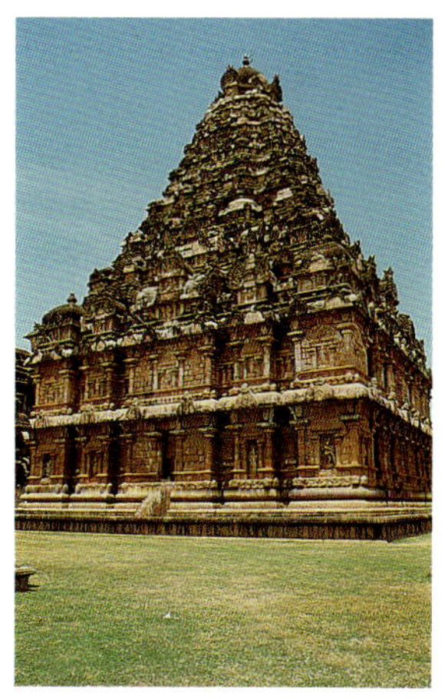

RAJENDRA CHOLA'S TEMPLE AT GANGAIKONDACHOLAPURAM. PHOTO VIDYA DEHEJIA
FIG. 12

In 1070, after three of Rajendra's sons and one grandson had succeeded him, a new line of Chalukya-Cholas was established. The Eastern Chalukya prince Rajendra II (r. 1070–1125), whose mother and grandmother were Chola princesses, ascended the throne assuming the title of Kulottunga (Star of the Dynasty). Although Sri Lanka gained its independence from Chola rule during his reign, trade flourished with Southeast Asia. A Tamil record from Loboe Toewa in Sumatra, dated to 1088, records the activities there of a guild known as the *ayiratti-ainutravar* or the Group of 1500, that was well-known in Chola territory.[21] A Chola embassy was sent once again to China, along with seventy-two merchants, and trade with Shrivijaya was active. Kulottunga renewed the grant of a village for the upkeep of the Shrivijaya Buddhist monastery at Nagapattinam, and in a gesture of appreciation, the Shrivijaya monarch commissioned jewels and temple lamps and presented them to a Nagapattinam Hindu temple in honor of the Chola monarch. Kulottunga seems to have been a charismatic leader, and his reign was one of peace and prosperity. His immediate successors were able leaders, and until the end of the reign of Kulottunga III in 1216, the Chola empire, though not as extensive as in the earlier days of Rajaraja I and Rajendra I, held together well.

By the thirteenth century—with the increasing strength of the Pandya monarchs to the south, and with a group of feudatory chieftains aggressively pursing power—the Chola empire shrank once again to the region around Tanjavur. Finally, when the Chola monarch Rajaraja III died in 1279, Chola territory was easily absorbed into Pandya domain and the dynasty came to an end. A flavor of the fluctuating fortunes of the Chola monarchs emerges from the preamble to royal inscriptions that is the subject of appendix 2.

REGIONAL CHOLA STYLES

Having surveyed the geographical vicissitudes of the Chola empire, it is proper to abandon the inexact word "provincial" I used previously to describe an image that was obviously not sculpted in the heart of the Chola country,[22] and to explore the possibility of perceiving stylistic distinctions between sculptures produced at the center of the Chola empire, i.e., the Kaveri Basin, and those from the three surrounding regions of Tondai-nadu to the north, Kongu-nadu to the west, and Pandi-nadu to the south. Is it feasible to assign a museum bronze from the period of the ninth to the thirteenth centuries, now out of its temple context, to one or the other of these regions? The first step toward understanding any indicative variations is to undertake a stylistic analysis of a Chola bronze image in situ in a typical temple in each of these regions; for this purpose, I have chosen to focus on female imagery, generally an image of the goddess, who is invariably featured in any temple bronze assemblage, but in one instance on a deified woman saint.

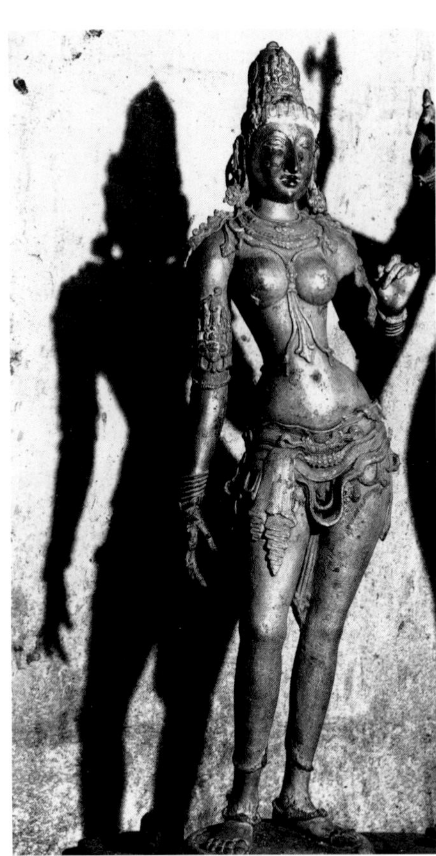

UMA, CA. 969, KONERIRAJAPURAM TEMPLE, CHOLA-NADU. REAR VIEW ON OPPOSITE PAGE
PHOTOS R. NAGASWAMY
FIG. 13

CHOLA-NADU

The Chola heartland, with its early capital at Tanjavur and later at Gangaikondacholapuram, is the stretch of land along the banks of the Kaveri River, the region in which the classic Chola artistic style was born. Bronzes in the temple at Konerirajapuram, some thirty miles east of Tanjavur, and belonging to the year 969 provide a starting point for this regional stylistic analysis.[23] Tall, slender, and of markedly sensuous modeling is an image of Uma (fig. 13), consort of Shiva as Tripuravijaya (Victor of the Three Cities). Her face, a perfect oval, is serene and remote, dignified and assured. A tall crown is placed above her headband. Gently sloping shoulders, long slender arms, softly modeled breasts placed high on her torso, slender calves, and elegant ankles complete the picture of elongated grace. The spread of her gently swelling stomach conveys the illusion of flesh as it contrasts with the details of the rich jewelry that adorns her. But she retains a sense of remote dignity and ethereal majesty. She is gorgeous, but it is impossible to treat her as a mere sensual figure—she has a majesty that alerts the viewer to her sacred status. This bronze reveals a heightened awareness of form, a sense of assurance, and a degree of technical accomplishment that is characteristic of the Chola-nadu style of the late tenth century.

TONDAI-NADU

The Madras region to the north of the Kaveri basin was captured by the second Chola monarch Aditya (r. ca. 871–907), who defeated the armies of the Pallavas of Kanchipuram and claimed all of Tondai-nadu as Chola territory. Aditya retained his interest in this northern region and, in fact, died at Tondaimannar near Kalahasti in the upper reaches of the Tondai region, where his son built him a funerary chapel *(pallippadai)*. Though the kingdom soon shrank into what was merely Chola-nadu, when Rajaraja ascended the throne in 985, he reconquered the Tondai area, which remained a prominent part of the empire when the new line of Chalukya-Cholas, headed by Kulottunga I, established their presence beginning in 1070. Between Tondai-nadu proper and Chola-nadu was a transitional region appropriately called Nadu-nadu (Middle-nadu).

In the Mylapur section of Tondai-nadu's city of Chennai, there stands today—in a modern temple dedicated to Koli Amman (Mother Kali)—a striking bronze image of a four-armed dancing Kali that

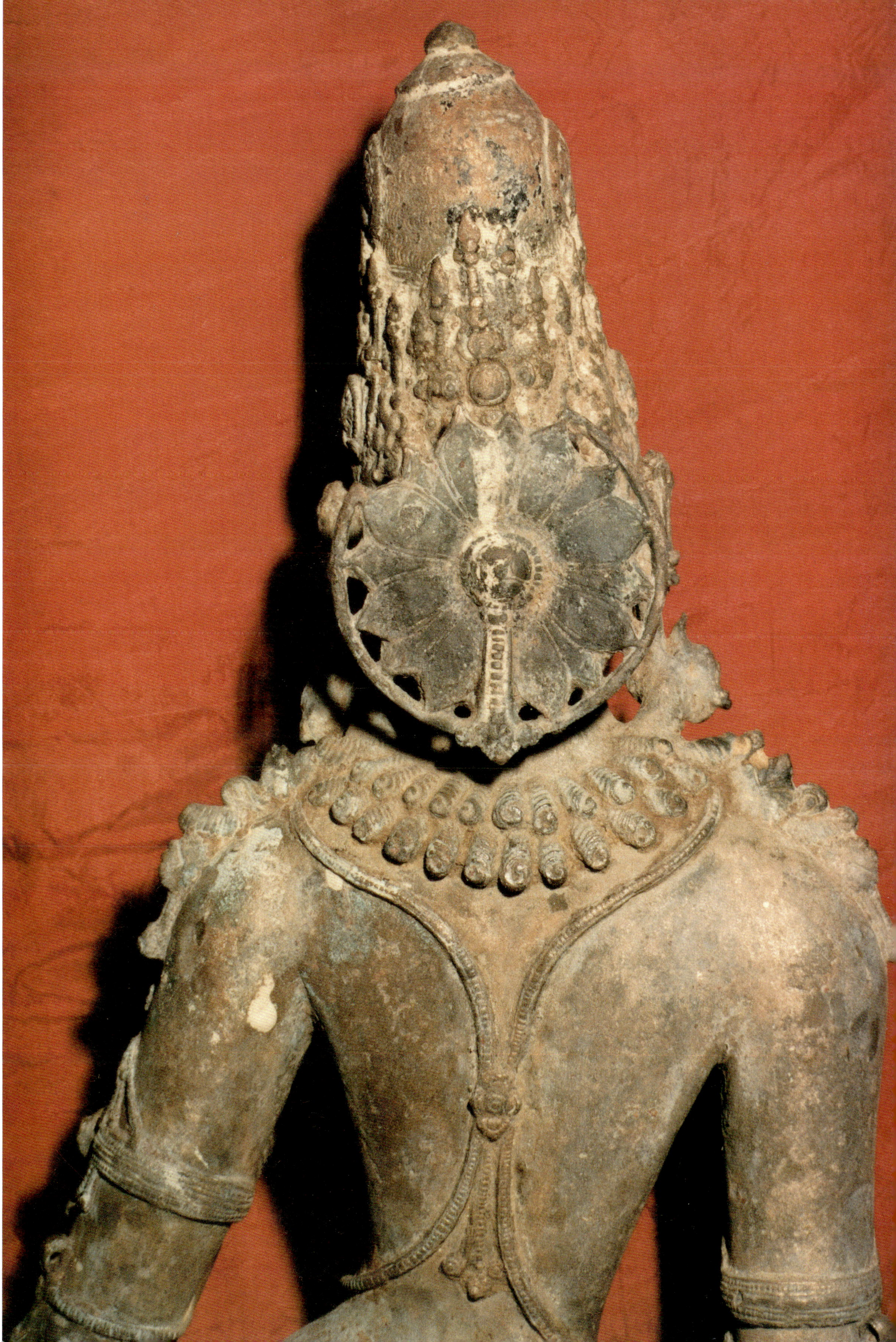

clearly dates to the tenth century (fig. 14). With her locks piled high upon her head, and wearing a breastband consisting of knotted snakes, Kali stands in the *chatura* dancing pose on her bent left foot with the toes of the right foot just touching the ground. Her short skirt, held by an ornamental girdle, is looped and knotted on both sides. Kali holds a *damaru* drum in her proper right rear hand, while her front right hand beckons the viewer; her left rear hand makes the gesture of wonder, and her left front hand moves in the gesture of dance. On examination one earring reveals itself as a human corpse, while a standard ring adorns the other ear. Her rich, jeweled adornment includes, across her chest, a beaded sacred thread, the "beads" of which are actually human skulls.

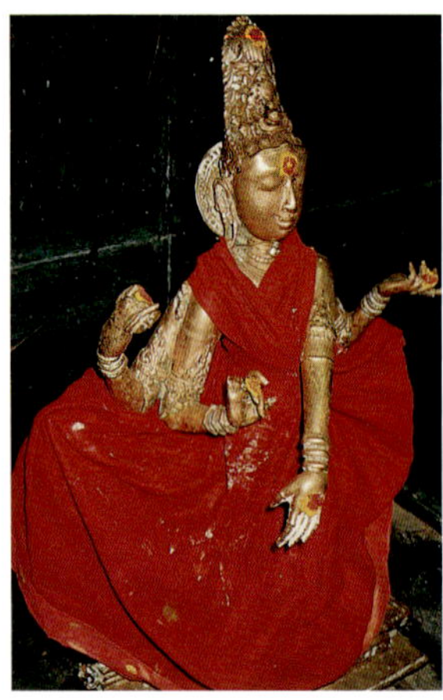

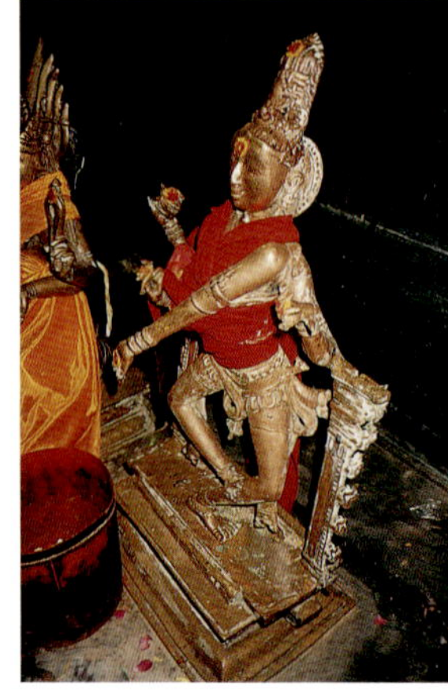

KALI, 10TH CENTURY, KOLI AMMAN TEMPLE, MYLAPURE, TONDAI-NADU
PHOTOS VIDYA DEHEJIA
FIG. 14

A comparison of this Tondai-nadu image of the goddess with the sensuously slender Uma of Chola-nadu's Konerirajapuram (fig. 13) reveals a definite distinction. The Tondai goddess has angular, slight limbs, and small, high breasts that result in a lean slenderness that is artistically distinct from the sensuous, majestic grace of the Chola-nadu figure. While the verbalization of this apparently subjective distinction may sound stretched, the variance is manifestly visible; it is akin to the difference between a budding adolescent and a nubile young woman.

KONGU-NADU

Kongu-nadu, the western region around Coimbatore, was at times in the hands of the Chera rulers of Kerala and at other times part of the Chola empire; the small Karaipottanaru River that runs from the town of Namakkal to join the Kaveri demarcates Kongu from Chola-nadu. The various regions of south India find occasional mention in the poems of the ancient poet-saints; in a poem dedicated to "The Lord who wanders through many a fair town," Appar speaks of Shiva as "He who lives at Kodumudi in Kongu," a temple renowned to this day.[24] Aditya Chola captured Kongu-nadu, but from 1004 onward, at the very height of Chola power, the area was governed by Kongu-Chola princes who were initially Chola governors but later became a line of independent, if subordinate, rulers.

A finely modeled, early-eleventh-century image of Uma from the temple at Avanashi near Coimbatore is a typical Kongu image, with a rounded face, broad nose, full lips, substantial rounded breasts, and a conical crown (fig. 15). A comparison with the Kaveri Delta Uma from Konerirajapuram (fig. 13) highlights the Kongu characteristics of the Avanasi image, which is not as elongated and displays different bodily proportions. Compared with the super-refined Chola-nadu images that rise tall and erect with majestic bearings, Kongu images of the goddess have an earthy touch. Whether male or female, all images from Kongu-nadu display shoulders of an exaggerated width, that barely slope downwards, and are almost parallel to the ground. These features are seen, for instance, in a standing Lakshmi from the Victoria & Albert Museum (cat. no. 42) as well as in a seated Vishnu from the British Museum (cat. no. 39). Female figures, in particular, display strikingly wide shoulders that contrast

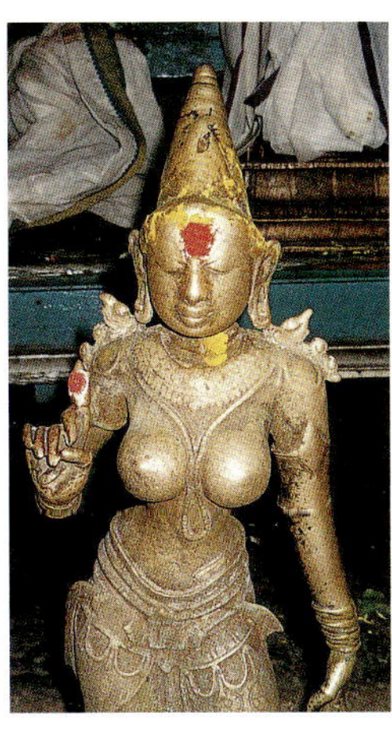

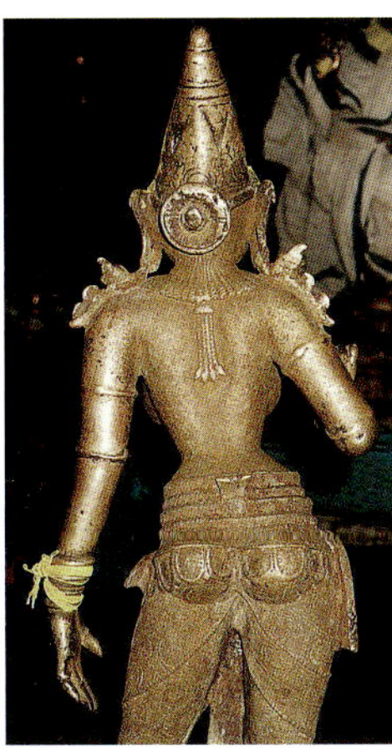

UMA, CA. 1020. AVANASHI TEMPLE, KONGU-NADU
PHOTOS VIDYA DEHEJIA
FIG. 15

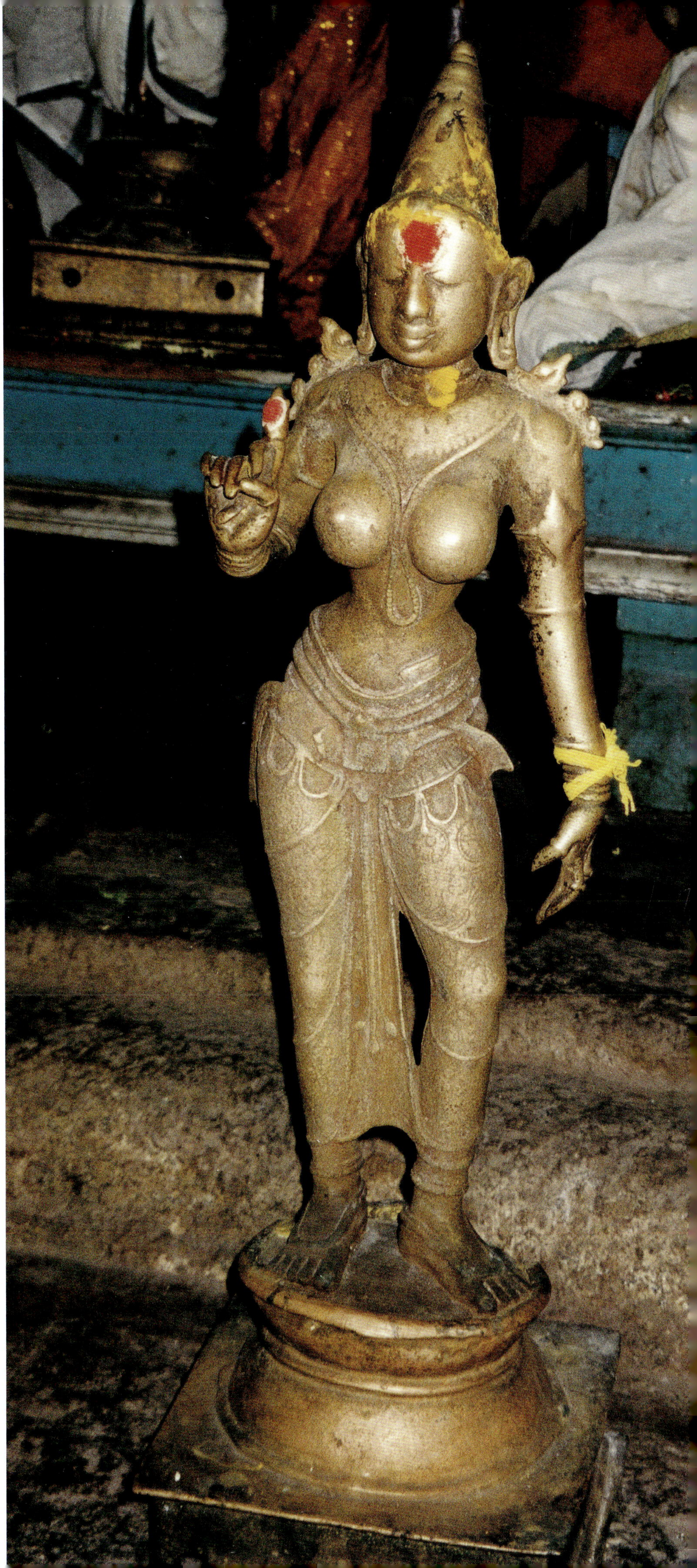

strongly with their narrowed waists and, together with the typical conical crown, enable identification as the work of Kongu craftsmen.[25]

PANDI-NADU

The southern Pandya territory was first captured by Aditya's son Parantaka (r. 907–55), who assumed the title of Maduraikonda or Capturer of Madurai, the Pandya capital. However, in the thirty-year period between the death of Parantaka and the accession of Rajaraja in 985, the Chola kingdom shrank in size so that Rajaraja had once again to conquer Pandi-nadu, which then remained part of the Chola empire for the better part of a century. It slipped out of direct Chola control only after the Chalukya-Cholas, with their more northern preoccupations, took over from the earlier line of Vijayalaya-Cholas in 1070.

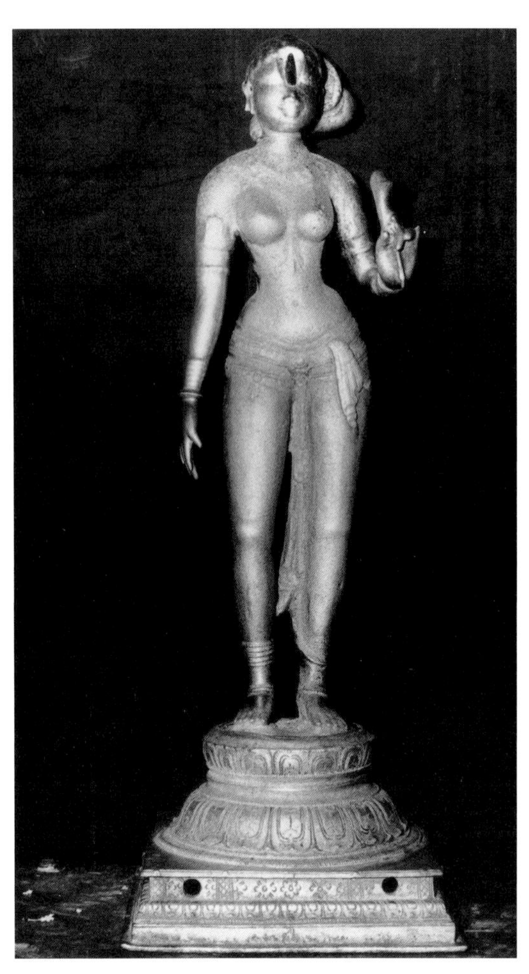

WOMAN-SAINT ANDAL, CA. 1000, RAJENDRA VINNAGAR TEMPLE, PANDI-NADU
PHOTO R. NAGASWAMY
FIG. 16

The modestly sized temple at Tiruvalishvaram, situated west of Tirunelveli in the heart of Pandi-nadu, bears striking similarities to a typical Chola temple, except that the niches along its plain stone walls are "false niches," never intended for the placement of images, as was customary in Chola-nadu. A single level of *shikhara*, topped by a large octagonal *stupi*, is adorned with exquisite little tableaux that feature lithe, elegant figures, closely akin to Chola-nadu imagery, charmingly poised to portray all the favorite myths of Shiva. A series of inscriptions on the temple provides interesting information; one on the sanctum wall tells us it was built by Emperor Rajaraja in his eleventh year (996). It would appear that Rajaraja not only broadcast Chola power across the length and breadth of his kingdom, but also transmitted Chola aesthetics and ideals—as indeed he did also in Karnataka and Sri Lanka. A second Tiruvalishvaram inscription speaks of a military regiment, the Muntukai Mahasenai, that was assigned to protect the temple (in a newly captured region), its treasury, and its servants. Subsequent inscriptions speak of a group of Chola-Pandya princes ruling the area, the dual name having been assigned presumably to persuade acceptance by the local population. The latest inscriptions belong to the Pandya monarchs of the thirteenth century and indicate their resumption of political control of the area.

The bronze image of the woman saint Andal from the Vishnu temple at Rajendra Vinnagar, some three kilometers from Tiruvalishvaram,[26] may be considered an example of the Pandi-nadu style (fig. 16; see also fig. 2). The simplified bodily contours of this image, which is only marginally later than Uma from Konerirajapuram in the heart of Chola-nadu (fig. 13), are striking. Yet, the similarities of the Andal image to the Konerirajapuram Uma, particularly in its elongated proportions, are also noteworthy. It would appear that though the location of the temple itself is in the heart of Pandi-nadu, the artist who sculpted this bronze image was familiar with, and admired, the work produced in the Chola heartland.[27]

This brief and preliminary examination of bronze images from temples in the different geographical regions of the Chola empire highlights the fact that thus far the focus of connoisseurship on Chola bronzes has been on the dating of images and not on their geographical affiliations. Neither have the stone sculptures associated with temples been the subject of a comparable study of regional artistic style (except for labeling them by their physical location), thus eliminating the possibility of assessing, by comparison, bronze and stone images in Kongu, Tondai, and Pandi styles. Into this complex picture must now be introduced the added possibility of royal and nonroyal styles coexisting in any one region, an issue given prominence for the first time by R. Nagaswamy's essay in this volume. The visual material he presents suggests, among other things, the contemporaneous use of differing proportional systems. Of relevance here might be Samuel Parker's observation that a harmonious project (read "image") is one that is integrally connected to the physical body of the patron in one way or another. This relationship, known as *ayati,* could be articulated through a measurement such as the middle joint of the middle finger of the patron's right hand, or a number derived from the patron's astrological chart or numerological system, taken in conjunction with values derived from the deity.[28] These possibilities are indeed pointers toward a major direction for future studies.

NOTES

1 These letters were found in the Cairo Geniza, attached to the synagogue, in which discarded writings that had the name of God on them were stored to protect them from desecration. The letters in question were written by Arabic-speaking Jews, and they give us considerable information on the India trade. See S. D. Goitein, *Letters of Medieval Jewish Traders* (Princeton: Princeton University Press, 1973), pp. 194–95.

2 Vidya Dehejia, *Antal and Her Path of Love: Poems of a Woman Saint from South India* (Albany: State University of New York Press, 1990), p. 113: Nachiyar Tirumoli 10.8 (hymn 10, verse 8).

3 Vidya Dehejia, *Slaves of the Lord: The Path of the Tamil Saints* (New Delhi: Munshiram Manoharlal, 1988), pp. 173–74.

4 Indira Viswanathan Peterson, *Poems to Siva: The Hymns of the Tamil Saints* (Princeton: Princeton University Press, 1989), pp. 184, 185: Appar 4.21.1,8 (Appar, Book IV, hymn 21, verses 1, 8).

5 Peterson, *Poems to Siva,* p. 183: Sambandar 1.71.5.

6 Peterson, *Poems to Siva,* pp. 186–89: Sambandar 2.47.3,6,7,9.

7 Vidya Dehejia, *Art of the Imperial Cholas* (New York: Columbia University Press, 1990), p. 100. Kulottunga's dates have been adjusted due to an epigraphical find that assigns him a reign of 55 years. See R. Nagaswamy's essay in this volume.

8 Paul Younger, *The Home of Dancing Sivan: The Traditions of the Hindu Temple in Citamparam* (New York: Oxford University Press, 1995), pp. 52–54.

9 Peterson, *Poems to Siva,* p. 183: Appar 4.50.2.

10 Vidya Dehejia, "Sculptures from Southern India," *Orientations* (March 1994): 44.

11 *Indian Archaeology—A Review*, 1959–60, p. 54; and *Indian Archaeology – A Review, 1958–59*, p. 8, record the consecration of a wooden image of *ashtabhujasvamin*, and the discovery of a conch shell inscribed with the words *bhagavato ashtabhujasvamin.*

12 E. Hultzsch, ed., *South Indian Inscriptions*, vol. 3 (New Delhi: Archaeological Survey of India, 1992 reprint), part 3, nos. 151, 151A, pp. 300–322.

13 *Madras Epigraphy Report,* 1930–31, inscription no. 36.

14 See, for instance, *Madras Epigraphy Report*, 1916, no. 345, in the Shiva temple at Tiruvalishvaram, dated in the fifth year of Sundara Pandya. It records a gift from the dancing girl Bhuvana Pandi for offerings to an image of Paravai (saint Sundarar's wife and also a dancing girl) that she had donated earlier.

15 Nicholas Dirks, *The Hollow Crown* (Cambridge: Cambridge University Press, 1987), has demonstrated that "no gift was given without reason, intention, and interest" (p. 129).

16 See Dirks, *The Hollow Crown.*

17 N. Sethuraman, "Date of Birth, Date of Coronation, & the Last Day of Raja Chola," in *Rajaraja The Great (Seminar Proceedings)* (Bombay: Ananthacharya Indological Research Institute, 1987), pp. 17–32.

18 S. R. Balasubrahmanyam, *Early Chola Temples: Parantaka I to Rajaraja I, A.D. 907–985* (Bombay: Orient Longman, 1971), p. 225.

19 Among the most useful studies are the following: Burton Stein, *Peasant, State, and Society in Medieval South India* (Delhi: Oxford University Press, 1980); R. Champakalakshmi, *Trade, Ideology, and Urbanization: South India 300 B.C. to A.D. 1300* (Delhi: Oxford University Press, 1996); Kesavan Veluthat, *The Political Structure of Early Medieval South India* (New Delhi: Orient Longman, 1993); Y. Subbarayalu, *Political Geography of the Chola Country* (Madras: State Department of Archaeology, 1973); and Kenneth R. Hall, *Trade and Statecraft in the Age of Colas* (New Delhi: Abhinav, 1980).

20 See Hall, *Trade and Statecraft in the Age of Colas*, especially chapter 4.

21 K. A. Nilakantha Sastri, "A Tamil Merchant Guild in Sumatra," *Tijdschrift voor Indische taal-, land-en volkenkunde* 63, no. 2 (1932): 314–27.

22 Dehejia, *Art of the Imperial Cholas*, p. 84.

23 Ibid., p. 4.

24 Peterson, *Poems to Siva*, p. 151: Appar 4.19.5.

25 While I hesitate to offer a simplistic solution, there could be an obvious explanation for such a distinctive feature. Artists tend to mold figures from what they perceive around them as much as they draw upon their imagination. In this context I would report the reaction of a Tamil woman from the Madras region (ancient Tondai-nadu) who had never traveled beyond her own area. She spoke of her first trip to Coimbatore and her amazement at the local broad-shouldered women!

26 This image is featured on the cover of my book *Antal and Her Path of Love,* where it is erroneously attributed to the temple at Srivilliputtur, also in Pandi-nadu, but somewhat further north. I have since photographed it in situ in the temple at Rajendra Vinnagar.

27 It would also appear that bronzes were taken from one part of the Chola empire to another. For instance, an image of Vishnu attributed to a Pandya artist was found as part of a treasure trove near Nagapattinam in Chola-nadu. See R. Nagaswamy, "Some Contributions of the Pandya to South India Art," *Artibus Asiae* 27, no. 3 (1964–65): 274 and fig. 10.

28 Samuel K. Parker, "Contemporary Temple Construction in South India: The Srirangam Rajagopuram," *Res* 21 (Spring 1992): 113.

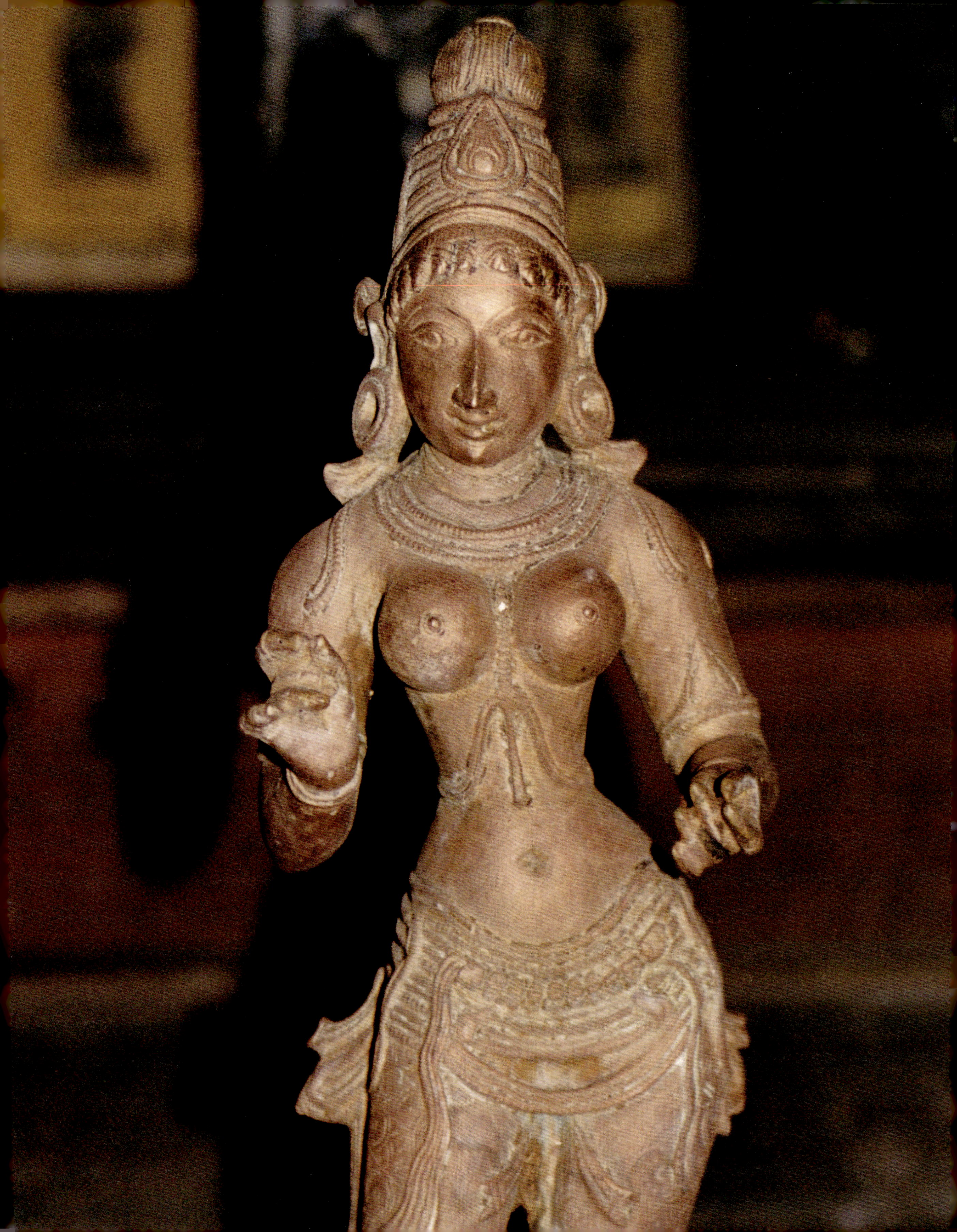

THE BRONZES OF EMPEROR KULOTTUNGA AND HIS SUCCESSORS

R. NAGASWAMY

The age of Kulottunga Chola (1070–1125)[1] marks both the midpoint in the political history of the Chola empire and an important epoch in the field of arts in which the personal touch of the emperor was apparent, as it had been in the earlier glorious age of Rajaraja I (985–1014). Kulottunga's son and successors continued the artistic tradition right up to 1250, when political disintegration and violent changes took place. Although the bronzes of this age of the later Cholas tend to be described vaguely as less refined, a detailed analysis reveals the commission of delicate and aesthetically successful images, particularly of Nataraja (Shiva as Lord of Dance) and his consort Uma, mostly in temples where inscriptions record the immediate involvement of the emperor himself or that of his high officers. Quite a number of these bronzes may be dated through epigraphic records, though in some instances style is still the only recourse. In order to recognize the classical refinement arising out of the emperor's presence, I propose to speak of a royal school that coexisted side by side with other, regional schools representing different village centers. The period covered in this essay extends from 1070 to 1250,[2] with an emphasis on the age of Kulottunga I.

It is of interest to mention here my recent discovery that the spiritual gurus of the Chola emperors, called *rajagurus* or royal gurus,

ATTENDANT GODDESS TO UMA AS TANI AMMAN, EARLY 12TH CENTURY, KULOTTUNGA I ERA, SHIVA TEMPLE, SHIVAPURAM
PHOTO R. NAGASWAMY
FIG. 1

all originally came from either southern Gujarat (then Lata), or Bengal (Gauda).[3] Rajaraja's guru, Ishana Shiva Pandita, and Rajendra's guru, Sarva Shiva Pandita, both perhaps from Lata, were active in temple construction and the donation of bronzes to such shrines. Thus Sarva Shiva Pandita built a Shiva temple at Esalam and requested his monarch Rajendra to issue a land grant for worship at the temple. Rajendra's copper-plate grant recording this gift devotes several verses to the praise of his guru. From the time of Kulottunga onward, *rajagurus* hailed exclusively from Bengal, commencing with Shrikantha Shiva, guru to both Kulottunga and his son Vikrama Chola (r. 1118–35). Elsewhere I have highlighted the superb bronze of dancing Shiva in Kulottunga's temple at Melaikadambur, quite unlike its southern counterpart and clearly an import from the Pala dynasty of Bengal, that may have been a gift to the temple from the Bengali *rajaguru* (fig. 2).[4] On occasion, the actual names of the gurus, as opposed to their honorific titles, give a clear indication of their Bengali origin. Thus Umapati Shiva, guru to Rajadhiraja Chola, was a Ganguli, a typical Bengali name to this day.

BRONZES FROM THE REIGN OF KULOTTUNGA I (1070–1125)

The artistic trends under Kulottunga I cannot be studied without a reference to the contribution of his commander Naralokaviran, a brahmin who served as prime minister and general under both Kulottunga I and Vikrama Chola. Hailing from Arumpakkam, near Chennai (Madras), he was called the chieftain of Tondai-nadu, the northern part of the Chola empire. His other titles include chief of Mylapur, today the center of the modern city of Chennai, and chief of Manavil, also near Chennai. Naralokaviran commanded the Chola army in wars against the Pandyas and Cheras in the extreme south, and in Vengi to the north (a part of eastern Andhra), gaining outstanding victories for Kulottunga I. Among his conquests, Kalinga (Orissa) is also prominently mentioned; it is not known whether Naralokaviran's title of *Kalingar ko* (chief of Kalinga) was assumed because he originally hailed from Kalinga, or whether he received it as a title for his signal victory over Kalinga.

Besides his conquests, Naralokaviran deserves to be remembered for his contribution to temple arts, especially bronzes. His most significant gifts are recorded in inscriptions at Chidambaram, where he consecrated a number of bronzes, several of which can be identified with images found in an underground hiding place, and now in locked storage within the temple. He was specially attached to the form of dancing Shiva, and in a number of places, including Chidambaram, Tiruvadigai, Tirupulivanam, and Siddhalingavadam, he made special gifts of Nataraja images.

Naralokaviran's contribution to Chidambaram merits discussion. His inscriptions there include a number of verses that seem to have been taken from a lengthy poetic composition dedicated to him. Naralokaviran consecrated a metal image of Nandikeshvara, (not Nandi, Shiva's bull vehicle), in human form with four hands; the two front hands have palms joined in the *anjali* gesture, while the rear ones hold axe and antelope.[5] Nandikeshvara is accompanied by his wife. Naralokaviran also set up a metal image of Patanjali in half-human and half-snake form.[6] Another dedication was a golden bull, to serve as the mount upon which the image of Shiva as the Enchanting Mendicant (Bhikshatana) was to be taken out in procession; the image now in the temple collection is the one referred to in the record.[7] Besides these three bronzes, a few more at Chidambaram may be assigned to the age of Kulottunga I, and one such is a fine image of child-saint Sambandar.[8] Naralokaviran's inscription mentions that he set up an image of Sambandar (referred to as Kumara or young one) and that he also built a shrine for this child-

DANCING SHIVA, BENGAL, PALA DYNASTY (8TH–12TH CENTURIES), NOW IN THE AMRITAGHATESHVARA TEMPLE, MELAIKADAMBUR, BUILT BY KULOTTUNGA I IN 1110
PHOTO R. NAGASWAMY
FIG. 2

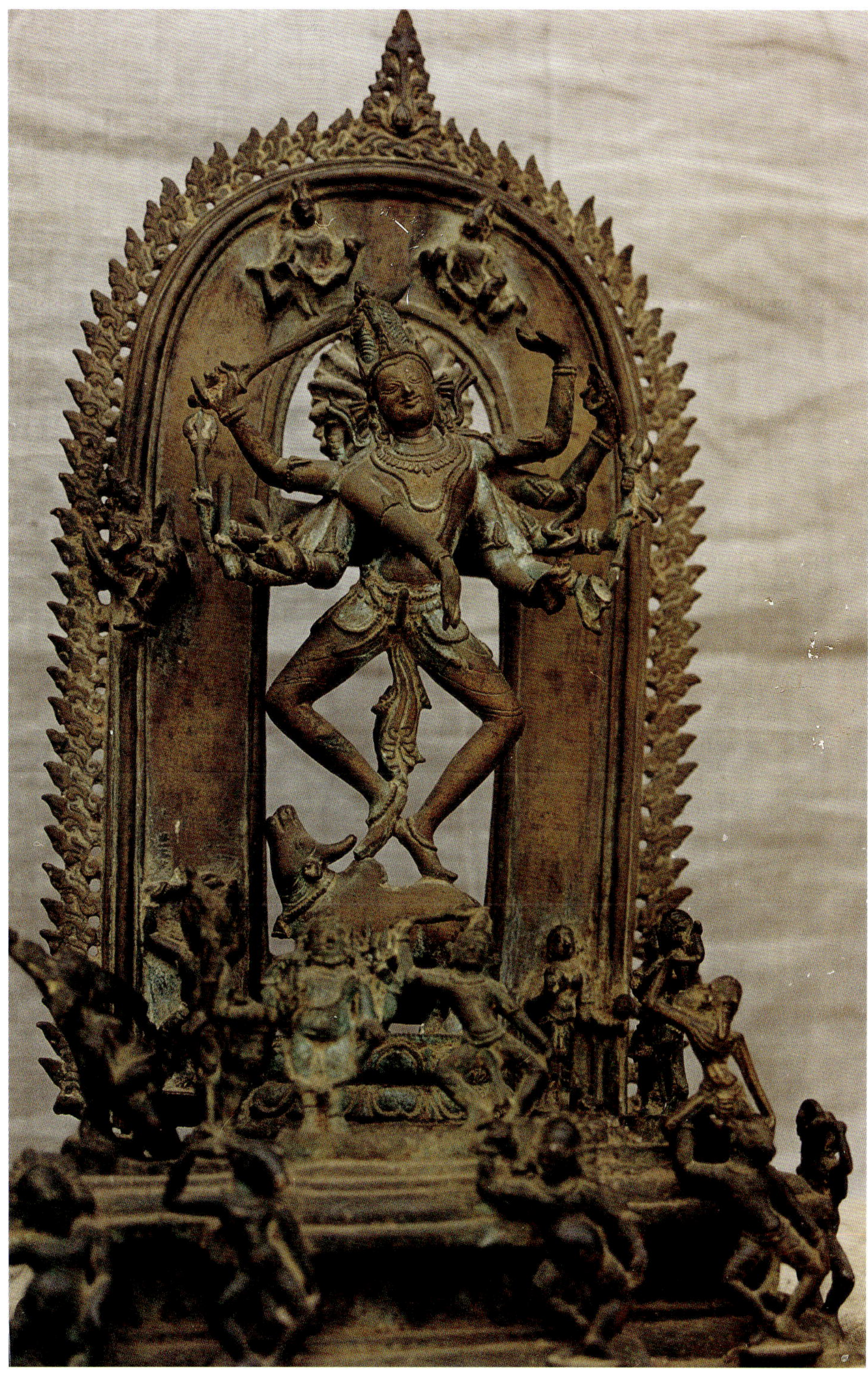

saint, covered it with gold, and arranged for the daily recitation of Sambandar's hymns, called *Kumarasthava* (the young one's praise) in the inscribed record.

Naralokaviran's inscriptions further mention his extensive contributions to the temple of Atikai Virattanam, in particular his gift of an image of Nataraja and his consort. A Nataraja bronze found beneath the *mandapa* in front of the main shrine at that temple is stylistically assignable to this age, and may be the one mentioned by Naralokaviran.[9] Bronzes associated with Naralokaviran constitute an important stylistic touchstone for firmly dating bronzes of the age of Kulottunga I.

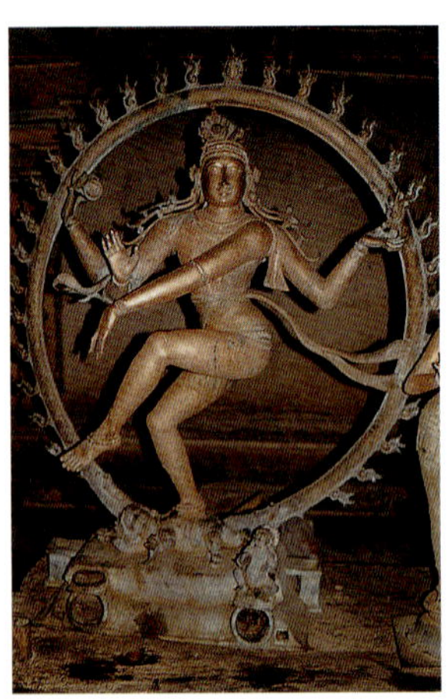

SHIVA AS LORD OF DANCE, NATARAJA 1 OF TIRUMANGALAKUDI, EARLY 12TH CENTURY, CHOLA DYNASTY, KULOTTUNGA I ERA, PURANA VITANKAR TEMPLE, TIRUMANGALAKUDI
PHOTO R. NAGASWAMY
FIG. 3

TIRUMANGALAKUDI

Tirumangalakudi is a small village near Kumbakonam on the northern bank of the Kaveri River. Its main Shiva temple was sung of by the saints Appar and Sambandar, both of whom address the deity as the primordial lord or *adippiran*. The earliest inscription found on the temple is that of Kulottunga, and it speaks of the deity as *purana vitankar* (ancient beauteous lord). There are two inscriptions on the temple of special historic interest. Toward the end of Kulottunga's reign, his Bengali *rajaguru* Shrikantha built a temple, named Kulottunga-cholishvaram after the emperor, to ensure the monarch's good health; Kulottunga was at this time of advanced age. A land grant dated to the following year makes provision for services and worship in the temple. A record dated in the reign of Kulottunga III, to around 1200, refers to continuing gifts to the temple.

The Tirumangalakudi temple houses a number of bronze images for processional ritual, among which are two images of dancing Shiva accompanied by his consort. For convenience, I will call the finer one Nataraja 1 and the other Nataraja 2. The Natarajas are almost identical except in some minor details. Thus Nataraja 1 (fig. 3) has an absolutely circular *prabha* (aureole), while in the other (fig. 5), the circle of the *prabha* issues from the mouth of *makaras* (mythical crocodile-like creatures) that rise up about nine inches, giving the *prabha* an oval appearance. Nataraja 1 and his consort are superb pieces of art with smooth and flowing lines. The matted locks on either side of Shiva's face hang below the shoulders at the back, and the crane feathers on his head are slightly tilted to the right of the centerline (see also detail on p. 90). The head faces directly to the front, and the fire in the upper-left hand is held in the tips of the fingers. The rim of the *prabha* is narrow, as are the flames issuing from its fringe, so that the *prabha* takes a subordinate role and does not distract from the beauty of the face. Gentleness is coupled with grandeur in this fine Nataraja. The dwarf beneath the foot of Shiva has his head on the ground. Originally there were *ganas* (Shiva's dwarfish attendants) on either side, but only the one on the left alone remains, playing cymbals. The accompanying image of Uma (Parvati) (fig. 4) is delightful and perfectly modeled. In terms of aesthetic quality, it is a superlative bronze that pulsates from delicate fashioning, with a gentle tilt of the head, a serene expression on the face, an evocative hand gesture, and a relaxed stance, all making it a pièce de résistance of Kulottunga's age (see also fig. 2 on p. 130). Each turn or bend of the body of this fine bronze is from the dexterous hands of a master craftsman. There is no *prabha* provided for this Uma; presumably there was one on its pedestal which is now lost.

Nataraja 2 (fig. 5) of the same temple is closely similar. Shiva's head turns slightly to the left, and river goddess Ganga (Ganges) appears in a loop of the lowest of his matted locks. The god's chin is a little more emphasized than in the other image. The dwarf lying beneath the dancing foot raises his head to look at the snake in his hand. The accompanying figure of Uma as Shivakami (fig. 6) is provided with

UMA AS SHIVAKAMI, CONSORT OF NATARAJA 1 OF TIRUMANGALAKUDI, EARLY 12TH CENTURY, KULOTTUNGA I ERA, PURANA VITANKAR TEMPLE, TIRUMANGALAKUDI
PHOTO R. NAGASWAMY
FIG 4

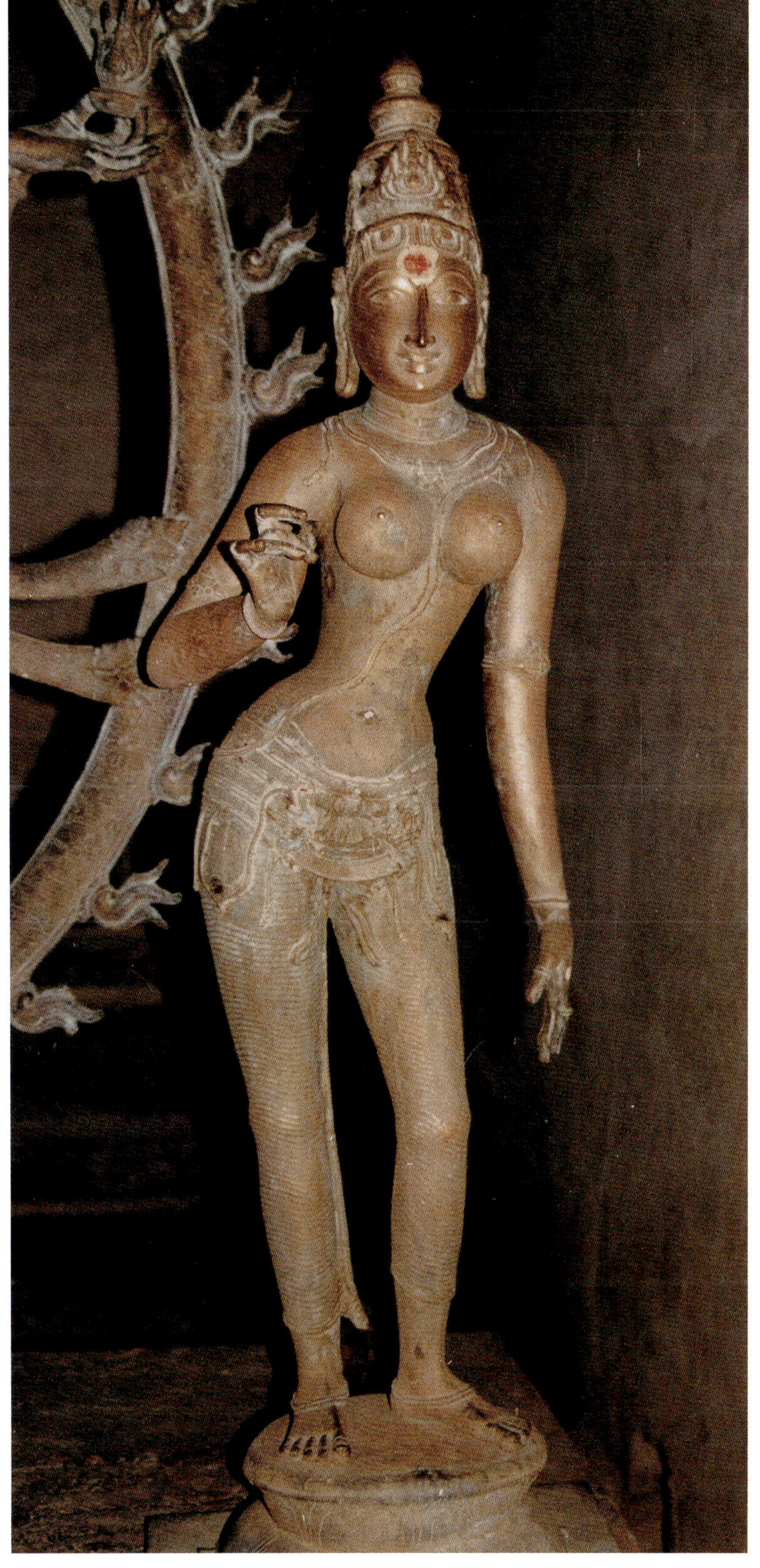

NATARAJA 2 OF TIRUMANGALAKUDI, EARLY 12TH CENTURY, KULOTTUNGA I ERA, PURANA VITANKAR TEMPLE, TIRUMANGALAKUDI
PHOTO R. NAGASWAMY
FIG. 5

UMA AS SHIVAKAMI, CONSORT OF NATARAJA 2 OF TIRUMANGALAKUDI, EARLY 12TH CENTURY, KULOTTUNGA I ERA, PURANA VITANKAR TEMPLE, TIRUMANGALAKUDI
PHOTO R. NAGASWAMY
FIG. 6

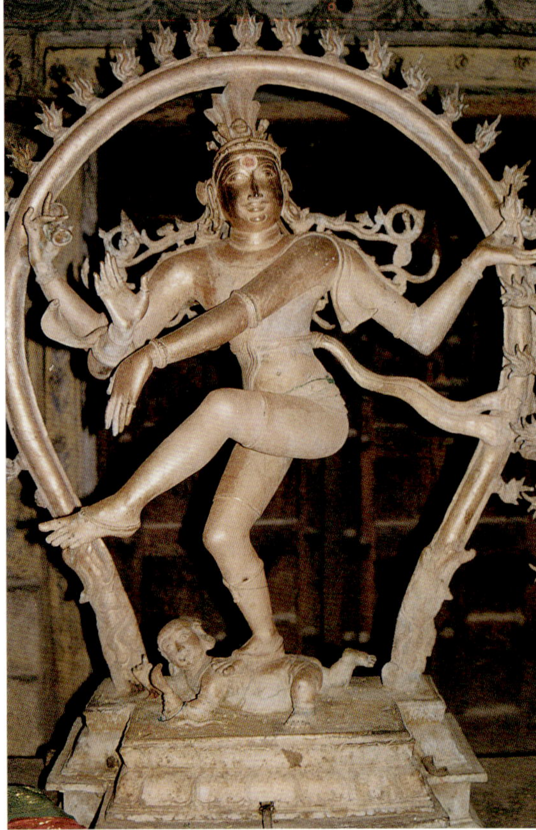

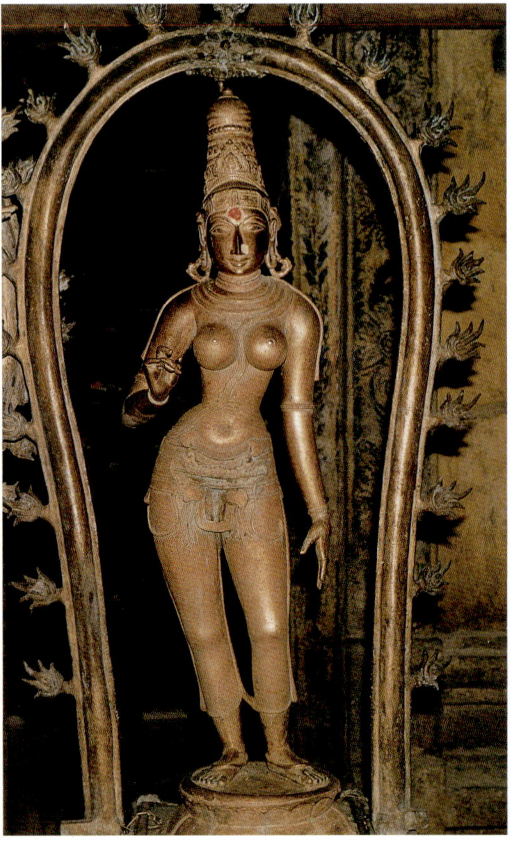

a *prabha*, and is modeled with less movement than the previous example. In the presence of the first group, these figures seem to take a back seat in quality. And yet there is no possibility of them being substantially removed in time from the first, the variation being only in artistic quality. Possibly Nataraja 1 and his consort were commissioned (from the royal workshop) for the Kulottunga-cholishvaram temple built by the *rajaguru* to honor the emperor, while Nataraja 2 and his consort were produced (by a local workshop) for the Tirumangalakudi Purana Vitankar temple.

A fine Somaskanda group (see fig. 1 on p. 128) and an Uma as Tani Amman (also called Adip-pooram Amman) are assignable to the same age. An arresting little bronze of Ganesha is also of the high Kulottunga style (see fig. 1 on p. 140).

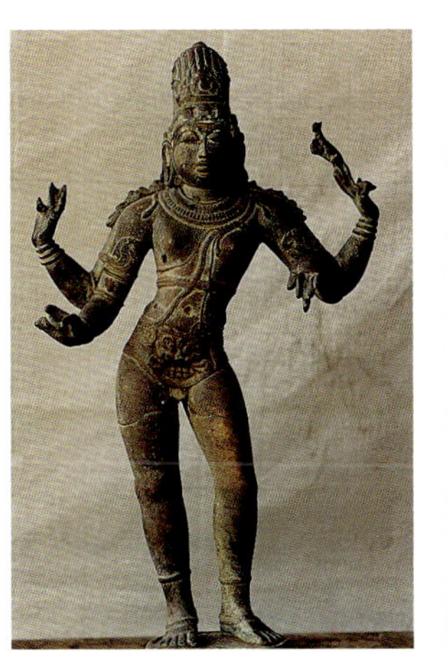

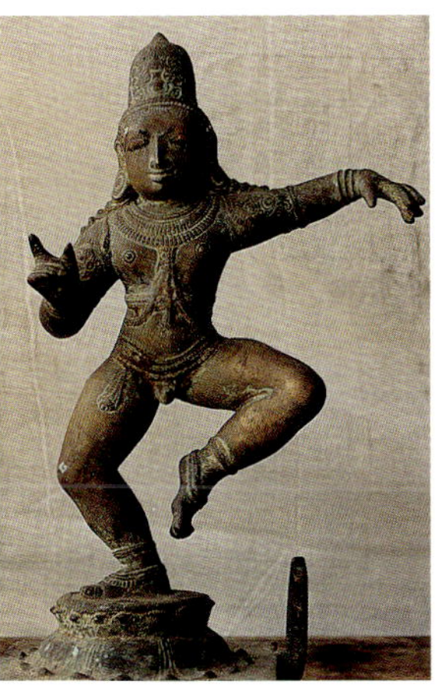

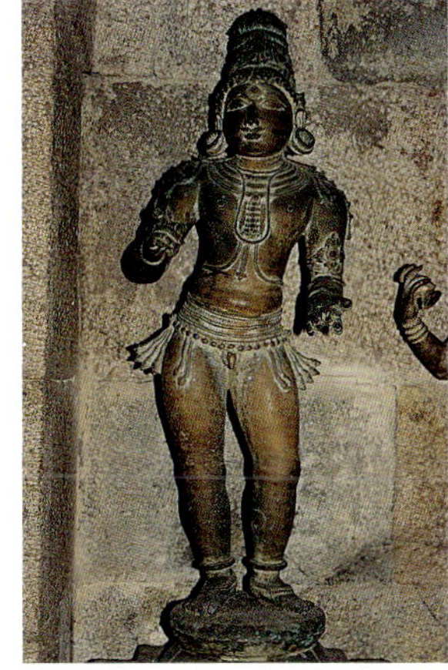

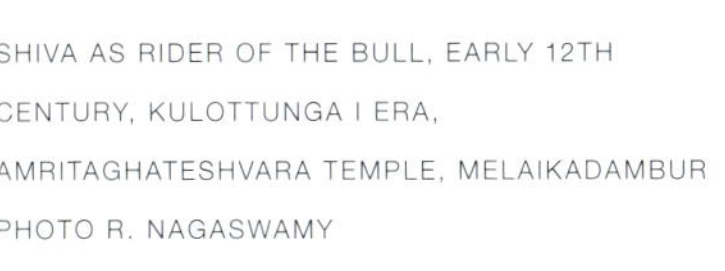

SHIVA AS RIDER OF THE BULL, EARLY 12TH CENTURY, KULOTTUNGA I ERA, AMRITAGHATESHVARA TEMPLE, MELAIKADAMBUR
PHOTO R. NAGASWAMY
FIG. 7

DANCING SAMBANDAR, EARLY 12TH CENTURY, KULOTTUNGA I ERA, AMRITAGHATESHVARA TEMPLE, MELAIKADAMBUR
PHOTO R. NAGASWAMY
FIG. 8

STANDING SAMBANDAR, EARLY 12TH CENTURY, KULOTTUNGA I ERA, AMRITAGHATESHVARA TEMPLE, MELAIKADAMBUR
PHOTO R. NAGASWAMY
FIG. 9

MELAIKADAMBUR

Melaikadambur is a unique and entrancing temple built in the form of a chariot on wheels, drawn by horses. Though the temple was celebrated in the seventh-century *Tevaram* hymns as *karakkoil* (stone temple), that early form has not survived. The first record on the temple walls belongs to Kulottunga I, dated to 1110, and its sculptural style also affirms that it is a Kulottunga foundation. There are some remarkable Chola bronzes in the temple, including an Ardhanari and a Bhikshatana of superb workmanship,[10] that are the products of the royal school. However, we will concentrate here on certain other Chola bronzes, including Shiva as Rider of the Bull (Vrishabhavahana) (fig. 7) and a dancing Sambandar (fig. 8), that are clearly products of a regional atelier. Compared with the exquisite royal Nataraja 1 of Tirumangalakudi, or the delicate Ardhanari and Bhikshatana at Melaikadambur, these images exhibit a certain rigidity and seem to be the work of artists who followed a somewhat different scheme of proportions. These bronzes of a local idiom perhaps postdate the royal images by a few years. An exercise in comparison between the work of the local (fig. 8) and the royal schools (fig. 9) is provided by comparing Melaikadambur's dancing Sambandar with its standing Sambandar; the differences in their proportional systems and the quality of their workmanship is striking.

UTTARAMERUR

The Subrahmanya temple at Uttaramerur, near Chennai, has an exquisite Nataraja and consort of the age of Kulottunga. The Nataraja is about three and a half feet in height, and is a perfect specimen (fig. 10) in both form and expression. The pose of the legs, hands, and head, and the balance achieved in the portrayal, make it one of the finest images of Nataraja to be assigned to the early years of Kulottunga, when the classical touch of the early Chola age was still in evidence. In terms of the rhythm of dance, the lifted leg is just level with the waist, the bend of the foreleg is smooth and fine, neither too close to the body nor too far in the front, making it an aesthetically successful image. The two front arms, one poised before the body and the other with hand in the gesture of protection, are in absolute symmetry, and the two rear hands hold the *damaru* drum and the fire, here in a cup. Some Nataraja bronzes have their matted locks spread out to either side, with intervening rows of flower garlands, which sometimes distract the viewer's attention from the face. But in this case, the locks are lowered, almost beneath the shoulders at the back. The smiling, rounded face results in a charming figure that recalls saint Appar's poem:

> *This mortal life too is worth living*
> *If only I could behold, Oh Lord of Dance!*
> *The enchanting smile on thy face*[11]

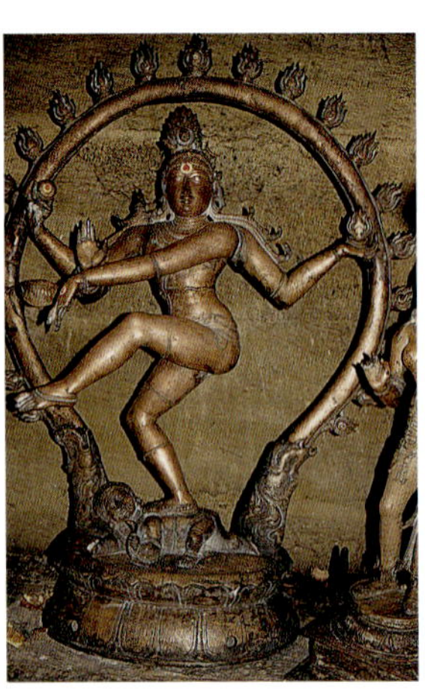

NATARAJA, LATE 11TH CENTURY, KULOTTUNGA I ERA, SUBRAHMANYA TEMPLE, UTTARAMERUR
PHOTO R. NAGASWAMY
FIG. 10

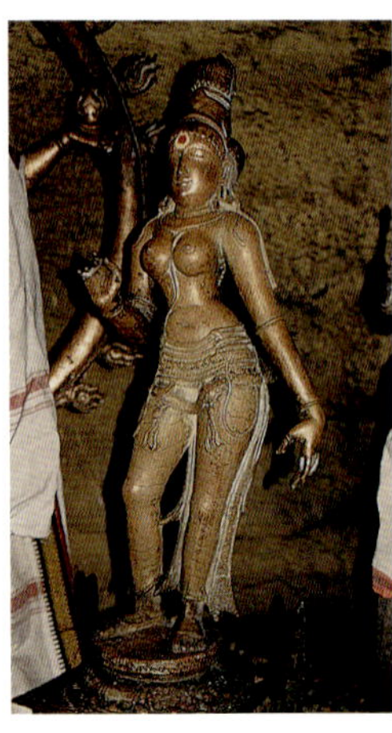

UMA AS SHIVAKAMI, LATE 11TH CENTURY, KULOTTUNGA I ERA, SUBRAHMANYA TEMPLE, UTTARAMERUR
PHOTO R. NAGASWAMY
FIG. 11

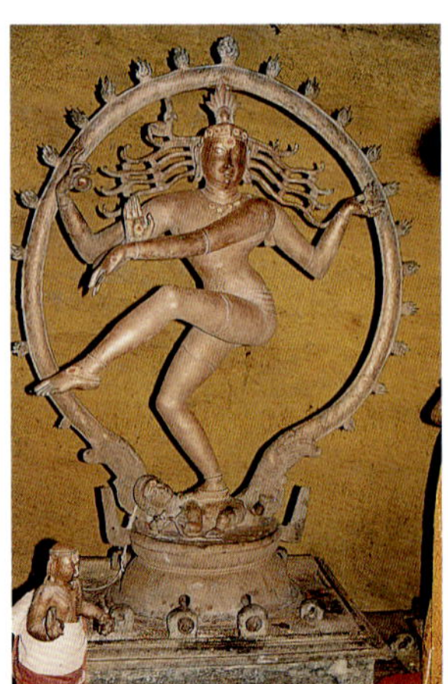

NATARAJA, EARLY 12TH CENTURY, KULOTTUNGA I ERA, SHIVA TEMPLE, TIRUPALAIVANAM
PHOTO R. NAGASWAMY
FIG. 12

Sekkilar, the minister to the Chola monarch Kulottunga II, sang this of the effect of seeing Shiva dance:

> *The faculties of perceptions, all*
> *Converge on the eyes, to behold*
> *The charm of the Dance of Lord*
> *Even as the mind is drowned in the waves of joy*
> *The very acme of immeasurable delight.*[12]

One must remember that when this image was made, the emotional and poetic ethos echoing on the temple premises would have had an electrifying impact on the artist. The feathers, arranged in a fan-shape above his locks, tilt to the right, creating the impression of a gentle turn to the head. Goddess Ganga, peeping out from the matted locks above the right shoulder, is counterbalanced by a serpent on the left. The crescent of the moon, resembling that of the third day of the bright fortnight, is a gem of an ornament. The aureole surrounding the figure issues from the mouth of the *makaras* and then forms a circle. The accompanying Uma (fig. 11) is a fitting consort, and the image undoubtedly came from the hand of the same artist. Her headdress consists of locks of hair raised as a crown, while curls are arranged to frame the face. The lively lines of the body, well-proportioned limbs, evocative glance, and position of the legs make it a memorable creation. A double *makara* clasp fastens the waistband, and an elegant chain, issuing from the mouth of the clasp, falls against each thigh as a loop.

In a number of temples dedicated to Shiva's son Subrahmanya (Skanda), metal images of Nataraja receive regular worship in festivals, and the Agamic texts confirm that the worship of Nataraja in Subrahmanya temples is a well-known tradition. Kulottunga's contribution to Uttaramerur is known through several inscriptions.[13] The Vaikuntaperumal temple in the center of the village, originally an assembly hall, was rebuilt as a Vishnu temple and called Chola-Narayana-Vinnagar after one of the emperor's titles. This rebuilding drew Kulottunga's attention to the site, and he rebuilt in stone, and on a large scale, a Shiva temple in Tirupulivanam, a hamlet of Uttaramerur.[14] The presence of the bronze Nataraja and consort of the Kulottunga I period in its Subrahmanya temple is in conformity with the history of the town. It should also be mentioned that Naralokaviran gifted gold for burning perpetual lamps in the shrine of Nataraja at Tirupulivanam in the year 1115, during Kulottunga's reign.[15]

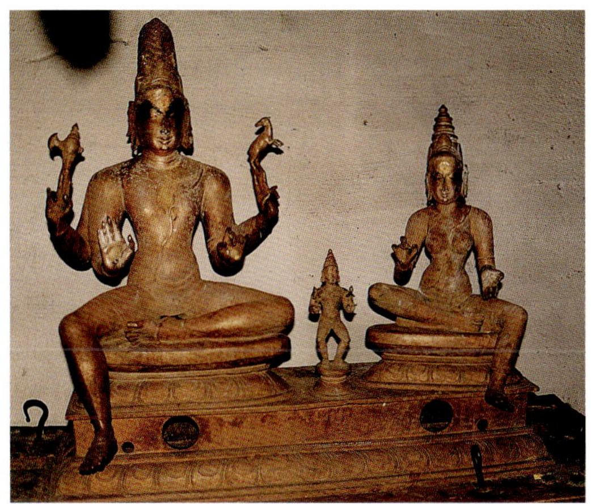

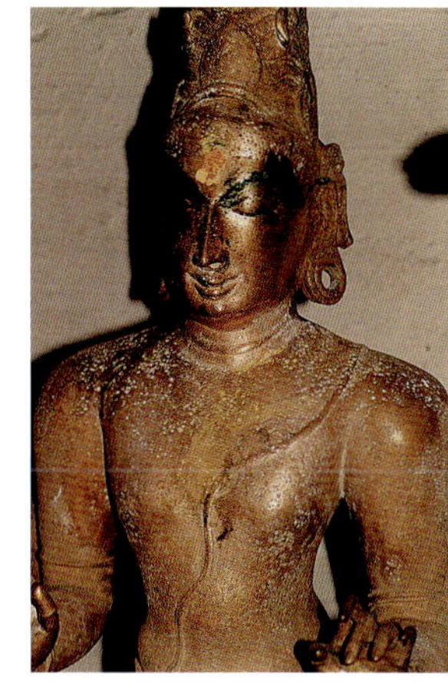

SOMASKANDA AND SHIVA, EARLY 12TH CENTURY,
KULOTTUNGA I ERA, SHIVA TEMPLE, TIRUPALAIVANAM
PHOTOS R. NAGASWAMY
FIG. 13

TIRUPALAIVANAM

The apsidal granite Shiva temple at Tirupalaivanam has a large number of inscriptions on its walls, mostly belonging to the time of Kulottunga III. However the earliest record, that of Vikrama Chola, speaks of a gift to the temple and not its construction[16]; clearly, the temple had come into existence in the time of Kulottunga I. Three bronzes in worship in the temple belong to the period of Kulottunga I and were apparently consecrated when the temple was built. A four-foot high Nataraja (fig. 12) is modeled in the same tradition as the dancing Shiva at Uttaramerur (fig. 10) except that here Shiva's matted locks are spread on either side and goddess Ganga appears in a prominent position. This dancing Shiva lacks the usual scarf that flies out from the waist. The Nataraja, together with its *prabha* and base plate, was clearly fitted at a later date onto the lotus and lower pedestal from another image, as this pedestal has prongs to receive a *prabha*. The local populace reports that the accompanying figure of the goddess Uma was stolen some years back; clearly a remarkable bronze has been lost. Of the same date is a Somaskanda (Shiva with Uma and Skanda) of impressive size (fig. 13). Shiva is very simply rendered with minimum ornamentation and jewels, but the treatment of face, lips, and limbs, and the dignified pose leave no doubt of its age, and the same is the case with Uma. A third bronze at the temple that is a classic piece of Kulottunga's age is a standing image of the goddess as Tani Amman.

TIRUVAVADUTURAI

Tiruvavaduturai is an important Shiva center that attracted attention by the seventh century, as evidenced by the poems of saint Appar. During the eleventh century, prior to the accession of Kulottunga I, the temple received great *rajagurus* during the reigns of Rajendra Chola I (r. 1012–44) and Rajadhiraja I (r. 1018–54). A superlative tenth-century bronze of Nataraja (fig. 14) testifies to the importance of the temple in the early Chola period. From the temple at Tiruvavaduturai comes a classic piece of the age of Kulottunga I, an image of Shiva with the goddess as Alingana Chandrashekhara (also called Pradoshamurti) that is about three feet in height (fig. 15). The exquisite treatment of the faces and the majesty of the portrayal in both figures reveal the hand of a royal artist.[17] The delicate oval faces and proportionally tall headgear lead us to conclude that they are of high Kulottunga style. Inscriptions of Kulottunga and his son Vikrama Chola reveal that from the beginning of his rule almost till his death Kulottunga took a personal interest in this temple, making donations and providing exemption from taxes.[18] A point of interest is the fact that three commanders under the Cholas, who all bore the title of *anantapala* (revealing their connection with Bengal's Pala dynasty) made major contributions to this temple during this period. It is not unlikely that the bronze Alingana Chandrashekhara was made during this phase of activity.

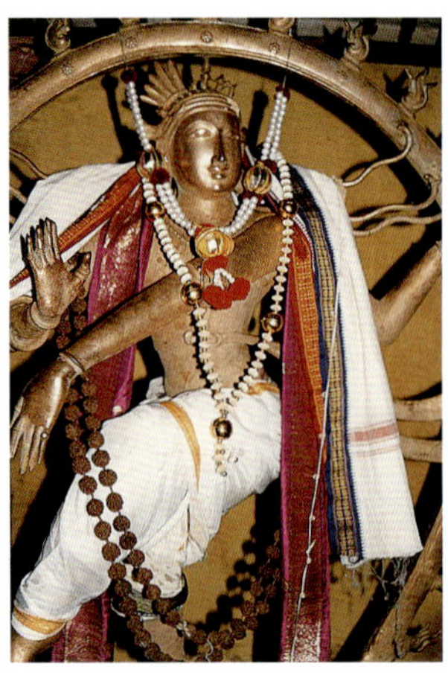

PARTIALLY ADORNED NATARAJA, 10TH CENTURY, EARLY CHOLA PERIOD, SHIVA TEMPLE, TIRUVAVADUTURAI
PHOTO R. NAGASWAMY
FIG. 14

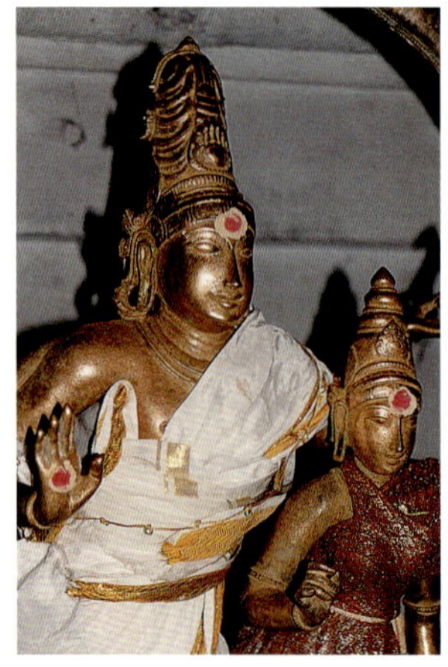

ALINGANA CHANDRASHEKHARA, EARLY 12TH CENTURY, KULOTTUNGA I ERA, SHIVA TEMPLE, TIRUVAVADUTURAI
PHOTO R. NAGASWAMY
FIG. 15

Of similar age is a Somaskanda group, with Skanda dancing between his parents, who are seated in quiet dignity. The faces of Shiva and Uma are less elongated, but nevertheless similar to those of the Alingana Chandrashekhara. An image of the goddess as Tani Amman, standing on a pedestal and encircled by a *prabha,* is of the same quality as the Somaskanda and has a face akin to that of Uma of the Alingana Chandrashekhara group; it clearly belongs to the Kulottunga I period. There are provisions on the pedestal to receive two attendant goddesses, one on either side, but both are missing today. Many temples in this region have Uma bronzes flanked by attendant goddesses (see Shivapuram below). It is important to note that small-scale figures of goddesses, whether in the Chidambaram group of bronzes or elsewhere, fulfill this attendant role not hitherto noticed.

SHIVAPURAM

Shivapuram, a small village near Chidambaram, is an ancient center celebrated in the *Tevaram* hymns of the Shaivite saints. Among the temple's bronzes, a Somaskanda, an Uma with attendant goddesses, and a saint Chandesha are of special interest. The Somaskanda image, with Uma sitting close to Shiva and the child Skanda dancing between but behind them, is a fine image displaying the features characteristic of the age of Kulottunga (fig. 16). The standing bronze of goddess Uma as Tani Amman (fig. 17) is also of the same school. Of utmost interest are the two flanking attendant goddesses that are half the size of Uma (fig. 1 on p. 28). Both standing goddesses are delicately modeled and stand in *tribhanga* (triple-bend) pose, with one hand poised to hold a flower and the other open to hold an ornamental jewel box for the goddess. Religious texts, hymns, and prayers describe the goddesses Sarasvati and Lakshmi as attendants of Uma who assist her in beautifying herself with jewels. A look at the exquisite modeling of these images suggests their placement around the year 1100; these two remarkable pieces, perfectly in Kulottunga idiom, are true gems. A bronze of Chandesha (fig. 18) has a certain rigidity, but its square face is similar to that of the standing Uma.

SOMASKANDA, EARLY 12TH CENTURY, KULOTTUNGA I ERA,
SHIVA TEMPLE, SHIVAPURAM
PHOTO R. NAGASWAMY
FIG. 16

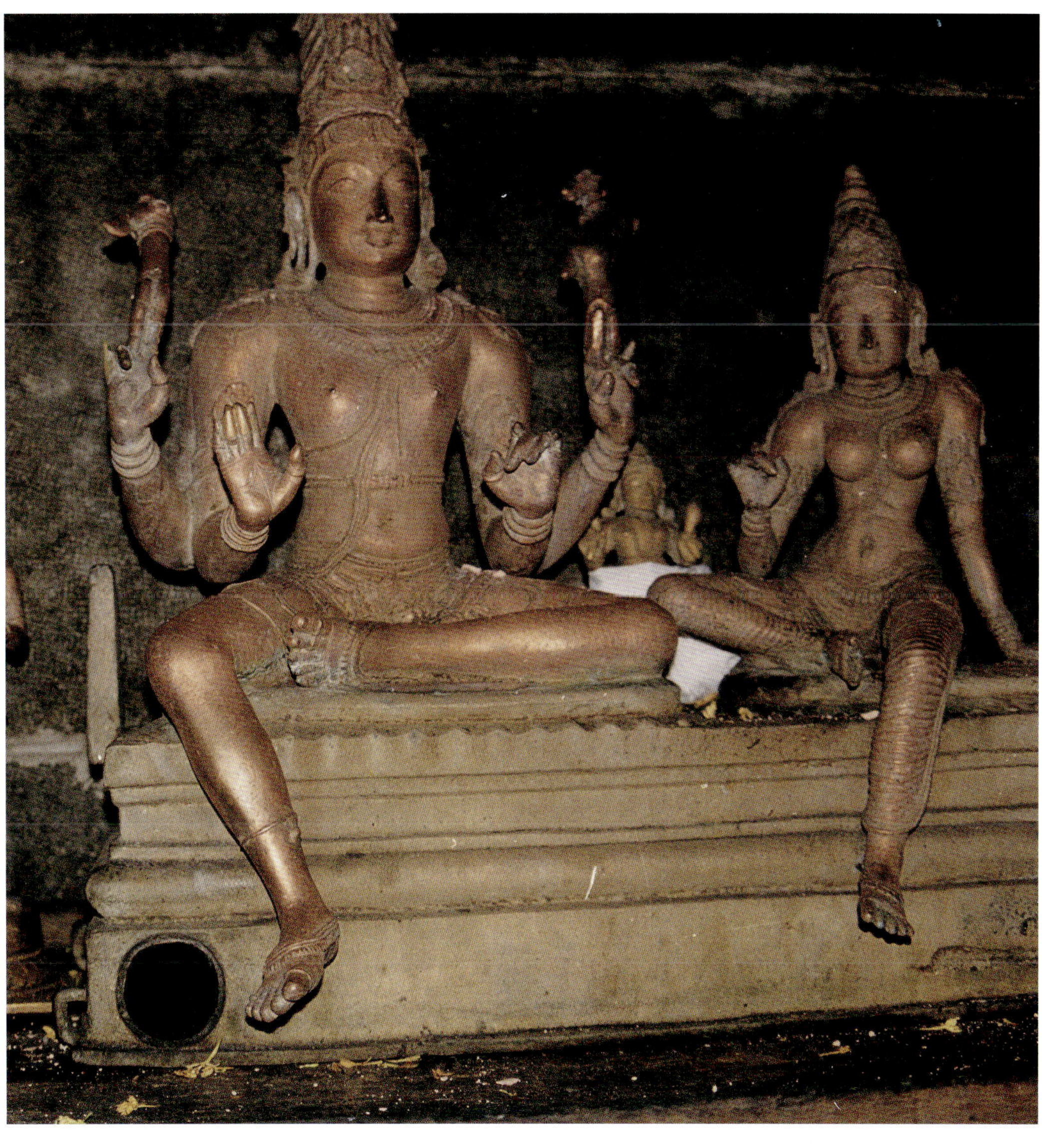

TIRUKALIPALAI

At Tirukalipalai, close to Shivapuram, is a once-famous Shiva temple that is not in its original locale; it was shifted to the present site about one hundred and fifty to two hundred years ago. Initially, it was located across the river but fell into ruins during a flood, after which the entire temple was shifted and re-erected. The original was probably built by the great Chola queen Sembiyan Mahadevi, as indicated by exquisite stone sculptures of Durga, Brahma, and *dvarapalas* (door guardians) of superlative workmanship. This temple has at least three bronzes in the Kulottunga idiom. One is a fine Somaskanda group (fig. 19) in which child Skanda, now missing, was placed in front on the lower part of the pedestal. Tall headdresses crown both Shiva and Uma, and the whole displays the somewhat linear and fine proportions that are stylistically close to those of the Alingana Chandrashekhara of Tiruvavaduturai (fig. 15). The face of Uma exhibits the same delicacy as the attendant goddess of Shivapuram just discussed. The second bronze is an excellent Uma (fig. 20, left) standing in a flowing *tribhanga* pose. The two-armed goddess, who is reminiscent of the Tiruvenkadu tradition of the earlier emperor Rajendra I, seems to be pre-Kulottunga and dates to the mid-eleventh century (ca. 1050). The third bronze is a trident that carries images of Shiva and Uma standing beside the bull (fig. 20, right). Such tridents, called *shuladevar*, are carried in procession in daily festivals. They also play a crucial role on the concluding day of various annual festivals when the trident is carried to a water source and ceremonially immersed in the waters.

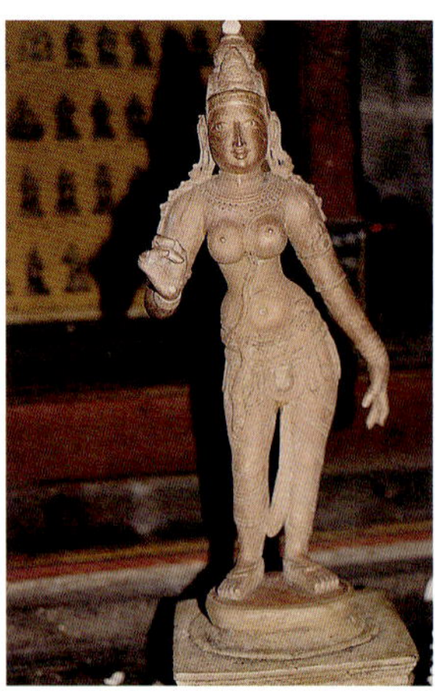

UMA AS TANI AMMAN, EARLY 12TH CENTURY, KULOTTUNGA I ERA, SHIVA TEMPLE, SHIVAPURAM
PHOTO R. NAGASWAMY
FIG. 17

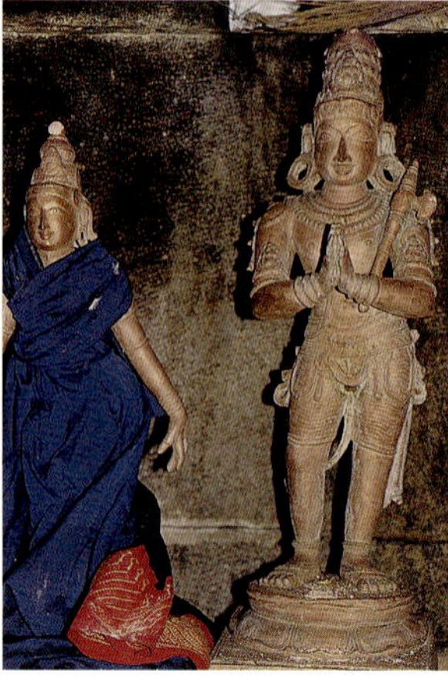

CHANDESHA, EARLY 12TH CENTURY, KULOTTUNGA I ERA, SHIVA TEMPLE, SHIVAPURAM
PHOTO R. NAGASWAMY
FIG. 18

It is worth noting that Chidambaram, which attracted the attention of the later Cholas from the time of Kulottunga, is hardly ten kilometers from Shivapuram and Tirukalipalai; the presence of such a fine group of later Chola bronzes in these Shiva temples should be considered against this background.

BRONZES FROM THE REIGN OF KULOTTUNGA II (1133–50)

KONULAMPALLAM

A group of bronzes that includes a Nataraja (fig. 21) and consort, a Somaskanda, Tani Amman, Chandesha, Sambandar, and Appar, along with some *puja* utensils, was found accidentally in a village named Konulampallam near the famous temple of Tiruvidaimarudur and is now preserved in the Tanjavur Art Gallery. The objects were found about two hundred yards from the remains of an ancient temple, and the bronzes belong stylistically to the later Chola period. Confirmation of their date comes from the fact that the ritual utensils carry inscriptions in Tamil Chola characters reading *edirili cholan* (the Chola with no challenger),[20] a significant title of Kulottunga II, who carried out extensive renovations at the Chidambaram temple. The bronzes in this group form a transitional phase within later Chola art, belonging between the images of Kulottunga I (ca. 1100) and those of Kulottunga III (ca. 1200).

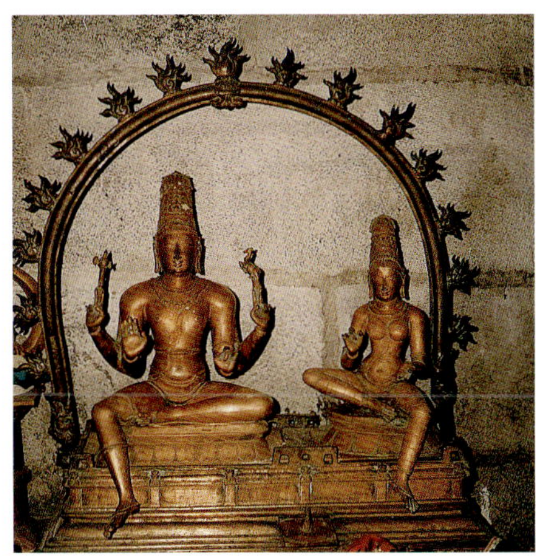

SOMASKANDA, EARLY 12TH CENTURY, KULOTTUNGA I ERA, SHIVA TEMPLE, TIRUKALIPALAI
PHOTO R. NAGASWAMY
FIG. 19

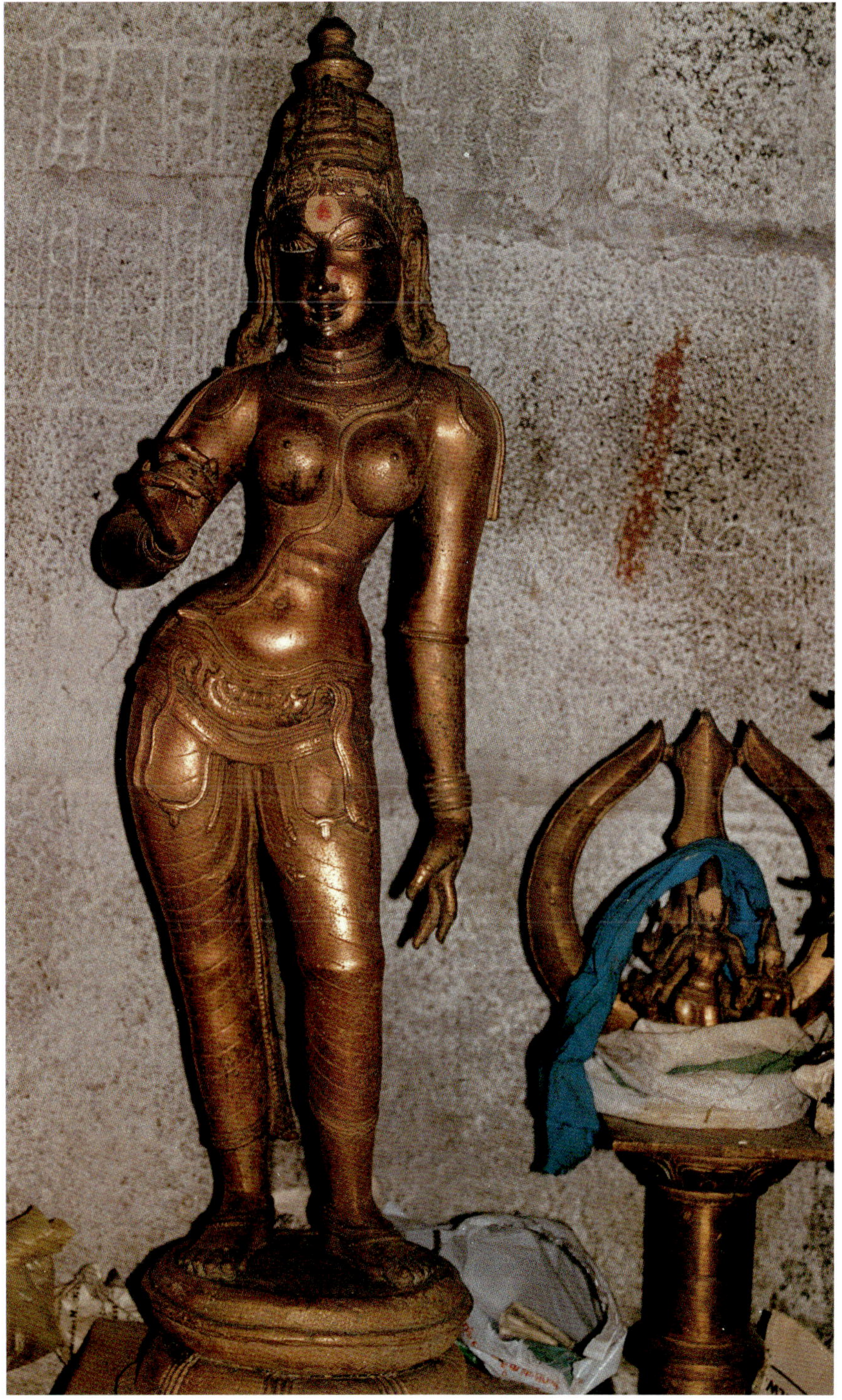

UMA NEXT TO A TRIDENT, SHIVA TEMPLE, TIRUKALIPALAI. UMA, MID-11TH CENTURY, BEFORE KULOTTUNGA I ERA; AND TRIDENT, EARLY 12TH CENTURY, KULOTTUNGA I ERA
PHOTO R. NAGASWAMY
FIG. 20

BRONZES FROM THE REIGN OF KULOTTUNGA III (1178–1216)

PAUNDARIKAPURAM

Paundarikapuram in the Tanjavur district, an important temple of the later Chola period, carries no inscription on its walls, but the iconographic choice of its sculptures and their style leave no doubt that it belongs to the later Chola period. Among its bronzes is a Somaskanda, a Nataraja and consort, and an Alingana Chandrashekhara, all clearly in later Chola style. The Somaskanda group, with a dancing child Skanda, is portrayed with fluid grace (fig. 22). An inscription on its pedestal in Grantha characters of the thirteenth century indicates that the original name of the temple was Somanatheshvaram or Anadi-mangalam (beginningless or ancient village).[21] This temple should be assigned to the end of twelfth century during the reign of Kulottunga III, whose royal preceptor, Somanatha, consecrated the Tribhuvanam temple.[22]

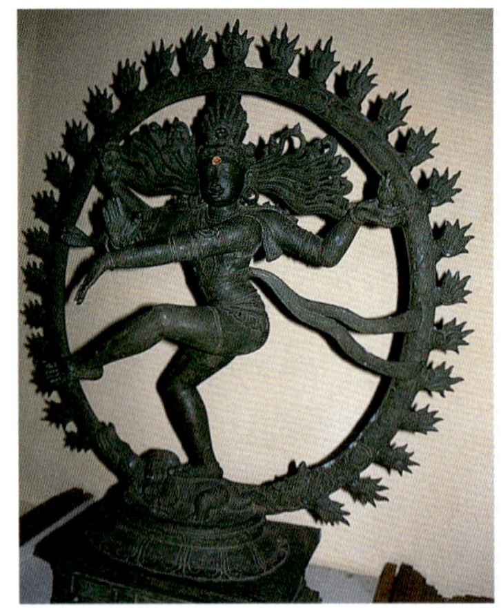

NATARAJA, MID-12TH CENTURY, KULOTTUNGA II ERA, SHIVA TEMPLE, KONULAMPALLAM
PHOTO R. NAGASWAMY
FIG. 21

Its Nataraja (fig. 23) has a broad circular *prabha* with flames that do not stand apart distinctly but are connected to each other to form another ring. Shiva's face is somewhat squarish, and his matted locks flow on either side onto the *prabha*. The crane feathers that decorate his headdress spread out like a fan, with the hood of a coiled snake at its root. River goddess Ganga is shown as a tiny mermaid on the locks to the right side of Nataraja's face. The image of his consort (fig. 24) follows the style of Nataraja, but is somewhat stiff. The other bronze of this period portrays Shiva and Uma together as Alingana Chandrashekhara (fig. 25). The square modeling of their faces is similar to that of Nataraja and Shivakami, and the bronzes belong to the final phase of Chola imagery.

A comparison of this group with a fine bronze of Shiva as the Enchanting Mendicant or Bhikshatana (fig. 26) in the Shiva temple at Tribhuvanam is instructive. Kulottunga III built this temple under the guidance of his guru Someshvara, also known as Ishvara Shiva. The Tribhuvanam Bhikshatana is a work of remarkable beauty and classical refinement, and true to the god's manifestation as a naked beggar, he is shown nude, with little ornament. The smooth contours, the perfect proportions, and the exquisite face suggest a royal commission. A comparison with the Vinadhara Bhikshatana of Melaperumpallam, cast twenty years earlier in 1178, under Rajadhiraja II, is instructive. It seems likely that the two images, though produced in the reigns of two different monarchs, were made by the same artist.[23] By contrast, the Paundarikapuram group, though belonging to the same period, reveals a different trend, confirming the existence of nonroyal, regional workshops that coexisted with a royal school.

BEYOND TAMIL FRONTIERS

The consecration of metal images of the Kulottunga period did not stop in Tamil Nadu but went beyond into Chola-controlled territory in Karnataka. A commander under Vikrama Chola—Udayamartanda Brahmarayan—built a temple named Someshvara at Kolar near Bangalore, and informs us in an inscription that he consecrated a metal image of seated Shiva and Uma (Uma-sahita). The record also states that at the insistence of the *rajaguru*, the chieftain brought Ganga water, and also sacred earth from the banks of the Ganga, dug a sacred tank in the village near the temple, and sanctified it.[24]

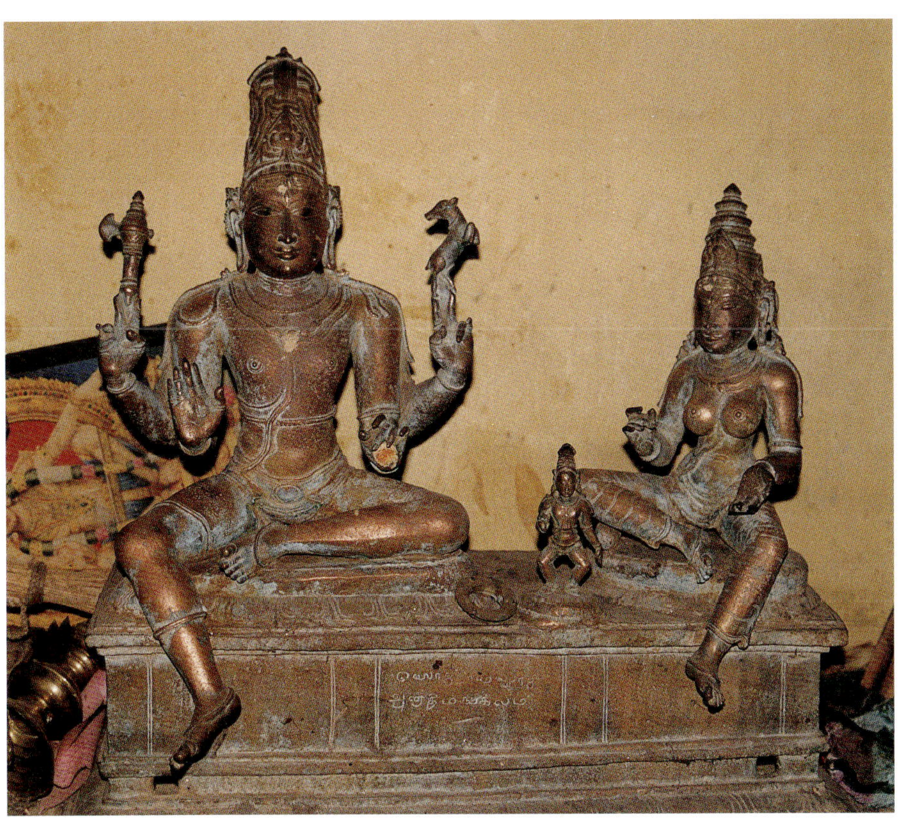

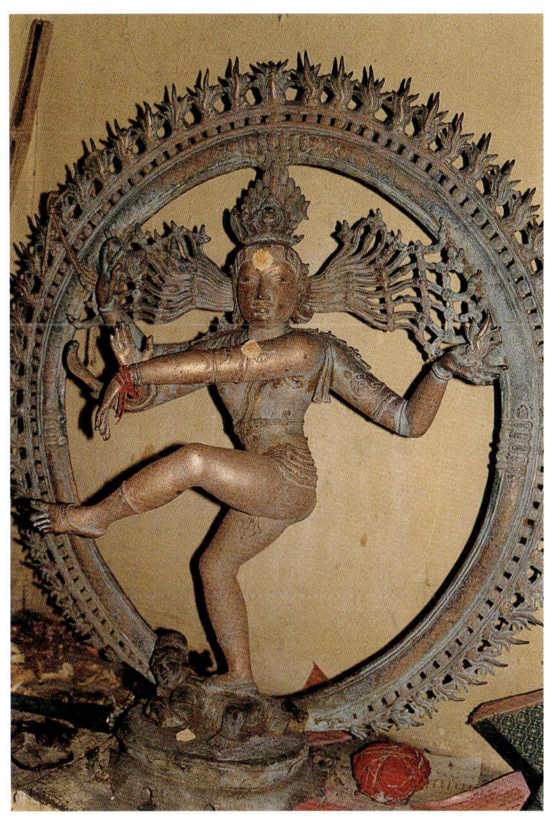

SOMASKANDA, LATE 12TH CENTURY,
KULOTTUNGA III ERA, SHIVA TEMPLE,
PAUNDARIKAPURAM
PHOTO R. NAGASWAMY
FIG. 22

NATARAJA, END OF 12TH CENTURY,
KULOTTUNGA III ERA, SHIVA TEMPLE,
PAUNDARIKAPURAM
PHOTO R. NAGASWAMY
FIG. 23

CONCLUSION

A quick look at the available inscriptional records, as well as actual bronzes still under worship in Tamil temples, reveals that during the late Chola period there was a wave of casting and consecrating bronzes of four particular types—Nataraja with his consort, Somaskanda, Uma on her own, and portraits of the four main Shaiva saints.[25] Forms popular in the earlier period, like Shiva as Tripuravijaya (Victor of the Three Cities), though seen occasionally, do not occupy the position of prominence that they once held. The particular emphasis on Nataraja and Somaskanda calls for an independent study, while the tremendous popularity of the *Tevaram* hymns is reflected in the commissioning of bronze portraits of the saints. The art of bronze-casting under Kulottunga I still retains the freshness, supple movement, and sinuous lines of the earlier Chola age, but it is now necessary to distinguish among the royal school and regional schools focused around village centers.

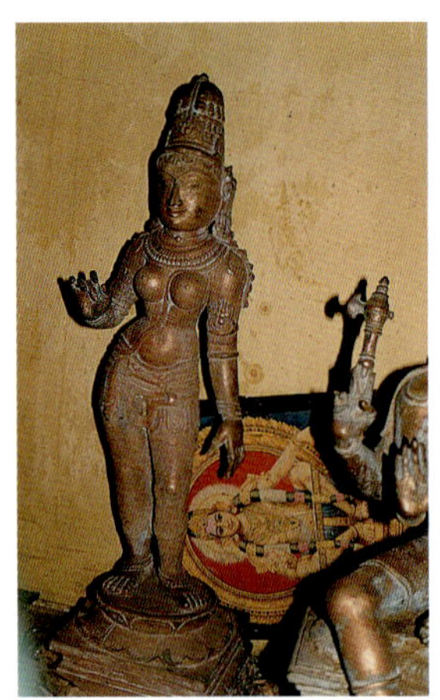

UMA AS SHIVAKAMI, END OF 12TH CENTURY,
KULOTTUNGA III ERA, SHIVA TEMPLE,
PAUNDARIKAPURAM
PHOTO R. NAGASWAMY
FIG. 24

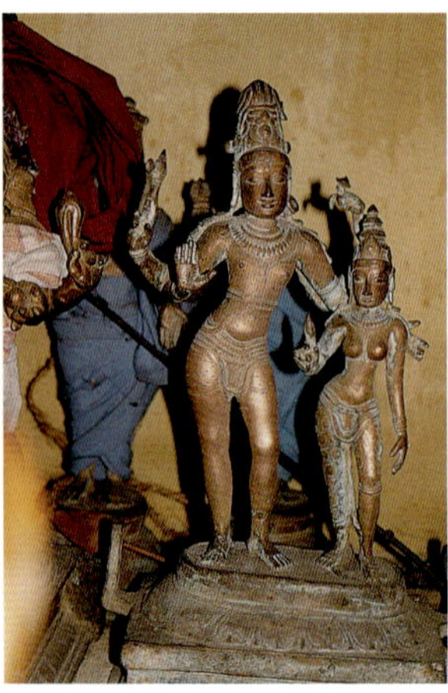

ALINGANA CHANDRASHEKHARA, END OF 12TH CENTURY,
KULOTTUNGA III ERA, SHIVA TEMPLE,
PAUNDARIKAPURAM
PHOTO R. NAGASWAMY
FIG. 25

NOTES

1 A recent epigraphical find gives 55 years of rule to Kulottunga I, and his dates are here revised.

2 The rulers and their respective reign periods are as follows: Kulottunga I (1070–1125); Vikrama (1118–35); Kulottunga II (1133–50); Rajaraja II (1146–73) Rajadhiraja II (r. 1166–80); Kulottunga III (1178–1216); Rajaraja III (1216–60).

3 R. Nagaswamy, "Eastern Indian Contact with Tamilnad," *Journal of Bengal Art* 3 (1998): 17–49. See also idem, "Bengal and Chidambaram," *Journal of Bengal Art* 4 (1999): 33–47; and idem, "Bengal's Contribution to Cola Temples," *Journal of Bengal Art* 5 (2000): 9–38.

4 Nagaswamy, "Eastern Indian Contact with Tamilnad," p. 44.

5 R. Nagaswamy, "On Dating South Indian Bronzes," in *Indian Art and Connoisseurship: Essays in Honour of Douglas Barrett*, ed. John Guy (Ahmedabad: Mapin Publishing, 1995), fig 19.

6 Ibid., fig. 21.

7 Ibid., fig. 20.

8 R. Nagaswamy, "Chidambaram Bronzes," *Lalit Kala* 19 (1979): figs. 62–63.

9 Marxia Gandhi, "Art Treasures of Thiruvadigai," in *South Indian Studies*, vol. 1, ed. R. Nagaswamy ([Madras]: Society for Archaeological, Historical, and Epigraphical Research, 1978), p. 151.

10 C. Sivaramamurti, *South Indian Bronzes* (New Delhi and Bombay: Lalit Kala Academy, 1963), fig. 98; Sivaramamurti cites it as "an image with a good deal yet of the grace of early Chola sculpture"; and Douglas Barrett, *Early Cola Bronzes* (Bombay: Bhulabai Memorial Institute, 1965), figs. 101–2.

11 Appar IV:81, v. 4. Translation is mine.

12 *Periya Puranam*, chapter 6, verse 105 (Chennai: Saiva Siddhanta Maha Samajam, 1950).

13 François Gros and R. Nagaswamy, *Uttaramerur: Légendes, histoire, monuments* (Pondicherry: Institut français d'indologie 1970), p. 69.

14 Ibid., p. 60.

15 Ibid., p. 63.

16 S. R. Balasubramaniyan, *Later Chola Temples: Kulottunga I to Rajendra III, A.D. 1070–1280* (Madras: Mudgala Trust, 1979), p. 322.

17 P. R. Srinivasan, *Bronzes of South India.* Bulletin of the Madras Government Museum (Madras: Controller of Stationery and Printing, 1963), fig. 302. Srinivasan compares this bronze with a Devi in Srirangam and assigns it to sixteenth century. His dating is way off the mark.

18 Nagaswamy, "Bengal's Contribution to Cola Temples," p. 24.

19 Nagaswamy, "Chidambaram Bronzes," figs. 54, 55.

20 When these bronzes were unearthed I was the first to inspect them, and I found them encrusted with earth. On cleaning I saw that they bore the inscription *edirili cholan*. I published a note on the find in all the dailies.

21 In my recent resurvey of this temple, I stumbled across an old man of the village who recalled that the village had traditionally been called Anadimangalam, and the Shiva temple called Somanatha temple. The change of name has occurred within living memory. There are a number of bronzes from this temple, which are kept in a nearby temple for safety.

22 H. Sarkar, *The Kampaharesvara Temple at Tribhuvanam* (Madras: Tamilnadu State Department of Archaeology, 1974), p. 23.

23 R. Nagaswamy, "Melapperumpallam Bronzes," in *Art and Culture of Tamil Nadu* (Delhi: Sundeep Prakashan, 1980), p. 99, pl. 42; and Vidya Dehejia, *Art of The Imperial Cholas* (New York: Columbia University Press, 1990), pp. 116–17.

24 *Epigraphia Carnatica*, vol. 10, p. 111.

25 There are a number of other temples in which bronzes of Nataraja and his consort and also Somaskanda are still worshiped, but they have not been included here as the list would be too long and might also be repetitive.

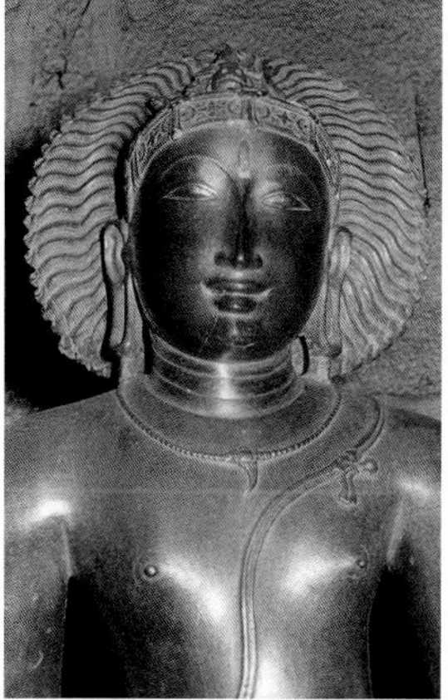

BHIKSHATANA, END OF 12TH CENTURY, KULOTTUNGA III ERA, ROYAL SHIVA TEMPLE, TRIBHUVANAM

PHOTO R. NAGASWAMY

FIG. 20

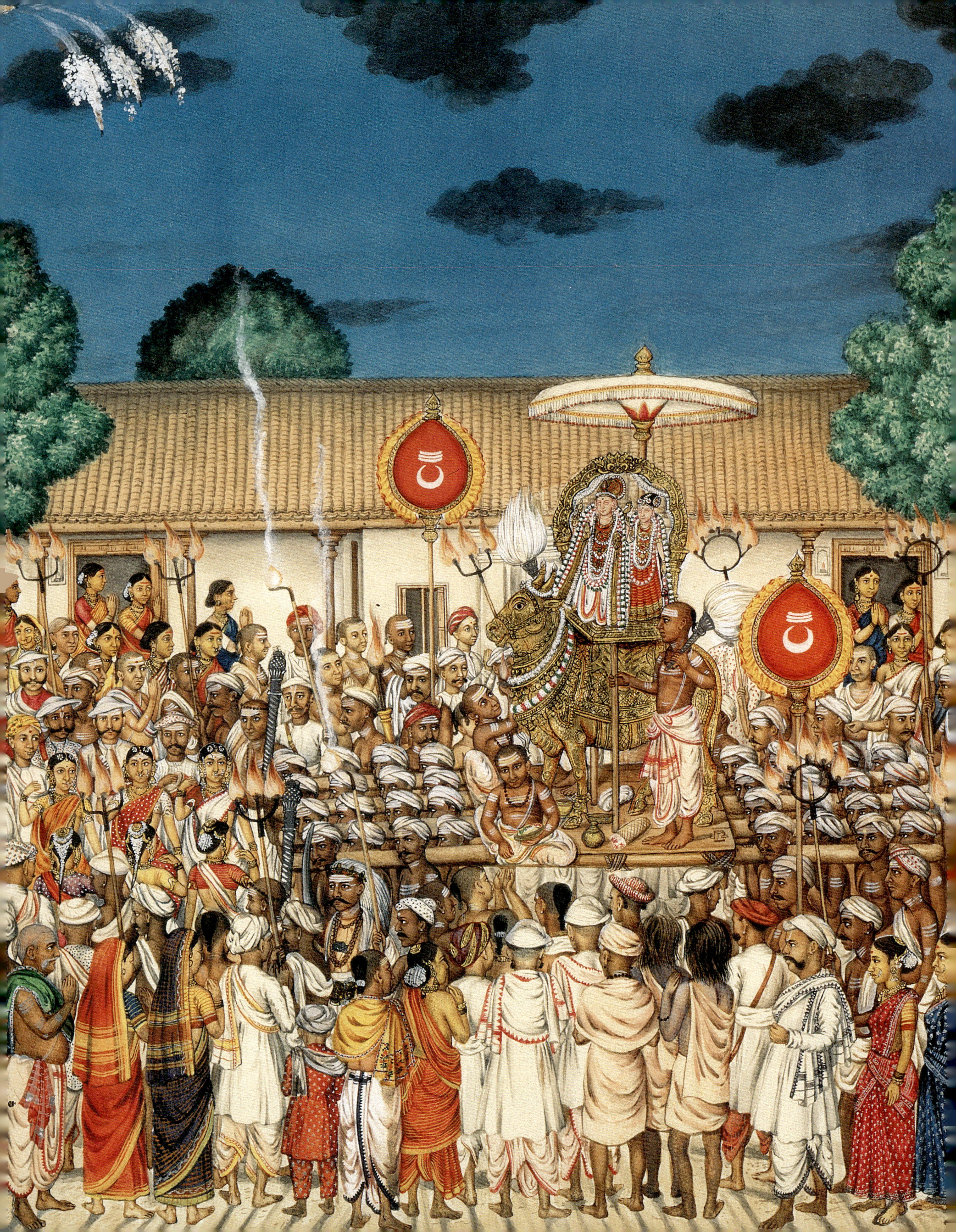

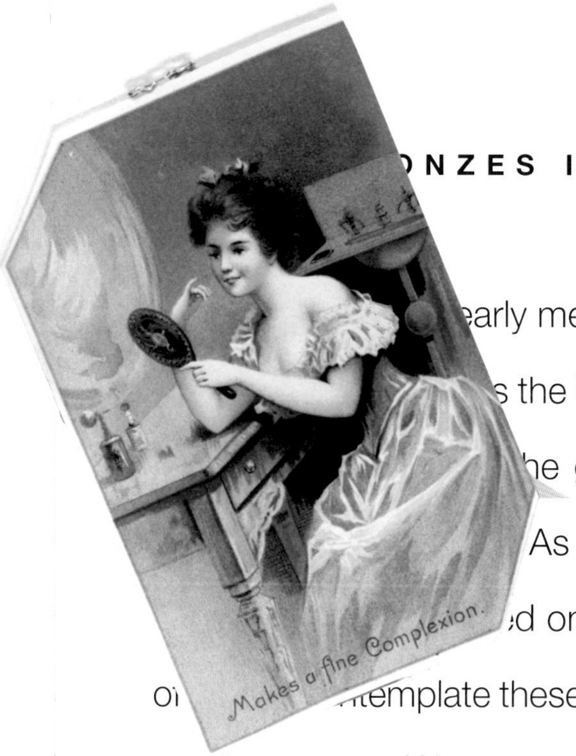

…NZES IN PROCESSION

RICHARD H. DAVIS

…early medieval south Indian bronze images trav-
…s the United States, American visitors have an
…he great artistry and religious passion that
… As we stand quietly in the enclosed exhibi-
…d only by like-minded museum-goers, each
o… …ntemplate these works of religious sculpture cast a thousand years ago. We encounter each image as it presents itself to us, unmoving, in the purity of its unadorned bronze form. In the luminous track lighting of the modern museum display, these ancient Indian bronze images may well seem to glow. Visitors are able, as one observer wrote of the Chola bronzes at another exhibition of Indian sculpture, "to luxuriantly bask in the supple, sensuous, sinuous beauty of these idealized forms."[1]

Viewers of these same images in Chola times would have seen them in a different light altogether. They would have heard, first of all, the exciting clamor of drums and the resounding tones of conch shells heralding the arrival of the images from far away (fig. 1). As the crowd approached, they would have first seen the leader of the parade on an ornamented, caparisoned elephant holding a banner aloft. Men chanting hymns and women dancers from the temple would pass by. Then, in the crush of people pushing to get closer to the action, they would have seen the bronze figures nearly hidden

A TEMPLE PROCESSION AT NIGHT (DETAIL OF FIG. 1)

beneath silk garments, gold ornaments, and garlands of flowers, shaded by parasols, parading forth from their temple palaces into the torch-lit streets of the town, riding on palanquins carried on the shoulders of temple workers or in four-wheeled wooden chariots pulled with ropes by scores of devotees. Alongside the palanquins would be attendants waving yak-tail fans to whisk away insects, and others collecting offerings. If fortunate enough to approach one of the sculptures, viewers would have stood with hands folded in respect, and they might have given it a coconut or another garland of jasmine as a gift of devotion to God. There would have been no time to bask, but they might well have rejoiced in the visible, physical presence of the deity and this opportunity to encounter God, as it were, face to garlanded face. For the Chola bronzes we see in this exhibition were originally created to serve as *utsavamurtis*, mobile forms or embodiments for deities to inhabit during the processions of temple festivals.

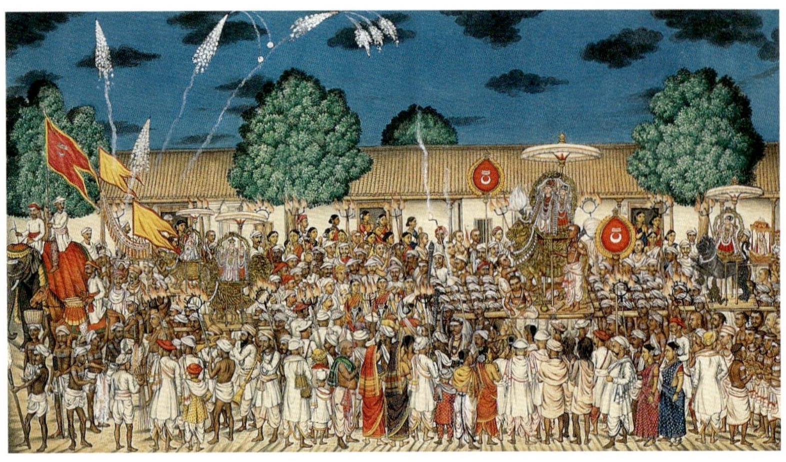

A TEMPLE PROCESSION AT NIGHT. COMPANY SCHOOL, TANJAVUR, TAMIL NADU, CA. 1830. VICTORIA & ALBERT MUSEUM PICTURE LIBRARY, LONDON
FIG. 1

No one expects museum curators to decorate the works of Indian sculpture, or guards to carry them out into the streets of Cleveland or down the Mall in Washington. Nor will visitors to the museum be expected to bring coconuts or garlands to the exhibition. We can, however, gain an initial glimpse of how an adorned processional image appears visually, in the decorated Nataraja from the Museum of Fine Arts, Boston (cat. no. 4) on view in the exhibition. We can hear the distinctive sounds of the temple *nagasvaram* and *tavil* by listening to a recording.[2] This is a start. But to recover more of how the original Hindu viewers of Chola times saw these divine icons in procession, and how they would have understood what they were seeing, we need to exercise our historical imagination further. We need first to consider some of the underlying theological premises of early medieval Hinduism, and then to consider Hindu temples and their festivals as social and religious institutions. To do this, there is no better place to start than with the Tamil devotional songs of the Vaishnava and Shaiva poet-saints, composed in the seventh through ninth centuries and widely sung in temples during the Chola period.[3]

GOD'S SUPREMACY AND ACCESSIBILITY

The lord, First in heaven
and in all other worlds,
the lord who defies the gods' comprehension,
the supreme lord
who swallowed all of creation
and razed the three cities,
the lord who gives knowledge even to the gods

was called Aran [Shiva]
when he destroyed,
and Ayan [Vishnu]
when he created the world.[4]

Nammalvar, greatest of the Tamil Vaishnava poet-saints, celebrated his lord Vishnu as a god who is beyond all understanding, and even beyond the comprehension of other gods. He is the lord above all others, creator and destroyer of the cosmos. And yet Nammalvar also sang repeatedly of seeing and even holding this vast, all-creating-and-destroying, incomprehensible lord.

Never parted from his three ardent ladies—
the goddess of riches, the Earth, and the simple cowherd maid,
the lord who rules the three worlds and swallows them whole,
our lord who rests on a banyan leaf
and conjures great illusion in the ocean

is Kannan
the child I carry on my hip.[5]

Large enough to swallow the three worlds, Vishnu paradoxically remains light enough to rest on a banyan leaf. And while remaining lord of all creation, Vishnu also takes on human forms or incarnations, such as Kannan or Krishna, a young child who grows up among the humble cowherders of Vraja (the land along the Jumna [Yamuna], south of Delhi). In this poem Nammalvar identifies himself as one of those "ardent ladies" never parted from their lord, Krishna's cowherd babysitter carrying the toddler-god about on her hip.

Whether they recognized Vishnu or Shiva as highest deity, Hindus of early medieval Tamil Nadu considered that this High God not only remained the transcendent Supreme, but also made himself present on earth, to intervene in the world process and in human affairs. Ramanuja, the preeminent Vaishnava religious philosopher of Chola times, spoke of this double nature of the Lord as Vishnu's simultaneous "supremacy" *(paratva)* and "accessibility" *(saulabhya).*[6] Just as Nammalvar celebrated Vishnu's overarching greatness, he also celebrated the accessible, reachable side of Vishnu's nature.

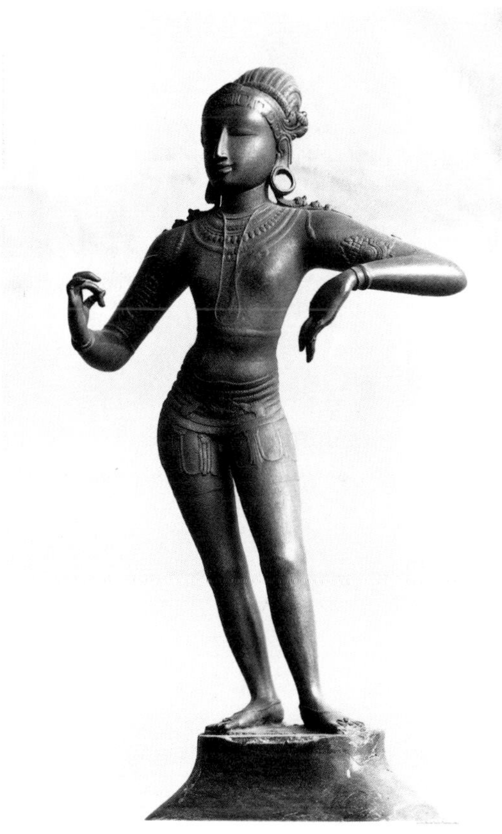

SUNDARAR, FROM KILAIYUR, CA. 950. RAJARAJA ART MUSEUM, TANJAVUR
PHOTO RICHARD H. DAVIS
FIG. 2

In birth after birth with no fixed place or boundary,
the lord comes within everyone's reach

ever radiant, filled with goodness,
with no origin or demise . . .[7]

The Tamil devotional poets sang of encountering their gods in a great variety of forms, often perplexing or paradoxical, sometimes demanding or challenging in the most fundamental way. Consider the experience of Sundarar, the Shaiva poet of the eighth century (fig. 2). According to his traditional biography as told by the Chola-period court poet Sekkilar, Sundarar was born in an honorable priestly family and raised in a king's palace.[8] When he came of age, his elders arranged his marriage with a beautiful young brahmin girl, and they celebrated it with all the pomp of a royal wedding. As the festivities went on, however, an aged, ash-covered hermit tottered up. The old man demanded that the ceremonies halt, for he had a contract with the bridegroom: Sundarar was to be his slave. How could a brahmin become a slave? These could only be the words of a madman, Sundarar accused. The old man pulled a document out from his tattered dhoti, but Sundarar caught him, grabbed the contract, and tore it to pieces. This was not enough to avert the hermit's demand, however, and the dispute was taken to court, where the old man produced yet another deed, signed by Sundarar's grandfather, pledging the servitude of his descendent to the old sage. The judge ruled that Sundarar would indeed have to become slave to the old man—who shortly led Sundarar to a nearby temple and revealed himself to be, in fact, Shiva.

Appropriately, Sundarar began his first hymn to Shiva with his accusatory charge:

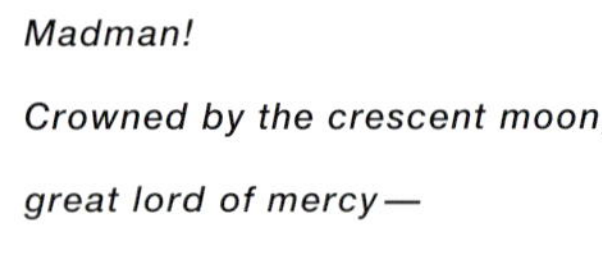

Madman!
Crowned by the crescent moon,
great lord of mercy—

you have placed yourself in my heart;
now nothing will let me
forget you.

Father in Arutturai of Venneynallur
to the south of the Pennai River—

how could I ever say
that I am not your slave?[9]

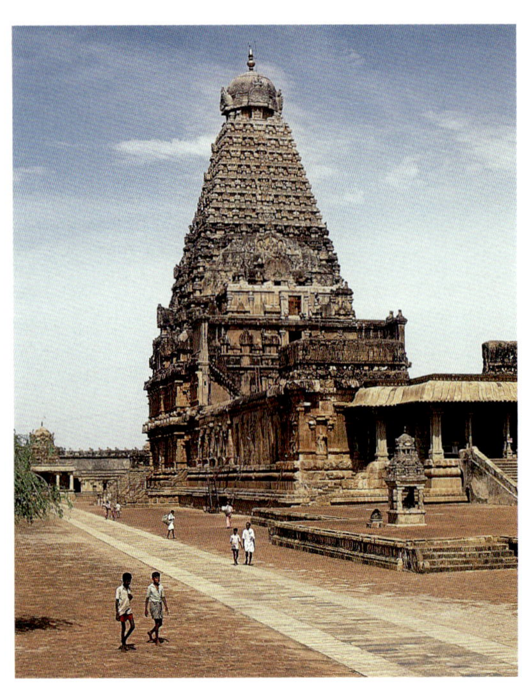

BRHADISHVARA OR RAJARAJESHVARA TEMPLE, TANJAVUR, COMPLETED IN 1013. PHOTOGRAPH TAKEN IN 1985 DURING CLEANING OF TEMPLE TOWER IN PREPARATION FOR ONE THOUSANDTH ANNIVERSARY OF RAJARAJA'S ACCESSION TO THE CHOLA THRONE.
PHOTO RICHARD H. DAVIS
FIG. 3

Shiva does indeed sometimes appear like a cantankerous madman as he interposes himself into the lives of his devotees. Confusing as they may initially appear, these appearances of God taking accessible bodily form are taken as acts of grace or mercy. So Sundarar immediately follows his opening "madman" with a recognition of Shiva as "great lord of mercy." Shiva's demands are signs of favor, for they lead the fortunate devotee to a greater degree of participation in his divine realm, however difficult that path may be, and insert Shiva's own presence still more intimately within the devotee's being. As Sundarar saw it, through his seemingly mad disruption of the wedding, Shiva had placed himself in Sundarar's heart, unforgettably.

The poet-saints also encountered their gods at shrines or temples throughout the Tamil countryside. Indeed, the lives of these saints were often dominated by continuous restless peregrinations in search of their lord.[10] At each place they sought to see and celebrate God in the specific, local form of a particular enshrined icon.

TEMPLES: ACCESS AND EXCLUSION

Medieval south Indian Hindus encountered their gods most readily in the form of images or icons located in public temples, as well as in the domestic shrines maintained by pious households. From the time of the devotional poet-saints through the Chola period, temples became an increasingly prominent part of the Tamil religious landscape. Chola royalty and local elites rebuilt older brick shrines in more durable stone. Chola rulers starting with the early-eleventh-century emperors Rajaraja I and Rajendra I constructed massive, towering imperial temples in their capitals of Tanjavur (fig. 3) and Gangaikondacholapuram. Such large temples took on the form of cosmic palaces, teeming with deities and all manner of creatures, rising like the mountains where the gods preferred to reside. Rajaraja even named his imperial temple Dakshinameru, the World-Mountain of the south. Important religious centers like the Shaiva temple at Chidambaram and the Vaishnava one at Srirangam expanded with more and more shrines and halls, until they seemed like veritable metropolai of the gods.

The temples were also, more humbly, homes of the gods, each one a place where human worshipers could encounter God in a material form. At each, the god took on a local identity. A Shaiva poet like Sundarar accordingly referred to the Shiva he found in each place by a distinctive name: "Father in Arutturai of Venneynallur," "Lord of Venkatu surrounded by sea," and the like. At the same time, the devotional poets reminded their audiences that each local form of Shiva was also simultaneously the one who carried out all those mythical deeds of the Great God. The relation of local to universal, the instantiation of the entirety of a god's being and all his divine acts within a particular material form, sometimes posed an unsolvable question for the poets. Once the devotee accepted this paradox, however, each particular icon offered a point of entry to the whole.[11]

As the scale of the temples grew in early medieval Tamil Nadu, priests developed increasingly elaborate liturgical practices. New genres of ritual texts, most notably the Vaishnava Samhitas and the Shaiva Agamas, prescribed how these rituals were to be performed. Priests would subject the icon at the center of the temple—most often an anthorpomorphic image of Vishnu for a Vaishnava temple or a Shiva-linga for a Shaiva one—to a lengthy ritual "establishment" *(pratistha)*, which gradually purified and transfigured the material substance of the icon and invoked the presence of the deity into it. Establishment ritually assisted God's entry into form, his divine movement, in Ramanuja's terms, from supremacy to accessibility. Once it was properly consecrated, the icon would receive the regular ritual attentions of worship *(puja)*. Once, twice, or up to eight times per day in a very active temple, priests would offer a series of devotional services *(upacharas)* to the iconic deity. Treating God as an honored guest and as a respected lord, priests would wash the feet of the icon, bathe it, anoint it, rub it with soothing sandal paste, dress and ornament it, feed it, entertain it with dance and song (including the hymns of the Tamil poet-saints), praise it, and bow humbly before it. All this the temple priests were to do on behalf of the entire community, for public worship would "increase the longevity, health, victory, and prosperity of the ruler," and also "make the villagers and others thrive."[12]

The devotional movements of medieval India often conveyed a message of religious equality. In Nammalvar's words, "the lord comes within everyone's reach," without regard to social status and without need of priestly mediation.[13] Yet temples, primary sites of devotional religion, were also inescapably social institutions. In tension with the theoretical egalitarianism of bhakti, temple practices also reflected and articulated a social hierarchy.

In a temple, God in his highest form dwelt in the sequestered center, the "womb-room" *(garbhagrha)*. Only highly qualified persons could enter and minister directly to this innermost iconic deity. Among Shaivas, only males of certain Adishaiva brahmin families, known as Shaiva-brahmanas, who had undergone a series of initiations, a lengthy period of training, and finally a special "consecration into priesthood" *(acharyabhisheka)* were eligible to perform worship in the sanctum. Enjoying this privileged access, they became mediators for the entire community by carrying out "worship on behalf of others" *(pararthapuja)*. Members of other social groups were limited in their access. Some could enter as far as the fore-pavilion just in front of the sanctum, others could come only into the main pavilion, while still others could come no further than the door of the entry-tower or *gopuram*.[14] The penalties for transgressing these limits and approaching too closely to the center could be stiff indeed.

RANGANATHA TEMPLE, SRIRANGAM. COMPANY SCHOOL PAINTING, SOUTH INDIA, EARLY 19TH CENTURY. TRUSTEES OF THE BRITISH MUSEUM, LONDON

FIG. 4

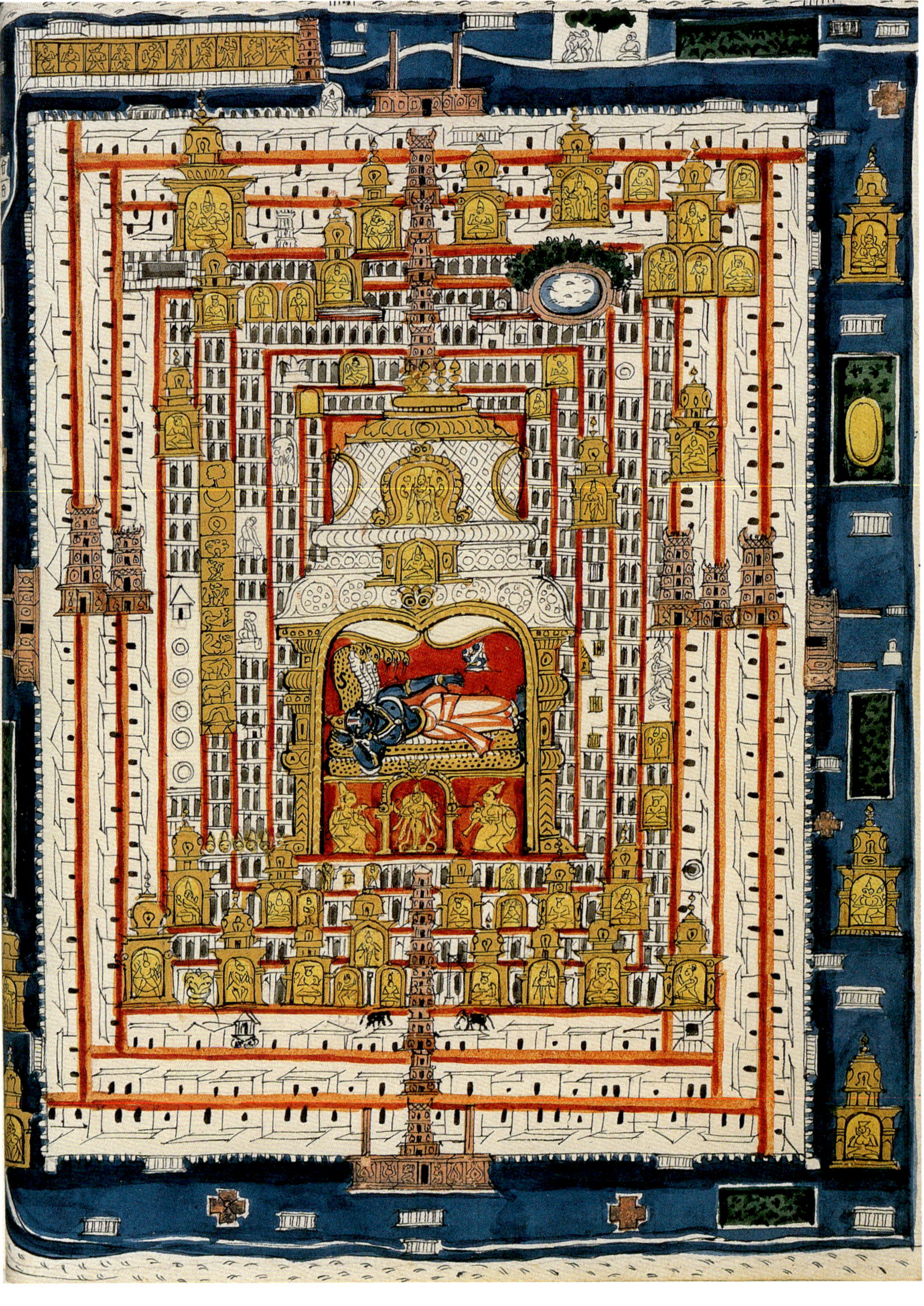

> The one who, out of perversity, leaves his own place and goes too far into the temple, although he has been told not to, will certainly go to hell, tossed there by Shiva. And even if one goes too far out of ignorance, there will nevertheless be some disturbance in the kingdom.[15]

Those at the lowest rungs of medieval south Indian society were excluded completely from entering the temple.

Temple exclusion did not preclude devotion to God, of course. The biographies of the Tamil devotional saints include stories of potters, leather workers, tribal huntsmen, and other outcastes whose passionate commitments to Shiva or Vishnu proved to be far greater than that of others who were more favored socially. Among Tamil worshipers of Vishnu, the untouchable saint Tiruppan served as a model for lower-class devotion. As Garudavahana Pandita relates in the twelfth-century *Divyasuricharita*, Tiruppan was born in the Panar caste, a group of traditional bards who had sunk to the social status of untouchables.[16] Yet he was a prodigy of emotional attachment to Vishnu. Everyday he would go to the southern bank of the Kaveri River and sing his hymns of praise to Vishnu, in the form of lord Ranganatha, who reclined in the sanctum of the Srirangam temple on the northern bank of the river (fig. 4). As an untouchable, Tiruppan was not allowed to approach any closer than this to the sacred shrine, though his words could. From the depths of the many-walled temple, Ranganatha heard and savored Tiruppan's pure songs of devotion. After some time, the story goes, Ranganatha's wife Lakshmi suggested that Tiruppan might be brought into the temple, and so Ranganatha ordered the chief priest of the temple to fetch the untouchable. The priest willingly crossed the river and returned carrying Tiruppan on his back, presumably so the untouchable's impure feet would not touch the pure grounds of the sanctuary. When Tiruppan entered the shrine and saw Vishnu Ranganatha face to face, he was overcome with unbearable emotion and spontaneously sang a hymn of ten stanzas that described the body of the lord from the feet up to his crown. It begins:

Pure primordial lord,
  radiant god who had made me a slave
of slaves; flawless
  overlord of angels
who lives in Venkata of fragrant groves;
  sinless dweller
in righteous heaven—
  our dear father,
here in Arangam of long high rampart walls:
It seems as if his lovely feet
  have come and entered
my eyes![17]

This is Tiruppan's one composition included in the Tamil Vaishnava canon. After his epiphany at Srirangam, according to later tellings of the saint's biography, Tiruppan disappeared physically into the holy body of his God.

In such paradigmatic stories, individual devotional intensity overcomes the constraints imposed by social class. Yet this was certainly not a model that all could follow. For many worshipers the gods remained concealed and unapproachable within their palatial temples most of the time. Fortunately, the temple gods themselves also sought to step across the boundaries that separated them from the mass of their devotees. In medieval times, as today, deities in south Indian temples would regularly venture out from their enclosed sanctuaries, to make themselves visible and accessible. During regular daily festivals *(nityotsava)* and periodic great festivals *(mahotsava)*, the primary gods of a temple are carried in procession to benefit all beings, including even "those rogues, birds, and animals who are not initiated, as well as for initiates and devotees."[18] In these processions we see the Hindu gods at their most accessible.

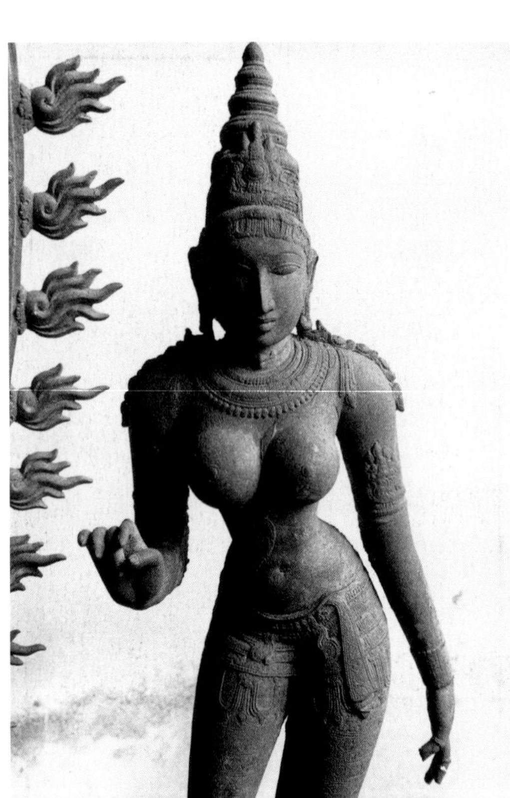

SHIVAKAMI (UMA ACCOMPANYING NATARAJA), FROM TIRUKALAMPUR, 11TH CENTURY. RAJARAJA ART MUSEUM, TANJAVUR
PHOTO RICHARD H. DAVIS
FIG. 5

PROCESSIONAL PRACTICES

In every Chola temple, God took on more than one form. The priestly texts that prescribe ritual practices for Chola-period temples, the Vaishnava Samhitas and the Shaiva Agamas, specify that each temple should provide its primary deity with both "immobile" and "mobile" bodies. The main icon, termed the "root body" *(mulamurti)*, was a fixed icon, most often stone, set permanently at the center of the central sanctum. Most of the time this principal form of God was the main recipient of worship. There would also be one or more portable icons for the same god, cast most often in bronze of a special five-metal *(panchaloha)* mixture. The texts designate these mobile icons as "processional bodies" (*utsavamurti),* for these were the forms in which god would venture out along with his entourage of other processional icons, beyond the confines of the inner sanctum. These processional bodies, we should remember, are the ones that have also traveled overseas to make themselves present to us in a museum.

Some of the ritual texts relate the two types of icons to the two levels or aspects of god's being. As the *Kashyapa Jnanakanda* puts it,

> The Lord has two forms: the unmoving and the moving one. The unmoving form is everywhere, is like the sky, to be characterized only by negative epitheta, unperceivable even by Brahma and the other gods, and indivisible.[19]

In other words, the primary immobile icon in the central sanctum represents the Lord "without attributes" *(nirguna)*, or in Ramanuja's terms, the supreme aspect of God. The moving form, by contrast, is finite in form, "with attributes" *(saguna)*, and so embodies the Lord in his more accessible aspect. In many cases this corresponds to a contrast in iconographic form as well. For example, at Srirangam the fixed form of Vishnu in the sanctum represents the lord reclining on his snake-couch, in the deep yogic sleep out of which all creation proceeds, while the processional icon has Vishnu standing, ready to move out into the world. In Shaiva temples the distinction is even more evident. The central icon of Shiva, in all but a very few cases, is an austere, unmarked cylindrical Shiva-linga which, according to the ritual texts, parallels Shiva's highest, most encompassing level of being. Processional images, by contrast, embody Shiva in more anthropomorphic form—as a family man (Somaskanda), a naked beggar (Bhikshatana), a great dancer (Nataraja), or other forms in which he acts physically on earth.[20]

Artisans made the processional icons for a temple following iconographic guidelines set out in priestly Samhitas and Agamas, and also in artisan handbooks known as Shilpashastras.[21] For a newly constructed Shaiva temple, the bronze-makers might well fabricate an entire suite of processional images, including Somaskanda, Bhikshatana, Nataraja, and other forms of Shiva, as well as Uma, Ganesha, Skanda and his two wives, Shiva's foremost devotee Chandesha, the bull Nandi, exemplary devotional saints, and more (figs. 5, 6). Such images would undergo elaborate rituals of establishment *(pratistha)*, just as would the primary temple icon and the temple itself, which infused into each one the appropriate divine presence. Once established, the processional icons would reside in the main sanctum or very near it, though clearly subordinate to the main temple icon. Since these icons were living embodiments of the deities they represented, each would receive at least a simple offering of worship each day. During festivals, however, they would come into their own.

The priestly texts speak of temple festivals as *utsava*, from a verb meaning "to stir up, to excite or agitate," and festivals certainly did excite and agitate all involved. They served many other purposes as well. The *Parameshvara Samhita* claims the *utsava* is so named because it removes *(ut)* suffering *(sava),* while the *Ajita Agama* states that the daily festival prevents all misfortune and grants worldly prosperity.[22] The texts also specify several different types of festivals. First, there are the daily festivals (*nityotsava*), performed each day as part of the regular services of worship, during which the processional image of the presiding temple deity makes a circumambulatory tour of the temple precincts. Some texts advise that special festivals of pacification *(shanti)* be held after unforeseen natural calamities and other ominous events. The *Parameshvara Samhita*, for example, lists the following occurrences as warranting a pacification festival: earthquakes, fires, public calamities, famine, epidemic, threats from enemies, drought, stars falling from the sky, the lord's icon laughing or moving its limbs or crying, the icon moving from its seat, the sun reversing its direction, and similarly inauspicous omens.[23] More positively, one might sponsor a festival to gain some personal goal, since festivals can yield any of the four aims of humans: love, material well-being, righteousness, and liberation. The most dramatic and most popular of celebrations, however, were the great annual festivals, or *mahotsavas*.

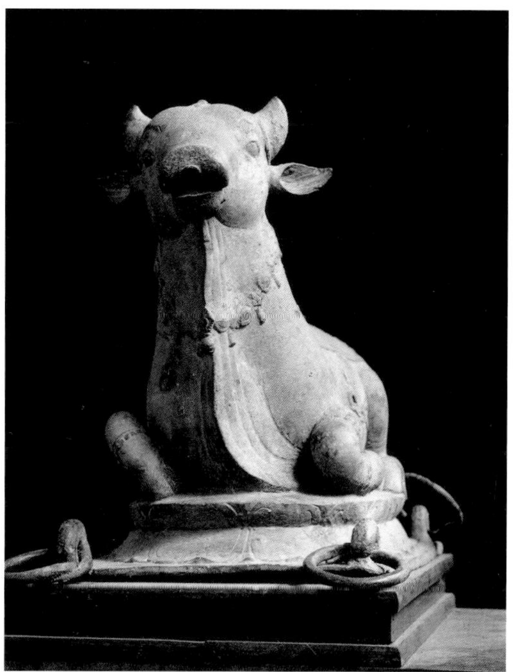

A *mahotsava* lasted for anywhere from one to thirty days, though most of the major annual festivals occupied eleven to fifteen days. Annual festivals were already common in Tamil Nadu during the time of the devotional saints, for several poets describe festivals and their processions. The scale of such ceremonies, however, expanded greatly in Chola times, along with the tremendous growth in the temples themselves. With this expansion of festivals, the demand for great numbers of larger and more beautiful processional icons enabled the bronze-casters of southern India to produce their finest work. Such great festivals have continued to the present, and some of the big temples in Tamil Nadu celebrate their annual festivals on a scale that even those ambitious Chola emperors Rajaraja I and Rajendra I would have envied. Though much has changed in the thousand years since Rajaraja, many of the ritual guidelines that modern-day priests follow in their festival practices adhere remarkably to the old prescriptions of the Samhitas, Agamas, and other ritual texts set down in Chola times.[24]

Temple festivals begin with several interrelated rites: sprouting seeds *(ankurarpana),* offering of tribute to all deities *(balidana)*, beating of the temple drum *(bheritadana)*, and especially raising the festival flag *(dhvajarohana)*. The ceremonial hoisting of the flag marks the opening of a festival, and its later lowering signifies the conclusion. A new white cotton cloth, proportional in size to the temple door, is first inscribed with an image of the animal mount of the presiding deity, the eagle Garuda for a Vishnu temple or the bull Nandi for Shiva. This does not remain a simple design for long. Priests subject the flag to a process of establishment similar to that which the principal and processional icons have previously undergone. These ritual acts infuse life into the flag, so that it too becomes a body for the divine to inhabit. The flag then makes its own procession around the temple, accompanied by music and dance. At the flagpole a drummer strikes the great temple-drum, over three feet in diameter, to address all the gods in all the worlds with the request that they honor the flag-raising. The officiating priest announces that "it is the special wish and command of the Lord that all the gods and mortals should be present not only at the *dhvajarohana*, but also stay there till the completion of the festival."[25] Then, while the priest recites appropriate mantras and auspicious music plays, temple servants hoist the flag. Festivals are inclusive, congregating affairs, and the elevated flag and echoing drum insure that all beings in the area, both human and divine, receive news of the event. The festival is officially underway.

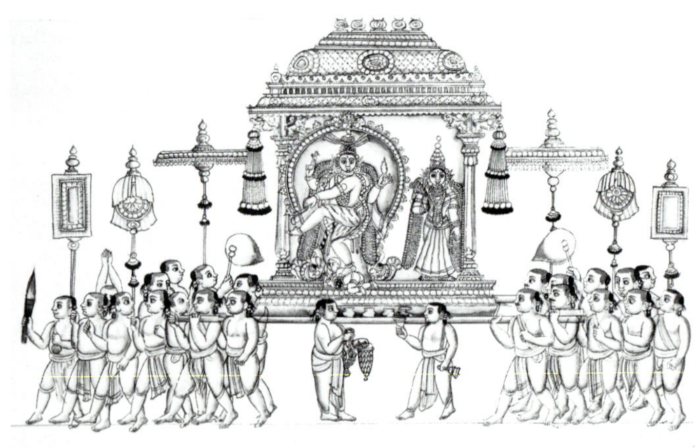

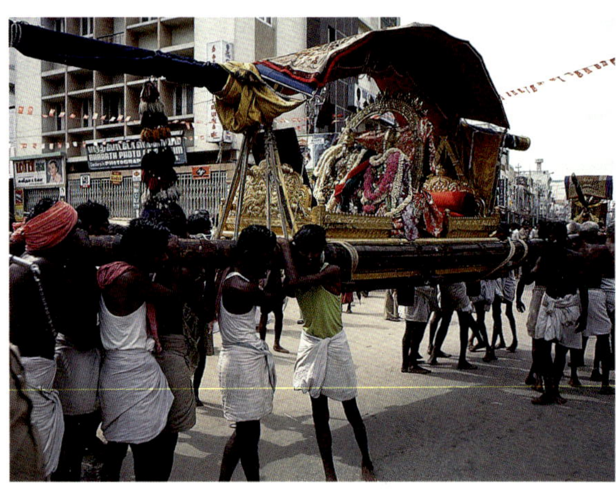

NATARAJA AND SHIVAKAMI ON PROCESSIONAL PALANQUINS. COMPANY SCHOOL DRAWING, TAMIL NADU, CA. 1820. THE TRUSTEES OFTHE BRITISH MUSEUM, LONDON
FIG. 7

SHIVA AND UMA ON PROCESSIONAL PALANQUINS, CHITRAI FESTIVAL, MINAKSHI-SUNDARESHVARA TEMPLE, MADURAI, 1982
PHOTO RICHARD H. DAVIS
FIG. 8

Meanwhile other festival preparations are in progress. "The officiating priest should adorn the temple everywhere with incense and lamps, canopies, banners, strings of darbha grass, pillar-coverings, garlands of flowers, and other ornaments," advises the *Kashyapa Jnankanda*, and "at the doors, he should deposit branches or nuts of the betel-nut tree, pots filled with water, and sprouts." Not just the temple, but also the surrounding neighborhood must look beautiful. "After cleaning the streets of the village, sprinkling them, and adorning them with branches of plantain and betel-nut trees, pots filled with water, sprouts, banners, etc., the people living in that village should adorn them also with ornaments and perfumed garlands."[26]

While a great many rites and celebratory activities occur in the course of a *mahotsava*, the defining public acts of the festival are the recurrent processions of the gods. Twice a day deities emerge from the temple and circumambulate around their own home through the surrounding streets of the town. On some occasions the deities may undertake a longer pilgrimage *(yatra)* to a holy bathing place, to undergo a purificatory bath.[27] In processions, the gods never appear in simple bronze form. They too must be decorated, just as the temple and town are. Each day, each processional icon is carefully washed and then suitably adorned for public appearance.

> Then the officiating priest should adorn the festival image . . . with garments, by preference silken, of white, yellow, or black colour, and with ornaments: crown, bracelets for the upper arms, necklace, breast-string, sacred thread, bracelets for the lower arms, finger rings, ear-rings in the shape of sea-monsters, hip-string, and belly-band, made of gold, and inlaid with pearls and jewels; and also with fragrant wreaths of flowers and with perfumes.[28]

In the view of the priestly guides, this adornment is not just extraneous decoration, but rather a crucial part of God's movement into form and becoming accessible. As the art historian A. K. Coomaraswamy observed in his essay on "Ornament":

> Whatever is unornamented is said to be "naked." God, "taken naked of all ornament" is "unconditioned" or "unqualified" *(nirguna)*: one, but inconceivable. Ornamented, He is endowed with qualities *(saguna)*, which are manifold in their relations and intelligible.[29]

The decorated mobile gods move about on palanquins (*sibika*) or chariots *(ratha)*. Palanquins are portable pedestals or sedans affixed to long bamboo poles hoisted on the shoulders of temple servants (figs. 7, 8). Chariots roll on four or more wooden wheels, pulled with long ropes. The festival chariots have superstructures above the throne of the images, so that they resemble moving temple towers. Chola-period guides like *Mayamata* prescribe relatively modest three-story chariot structures.[30] The massive wooden chariots employed nowadays by large institutions in Tamil Nadu like the Minakshi-Sundareshvara temple in Madurai date from a later period (fig. 9).

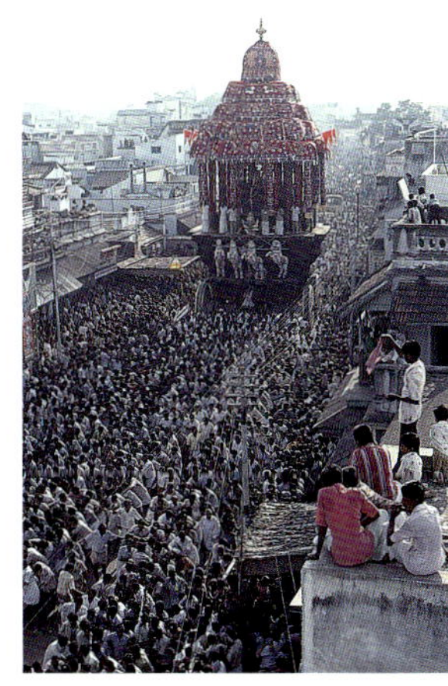

CHARIOT PROCESSION, CHITRAI FESTIVAL, MINAKSHI-SUNDARESHVARA TEMPLE, MADURAI, 1982
PHOTO RICHARD H. DAVIS
FIG. 9

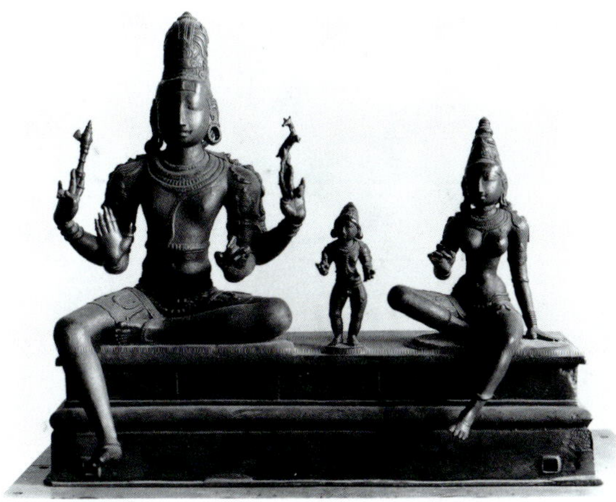

SOMASKANDA, FROM PATTISHVARAM, 10TH CENTURY. RAJARAJA ART MUSEUM, TANJAVUR
PHOTO RICHARD H. DAVIS
FIG. 10

God never travels alone in procession. In Shaiva *mahotsavas*, typically Shiva parades with other members of his innermost family, in five separate vehicles. First comes his son Ganesha; then Shiva as loving family man with wife Uma and son Skanda (Somaskanda) (fig 10); Uma alone; next Skanda with his two wives; and finally Shiva's "foremost devotee" Chandesha brings up the rear. Yet this is not just any household on tour. The lord travels surrounded by all the paraphernalia of royalty, appropriate to his status as Ruler of the Cosmos: the elephant leading the way, the great drum heralding his approach, the parasols and yak-tail fans, and his foremost weapon, the trident. Completing the entourage is the retinue of human followers. Brahmins recite mantras, temple servants carry the palanquins, temple women dance, musicians play on *nagasvarams* and drums, devotees sing the Tamil hymns, and others just follow along. As the parade circles through the town, it is as if the lord's royal court moves about with him. Indian processions always speak in the vocabulary of lordship.

Over the course of a lengthy *mahotsava*, the processions will vary. The route may change from day to day. The images may be decorated in new colors and styles. The principal deity rides atop a different vehicle each day. At a typical Vaishnava temple, for example, Vishnu might appear over the course of an eleven-day festival mounted on a lion, Garuda, Hanuman, the snake Shesha, a swan *(hamsa)*, an elephant, a chariot, and a horse, as well as the normal palanquin.[31] The deity himself may appear in different manifestations. In Shaiva processions, the lord will appear most commonly in the form of Somaskanda, but may on certain occasions manifest himself instead as Bhikshatana or as Nataraja. On other nights, the devotional saints themselves, in icon form, may also join in the procession (cat. nos. 27, 29, 31). At many temples these variations fit into a narrative, such that the overall festival re-enacts a mythical story of past divine activities specific to that locality. All this makes the *mahotsavas* of every temple in Tamil Nadu distinctive, adding interest and local color to each one. However, the most abiding feature of all festival processions is the self-presentation of God, in an accessible and beautiful form, to see and be seen by all living beings who are his subjects and devotees.

The Vaishnava Samhitas and Shaiva Agamas set out in detail the ritual procedures for the specialists who conducted temple ceremonies, but they offer less insight into how ordinary medieval Hindus might have seen and acted in these festivals. To some extent we can postulate from contemporary practice. Medieval viewers, like devout Hindus in modern India, would have viewed the bronze icons that came out from their temples with such pomp as living embodiments or manifestations of the gods who normally resided within. They would have received the mobile deities with all the proper gestures of respect due to a superior, and some might well have felt more profound religious emotions. Others might have arranged to give material offerings to a deity as the procession came by, or even to host the deity at a rest stop along its route, as wealthy devotees and businesses do these days (fig. 11). For a perspective closer to the time of the Cholas, however, we need to turn back again to the medieval Tamil poets.

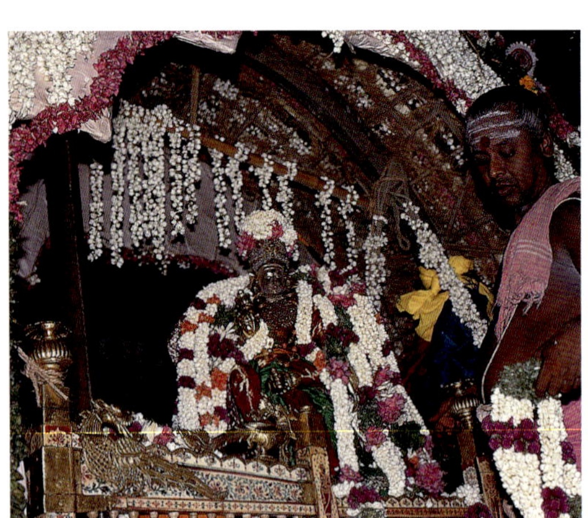

PRIEST RECEIVES GARLANDS FOR DEITIES, DURING FLOWER PALANQUIN PROCESSION, CHITRAI FESTIVAL, MINAKSHI-SUNDARESHVARA TEMPLE, MADURAI
PHOTO RICHARD H. DAVIS
FIG. 11

A MEDIEVAL PROCESSION OBSERVED

Festival processions have been a dramatic and joyous feature of south Indian temple life since before the Chola period. One of the earliest eyewitness accounts comes from the seventh-century Shaiva poet-saint Appar, who praises the Tiruvadirai celebration at Tiruvarur in a decade of stanzas. In our attempt to reimagine Chola bronzes in their original processional setting, it is fitting to give the final word to Appar's vivid description.[32]

Throughout his poem, Appar emphasizes the magnificent appearance of Tiruvarur (Arur) during the Tiruvadira (Atirai) festival, repeating in each stanza the refrain:

> *Such is the splendor of Atirai day*
> *in Arur, our Father's town.*

Appar repeats this refrain in each stanza, with slight variations. He describes the lavish decorations that adorn the town.

> *On every street, white flags flutter,*
> *canopies studded with great bright gems*
> *glitter, festooned with strands*
> *of priceless coral and pearl.*

The town is filled with people, both locals and pilgrims from far away, both "good men and rogues." Wandering ascetics likewise have streamed into town, and Appar particularly notes the "Virati" ascetics:

> *Devoted men and women follow him,*
> *along with Virati ascetics in bizarre garb*
> *garlanded with white skulls.*

These are probably the Shaiva anchorites known as Kapalikas, on account of their skull *(kapala)* begging bowls, who undertake a "great vow" *(mahavrata*, Tamil *viratta).*[33] Appar observes that gods and other divine figures are likewise in attendance, for the festival at Tiruvarur is an inclusive celebration for all beings, divine, human, and animal.

As the parade starts up, Appar hears the tumult of the processional ensemble, the percussive sounds of conches, drums, and jangling anklets.

As the blare of the moon-white conch,
the parai *drum's beat,*
and the jingle of the cymbals of dancing devotees,
spread everywhere, peacocks,
thinking that the rains have come,
dance in delight.

So thunderous is the procession that peacocks believe the monsoon is arriving, even though the Tiruvadirai festival takes place in the cool month of Markali (December–January), and the birds join in the general mood of excitement and dance.

On this festival day, Shiva comes forth from the main shrine in the guise of a beggar. The iconographic form of this bronze is known as Bhikshatana or Enchanting Mendicant (fig. 12), and it refers to a well-known narrative of Shiva's manifestation in the Pine Forest hermitage.[34] In order to convert a group of Vedic forest-dwellers to a more efficacious form of worship, the story goes, Shiva once took on the appearance of a naked, ash-smeared beggar and showed up unexpectedly in their ashram. Despite his unprepossessing appearance, the mendicant proved irresistible to the wives of the Pine Forest sages. The women sang, danced, and clung to him in erotic abandon. Failing to recognize the disguised deity, and enraged by this invasion of their austere lives, the sages tried to attack the beggar, but all their curses and sacrificial weapons were useless against the god. Finally, in a verbal confrontation, Shiva tore off and threw down his penis *(linga)* before the astonished hermits and disappeared. In the end, the sages became successful practitioners of the new rites of worshiping the Shiva-*linga*.

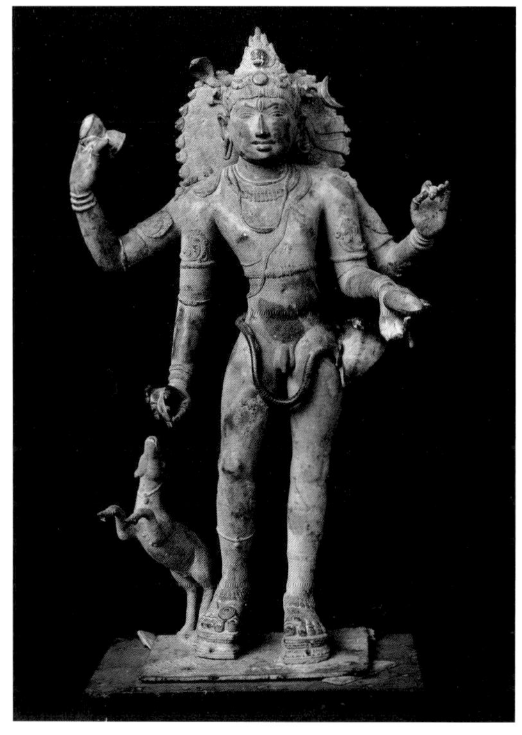

BHIKSHATANA (SHIVA AS ENCHANTING MENDICANT), FROM TIRUVENKADU, EARLY 11TH CENTURY. RAJARAJA ART MUSEUM, TANJAVUR
PHOTO RICHARD H. DAVIS
FIG. 12

Shiva's manifestation as a seductive beggar is particularly suitable for a processional image, for in contrast to the immovable *linga*, Shiva actively roamed the world in this form. In another song, Appar adopts the perspective of one of the seduced wives of the Pine Forest. Shiva has appeared at her door, entered her house, taken her by force, and made her sick with love, cries the female poetic voice in ironic lament.[35] For worshipers, Shiva's form as a beggar suggests his active intervention and engagement in the world, his vigorous pursuit and testing of devotees, and his insinuating power over their emotional lives.

In the Tiruvarur festival, however, Appar sees another irony in Shiva's appearance as Bhikshatana. He begins the poem:

He goes on his begging rounds
amid the glitter of a pearl canopy
and gem-encrusted golden fans.

The naked beggar is covered over and adorned with all the ornaments and sumptuous raiment proper to a lord in procession, and the austere but nearly hidden underlying mendicant form contrasts dramatically with the lush royal display Appar sees in the palanquin before him.[36] This is another paradox in Shiva's character, simultaneously lord of all and naked, ash-covered beggar.

Shiva Bhikshatana, the ascetic god, sets out on his procession with an entire retinue of divine and human followers as any lord would.

The ascetic god goes in procession,
led by the immortal gods
whose heads are bowed low to him,
while lovely celestial women
with shoulders graceful as the bamboo
follow behind, and ash-smeared devotees
surround him, singing his praise.

It is important to notice that Appar here simply refers to "the ascetic god," not to "the image of the ascetic god," because to the poet they are at this moment one and the same. Appar does not specify which "immortal gods" lead the cavalcade, but we might postulate, based on the medieval priestly texts and modern practice, that these would include Ganesha, Skanda, Uma, Nandi, and others. Elsewhere in the poem Appar mentions other humans also following Shiva in the parade, including devotees both male and female, and the Virati ascetics who perhaps look a bit like Bhikshatana themselves. Appar stresses that many in this entourage sing Shiva's praises as they march. We can imagine Appar himself joining in the procession, singing his own hymns such as this one, much as in later times the chanting of his devotional hymns came to be a regular part of processional ceremonies.[37]

Through his appearance in this festival, Shiva makes himself available and visible to all who have assembled in Tiruvarur for the occasion. Appar points to Shiva's accessibility here in the idiom of kinship:

our Lord of Arur is kinsman
to all those who cry,
"O my jewel, golden one, dear husband! My son!"

Clearly these responses are far from the more detached, dispassionate visual attention that we might pay to the same south Indian bronzes in a modern museum. But it is central to the devotional ethos of medieval Tamil Nadu to seek to place oneself in close proximity to the lord, to participate as intimately as possible in the life of God. These relations of intimacy with God are often figured in terms of intimate human relations. Appar notes the fervent emotional responses that go with this proximity to the divine. The temple women with their coral-red lips, meditators, young lovers, even gods all sing his praises.

Gathered together, his servants sing him;
now they praise his virtues,
now quarrel amongst themselves,
babbling like madmen, . . .

Not only verbal reactions, but also dancing and even more violent, uncontrollable bodily movements break out in the crowd of devotees.

They sob and tremble,
they stare and shout.
They frighten others, forget themselves,
and go wild. Dashing their heads,
they cry, "My Lord! God! Elder kinsman! O Father!"

Far from suggesting moral censure toward these outbursts of uncontrolled feeling, Appar portrays them as appropriate and valued emotional responses to Shiva's overwhelming presence as he approaches in procession.[38]

Appar returns, in the final stanza of the hymn, to the leitmotif of splendor and glory that suffuses Tiruvarur on this festival day.

> *It is glorious with unceasing*
> *singing and dancing about the Lord's glory,*
> *as devotees worship and sing the praise*
> *of the god who stood revealed*
> *in the cosmic flood that engulfed the earth.*
> *Such is the splendor of Arur, which place*
> *every town in the world praises in song.*

In concluding his encomium to this particular festival of Shiva, though, Appar also reminds his audience that the same god who makes himself accessible as a beggar is also an awesome, incomprehensible, Supreme God. In another manifestation during the cosmic flood, Shiva stood revealed in a *linga* of pure light so extensive that neither Vishnu nor Brahma could find the bottom or top even in ten thousand years.[39]

Appar's song of the Tiruvadirai celebration brings together the most important themes and features of medieval south Indian festival processions. Festivals are inclusive events intended for the participation of all beings. Festivals are occasions when the town, the temple, the residents, and the deities all appear at their most splendid. Festivals center around moments of divine appearance, when the Supreme Lord becomes most accessible, when a temple icon emerges from the innermost sanctum of its palatial temple to see and be seen by all worshipers. Festival processions dramatize the divine sovereignty of Vishnu or Shiva for all present. And festivals provide moments when, in the face of the divine, viewers may find themselves overwhelmed with devotional emotion. Appar recreates for us the kind of processional scene for which Chola artisans created their works of bronze statuary and within which south Indians of medieval times viewed these divinized icons. The images have made a still longer procession to appear before us, in North American museums, some ten centuries later.

NOTES

Work on this essay was aided materially by research grants from the National Endowment for the Humanities and the Bard College Research Fund, and I am grateful to both institutions. I am also grateful to esteemed scholars N. R. Bhatt and R. Nagaswamy for extensive conversations and valuable guidance during my research visit to Chennai in 2000. I thank friends at the Kuppuswami Sastri Research Institute for much help, Arunasundaram Gurukkal at the Sanskrit College and Kapalishvara temple for further conversations on temple processions from a priest's point of view, and Martha Selby for a place to stay. I owe a continuing debt to the late Dr. S. S. Janaki and the late Sri K. A. Sabharatna Sivacarya for initiating me into the world of the Shaiva Agamas.

1 Kenneth X. Robbins, "The Sculpture of India, 3000 B.C.–1300 A.D.," *Arts of Asia* 15, no. 5 (1985): 104.

2 The most striking and characteristic musical sound of contemporary south Indian temple festivals, played by the raucous double-reeded *nagasvaram* (or *nadasvaram*) and stick-beaten *tavil* drum, was evidently introduced after the Chola period, perhaps as early as the thirteenth century. See R. Rangaramanuja Ayyangar, "Music in Temple Rituals," in K. K. A. Venkatachari, ed., *Proceedings of the Seminar on Temple Art and Architecture* (Bombay: Ananthacharya Indological Research Institute, 1981), pp. 47–52.

3 Buddhists and Jains of medieval south India also celebrated festivals by carrying images in processions, and as a result fine bronze *utsavamurtis* depicting figures such as the Buddha Shakyamuni and Mahavira the Jain *tirthankara* are also found in southern India, along with the more numerous Hindu icons. However, the somewhat different theological premises and ceremonial practices of these other religious groups falls beyond the scope of this essay. For an evocative narrative of a Jain festival procession, composed by the court poet Henachandra of the Solanki dynasty in Gujarat contemporaneous with the Cholas, see R. C. C. Fynes, *The Lives of the Jain Elders* (Oxford: Oxford University Press, 1998), pp. 201–14.

4 Nammalvar, *Tiruvaymoli* 1.1.8, trans. in Norman Cutler, *Songs of Experience: The Poetics of Tamil Devotion*, Religion in Asia and Africa series (Bloomington: Indiana University Press, 1987), p. 133. For further translations of the poetry of Nammalvar, see A. K. Ramanujan, *Hymns for the Drowning: Poems for Visnu by Nammalvar*, Princeton Library of Asian Translations (Princeton: Princeton University Press, 1981). Modern scholars generally date Nammalvar's poetry to the ninth century.

5 Nammalvar, *Tiruvaymoli* 1.9.4, trans. in Cutler, *Songs of Experience,* p. 140.

6 For a full discussion of these two terms within Ramanuja's theology, see John Braisted Carman, *The Theology of Ramanuja: An Essay in Interreligious Understanding* (New Haven: Yale University Press), pp. 77–87. In their *The Tamil Veda: Pillan's Interpretation of the Tiruvaymoli* (Chicago: University of Chicago Press, 1989), John Carman and Vasudha Narayanan discuss Nammalvar's poetry as it was interpreted within the parameters of Ramanuja's philosophy.

7 Nammalvar, *Tiruvaymoli*, 1.3.2, trans. in Cutler, *Songs of Experience,* p. 135.

8 Sekkilar, *Periyapuranam* vs. 147–349, in T. N. Ramachandran, trans., *St. Sekkizhar's Periya Purana* (Tanjavur: Tamil University, 1990), pp. 41–73. David Dean Shulman dramatically retells the wedding incident in the introduction to his full translation of Sundarar's *Tevaram* (*Songs of the Harsh Devotee: The Tevaram of Cuntaramurttinayanar*, University of Pennsylvania Studies on South Asia [Philadelphia: Department of South Asia Regional Studies, University of Pennsylvania, 1990], pp. xv–xvii). Sekkilar probably served as court poet for the Chola ruler Kulottunga II (r. 1133–50).

9 Sundarar, *Tevaram* 1,. in Shulman, trans., *Songs of the Harsh Devotee,* p. 1. Sekkilar, *Periyapuranam* vs. 219–20, narrates the circumstances of Sundarar's first poem (trans. in Ramachandran, *St. Sekkizhar's Periya Purana*, p. 51).

10 George Spencer, "The Sacred Geography of the Tamil Shaivite Hymns," *Numen* 17 (1970): 232–44; and Indira Viswanathan Peterson, "Lives of the Wandering Singers: Pilgrimage and Poetry in Tamil Saivite Hagiography," *History of Religions* 22 (1983): 338–60, discuss the pilgrimages of the early medieval Tamil Shaiva saints and their role in establishing a "sacred geography" in southern India.

11 See the discussion of the "devotional eye" in Richard H. Davis, *Lives of Indian Images* (Princeton: Princeton University Press, 1997), pp. 37–44.

12 *Purvakamikagama* 4.6. See Richard H. Davis, *Ritual in an Oscillating Universe: Worshiping Siva in Medieval India* (Princeton: Princeton University Press, 1991), for a detailed discussion of Shaiva temple *puja*, based on Shaiva Agama texts of the Chola period.

13 Cutler, *Songs of Experience*, p.135. The Virashaivas of eleventh- and twelfth-century Karnataka furnish perhaps the most vivid example of devotional egalitarian or "anti-structural" rhetoric. See A. K. Ramanujan, *Speaking of Siva* (Harmondsworth, England: Penguin Books, 1973).

14 Ramakantha's *Jatinirnayapurvakalayapravesavidhi* of the tenth century sets out a full hierarchy of temple spaces and rules of access (Pierre-Sylvain Filliozat, "Le droit d'entrer dans les temples de Siva au XIe siècle," *Journal asiatique* 263 [1975]: 103–17). See Davis, *Ritual in an Oscillating Universe,* pp. 60–72, for a general discussion of temple space in medieval Shaiva temples. For a discussion of the issue of differentiated access in medieval temple Hinduism, see Ronald Iden, "The Temple and the Hindu Great Chain of Being," *Purusartha* 8 (1985): 53-73.

15 Samakantha, *Alayapravesavidhi*, quoted in Davis, *Ritual in an Oscillating Universe*, p. 70.

16 Garudavahana Pandita, *Divyasuricarita*, ch. 7, trans. in Friedhelm Hardy, "TirupPan-Alvar: The Untouchable Who Rode Piggy-Back on the Brahmin," in *Devotion Divine: Bhakti Traditions from the Regions of India; Studies in Honour of Charlotte Vaudeville*, ed. Diana L. Eck and Françoise Mallison, Groningen Oriental Studies 8 (Groningen: Egbert Forsten, 1991), p. 134. Tiruppan's story is retold many times in later Vaishnava hagiographies. A parallel story is told in the Shaiva *Periyapuranam* of the Panar Nilakanta Nayanmar, who was similarly brought into temples at Madurai and Tiruvarur.

17 Tiruppan Alvar, "Amalanatipiran," in *Nalayirattivviyappirapantam* 927–36, trans. in Steven P. Hopkins, "In Love with the Body of God: Eros and the Praise of Icons in South Indian Devotion," *Journal of Vaisnava Studies* 2 (1993): 24–28.

18 *Purvakaranagama* 24.95, trans. in Davis, *Ritual in an Oscillating Universe*, p. 72.

19 *Kashyapa Jnanakanda* 55.1–3, trans. in Goudriaan Teun, *Kasyapa's Book of Wisdom (Kasyapa-jnanakandah): A Ritual Handbook of the Vaikhanasas.* Disputationes Rheno-Trajectinae 10 (The Hague: Mouton & Co., 1965), p. 162. The *Kashyapa Jnanakanda* is a text of the Vaishnava Vaikhanasa school, probably composed between C.E. 800 and 1000 in southern India, according to Goudriaan's estimate.

20 On Shiva's levels of being in relation to the supports of Shiva's presence, see Davis, *Ritual in an Oscillating Universe*, pp. 112–22.

21 For one example, *Mayamata* is a Shaiva Shilpashastra of the Chola period. See Bruno Dagens, ed. and trans., *Mayamatam: Treatise of Housing, Architecture, and Iconography*, Kalamulasastra Granthamala series 14–15 (New Delhi: Indira Gandhi National Centre for the Arts and Motilal Banarsidass, 1994), for iconographic prescriptions for Shiva's main processional forms. As Dagens notes, the prescriptions set out in this artisans' guidebook correspond closely to major Shaiva Agamas of the same period such as *Kamikagama*.

22 *Paramesvara Samhita kriya* 16.2–3, ed. U. V. Govindacarya; *Ajitagama* 27.1, ed. N. R. Bhatt.

23 *Paramesvara Samhita kriya* 16.4–7.

24 There are a number of excellent studies of modern south Indian temple festivals. Some noteworthy examples are: K. Rangachari, *The Sri Vaisnava Brahmans*, Bulletin of the Madras Government Museum (Madras: Government Press, 1931), on festivals in Kanchipuram; Dennis Hudson, "Siva, Minaksi, Visnu—Reflections on a Popular Myth in Madurai," *Indian Economic and Social History Review* 14 (1977): 107–18; William P. Harman, *The Sacred Marriage of a Hindu Goddess*, Religion in Asia and Africa series (Bloomington: Indiana University Press, 1989), on the Chitrai festival in Madurai; Paul Younger, "Ten Days of Wandering and Romance with Lord Ranganathan: The Pankuni Festival in Srirankam Temple, South India," *Modern Asian Studies* 16, no. 4 (1982): 623–56, on Srirangam festivals; Glenn Yocum, "Brahmin, King, Sannyasi, and the Goddess in a Cage: Reflections on the 'Conceptual Order of Hinduism' at a Tamil Saiva Temple," *Contributions to Indian Sociology* n.s. 20, no. 1 (1986): 15–39, on the Avadayarkoyil festival in Ramnad district; Joanne Punzo Waghorne, "Dressing the Body of God: South Indian Bronze Sculpture in Its Temple Setting," *Asian Art* 5, no. 3 (September 1992): 9–33, focusing on the Kapalishvara temple in Chennai; and Paul Younger, *The Home of Dancing Sivan: The Traditions of the Hindu Temple in Citamparam* (Oxford: Oxford University Press, 1995), on the Chidambaram Nataraja temple.

25 S. S. Janaki, *Dhvaja-Stambha (Critical Account of Its Structural and Ritualistic Details)* (Madras: Kuppuswami Sastri Research Institute, 1988), p. 45. Janaki's excellent work offers a comprehensive overview of the rites of temple flag-raising and its interpretations within a Shaiva context.

26 *Kashyapa Jnanakanda*, ch. 89, trans. in Goudriaan, *Kasyapa's Book of Wisdom*, pp. 275–76.

27 For instance, *Parama Samhita*, one of the earliest Vaishnava Samhitas, treats festival processions exclusively in terms of an image pilgrimage to a bathing place. It may well be, as Paul Younger suggests in his study of Chidambaram *(The Home of Dancing Sivan)*, that such back-and-forth trips were more typical of early temple processions in south India, while the more regal circumambulatory tours were institutionalized particularly during the Chola period.

28 *Kashyapa Jnanakanda*, ch. 89, translated by Goudriaan, *Kasyapa's Book of Wisdom,* p. 278.

29 A. K. Coomaraswamy, "Ornament," *Art Bulletin* 1939, quoted in Waghorne, "Dressing the Body of God," p. 13. See Waghorne's essay for an insightful treatment of these issues of adornment and appearance of festival icons. For a parallel descriptions of the aesthetics of Jain image adornment, see John E. Cort, "King or Ascetic? Ornamentation of Jain Temple Images," ACSAA Symposium, Minneapolis, 12 May 1996.

30 *Mayamata,* ch. 31 contains directions for constructing suitable palanquins and chariots.

31 Rangachari, *The Sri Vaisnava Brahmans,* based on Shri Vaishnava temples at Kanchipuram and Lakshmanapuram.

32 Appar, *Tevaram* 4.21, "Tiruvatirait Tiruppatikam," trans. in Indira Viswanathan Peterson, *Poems to Siva: The Hymns of the Tamil Saints,* Princeton Library of Asian Translations (Princeton: Princeton University Press, 1989), pp. 184–86. I take the liberty here of rearranging the order of Appar's own presentation. For those who wish to see the original, I recommend Peterson's excellent translation. Also useful is R. Nagaswamy's discussion of the poem in his *Siva-Bhakti* (New Delhi: Navrang, 1989), pp. 155–56.

33 On the Kapalikas and their "great vow," see esp. David N. Lorenzen, *The Kapalikas and Kalamukhas: Two Lost Saivite Sects,* Australian National University Centre of Oriental Studies Oriental Monograph 12 (New Delhi: Thomson Press [India], 1972), pp. 73–82. In the *Mattavilasaprahasana*, a Sanskrit play composed by the Pallava king who was Appar's contemporary and patron, we find a satiric account of Kapalikas. However, the Viratis may also designate a distinct group of Shaiva ascetics, for in another poem Appar refers to several categories of Shaiva religious specialists dwelling at Tiruvarur: Virati ascetics, brahmins, Shaivas, Pashupatas, and Kapalikas (*Tevaram* 4.20.3, trans. in Peterson, *Poems to Siva*, p. 182).

34 For a translation of one of the many versions of this story, from the *Kurma Purana*, see Richard H. Davis, "The Origin of Linga Worship," in *Religions of India in Practice*, ed. Donald S. Lopez (Princeton: Princeton University Press, 1995), pp. 637–48. A general discussion of the myth in its many variants is provided in Wendy Doniger O'Flaherty, *Siva: The Erotic Ascetic* (Oxford: Oxford University Press, 1981).

35 Appar, *Tevaram* 4.223, trans. in Peterson, *Poems to Siva*, pp. 124–26.

36 Younger *(The Home of Dancing Sivan)* points to this contrast in his description of the popular Chidambaram procession featuring Bhikshatana, also celebrated on Tiruvadirai day.

37 Peterson (*Poems to Siva*, pp. 56–58) discusses the singing of Tamil devotional hymns in contemporary processions. Vedic brahmins chanting passages from the Veda head the procession, while the *otuvars* who sing the Tamil *Tevaram* songs bring up the rear.

38 Friedhelm Hardy (*Viraha-Bhakti: The Early History of Krsna Devotion in South India* [Delhi: Oxford University Press, 1983]) uses the apt term "emotional bhakti" to describe this devotional ethos in medieval South India, and traces its historical development within the Vaishnava tradition. On the suitability of possession within bhakti, see also Ramanujan, *Hymns for the Drowning*.

39 One of the many tellings of this myth, from the *Kurma Purana*, is translated in Cornelia Dimmitt and J. A. B. van Buitenen, *Classical Hindu Mythology: A Reader in the Sanskrit Puranas* (Philadelphia: Temple University Press, 1978), pp. 205–6.

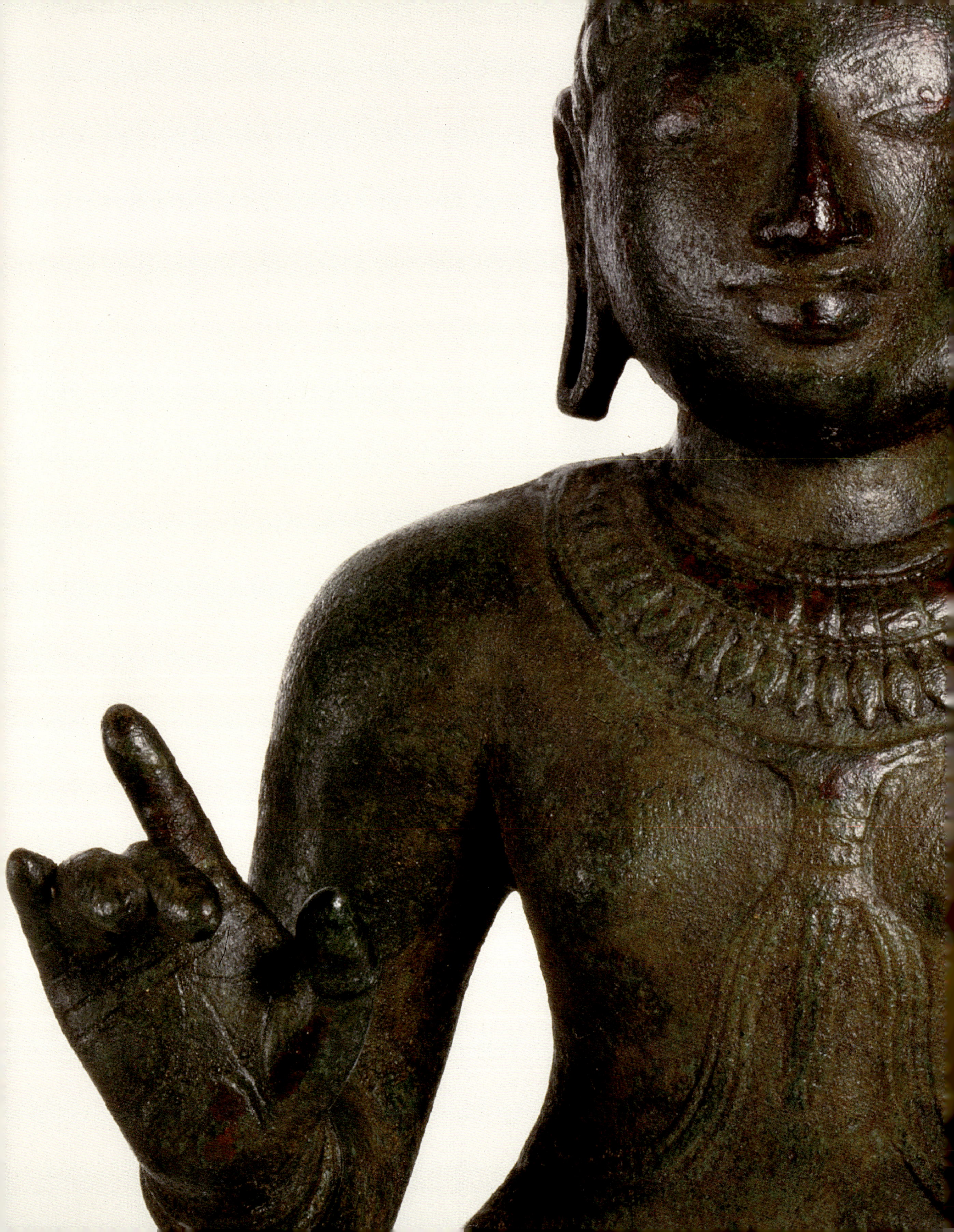

JOYOUS ENCOUNTERS: TAMIL BHAKTI POETS AND IMAGES OF THE DIVINE

KAREN PECHILIS PRENTISS

Sacred images in Hindu culture are "visual theologies"[1]; they are encoded with symbolic references that point the viewer toward specific meanings, especially the powers associated with the sacred subject. As this exhibition makes abundantly clear, the vast majority of these sacred images are iconic images of gods; however, there are also aniconic images of gods, as well as images of human saints, both of which are also symbolically rendered.[2] It is the iconic images of gods, though, that are especially related to Hinduism's huge corpus of classical mythology in the popular imagination, for these myths are stories that Hindus bring to their viewing of the images, providing them with "manageable models" for understanding and interpreting the images.[3]

A case in point is provided by Shiva as Nataraja, or Lord of Dance, which is understood to represent the cosmic dance of Shiva, by which he alternatively creates and destroys the world (cat. nos. 1–4). The density of symbolic meaning lies in the union of these and other opposing forces in a single image.

> The flaming circle in which he dances is the circle of creation and destruction called *samsara* (the earthly round of birth and death) or *maya* (the illusory world). The Lord who dances in the circle of this changing world holds in two of his hands the drum

CHILD-SAINT SAMBANDAR (DETAIL OF CAT. NO. 27)

> of creation and the fire of destruction. He displays his strength by crushing the bewildered demon underfoot. Simultaneously, he shows his mercy by raising his palm to the worshiper in the "fear-not" gesture and, with another hand, by pointing to his upraised foot, where the worshiper may take refuge. It is a wild dance, for the coils of his ascetic's hair are flying in both directions, and yet the facial countenance of the Lord is utterly peaceful and his limbs in complete balance. Around one arm twines the *naga*, the ancient serpent which he has incorporated into his sphere of power and wears now as an ornament. In his hair sits the mermaid River Ganga, who landed first on Siva's hair when she fell from heaven to earth.[4]

The simultaneity of image and mythology informs the popular appreciation of the image and, generally speaking, provides a gentle consensus of meaning in contemporary Hindu interpretation and practice.

Although mythological stories are the most common reservoir of meaning that Hindus draw upon to interpret sacred visual images, the myths are by no means the only type of theology that may inform them. Hinduism is pluralistic in nature; in its long history many philosophies and practices have been developed that may take very different interpretive stances on sacred images. Thus, one must ask *which* theology a viewer is using to interpret the image, for sacred images are actually a contested locus of meaning for many Hindu theologies.

The Tamil bhakti poets (ca. sixth–ninth centuries), who lived several centuries prior to the dominance of the Chola dynasty, sought to imbue sacred images with their own distinctive theology. Bhakti is often translated into English as "devotion," although this term does not quite capture the wholehearted dedication of the poets to their chosen deities. The poets composed thousands of poems; tradition represents the poets as having sung them as hymns in praise of the Lord. The bhakti poems devoted to Shiva were collected as the seven-volume *Tevaram*, which was incorporated in the Shaiva canon, the *Tirumurai*; and the bhakti poems devoted to Vishnu were collected in the Vaishnava canon, the *Nalayira-Divya-Prabandam*. The poets' approach was joyous and engaged, and remains influential in the present day.

The term "devotion" does not necessarily convey that the bhakti poets developed a distinctive theology; their act of reasoning, as well as the experience of emotion, is constitutive of their bhakti. The bhakti poets' special contribution was a theology of embodiment. In this theology, they foregrounded the human appreciation of God. For example, consider this hymn of the Shaiva saint Appar (cat. no. 29) on Shiva as Nataraja:

> *If you could see*
> *the arch of his brow,*
> *the budding smile*
> *on lips red as the* kovvai *fruit,*
> *cool matted hair,*
> *the milk-white ash on coral skin,*
> *and the sweet golden foot*
> *raised up in dance,*
> *then even human birth on this wide earth*
> *would become a thing worth having.*[5]

In Appar's vision, God is alive: his lips are red, emerging into a smile, and the colors of his body are vivid. His dance has cosmic significance, as per the mythological story, but it is also personally meaningful. The poet addresses his fellow humankind with "if you could see," and he assures them that their unmediated vision of the living Lord is worth the price of birth in this world. Significantly, the poet makes this assertion in contrast to the dominant Hindu philosophical axiom that birth and rebirth are a condition of humankind that must be escaped. Thus, bhakti to the Lord transforms the very quality of life itself. Similarly, although the poem alludes to the cosmic dance of the Lord, it foregrounds the live encounter with the Lord.

Appar's hypothetical "if" raises an interesting issue: can humankind see the Lord? Surely that is what images of the Lord displayed in the ritual context of temples, such as those represented in the exhibition, were intended to affirm. On one level, as Norman Cutler has discussed, the theology of the poet-saints effectively matched the theology that guided the ritual honoring of sacred images in temples.

> It is useful to think of Tamil bhakti poetry as a poetic corollary of a theology of embodiment. . . . The poetics of bhakti . . . mirrors the religious ideology implicit in temple worship, for just as the presence of divinity is thought to be literally embodied in a properly consecrated stone or metal image of god, similarly the saint's communion with divinity is literally embodied in the recitation of his or her poetry in a consecrated ritual environment.[6]

This sense of bhakti as a theology of embodiment was especially operative in the ritual context of the temple, where the saints' poems became established as performed liturgy by the eleventh century. However, the grand imperial stone temples were themselves contested space, in which attempts were made to harmonize hierarchically distinctive modes of knowledge and practice; in this context, the performance of the bhakti hymns was cast in a supporting role to the main traditions of ritual worship.[7]

In contrast, the saints' depictions of the path of bhakti in their poems do not suggest that it has a limited role: they represent bhakti as a primary way to understand God, humankind, and the relationship between them. Appar's use of "if" seemingly acknowledges this difference in theology. Thus, on another level, bhakti's theology of embodiment is an encompassing worldview that seeks to locate other modes of religiosity within itself. For the saints, bhakti is the map, and aspects of religious practice, such as mythology, images, and ritual, are points on it. The Shaiva saint Appar represents the practice of temple worship as a metaphor that signifies the inner engagement of bhakti:

Inside this house called the body
the heart is the lamp;
pour knowledge that dispels ignorance as the ghee,
fashion the soul as the wick,
take the supreme fire of nana as the flame
and the vision of the One
    whose feet have anklets
    and whose son enjoys the katampu tree
will be yours.[8]

More than a way of worship, bhakti for the Tamil saints is a way of being. In this poem, Appar urges the bhakta (one who practices bhakti) to commit his or her inner core to Shiva: the heart is the locus of the commitment, knowledge is the fuel, the soul is the agency, and higher wisdom *(nana*, Sanskrit *jnana)*, which is spiritual insight resulting from inner contemplation, is the conflagration of truth. Note that, as with the poem by Appar cited earlier, the one who embodies bhakti through emotional and mental commitment to the Lord is rewarded by a direct, unmediated vision of the Lord himself.

The vision of the Lord as portrayed in this poem has both iconographical and mythological dimensions: the poem's attention to the anklets on the Lord's feet calls to mind the image of Shiva as Lord of Dance, and the reference to the Lord's son calls to mind the aspect of Shiva as a family man, as portrayed in the Somaskanda image (Shiva with Uma and Skanda) (cat. nos. 15, 16). Further, association of Shiva's son with the *katampu* tree localizes the image in Tamil mythology, for Skanda is identified with the Tamil god Murugan, who resides in the hills covered with *katampu* trees. However, the poem frames these images and their mythologies with the assertion that humankind must embody bhakti: the body is the "house" where we live, and all of its components must be actively dedicated to the Lord. The Tamil bhakti poets mapped images of the Lord with the love of the human heart, and the spiritual insight of the human mind.

Similar imagery occurs in bhakti poetry to Vishnu. One of the earliest poets in the Vaishnava group of bhakti poets also homologized internal dedication with the external features of ritual practice, in this case linking the experience of knowledge to the poet's craft of writing:

> *With love as bowl,*
> *ardor as oil,*
> *and a joyful mind as wick,*
> *I swooned*
> *and lit a blazing lamp of knowledge*
> *for Naranan,*
>
> *even as I delight in the sage Tamil tongue.*[9]

For all of the Tamil bhakti poets, so great is the beauty of the Lord when experienced through the language of Tamil that life itself becomes beautiful.

The Tamil Shaiva and Vaishnava bhakti poets illuminated images of Shiva and Vishnu in their poetry, through which they gave voice in their mother tongue to their ongoing and encompassing engagement with the Lord. Furthermore, they designed their poems to provide others with a way to experience bhakti for the Lord; for example, Appar's poem promises that a vision of the Lord "will be yours" if "you" approach the Lord with bhakti.

In this way, the Tamil Shaiva and Vaishnava bhakti poets' compositions enhance the sacred images found in the temples, such as the bronzes in this exhibition; yet the poets are not bound by these sculpted images, as their emphasis on personal encounter in the context of a theology of embodiment makes clear. This point has been somewhat obscured in some modern scholarship on the Tamil Shiva-bhakti poets, which makes the argument that, since the epigraphical records of the Cholas describe images of the Lord in specific temples that "match" the image of the Lord in the poems, then the poets must have been describing what they saw. It is the case that in major centers, such as the temple town of Arur, where the Cholas resided long before their dominance over the Tamil region, internal evidence from some of the poets' compositions does seem to suggest that they were describing an established temple culture. However, this is probably more the exception than the rule, for it is also the case that when the Cholas, who were mostly Shaiva, came to reign, they used the poets' compositions as a template in order to establish imperial stone temples throughout the Tamil region.[10] Thus, the poets' imagination became concretized by the Cholas, not the other way around. To illuminate further the nature of the poets' imagination, I will discuss selected poems under themes of the human perspective especially prominent in the poems of the Tamil saints.

BEHOLDING THE LORD

As we follow the poets' gaze of awe toward the Lord, the visibly breathtaking beauty of the Lord actually points us beyond his image to intuit his awesome, complete power. The first poem, on Shiva, presents us with a "Portrait in Silver" and provides the viewer with the colors of white, silver, and coral to enhance the bronze image. In its emphasis on the cool beauty of silver, the poem transforms the image of Shiva as a frightful beggar into a luminous embodiment of ultimate beauty. The second poem, which is on Vishnu, shows us "The Lord at Play," linking the beautiful form of the Lord to his cosmic powers.

He bears a skull
like a silver conch shell.
His twisted white sacred thread
shines like a strand of silver rope.
Matted hair crowned with the white moon
bright as beaten silver leaf,
wearing white bones,
the brahmin has smeared silver ash
on his coral skin.[11]

O lord unending
wearing honey flowers
and basil leaf
in your hair

tell us this:

as moon
as sun
as the amazing numberless stars

as darkness
and as torrents of rain

as honor
as shame

and as death
with his cruel eyes
how fantastic
can you get?[12]

PRAISING THE LORD'S DEEDS

Here we follow the poets' gaze of celebration toward the Lord, especially his heroic deeds. This category of poem draws heavily on the mythology of Shiva and Vishnu, and its visualization of the Lord and his deeds often correlates with the established iconography of rendering the images into bronze. However, as important as the Lord's deeds are in defining his nature and the ways in which he has bestowed grace on humankind throughout the ages, of equal importance to the bhakti saints is the ongoing relationship of humankind to the Lord. To address this dimension, they frame the mythological deeds of the Lord with their very local, present-day concerns. The well-known, official mythologies of the Lord in classical Sanskrit texts are thus celebrated by the Tamil poets both for their once-upon-a-time quality and for their relevance to those who dedicate themselves to the Lord today.

The story of Shiva as the swallower of poison (Vishapaharana- or Shrikantha-murti; cat. no. 9) is a famous image from the classical Sanskrit Puranas, or mythological texts, and it finds mention in the poetry of each of the three prominent Shiva-bhakti saints, Sambandar, Appar, and Sundarar. A summary of the Sanskrit myth is as follows:

> The gods and demons decided to churn the celestial ocean of milk in order to bring forth *amta* (ambrosia), the elixir of immortality. With Mount Mandara for their churning stick and the world-snake Sesa or Vasuki for the rope, they began churning the ocean. To their dismay, the first substance to rise from the ocean was a black mass of Kalakuta, the world-poison. The frightened gods and demons appealed to Siva Mahadeva to rescue them. Siva at once seized the poison and drank it, retaining it in his throat, which turned blue-black on account of the poison.[13]

A poem by the child-saint Sambandar (cat. nos. 27, 28) on this theme locates this very Lord in the Tamil town of Valitayam:

The Lord who swallowed the poison
in the primordial sea
as though it were water;
who danced while the celestials worshipped
and praised Him;
who gracefully subdued the power
of the mighty king of Lanka
lives in the temple at Valitayam
  which abounds with the sweet sap
  of the jack tree and the shiny-leaved betel nut tree.
If one worships Him
for as long as the soul shines in the body
the troubles of the mind will be gone.[14]

The Lord's beneficial powers subdue destructive powers (poison, king of Lanka), and the celestials praise his cosmic dance as a manifestation of his strength. The poem's allusion to these myths demonstrates Shiva's cosmic powers; however, the poem asserts that he "lives" in Tamil country, at the temple at Valitayam. Here, the Lord's beneficial powers apply locally: just as he cosmically swallowed the poison so that the divine ambrosia could flow, he makes possible the flow of sweet sap in the town, which renders the land fertile for cultivation. Similarly, those who worship Shiva at the temple will gain a free-flowing mind, which is peace of mind.

A poem by the older saint, Appar, whose familiar name of "Father" *(appar)* is said to have been bestowed by the child-saint Sambandar, speaks of the poet's mystical experience with the Lord who swallowed the poison:

> *Can I who am prone to deception henceforth forget*
> *the light that shone even while I slept,*
> *the virtue that remains in my mind, causing me to remember*
> *the Lord who subdued the poison in His throat?*[15]

Here, the poet critiques his very human tendency to forget the Lord; yet the Lord prods him to know their shared divine nature through a dazzling display of light while the poet is in an unconscious state. It is up to the poet to retain this light, the ultimate virtue, when he is awake; a way to do this is to remember, and to meditate on, the image of the Lord who subdued the poison in his throat.

The image of the Lord who swallowed poison occurs with great frequency in the poetry of Sundarar (cat. nos. 31, 32). This poet is famous for his loving, yet argumentative tone toward the Lord in his poetry, of which the following poem is a representative example:

> *Except when I'm in trouble,*
> *I don't realize how much I need him.*
> *I used to think*
> *my heart*
> *would be enough.*
>
> *He destroyed by fire*
> *the Triple City of his enemies,*
>
> *the lord of Paccilacciramam*
> *with his red matted hair*
> *and throat filled with poison*
> *who has mercy*
> *on those who have nothing.*
>
> *Say what you will,*
> *we can rejoice when he gives us gifts*
> *or curse him when he doesn't, but*
>
> *can't we find some other god?*[16]

This poem brings together opposing emotions: it is "at once plaintive and acrimonious," and "the underlying emotion is an explosive combination of fear and love for the deity."[17] This is a combination most characteristic of Sundarar's poetry; however, it can easily be extended, as the poet does, to represent humankind's ongoing oscillation of emotions toward the Lord.

The Vishnu-bhakti poet Nammalvar explores the ten avatars (incarnations) of Vishnu in his poetry. These avatars performed heroic deeds for the benefit of humankind in remote times, beginning with creation. For example, the boar (Varaha) is Vishnu's third incarnation, by which he rescued the earth from a demon's submergence of it under the waters of the ocean (cat. no. 44). In the poet's vision, the Lord saved the earth by keeping it whole.

No, they did not come apart:

the seven islands of the earth,
they stayed in place;

and the seven mountains,
they stayed in place;

and the seven seas
did not go wild
but stayed in one place

miraculously,
    that day

our lord pitchforked them out
with his tusks
from the deep.[18]

In another poem on the same theme, the poet frames allusions to Vishnu's heroic deeds with humankind's inability to grasp fully the cosmic cycles of time that the Lord maintains:

Who can fathom the illusions
conjured by Mal
on this earth,
the woman with long arms
locked tightly in his embrace?

he measured the world with his strides,
he became a boar
and scooped the earth from the depths of the sea,

he reclines, sits, and stands
on the very earth he swallowed and spewed up once more.[19]

The famous hero Rama, whose exploits are detailed in the epic *Ramayana*, is another avatar of Vishnu (cat. no. 46). Poems by Nammalvar praise his prowess in battle as he defeats the demon army of Lanka, as well as his grace when he rules righteously in his re-established kingdom in Ayodhya.

Crowding each other
face to face
as the arrows sang
and jangled
demon carcasses fell
in hundreds
rolled over
like hills
the sea stained with blood
backed up into the rivers
when our lord and father
ravaged the island
and left it
a heap of ash.

Why would anyone want
to learn anything but Rama?

Beginning with the low grass
and the creeping ant
with nothing
whatever,

he took everything in his city,
everything moving,
everything still,
he took everything,
everything born
of the lord
of four faces,

he took them all
to the very best of states.[20]

LONGING FOR THE LORD

We follow the poets' gaze of longing toward the Lord. As a theology of embodiment, bhakti acknowledges that humankind is separate and distinct from the pure essence of divinity that is the Lord; and yet, in its inner nature humankind shares in the divinity of the Lord. This tension is dramatized in bhakti poems through the poets' poignant emotion of longing for the Lord, simultaneously affirming the identity between and the separation of humankind and God.

For example, one of the poems of Sundarar juxtaposes the heroic Shiva from classical Sanskrit mythology, in this case the Lord Who Destroyed the Three Cities, also known as Victor of the Three Cities (Tripuravijaya; cat. nos. 5, 6), with the poet's own longing.

The Lord who burned the cities
drawing against His body
the mountain as the bow, the strong cobra as the bowstring,
and Agni and Hari as the arrow—
I am a fool not to think of Him first.
Bearing this body,
How long can I remain separate
from my Lord of Arur?[21]

In the mythological story, Shiva heroically rids the world of three demons who, by a boon from Brahma, are invincible unless they are killed with a single arrow. Shiva developed a potent arrow from a composite of other gods' powers; here, Agni (fire, perhaps as the tip), and Hari (Vishnu, perhaps as the shaft). The majestic power of the Lord as a victor in cosmic battles sets him apart from the humble and fallible poet, who forgets to think of the Lord first; Shiva's body is an emblem of strength, while the human body is one of weakness. And yet, when the poet sets his mind to it, intimacy is possible, as in the vividness of his description of the Lord.

Sometimes the voice of the poem can be that of a lovelorn woman; in this case, the longing is of a passionate nature. Many of these poems draw on the *akam* (interior) genre of classical Tamil poetry, in which a heroine speaks longingly of her absent male lover. The bhakti poets adapted this genre to their theology of embodiment, by imagining the Lord to be the absent male lover. For example, the woman poet Andal, the only woman poet included among the twelve prominent Vishnu-bhakti poets *(alvars)*, expressed her love for the Lord by contrasting it to marriage with a mortal man:

I dedicated my swelling breasts
to the lord who holds
the conch and flaming discus.
If there is even a whisper
of giving me to a mortal,
I shall not live.
O Manmatha,
would you permit a roving jackal
to sniff and eat
the sacrificial food
that brahmins offer
to celestial gods?[22]

For Andal, her sublime love for the Lord is a matter of life or death: her motive and her body are as pure as food ritually offered to the gods. She uses the stark imagery of the sly jackal, taking what does not belong to him, as a metaphor for her defilement if she married a mortal man.

Male poets also write in the voice of the lovelorn heroine; in these cases, the poet takes on a female persona. In the following poem by Nammalvar, the poet formally draws on the *akam* genre of love poetry, in which the audience overhears the heroine's longing for her lover; although in this case she is pining for Krishna (cat. no. 52A). In keeping with the genre, elements of the landscape are used to create the mood of yearning, as the heroine's distracted mind reads imagined messages into her surroundings. As with Andal's poem, the longing is represented as a life or death situation.

WHAT SHE SAID

Evening has come,
but not the Dark One.

The bulls,
their bells jingling,
have mated with the cows
and the cows are frisky.

The flutes play cruel songs,
bees flutter in their bright
white jasmine
and the blue-black lily.

The sea leaps into the sky
and cries aloud.

Without him here,
what shall I say?
how shall I survive?[23]

The Shiva-bhakti poet Sambandar also explored the emotional realm of a woman who longs to be with her Lord. One of his poems concerns the form of Shiva as the Lord who plays the *vina,* a mellow stringed instrument that continues to be popular today in performances of classical south Indian (Karnatic) music. The Tamils say that this form of the Lord is "'Talam vinai panni'; literally, 'strumming the *vina* to keep time [to his song].'"[24] The female persona in the poem is recalling happy times that she and the Lord spent together pursuing the Tamil arts of poetry and music; when he left, he took away the aesthetic dimension of her life, including her own beauty.

The coral-red Lord
who loves to dwell in Kanur of fragrant groves
came to me chanting sweet Tamil poems.
He stayed,
playing the lute, singing songs
to the beat of the mulavam *and* montai *drums.*
Now he is gone,
taking my beauty with him,
leaving me pale as the kumil *flower.*[25]

ASSURANCE OF SALVATION

We follow the poets' gaze of assurance toward the Lord. As much as the human struggle is represented in the Tamil bhakti poems, especially the struggle of forgetful humankind to remember the Lord continuously, the certainty of salvation is also a prominent theme. It is the ultimate act of grace that the Lord frees his bhaktas from the cycle of birth and rebirth. The hagiographies of the saints who composed the poems offer two types of images of their salvation: a more philosophically oriented image of the saint merging into the Lord, thus achieving the union of the soul with divinity; and a more mythologically oriented image of the saint as evermore living with the Lord in his abode.

The following poem by the Shiva-bhakti saint Manikkavachakar (cat. no. 36) has a number of very interesting features. In the first place, the speaker urges a parrot, a colorful and talkative feature of the landscape, to sing the praises of Lord Shiva. In particular, he urges the parrot to praise aspects of the kingdom of the Lord; here, the trident weapon of the Lord, which is a prominent part of his iconography, is being praised in terms that recall his cosmic destruction of the triple cities.

> ***Parrot who speaks words sweet as wild honey,***
> ***sing of the weapon***
> ***that crushes the foes of the faultless King***
> ***who rules Perunturai.***
> ***Don't you see?***
> ***The weapon he wields is the trident***
> ***that drives off the three taints***
> ***so the spotless hearts of his servants***
> ***will melt with love.***[26]

In this case, the enemies that the Lord spears with his trident are not the three cosmic demons, but instead the three aspects of the human condition that serve to deprive humankind of salvation:

> "The three taints" *(mu-malam)* figure prominently in Tamil Saiva theology. These three psycho-metaphysical entities cloud the intelligence of human beings and keep them mired in the cycle of birth and death. The three taints (*malam* literally means "dirt") are *anavam*, "egoism," *mayai*, the power of illusion, which causes people to believe in the reality of the empirical world; and *kanmam* or karma, the accumulated effects of action, which entraps living beings in *samsara*, the cycle of births and deaths.[27]

Human beings are deprived of salvation, that is, until they become bhaktas to Shiva, and allow his grace to pierce the three faults and thus neutralize their effect.

Sometimes, however, "salvation" does not look like the "heaven" we might imagine; this is particularly the case with the god Shiva, who is famous for bringing together seemingly opposing forces, as discussed above in terms of creation and destruction and the dancing Shiva. For example, the Shiva-bhakti woman saint Karaikkal Ammaiyar imagines her salvation to be in a cremation ground. Karaikkal Ammaiyar is one of three women saints in Tamil Shiva-bhakti; the other two are Mangaiyarkkarasi, a Pandyan dynasty queen, and Isainani Ammaiyar, the mother of the poet Sundarar. However, Karaikkal Ammaiyar is the only author among these women saints, and her works are included in the Shiva-bhakti canon, the *Tirumurai*.

The hagiography of Karaikkal Ammaiyar (cat. no. 35) tells us that her special relationship with Shiva (he gave her a mango immediately upon her request) frightened her husband, who abandoned his beautiful young wife. Subsequently, she prayed to Shiva that she might abandon her beauty and become a bhakta to him forever. Karaikkal Ammaiyar may be one of the earliest women in history to recognize that a young and beautiful woman is indeed a contested social entity. Thus, she sought to renounce her beauty as she departed from wifely duties, transforming her body into the socially undesirable form of a ghoul. Further, she sought to witness the Lord's dance of destruction at the cremation ground. The cremation ground is also uncontested space, for humankind avoids this inauspicious arena. In a stunning self-portrait, Karaikkal Ammaiyar represents these features, which are ordinarily understood to be inauspicious, as her salvation granted by Shiva.

She has shriveled breasts
and bulging veins,
in place of white teeth
empty cavities gape.
With ruddy hair on her belly,
a pair of fangs, knobby ankles and long shins
the demon-woman wails at the desolate cremation ground
where our lord,
whose hanging matted hair
blows in all eight directions,
dances among the flames
and refreshes his limbs.

His home is Alankatu.[28]

In a more normative description of salvation, the Shiva-bhakti poet Appar assures himself and others that the Lord will bring freedom from death and rebirth, from actions and their results (karma), from mental distress and disease of the body, and from debasement.

The severe punishments of Yama will not approach us
the fierce enemy karma will gradually be reduced
we are cured of our distress
we have no afflictions
we are not lowly;
where will the sun arise for us?
The Lord is in my mind
crowned by the river through His beautiful red matted locks
dancing with fire
pleased by bathing with the five substances of the cow
bearing a red complexion like coral, the hills, the heavens.[29]

In the following poem, the Vishnu-bhakti poet Nammalvar expresses the assurance of salvation with an image of the union of himself with the deity in this very lifetime. This personal salvation is framed by the cosmic majesty of the Lord as one who claims the universe and all people for himself.

He who devoured all seven worlds
  happily came
  and entered me
and he will not leave now;

from now on
  what's not possible
    for me?

At one stroke
seven generations below
and seven above
have cleared a wilderness
of trouble,

and escaped hell,
hot, endless hell.[30]

The hallmark of the Tamil bhakti poets is that they foreground human responses to God, such as awe, celebration, longing, and assurance, while simultaneously offering praise to the Lord in their compositions. Their promotion of emotional experience in the context of a theology of embodiment points their audience in two overlapping directions. On the one hand, the poets' compositions imbue sacred images of the Lord, such as those in this exhibition, with heartfelt human relevance, and thus enhance the aesthetics of the images with the living relationship between humankind and God. On the other hand, the poets encourage their audience to encounter the Lord for themselves, which may be better experienced and expressed through the imagination than through material culture.

ASSEMBLAGES OF SACRED BRONZES

VIDYA DEHEJIA

From the time of their ascent to power in the mid-ninth century, Chola monarchs built finely proportioned temples adorned with elegant stone sculptures, and commissioned assemblages of sacred bronzes to meet the requirements of ritual worship. Several of these Chola temples are still intact, but many have been accommodated within courtyards of later date added in response to the expanding needs of temple complexes in Tamil Nadu (fig. 2). Similarly, the bronze groupings in evidence in the temples today are the result of accretion over time, with new images commissioned to replace damaged bronzes or those missing from temples because they were buried to save them from the iconoclasm of the approaching armies of the Delhi Sultanate. A glimpse into the character, number, and size of the sacred bronzes that was considered adequate to satisfy the ritual requirements of a Chola shrine comes from two sets of ancient inscriptions. One, inscribed in the modestly sized Shiva temple at Tiruvaduturai,[1] and the other from the grand royal temple for Shiva at Tanjavur, together form the basis for the collection of sacred bronzes brought together for this exhibition. Current groupings in Shiva temples (fig. 1), also considered in this context, compare surprisingly well with the assemblage of bronzes in the Tiruvaduturai temple, revealing the remarkable continuity in the range and character of temple festivals over a period of more than a thousand years. No comparable

GROUP OF ANCIENT BRONZES,
SHIVA TEMPLE, KILAIPALAVUR
PHOTO VIDYA DEHEJIA
FIG. 1

inscription was found for a Vishnu temple,[2] and the exhibition's grouping of Vaishnava bronzes has been made largely on the basis of the images seen today in such temples. I have assumed that, as with Shaiva bronzes, present-day Vaishnava bronze groupings are similar to their ancient assemblages.

THE GOMUKTISHVARA TEMPLE AT TIRUVADUTURAI

This early Chola shrine of modest proportions, today enclosed within a later construction, was commenced in the year 932 by a private individual named Karrali Picchan (madman of the stone temple), but completed by the Chola king Parantaka (r. 907–55) in the year 945 with a gift of gold.[3] Some time thereafter, a series of bronzes was gifted to the temple to enable it to celebrate a complete annual cycle of festivals and rituals. While the inscription that mentions these images belongs to the year 1018, the bronzes are spoken of not as new donations, but as images already existing in the temple. Since the full-fledged ritual functioning of a temple necessitates portable images and festival processions, we may assume that the images were presented closer in date to the completion of the temple than to the year 1018. The purpose of the 1018 inscription is to record that four individuals—the mother-in-law of Emperor Rajendra (r. 1012–44), the preceptor of his son Rajadhiraja, and two palace maidservants—donated jewels for certain temple bronzes, as well as gold for ritual vessels. In the course of recording this information, the inscription provides a complete list, together with measurements, of the twenty-five bronzes in the Tiruvaduturai temple.[4] Sadly, none of these original images remains in the temple today.

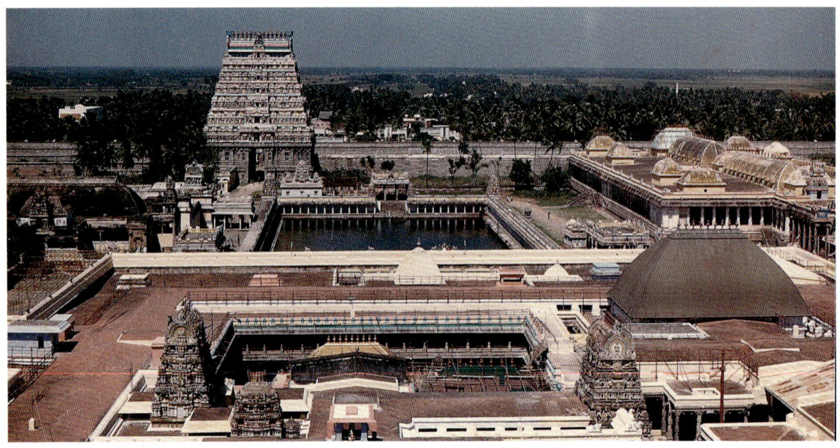

TEMPLE AT CHIDAMBARAM
PHOTO NEIL GREENTREE, 1998
FIG. 2

The Tiruvaduturai bronzes were a group of impressive size, and the inscription specifies that the measurement given for the height of each image includes both pedestal and *prabha* or aureole. The largest images—dancing Shiva, the goddess as Tripurasundari or Beauty of the Three Cities, and the group featuring Shiva as Vrishabhavahana or Rider of the Bull—are almost three and one-half feet in height. If we discount the aureole for comparison with the bronzes assembled in this exhibition (only four have their *prabha* intact), these images were around three feet high. In addition to a range of forms of Shiva, there are four images of Uma (or Parvati) on her own, and one in which she is with her infant son Skanda. The group includes four Shaiva saints *(nayanmars),* the bull, the trident, and two donor-type portraits, one in the form of a lamp. Measurements given below in centimeters are approximations of the ancient measures of *torai* (rice grain), *viral* (finger), *shan* (span), and *muram* (elbow to fingertips). The precision of these measurements is indeed striking, considering that a *torai* is a mere 18 millimeters.

1	Dancing Shiva (*adiyarulumudaiyar,* lord who gives grace by dancing)	103.6 cm
2	His consort (*nampirattiyar,* our lady)	36.0 cm[5]
3	Shiva as the Lord Who Sports a Crescent Moon (Chandrashekhara)	69.1 cm
4	His consort (*tampirattiyar*, his lady)	34.5 cm
5	Chandrashekhara	18.7 cm

6	Uma as Beauty of the Three Worlds (Tribhuvanasundari)	103.6 cm
7	Ganesha	34.5 cm
8	Shiva as Guardian of the Site (Kshetrapala)	34.5 cm
9	Kshetrapala	23.0 cm
10–12	Shiva as Rider of the Bull (Vrishabhavahana), with consort and bull	103.6 cm
13	Shiva as Enchanting Mendicant (Bhikshatana) with deer and dwarf	73.4 cm
14	Shiva as Half-Woman (Ardhanari)	34.5 cm[6]
15	Shiva as Teacher (Dakshinamurti) with tree	34.5 cm
16	Uma as Devi of the bedroom *(palli-arai devi)*	69.1 cm
17	Uma with Skanda	69.1 cm
18	Trident *(astra devar)*	not available
19	Bull	not available
20	Seated saint Chandeshvara	34.5 cm
21	Saint Appar	40.3 cm
22	Child-Saint Sambandar	43.2 cm
23	Saint Sundarar	43.2 cm
24	Portrait *(tammaiyaka varta)* of mother of Kalahasti-picchar (madman of Kalahasti)	34.5 cm
25	Portrait lamp *(tanaku varta vilakku)* of Kaviniyan Mahendra Neelan	not available

THE GREAT TEMPLE AT TANJAVUR

Rajaraja's monumental royal temple at Tanjavur, completed in the year 1010, contained at least sixty different sacred metal images (the actual number is greater because several—such as the marriage group of Shiva, Uma, Vishnu, and Brahma consist of more than one independent image), mostly of copper alloy (referred to in inscriptions as *ceppu,* "copper"), although two are of gold and four of silver.[7] Twenty-two of the images were given by the emperor himself, seventeen came from his sister and his queens, and the remaining twenty-one from officials and nobles at the Chola court. The images encompass a wide range of iconographic types, but a study of the list given below reveals the donation of multiple examples of certain popular images. There are two images of dancing Shiva accompanied by his consort, two images of Shiva as Tripuravijaya (Victor of the Three Cities) together with consort, and nine independent images of Ganesha, although several are diminutive in size. In addition, six standing images of Uma accompany various forms of Shiva, while three seated images are part of Shiva groupings. The Tanjavur bronzes included six saints plus members of their families, four royal portraits, and one of a revered guru. The largest image is of Shiva as Tripuravijaya (97.9 cm, or a little over 3 feet) together with his consort (86.4 cm), saint Patanjali as half-man and half-snake, Shiva as Enchanting Mendicant, and Shiva as Rider of the Bull. Measurements are not available for eleven bronzes, including a dancing Shiva, since these images are mentioned solely in the context of donations of rich jewelry for their adornment.[8] Measurements for height given below include the lotus and pedestal, but not the *prabha,* for which only the circumference is specified; we have given a parallel height measurement in the catalogue entries. One may note that almost every image, with the exception of the small Ganeshas, had a *prabha*; in several instances it is specified that this was cast in three pieces, consisting of two pillars and one crescent-shaped top piece. With the exception of a single large image of dancing Shiva (fig. 3), which, from its large size, appears to have been the principal bronze of the temple (no 3: *adavallar dakshina meru vitankar*), the images listed below are lost to us and not available for study.

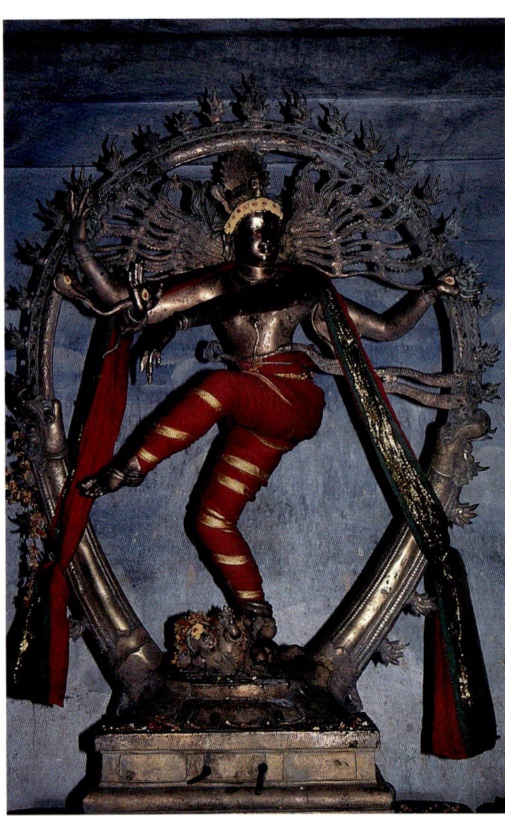

DANCING SHIVA, CA. 1010, TANJAVUR TEMPLE
PHOTO VIDYA DEHEJIA
FIG. 3

1	Golakai devar in gold (*linga* set with five gems for the five aspects of Shiva)	size not available; weight approx. 4.4 kilos
2	Kshetrapala in gold	5.9 cm, weight ⅓ kilo
3	Dancing Shiva *(adavallar dakshina meru vitankar)*	not available
4	His consort Uma	not available
5	Dancing Shiva *(adavallar)*	41.5 cm
6	His consort Uma	33.4 cm
7	Tripuravijaya (*tanjai alagar* with Mushalagan at his feet) and his consort Uma, on common pedestal	97.9 cm[9] 86.4 cm
8	Tripuravijaya *(tanjai vitankar)*	not available
9	His consort Uma	not available
10	Mahameru vitankar (Shiva and Uma on Mount Meru with Ganesha, Skanda, and others)	Shiva not available, Uma 19.44 cm from mountain to her head[10]
11	Bhikshatana[11]	74.1 cm
12	Group of seven images celebrating story of saint Chandesha[12]	33.4 cm
13	Five-bodied Shiva *(panchadehamurti)*[13] four surrounding figures	central image 37.4 cm 25.2 cm
14	Dakshinamurti with Mushalagan at his feet (four-armed Shiva as Teacher seated on a mountain with sages) Shiva rises 25.9 cm above mountain[14]	mountain 17.2 cm
15	Shiva as Rider of the Bull (Vrishabhavahana)	68.5 cm; bull 58.14 cm
16	His consort	59.9 cm
17	Shiva as Drinker of Poison *(Shrikantha)*	46.7 cm
18	Marriage group of Shiva, Uma, Vishnu, and Brahma common pedestal	Shiva 70.5 cm; Uma 57.6 cm 12.9 cm
19	Shiva manifesting within the *linga*, with Vishnu and Brahma[15]	42.4 cm
20	Shiva as Lord of Beasts (Pasupata)	not available
21	Shiva as Half-Woman (Ardhanari), with Uma half plated with brass	38.1 cm
22	Eight-armed Kshetrapala	43 cm
23	Two-armed dancing Bhairava	38.8 cm
24	Shiva as Divine Hunter *(kirata-arjuniya)*	not available
25	Seated Shiva and Uma with Skanda and Ganesha heights from top of pedestal to top of head	20.8 cm, 16.5 cm, 7.9 cm; 7.2 cm
26	Durga Parameshvari	48.9 cm
27	Seated Kali *(kala pidari)*	34.9 cm
28–31	Vasudeva (4 images in silver)	size not available, largest weight 1 kilo, next ½ kilo; two much smaller
32	Maha Vishnu	40.3 cm
33	Surya	37.4 cm
34	Four-armed Subrahmanya [or Skanda]	34.7 cm
35	Ganesha standing	25.9 cm
36	Ganesha standing	14.4 cm
37	Ganesha standing	26.9 cm
38	Ganesha standing (four-armed)	40.86 cm
39	Ganesha seated with shrub (.9 cm)	12.9 cm
40	Ganesha seated	5 cm
41	Ganesha seated	2.8 cm
42	Ganesha dancing	6.4 cm
43	Ganesha dancing	27.7 cm
44	Sundara Chola, Rajaraja's father[16]	not available
45	Vanavan Mahadevi, Rajaraja's mother	not available

46	King Rajaraja *(periya perumal)*	56.8 cm
47	Queen Lokamahadevi	46.8 cm
48	Saint Patanjali (Half-Man, Half-Snake)	78.3 cm
49	Three-legged mythical devotee Bhringi	(plant 1.4 cm) 58.1 cm
50	Four-armed Chandrashekhara as Lord of the Tevaram *(tevara-devar)*, in brass	11.1 cm
51	Saint Chandesha	59 cm; ax 18.7 cm
52	Saint Sundarar	31.6 cm
53	His wife Paravai	30.6 cm
54	Saint Appar	41.7 cm
55	Child-Saint Sambandar	41 cm
56	Saint Miladu-Udaiyar	40.3 cm
57–59	Saint Siruttondar, wife, son Sirala	36 cm, 33.1 cm, 28.8 cm
60	Guru of Isana Shiva Pandita	not available

In recreating groupings for this exhibition, the repetition of images at the Tanjavur temple has been kept in mind and more than one image of popular forms of Shiva—such as Nataraja and Tripuravijaya, as well as three independent images of Uma and two further seated images that feature her with Shiva—have been included. Similarly, the Vaishnava grouping includes multiple images of Vishnu, as well as the popular monkey general Hanuman. Certain important images, such as Shiva accompanied by his bull, Shiva as Half-Woman, and the marriage group of Shiva and Uma, do not exist in western collections. Since loans from India were not feasible, the exhibition grouping cannot be totally representative of the ancient scenario; however, Shiva with his bull and as Half-Woman are represented partially, insofar as their images are portrayed against the tridents on view in the exhibition.

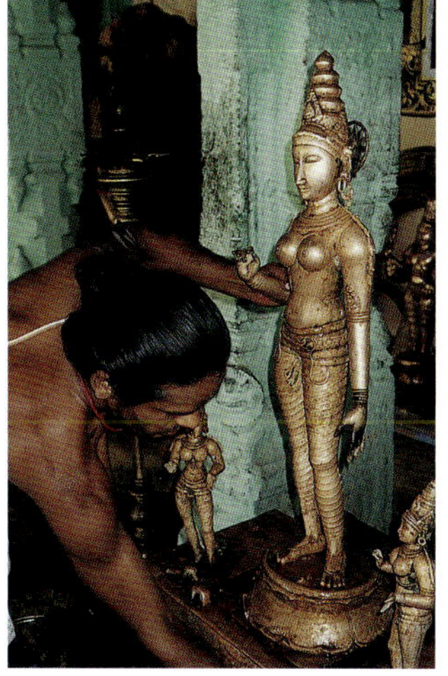

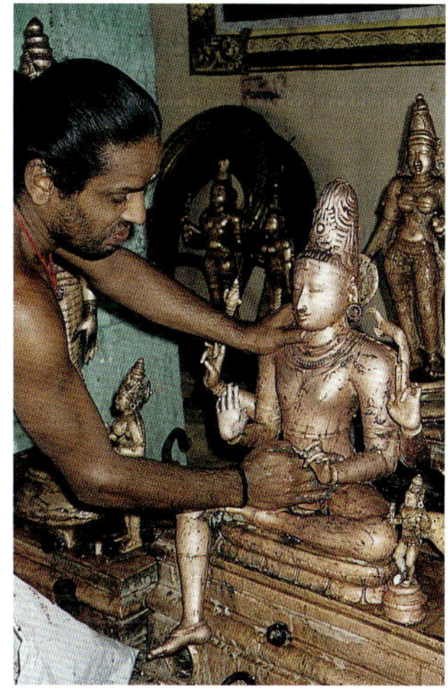

PRIEST AT TIRUVENKADU TEMPLE PERFORMING RITUAL PURIFICATION OF BRONZE IMAGES AFTER A MAJOR FESTIVAL
PHOTOS VIDYA DEHEJIA
FIG. 4

RITUAL WORSHIP AND THE SURFACES OF BRONZES

Several images in the exhibition reveal a degree of wear on their surfaces that is the result of having been in continuous use down the centuries. In preparation for daily worship, the images are ritually anointed *(abhishekha)*[17] by smoothing over them a range of substances that might include milk, honey, curds, ghee, sugar, and jaggery, followed by water, after which cooling, fragrant sandal paste and turmeric are applied. There is, however, the far more telling effect of the *prayaschitta abhishekha* or atonement ritual bath conducted at the close of each major festival. Since the bronze images have been paraded through the town and its environs for three to ten days, it is believed that they have been exposed to pollution. In order to repurify them before they enter the sacred premises of the temple, they must undergo a purifying ceremony that is carried out in an outer pavilion. Tamarind or palm-olive *(boondi kottai)* are softened in water and then used, together with the seed and stringy pulp, to rub down the bronzes; such repeated application over the centuries quite naturally wears away details. Then follows an equally vigorous cleansing with sacred ash (fig. 4). During this process, the images are treated as mere metal likenesses, bereft of all divine associations, and they are cleaned much as one might clean any metal object. The priests are astoundingly casual about scrubbing body parts of the deities, male and female. Once this cleansing is complete, and the first pot of ritual water is poured over the bronzes, the images return to being pure, sacred objects that one may worship but no longer photograph.

When the eyes of sacred bronzes wear down so as to blur the detail, temple authorities often feel the need to have the eyes recut and restore a degree of precision. The Indian concept of *darshan,* or sacred "seeing," involves devotees in gazing at the image, as well as receiving divine grace through the return gaze of the deity. The recutting of eyes, apparent on a few images in the exhibition (cat. nos. 5, 11, 15, 18, 51), indicates their regular participation in temple ritual; their continued usage and importance in the festival cycle required the eyes to be renewed for *darshan.* Similar wear apparent on other surfaces of images is not considered significant and remains untreated.

Large numbers of Chola bronzes were hidden underground in the year 1310 when news reached the southern temples of the approach of the armies of Malik Kafur, commander-in-chief of the Delhi Sultanate, who had heard of the fabled wealth of the Tamil temples. Rather than risk the desecration of their sacred images, temple authorities buried them, fully intending to bring them out and reconsecrate them once the Muslims had retreated. However, a Muslim sultanate established at Madurai survived for close to eighty years, during which time trusted priests had died and many temples had no clues to the locations of secret hiding spots. While inscriptions report that some temples retrieved and reconsecrated their images,[18] many others merely commissioned new images, so that the bronzes seen today in Tamil temples often belong to the late fourteenth or early fifteenth centuries. Buried bronzes that display green patina evoke the admiration of art lovers but are anathema to temple authorities, who would prefer to restore the images to their original luster.[19] Bronzes that appear in close-to-pristine condition are mostly those subjected to ritual worship for a relatively short period of time, buried for protection, and recently recovered from treasure troves in the course of twentieth-century construction within temple grounds.

NOTES

1 Also known as Tiruvavaduturai.

2 Dr. Marxia Gandhi, epigraphist at the Tamil Nadu State Department of Archaeology, confirms that she has never come across such a record.

3 Inscriptions of Parantaka's second and third year (908, 909) that speak of the maintenance of the temple gardens and of hymnists, pipers, and carriers of sacred water for the ritual bath of the deity suggest that an earlier consecrated shrine, perhaps of brick, was already in place.

4 I am grateful to Dr. Marxia Gandhi for help in translating the inscription and clarifying a number of details. Dr. M. D. Sampath of the Epigraphical Survey of India, Mysore, very kindly made available to me a transcript of the two inscriptions, copied in 1911 and 1913. The conversion is made here on the basis of 1 *muram* = 34.56 cm; 1 *shan* = 17.28 cm; 1 *viral* = 1.44 cm; 1 *torai* = 18 mm. It is intriguing to ponder the reasons for such detail and to wonder if, for instance, there was worry over the possibility of bronzes being stolen.

5 Measurement given as 1 *muram* + 1 *viral.*

6 *Ottai,* an unknown measurement, is mentioned for this image and number 19, the bull. This has not been taken into account in the calculations.

7 The information on the Tanjavur bronzes is the result of a thorough re-examination of the Tanjavur inscriptions by Dr. Marxia Gandhi, who checked the original Tamil, not relying on the partly corrupt and incomplete English translations previously published.The chapter in B. Venkataraman's *Rajarajesvaram: The Pinnacle of Chola Art* (Madras: Mudgala Trust, 1985), while extremely useful, does not contain details included here.

8 The inscriptions providing this information are located in various parts of the Tanjavur temple. They are listed in E. Hultzsch, ed., *South Indian Inscriptions*, vol. 2 (New Delhi: Archaeological Survey of India, 1992 reprint), parts 1–4, nos. 6, 8, 9, 11, 29, 30, 32, 34, 35, 38, 39, 40, 42, 44, 46, 47, 49, 50, 51, 53, 55, 79, 80, 81, 83, 84, 91, 95, 96.

9 The image itself measured 2 *muram* + 4 *viral;* the lotus was 5 *viral* high, the pedestal was 11 *viral* high.

10 Ganesha 12.9 cm; Subrahmanya 9 cm; bull 16.3 cm; tree 14.9 cm; Surya and Chandra 2.8 cm; plant 2.8 cm.

11 Antelope 27.3 cm; *bhuta* 7.9 cm; *prabha* (three pieces, 2 pillars and 1 crescent) 210.2 cm in circumference.

12 This group of copper images appears to depict two distinct episodes in the story of Chandesha. The first: (1) four-armed seated Shiva 29.5 cm from pendent foot on Mushalagan to hair, (2) Uma 22.1 cm from pendent foot to hair, both (1) and (2) on a common pedestal 8.6 cm high; (3) Chandesha 8.1 cm. The second: (4) Shiva *linga* with single arm 4.6 cm, (5) father on ground 9.9 cm long, (6) Chandesha 12.9 cm, (7) garland 23.7 cm long. A *prabha* for the entirety with a circumference of 73.4 cm.

13 An image with ten arms has attached to it four solid images, each with four arms.

14 Myriad details include: two flanking peaks 17.2 cm; banyan tree 46.8 cm; *kinnaras* 5.7 cm; *kinnaris* 5 cm; Mushalagan 14.4 cm long; *rishis* 17.2 cm and 11.5 cm; serpent 8.6 cm long; tiger 7.9 cm long.

15 Shiva within *linga* 18 cm; Brahma 10 cm; Vishnu 10 cm.

16 The phrase used is *ponmaligai tunjina devar* or lord who sleeps in the gold mansion. In the case of these royal portraits, as also with the saints, the bronzes are specifically referred to as *pratima* or portrait.

17 A list of *abhisheka* possibilities and their rewards, as posted in the late Chola temple of Kashivishvanatha in Kumbhakonam include oil (bodily comfort), turmeric (easing of debt), *panchamrta*, a mixture of five delicious substances, usually banana, sugar, honey, ghee and grape (bodily comfort), milk *panchamrta* (increase of wealth), milk (love life), curds (children), ghee (house), honey (sweet voice), sugarcane juice (bodily comfort), coconut water (fortune), lemon (enmity ceases), sacred ash (fortune and house), sandal paste (children's fortunes), rose water (children's fortune), gold cloth (acquisition), gold (acquisition), conch (good life), water pot (all one's desires). In the year 2000, to perform all eighteen *abhishekhas* would cost somewhat more than 3000 rupees or roughly $75; however, devotees may pick how many, and which specific ones, they wish to perform.

18 A fifteenth-century inscription (*Madras Epigraphy Report,* 1935–36, no. 144) informs us that the image of Vishnu at the Kannanur temple to Vishnu that had been hidden away due to the Muslim incursions was reconsecrated and restored to its place of glory.

19 When the image of Shiva as Enchanting Mendicant of Molaperumpallam was recently discovered in the now-dry temple tank, the temple authorities rubbed it down with palm-olive and restored it to its original coppery sheen before reconsecrating it and returning it to its place in the temple.

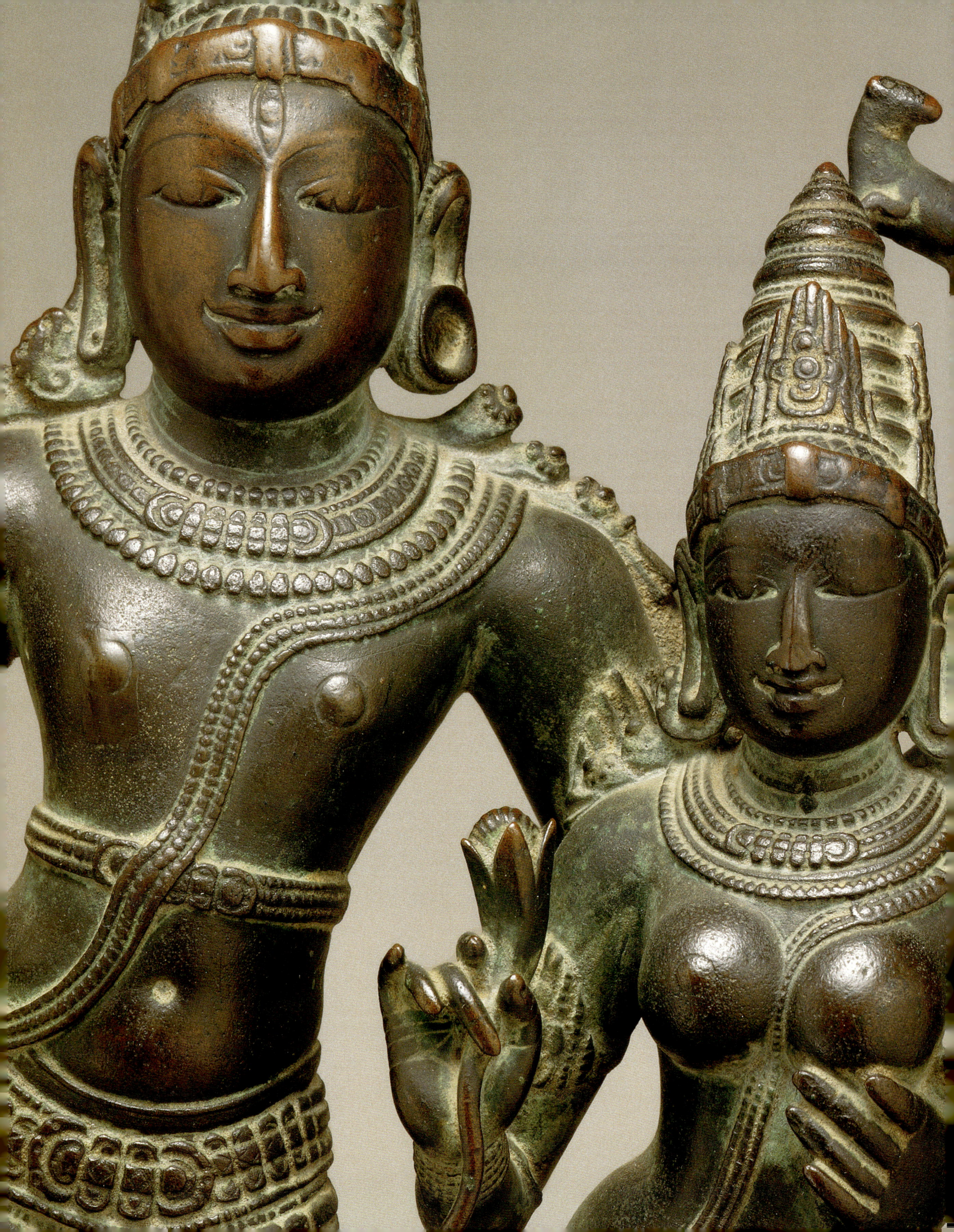

CATALOGUE

VIDYA DEHEJIA

Shiva—His Temples, His Images

Shaiva Saints

Vishnu—His Temples, His Images

Buddhist and Jain Shrines

Ritual Lamps

Jewels for Temple Bronzes

ALINGANA CHANDRASHEKHARA (DETAIL OF CAT. NO. 8)

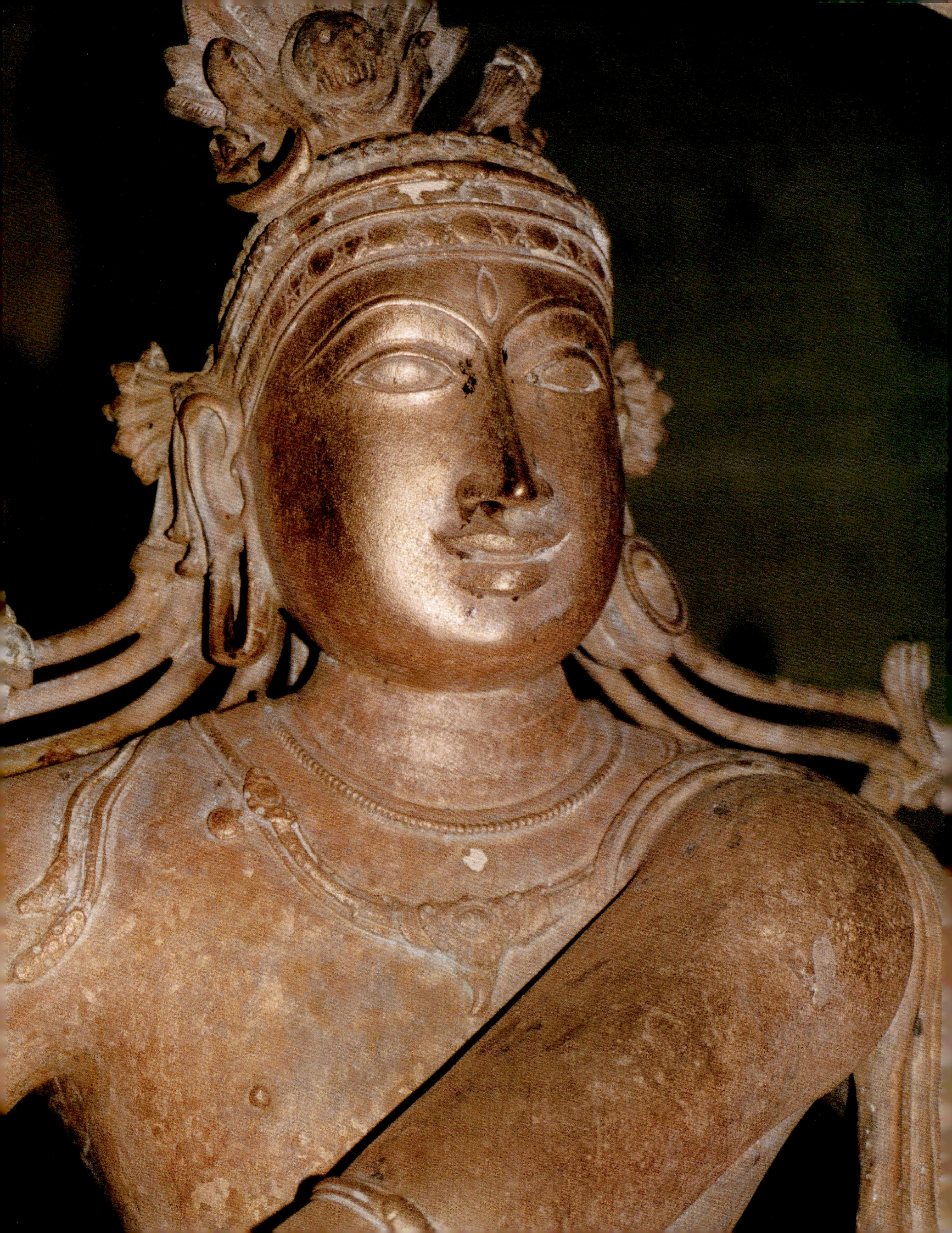

SHIVA—HIS TEMPLES, HIS IMAGES

The Shaiva Siddhanta school of south India, which originated around the ninth century at the very start of Chola rule, conceives of Shiva on two very different levels.[1] The first is Paramashiva, the infinite and supreme aspect of Shiva that cannot be visualized or worshiped. The second level is the one in which Shiva manifests, and through which humans can comprehend him. The temple is the place where Shiva's manifestations may be seen, admired, and approached in worship by priests and devotees. The sanctum of a Shiva temple never contains an anthropomorphic image of the deity. Invariably enshrined therein is Shiva's manifestation as the pillarlike *linga* (literally "sign"), his aniconic emblem, originally conceived as a shaft of light and glory. Over the course of time, the *linga* was transformed into a phallic symbol,[2] and later still the pillarlike shaft was placed on a pedestal shaped as the *yoni* emblem of the goddess, thereby representing the inseparable fusion of male and female principles. While scholars of myth and legend may profitably explore the complexities of the *linga*'s phallic symbolism, this aspect has no resonance at all with Shaiva worshipers. As far as temple worship is concerned, the *linga's* phallic symbolism is largely irrelevant.

Shiva's many enthralling anthropomorphic manifestations—as Nataraja (Lord of Dance), Tripuravijaya (Victor of the Three Cities), Somaskanda (with Uma and infant Skanda), Chandrashekhara (Moon-Crowned Lord), and a host of other forms—are portrayed in stone sculptures that decorate the outer walls of temples and in a temple's many festival bronzes. Shaiva Siddhantins hold that the most comprehensive of manifestations is five-fold Sadashiva, often visualized as five faces against the *linga.* Emperor Rajaraja Chola (r. 985–1016) commissioned two images of this form for his Tanjavur temple. One was in the form of a gold *linga* that was embedded with five jewels to represent the five aspects *(golakai devar)*; the second was a bronze of anthropomorphic type (*panchadehamurti* or image with five bodies) consisting of a central standing image surrounded by four smaller standing figures.[3]

In considering the manifestations of Shiva, one may note certain features common to all images of him. He is always portrayed as the bold god sporting a vertical third eye in the middle of his forehead (fig. 1), the origin of which saint Sundarar attributes to Uma's playful action:

> *Once the Mountain Girl was playing:*
> *happily,*
> *as a game,*
> *she covered his eyes with her hands.*
> *At once thick darkness swallowed the world.*
> *To dispel that darkness, the supreme god*
> *created in joy*
> *the single eye on his forehead.*[4]

Shiva is as much the lord of the matted locks; these dreadlocks are knotted together, piled elegantly upon his head, and adorned with the crescent moon, a skull, and a serpent. Blossoms of *konrai* or wild cassia are Shiva's favorite, as is the *unmattai* or horn-blower flower.

NATARAJA, CA. 1100,
PURANA VITANKAR TEMPLE,
TIRUMANGALAKUDI
PHOTO R. NAGASWAMY
FIG. 1

A bleached skull,
the crescent moon,
konrai *and serpent*
umattam *flowers dripping with honey,*
great intai *blossoms —*
all these, thrown together,
crown the red, matted hair
of the lord
who pervades the universe
in Tiruvavatuturai.[5]

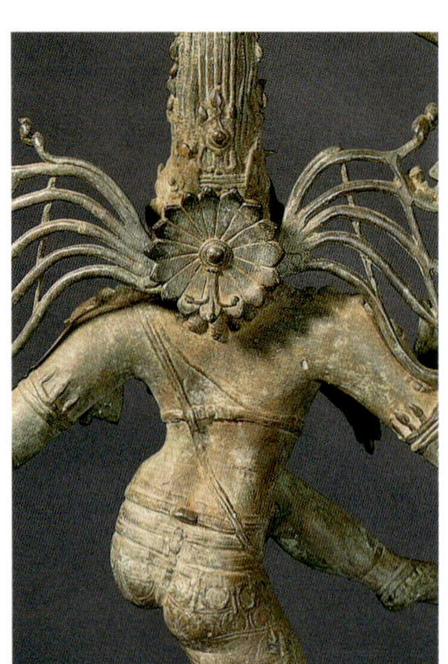

SIRASCHAKRA ADORNING HEAD OF SHIVA AS NATARAJA (DETAIL OF CAT. NO. 1)

In another verse, Sundarar includes the river Ganga in his list. Originally a celestial river, the Ganga, personified as a goddess, agreed to descend to earth so that human beings might attain grace by immersion in her holy waters. Since the force of her descent would be too much for the earth to bear, the god Shiva agreed to receive her in his matted locks and then gently let her down on the earth.

A splinter of moon,
konrai *from the uplands*
and the Water
adorn your crest,
auspicious god,
brilliant light
shining through a ring of serpents.[6]

As these verses indicate, Shiva is the lord adorned with serpents; he uses them as a loincloth, as a belt for holding his lower garment, as a hair ornament, and as necklaces, armlets, and wristband. Saint Sundarar describes with fond mockery this eccentric form of adornment, highlighting the paradoxical nature of Shiva.

In your hand: one snake;
another snake tied to your waist;
a snake on your neck —
they are crawling all over your back,
down your body smeared with ash![7]

Shiva usually wears different kinds of earrings in his two ears, symbolizing the fact that both male and female aspects are incorporated in the godhead. His left ear is adorned with a large circular ring *(patra kundala)* or a round stud set with gems *(ratna kundala)*, both worn by women, while his right ear sports an earring shaped as the aquatic mythical *makara*, a lion, or a serpent. Adorning the rear of Shiva's head, and indeed of all Chola bronze images of deities, male or female, is a small halo-like ornament known as a *siraschakra*, literally "head-wheel" (see detail on this page). It appears to have been created to cover the knot that secured the headband worn by all the deities. At any rate, it is only when the knot itself is treated as a decorative feature, as with the image of Chandesha in the exhibition (cat. no. 33), or with the Nataraja from Tiruvedikudi (fig. 2), that the *siraschakra* is absent.

Clothing for the gods, as indeed for priests and devotees, consists of a lower garment *(veshti)* wrapped saronglike around the waist; it is customary for the male torso to be bare with only a scarflike *angavastra* over one shoulder. Shiva wears the sacred thread that marks the brahmin caste, and since he is the lord of coral hue, the contrast with the white thread led poets to eloquent description.

> ***Like a stream of crystal***
> ***plunging***
> ***down a coral mountain:***
> ***the thread he wears***
> ***upon his breast.***[8]

Shiva's attributes include the deer, the battle-ax, and the trident. The dwarflike figure of Mushalagan, representing darkness and ignorance, often appears beneath Shiva's foot. His appearance is not restricted, as is sometimes thought, to Shiva's form of Nataraja or Lord of Dance. Mushalagan frequently appears with Shiva in his form as Tripuravijaya (Victor of the Three Cities) and is invariably present in Shiva's manifestation as Dakshinamurti, the great teacher, who rests one foot on him while sages and creatures of the forest listen to Shiva's exposition of the truth. Occasionally, Mushalagan is seen beneath Shiva's foot when he appears, accompanied by Uma, to confer his grace upon saint Chandesha.[9]

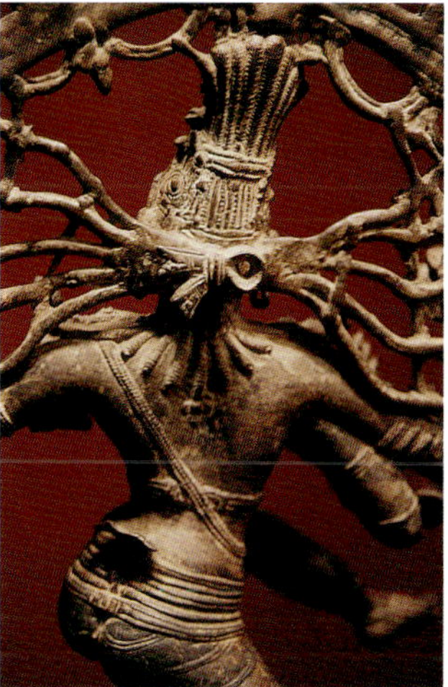

DECORATIVE KNOT OF HEADBAND ON NATARAJA, CA. 970. ASIA SOCIETY, NEW YORK; MR. AND MRS. JOHN D. ROCKEFELLER 3RD COLLECTION (1979.20) PHOTO VIDYA DEHEJIA
FIG. 2

Shaivas do not believe that Shiva is permanently present in any temple image, whether it is the sanctum *linga* or a movable bronze sculpture. The devotee does not worship an image *as* Shiva, or even as *representing* Shiva; rather, the image, exquisite as it needs to be, is little more than an appropriate physical conduit for Shiva's special presence. An invocation known as *avahana* or invitation, performed by a priest, is necessary to summon Shiva into the *linga,* or into the anthropomorphic icon, for the duration of any ritual. When worship has been completed, a rite known as *visarjana* or sending away is performed to allow Shiva to leave the image. When this has been done, the image returns to being an inanimate object, bereft of any spark of divinity.

The ritual bronzes of a Shiva temple—whether they are around twenty-five in number as in a medium-sized temple, or up to fifty as in a major shrine—generally reside in the hall immediately surrounding the sanctum that enshrines the stone Shiva *linga.* Such a configuration is seen today in numerous temples from Kodumudi in the western Kongu region to Tiruvarur at the eastern end of the Kaveri Delta. On occasion, however, as in the temples at Avanashi in Kongu, or Chidambaram north of the Kaveri Delta, the bronzes may be placed in a hall further away within the temple grounds.

NOTES

1 For a full explication of the ideas presented all too briefly here, see Richard Davis, *Ritual in an Oscillating Universe: Worshiping Siva in Medieval India* (Princeton: Princeton University Press, 1991), especially chapter 4, "Summoning the Lord," pp. 112–36; and chapter 5, "Relations of Worship," pp. 137–62.

2 As at Gudimallam, where the shaft, with clearly depicted foreskin, has a standing image of Shiva carved against it.

3 See above, "The Assemblage of Sacred Bronzes," Tanjavur list nos. 1, 13. For a drawing of the latter, see R. Nagaswamy, "Iconography and Significance of the Brhadisvara Temple, Tanjavur," in *Discourses on Siva: Proceedings of a Symposium on the Nature of Religious Imagery*, ed. Michael W. Meister (Philadelphia: University of Pennsylvania Press, 1984), p. 178, fig. 2.

4 David Dean Shulman, trans., *Songs of the Harsh Devotee: The Tevaram of Cuntaramurtinayanar* (Philadelphia: University of Pennsylvania Press, 1990), p. 101: Sundarar hymn 16, verse 4.

5 Ibid., p. 455: Sundarar 70.10.

6 Ibid., p. 496: Sundarar 77.8.

7 Ibid., p. 222: Sundarar 36.10.

8 Ibid., p. 590: Sundarar 94.5.

9 See above, "Assemblages of Sacred Bronzes," note 12.

1 **SHIVA AS NATARAJA, LORD OF DANCE**
CHOLA PERIOD, CA. 990
BRONZE, 28 IN. (71.12 CM)
PRIVATE COLLECTION (SCHEDULED ACQUISITION BY THE FREER GALLERY OF ART, SMITHSONIAN INSTITUTION)

2 **SHIVA AS NATARAJA, LORD OF DANCE**
CHOLA PERIOD, CA. 1100
BRONZE, 35 IN. (88.9 CM)
DALLAS MUSEUM OF ART; GIFT OF MRS. EUGENE MCDERMOTT, THE HAMON CHARITABLE FOUNDATION, AND AN ANONYMOUS DONOR IN HONOR OF DAVID T. OWSLEY, WITH ADDITIONAL FUNDING FROM THE CECIL AND IDA GREEN FOUNDATION AND THE CECIL AND IDA GREEN ACQUISITION FUND (2000.377)

3 **SHIVA AS NATARAJA, LORD OF DANCE**
CHOLA PERIOD, CA. 1150
BRONZE, 60 1/4 IN. (153 CM)
RIJKSMUSEUM, AMSTERDAM; LONG-TERM LOAN OF THE SOCIETY OF FRIENDS OF ASIATIC ART (AK-MAK-187)

4 **SHIVA AS NATARAJA, LORD OF DANCE**
18TH CENTURY
BRONZE, 40 1/2 IN. (103 CM)
MUSEUM OF FINE ARTS, BOSTON; MARIANNE BRIMMER FUND (21.1828)

He dances, a whirl
of motion,
the great lord
bearing fire, crowned
with the crescent and with Ganga,
as his golden anklets chime
and his serpents dance, too.[1]

Shiva as Nataraja, Lord of Dance, standing in dramatic splendor on his bent right leg with left foot raised high across his body is the quintessential deity of the Tamil country of south India. The four-armed divine dancer holds fire in one rear hand and a *damaru* drum in the other, while his front right hand is in the gesture of protection and the left gracefully extended in a dance gesture. With his matted locks splayed by the swaying of the dance, and the scarf and serpents wrapped around him likewise responding, Shiva rests upon a dwarflike figure. The image—the perfect embodiment of rhythmic movement according to French sculptor Auguste Rodin—was the creation of the early Chola period. The names by which dancing Shiva was addressed are compounds that include either the Tamil noun *kuttu* (dance) or the Tamil verb *adu* (to dance). Prior to the thirteenth century, no Tamil Nadu inscription—whether of the Cholas, Pandyas, or any chieftains—contains the Sanskrit word Nataraja.[2] Dancing Shiva was known in Chola territory as *adavallan* (master of dance), *kuttadavallan* (master who dances the dance), *tillai ambalattu kuttan* (dancer in the hall of Tillai), *chittrambalattu kuttan* (dancer of Chidambaram), and *kuttu-perumal* (lord of dance). For instance, an inscription of the year 945 records that a merchant of Tirunavalur gifted a lamp to *kuttu-perumal* at the local temple; another record of the year 985 mentions a shrine to *kuttu-perumal* in the temple of Udaiyargudi.[3] The Sanskrit Nataraja was adopted into the Tamil language as late as the thirteenth century, some three to four centuries after the creation of images of this form.[4] But this later term gained immense popularity, superseded the Tamil titles, and is used today by one and all to refer to this image.

Extant remains in stone and bronze suggest that the artistic formulation of the Nataraja icon was achieved only in the early tenth century. However, the devotional *bhakti* hymns of the *nayanmars* (the Shaiva saints of the Tamil country who largely date between the sixth and ninth centuries) speak of Shiva's raised dancing foot, the fire in his hand, the locks of his hair fanned out by his movement, and the snake dancing upon his form.[5] Poems sung by Sambandar and Appar, both of the seventh century, speak specifically of Shiva's lifted foot, suggesting the distinct possibility of a dancing posture similar to that seen in the Chola images of Nataraja. Appar, for instance, sang thus in a poem dedicated to dancing Shiva in the shrine at Tillai (Chidambaram):

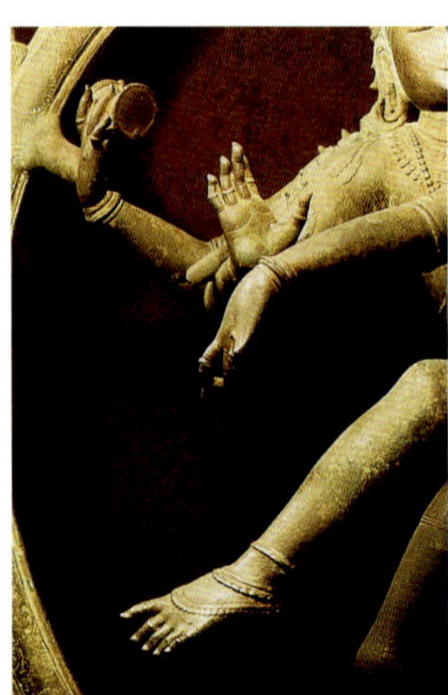
RAISED FOOT OF NATARAJA, 11TH CENTURY. THE CLEVELAND MUSEUM OF ART; PURCHASE FROM THE S. H. WADE FUND (1930.331)
FIG. 1

If you could see
the arch of his brow,
the budding smile
on lips red as the kovvai *fruit,*
cool matted hair,
the milk-white ash on coral skin,
and the sweet golden foot
raised up in dance,
then even human birth on this wide earth
would become a thing worth having.[6]

In the same poem, Appar refers to the raised foot of Shiva that enslaved him (fig. 1).

The very foot he raised
to dance the dance
in the little hall of Tillai—
It claimed me as a slave.[7]

Saint Sundarar's (ca. 800) hymn on Chidambaram commences with a reference to the lifted foot:

Those days that you live
my heart
not serving
the foot that is bent in dance,
he will stop you
shake you up . . .[8]

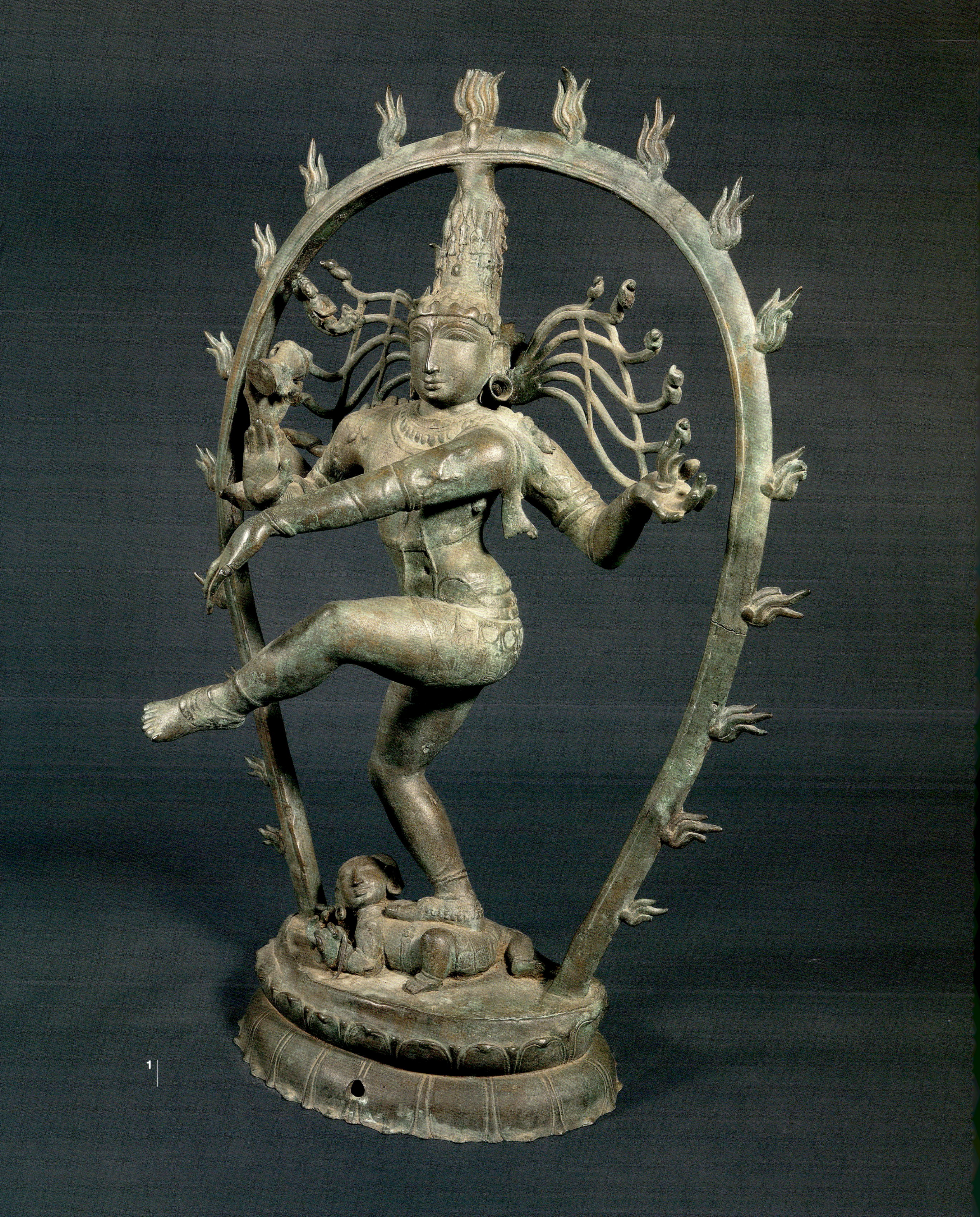

1

The collection of hymns by saint Manikkavachakar (ninth century), the *Tiruvachakam* (sacred utterance), commences with this verse that repeatedly praises the foot (not feet) of Shiva.

Glory be to the syllables five
glory to that foot of the lord—
hail foot of him
who even a trice leaves not my heart—
hail foot of the guru-gem who reigns in Gogari—
glory be to the foot of him
who as essence of agama draws near and abides—
glory to the foot
of the One, the Many
the lord supreme.[9]

The pose indicated in these verses is clearly not that of Shiva's other dances, such as the *chatura tandava*, representations of which are seen in most other parts of India (in a few instances in the Tamil country too), in which both of Shiva's feet are elegantly planted on the ground.

A poem by Sambandar dedicated to dancing Shiva in the shrine of Atikai Virattanam is important in this context. While five verses are dedicated solely to dancing Shiva, the other five describe Shiva as Tripurantaka who destroyed the demon cities, as Bhikshatana on his begging rounds, as Ardhanari or half-woman, as Lingodhava who manifested within the boundless *linga,* and as the lord who imprisoned Ravana beneath Mount Kailasa; but the poem does so to maintain that these are but forms of the supreme Shiva who dances in the Virattanam shrine. It further identifies the Shiva who dances in the cremation grounds as the lord who dances also in the Virattanam shrine. In this poem's description of Shiva's dancing form, Sambandar makes repeated reference to the fire in Shiva's hand, the splayed locks of his matted hair, the crescent moon, and the river Ganga (Ganges) in his locks.

He waves the fire lifted up in his hand;
the strands of flame-red hair
adorned with konrai blossoms thick with bees
sway, as he dances[10]

Again:

The Lord who holds fire
and bears the broad river on his head
dances, trailing strands of fire-red matted hair,[11]

And again:

The god crowned with the bright moon
dances, playing with flickering fire
in the hollow of his hand.[12]

In the same poem, Sambandar speaks of the swaying serpent:

The great deadly snake at his waist
dances along
as he . . .
dances in the Virattanam shrine at Atikai[13]

It would appear that a pose not dissimilar to that of the Chola Nataraja had already been visualized during the late seventh century. As Kamil Zvelebil suggests, this might have been one of three

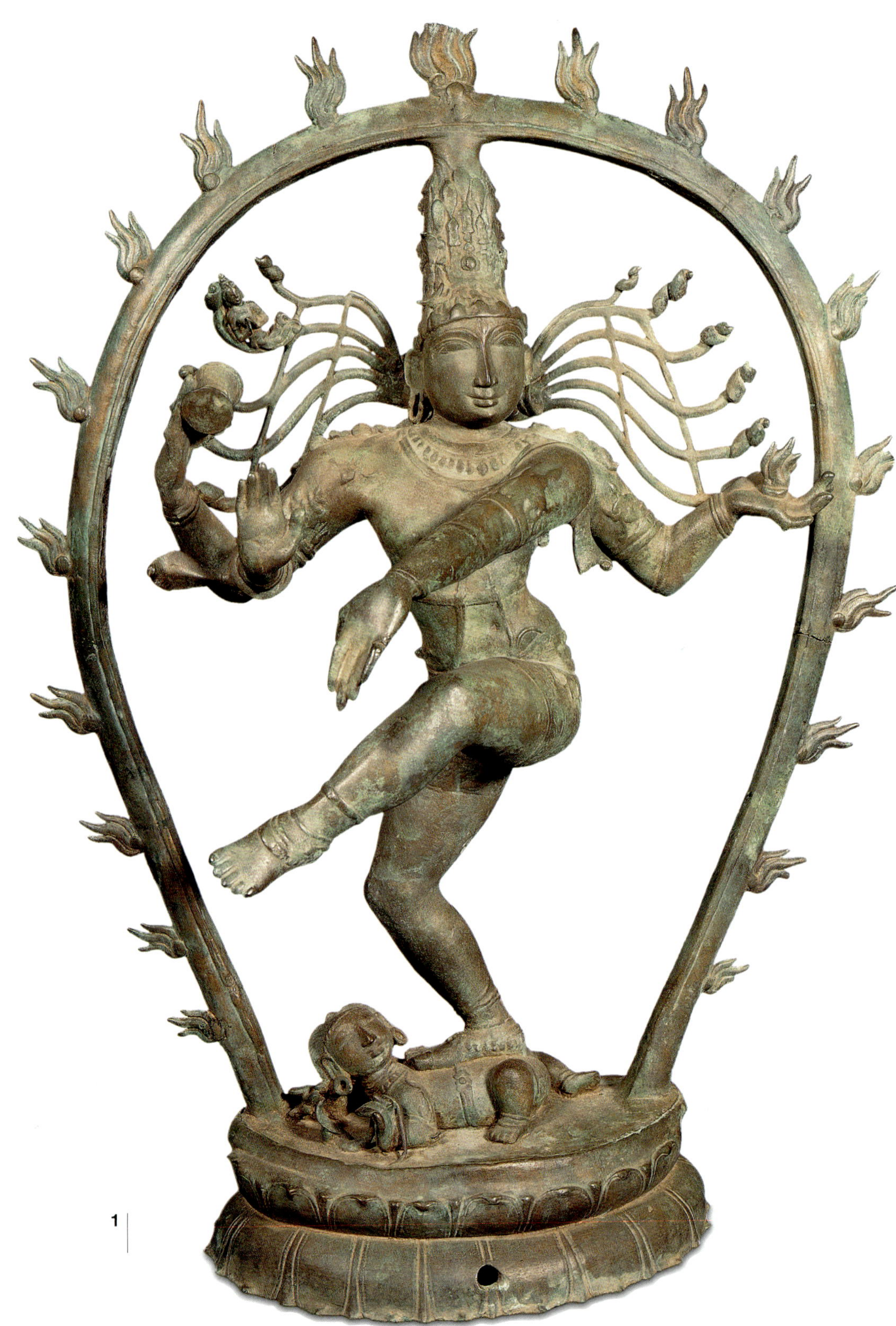

1

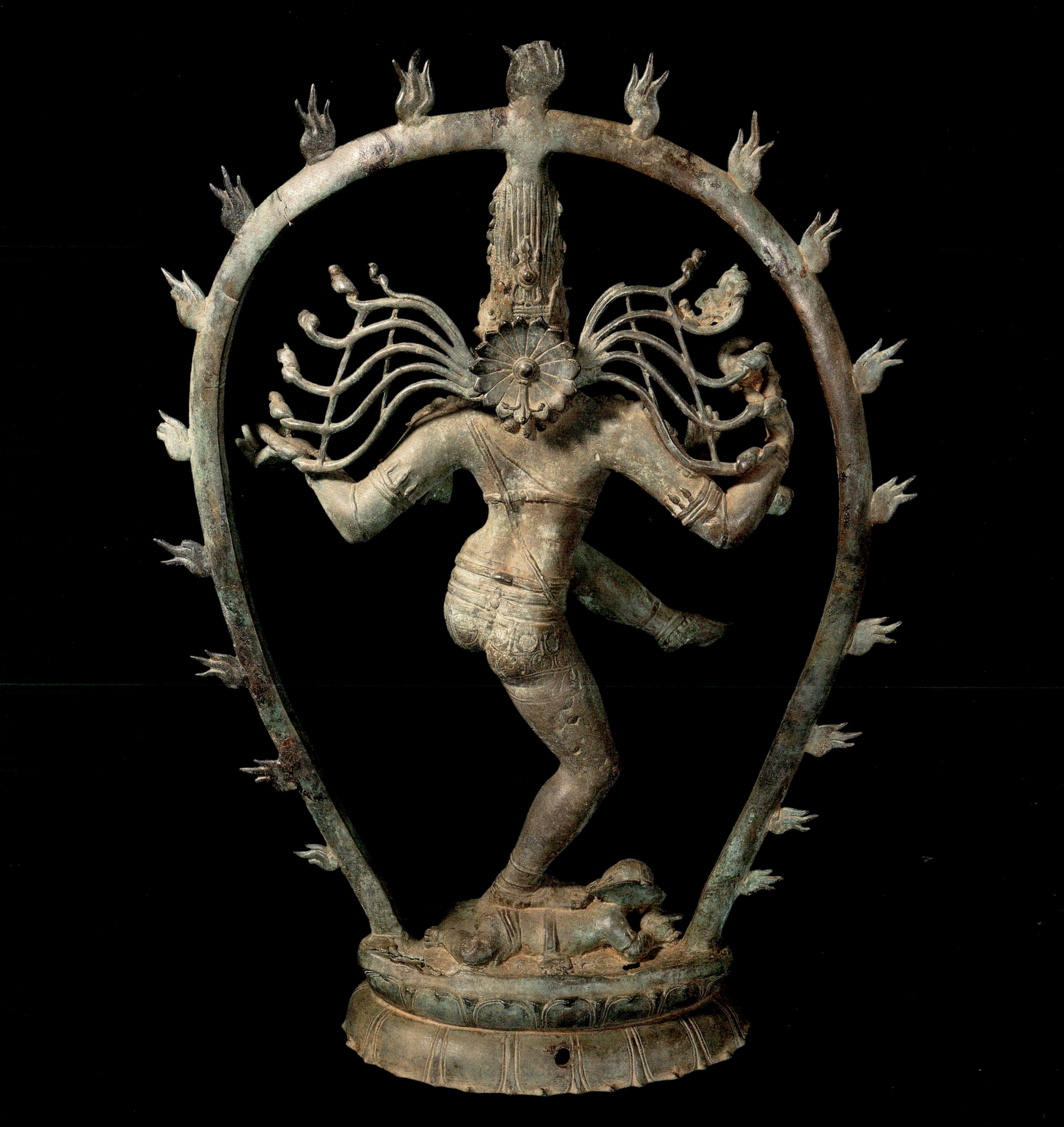

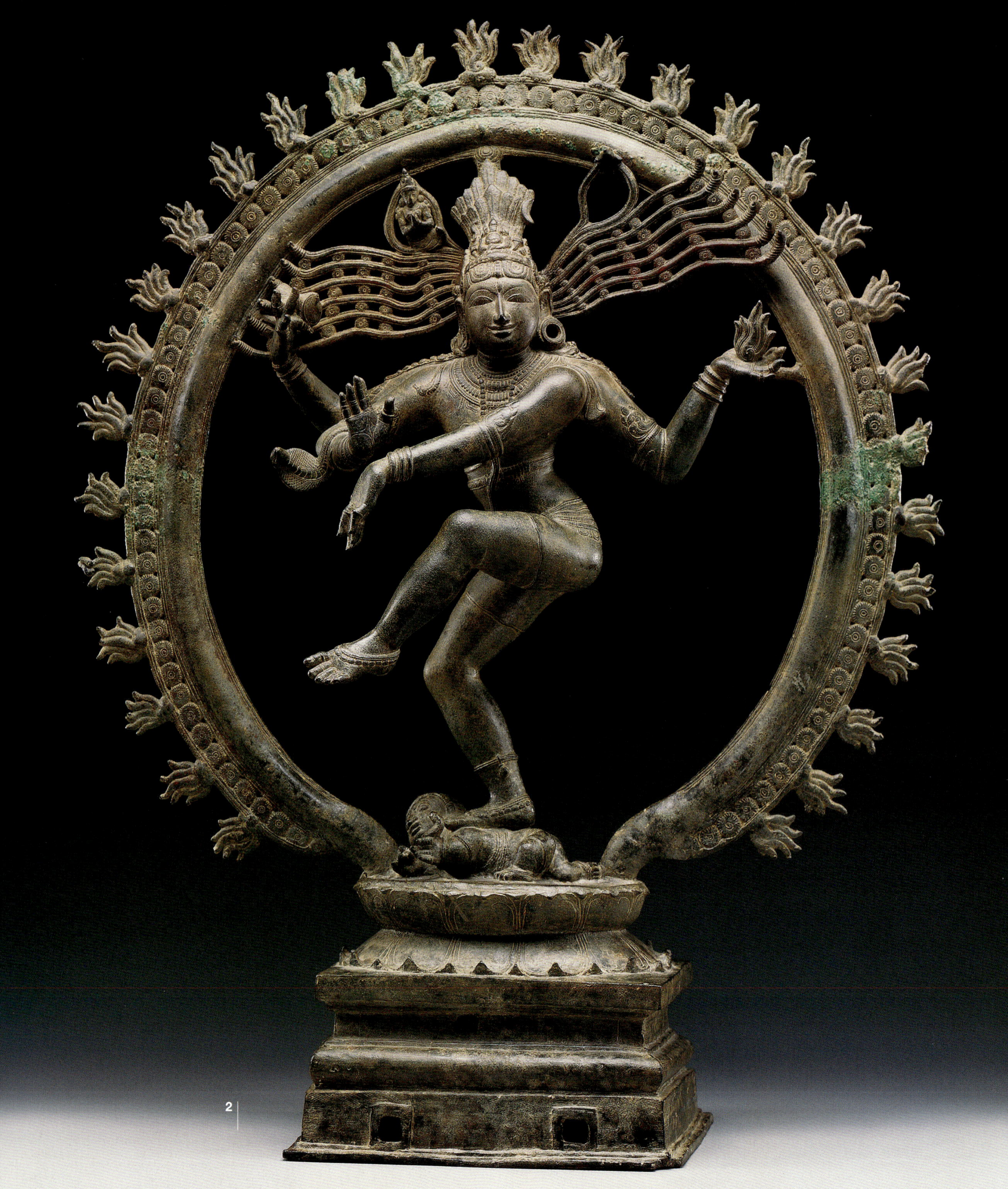

2

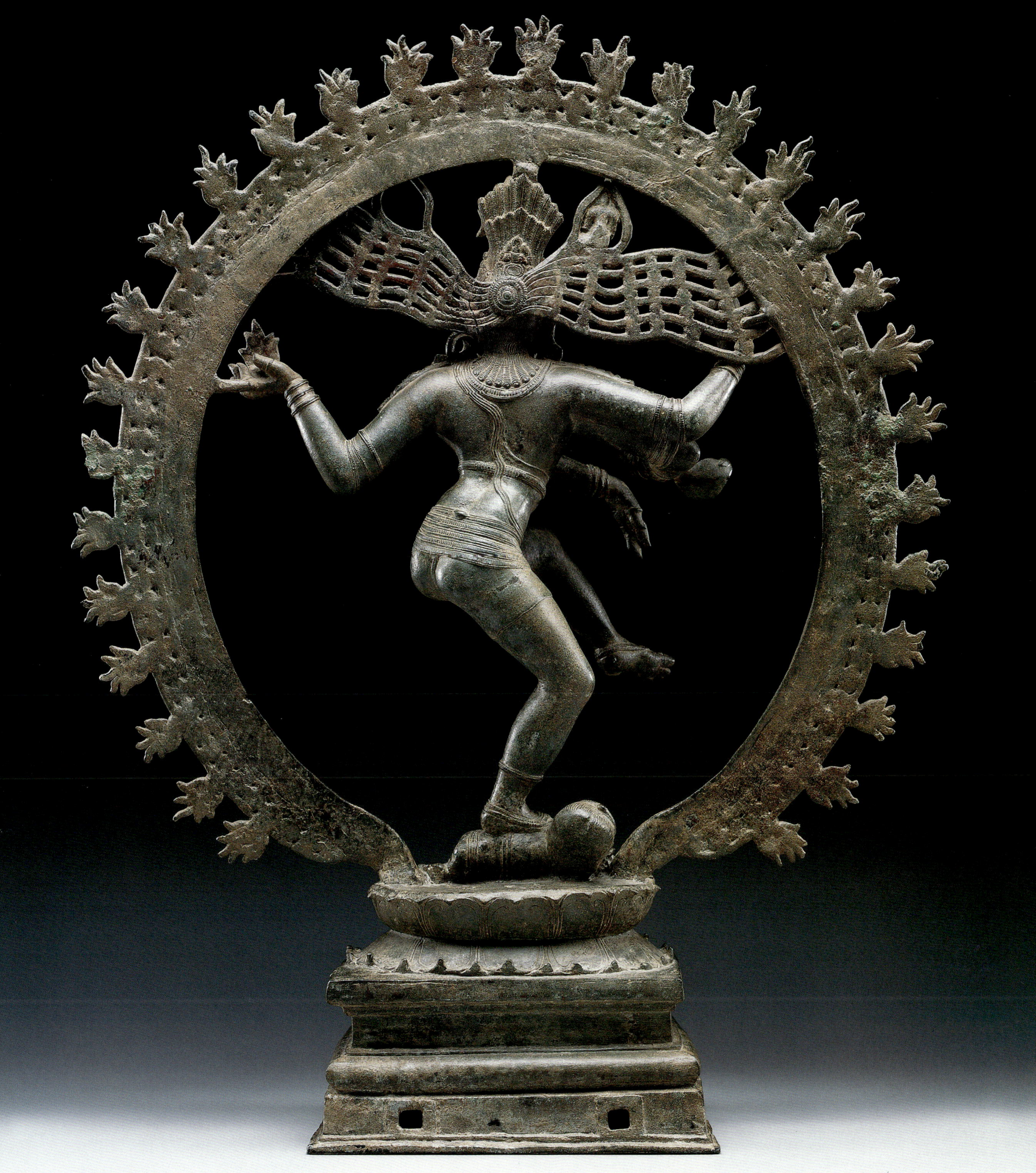

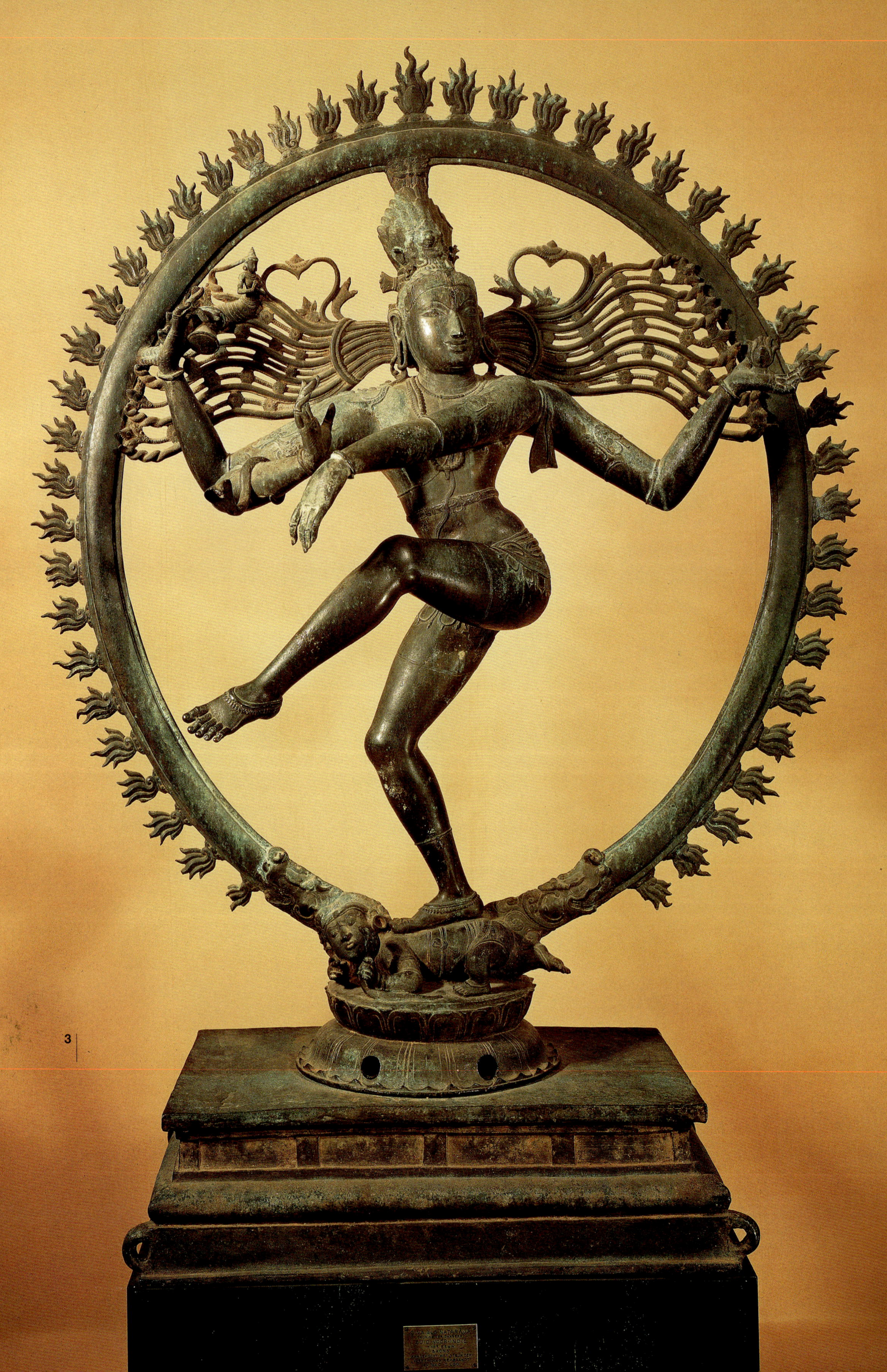

3

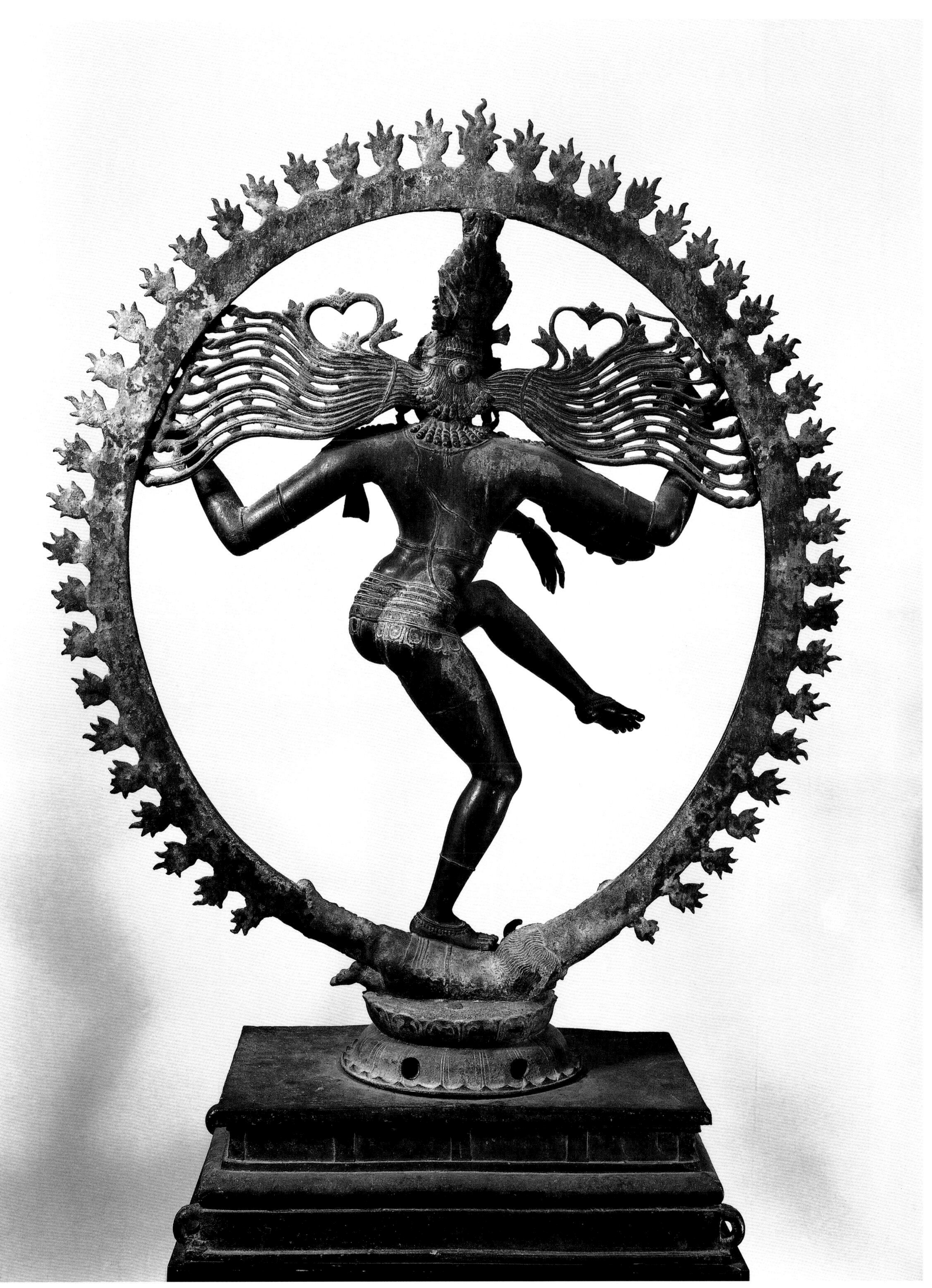

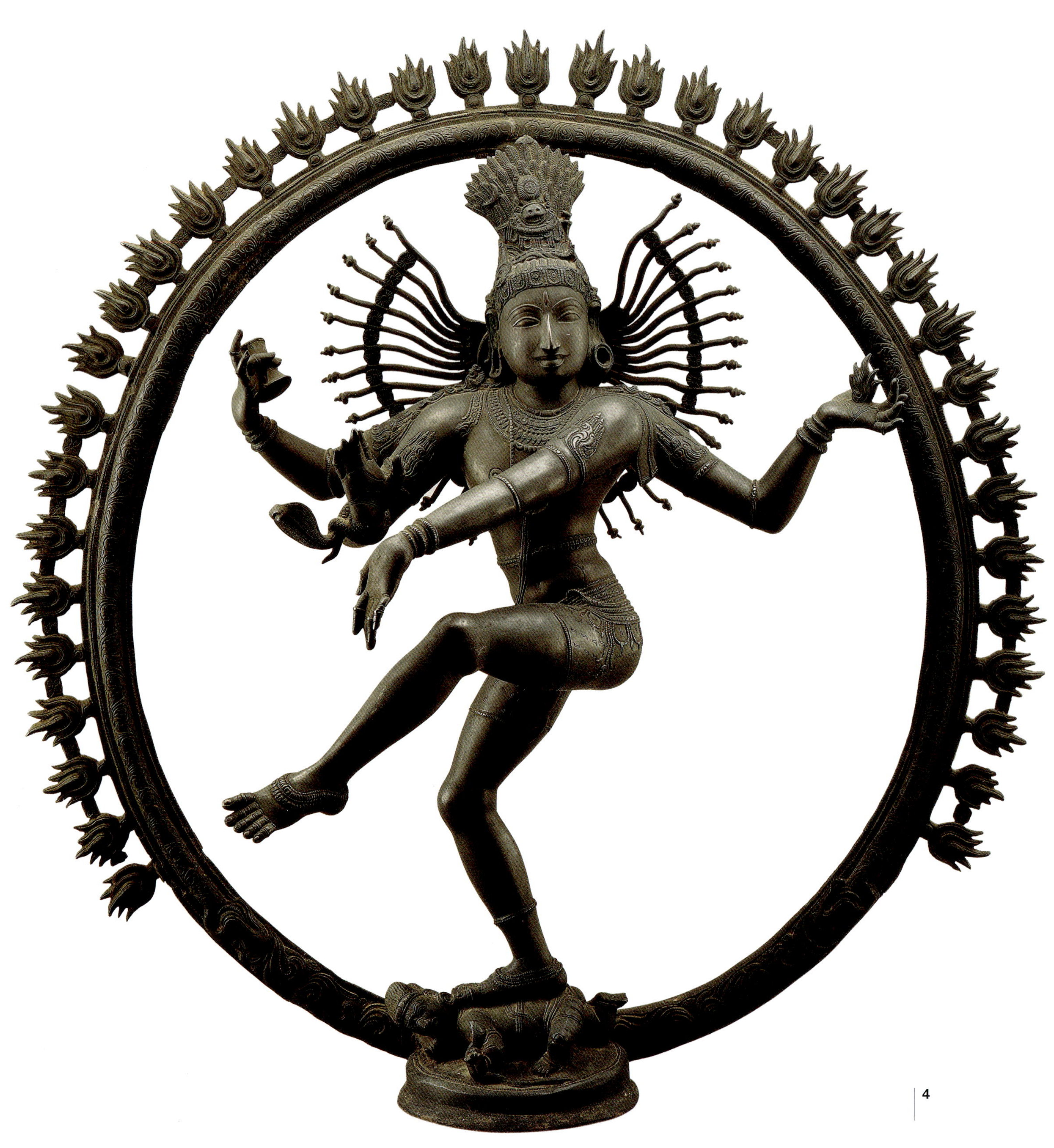

4

known poses described in a manual on dance, the *Natyashashtra* of around 400, which are clear forerunners of the full-fledged iconography of the pose known as *ananda tandava* or dance of bliss.[14] Was this merely a verbal picture or could it possibly have been executed in a three-dimensional medium?

Several hymns of the *bhakti* saints, reviewed in my introductory chapter to this volume, speak of temple processions centered on images that were clearly portable, raising the possibility of the early execution, perhaps in the medium of wood, of an image of dancing Shiva. One of Appar's verses, which refers to the monthly festival of Asthami (the eighth day of the bright fortnight of the moon) in the temple of Kurukkai Virattam, speaks specifically of an image of dancing Shiva *(kuttar)* being taken in procession.

> ***For seven holy days before***
> ***the festival of Attami, the Eighth Day,***
> ***the Lord of Kurukkai Virattam***
> ***goes in procession in his dancing form*** **[kuttar],**
> ***as Ayan [Brahma] and Mal [Vishnu] and all the gods***
> ***bow to him and praise him,***
> ***calling him their Lord.***[15]

A second verse speaks thus of a processional image:

> ***The Lord of Citticcaram shrine in Naraiyur,***
> ***who has the river in his hair,***
> ***the poison stain on his throat,***
> ***and the Veda on his tongue,***
> ***goes resplendent in ceremonial dress . . .***[16]

It is evident that portable festival images, including dancing Shiva, existed during the late seventh century. If these were made of wood, as seems most likely, then the entire reasoning behind the resplendent ceremonial dress referred to in the quoted verse becomes clear. Silks, jewelry, and flower garlands were necessary to enhance the appearance of the early wooden images; when bronze replaced wood, the established practice of more than two centuries duration was directly transferred to the metal images.

In an evocative and poetic essay originally published in 1912 titled "The Dance of Shiva," Ananda Coomaraswamy presented an eloquent explication of the philosophical basis for Nataraja's dance of bliss as signifying Shiva's destruction of the universe only in order to recreate it in India's cyclical concept of time.[17] He explained that the fire in one hand of Shiva signifies cosmic destruction, the drum in another hand indicates the rhythm of creation, the upraised open palm means protection, while the raised foot signifies deliverance. The circle of flames enclosing the image represents the material cosmos that Shiva keeps in perpetual oscillating motion.[18] While Coomaraswamy may have drawn directly on texts composed no earlier than the thirteenth century, the philosophic and cosmic dimensions of Shiva's dance appears to have been present in nascent, if not explicit, form as early as the ninth or tenth century, at the time of the creation of the first Nataraja images in stone and bronze.[19] Consider, for instance, this verse in a poem by Manikkavachakar, who does not belong to the group of *nayanmars* but postdates them by a century or so. Sometime during the ninth century, just as the Nataraja icon in its classic form came to be, he sang thus:

> ***Let us praise***
> ***the Dancer*** **[kuttan]**
> ***who in good Tillai's hall***
> ***dances with fire,***
>
> ***who sports*** **[vilaiyatu]**
> ***creating***
> ***destroying***
> ***this heaven and earth***
> ***and all else.***[20]

One may ponder the reference to creating, protecting, and destroying; is it merely a generic reference to Shiva as the supreme source of all existence, or does it in fact foreshadow the ideas clearly and directly expressed soon after in a Tamil text known as *Tirumantiram and* attributed to Tirumular? The date and identity of Tirumular is disputed, but recent research makes it difficult to uphold the claim that he is the same Tirumular of pre-eighth-century date who is one of the sixty-three *nayanmars*.[21] Current thinking suggests that the philosopher-poet who composed the *Tirumantiram* belonged to "approximately 1000 A.D.," and no later than "the first half of the eleventh century."[22] In a section of seventy-nine verses referred to as *Shivananda-kuttu* or Shiva's dance of bliss *(ananda-tandava)*,[23] Tirumular explains:

> ***Hara's drum is creation;***
> ***Hara's hand gesturing posture is preservation;***
> ***Hara's fire is dissolution;***
> ***Hara's foot planted down is Obfuscation (tirodhayi);***
> ***Hara's foot, raised in dance, is Grace (redemption)***
> ***abiding.***
>
> ***Verse 2799***[24]

While there is no reference here to the dwarflike figure upon whom Shiva dances, an earlier verse in the same work, which pictures Shiva's body as space itself, specifies that Mushalagan (the demon on whom Shiva dances) is darkness in that space.[25]

Tirumular may have composed these explanatory verses at the very time the first images were created, or anywhere from fifty to a hundred years after, depending on the date assigned to him. It would be useful to keep in mind that a complex philosophy rarely dates from the time of its first articulation in a text. Rather, it is likely that such ideas had been discussed and refined in intellectual circles for some time before they were included in a poetic text. In other words, an explanation very similar to that enunciated in thirteenth-century Chidambaram, and popularized in the twentieth century by Ananda Coomaraswamy, was likely current at the time of the creation of the first Chola images of dancing Shiva. Certainly, as Zvelebil so aptly puts it, "one thing is beyond doubt: the cult is syncretistic, a complex amalgam of many trends, concepts, and elements, not a 'straight-forward' unilinear development derived 'directly' from any one single impetus."[26]

Emerging as an icon of significance during the tenth century, especially in the temples built by Queen Sembiyan Mahadevi (active 941–1001), Nataraja seems to have rapidly become an indispensable icon for the Chola dynasty. Ultimately, five sites in Tamil Nadu became specially famous for their images of the dancing lord. Tiruvalangadu in Tondai-nadu was known as *ratna sabha* or hall of gems; Chidambaram in the heart of Chola territory was the *kanaka sabha* or golden hall; Madurai in Pandi-nadu was the *velli sabha* or silver hall; Tirunelveli in Pandi-nadu was the *tamra sabha* or copper hall; and Courtallam, also in Pandi-nadu, was the *chitra sabha* or painted hall. In each of these sites, dancing Shiva was known as the lord *(pati)* of the hall, for example, as *ratna-sabha-pati* at Tiruvalangadu. The first four temples had Nataraja images of gems, gold, silver, and copper, while the fifth had a painted image.

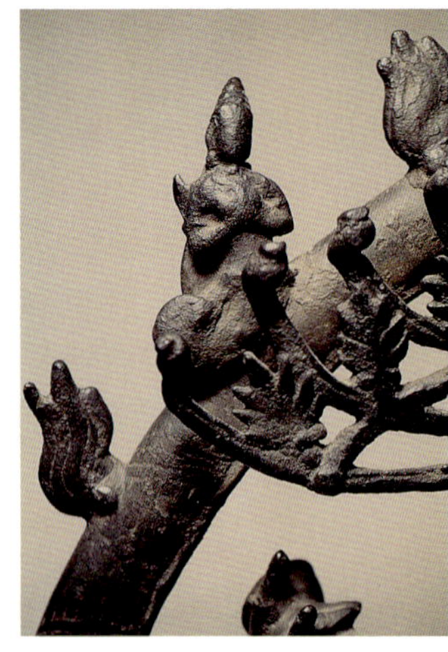

GODDESS GANGA ON *PRABHA* OF NATARAJA, CA. 990. VICTORIA & ALBERT PICTURE LIBRARY
PHOTO VIDYA DEHEJIA
FIG. 2

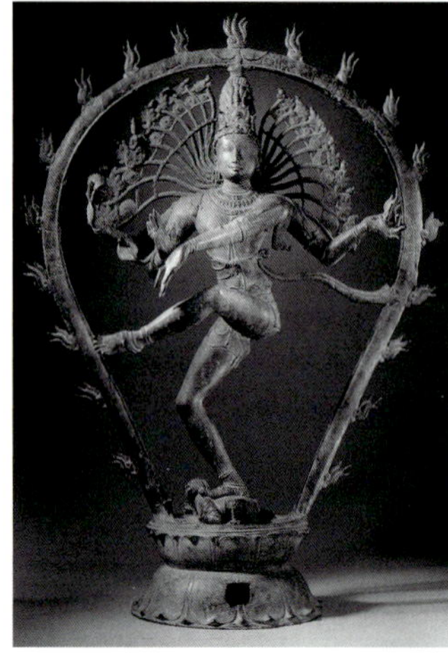

NATARAJA, CA. 950-1000. LOS ANGELES COUNTY MUSEUM OF ART; ANONYMOUS GIFT OF MR. AND MRS. HARRY LENART
PHOTO MUSEUM ASSOCIATES/LACMA
FIG. 3

The images of dancing Shiva in the exhibition display all the features typical of the dance of bliss. Elsewhere I have demonstrated the evolution of a set of features that generally distinguish an eleventh-century Nataraja from one of the tenth century. These include a circular rather than oval *prabha*, a five-tipped flame decoration as against three-tipped flames, the fire in Shiva's hand descending from the bowl into his palm, and goddess Ganga nestling in Shiva's locks (she is absent initially and first appears on the *prabha* [fig. 2]).[27]

The image of Shiva from a private collection (cat. no. 1) is a fine example of bronze-casting belonging to the very end of the tenth century, before the fully circular aureole for the image became the standard. Framed by an oval *prabha* that rises straight out of the lotus base and is adorned with three-tipped flames, Shiva dances gracefully with a serpent wrapped around his wrist. Goddess Ganga, her lower half depicted as flowing water, is positioned in the matted locks that sway with the movement of Shiva's dance. His waist-cloth *(veshti)* is partially thrown over his left shoulder, and his right foot rests lightly upon the dwarflike form of Mushalagan, who raises his head to look up adoringly at the dancing lord. Shiva smiles benignly at his devotees; here is not the regal detachment seen in an image of approximately the same date, now in the Los Angeles County Museum of Art (fig. 3), but a divine dancer who is approachable and accessible. The master artist created an image, bewitching from both front and rear, that conveys magnificently the swaying movement of dance.

Created some one hundred and fifty years later is the Nataraja from the Dallas Museum of Art (cat. no. 2). The *prabha* has now assumed its standard circular shape and here consists of two circular bands, the inner plain and the outer carved with rosettes—the whole framed with five-tipped flames. The uppermost of Shiva's flowing locks creates a loop on both sides, and the loop to the viewers' left encloses the figure of the goddess Ganga. From the rear it is possible to discern that the locks were cast separately and riveted to the head, a characteristic typical of the twelfth century. The flame in Shiva's rear left hand, clearly contained within a small bowl in the earlier image, now appears to rise directly from his palm. The details are exquisite—the skull in Shiva's headdress is large and expressive, the crescent moon is clearly delineated, as are the crane feathers crowning his locks. Shiva wears abundant jewelry that includes many strands of necklaces, armlets, and foot ornaments, and his locks are threaded with *konrai* blossoms. The image is similar in style and treatment to two Nataraja images of the twelfth century from Kumbhakonam and Tiruvanaikka.[28]

From some fifty years later is the monumental image from the Rijksmuseum that reveals absolute mastery of the art of bronze-casting (cat. no. 3). Shiva, the master of the universe, stands balanced and serene, resting his right foot on the back of a playful Mushalagan who has his knees planted as if attempting to adjust his position. The circular *prabha* no longer rises straight out of the lotus base, but from the mouths of hybrid aquatic creatures known as *makaras* that henceforth become the traditional embellishment. The manner in which two plaited strands connect the hands holding drum and fire to the edges of the *prabha*, and the introduction of a *kirtimukha* or face of glory to connect the locks piled upon Shiva's head with the aureole are interesting details of technique. This image exemplifies the final perfected iconography for Nataraja that has remained the model into the twenty-first century.

The image of dancing Shiva from the collection of the Museum of Fine Arts in Boston, belonging to the end of the eighteenth century (cat. no. 4) demonstrates the persistence of well-tested iconography. The image is finely constructed, the facial features clearly delineated, and there is an elegant tilt to the head that is crowned with crane feathers. The matted locks are now exceedingly stylized and somewhat mechanical in arrangement, and Mushalagan is a fierce figure. The *makaras* from whose mouth the circular *prabha* once emerged have now become stylized wavelike motifs, and the perfectly symmetrical flames decorating the *prabha's* rim are joined one to the other with an outer circular band. The image demonstrates the manner in which a well-established sacred iconography carries lasting power through the centuries.

NOTES

1 David Dean Shulman, trans., *Songs of the Harsh Devotee: The Tevaram of Cuntaramurtinayanar* (Philadelphia: University of Pennsylvania Press, 1990), p. 544: 82.2.

2 V. Vedachalam, "Pandiya nattil Natarajisvaram," in *Tolliyal Nokkil Tamilakam* (Chennai: Tolpural Ayva Turai, 1999), pp. 274–79. Vedachalam, epigraphist with the Tamil Nadu State Department of Archaeology, points to the very first use of the term Nataraja in any inscription from Tamil Nadu. A Pandya record from the town of Tiruvekampattu near Shivaganga records the dedication of a temple named Natarjishvaram that enshrined an image of Nataraja. The donor was a certain Somanathadevar, the family guru of the monarch Vikrama Pandya, and the inscription dates to the year 1245.

3 S. R. Balasubrahmanyam, *Early Chola Temples: Parantaka I to Rajaraja I,* A.D. *907–985* (Bombay: Orient Longman, 1971), pp. 65, 74.

4 Padma Kaimal, "Shiva Nataraja: Shifting Meanings of an Icon," *Art Bulletin* 81, no. 3 (1999): 390–419, points out that transformations or "Sanskritization," occurred at Chidambaram during the tenth century, including the new Sanskrit name of Chidambaram for what had thus far been known as Tillai, as well as a mythic identity for the Nataraja icon. However, the Sanskrit term Nataraja did not enter Tamil vocabulary until the thirteenth century.

5 Ibid., p. 394, states that none of the seventh- and eighth-century *bhakti* hymns mention "the circle of flame, the flying sashes, the leg lifted across the body, or locks of hair that fly or fan out." She seems to have missed the frequent references (quoted below) to Shiva's lifted leg, the locks of hair that fan out with the movement of his dance, and the flying serpent (though not flying sashes) that accompany his movement.

6 Indira Viswanathan Peterson, *Poems to Siva: The Hymns of the Tamil Saints* (Princeton: Princeton University Press, 1989), p. 118: Appar 4.81.4, dedicated to the Shiva of Tillai or Chidambaram.

7 T. V. Gopal Iyer and François Gros, eds., *Tevaram: Hymnes Sivaites du pays Tamoul,* vol. 2 (Pondicherry: Institut français d'indologie, 1985), p. 8: Appar 4.81.10. Translation is mine.

8 Shulman, *Songs of the Harsh Devotee*, p. 567: Sundarar 90.1.

9 G. U. Pope, *The Tiruvacagam* (Oxford: Clarendon Press, 1900), p. 1: 1.1. Translation is mine.

10 Peterson, *Poems to Siva*, p. 120: Sambandar 1.46.2.

11 Ibid., p. 121: Sambandar 1.46.5.

12 Ibid., Sambandar 1.46.6.

13 Ibid., Sambandar 1.46.3.

14 Kamil V. Zvelebil, *Ananda-Tandava of Siva-Sadanrttamurti* (Madras: Institute of Asian Studies, 1985), pp. 7–20.

15 Peterson, *Poems to Siva*, p. 183: Appar 4.50.2.

16 Ibid.: Sambandar 1.71.5.

17 Ananda K. Coomaraswamy, "The Dance of Shiva" (1912), in *The Dance of Shiva: Fourteen Indian Essays,* 2d ed. (New Delhi: Munshiram Manoharlal, 1970), pp. 83–95.

18 See the title of Richard Davis's book on Shaiva theology: *Ritual in an Oscillating Universe* (Princeton: Princeton University Press, 1991).

19 Kaimal, "Shiva Nataraja," pp. 390–94, in critiquing Coomaraswamy for relying on later texts, emphasizes the need for a more historically grounded analysis. But her assumption that the ideas contained in thirteenth-century texts evolved only in the thirteenth century ignores the textual evidence that locates these concepts in earlier texts. The increasingly popular discipline of historiography more often than not provides a much-needed corrective to a range of outdated approaches of earlier traditional scholarship. It is useful to remind oneself that such scholars were working in a different historical framework, without the benefit of the half or full century of information, discovery, scholarship, and theory that is our heritage.

20 Glenn Yocum, *Hymns to the Dancing Siva: A Study of Manikkava-cakar's Tiruvachakam* (New Delhi: Heritage Publishers, 1982), p. 158. This is from hymn 7, the "Tiruvempavai," v. 12. See also Pope, *The Tiruvacagam*, p. 110.

21 Earlier, I too subscribed to this view.

22 W. Graefe, "Legends as Mile-Stones in the History of Tamil Literature," in H. L. Hariyuppa and M. M. Patkar, eds., *Professor P. K. Gode Commemmoration Volume* (Poona: Oriental Book Agency, 1960), p. 145.

23 The dictionary meaning of Tamil *kuttu* is a dance or drama; Tamil *adu[tal]* means to dance, to act, to play, to sport. The dictionary meaning of Sanskrit *tandava* is dance and the art of dancing; and the meaning of both Tamil and Sanskrit *ananda* is bliss. Sanskrit *ananda tandava* and Tamil *ananda kuttu* do not translate as "dance of furious bliss" (see Kaimal, "Shiva Nataraja," p. 392) except by an act of interpretation not contained in the words themselves. Zvelebil, *Ananda-Tandava of Siva-Sadanrttamurti*, p. 2, cites the *Dravidian Etymological Dictionary* to give us what he calls "the hard philological truth." *Tandavam* is simply derived from the Tamil *tantu*—"to jump, leap across, jump over, dance." As such, Zvelebil variously translates *ananda tandavam* as "awesome dance of bliss" (p. 2), "dynamic dance of bliss" (p. 3), and "vigorous/awesome dance of bliss" (p. 9).

24 B. Natarajan, trans., *Tirumantiram: A Tamil Scriptural Classic—By Tirumular* (Madras: Sri Ramakrishna Math, 1991), p. 430.

25 Kaimal, "Shiva Nataraja," p. 394, citing this same verse, states that the Tirumantiram describes the dwarf as a terrifying creature with eight arms. Lines 2 and 3 of the verse in question, no. 2774, refer to Shiva's awesome presence, not to Mushalagan, and reads thus in Zvelebil, *Ananda-Tandava of Siva-Sadanrttamurti*, p. 49:

> His body is *akasa*, the dark cloud therein is Muyalakan,
> The eight quarters are his eight hands,
> The three lights are his three eyes—
> Thus he alone dances in our body as the Hall.

26 Zvelebil, *Ananda-Tandava of Siva-Sadanrttamurti*, p. 55. Kaimal, "Shiva Nataraja," highlights the importance of the Pine Forest myth as an iconographic source for the imagery.

27 Vidya Dehejia, *Art of the Imperial Cholas* (New York: Columbia University Press, 1990), pp. 42–47.

28 R. Nagaswamy, *Masterpieces of South Indian Bronzes* (New Delhi: National Museum, 1983), figs. 56, 62.

5 **SHIVA AS TRIPURAVIJAYA, VICTOR OF THE THREE CITIES, AND CONSORT**
CHOLA PERIOD, CA. 950–60
BRONZE, 32 1/4 AND 25 5/8 IN.
(81.9 CM AND 65.1 CM)
THE CLEVELAND MUSEUM OF ART;
JOHN L. SEVERANCE FUND (1961.94)

6 **SHIVA AS TRIPURAVIJAYA, VICTOR OF THE THREE CITIES, AND CONSORT**
CHOLA PERIOD, CA. 990–1000
BRONZE, 22 1/4 IN. (56.5 CM)
COLLECTION ROBERT HATFIELD ELLSWORTH

In Tamil Nadu, worshipers of Shiva celebrate his eight great heroic feats at eight heroic sites (Sanskrit *vira-sthanam*, Tamil *virattanam*). Tiruvadigai Virattanam is the temple where Shiva is celebrated in his form of Tripurantaka (Destroyer of the Three Cities). The festival to mark the exploit of Shiva destroying the fortified cities of three demons with a single arrow has been held annually since ancient times, and its performance is believed to ensure the protection of the town.

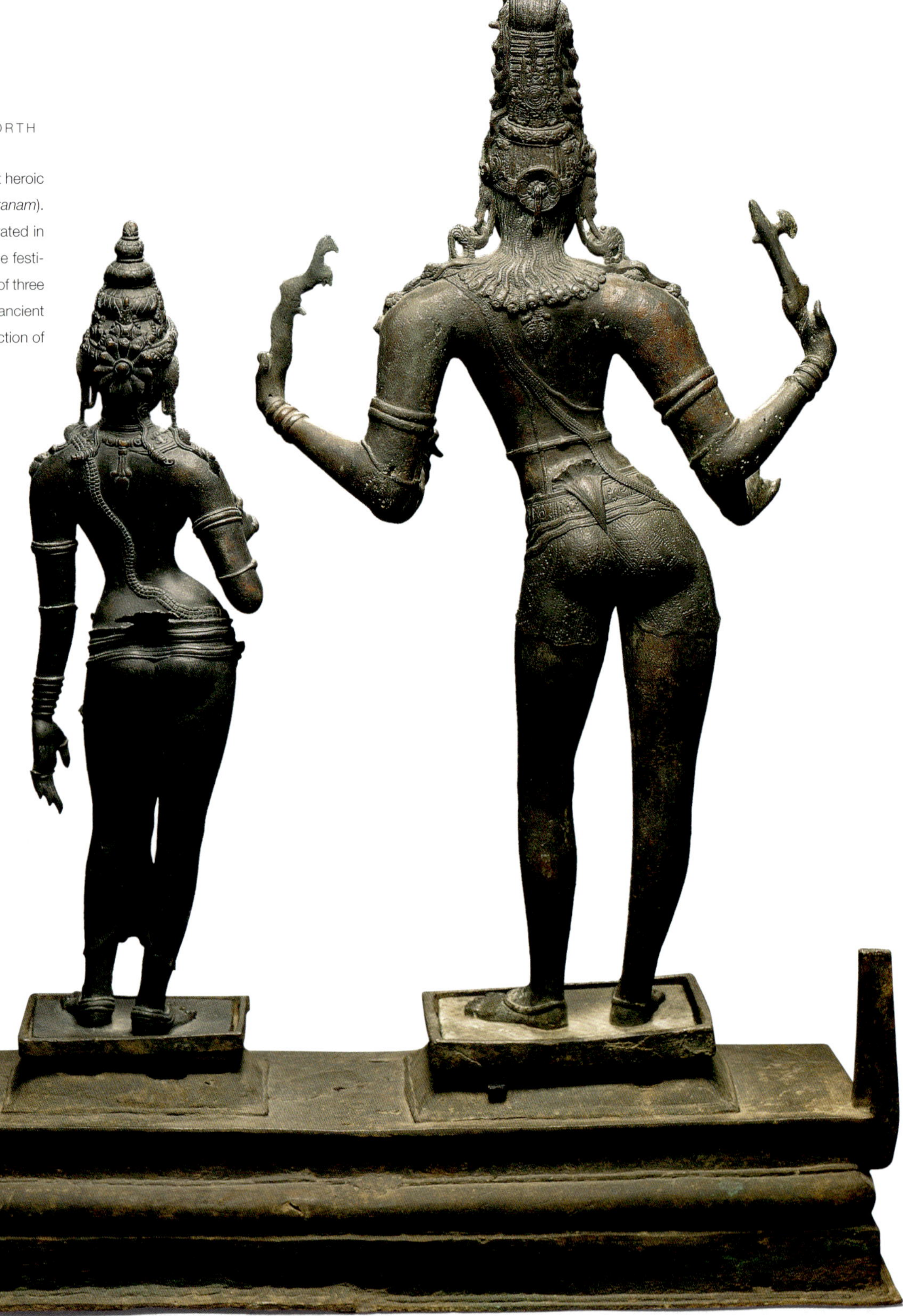

5

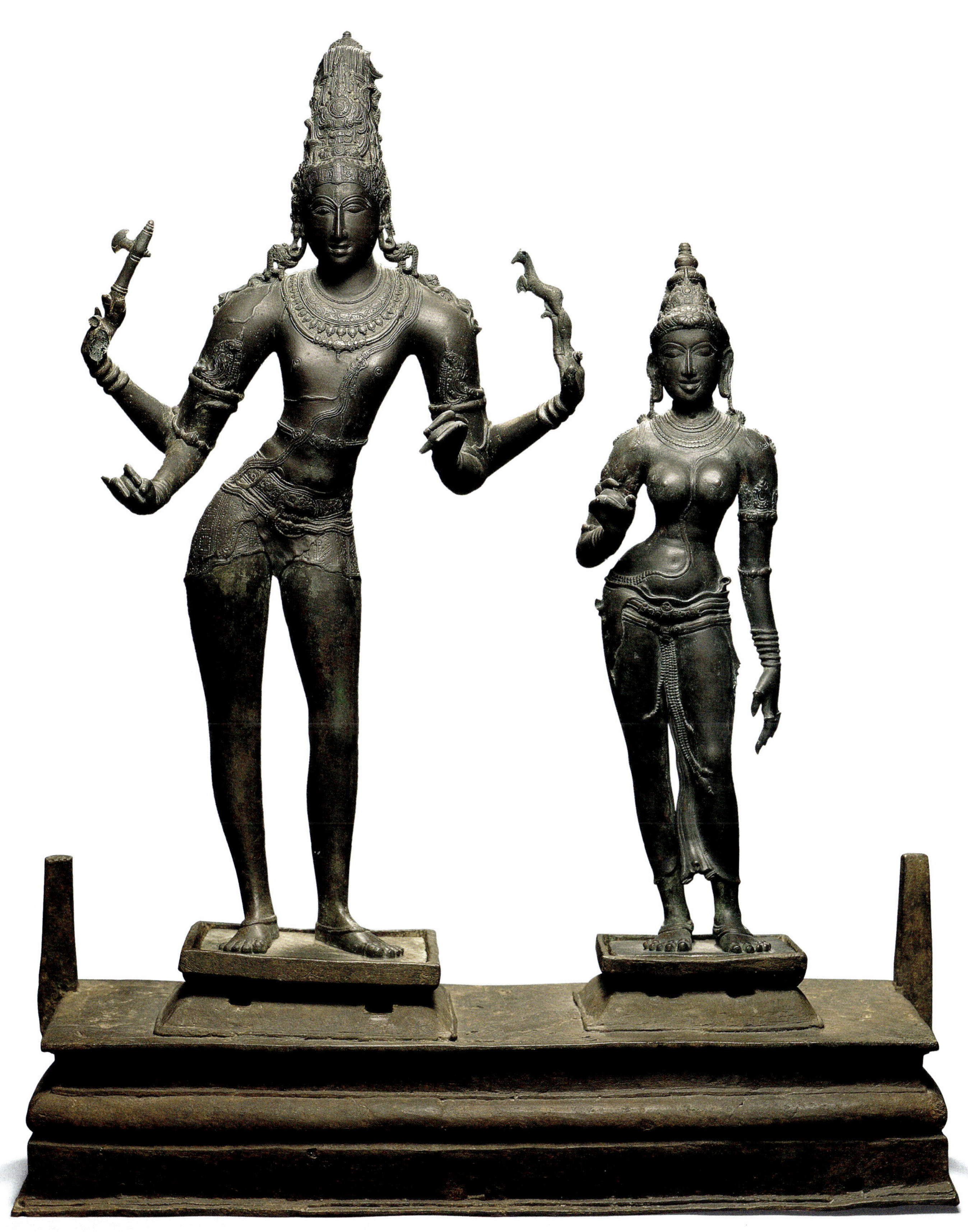

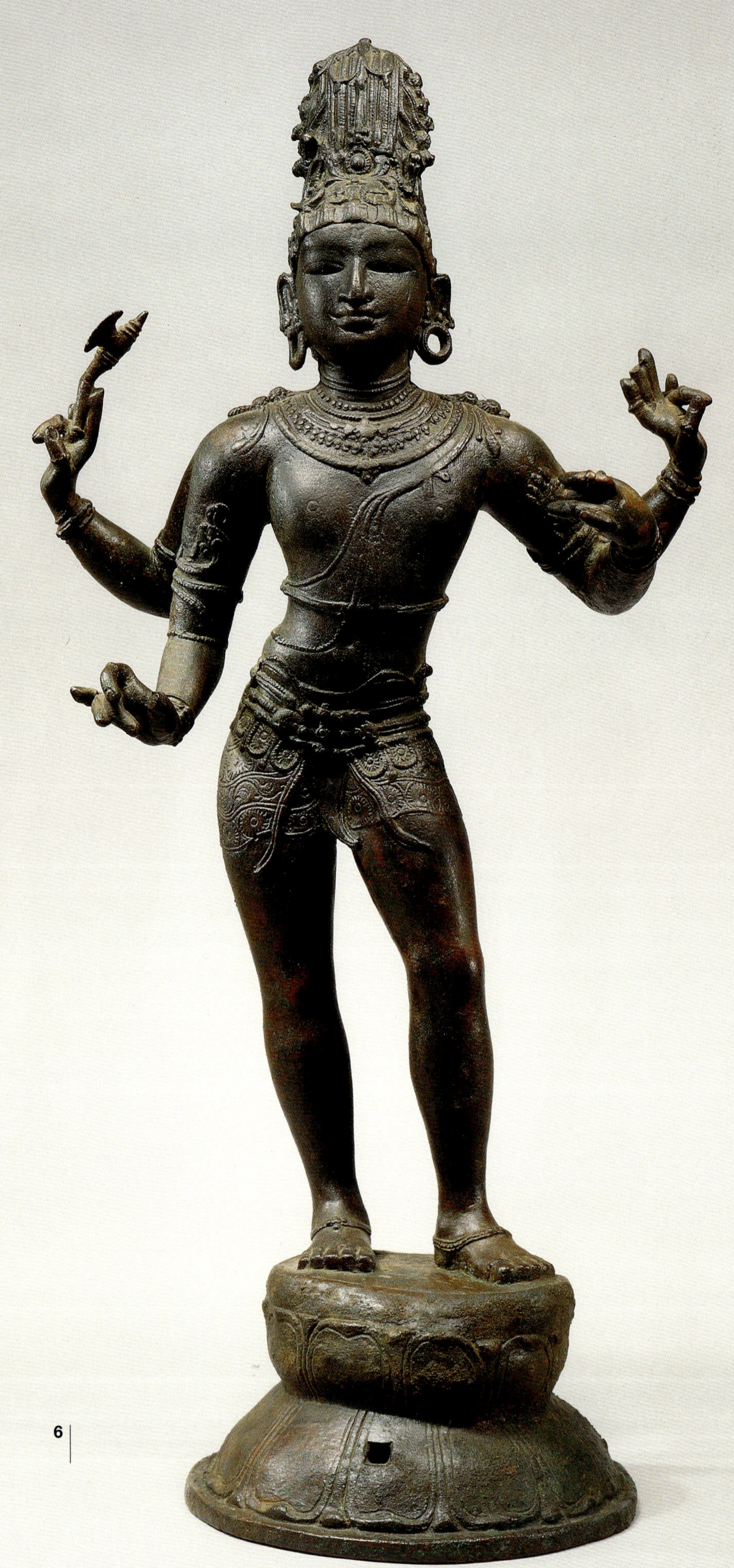

6

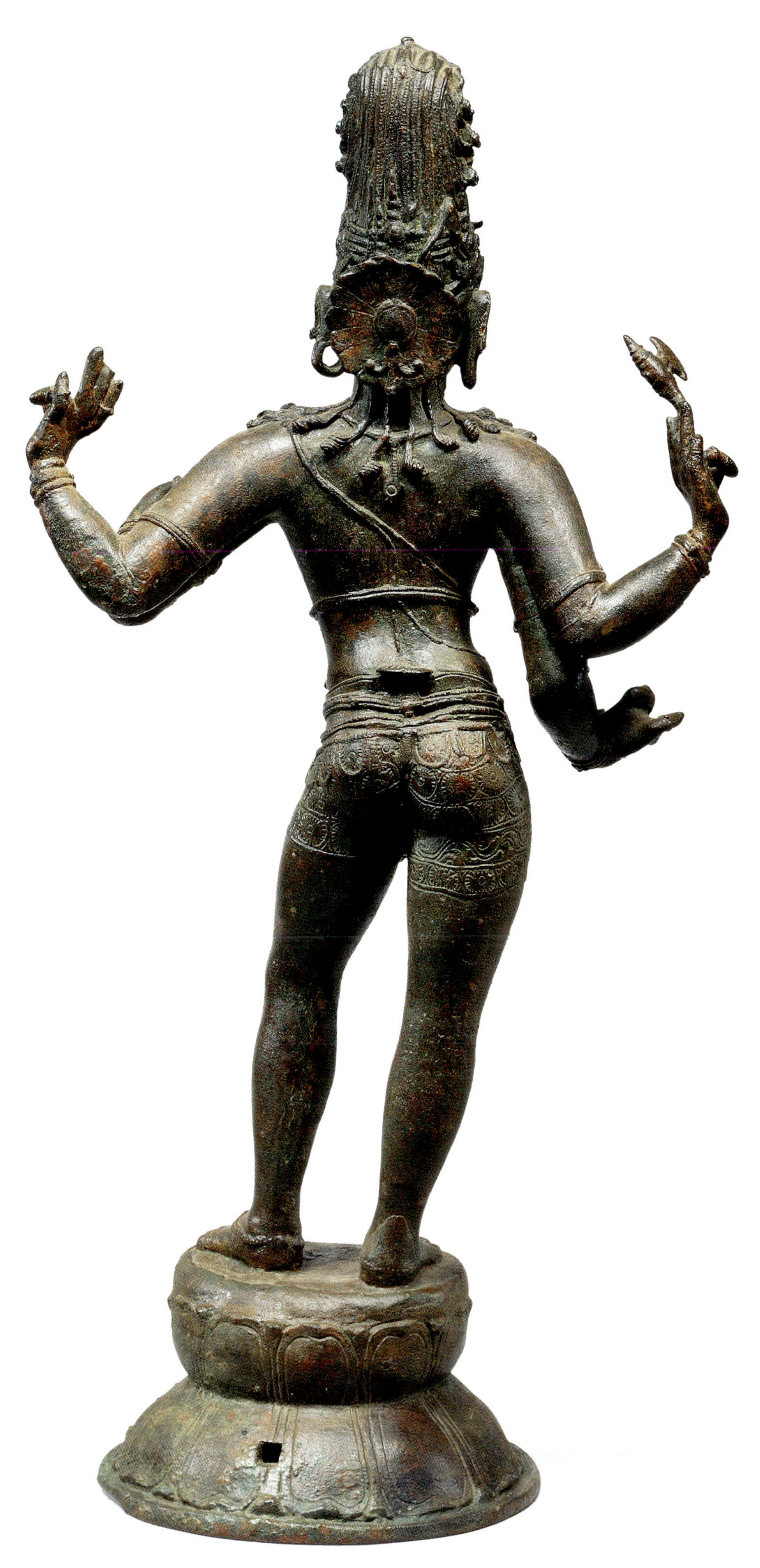

Legend speaks of powerful demons who propitiated Shiva until, pleased by their worship, he granted them a boon whereby they would live and rule over three cities *(tri-pura)*, made of gold, silver, and iron and placed respectively in the heavens, in the air, and on the earth. For a thousand years the demons lived in these cities, creating havoc while augmenting their powers to such an aggravating degree as to cause consternation among humans and gods alike. Unable to vanquish them (only a single arrow could be used), the gods appealed to Shiva, who assumed a form of great strength and beauty.

When the three citadels, unmoored,
flew about wreaking destruction
in heaven and on earth,
oppressed by their assault,
the frightened gods, led by Ari [Vishnu] himself,
sought his protection.
Then, moved by compassion, the gracious saviour
kindled his deadly arrow with fire,
shot fire from the snake that was his bowstring,
bent his mountain-bow to its fullest,
and reduced the citadels to ashes—[1]

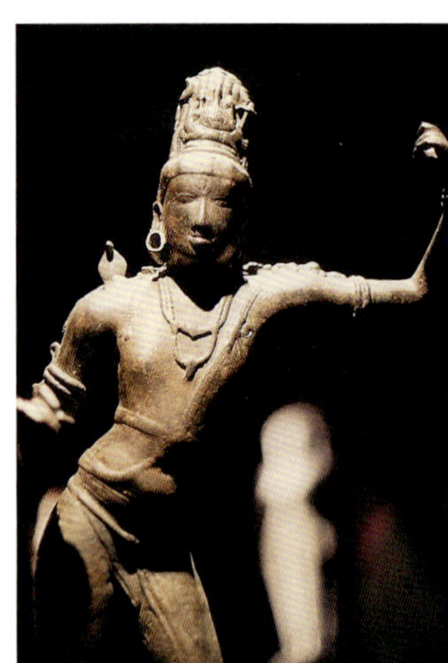

TRIPURAVIJAYA, CA. 925. THE NORTON SIMON FOUNDATION, PASADENA
PHOTO VIDYA DEHEJIA
FIG. 1

Thus Shiva came to be worshiped as *tri-pura-antaka* or destroyer of the three cities. While lay devotees accept the legend at face value and hail Tripurantaka as the victorious warrior who affords protection to those who worship him, the deeper meaning of this form revolves around Shiva's revelation of the significance of the Pasupata mode of worshiping the *linga*.[2]

The legend of Tripurantaka caught the imagination of devotees, and the ninth-century saint Manikkavachakar used it for the opening verses of a popular song that normally accompanied a game played with a small ball or shuttlecock known as an *unthi;* Manikkavachakar adapted the song to proclaim the glory of Shiva, here addressed as Ekambar.

Bent was the bow, arose tumult and uproar,
burned were three cities—fly unthi *fly!*
as one flame they burned—O fly unthi *high!*

Two arrows we saw not in Ekambar's hand,
only one arrow, three cities—fly unthi *fly!*
one was too many—O fly unthi *high!*[3]

It is only in painted murals and stone relief sculptures that an actual battle is portrayed. The image in bronze is better described as Tripuravijaya or Victor of the Three Cities, and is recognized from the stance of Shiva poised gracefully as the redeeming victor in the aftermath of the conflagration. It is this term that is used in an inscription of the year 976 of the Dowager Queen Sembiyan Mahadevi that speaks of an endowment to the temple at Koneri-rajapuram for the ritual worship of three groups of bronze images, one of which is Tripuravijaya.[4]

The earlier of the two images of Tripuravijaya is the sinuously elegant Shiva with his consort from the Cleveland Museum of Art (cat. no. 5). This image is not of Chandrashekhara and consort, but rather Tripuravijaya with Uma. Iconographic texts such as the *Mayamata* always speak of Chandrashekhara as standing straight upright (see cat. no. 7); it is Tripuravijaya who stands in the contrapposto position.[5] The images of Tripuravijaya and Uma are cast to stand together on a single pedestal, as indeed was Rajaraja Chola's slightly larger Shiva (with his foot on Mushalagan) together with Uma, commissioned for his Tanjavur temple.[6] The assured and confident handling of the image from the Cleveland Museum suggests the hand of a master in the early days of Queen Sembiyan's workshop. Yet, the slender sinuousness of Shiva's torso links the image to the Tripuravijaya of around 920 from the Norton Simon collection (fig. 1). His short, patterned lower garment, held in place with a lion-head buckle, is arranged with a triangular fold in front, and tucked into the waistband at the rear with a fan-shaped fold, reminiscent of the Rama bronze from Tirucherai.[7] Shiva's matted hairdo, the rich ornamentation, the soft handling of the form of slender Uma, and the petaled *siraschakra* at the rear of her head all suggest a date of around 950–60. The eyes have, unfortunately, been subjected to recutting. Clearly, the extensive bathing and anointing of the figures over several centuries of ritual worship resulted in the features being worn down. The recutting was necessary to make the images suitably potent both to receive the gaze of devotees and to focus a return-gaze in the complex process of *darshan,* or ritual seeing.

The four-armed Tripuravijaya from a private collection, dating to the very end of the tenth century, perhaps to around 990–1000 (cat. no. 6), exhibits the maturity of style seen during the reign of Emperor Rajaraja Chola (r. 985–1016). There is some evidence to indicate that Rajaraja, himself a great conqueror, personally related to the victorious form of Tripuravijaya, who provided the emperor with a divine archetype whose blessings would ensure him victory.[8] While the niches on the lower level of the walls of his great temple at Tanjavur house images of varying forms of Shiva, all eighteen upper niches carry identical images of Shiva as Tripuravijaya. The emphatic repetition is noteworthy.

This majestic bronze image stands on a lotus pedestal with his left foot gracefully bent. Two front hands are poised to hold the bow and arrow, while one rear hand holds a battle-ax and the fingers of the other once supported his little deer companion. While the earliest images depict Tripuravijaya with either two or four hands, the two-handed version was soon abandoned. Shiva is richly ornamented. A serpent peeps out from the matted locks piled high upon his head and held in place with an ornamental band. A triple-strand sacred thread circles his torso, and he wears multiple necklaces, armlets, and bracelets. His short, patterned lower garment *(veshti)*, secured with an ornamental girdle, reveals powerful muscular legs. The image is of slightly later date than the Tripuravijaya currently in the National Museum, New Delhi.[9] It is intriguing to note that the list of more than sixty bronzes in the inscriptions of the Tanjavur temple, all gifts from the royal family or high officials, does not include one specifically described by the term Tripuravijaya. However, there is no doubt that the image called *tanjai* (Tanjavur) *alaghar* (handsome one), described as standing with one foot upon the dwarf Mushalagan, is none other than Tripuravijaya. R. Nagaswamy has identified an image now in the Tanjavur Art Gallery as the bronze Tripuravijaya dedicated by the emperor.[10] Perhaps because of its personal significance to him, Rajaraja referred to Tripuravijaya by the familiar nickname of "handsome one of Tanjavur," his capital.

A certain degree of confusion persists between images of Tripuravijaya and those of Shiva as Player of the Vina (Vinadhara), since the positioning of the hands is so similar. In the case of Vinadhara, the two front hands would be playing the vina instrument (always missing in bronzes); in the case of Tripurantaka, those same hands would be holding a bow and an arrow (also invariably missing). While a thorough study of Chola inscriptions would throw further light on this issue, those records that are easily accessible have not, thus far, revealed evidence of the donation to temples of bronze images of Vinadhara.[11] In addition, Nagaswamy points out that two important Agamic texts that list festival bronzes, *Suprabheda Agama* and *Ajita Agama,* mention the image of Tripurantaka but not of Vinadhara.[12] However, Chola stone relief carvings include several depictions of Shiva with the vina in hand.

Both images of Tripuravijaya in the exhibition stand with their feet resting on the ground. But a variant form (fig. 2) follows the Tanjavur inscription model and portrays Shiva with his left leg raised and placed upon the back of dwarflike Mushalagan, while the other is placed on a small lotus pedestal. The image was then mounted on a compact rectangular platform with two metal rods to hold the *prabha,* while the lugs along the base were intended for the insertion of poles used to carry the image during temple festivities. (The eyes, including the third eye in the forehead, as well as the nose of this particular image have been recut, as was frequently done when centuries of ritual temple worship blurred the details of the sacred bronzes.)

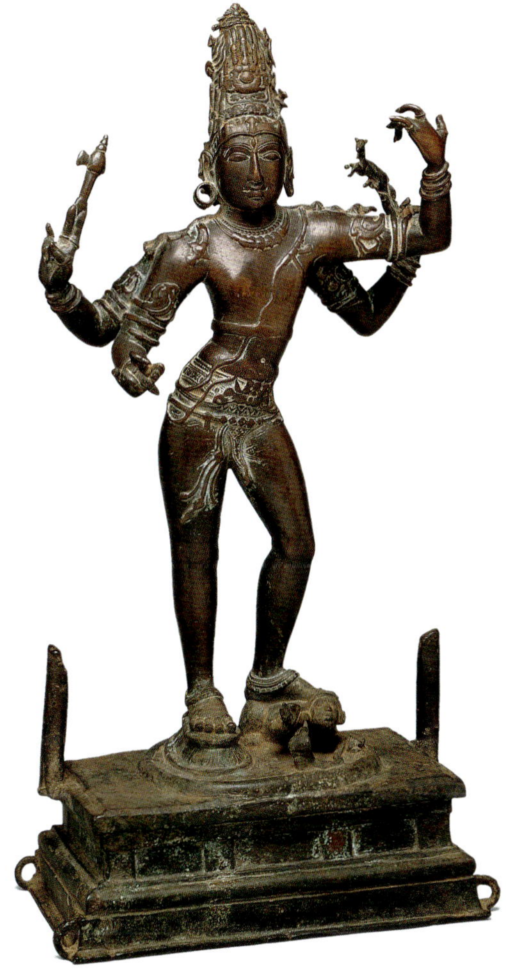

TRIPURAVIJAYA, 11TH CENTURY. THE JAMES W. AND MARILYNN ASLDORF COLLECTION COPYRIGHT THE ART INSTITUTE OF CHICAGO PHOTO MICHAEL TROPEA

FIG. 2

NOTES

1 Indira Viswanathan Peterson, *Poems to Shiva: The Hymns of the Tamil Saints* (Princeton: Princeton University Press, 1989), p. 134: Appar 4.14.5. The original verse specifies that Meru is the bow and Vasuki is the bowstring.

2 R. Nagaswamy, "Tripurantaka, Vinadhara Dakshinamurti, or Kiratamurti?" in R. Nagaswamy, *Aspects of Art and Architecture of South India* (New Delhi: Aryan Books, forthcoming). An alternative explanation is that the three cities are the three states of waking, dream, and deep sleep, and when Shiva reveals himself, the redemption is instantaneous and cuts through these three *puras* in one flash (the arrow).

3 G. U. Pope, *The Tiruvacagam* (Oxford: Clarendon Press, 1900), p. 178: 16.1,2. Translation is mine.

4 Vidya Dehejia, *Art of the Imperial Cholas* (New York: Columbia University Press, 1990), pp. 8–10. The other bronzes mentioned are Shiva with his bull accompanied by his consort, and Ganesha. For details, see inscriptions 151 and 151A in E. Hultzsch, ed., *South Indian Inscriptions,* vol. 3 (New Delhi: Archaeological Survey of India, 1992 reprint), part 3, pp. 300–322.

5 Bruno Dagens, in *Mayamata* (New Delhi: Sitaram Bhatia Inst, 1985) says that *Tripurantaka* "is balanced on one leg, the other being bent" (p. 348); and of *Chandrashekhara*, "the god who-has-the-moon-as-crest is represented standing perfectly upright" (p. 349). While labeling the image of Chandrashekhara, Stella Kramrisch commented upon the contrapposto versus straight stance. See her *Manifestations of Shiva* (Philadelphia: Philadelphia Museum of Art, 1981), p. 122.

6 See "Assemblage of Sacred Bronzes" in this volume.

7 Douglas Barrett, *Early Cola Bronzes* (Bombay: Bhulabhai Memorial Institute, 1965), fig. 43.

8 Gary Schwindler, "Speculations on the Theme of Siva as Tripurantaka as It Appears During the Reign of Raja I in the Tanjore Area, ca. A.D. 1000," *Ars Orientalis* 17 (1987): 163–78.

9 R. Nagaswamy, *Masterpieces of Early South Indian Bronzes* (New Delhi: National Museum, 1983), fig. 70, p. 83.

10 Barrett, *Early Cola Bronzes*, fig. 16. On page 20 Barrett cites a newspaper article by R. Nagaswamy, "Thanjai Azhagar," *The Hindu*, March 4, 1962.

11 Several images in museums have been identified as Vinadhara, some incorrectly so.

12 Nagaswamy, "Tripurantaka, Vinadhara Dakshinamurti or Kiratamurti?"

7 **SHIVA AS CHANDRASHEKHARA, LORD CROWNED WITH THE MOON**
CHOLA PERIOD, 990–1000
BRONZE, 20 IN. (51 CM)
TRUSTEES OF THE BRITISH MUSEUM; DONATED BY PT BROOKE SEWELL, ESQ. (OA 1958.7-15.1)

8 **ALINGANA CHANDRASHEKHARA, MOON-CROWNED SHIVA EMBRACING UMA**
CHOLA PERIOD, CA. 1150
BRONZE, 15 AND 8 IN. (38.1 AND 20.3 CM)
THE METROPOLITAN MUSEUM OF ART; SAMUEL EILENBERG COLLECTION, BEQUEST OF SAMUEL EILENBERG, 1998 (2000.284.2)

He bears a skull
like a silver conch shell.
His twisted white sacred thread
shines like a strand of silver rope.
Matted hair crowned with the white moon
bright as beaten silver leaf,
wearing white bones,
the brahmin has smeared silver ash
on his coral skin.[1]

Chandrashekhara, the Lord Crowned with the Moon, is Shiva in his most benign of forms. He may be portrayed on his own as *kevala* Chandrashekhara, or accompanied by his consort whom he gently embraces, in which case he is known as *alingana,* "embracing," Chandrashekhara.

The British Museum Chandrashekhara (cat. no. 7), apparently a *kevala* image on its own, is an exquisite bronze that displays the stylistic maturity characteristic of the workshop of Emperor Rajaraja (r. 985–1014), and resembles a Chandrashekhara image from the Konerirajapuram temple.[2] Although the attributes held in the hands are damaged, we would expect to see the battle-ax and deer in Shiva's two rear hands; one front hand reveals remnants of a flower stem, while the other is in the *abhaya* gesture of protection. Shiva's matted hair is piled elegantly on his head in three distinct tiers, marked on either side by the twisted ends of the matted locks, and the entire arrangement is crowned with a multi-petaled flower. A single set of locks ending in a curl rests along each shoulder, while the locks on the rear extend down to cover the shoulder blades. His face, with a gentle smile, has a third eye on the forehead, and he wears the usual headband. A large rounded ring adorns one ear but the *makara* earring in the other is missing. Multiple necklaces, richly ornamented armlets, a sacred thread, and a waistband *(kati sutra)* adorn him, while the girdle holding the lower garment is ornamented with a large lion-head clasp. His armlets are each clearly mounted on a cloth band that is tied at the back of the arm in a simple knot similar to that seen on the consort of a Shiva of around 940 in the Pallavanishvara temple.[3]

Cast together to stand upon a single lotus pedestal, with tangs to support a *prabha*, are the smiling joyous images of Shiva and Uma as a loving couple, with one of Shiva's hands gently caressing Uma's form (cat. no. 8). Shiva holds the typical attributes of Chandrashekhara, and Uma holds a lotus in one hand as she stands close to her lord; the interaction between the figures is sensitively and delicately rendered. This juxtaposition of the divine couple is addressed in the temples as Pradoshamurti or Twilight Image (fig. 1). Every evening, prior to the final *puja* of the day, this twosome is placed on a palanquin carried on the shoulders of priests and taken in procession, followed by devotees, so that Shiva and his consort may inspect the inner premises of the temple. The graceful example in the exhibition bear similarities to the pair from Tiruvavaduturai that R. Nagaswamy dates to the period of Kulottunga I in his essay in this volume (fig. 15 on p. 38).

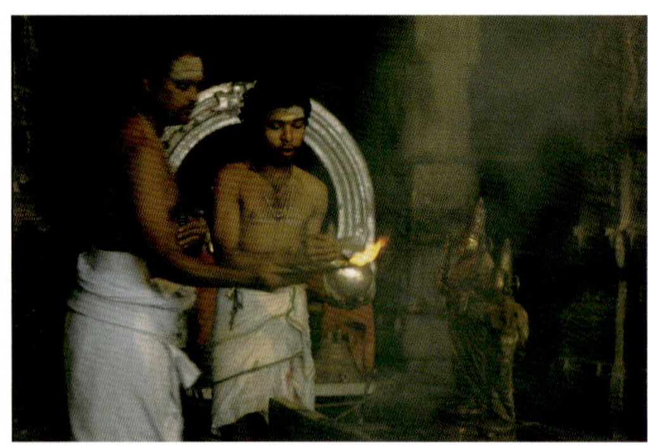

PRIESTS PERFORMING *PUJA* BEFORE ALINGANA CHANDRASHEKARA IMAGE, KANCHIPURAM
PHOTO NEIL GREENTREE, 1998
FIG.1

NOTES

1 Indira Viswanathan Peterson, *Poems to Shiva: The Hymns of the Tamil Saints* (Princeton: Princeton University Press, 1989), p. 103: Appar 4.113.1.
2 Douglas Barrett, *Early Cola Bronzes* (Bombay: Bhulabhai Memorial Institute, 1985), pl. 21.
3 Ibid., pl. 24.

SHIVA AS CHANDRASHEKHARA (DETAIL OF CAT. NO. 7)

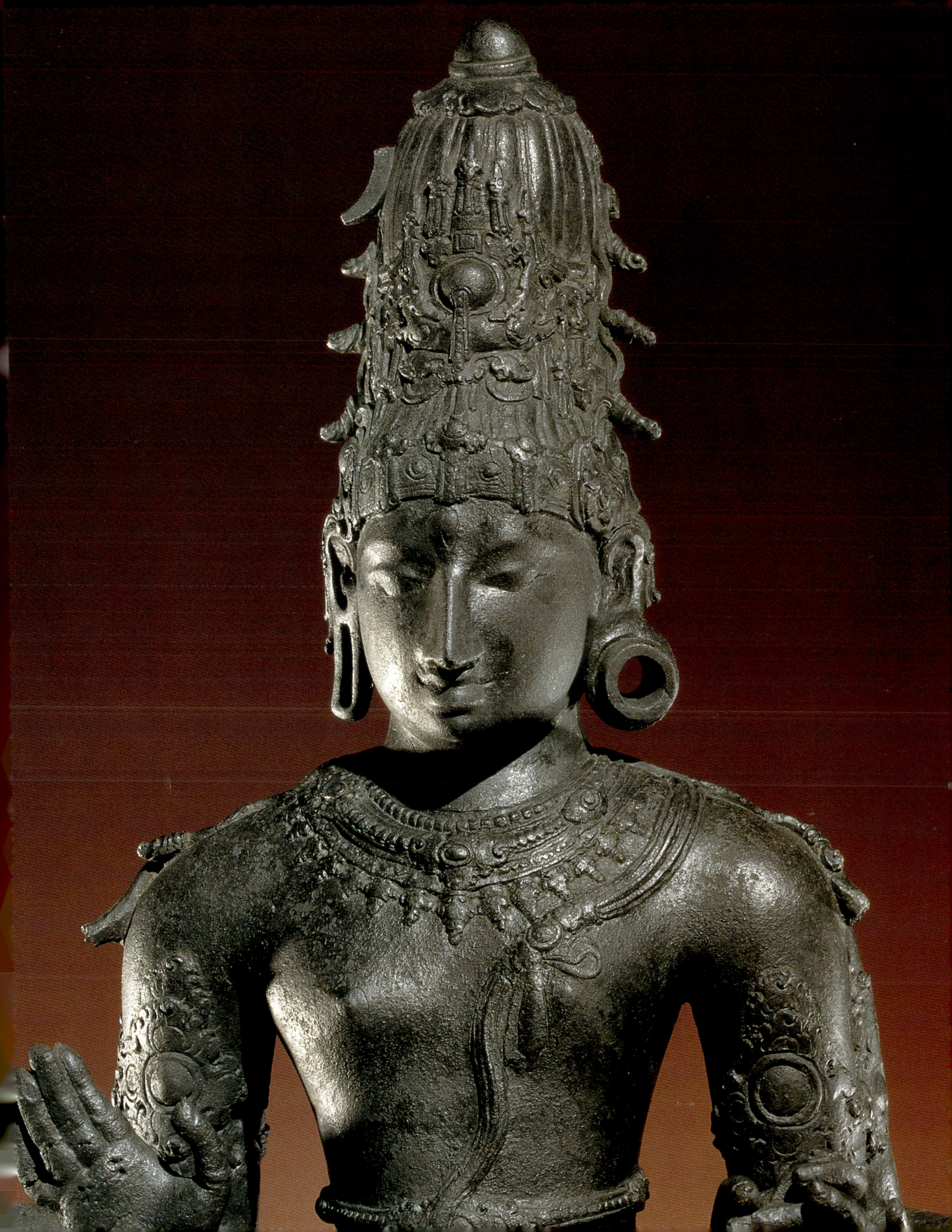

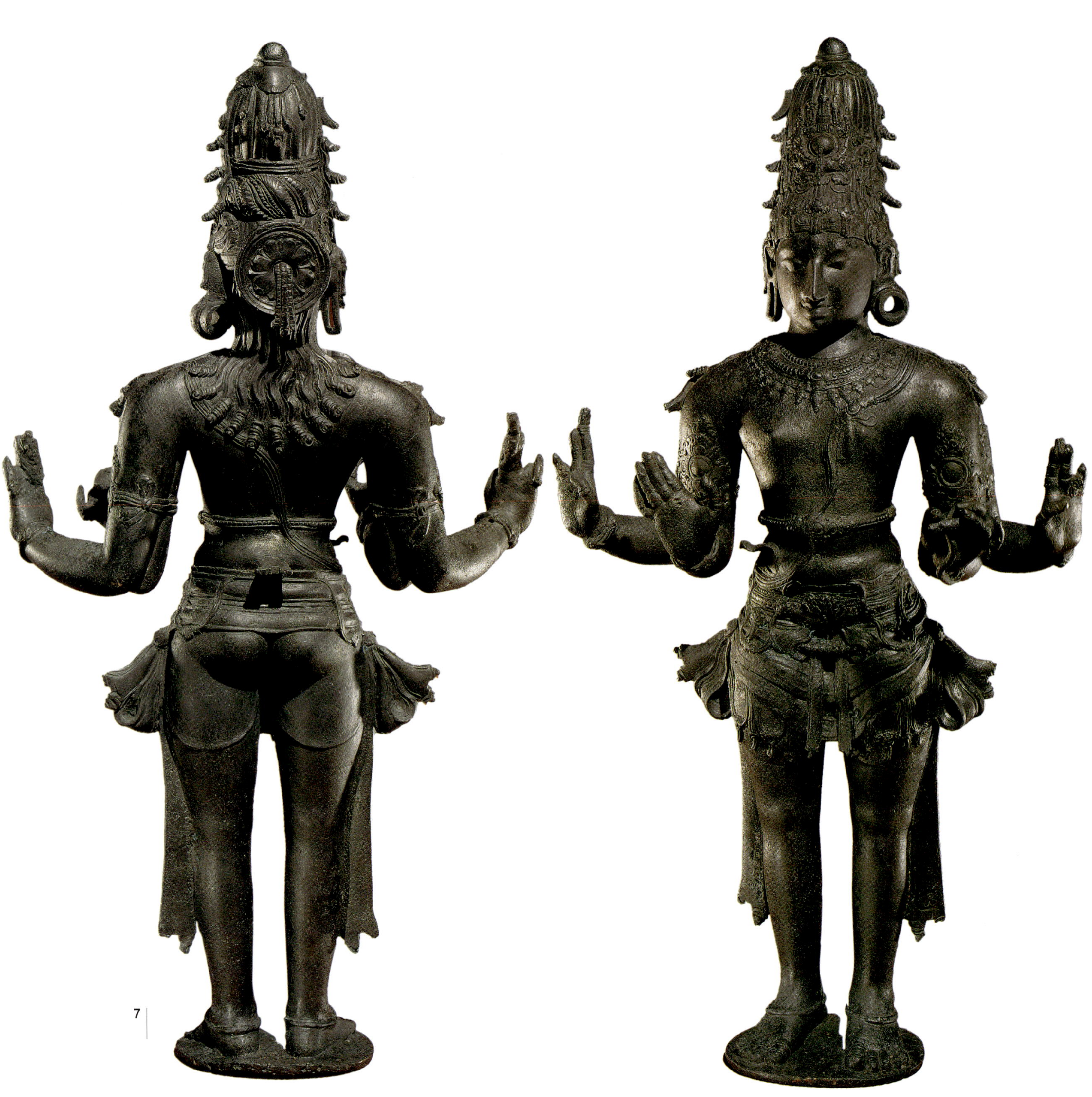

7

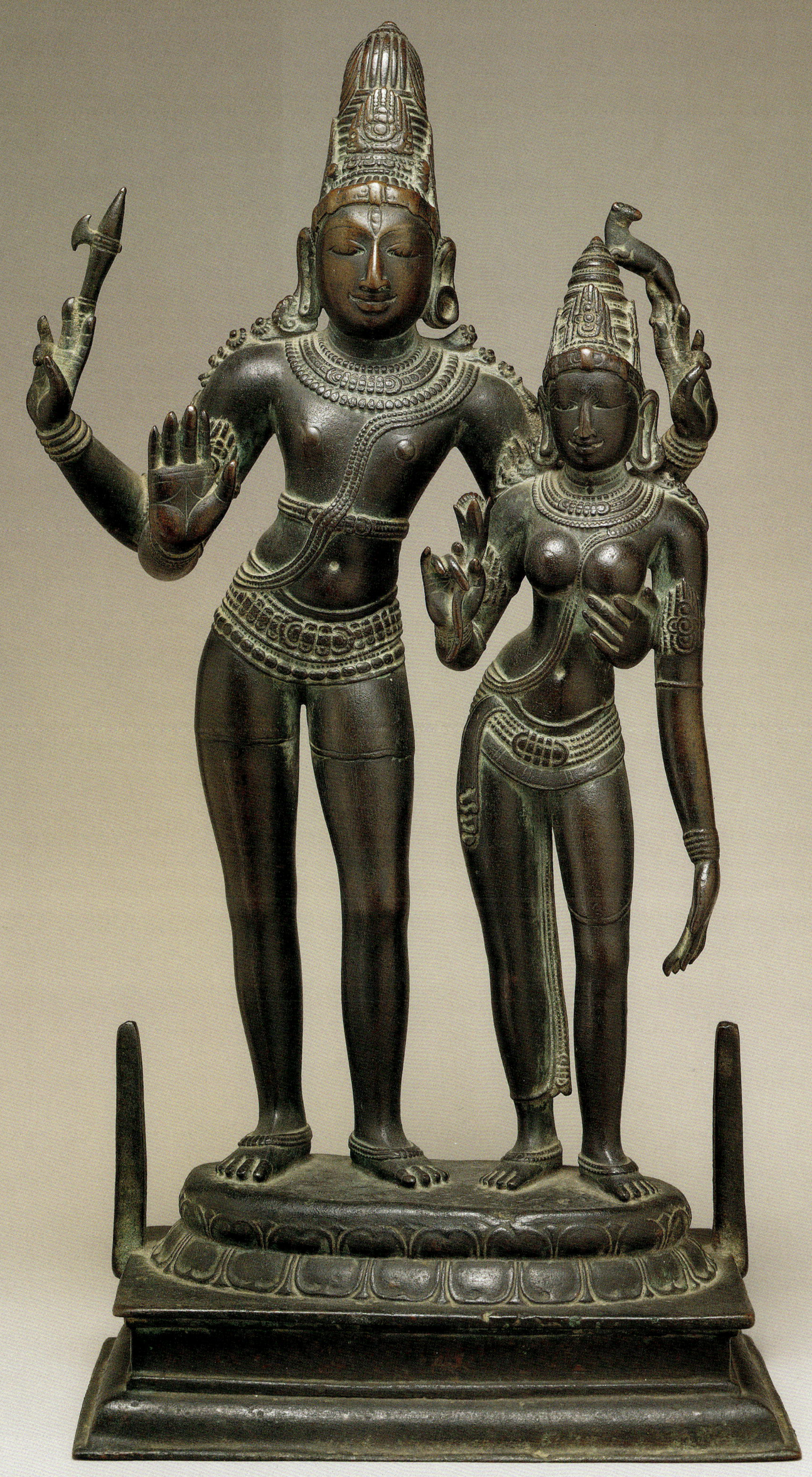

8

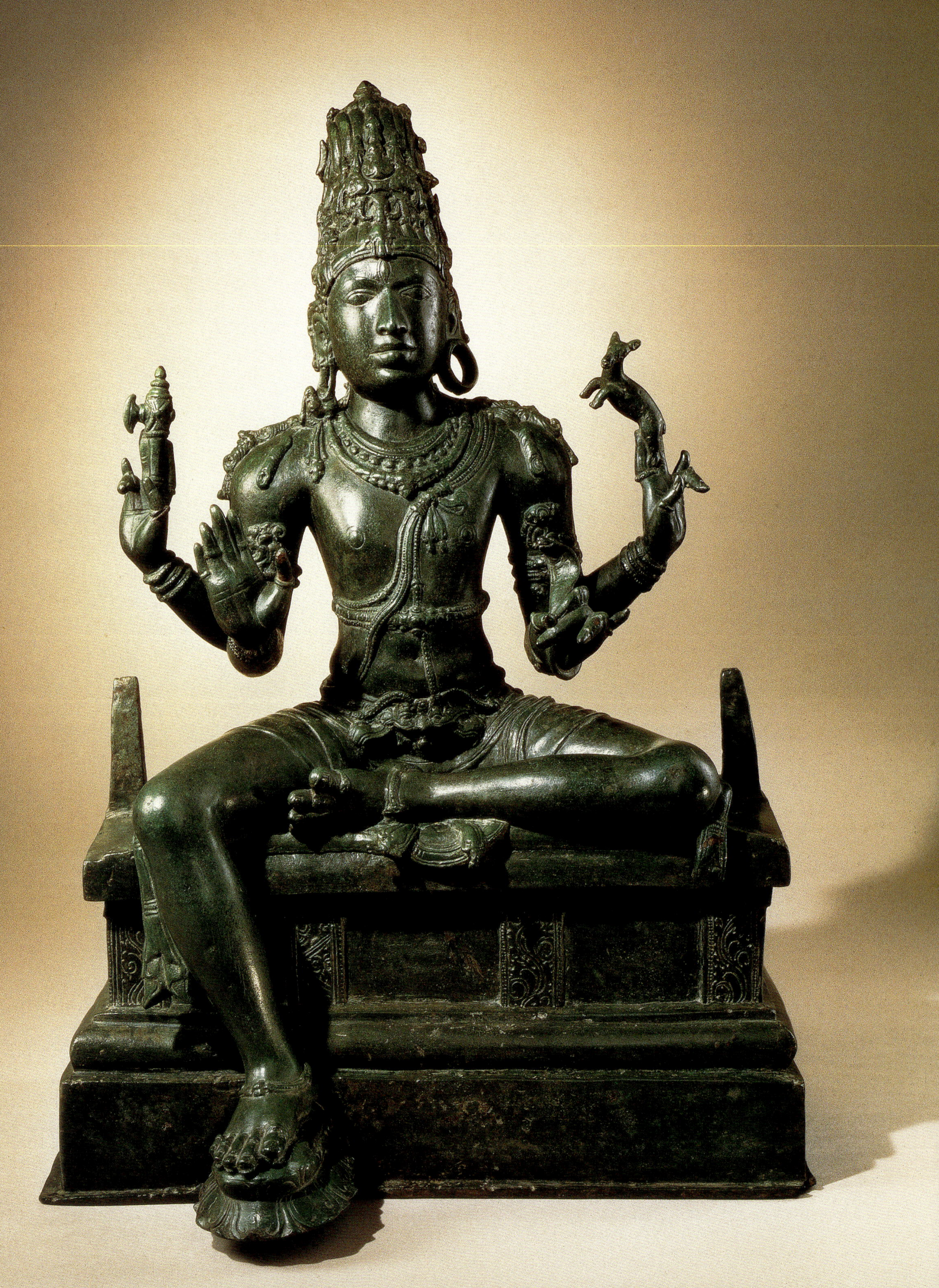

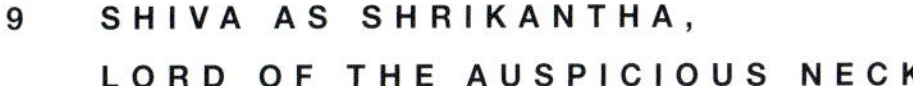

9 **SHIVA AS SHRIKANTHA, LORD OF THE AUSPICIOUS NECK**

CHOLA PERIOD, CA. 970
BRONZE, 23¼ IN. (59 CM)
TRUSTEES OF THE BRITISH MUSEUM;
BROOKE SEWELL PERMANENT FUND
(1970.9–21.1)

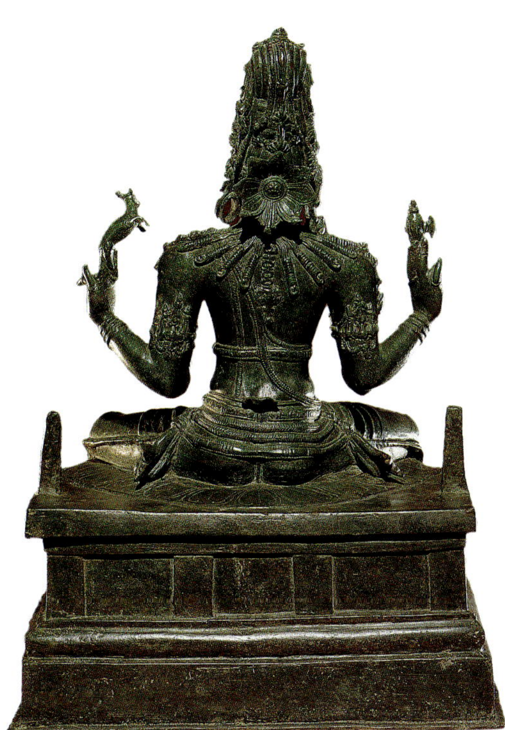

You whose brilliance
is like a coral-hued mountain
You have taken me captive.
Did you not,
out of compassion for the lowly
so all may taste your ambrosia,
gulp and hold
the burning poison?

—*Manikkavachakar*[1]

Shiva appears in his redeeming role of destroyer of poison at the time of the universal deluge of Hindu myth, which subsumed the earth and everything on it, including the divine nectar of immortality and the deadly *halahala* poison. When the ocean had to be churned to secure the nectar for the gods, Vishnu incarnated as a gigantic tortoise to provide a secure base for the sacred mountain Mandara that was used by the gods as a churning stick. It was not the nectar that emerged first, but the *halahala* poison, too lethal to let rest on earth or in the heavens. The gods fled to Shiva and beseeched him to save them, and this he did by imbibing the annihilating poison and retaining it in his throat. At the same time Shiva became the bestower of immortality on the gods by allowing the upsurge of the nectar of immortality from the waters.

When the Himalayan gods let go
of the snake coiled around the great hill,
and ran in fear as the poison,
darker than Tirumal's [Vishnu's] body,
shot out in a powerful stream
and burned the sky,
they cried: "Save us, O Lord!"
The one who was moved to compassion,
and devoured the deadly poison,
to shield them from harm,
is the King of the highest gods.[2]

For this feat Shiva is known as Shrikantha (lord of the auspicious neck), Nilakantha (Blue-Throated One), or Vishapaharana (One who Captured the Poison). According to the inscriptions in Rajaraja's royal temple at Tanjavur, one of its more than sixty gifted images was a four-armed copper-alloy image of Shrikantha, seated upon a jeweled pedestal. It measured approximately 55 centimeters in height, and was thus remarkably close in size to this image from the British Museum, whose heavy rectangular pedestal has panels of incised scrollwork, with two vertical tangs to support a *prabha*.

This exquisite Shrikantha sits in the position of royal ease known as *lalitasana*, with one foot crossed before him and the other pendant and resting upon a lotus flower. Impassive and regal, with the vertical third eye in his forehead open, Shiva is the gracious savior of the world. In three hands he holds the battle-ax, the deer, and a rearing serpent, while the fourth hand is in the *abhaya* gesture of protection. His matted locks, adorned with the crescent moon, are piled high on his head, while escaping locks are arranged in long ringletlike curls down the nape of his neck and across his back and shoulders. He wears a triple-strand sacred thread, a heavy necklace, high waist-band, armlets, bangles, rings, and anklets; a circular ring adorns one ear while the other has a *makara* earring. His short, lower garment is held in place by a jeweled girdle with a distinctive lion-head clasp, and the extra length of fabric is arranged in stylized folds on both sides and at the center. In the treatment of bodily form, as also in the depiction of details, such as the lion-head buckle, the stylized ends of the garment, the jewelry, the petaled *siraschakra*, and the manner in which the hair is piled upon the head, the figure is closest to the Sembiyan-period bronzes in the Konerirajapuram temple, in particular Shiva as Tripuravijaya (fig.1). This Shrikantha seems to have been made by a master craftsman from Queen Sembiyan's workshop, perhaps around 970.

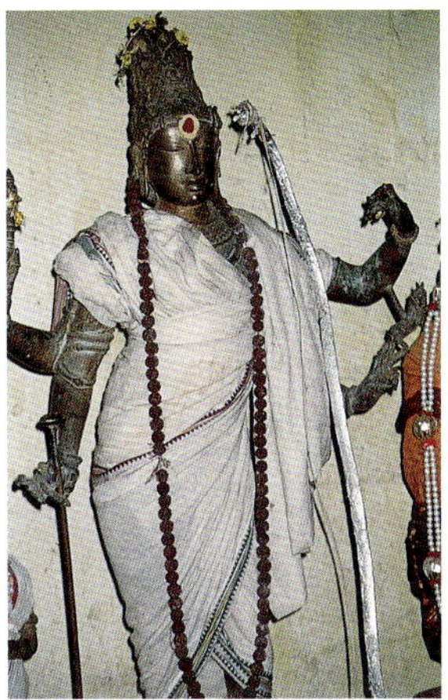

SHIVA AS TRIPURAVIJAYA,
CA. 969,
KONERIRAJAPURAM
PHOTO VIDYA DEHEJIA
FIG. 1

The form of Shiva as Shrikantha is of deep significance in Shaiva Siddhanta philosophy; it is Shrikantha who explicates knowledge of the system in the text of the *Kamika Agama*.[3]

NOTES

1 "Nital Vinnappam" 6.50; translation is mine. Glenn Yocum, in *Hymns to the Dancing Siva: A Study of Manikkavacakar's Tiruvachakam* (New Delhi: Heritage Publishers, 1982), points out that Manikkavachakar alludes several times to this manifestation of Shiva (6.7,32,46; 23.7).
2 Indira Viswanathan Peterson, *Poems to Shiva: The Hymns of the Tamil Saints* (Princeton: Princeton University Press, 1989), pp. 132–33: Appar 4.14.1.
3 Richard Davis, *Ritual in an Oscillating Universe: Worshiping Siva in Medieval India* (Princeton: Princeton University Press, 1991), p. 11.

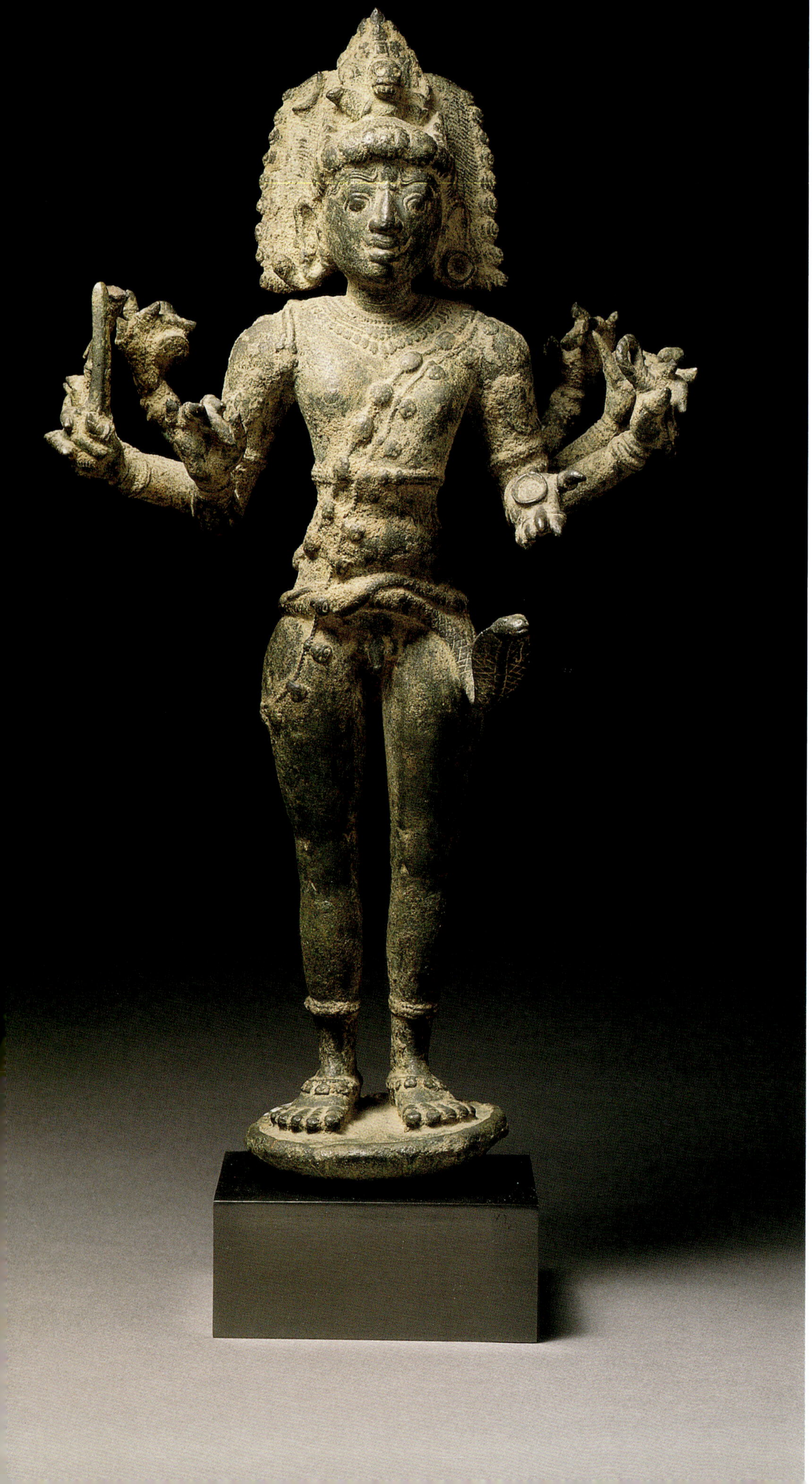

10 SHIVA AS KSHETRAPALA, GUARDIAN OF THE SACRED SITE, OR BHAIRAVA

CHOLA PERIOD, CA. 1100
BRONZE, 16 1/4 IN. (41.4 CM)
MUSEE NATIONAL DES ARTS ASIATIQUES-GUIMET, PARIS (MG 18571)

Holding the trident
its prongs flashing like the rays of the sun
with resounding drum in hand
he came in the guise of Kala-Bhairava
he ripped apart the elephant's skin—
seeing Uma shrink in fear
his beautiful mouth widened into laughter. . .
thus did he shower his grace
the beauteous lord of Tirucherai
goal of the Vedas.

—*Appar*[1]

The verse quoted praises Bhairava, the fierce form Shiva adopted to wander the earth with begging bowl in hand after he cut off arrogant Brahma's fifth head. Closely allied is Kshetrapala, a fearsome manifestation that Shiva assumed to ensure the protection of a *kshetra* or sacred site. Though iconographically similar, Bhairava is a destructive *(samhara)* form, while Kshetrapala is a protective, beneficent *(anugraha)* form. According to texts, Kshetrapala is to be worshiped for protection from destruction, to prevent suffering, to remove impediments, for the fertility of the soil, and for abundance of grain.[2] When an image is found out of its ritual context, as in the present instance, it is close to impossible to determine whether it is Bhairava or Kshetrapala. However, the balance tilts in favor of the latter. As a protective deity, Kshetrapala is worshiped in temples each day at the end of the day's ritual *pujas* and, as such, images of Kshetrapala were cast in far larger numbers than those of Bhairava. One may note that the Tiruvaduturai list of bronzes considered earlier mentions only Kshetrapala, not Bhairava, while the great temple at Tanjavur lists two images of Kshetrapala and one image of dancing Bhairava.[3] The first Tanjavur Kshetrapala, a four-armed figure, was a gold image gifted by Emperor Rajaraja that weighed a third of a kilo, while the second was an eight-armed copper image. R. Nagaswamy suggests that the famous Tiruvenkadu image, identified thus far as Bhairava (fig. 1), is more likely to be that of Kshetrapala.[4]

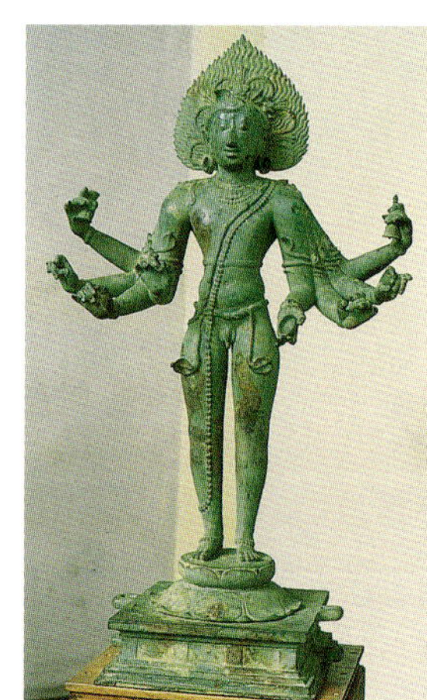

BHAIRAVA OR KSHETRAPALA, FROM TIRUVENKADU TEMPLE, CA. 1048. TANJAVUR ART GALLERY
PHOTO VIDYA DEHEJIA
FIG. 1

This image of Shiva—whether in his fierce form as Bhairava or, more likely, in his manifestation as Kshetrapala—combines harmoniously, and with remarkable balance and symmetry of proportions, the eight arms with the direct frontal view demanded by the iconography. In seven of his eight hands he holds the *damaru* drum, the club topped with a human skull *(khatvanga)*, a sword, a serpent, a noose, a skull-cup, and a now-missing object, while the eighth hand is posed in a graceful gesture. Shiva's loincloth is a rearing snake that, however, does little to conceal his nudity. In fact, child-saint Sambandar, with fond mockery, sang thus of this artifice:

> ***With perfect touch***
> ***he tied***
> ***upon his waist***
> ***the angry hissing serpent,***
> ***to serve in place***
> ***of loincloth***
> ***as only he could do.***[5]

Each of Kshetrapala's two sacred threads is strung with human skulls threaded together like beads. A diadem of rosettes circles his forehead, while the matted locks that terminate in ringletlike curls and stand up around his head in fearsome array—somewhat resembling a halo—are decorated with a skull, a serpent, and the crescent moon. He wears abundant jewelry; a serpent serves as earring in his right ear, while a circular ring *(patra kundala)* adorns the left. Round bulging eyes, fearsomely curved eyebrows, and fangs complete the picture. The image, imbued with grace and dignity despite its menacing attributes, is a powerful piece of the Kulottunga I period.

NOTES

1 T. V. Gopal Iyer and François Gros, eds., *Tevaram: Hymnes Sivaites du pays Tamoul*, vol. 2 (Pondicherry: Institut français d'indologie, 1985), p. 73: Appar 4.73.6. Translation is mine.

2 According to the *Amsumabhedagama*, as quoted in R. Nagaswamy, "Kshetrapala," in R. Nagaswamy, *Aspects of Art and Architecture of South India* (New Delhi: Aryan Books, forthcoming).

3 The lists are discussed above in "Assemblages of Sacred Bronzes."

4 Personal communication.

5 Vidya Dehejia, *Art of the Imperial Cholas* (New York: Columbia University Press, 1990), p. 60: Sambandar 1.87.5. The verse was sung in the context of Shiva as the nude Enchanting Mendicant, but could equally be applied to this image.

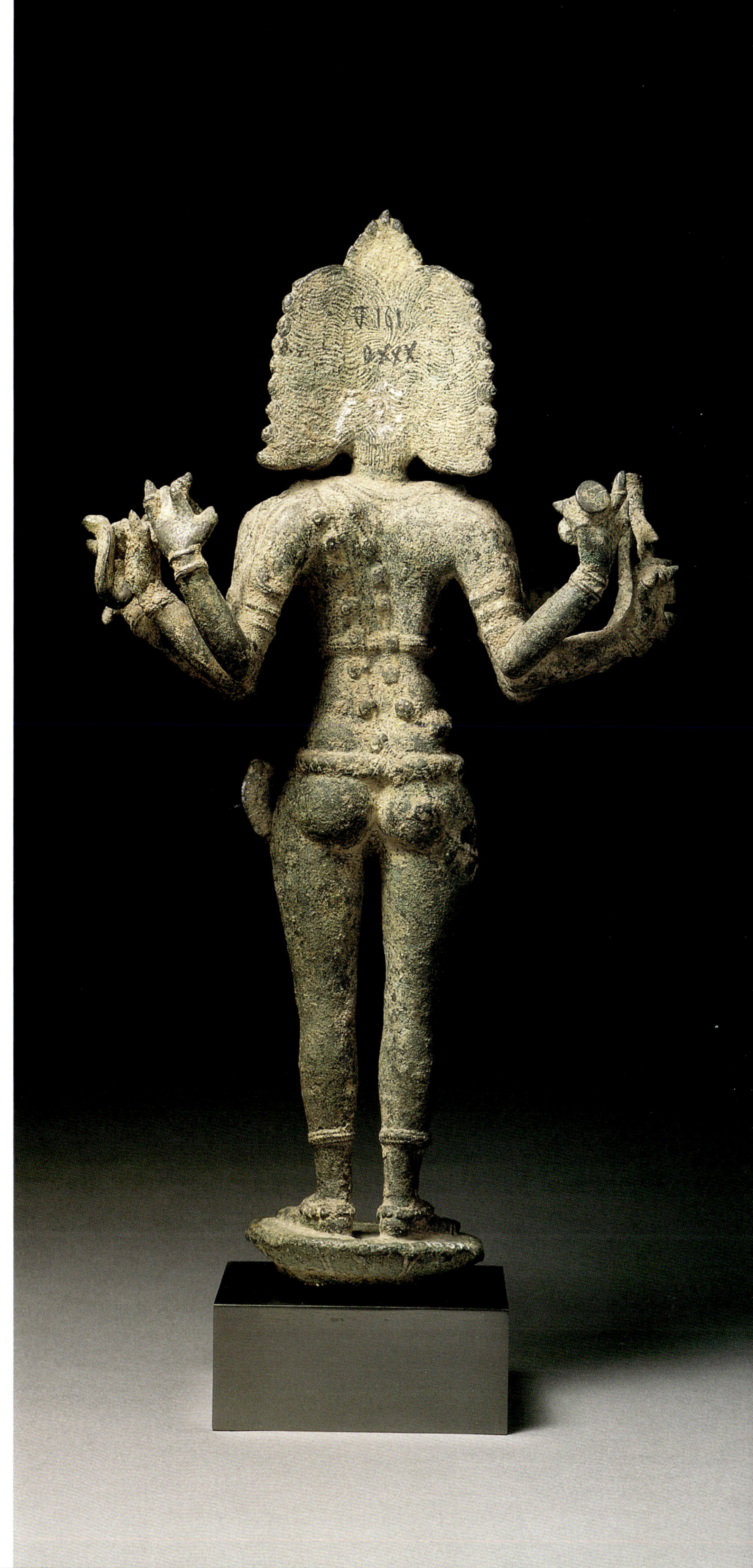

11 BRAHMA

CHOLA PERIOD, 11TH CENTURY
BRONZE, 15 5/8 IN. (39.7 CM)
ASIA SOCIETY, NEW YORK; THE MR. AND MRS. JOHN D. ROCKEFELLER 3RD COLLECTION (1979.25)

In this impressive bronze, a seated Brahma holds his signature attribute, the *kamandalu* or ritual water jar, in one rear hand; the other rear hand, now damaged, might have held a bunch of *kusha* grass, which is used in ritual. In his two front hands he holds a manuscript and the ritual ladle, the *sruk*. His hair is piled elegantly upon his head and adorned with a tiara. He wears elaborate necklaces, a sacred thread composed of pearls, armlets, and a long waist-cloth. The eyebrows and eyes on all four faces were apparently much worn through generations of ritual worship and have been subject to later recutting to return the image to its potency as an object of *darshan*.

Brahma is a deity featured regularly in one of the three central niches on the exterior sanctum walls of the earliest Chola temples. Aditya Chola's twin temples at Kilaiyur and his shrine at Srinivasanallur, and his successor Parantaka's temple at Pullamangai, feature standing images of Brahma in this location. When carved in stone to occupy a temple niche, the god is shown with three heads, with the fourth understood to be facing the rear; when cast in bronze, it was possible to depict the fourth head. Bronze images of Brahma are relatively rare and were created primarily to be part of the marriage group of Shiva and Uma. According to one version of the legend of the divine wedding, Brahma served as the officiating priest who performed the actual ceremony. The ritual ladle seen in Brahma's hand in this bronze is entirely appropriate for this function. The image is a fine example of eleventh-century bronze-casting, and its size suggests a marriage group of substantial proportions.

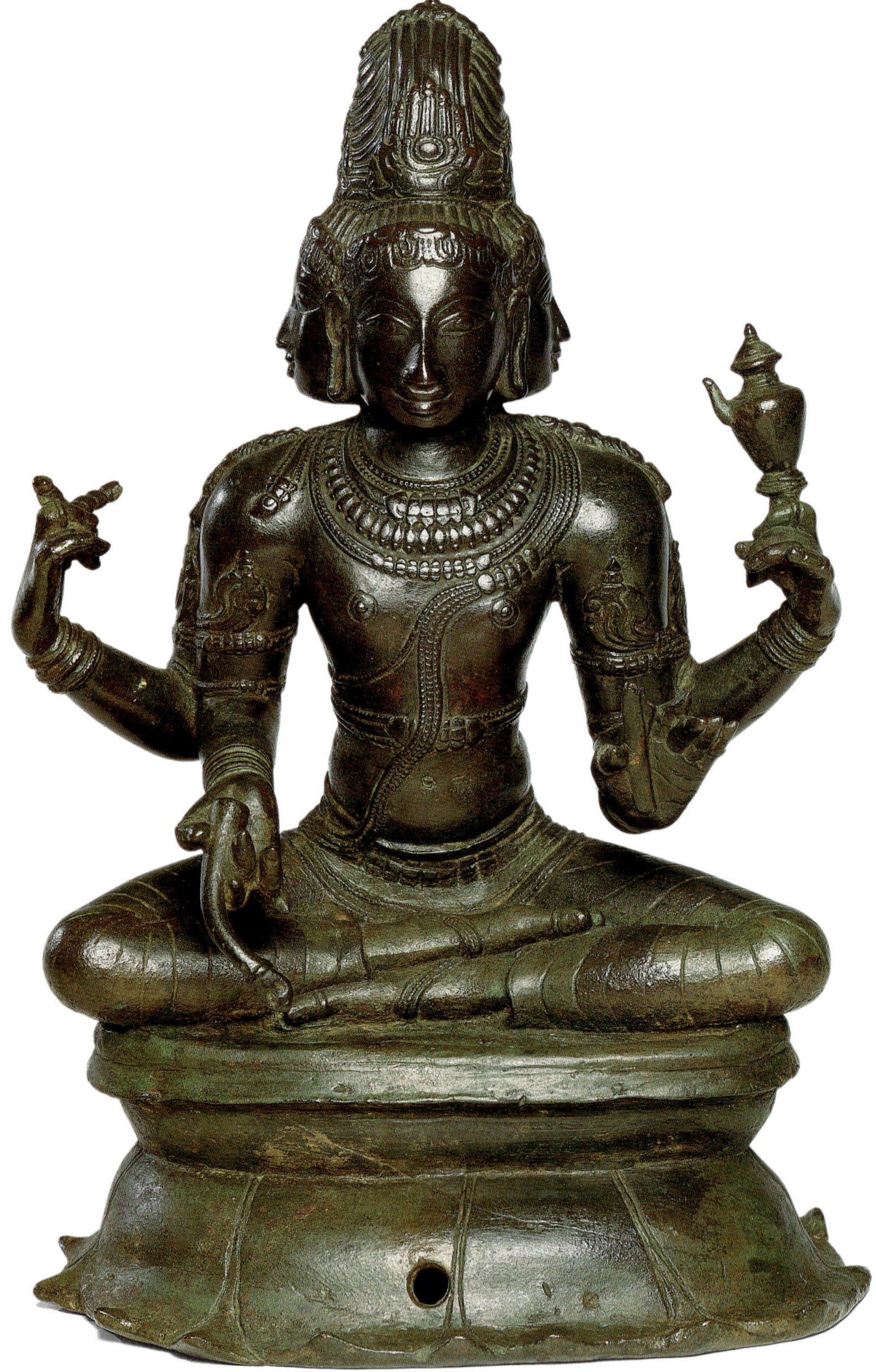

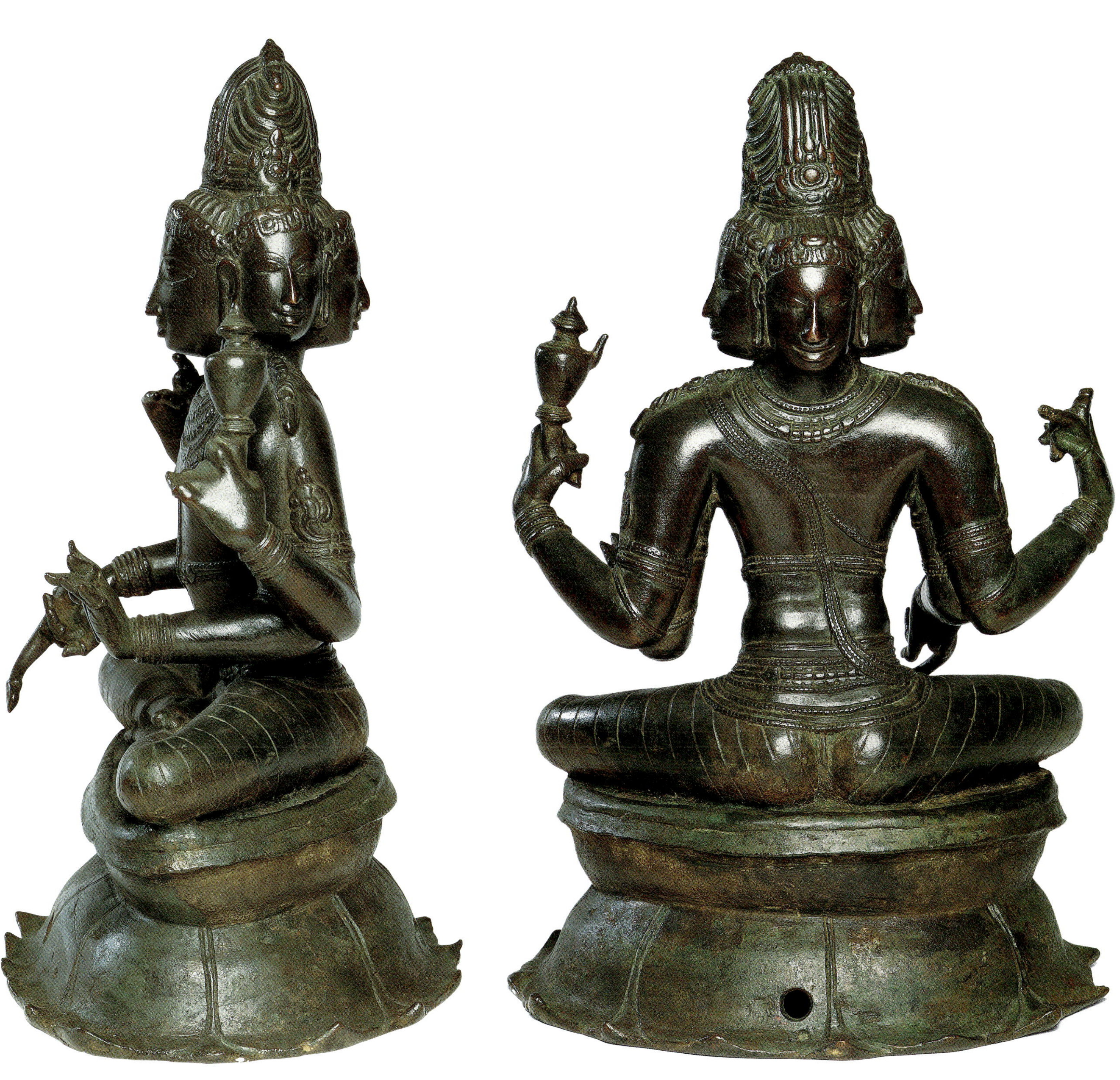

12 **DEVI UMA PARAMESHVARI, GREAT GODDESS UMA**
CHOLA PERIOD, CA. 950
BRONZE, 25 1/4 IN. (64.1 CM)
THE CLEVELAND MUSEUM OF ART;
LEONARD C. HANNA, JR. FUND (1984.2)

13 **UMA AS TRIPURAVIJAYI OR BHOGESHVARI, WITH ATTENDANT**
CHOLA PERIOD, CA. 950
BRONZE, 28 1/2 IN. (72.5 CM)
PRIVATE COLLECTION

14 **UMA AS QUEEN SEMBIYAN MAHADEVI**
CHOLA PERIOD, CA. 990
BRONZE, 24 3/8 IN. (62 CM)
FREER GALLERY OF ART, SMITHSONIAN INSTITUTION, WASHINGTON, D.C.;
PURCHASE (F1929.84)

Uma, the great goddess, consort of Shiva, is invariably portrayed in art as a slender, voluptuous woman of exquisite beauty. But the unabashedly sensual language used by the saints to describe her may come as a surprise to many. This sensuous visualization is well exemplified by saint Sundarar in a song in which each verse commences "He [Shiva] passed this way," followed by a phrase that describes Uma who accompanied Shiva.

He passed this way—

with the young woman
whose mound of Venus is like a cobra's
spreading hood

together with the woman whose soft breasts
fill her taut bodice

together with the woman
whose smile is white
as pearl

together with the woman, perfectly adorned
whose mound of Venus is veiled in cloth . . .

with the woman whose brow
is the crescent moon

together with his woman
her waist thin as a vine[1]

Consort of Shiva, and mother of two sons, Ganesha and Skanda, Uma Parameshvari, or Great Goddess Uma as she is addressed in Tamil Nadu, is represented in bronze temple assemblages by multiple images, both on her own and accompaning Shiva in one or other of his aspects. Since Parvati is a more northern appellation, I have chosen to refer to her as Uma in this volume that is devoted exclusively to the southern Chola ethos. The corpus of sixty-six bronzes in Rajaraja Chola's royal edifice at Tanjavur includes nine images of Uma (around a seventh of its bronzes), while at the modest Shiva shrine at Tiruvaduturai a quarter of the bronzes are those of the goddess (six of its total of twenty-three images). The various images of Uma are quite similar in their iconography, and depict the goddess standing in a graceful *tribhanga,* or triple-bend, posture with one hand raised to hold a lotus or blue lily blossom, while the other rests gracefully at her side. However, each image tends to be addressed by a distinct name that is dictated by the placement of the icon and hence the significance of the image in Shaiva temple ceremonies; without Uma's constant and repeated presence, the ritual cycle is incomplete.

Bhogeshvari or Goddess of Pleasure is the name given to the bronze image of Uma that stands within the sanctum to accompany the immovable *(achala)* stone *linga* of Shiva. This image is usually the largest and most impressive of the bronze figures of Uma in any temple and is recognizable solely by its size. An image of similar iconography stands within the celestial bedroom *(palli-arai)* located in the hall immediately adjoining the sanctum. Here Uma is referred to as Palli-arai Nacchiyar or Lady of the Bedroom, and she is joined each night, after the last *puja (ardhajama)* by an image (or merely the feet) of god Shiva. Frequently, a standing image of Uma is placed beside the Somaskanda group of seated Shiva and Uma with their infant son Skanda, as if watching over the group. In that position and function, Uma is spoken of as Tani Amman or Lone Goddess. Bhogeshvari, Palli-arai Nacchiyar, and Tani Amman are indistinguishable from one another in iconographic treatment: it is their placement alone that enables the priest, devotee, or art historian to give them a name that is more than generic.

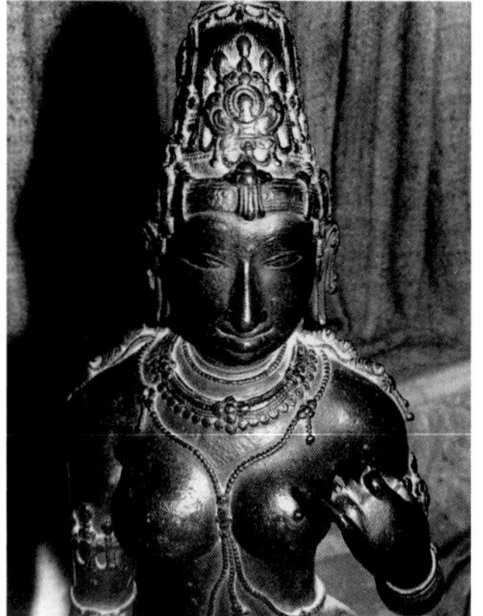

UMA, FROM KONERIRAJAPURAM TEMPLE, CA. 969.
COLLECTION GAUTAM SARABHAI, AHMEDABAD
PHOTO VIDYA DEHEJIA
FIG. 1

In addition to these images of Uma on her own, she accompanies Shiva in several of his manifestations; these images too would be given a mere generic appellation if they were not placed beside specific Shiva images. Dancing Shiva as Nataraja is invariably accompanied by a standing image of the goddess known today as Shivakami or Beloved of Shiva, but in ancient inscriptions as *nam pirattiyar* or our lady. Similar standing images accompany Shiva as Chandrashekhara (Crowned with the Moon), and as Vrishabhavana (Rider of the Bull); and in both these instances the term *tam pirattiyar* or his lady seems to be used. When standing Uma accompanies Shiva as Tripuravijaya (Victor of the Three Cities), she may be addressed as Tripurasundari (Beauty of the Three Cities) or perhaps as Tripuravijayi (Victress of the Three Cities). The only standing image of Uma that is iconographically specific depicts her as bride in the marriage group known as Kalyanasundarar (Handsome Bridegroom), where she demurely gives Shiva her hand in marriage. Images of the goddess in her warrior aspect as Durga, or in her fearsome aspect as Kali, are in a category apart (see cat. nos. 19–21).

All three Uma images presented here belong to the distinctive workshop of Chola Queen Sembiyan Mahadevi, who was an active patron of the arts, building temples and commissioning bronzes, for a period of sixty years between 941 and 1001.[2] The finest and largest group of tenth-century bronzes, revealing a mature and assured style, are those commissioned by this queen, who was widowed when she was barely thirty years of age. She witnessed the kingdom pass into the hands of her husband's brother, then to his son, before returning to her own son and rightful heir, Uttama Chola.

The Uma from the collection of the Cleveland Museum of Art (cat. no. 12) embodies the plastic quality that characterizes the early days of the Sembiyan workshop, and it predates the two Uma images commissioned by the queen for the Konerirajapuram temple (fig. 1). The group of Konerirajapuram bronzes, specifically mentioned in a temple inscription that makes provisions for their ritual worship and processional activities from the queen's endowment, were probably commissioned around 969, the year in which the temple was built. The Cleveland Uma, belonging to the mid-

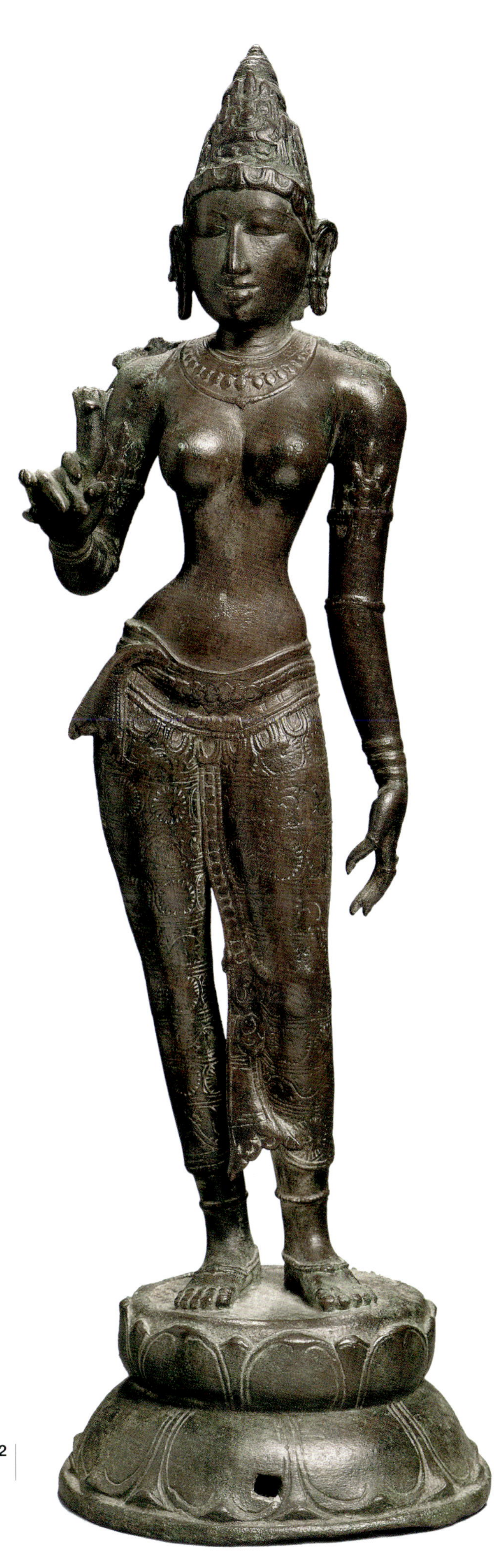

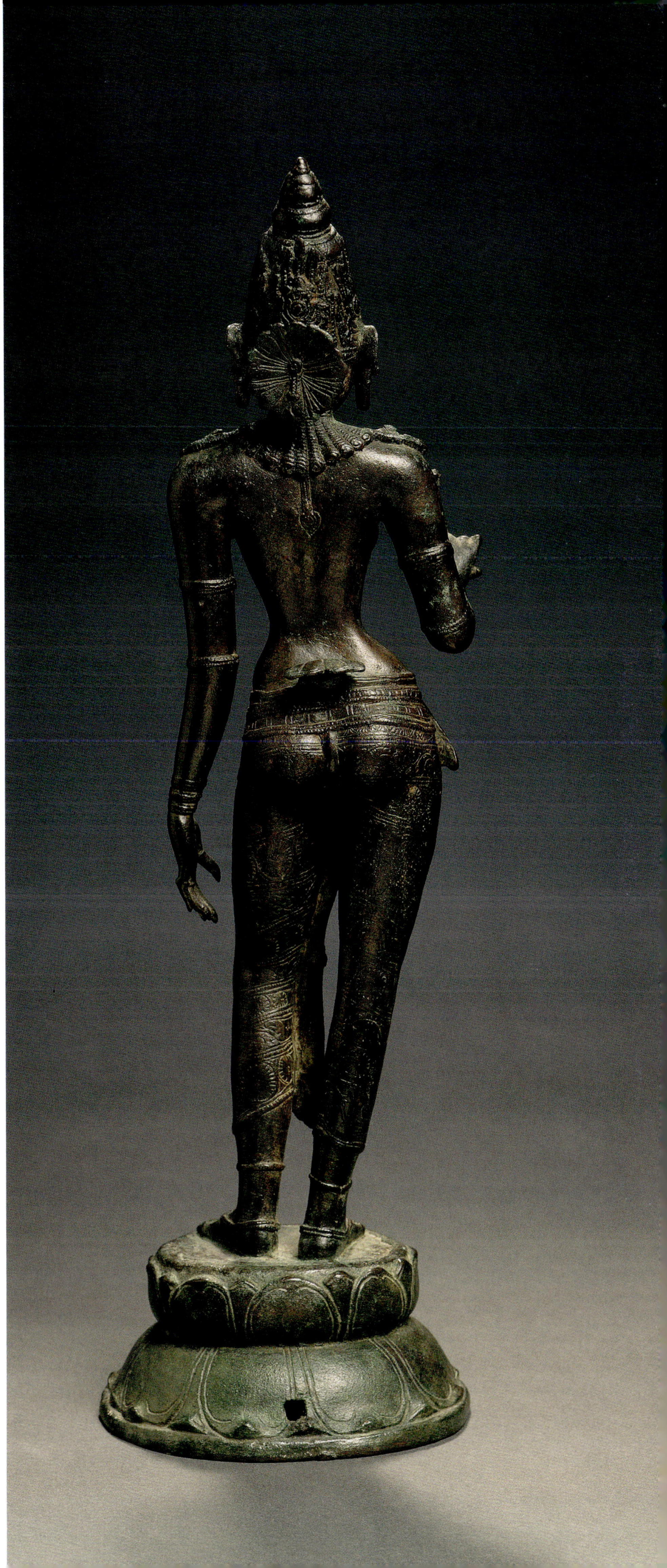

tenth century, is a slender figure of sensuous modeling. Her breasts are softly sculptured and the spread of the swelling stomach almost has the illusion of flesh, contrasting with the sharp details of the abundant jewelry that adorns her. The piece conveys a swaying sense of movement and a heightened awareness of form. The pattern of the drapery—a band of wavy lines and one of floral circles—is similar though not identical with that used by the Sembiyan sculptor responsible for an Uma from Konerirajapuram (now in the Gautam Sarabhai collection), and the Nallur temple Devi. Also similar is the treatment of the stylized inner fold of the skirt as it rests upon her thigh, the prominent fan-shaped *koshuvam* folds of the garment at the rear, and the manner in which the extra length of the skirt is pleated to fall between the legs.

Also from the early days of the Sembiyan workshop comes an image of Uma holding a lotus in one hand and resting the other on the head of a diminutive attendant (cat. no. 13). While the explanation for this iconography is not clearly understood, such images are variously seen today in Tamil temples either as consort of Tripuravijaya,[3] or as Bhogeshvari within the sanctum.[4] The image has the vertical tangs that support a *prabha*. Uma wears a conical ornamental crown, a forehead band whose tie at the rear is covered by a *siraschakra*, with a crisscross-patterned band between the two. Her long skirt wraps around to the rear, and its end as a triple wave is almost horizontally rendered. The contours of the body, the meticulous details of her jewelry, the sinuously slender form, the tasseled armbands, and the manner in which the inner folds of the skirt rest against the thigh are all indicative of the early Sembiyan workshop. Additional details seen in other late-tenth-century images, including an image of Bhogeshvari from the Pallavanishvara temple,[5] is the pendant on a thread that fits snugly around her throat *(ukkattu)* and ends with a pipal-leaf-shaped *kunjalam* tassel that rests between the shoulder blades,[6] a chainlike pendant suspended within the central pleated folds of the skirt, as well as the tasseled elbow band. Her face, in particular, is much worn through centuries of worship.[7] Uma's attendant is dressed like her mistress and carries a box in one hand while the other hand partially points upward with the thumb and middle finger joined. The attendant's hair is arranged in two distinct coiled rounds with floral adornment.

Created perhaps forty years later, during the closing days of the Sembiyan workshop, is the famous Freer image (cat. no. 14) that I have elsewhere suggested is a "portrait" of Queen Sembiyan Mahadevi as Uma Parameshvari, commissioned for the queen's Shiva temple in the town named after her.[8] Inscriptions indicate that a metal portrait of the queen was presented to the temple in the town of Sembiyan Mahadevi, and although we do not know the date of its commission, one may assume that it was presented while the queen was living. Certainly portraits of Emperor Rajaraja (r. 985–1014) and his chief queen were commissioned for his temple at Tanjavur while he was the ruling monarch. At any rate, we know that special arrangements were made in the temple for the celebration of Queen Sembiyan's birthday in the month of Chittarai that corresponds to March–April. The inscription that gives us this information is of the time of her great grand-nephew, Emperor Rajendra, and makes provision for the worship of her image alongside those of the gods and goddesses,[9] testifying to the great honor and respect accorded to her.

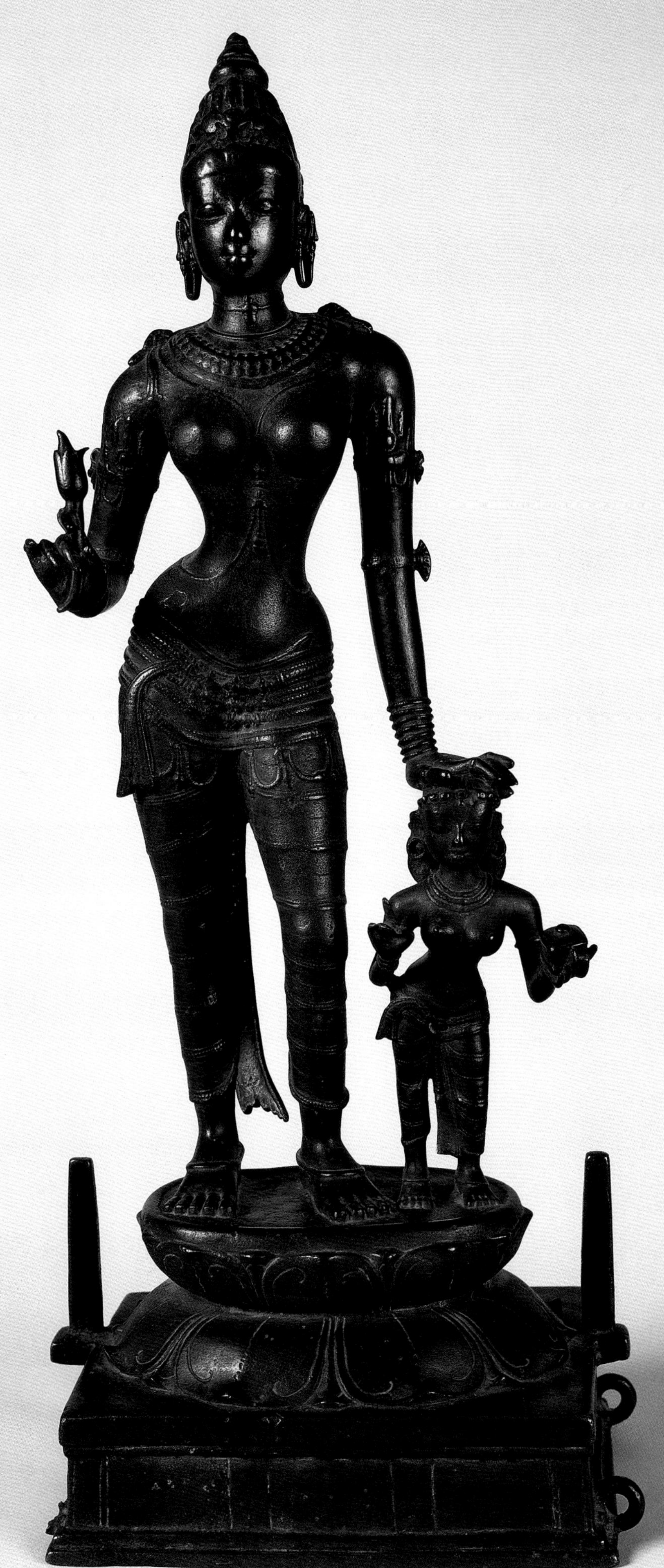

13

The Freer Uma comes from the Chola heartland and may be compared with a group of Uma images of the late tenth century, from the temples at Peruntottam (fig. 2), Kuttalam, and Pallavanishvaram, that appear to belong to the height of the Sembiyan workshop.[10] The bodily contours of these images compare closely to those of the Freer image, and the Bhogeshvari bronze from Pallavanishvaram displays a trellis pattern on the crown at the rear of the head that is found also on the Freer figure. However, the gravity of expression, the remarkable dignity of bearing, and the exaggerated slope of the shoulders have led me to raise the possibility of its being a portrait sculpture. Royal portraits, in ancient times, were modeled on deities. Consider the fourth-century play *Pratima-nataka*, in which prince Bharata prepares to bow before a set of four statues in a chapel, assuming that they are deities, only to be informed by its keeper that they are portrait statues of his own deceased father and three prior generations of ancestors.[11] If the audience watching the play did not think Bharata, or the playwright Bhasa, were extraordinarily foolish, it was because it was the accepted norm for artists to blur the boundaries, and overlap the categories, of the royal and the divine. It is highly unlikely that Queen Sembiyan would have been recognized from this portrait. But the ritual usage of the image would have given devotees the necessary clue; when it was carried in procession on Queen Sembiyan's birthday, there would have been little confusion over its identity.

The group of Uma images here testifies to the assured and mature style of the bronze workshop of Queen Sembiyan Mahadevi, whose remarkable and extended patronage of art during the tenth century was unsurpassed by other Chola luminaries.

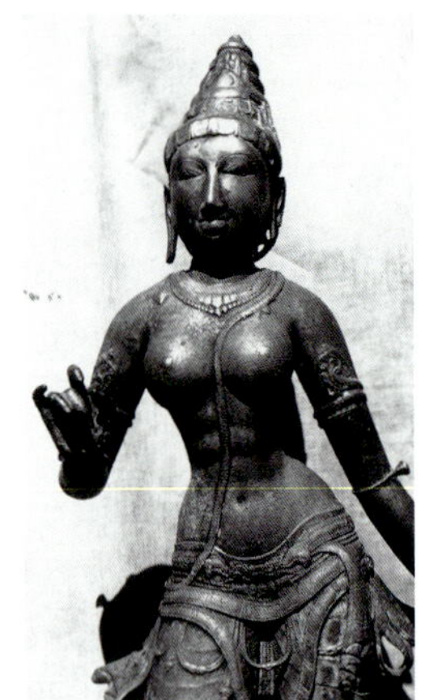

UMA, CA. 975, PERUNTOTTAM TEMPLE, PERUNTOTAM
PHOTO VIDYA DEHEJIA
FIG. 2

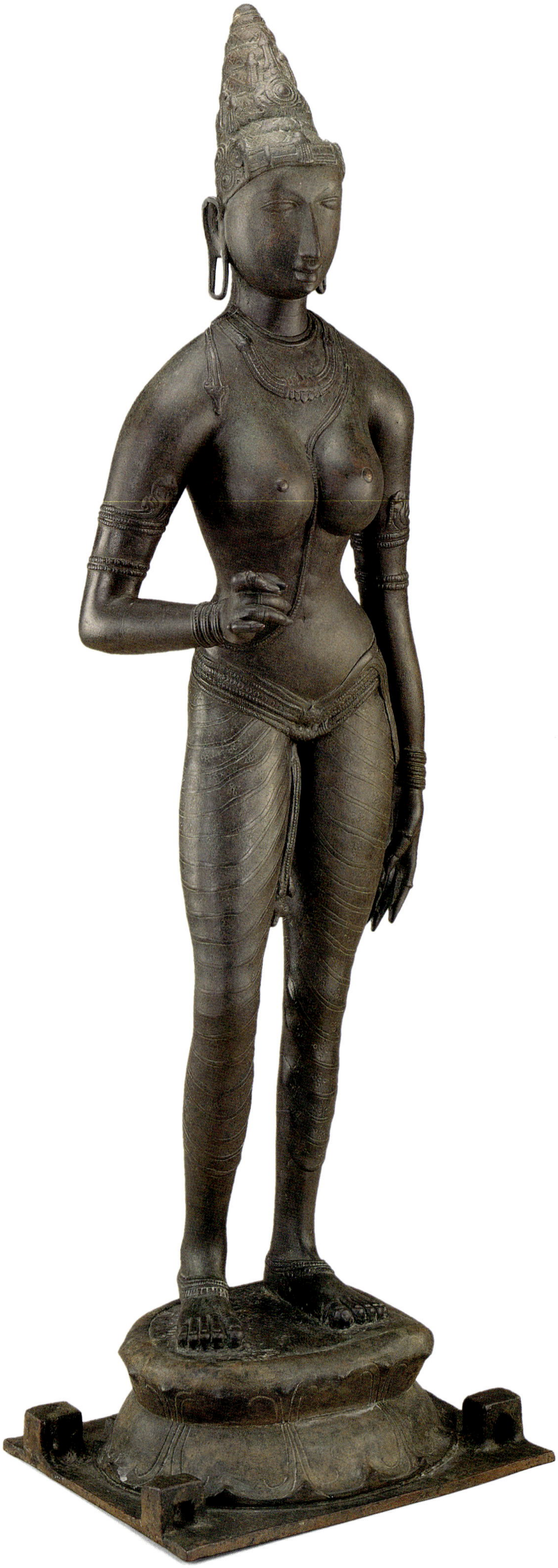

NOTES

1 David Dean Shulman, trans., *Songs of the Harsh Devotee: The Tevaram of Cuntaramurtinayanar* (Philadelphia: University of Pennsylvania Press, 1990), pp. 539–42: Sundarar 85.2,3,6,7,8,10.

2 Her first inscribed temple donation belongs to the year 941, while she was yet crown princess, while the last commission belongs to the year 1001 in the reign of her grandson Rajaraja Chola. See Vidya Dehejia, *Art of the Imperial Cholas* (New York: Columbia University Press, 1990), p. 2.

3 At Kodumudi. See R. Nagaswamy, "Rare Bronzes from Kongu Country," *Lalit Kala* 9 (1961): 7–10, pl. I, fig. 1.

4 At Konerirajapuram. See S. R. Balasubrahmanyam, "Konerirajapuram Bhogasakti," *Lalit Kala* 16 (1971): 51 and pl. XX. See also V. N. Srinivasa Desikan, "A Note on Two Metal Images in the Madras Museum," *Lalit Kala* 18 (1977): 40, pls. XIX, XX.

5 Douglas Barrett, *Early Cola Bronzes* (Bombay: Bhulabha: Memorial Institute, 1965), pl. 33.

5 This is seen earliest on the Karaiviram Devi with an inscribed date of 917. See R. Nagaswamy, "A Nataraja Bronze and an Inscribed Uma from Karaiviram Village," *Lalit Kala* 19 (1979): 17–19 and pls. XXXIII–XXXVII.

7 A recent application of wax to the eyes has lessened the worn effect.

8 Dehejia, *Art of the Imperial Cholas*, pp. 4, 36–39; also Vidya Dehejia, "The Very Idea of a Portrait," *Ars Orientalis* 28 (1998): 41–48. Padma Kaimal, "The Problem of Portraiture in South India, circa 970-1000 A.D." *Artibus Asiae* 60, no. 1 (2000): 139–79, rightly points out that this suggestion cannot be proven.

9 Dehejia, *Art of the Imperial Cholas*, p. 2f.

10 Barrett, *Early Cola Bronzes*, pls. 22, 29–32, 34, 44.

11 Dehejia, "The Very Idea of a Portrait," pp. 41–48.

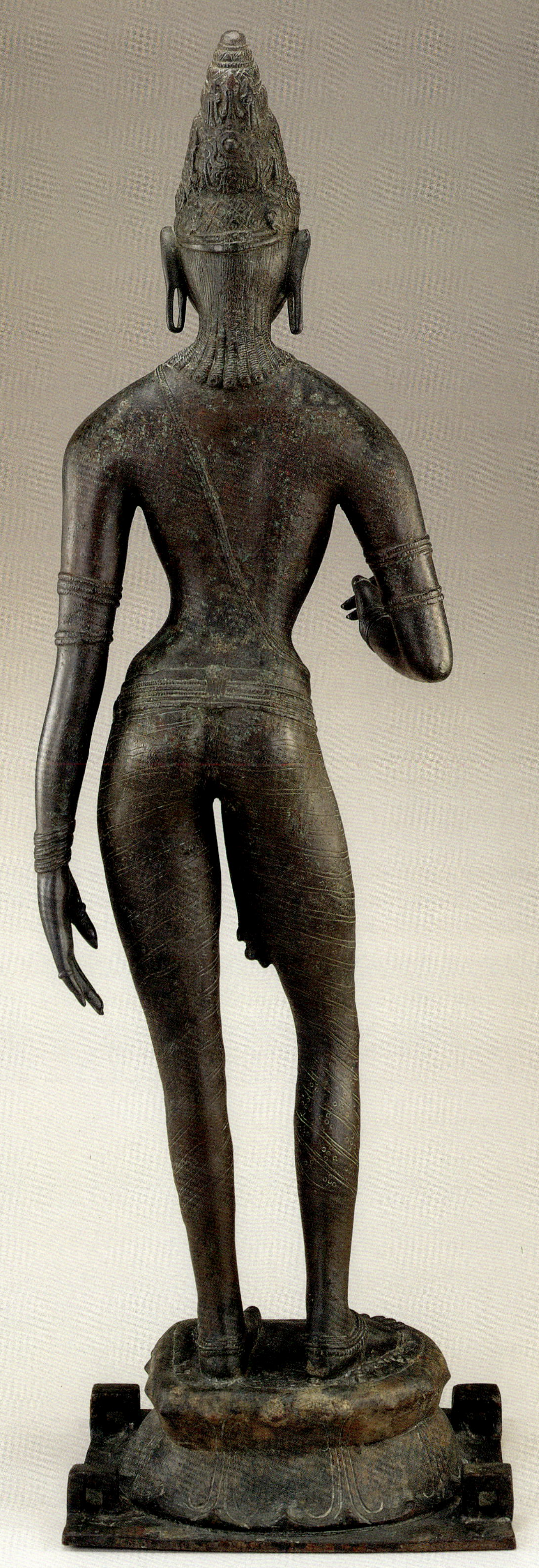

15 SOMASKANDA, SHIVA WITH UMA AND SKANDA
CHOLA PERIOD, CA. 1070–1100
BRONZE, 19 1/8 IN. (48.5 CM)
WORCESTER ART MUSEUM, WORCESTER, MASSACHUSETTS; MUSEUM PURCHASE (1951.93)

16 SOMASKANDA, SHIVA WITH UMA AND SKANDA
CHOLA PERIOD, CA. 1100
BRONZE, 18 5/8 IN. (47.3 CM)
COLLECTION DORIS WIENER, NEW YORK

17 SEATED UMA
CHOLA PERIOD, CA. 1100
BRONZE, 15 IN. (38.1 CM)
PRIVATE COLLECTION

18 SEATED SHIVA AND UMA FROM A SOMASKANDA GROUP
CHOLA PERIOD, 13TH CENTURY
BRONZE, 21 1/2 AND 16 3/4 IN.
(54.6 CM AND 42.5 CM)
PRIVATE COLLECTION

Here, on this good earth
you may lead a life of joy
living each day in fullness—
indeed this comes not in the way of liberation.
In the green and plenteous plains of Sirkali
thus too did the lord dwell,
beside him
the fairest of women.[1]

The *linga* enshrined within the temple sanctum is regarded as an abstract form of Shiva, while the image of Shiva seated with consort Uma and son Skanda (Somaskanda, *sa-uma-skanda* or with Uma and Skanda) is viewed as his main manifest form. In the temples of the Pallava dynasty that preceded the Chola, the sanctum routinely contained both forms; the *linga* occupied the center of the sanctum while a Somaskanda was carved as a relief image into its inner rear wall. The Somaskanda bronze is of such importance that it is often named after the temple itself.

According to Shaiva Siddhanta philosophy, only when he is in the company of his consort Uma does Shiva bestow grace upon an individual soul. A metal image of the god together with Uma and their son Skanda is thus the principal image of such individual grace, and every single temple, wealthy or otherwise, possesses a Somaskanda image. Today the chief festival of a Shiva temple is referred to as the *Brahmotsava* or Brahma festival (it is believed that Brahma conducts the rite), and five sets of images, known as the *panchamurti,* participate in it. The prime image is that of Somaskanda; the other four are Uma, youth Skanda with his two wives Valli and Devayani, Ganesha, and saint Chandesha, who is considered the guardian of all Shiva temples.

Large numbers of Somaskanda images exist, in part because a range of Agamic texts like the *Ajita Agama* specify that if a temple does not possess the exact image required for a specific ritual procession, a Somaskanda bronze may be used as a substitute.[2] Nagaswamy points out too that the *Linga Purana* specifies that a Somaskanda group could be commissioned by an individual and worshiped each year for a period of twelve years, after which he could gift it to a Shiva temple, consecrating it and thereby acquiring great merit. It is curious, though, that there is no typical Somaskanda group among the Tanjavur bronzes; instead there are two complete family groups including also the elder son Ganesha; one of these, in a most unusual format, presents the divine family seated on a mountain.[3]

The elegant Somaskanda of the age of Kulottunga I (r. 1070–1125), now in the Worcester Art Museum (cat. no. 15), is unusual in the manner in which it portrays the infant seated cross-legged between his parents, but on a separate projecting base. Generally, whether he is seated or standing, Skanda is merely positioned on the regular rectangular base between the two other figures. Shiva, with his matted locks piled high upon his head, holds battle-ax and antelope in two rear hands; one front hand is poised to hold a lotus, while the other, in the *abhaya* gesture of protection, blesses the individual devotee. Uma is poised, in three-quarter view, turning toward Skanda and Shiva. Noteworthy are the richly patterned garments of both Shiva and Uma, as well as the stylized curve of the upper edge of Uma's skirt, the rounded profile of her breasts, and the circle incised around her nipples. Rich, heavy jewelry adorns the figures. Both Shiva and Uma bear a close resemblance to images of the Kulottunga I period seen in temples examined by R. Nagaswamy in his essay for this volume (figs.15 and 16 on pp. 38 and 39). However, the "archaistic" treatment of Shiva's high matted locks, which resembles that of the mid-tenth-century image of Shrikantha (cat. no. 9), shows a reference to, or preference for, the style of an earlier period. The Worcester image has lugs for processional usage, as well as tangs to support an aureole. The eyes of the images have been recut to return them to a state of potency whereby they are ready, once again, for ritual worship and *darshan*.

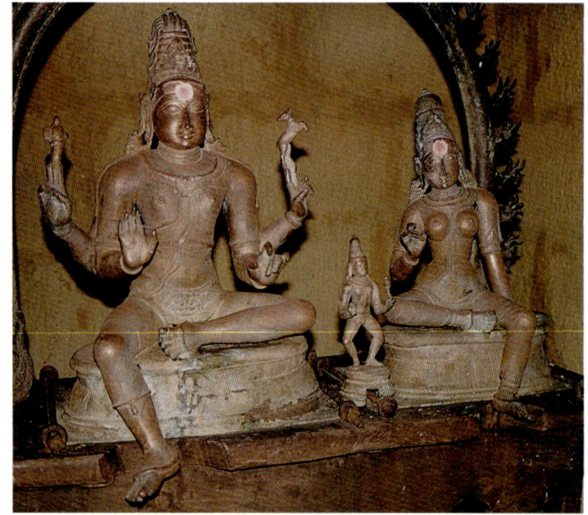

SOMASKANDA, CA. 1100, PURANA VITANKAR TEMPLE, TIRUMANGALAKUDI
PHOTO R. NAGASWAMY
FIG. 1

A Somaskanda with a charming image of infant Skanda dancing on the seat between his parents (cat. no. 16) is a fine composition dating from around the year 1100. Shiva, facing the devotee in direct frontal view, sits in stately dignity, while gentle Uma, placed in three-quarter view, watches over the infant. Shiva holds battle-ax and antelope in two rear hands, while his right front hand makes the gesture of protection and the left is held in a graceful gesture. A serpent peeps out from Shiva's tall matted locks, and he is richly adorned with multiple ornaments that include one *makara* and one round earring, several necklaces, a triple-strand sacred thread, armlets, and anklets. Uma is equally richly adorned, and while Shiva sits in the posture of ease known as *lalitasana*, with one leg folded and placed on the seat and the other pendant, Uma sits in a variation of this pose with her folded leg raised up at an angle. Little Skanda dances with lotus buds in both hands. The image bears a strong resemblance to the Somaskanda image in situ in the Tirumangalakdi temple that R. Nagaswamy dates to the period of Kulottunga I (fig. 1).[4]

Also belonging around the year 1100, and of exquisite finish, is a seated Uma from a private collection (cat. no. 17). While it is possible that she was part of a Somaskanda grouping, her position along the proper right side of the pedestal, where Skanda would normally be placed, suggests that she might be part of a Shiva-Uma grouping without the child. Such seated images were known merely as Uma-sahita (with Uma). A tiara with a triple medallion ornament holds in place the hair piled high upon her head and adorned with three strings of blossoms. She wears large round earrings, and the *siraschakra* is adorned with a triple tassel. Three lightly incised lines along her waist point to her beauty as *trivali tarangini,* or she with three rows of waves, a phrase sug-

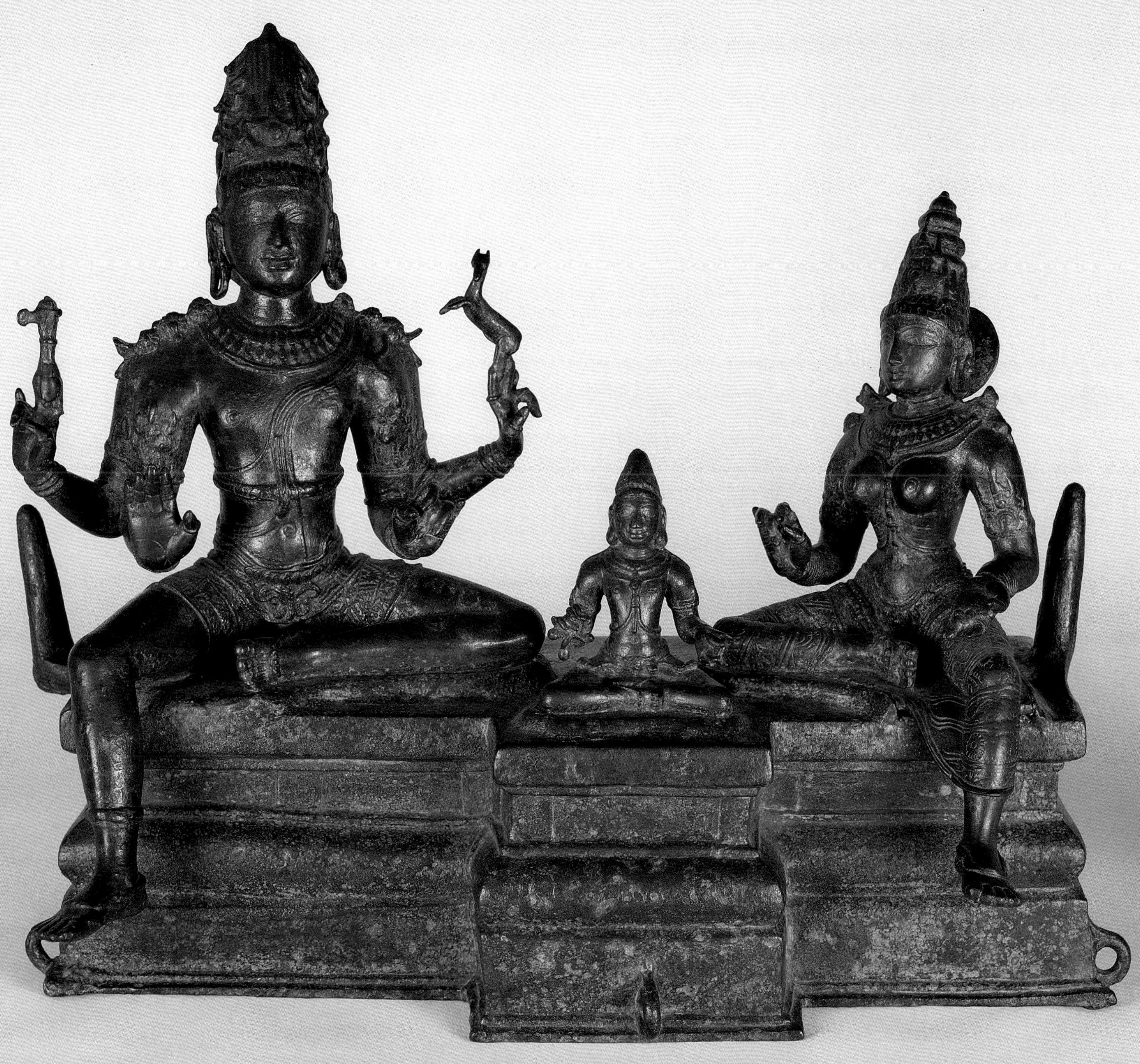

15

gestive of ample beauty. Her garment is held in place with a *makara*-clasped girdle. The treatment of bodily form resembles the image of Uma of Kulottunga I date from the Tirumangalakudi temple (fig. 2), which R. Nagaswamy discusses in his essay in this volume, and is also closely akin to an elegant Uma from the Chidambaram temple hoard, that this Uma resembles closely in many respects.[5] The bronze is much prior to the stylization seen in the thirteenth-century image of Satyabhama who is part of the four-piece Krishna group now in the Los Angeles County Museum of Art (see cat. no. 52b). An inscription of nineteenth-century date along the lotus seat of seated Uma reads *Shri Tali* and is, presumably, an abbreviated reference to the temple that once housed the image.

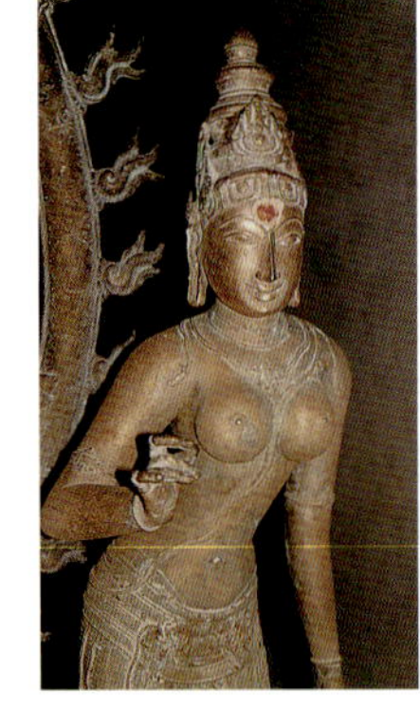

DETAIL OF UMA AS SHIVAKAMI, CONSORT OF NATARAJA 1 OF TIRUMANGALAKUDI, CA. 1100, PURANA VITANKAR TEMPLE, TIRUMANGALAKUDI
PHOTO R. NAGASWAMY
FIG. 2

The fine late-Chola images of Shiva and Uma on two separate lotus pedestals (cat. no. 18) were almost certainly part of a Somaskanda group. Skanda may have been attached to the base of the Uma bronze, as seen in a twelfth-century image from Kulashekharanallur (fig. 3), or an independent image of the child may have been placed between his parents. Shiva and Uma are seated on double lotuses in the *lalitasana* posture of ease. Shiva's piled-up, matted locks display a serpent and the crescent moon, and are held in place by a patterned forehead band and a tiara. Seven *konrai* (wild cassia) blossoms adorn the very top of his locks. Shiva's two rear hands hold the battle-ax and antelope; one front hand is in the *abhaya* gesture of protection while the other is held in an elegant frontal gesture. Uma holds a lotus flower in one hand while the second is open in a gesture that resembles the *varada* that grants wishes. She sports a forehead band and a crown, and blossoms decorate the strands of hair that rest along her shoulders. Both pieces have had their eyes recut to reinvigorate them for temple worship. The bronzes bear a strong resemblance to the images of Shiva and Uma as Alingana Chandrashekhara from the temple at Tirthanagari that bear an inscription of Kopperunjingan, a chieftain who ruled from 1243 to 1279.[6] The Somaskanda Shiva and Uma may likewise be assigned to this final phase of the Chola period.

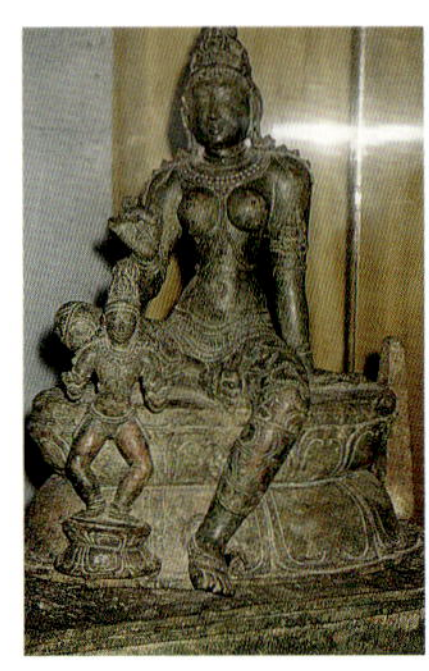

UMA AND SKANDA FROM A SOMASKANDA GROUP, FROM KULASHEKHARANALLUR, 12TH CENTURY, TANJAVUR ART GALLERY
PHOTO VIDYA DEHEJIA
FIG. 3

NOTES

1 T. V. Gopal Iyer and François Gros, eds., *Tevaram: Hymnes Sivaites du pays Tamoul,* vol. 1 (Pondicherry: Institut français d'indologie, 1985), p. 303: Sambandar 3.24.1, *mannil nalla vannam valalam* sung at the Tirukalamalam temple. Translation is mine.

2 R. Nagaswamy, "Tripurantaka, Vinadhara Dakshinamurti, or Kiratamurti?" in R. Nagaswamy, *Aspects of Art and Architecture in South India* (New Delhi: Aryan Books, forthcoming).

3 See in this catalogue "Assemblages of Sacred Bronzes," Tanjavur bronzes nos. 15 and 10.

4 See his essay in this volume.

5 R. Nagaswamy, "Chidambaram Bronzes," *Lalit Kala* 19 (1979): figs. 56, 57.

6 R. Nagaswamy, "On Dating South Indian Bronzes," in *Indian Art and Connoisseurship: Essays in Honour of Douglas Barrett,* ed. John Guy (Ahmedabad: Mapin Publishing, 1995), fig. 24 on p. 126.

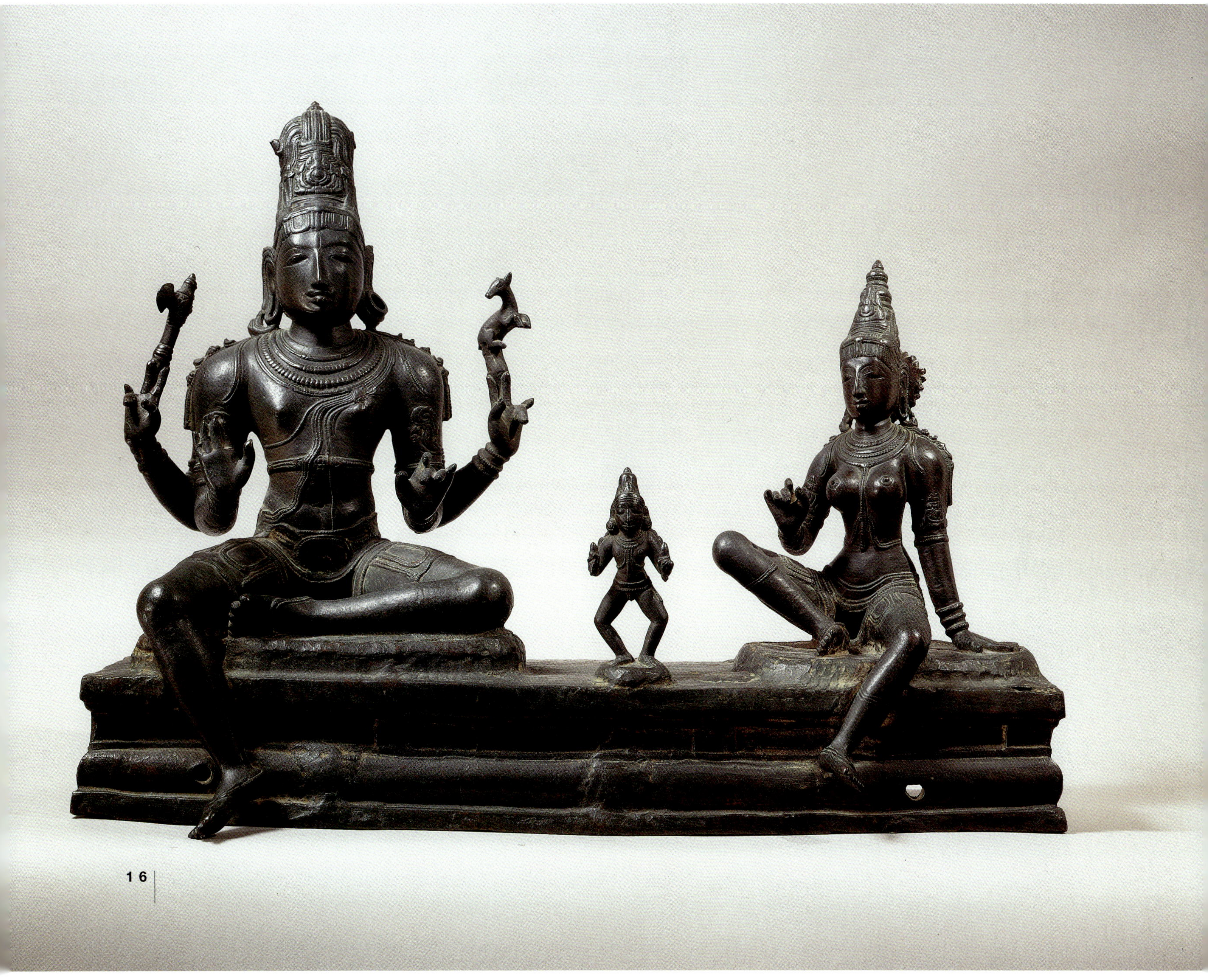

16

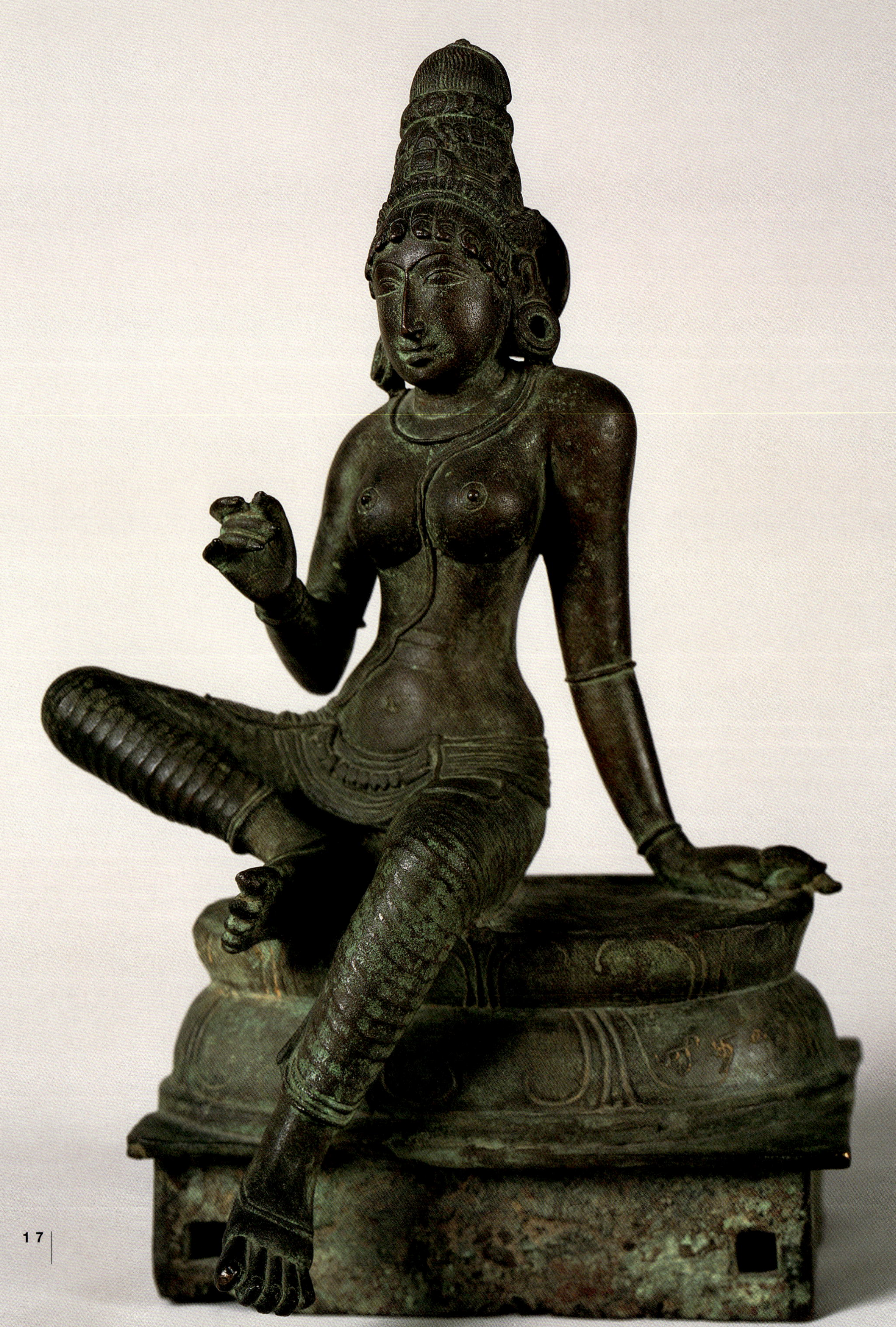

17

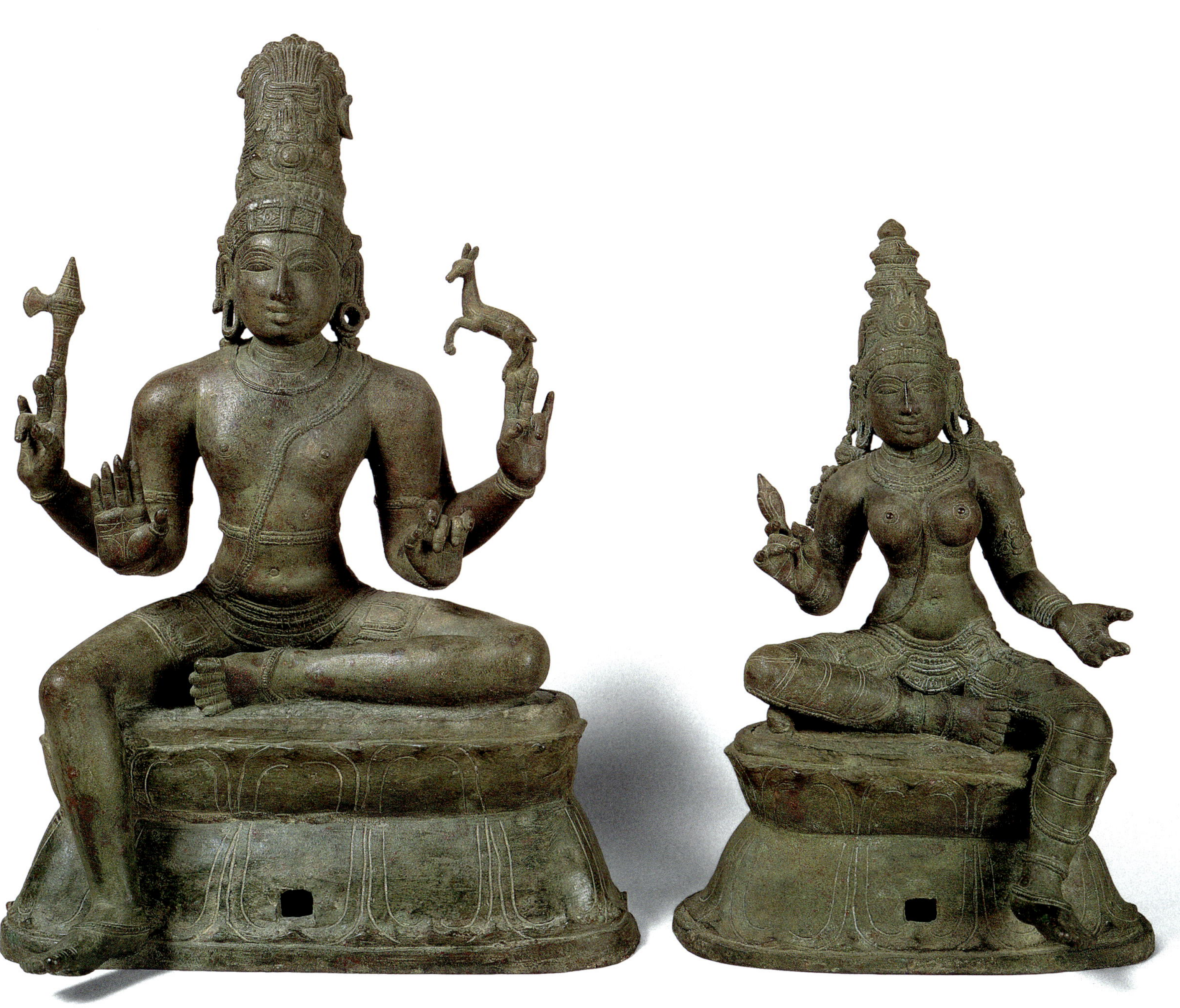

19 DURGA
CHOLA PERIOD, CA. 970
BRONZE, 22 1/2 IN. (57.1 CM)
THE BROOKLYN MUSEUM OF ART;
ANONYMOUS GIFT IN HONOR OF
WILLIAM H. WOLFF (1992.142)

20 DURGA
CHOLA PERIOD, CA. 1200–1250
BRONZE, 27 1/8 IN. (69 CM)
PRIVATE COLLECTION

You once stood on the back of a lion
With red, angry eyes, holding
The conch shell and wheel in your lotus hand.
Now you stand praised by the Vedas . . . [1]

When the goddess is visualized solely as consort and constant companion of Shiva, she is addressed as Uma Parameshvari or Great Goddess Uma. But in her own right, she is the powerful warrior goddess Durga, destroyer of demons. In Tamil Nadu she is also widely perceived as the sister of the god Vishnu, whose attributes of discus *(chakra)* and conch shell *(shankha)* she frequently assumes.

In the sacred courtyard of the goddess,
The younger sister of Tirumal [Vishnu], the cadamba *oak,*
Begonia and laurel are fragrant,
The bottle-flower and ironwood blossom.
On their boughs swarms of bees
Hum as if playing the lute.

So commences a section on Durga in the ancient *Shilappadikaram* text of around 450, and it continues with the verse quoted at the start that speaks of her holding discus and conch, and proceeds to make reference to her feat of destroying the buffalo demon:

You once stood on the black head
Of the wild buffalo robed
In elephant skin and tiger skin.
Now you stand, unwearied,
The sprout of wisdom, the Veda *beyond*
Vedas, *adored by the gods.*[2]

Durga, meaning Impassable One, is frequently invoked as protector, and this explains her repeated placement at the entrance to forts, and on the *gopuram* gateways of southern temples. While images of Durga, and shrines dedicated to her, are found more often in the context of a Shiva temple, inscriptions suggest that she is also at home in a Vaishnava context.[3]

The exquisite early image of Durga from the collection of the Brooklyn Museum (cat. no. 19) presents a lithe, youthful goddess, whose bodily form is almost adolescent, particularly in rear view. She holds Vishnu's conch-shell and discus in two rear hands, giving rise to her popular name in Tamil Nadu of Vishnu-Durgai. One front hand is raised in the *abhaya* gesture of protection while the other rests gracefully against her thigh in a gesture of ease *(katyavalambita)*. Her short, patterned lower garment is knotted with bowlike ties on both sides and held in place with a jeweled girdle, while a band of the garment forms a loop below the girdle clasp. Her breasts are softly modeled and naturalistic in profile, with a sacred thread that snakes between them; rich necklaces, armlets, bangles, and anklets complete her adornment. Beneath a tall

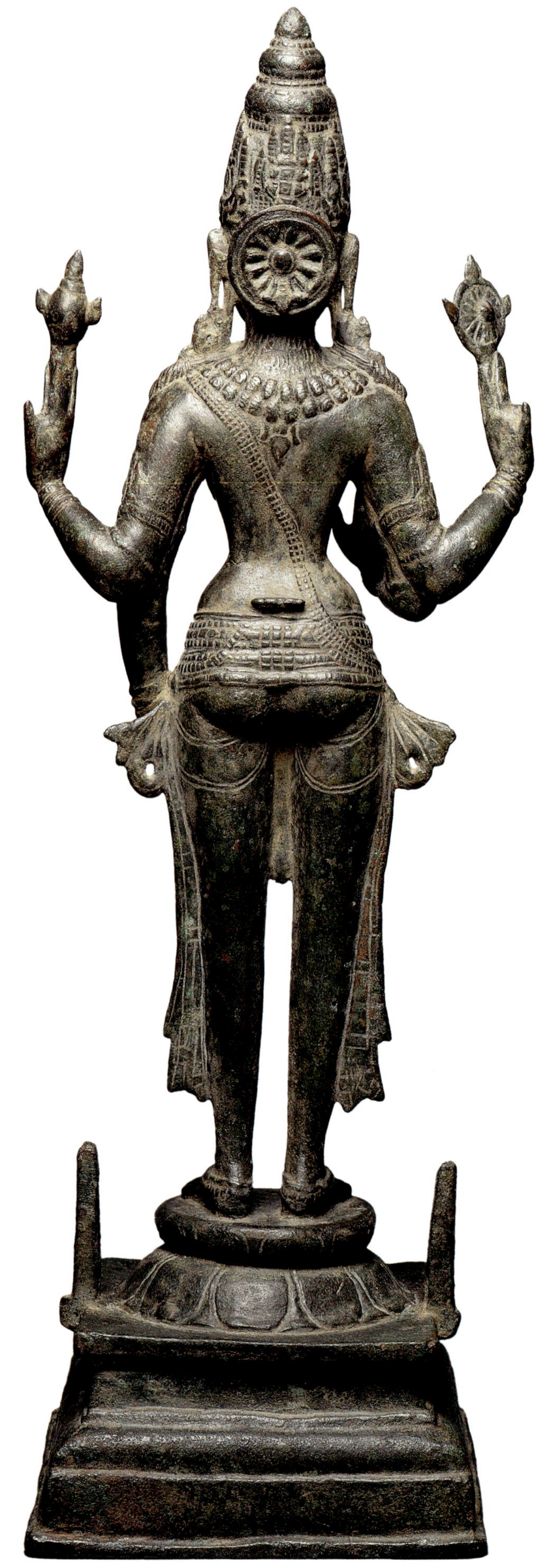

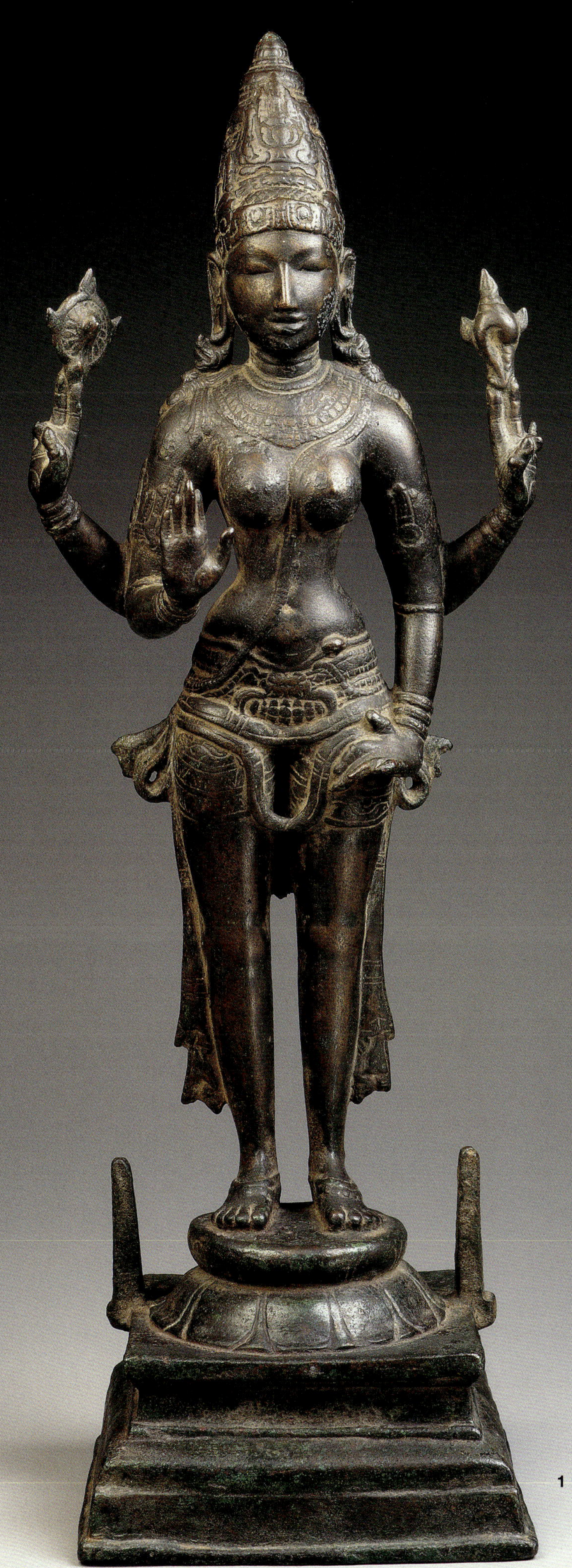

19

conical crown, her face is gentle, introspective, and quite exquisite. She stands on a lotus base placed on a rectangular pedestal with vertical tangs to support a *prabha.*

It is instructive to compare her with a much earlier image of Durga, belonging to the Pallava-Chola transition phase, that is now in the Sarabhai collection in Ahmedabad. In that image, a lithe Durga, slender as a reed, exemplifies the *Shilappadikaram* verse quoted above in standing firmly upon the decapitated buffalo head that is modeled as part of the circular plate on which she is cast. The richly adorned image wears a conical crown, a breast-band, and a skirt held in place by a girdle with a lion-head clasp and forming loops on both sides. In her demure look and bearing, and in the outline of her form, the Sarabhai Durga resembles the Uma of around 875 from the Vadakkalathur marriage group.[4] The Brooklyn Durga displays features that place her later than the 917 dated and inscribed Uma from Karaiviram.[5] In the treatment of bodily contours, as in details of clothing and ornamentation, the Brooklyn image seems also to belong to a period later than that of the Sita from Tirucherai or the seated Uma from Pallavanishvaram.[6] She appears to belong to the Sembiyan workshop and likely dates from around the year 970.

The statuesque image of Durga from a private collection (cat. no. 20), standing upright with both feet planted firmly on the ground, and not a hint of the *tribhanga* or triple-bent posture seen in images of Uma, appears to belong to the first half of the thirteenth century. Durga holds the discus and conch shell in two rear hands, has the right front hand raised in the *abhaya* gesture, and the left lowered in an elegant gesture with a parrot perched upon its wrist. She wears a tall crown, has a breast-band, and a broad ornamental girdle encircles her long skirt with a chain ornament hanging from the clasp along the centerfold. Her abundant jewelry includes *makara* earrings, multiple necklaces, a *channavira* suspended from a necklace to rest between her breasts and encircle the torso, elaborate armlets, and two sets of anklets. Her loose hair ending in ringlet curls is arranged along the nape of her neck, with strands resting along her shoulder and upper arms.

There is a popular misconception that the only sacred figures with a parrot on the wrist are goddess Meenakshi at Madurai, and Vaishnava woman saint Andal. However, goddess Durga definitely, if only occasionally, sports a parrot on her wrist, and one such image may be seen at the Pallava site of Mamallapuram, south of Chennai, where relief sculptures frequently feature Durga, often in a Vaishnava context. The eighth-century Adivaraha cave temple dedicated to Vishnu in his incarnation as the giant boar Varaha—and closed today to tourists because it has been reclaimed for active worship—contains a large relief panel that depicts an elegant, svelte Durga standing upon the buffalo head. The eight-armed goddess holds a discus and conch, sword and shield, bell, bow, and skull-cup, while perched upon her lowered front left hand is a parrot.[7] The ninth-century Chola temple of Tyagaraja at Tiruvarur presents an unusual configuration in which a parrot perched upon a stand is placed to the proper right of Durga.[8] In the tenth-century Chola temple of Tyagaraja at Tanjavur, the parrot is once again seen perched on Durga's wrist.[9] Additionally, Uma Parameshvari is sometimes given the parrot as an attribute; in Rajaraja's royal temple at Tanjavur, his sister Kundavai gifted to the bronze of Uma who is consort of dancing Shiva a gold parrot weighing 190.2 grams (7/16 lb.), with precious stones for eyes.[10] There is also textual association of the parrot with Uma; for instance, the *Tirumandiram*, in its section devoted to the worship of nine forms of the goddess *(shaktis),* describes three with a parrot perched on a lowered hand.[11]

NOTES

1 R. Parthasarathy, trans., *The Tale of an Anklet: An Epic of South India—The Cilappatikaram of Ilanko Atikal* (New York: Columbia University Press, 1993), p. 125: "The Book of Maturai," *In Praise of the Goddess,* verse 10.

2 Ibid., pp. 123, 124.

3 For instance, a lamp was gifted to a Durga shrine in the Lakshmi Narayana Perumal temple at Sinnanur. See R. Nagaswamy, *Tantric Cult in Tamil Nadu* (New Delhi: Agam Kala Prakashan, 1982), p. 217.

4 See R. Nagaswamy, *Masterpieces of Early South Indian Bronzes* (New Delhi: National Museum, 1983), pp. 44–45.

5 R. Nagaswamy, "A Nataraja Bronze and an Inscribed Uma from Karaiviram Village," *Lalit Kala* 19 (1979): pls. XXXIV, XXXV.

6 Douglas Barrett, *Early Cola Bronzes* (Bombay: Bhulabhai Memorial Institute, 1965), pls. 44, 35–36.

7 See line drawing in T. A. Gopinatha Rao, *Elements of Hindu Iconography*, vol. 1, part II, reprint (Delhi: Motilal Banarasidass, 1968), pl. CI facing p. 343.

8 R. Nagaswamy, *Tantric Cult in South India*, fig. 50.

9 Ibid., fig. 51.

10 E. Hultzsch, ed., *South Indian Inscriptions,* vol. 2 (New Delhi: Archaeological Survey of India, 1992 reprint), part 1, no. 2, p. 18.

11 B. Natarajan, trans., *Tirumantiram: A Tamil Classic by Tirumular* (Madras: Sri Ramakrishna Math, 1991). See tantra four, chapter 13, verses 1383, 1393, 1399.

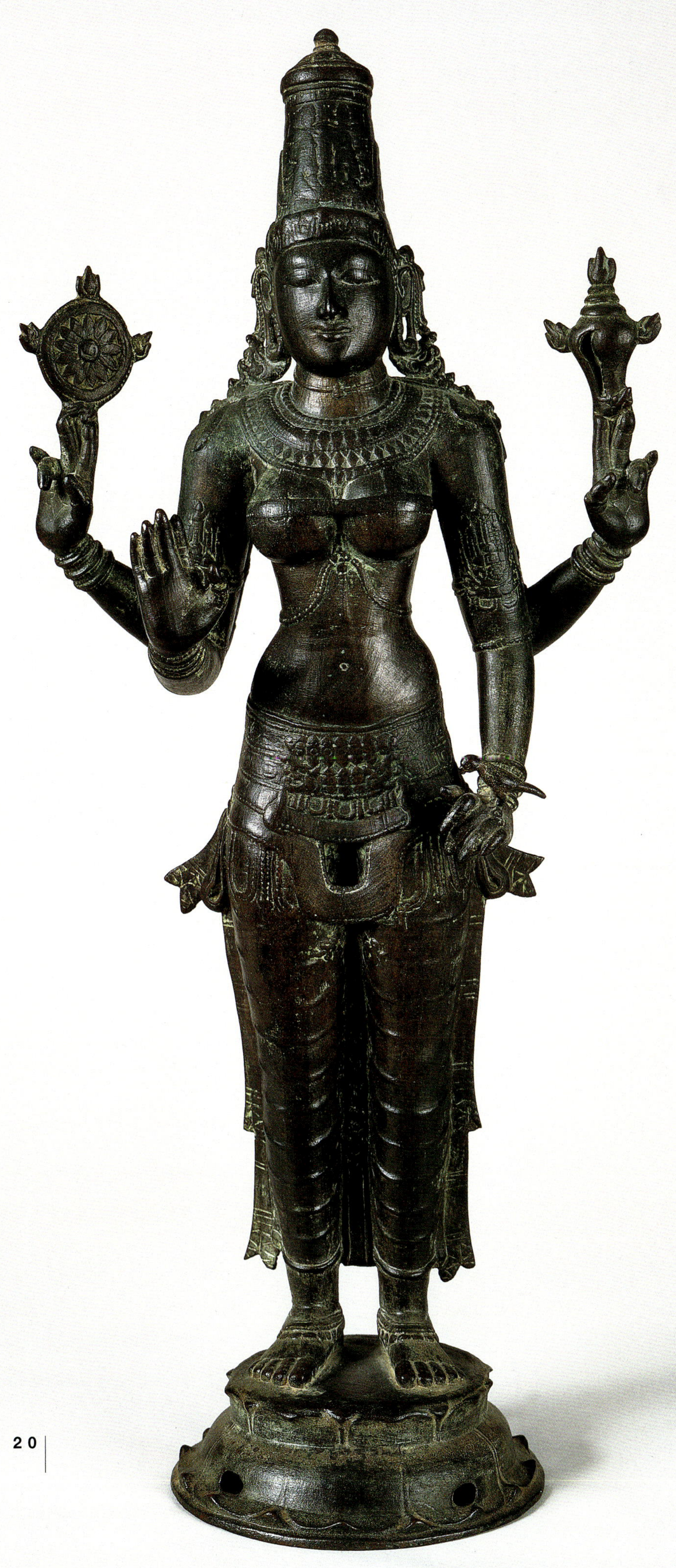

20

21 KALI

CHOLA PERIOD, CA. 940
BRONZE, 16 IN. (40.5 CM)
RIETBERG MUSEUM, ZURICH;
EDUARD VON DER HEYDT COLLECTION

Beginningless
she is the beginning too . . .
Kali, the boundless lake of bliss
is joy incarnate
the cause of pain too —[1]

This powerful image presents Uma in her fierce form of Kali, or Kala pidari as she is known in Rajaraja's Tanjavur inscription. Seated in the posture of royal ease known as *lalitasana,* with one foot crossed in front of her and the other pendant, this four-armed Kali holds a noose, a bell with a trident handle, and a skull-cup in three of her hands, while the fourth is in the *abhaya* gesture of protection. Her short skirt, fastened with an ornamental girdle, is knotted with loops at the sides and the extra folds of her garment are pleated to hang down both sides and in the front. Kali is exceedingly slender of torso with high, softly modeled breasts encircled with a knotted snake that serves as her breast-band. Her sacred thread consists of a garland of skulls, and she is adorned with necklaces, armlets, bangles, and anklets. Her serene face is framed by matted hair that rises like a halo behind her head, with a central ornament of a skull atop two snakes. Although the form contains several fierce allusions, Kali is here presented as the tranquil protector.

This finely sculpted image of great sensitivity belongs early in the tenth century. The modeling of bodily form reveals a close resemblance to the treatment of the bronze of the goddess destroying the demon Nishumba from the Turaikadu temple, now in the Government Museum, Chennai (fig. 1). The Rietberg Kali's exceedingly slender torso, even more strikingly apparent from the rear, points to her as the successor to images such as the Sita from Tirucherai, or the seated Uma from Pallavanishvaram. The face has the smooth wear of an image that has been in worship for centuries, but its patina clearly indicates that it was recovered from a treasure trove. Clearly the image was buried around the year 1310, after some 370 years of loving worship, when news of the approaching Muslim armies reached the Tamil temples.

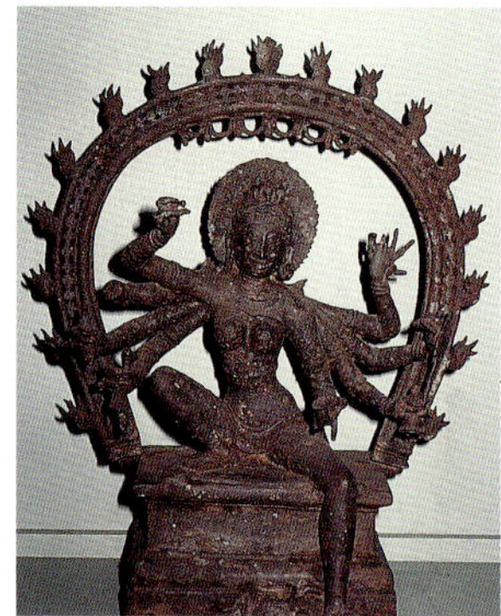

THE GODDESS AS NISHUMBA-SUDANI (DESTROYER OF NISHUMBA), 10TH CENTURY, FROM TURAIKADU TEMPLE. GOVERNMENT MUSEUM, CHENNAI
PHOTO VIDYA DEHEJIA
FIG. 1

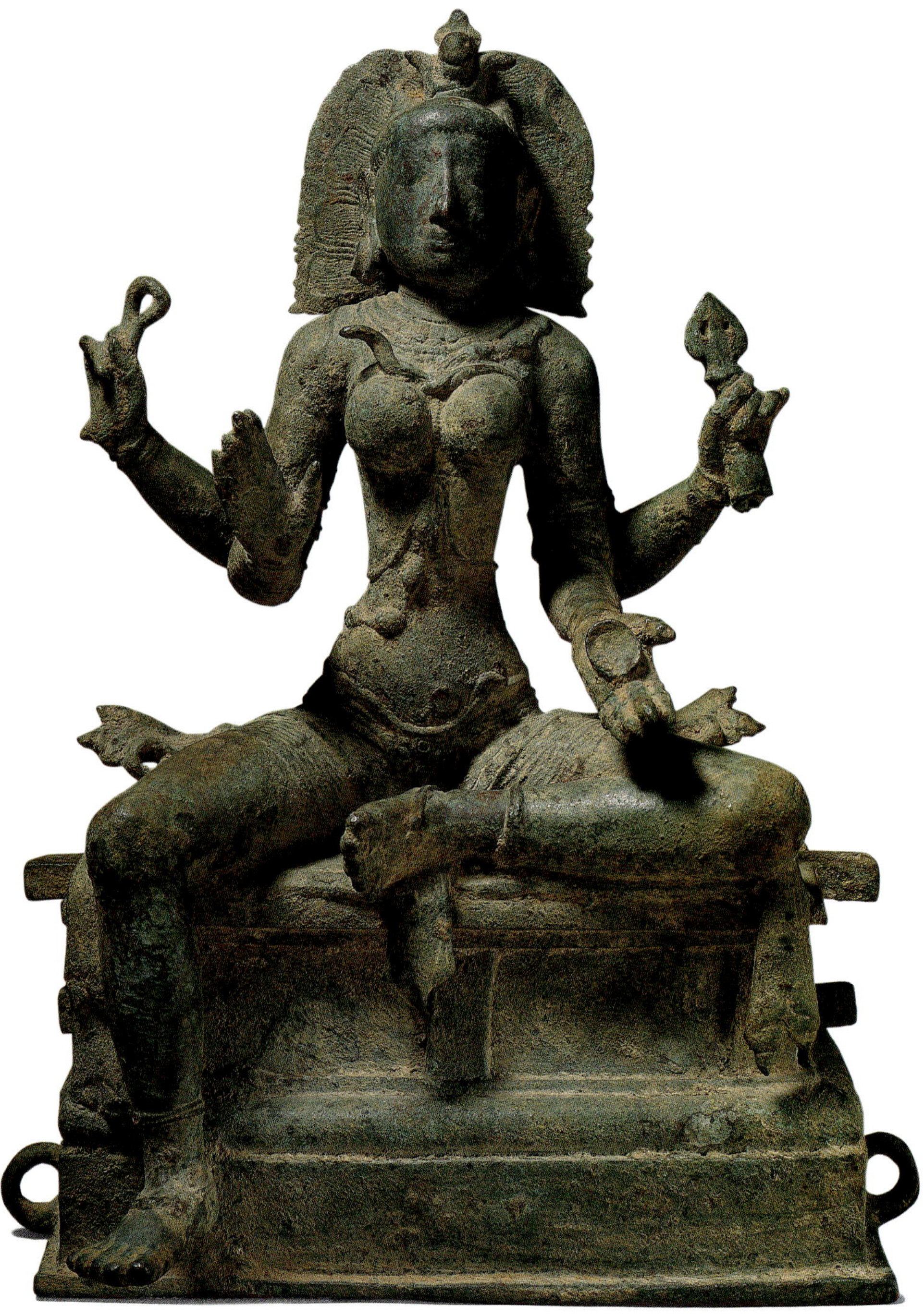

NOTE

1 Translation of Subrahmania Bharati's "The Mystique of Mahakali" is mine, in *Devi: The Great Goddess*, ed. Vidya Dehejia (Washington, D.C., Ahmedabad, and Cologne: Arthur M. Sackler Gallery, Mapin Publishing, and Prestel Verlag, 1999), p. 103.

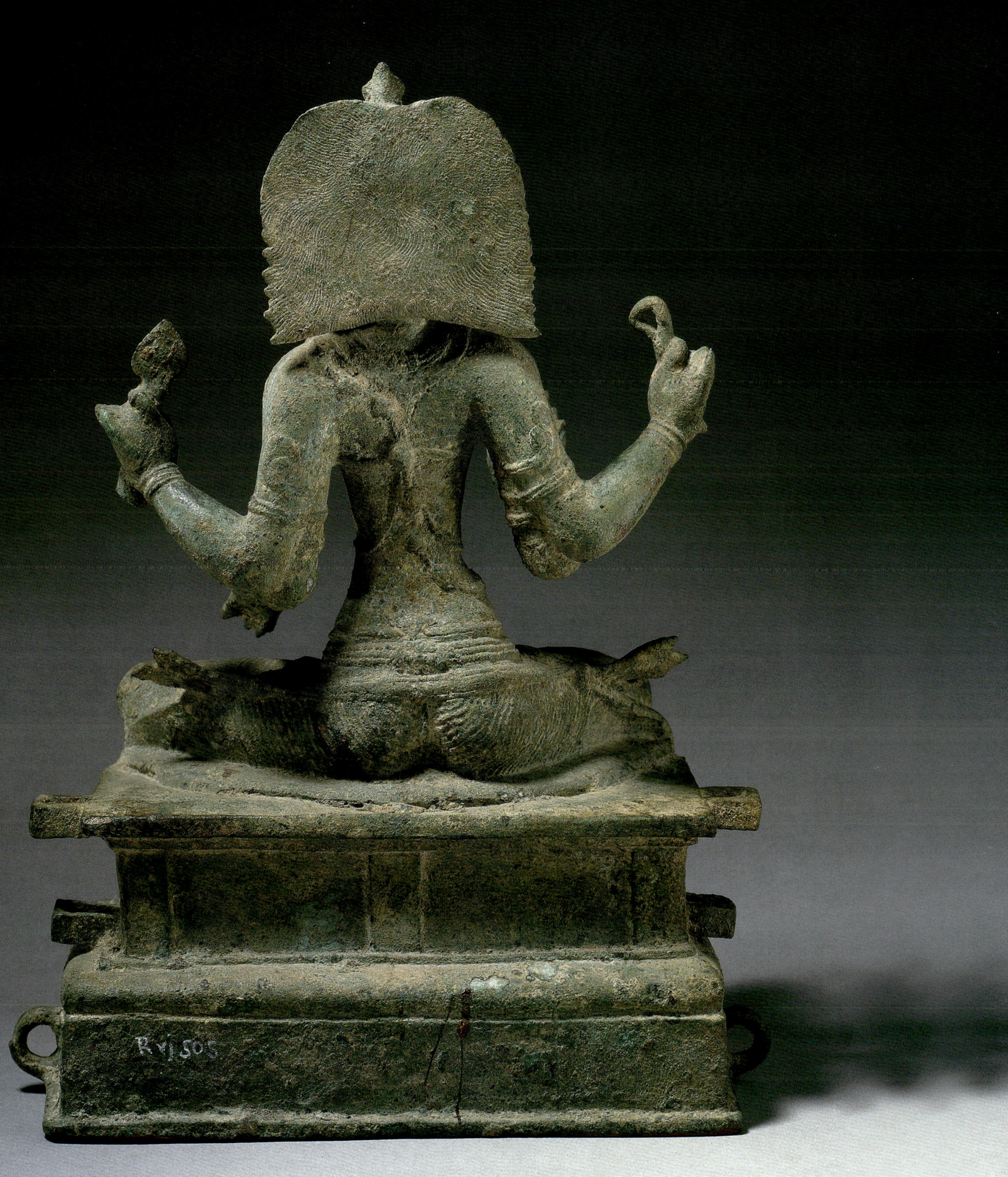
RV1505

22 GANESHA
CHOLA PERIOD, CA. 1070
BRONZE, 19 3/4 IN. (50.2 CM)
THE CLEVELAND MUSEUM OF ART;
GIFT OF KATHARINE HOLDEN THAYER
(1970.62)

23 GANESHA
CHOLA PERIOD, CA. 1170
BRONZE, 17 3/8 IN. (44 CM)
PRIVATE COLLECTION

Perhaps the most beloved of gods, elephant-headed Ganesha, son of Shiva and Uma, is known in Tamil Nadu as Pillaiyar *(pillai*, son [of Shiva]). He is also addressed as Ganapati or leader *(pati)* of Shiva's dwarflike *gana* attendants (Ganesha also means lord [*isha*] of *ganas*), and since Shiva's *ganas* tend to have the heads of various animals and birds, the elephant-headed god is indeed their appropriate leader. The most frequently repeated story of the elephant head speaks of the child having been left to guard the front door while his mother Uma went for a bath. Told not to allow anyone in, Ganesha followed instructions to the letter, obstinately refusing entry even to his father. An outraged Shiva cut off his head, immediately repenting and promising he would replace it with the head of the first living being that came by, which happened to be an elephant. Ganesha is entirely benign and is renowned for his practical astuteness and insight. The story is often narrated of how, despite being a clumsy, potbellied figure, he outwitted his lithe younger brother Skanda in a race. When Shiva and Uma challenged their sons and promised a special prize to the one who circled the world first, it was Ganesha who won. As Skanda sped off on his peacock mount, Ganesha and his mouse mount merely circumambulated his parents, claiming that they constituted the entire world.

Ganesha is also known as Vighneshvara or one who wards off obstacles *(vighna)*. He is the god of new beginnings, to be worshiped at the start of any new undertaking. To this day in India, he is invoked by students commencing an exam, by those starting to make a new batch of sweets, by accountants commencing the books for the new year. Ganesha's popularity may be gauged from the fact that as many as ten of the sixty-six bronzes set up around the year 1000 in Rajaraja's royal temple at Tanjavur were of this deity. Rajaraja himself set up seven images, of which two were standing, two dancing, and three seated comfortably, one beneath a tree (three of these were small images for private rather than temple worship). The remaining three Tanjavur temple images of Ganesha were dedications from two of Rajaraja's queens and from a court noble.

It is necessary for every temple to possess at least one bronze image of Ganesha since it is imperative that he be carried at the head of all festival processions that parade through the town, ahead of the chief deity of that festivity. By virtue of this function, the largest number of Ganesha images are standing images, such as the two included in this exhibition. Ganesha generally carries the battle-ax, and the noose or rosary in two rear hands, while the two front hands hold his own broken tusk (broken off in a victorious battle against a mighty demon) and sweets *(modaka)*. His love of sweets is proverbial, and sculptors frequently indicate this by depicting his trunk touching the sweets.

The Cleveland image displays powerful modeling and depicts the standing god with all his characteristic attributes (cat. no. 22). His short lower garment is tied below his gently swelling, yet flattened, belly so that the clasp of the girdle is hidden. The decorative treatment of the crown, the flattened ringlet curls arranged on the shoulders at the rear, the decoration of the rear of the girdle immediately below the fluted fan-shaped garment end, and the general treatment of bodily form resemble an image in the temple of Tirumangalakudi (fig. 1) of the reign of Kulottunga I, discussed by R. Nagaswamy in his essay in this volume.

Belonging to a century later is the impressive Ganesha whose waist-band forms a U-shape between the thighs (cat. no. 23). Ganesha holds battle-ax, tusk, and *modaka* sweet and wears a double-strand sacred thread and a patterned forehead band. A *kati sutra* band rests above his navel, while waist-cloth and girdle are slung below his gentle paunch. At the rear, the end of his *veshti* protrudes gently at his waist.

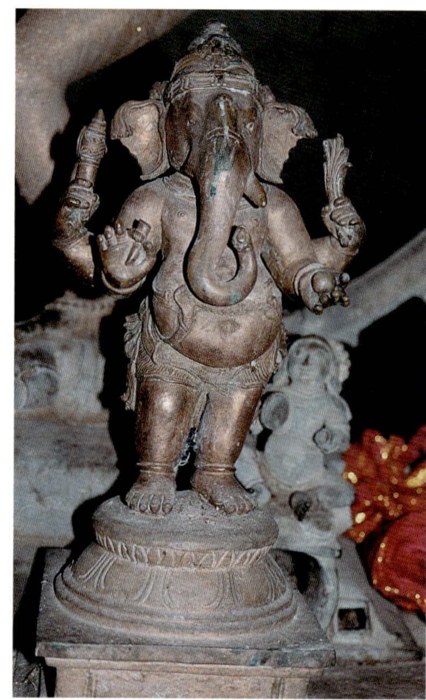

GANESHA, CA. 1100, PURANA VITANKAR TEMPLE, TIRUMANGALAKUDI
PHOTO R. NAGASWAMY
FIG. 1

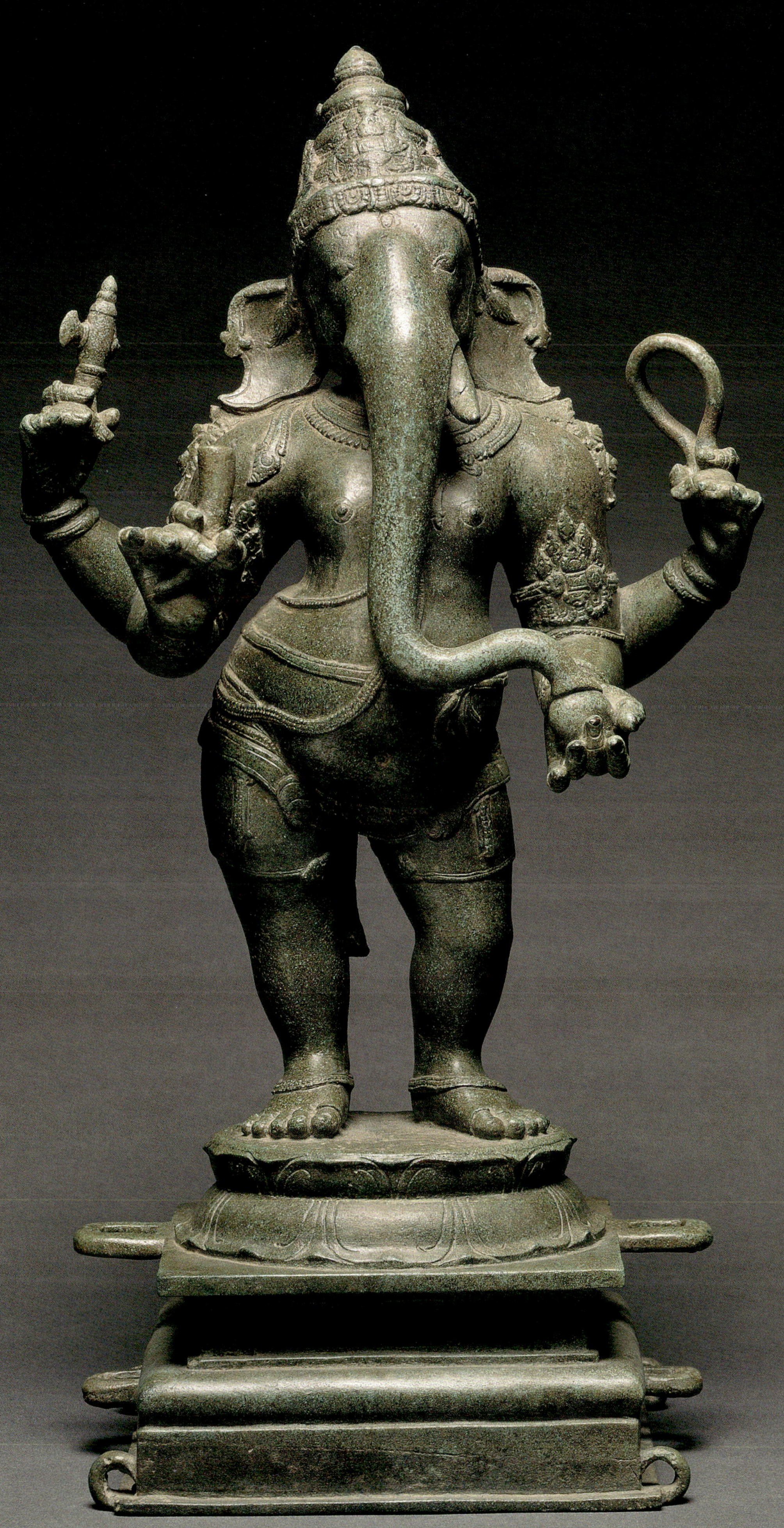

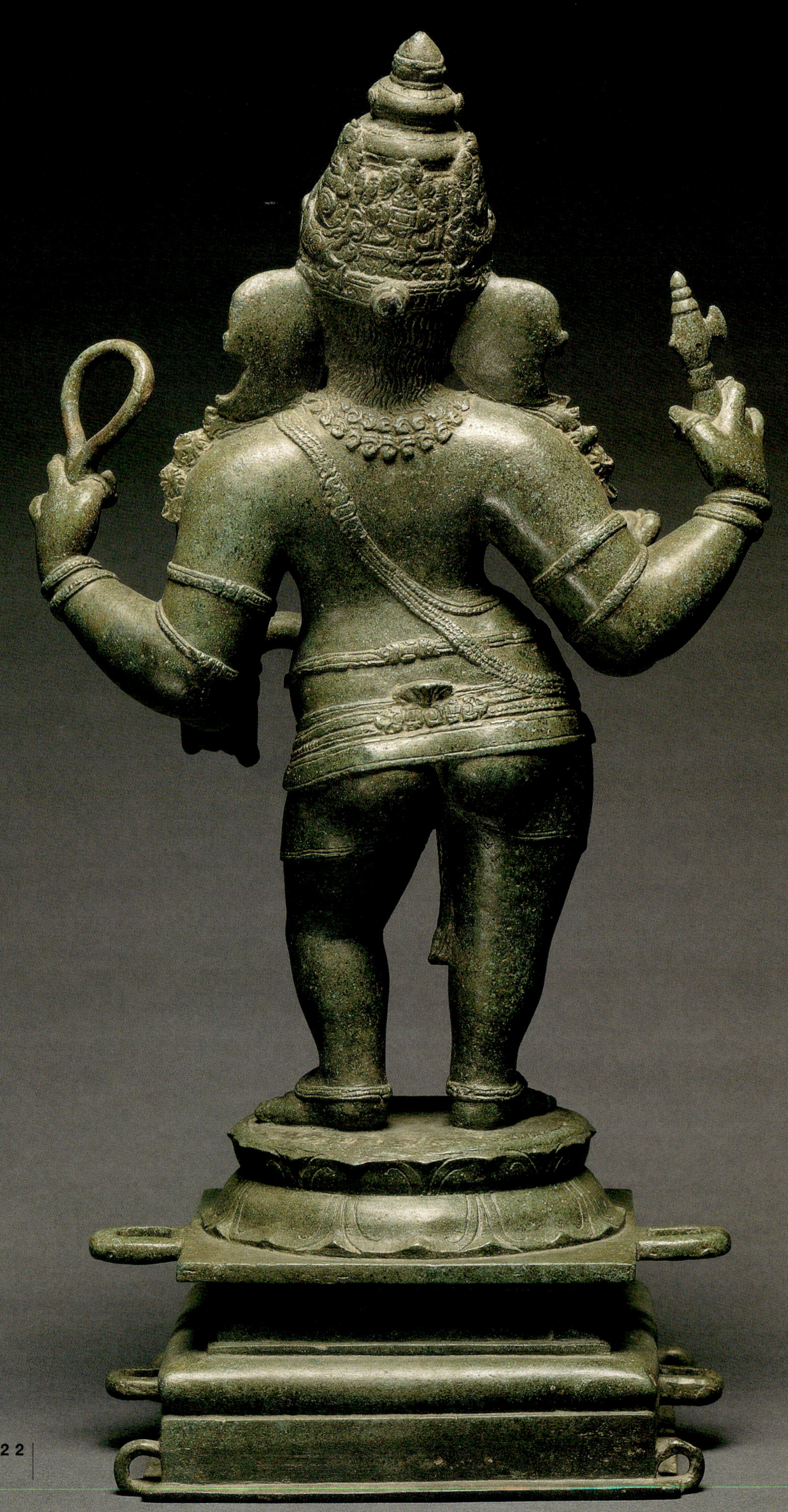

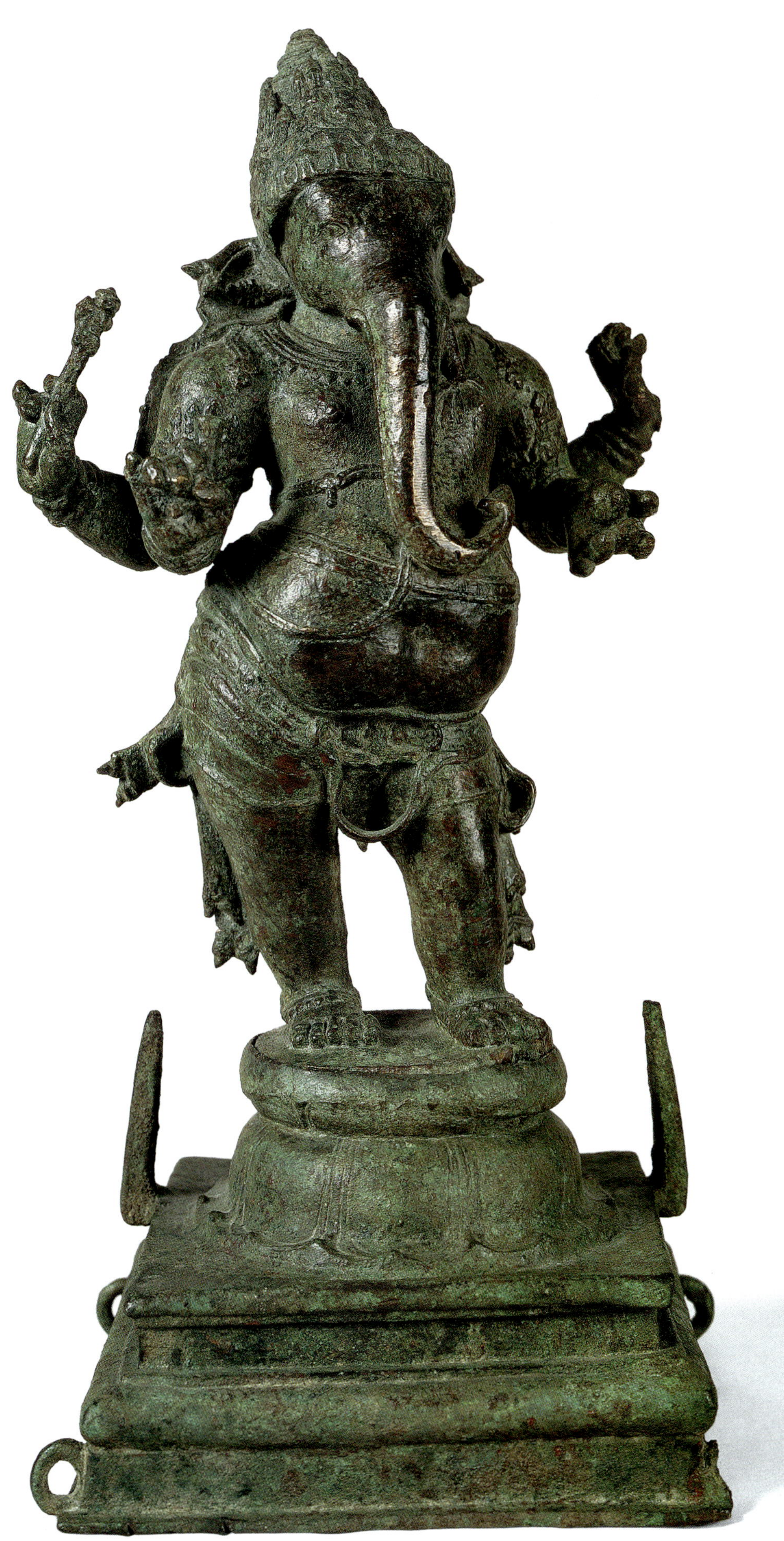

23

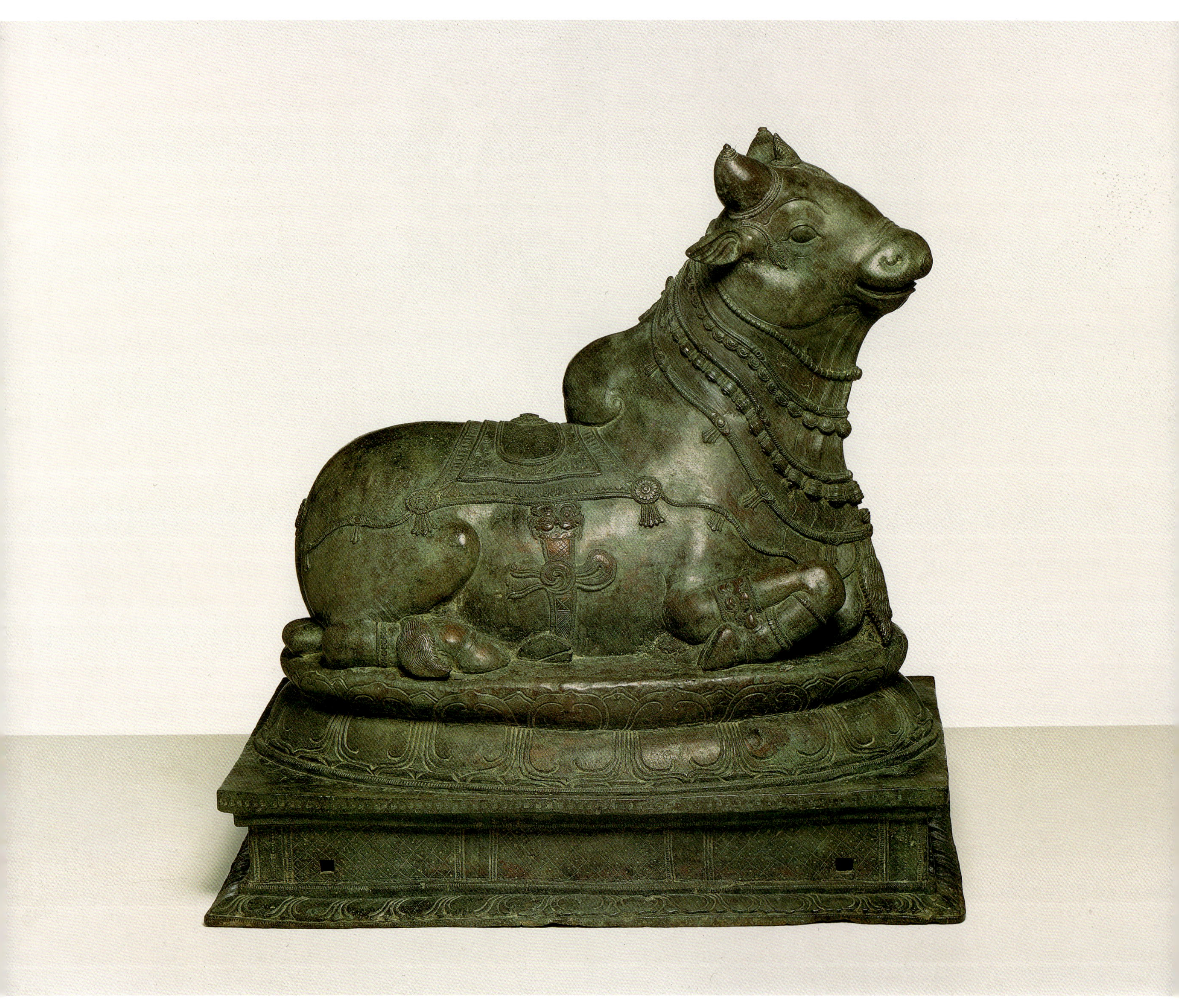

24 NANDI, SHIVA'S BULL MOUNT

CHOLA PERIOD, CA. 1200;
KONGU-KARNATAKA REGION
BRONZE, 20¼ IN. (51.4 CM)
ASIA SOCIETY, NEW YORK; THE MR. AND MRS. JOHN D. ROCKEFELLER 3RD COLLECTION (1979.30)

Will you not move just a little bit to one side?
Your form blocks my view of the sanctum lord.[1]

Thus did the saint Nandanar address the bull Nandi since, as an untouchable *(paraiyan),* he was not allowed access to the inner areas of the temple, but had to peer through the gateway for a glimpse of Shiva. As Shiva is the rider of the bull, every Shiva temple contains a shrine for a stone image of the bull Nandi, literally "joyous one," that is placed directly in front of the sanctum so the bull may face his master. Bronze images of Nandi are not common and seem, in general, to have been placed beside the stone bull rather than taken out for festival processions. However, the holes in the rectangular base of this image indicate that it was indeed a processional image that accompanied a festival image of Shiva. One may note too that while the inscription from the Tiruvaduturai temple lists a bull among its processional images, the Tanjavur temple's more than sixty bronzes did not include Nandi.

Nandi rests casually on a double lotus pedestal with his tail folded over his hind legs, his two front legs partially bent in typical fashion, and his tongue licking the tip of his nose. He has the distinctive hump of an Indian bull and is lavishly adorned with jewelry in a manner befitting his stature, from the metal covers on his horns to his range of foot ornaments. Four garlands adorn his neck, and an ornate saddlecloth is secured to his back with a decorative metal strap, while additional cords at its ends circle the body. This is an endearing image dating to around 1200; the long slender neck that the image shares with those from the Karnataka region suggests that it may have come from a temple from the western boundaries of the Chola empire.

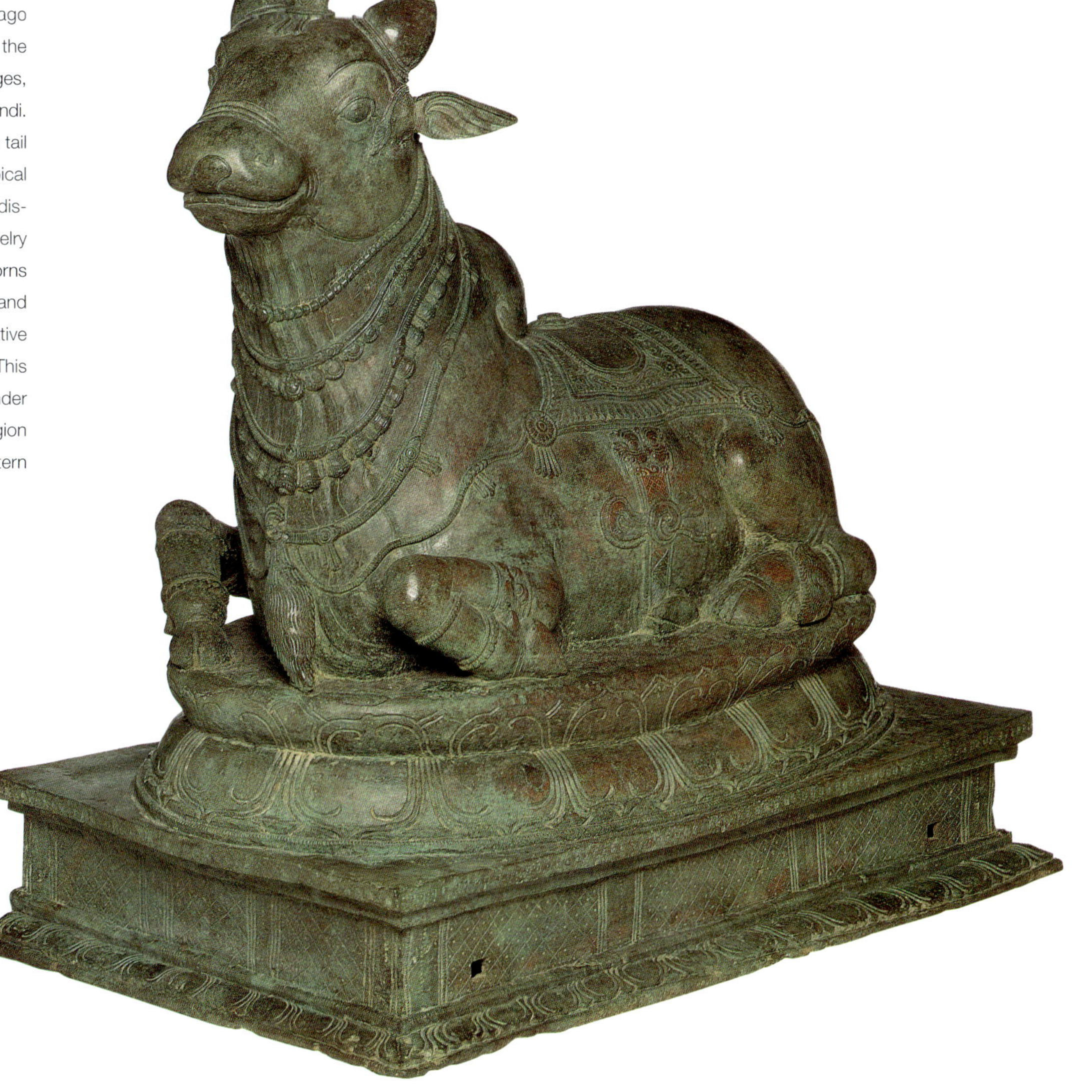

NOTE

1 Anonymous verse from popular performance of the life of Nandanar.

25 TRIDENT WITH SHIVA AS VRISHABHAVANA, RIDER OF THE BULL
CHOLA PERIOD, CA. 950
BRONZE, 32 7/8 IN. (83.6 CM)
TRUSTEES OF THE BRITISH MUSEUM; BEQUEATHED BY PROFESSOR SAMUEL EILENBERG (OA 2001.11-26.1)

26 TRIDENT WITH SHIVA AS ARDHANARI, HALF-WOMAN
CHOLA PERIOD, CA. 1050
BRONZE, 13 3/4 IN. (35 CM)
THE CLEVELAND MUSEUM OF ART; PURCHASE FROM THE J.H. WADE FUND (1969.117)

The trident, Shiva's prime attribute, serves him as a weapon in feats of cosmic destruction, but, in addition, it is invested with deep philosophical meaning. It is this layer of meaning that led to the production of bronze tridents and to the ritual of *ayudha puja* or weapon worship that is a regular feature of temple rites. A variety of Shaiva texts instruct worshipers to think of the trident and other *ayudhas* not as everyday tools of violence but rather as weapons of grace, whereby Shiva destroys the bonds that ensnare the human soul.[1] For instance, the text of the eleventh-century *Kamika Agama* states that the trident's three prongs stand for the three *gunas*, or qualities, of purity *(sattva)*, activity *(rajas)*, and lethargy *(tamas)*.[2]

Juxtaposed against the smoothly fashioned trident from the British Museum (cat. no. 25) is an exquisite image of Shiva as Rider of the Bull, which depicts him leaning gracefully against his bull mount, Nandi, with one hand resting upon its back. Shiva crosses one foot in front of the other in the manner of the famous image from Tiruvenkadu (fig. 1), and the hair of this image is also styled on that model and not on earlier crowned images of the tenth century at Konerirajapuram, Pallavanishvaram, Tirukkaravasal, and other sites.[3] Yet, the smooth fashioning of the form, and its slender elegance, suggests a date in the mid-tenth century. The abraded nature of the image, with the facial features of Shiva almost entirely obliterated, testifies to the centuries of ritual worship in which the trident would have been ritually bathed and anointed in a manner similar to that undertaken currently by the priests at the Chidambaram temple (fig. 2).

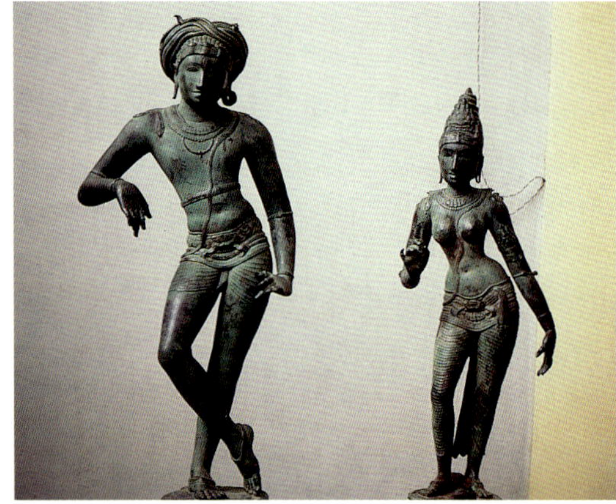

SHIVA AS RIDER OF THE BULL, FROM TIRUVENKADU TEMPLE, CA. 1012. TANJAVUR ART GALLERY
PHOTO VIDYA DEHEJIA
FIG. 1

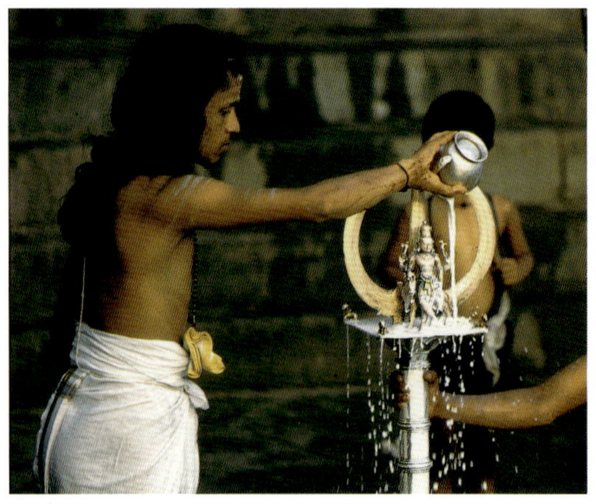

TRIDENT ANOINTED WITH MILK BY PRIESTS, CHIDAMBARAM
PHOTO NEIL GREENTREE, 1998
FIG. 2

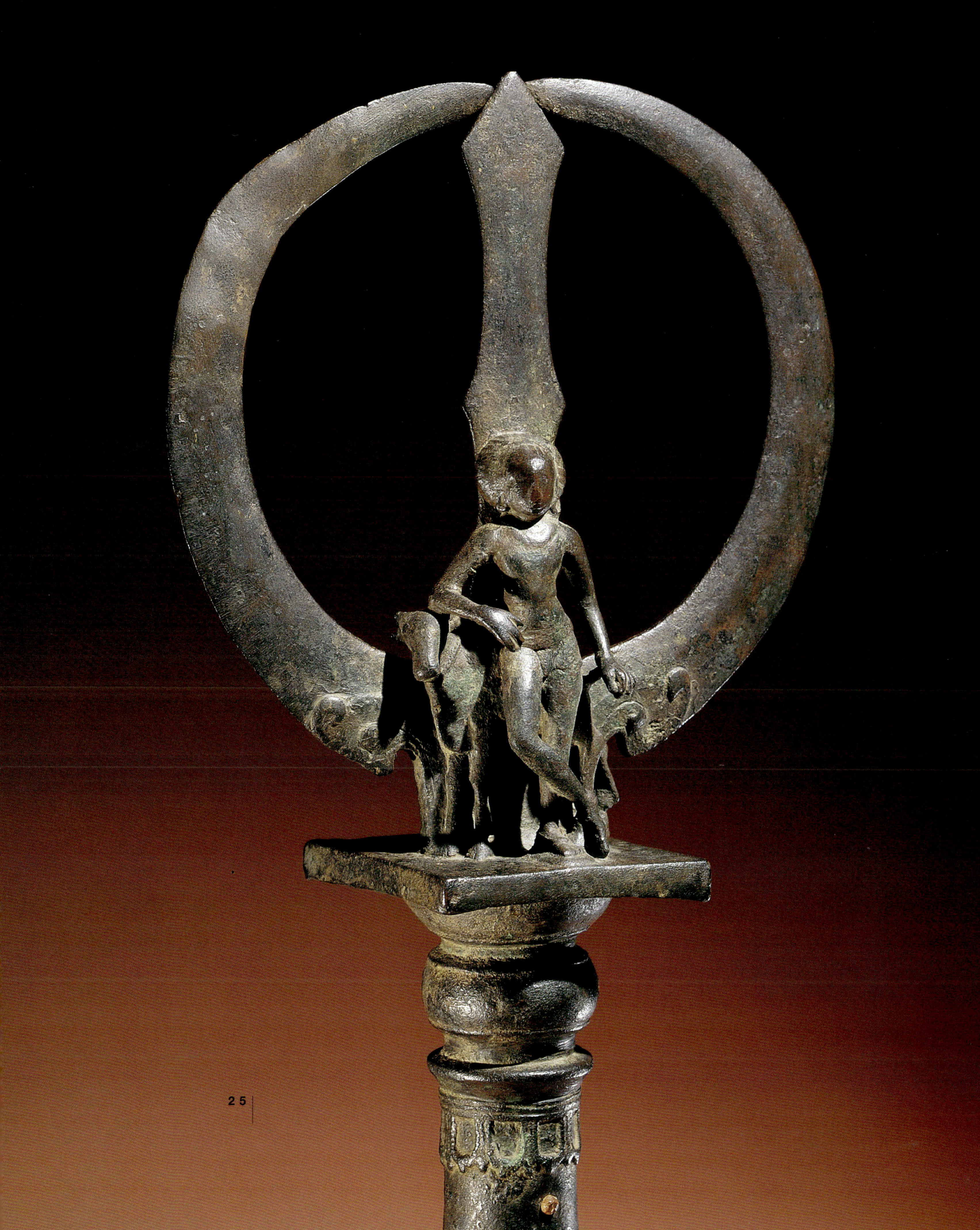

25

Of exceptional quality is a trident from the collection of the Cleveland Museum of Art that features Shiva in his form of Half-Woman or Ardhanari (cat. no. 26). While emphasizing the essential nonduality of the supreme principle, the image is remarkable for the precision with which it distinguishes the male and female aspects of the deity while harmoniously fusing them into a single form. The right half depicting Shiva has two arms, one resting against his bull mount, Nandi, and the other holding a battle-ax. Uma occupies the left half and her single hand probably once held a flower. Details of drapery, jewelry, crown, and bodily construction distinguish the two halves. Even facial features reflect the difference; Uma has a gently curved aspect to her jawline while Shiva has a firm, straight profile. The feminine aspect of this image, with its softly rounded breast and the smooth wide curve of the hip calls to mind child-saint Sambandar's verses on this androgynous form in which he celebrates the beauty of the feminine half:

Smooth and curved
her stomach
like the snake's
dancing hood
her flawless gait
mocks the peacock's grace
with feet soft
as cotton down
and waist
a slender creeper
Uma devi is one half of Siva
lord of sacred Pundarai.[4]

The treatment of bodily form, as well as details such as the pleated fold of the lower garment as it rests against Uma's thigh, closely resembles the famous Tiruvenkadu Ardhanari of around 1048 (fig. 4). The shape of the trident's prongs are also more stylistically advanced than that seen in the example from the British Museum and suggests its creation around the year 1050.

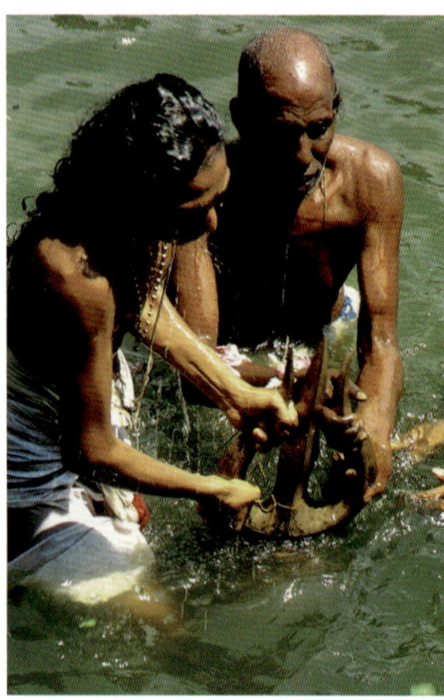

TRIDENT BEING GIVEN A RITUAL DIP IN TEMPLE TANK, CHIDAMBARAM
PHOTO NEIL GREENTREE, 1998
FIG. 3

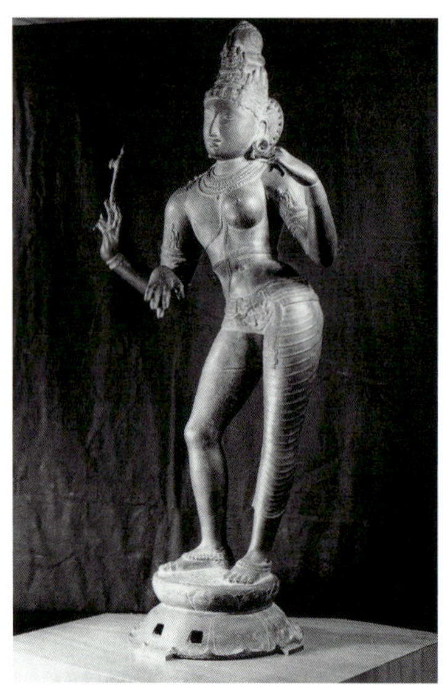

ARDHANARI, FROM TIRUVENKADU TEMPLE, CA. 1048. TANJAVUR ART GALLERY
PHOTO VIDYA DEHEJIA
FIG. 4

NOTES

1 Richard Davis, *Ritual in an Oscillating Universe* (Princeton: Princeton University Press, 1991), p. 117.
2 Ibid.
3 Douglas Barrett, *Early Cola Bronzes* (Bombay: Bhulabhai Memorial Institute, 1965), pls. 1–2, 23–24, 40, 4.
4 T. V. Gopal Iyer and François Gros, eds., *Tevaram: Hymnes Sivaites du pays Tamoul,* vol. 1 (Pondicherry: Institut français d'indologie, 1984), p. 280: Sambandar 3.20.3. Translation is mine. See Dehejia, *Art of the Imperial Cholas*, p. 86.

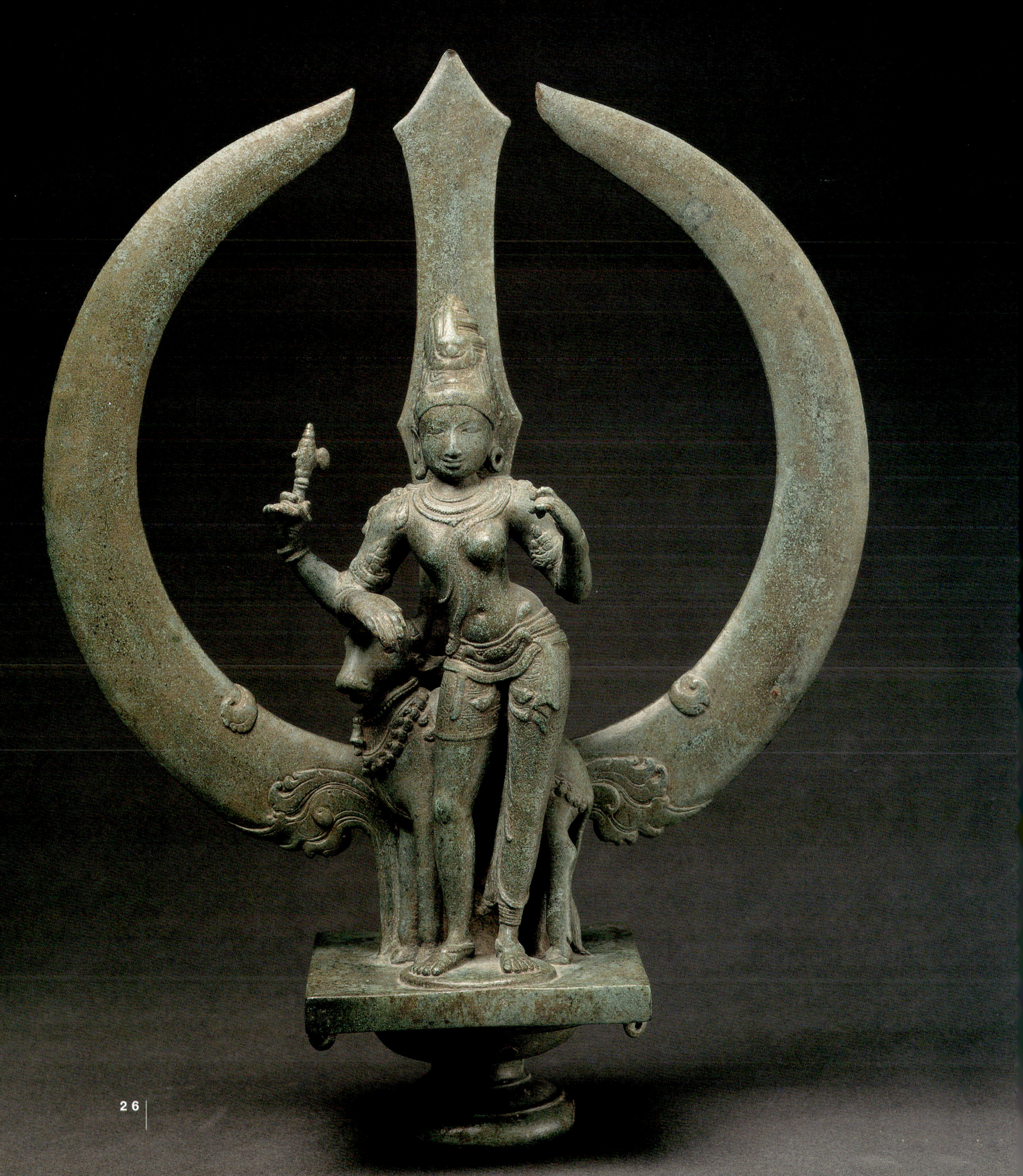

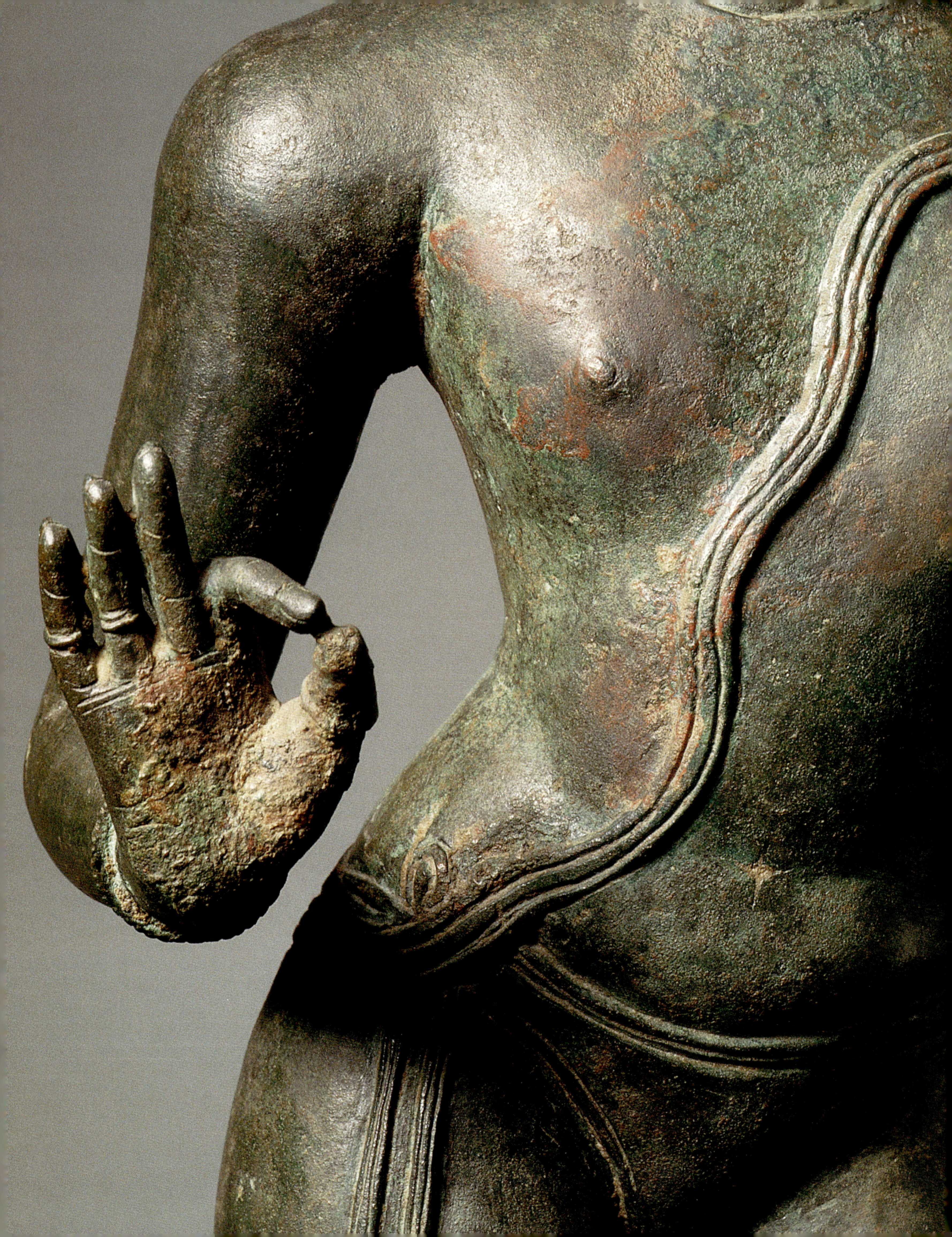

SHAIVA SAINTS

An interesting facet of Hinduism in the Tamil-speaking region of south India is the emphasis given to the worship of a group of saints who dedicated their lives to either Shiva or Vishnu. The Shaiva saints, a group of sixty-three, were known as *nayanmars* or leaders, and they referred to themselves as *adiyar* or *tontar,* both words meaning slave or servant [of the lord]. The Vaishnava saints, twelve in number, were known as *alvars* or those dived/plunged [into the divine].

The Shaiva saints, who lived between the sixth and ninth centuries, were part of a community of holy persons who traveled together across the Tamil countryside, stopping at each temple site to sing the glories of the deity enshrined therein. Renunciation and solitude were never themes for the *nayanmars*. Indeed, the majority acknowledged the normal bonds of family life and marriage was not something to be renounced. Was not lord Shiva himself always accompanied by his beautiful consort Uma? According to the legends that surrounded the lives of the saints, none of them died a normal death. Rather, each one was received into a sacred effulgence when his or her time was due. Thus, death anniversaries are occasions for celebration, to rejoice that the *nayanmar* was received directly into Shiva's presence.

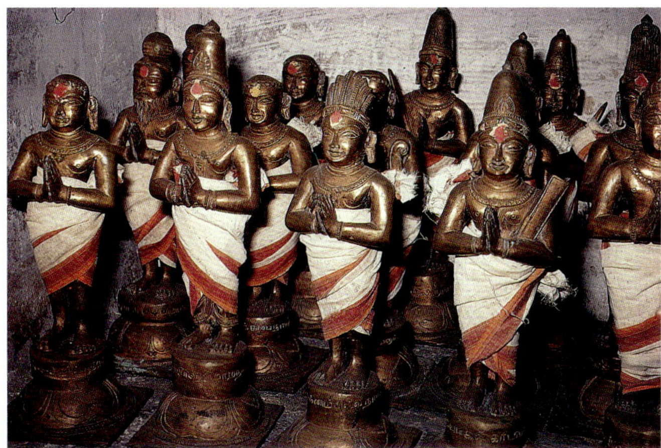

SIXTY-THREE *NAYANMARS*, 20TH CENTURY, KUVOOR TEMPLE NEAR CHENNAI
PHOTO VIDYA DEHEJIA
FIG. 1

The group of sixty-three *nayanmars* was consolidated around the year 800 by saint Sundarar, who composed a song in which he named sixty-two holy persons; he himself was added to the list to create the group of sixty-three. Three among them—child-saint Sambandar, Appar, and Sundarar—composed some seven hundred hymns that form a corpus known as *Tevaram*; these three saints are referred to as *muvar* or the Revered Three. During the ninth century, saint Manikkavachakar made such a tremendous impact that it became imperative to accommodate him within the group of saints. Devotees sometimes spoke of sixty-four to include this last great figure, and, an additional grouping known as the *nalvar* or Revered Four was formed by adding Manikkavachakar to the Revered Three.

In Tamil Nadu, to this day, the *nayanmars* evoke an immediate and spontaneous response. A Tamilian will speak with enthusiasm of the mystique of the innocent child-saint Sambandar, or the charisma of the impudent saint Sundarar, who so frequently bargained with the lord. In Shiva temples, bronze images of all sixty-three *nayanmars* are placed in a hall immediately surrounding the sanctum (fig. 1). Here they are lustrated, clothed, and ornamented in a manner similar to the deity himself. As early as the year 1040, during the reign of Emperor Rajendra, a festival of the sixty-three *(aravatti-muvar-ula)* was celebrated at the Tiruvottiyur temple just outside Chennai.[1] Similar festivals are still celebrated. At Mylapur, in the heart of Chennai, for instance, the festival of the sixty-three, celebrated on the eighth day of the ten-day Brahmotsavam festival, draws vast crowds of devotees who converge on the city from surrounding towns and villages. Bronze images of all sixty-three saints are bathed, clothed in silks, decorated with garlands, placed on palanquins, and carried through the streets to rest finally in the

SAINT MANIKKAVACHAKAR (DETAIL OF CAT. NO. 36)

square in front of the temple (fig. 2). Many temples also hold a festival of the Revered Three or the Revered Four to honor these specially venerated saints.

The sacred canon of south India (a total of twelve books) consists largely of the hymns of these saints, to which was added the *Periya Purana*, their official hagiography. The saints' hymns are chanted daily in the temples, and devout Tamilians are familiar with the better-known verses that are sung at festival and in homes. Through their songs, the Tamil saints humanized the figure of a distant godhead, a need specially felt in the case of Shiva, who had thus far been worshiped largely in the symbolic form of the *linga*. The deep mystic consciousness of the saints enabled them to visualize Shiva as the Rider of the Bull, as the Divine Dancer, as Crowned with the Moon, as the Enchanting Mendicant. From being a distant symbolic godhead, Shiva was transformed into a colorful, almost human personality. The "distant" attribute of godhead applied to Shiva in a literal way too since his home, Mount Kailasa in the Himalayas, is a thousand miles away from the Tamil country. The saints brought in this distant Shiva and located him in every town and village temple in the lush plains of the south.

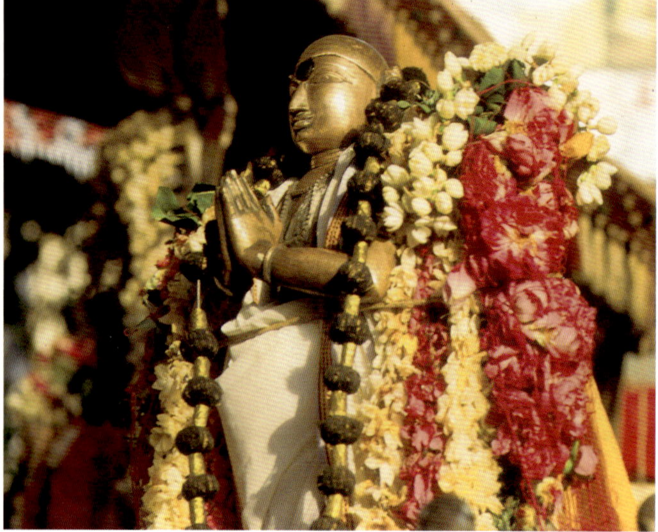

ADORNED PROCESSIONAL IMAGE OF APPAR, CHENNAI
PHOTO NEIL GREENTREE, 1984
FIG. 2

NOTE

1 *Madras Epigraphy Report,* 1912, no. 137.

27 CHILD-SAINT SAMBANDAR
CHOLA PERIOD, CA. 1050–75; PANDI-NADU
BRONZE, 17 IN. (43.2 CM)
VICTORIA & ALBERT MUSEUM (IM 75-1935)

28 DANCING CHILD-SAINT SAMBANDAR
CHOLA PERIOD, CA. 1250
BRONZE, 16½ IN. (42 CM)
LINDEN-MUSEUM, STUTTGART (SA 33588L)

Born of brahmin parents in the town of Sirkali, south of Chidambaram, Sambandar frequently accompanied his father to the temple. One day, left on the steps of the temple tank while his father went in for a ritual dip, the hungry child began to cry. When the father returned to find the child playing contentedly with a golden cup while trickles of milk ran down his chin, he was concerned about the source of the milk. By way of answer, the child raised his hand and pointed toward the temple tower that bore an image of the goddess seated beside Shiva. This incident is commemorated in bronze images of Sambandar that depict the child with an empty cup in one hand, and with the finger of the other pointing upwards. Having drunk this cup of divine milk, the child is said to have burst into song, praising Shiva and Uma. Historical allusions in his poems suggest that Sambandar lived toward the end of the seventh century.

The image of standing Sambandar from the Victoria & Albert Museum (cat. no. 27) commemorates this early episode in Sambandar's life and depicts the naked child adorned with the infant's traditional girdle of bells *(kinkini sara)*. Sambandar wears a heavy necklace and a sacred thread that descend from a neck-band to circle both sides of his body. The image belongs to the mid-eleventh century and is typical of the Kaveri Delta style even though it comes from Tirunelveli in Pandi-nadu; it belongs soon after the time of the typical Kaveri Delta–style temple constructed by Rajaraja at Tiruvalishvaram, not far from Tirunelveli, that was discussed in the introductory essay to this volume. It seems that images of the tenth and eleventh centuries from this area of Pandi-nadu, captured by Rajaraja, might have been commissioned in the Kaveri Delta.

Sambandar's songs are a joyous expression of the beauty and glory of Shiva and Uma in the context of the beauty of nature—of cool lotus ponds and rich green paddy fields, cloud-capped mountains and shady groves of coconut palms abounding in peacocks, parrots, and koels. The birds, bees, and insects participate in his paean to Shiva:

O devotees!
Kurralam, in whose spacious groves
the peacock dances with his mate
is the fair town of our trident bearer,
the god who quelled Death
with his foot.[1]

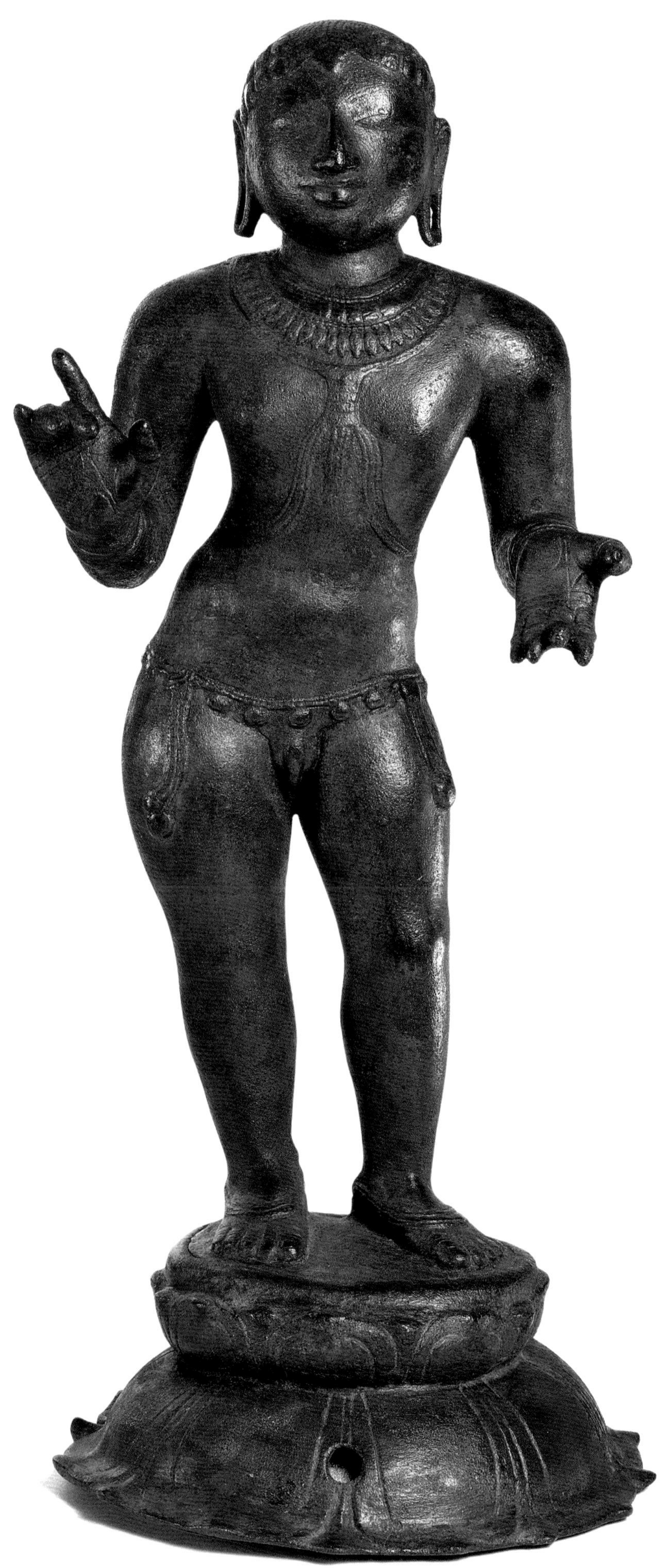

27

Sambandar set to music all four thousand of his verses, and a brother saint provided musical accompaniment on an instrument called the *yal.* Perhaps it was the joyous participation evoked by Sambandar's approach to Shiva and Uma, and his love of music, that caused artists to portray him as a dancing child. However, it is also probable that the existing iconography of dancing child-god Krishna (cat. no. 51), and his immense popularity, gave artists the added impetus to create an image of equal appeal in a Shaiva context.[2] Even Krishna's crown was adapted to create dancing Sambandar's towering hair style, which is absent in the regular standing images of the child-saint. The dancing image from the collection of the Linden-Museum is an exquisite piece of the thirteenth century (cat. no. 28). While iconographically close to dancing Krishna, Sambandar always has the finger of one hand pointing upward, while Krishna's hand is in the divine *abhaya* gesture of protection (cf. cat. no. 51). The image is later in style than a dancing Sambandar of the Kulottunga I period that stands in the Melakadambur temple, and is probably to be placed a good hundred years later.

NOTES

1 Indira Viswanathan Peterson, *Poems to Siva: The Hymns of the Tamil Saints* (Princeton: Princeton University Press, 1989), p. 172: Sambandar 1.99.7.

2 Vidya Dehejia, "Iconographic Transference Between Krsna and Three Saiva Saints," in *Indian Art and Connoisseurship: Essays in Honour of Douglas Barrett*, ed. John Guy (Ahmedabad: Mapin Publishing, 1995), especially pp. 142–45.

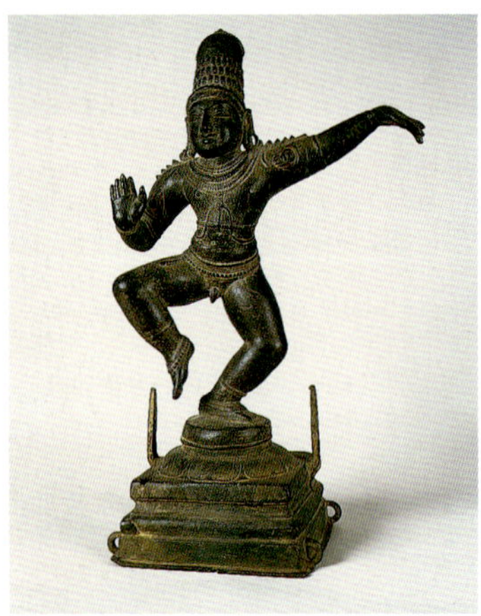

DANCING CHILD KRISHNA (CAT. NO. 51)

28

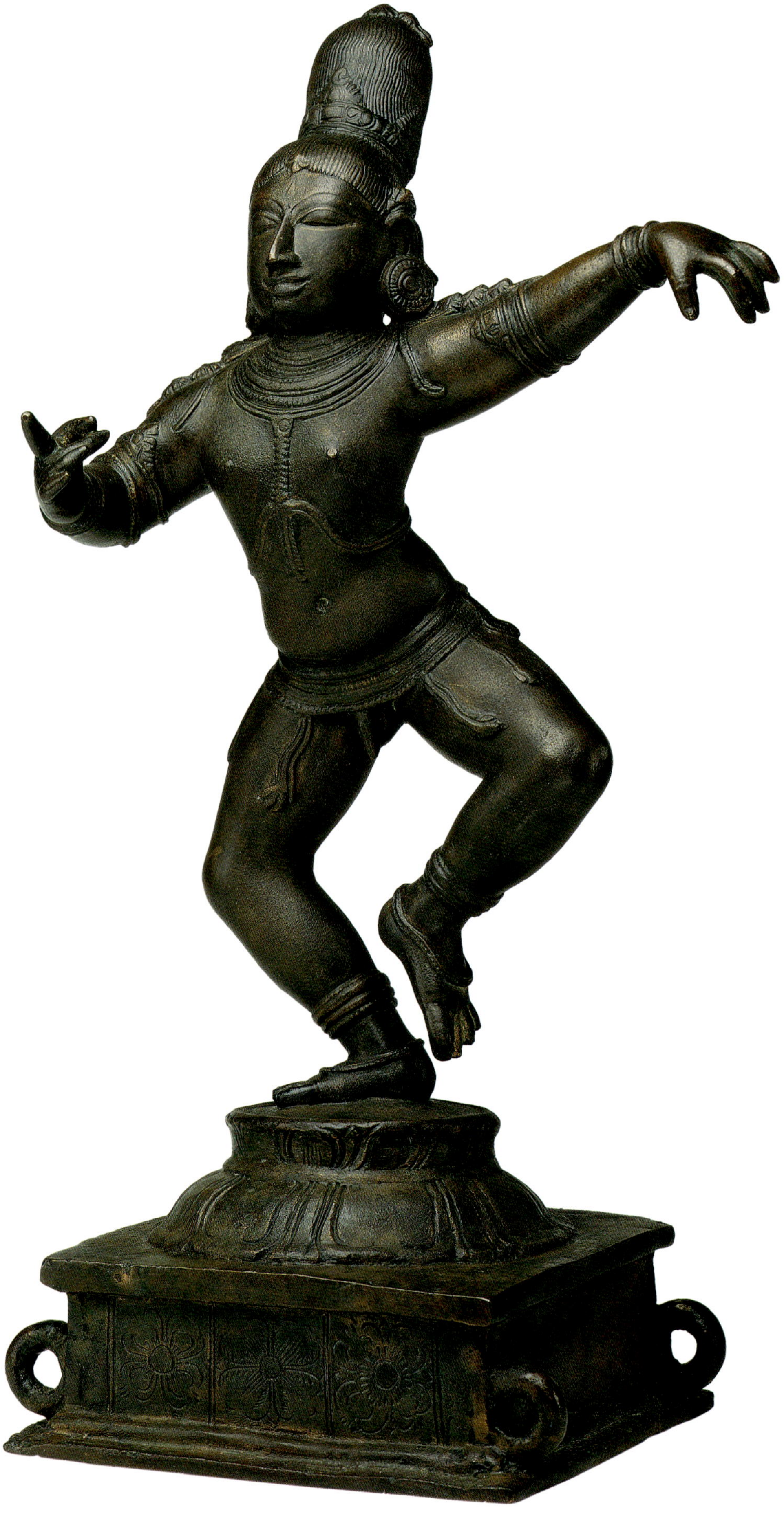

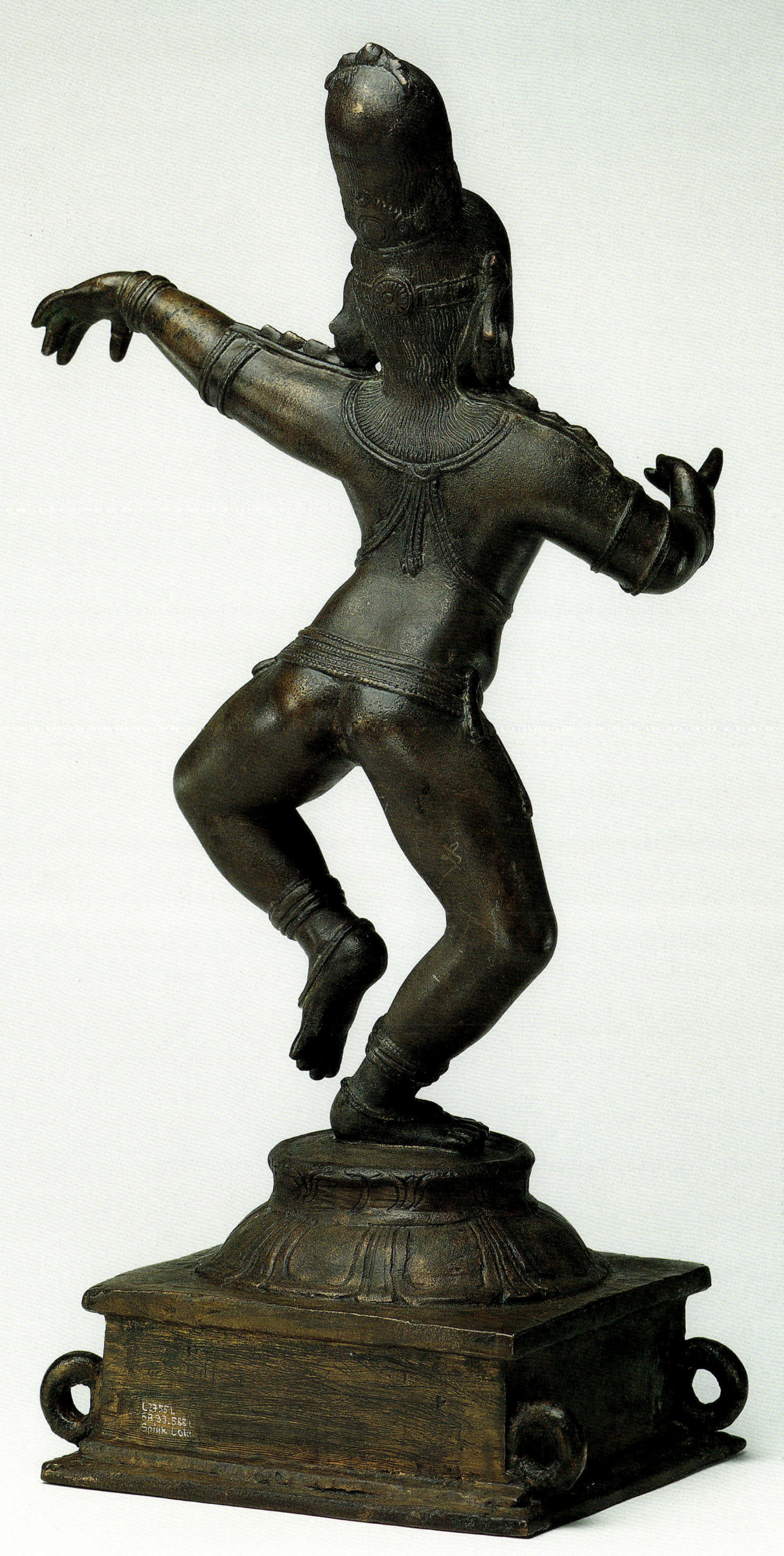

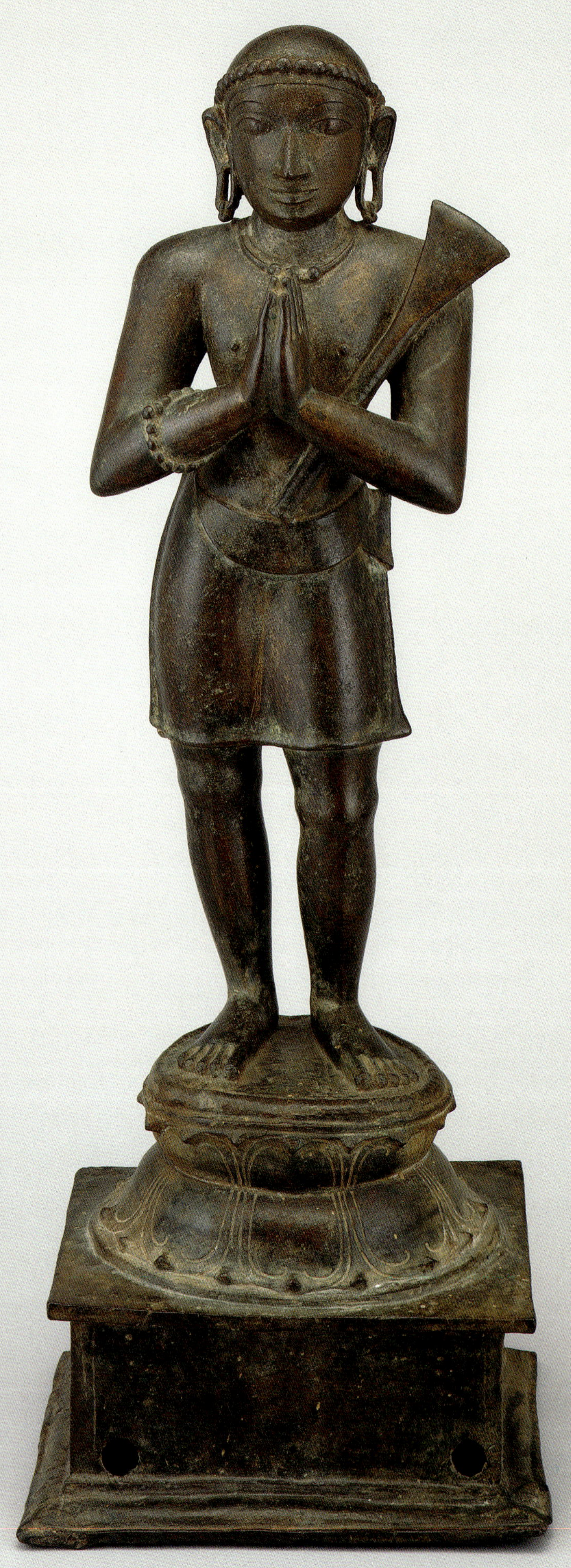

29 SAINT APPAR

CHOLA PERIOD, CA. 1200
BRONZE, $23^{3}/_{4}$ IN. (60.3 CM)
THE ART INSTITUTE OF CHICAGO;
BERTHA EVANS BROWN COLLECTION
(1970.552)

Appar was an elder contemporary of Sambandar, and his title of revered father *(appar)* was given to him by the child-saint. Converted from Jainism to the worship of Shiva, Appar approached Shiva as a humble servant, referring often in his songs to his erstwhile days as a Jain monk.

O god who pierced the delusion
that afflicted me
when I joined the Jains
and became a wicked monk!
O bright flame, celestial being
who stands as the pure path,
bull among immortals,
honey who dwells in Tiruvaiyaru!
I wander as your servant,
worshipping and singing your feet.[1]

Appar is invariably depicted as a standing figure with palms joined in adoration and holding the hoe in the crook of his arm. The hoe is the emblem that identifies him, and it stands for his ready performance of menial services in the temple, in particular clearing the weeds that sprang up within the temple premises. In early images, the hoe is part of the same casting as the figure; later on, it became customary to cast the hoe separately and place it in the crook of the arm. Appar is clothed simply in a short waist-cloth with a knotted band resting on his thigh. He wears a strand of *rudraksha* beads around his head, and a strand of the beads also serves as a bracelet. This bronze is somewhat later than an image from Jambavanodai, now in the Tanjavur Art Gallery.[2]

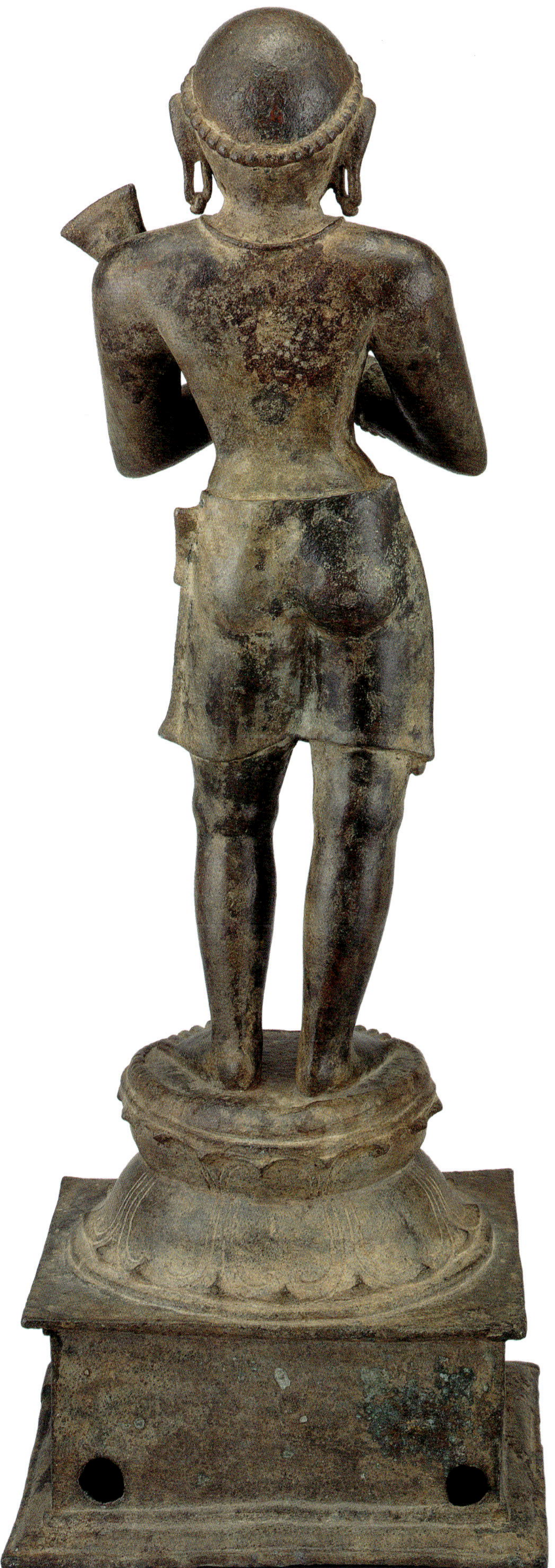

NOTES

1 Indira Viswanathan Peterson, *Poems to Siva: The Hymns of the Tamil Saints* (Princeton: Princeton University Press, 1989), p. 286: Appar 4.39.1.
2 Vidya Dehejia, *Slaves of the Lord: The Path of the Tamil Saints* (Delhi: Munshiram Manoharlal, 1988), fig. 8.

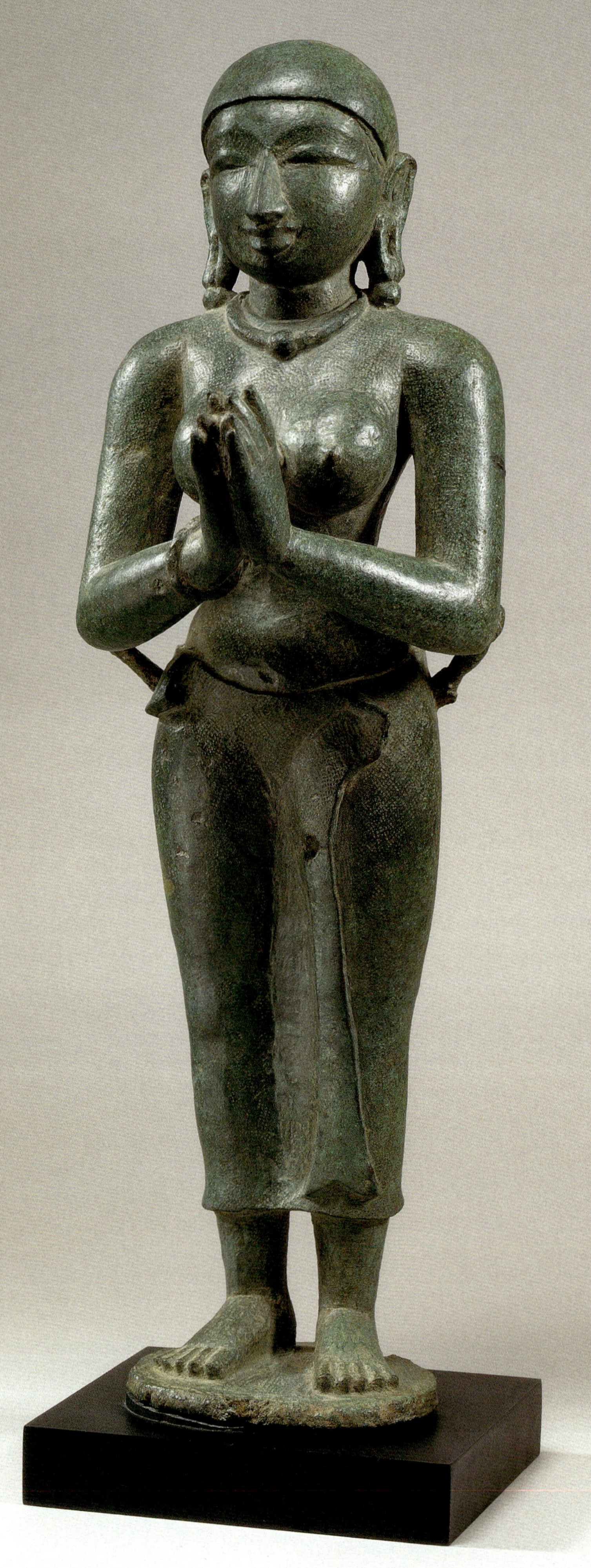

30 SHAIVA DEVOTEE (PERHAPS APPAR'S SISTER TILAKAVATI)

CHOLA PERIOD, CA. 980
BRONZE, 15 IN. (38.1 CM)
COLLECTION ZINA AND ERNEST STERN, NEW YORK

With a blissful expression on her face, which is topped by a shaven pate, this female devotee stands with palms joined in adoration, wearing a simple long skirt and the simplest of jewelry. She has no attributes to help identify her, and she does not seem to be one of the three women *nayanmars*, one of whom is a queen, another is emaciated, and the third is the mother of saint Sundarar. Yet, this figure appears to belong with such a group, and it seems possible that she is Tilakavati, sister of Appar, a devout Shaivite who played a major role in her brother's conversion from Jainism to the worship of Shiva. This evocative bronze appears to have been cast toward the end of the tenth century, around the year 980. The fact that the channels connecting the arms to the torso have not been cut away suggests that the image remained unfinished and may never have entered the ritual cycle.

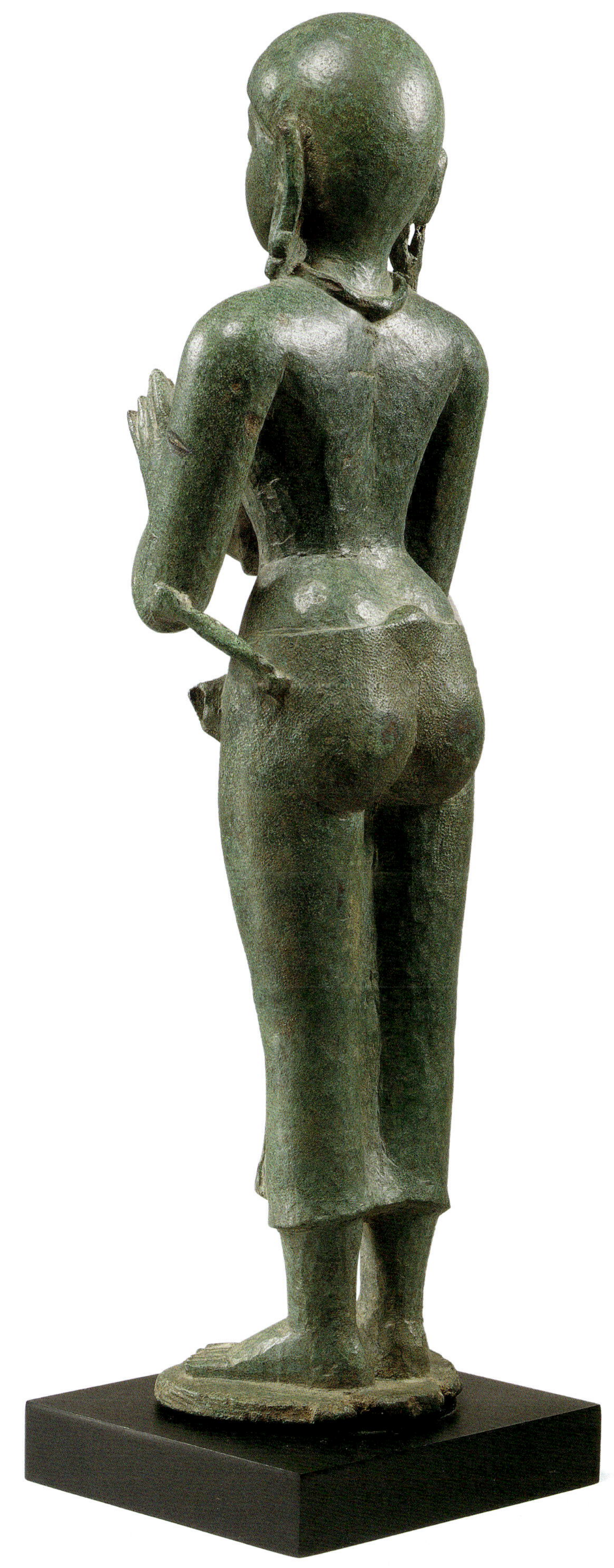

31 SAINT SUNDARAR
CHOLA PERIOD, CA. 1300
BRONZE, 20 IN. (50.8 CM)
ERIE ART MUSEUM; JAMES D. BALDWIN BEQUEST (1987.001.0168)

32 SAINT SUNDARAR
CHOLA PERIOD, CA. 1300
BRONZE, 31 1/2 IN. (80 CM)
CARNEGIE MUSEUM OF ART, PITTSBURGH; PURCHASE: GRETA S. HECKETT BEQUEST (77.73)

Saint Sundarar (handsome one) lived in the early years of the eighth century and acquired the epithets of "insolent devotee" and "the lord's friend" because of the familiar tone toward Shiva that he adopted in his songs. His mode ranges from gentle ridicule through impudence to almost abusive demand. The story of Sundarar's bondage to Shiva reads like a fairy tale. The youthful Sundarar, born of brahmin parents, stood decked as a bridegroom when an aged man intervened and stopped the wedding, claiming that Sundarar was his bonded slave. Sundarar responded by repeatedly calling him a madman, but when papers confirming his bondage were produced and validated by the village council, Sundarar had no choice but to follow his new master. The "madman" walked faster and faster, entered the sanctum of Vennai Nallur's temple, and vanished. As Sundarar stood transfixed, realizing the madman was none other than god Shiva, he heard a voice command him:

You are an insolent devotee. Worship me with song.
How shall I sing of you my Lord?
You called me madman many times. Let your first song start with that word.

And Sundarar obeyed, commencing his song thus:

Madman!
Crowned by the crescent moon,
great lord of mercy . . .[1]

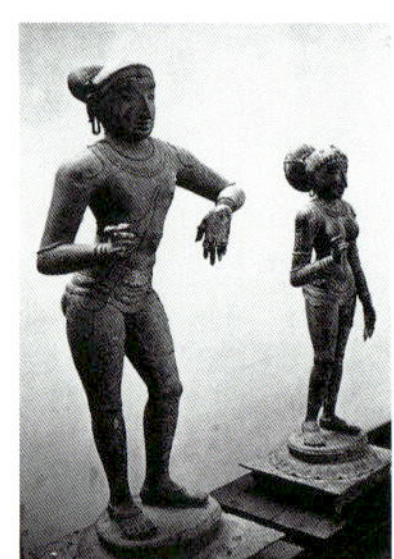

SUNDARAR AND WIFE PARAVAI, FROM TIRUVENKADU TEMPLE, CA. 1012. TANJAVUR ART GALLERY
PHOTO VIDYA DEHEJIA
FIG. 1

Sundarar is most frequently portrayed as the handsome bridegroom, with lotus flower in one hand and a staff in the other. In this mode, seen in the Erie Art Museum bronze (cat. no. 31), the image would have been one of the set of sixty-three *nayanmars*, or one of the smaller group of the *muvar* or *nalvar*. His hair coiffed in an elaborate knot, Sundarar wears large circular earrings, several necklaces, and a short waist-cloth held in place with a girdle and a large clasp. The image belongs around the year 1300.

The bronze from the Carnegie Museum of Art, also belonging to around 1300 (cat. no. 32), would have been part of a group depicting Sundarar with one hand raised to rest against the shoulder of his wife Paravai, as in the images from Tiruvenkadu of mid-eleventh-century date (fig. 1). Although claimed as a slave at his wedding ceremony, Sundarar later married the lovely dancing girl Paravai at Tiruvarur, and later still married a second wife, Shangili, at Tiruvottiyur. As he encountered problems with two wives, in one of his songs he addressed Shiva with familiarity as one who should understand his problems since he too married Uma but did not hesitate to dally with the river goddess Ganga on the side.[2]

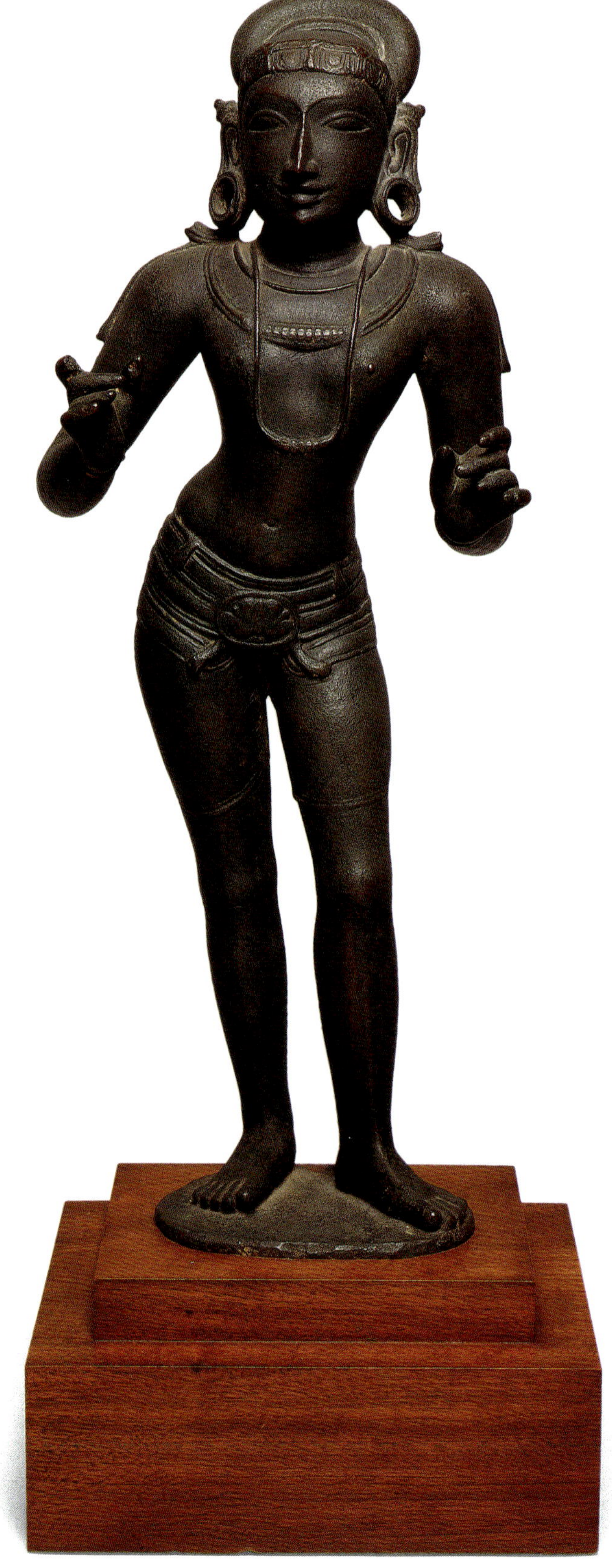

31

NOTES

1 David Dean Shulman, trans., *Songs of the Harsh Devotee: The Tevaram of Cuntaramurttinayanar* (Philadelphia: University of Pennsylvania Press, 1990), p. 1: 1.1.

2 Ibid., p. 132: 54.8.

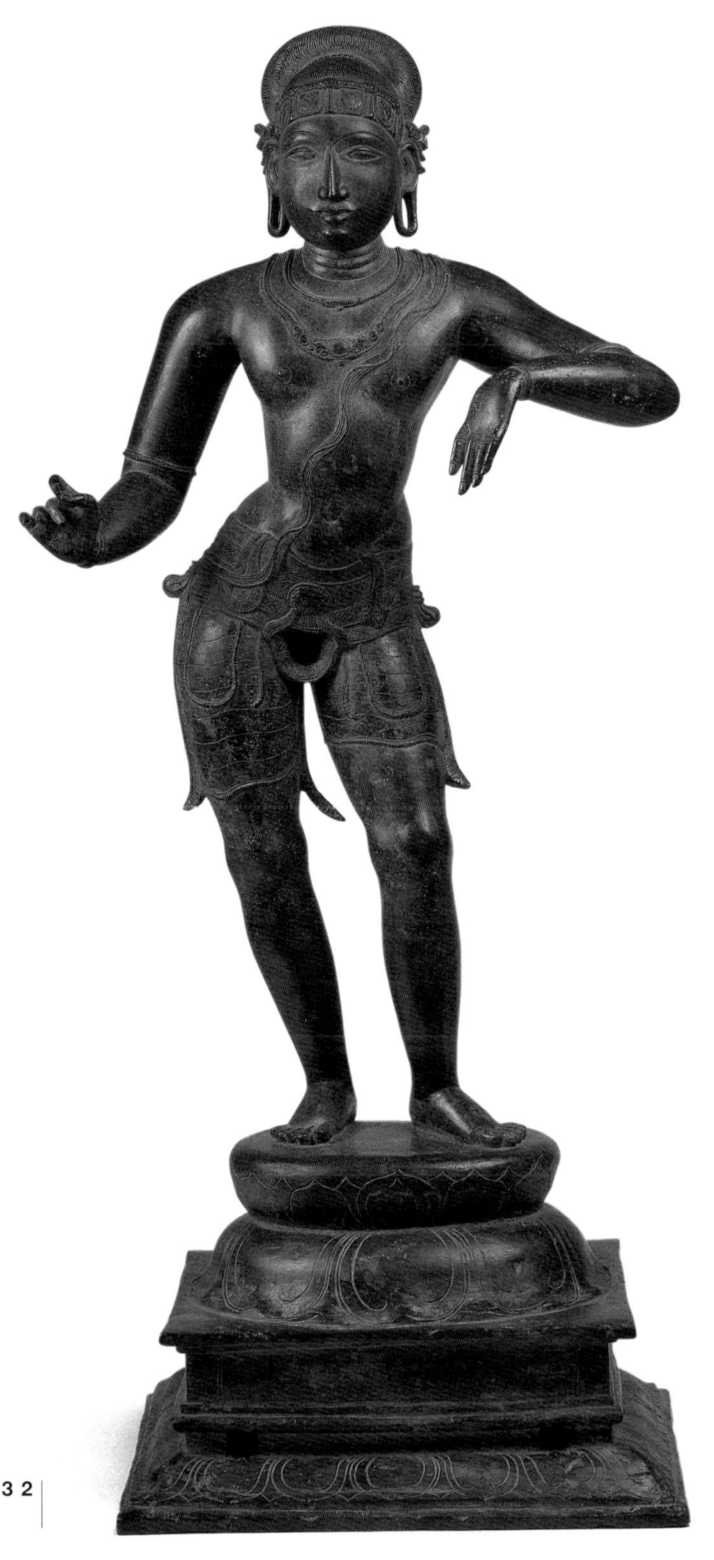

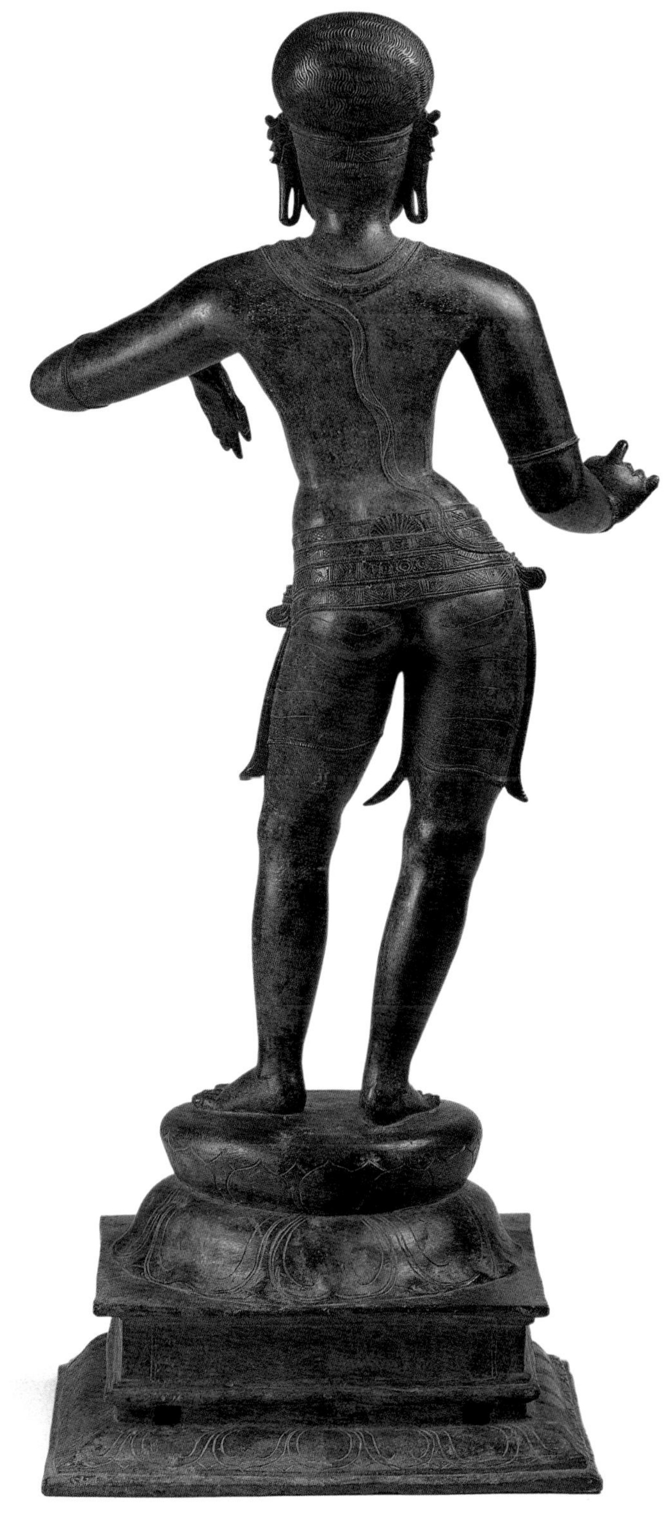

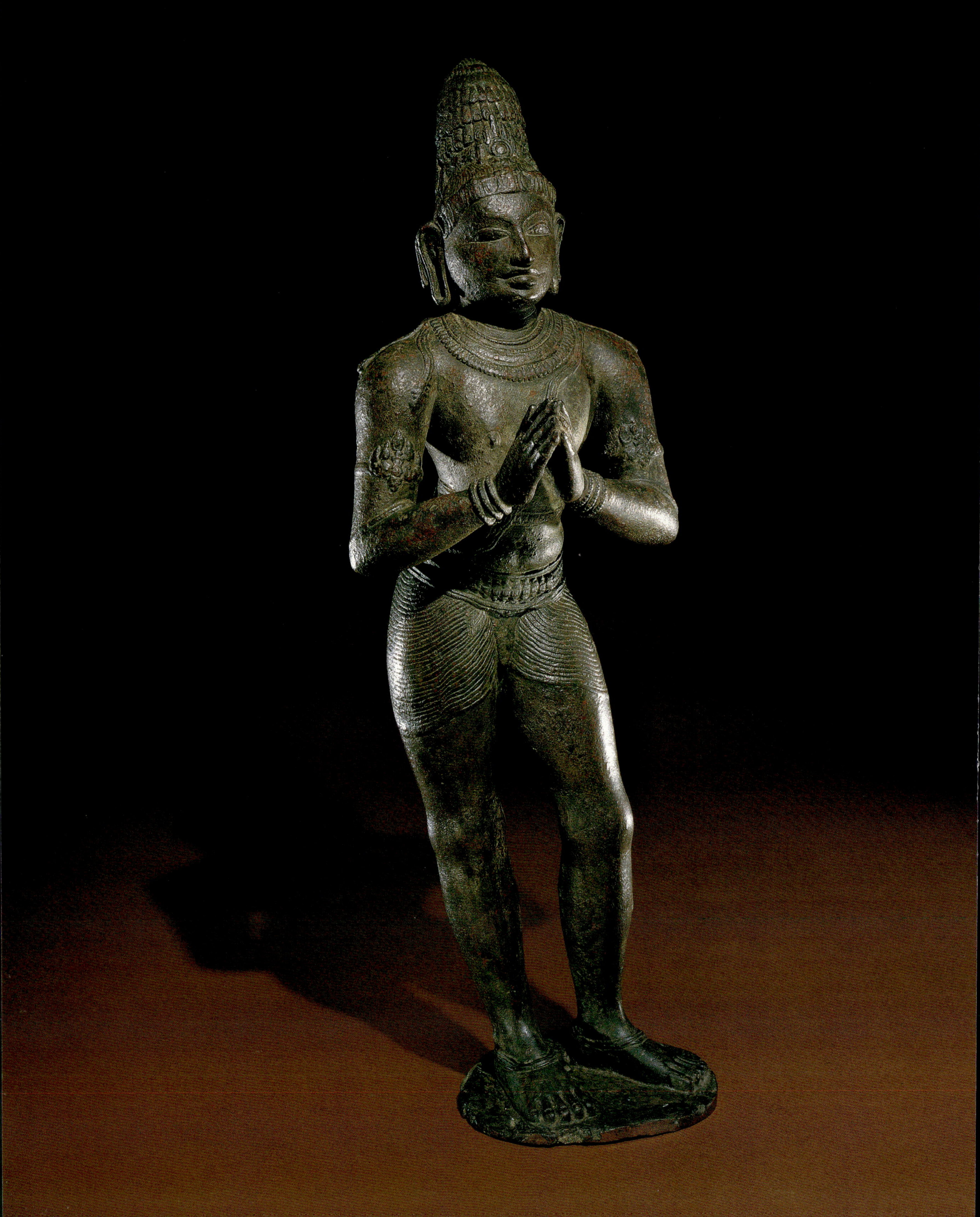

33 SAINT CHANDESHA
CHOLA PERIOD, CA. 970
BRONZE, 18 7/8 IN. (48 CM)
TRUSTEES OF THE BRITISH MUSEUM;
DONATED BY ETON COLLEGE, WINDSOR
(OA 1988.4-25.1)

34 SAINT CHANDESHA
CHOLA PERIOD, CA. 1100
BRONZE, 18 1/2 IN. (47 CM)
THE NELSON-ATKINS MUSEUM OF ART,
KANSAS CITY, MISSOURI; PURCHASE:
NELSON TRUST (50-19)

Chandesha, a cowherd saint who wrote no poetry, attained to sainthood through one single dramatic incident. Each day, as he tended his cows, the young lad Chandesha had used some of their milk for ritual lustration of a mud *linga* that he worshiped devoutly. Hearing complaints about the misuse of milk, Chandesha's father came out to investigate. The devout cowherd was so absorbed in his worship of Shiva that he remained unaware of his father's reproachful words. The enraged father kicked the mud *linga*, and Chandesha lashed out with his cowherd staff, which miraculously turned into Shiva's sacred ax, felling the father to the ground. Pleased by Chandesha's single-minded devotion, Shiva and Uma appeared to bless him with a divine garland.

This story seems to have left a deep imprint on Emperor Rajaraja Chola, who himself presented to the Tanjavur temple a seven-piece copper-alloy group commemorating the story. To portray its first phase, the group included a Shiva *linga* from which a hand emerged, a standing Chandesha, and the prostrate father. The culmination was indicated by a kneeling Chandesha, a four-armed Shiva with foot on Mushalagan accompanied by Uma, and the garland given as blessing. Unfortunately this group does not survive, and no similar one is known. The Chandesha legend is featured in stone on the outer walls of Rajendra Chola's temple at Gangaikondacholapuram. The niche itself carries a large, deeply cut relief of seated Shiva and Uma blessing Chandesha with a garland, while shallow relief vignettes on either side feature earlier episodes from the story (fig. 1).

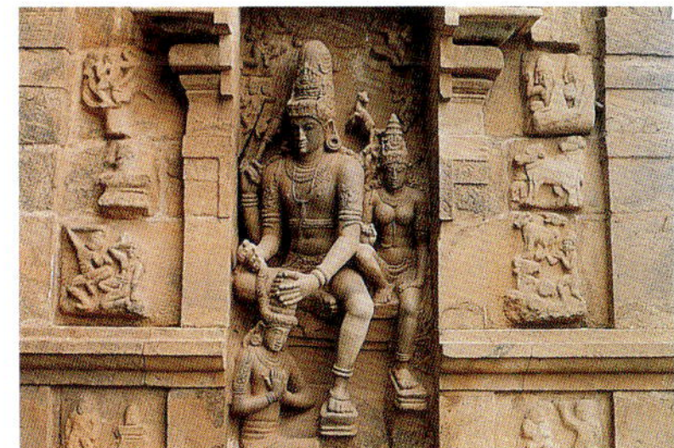

CHANDESHA LEGEND, CA. 1030,
GANGAIKONDACHOLAPURAM TEMPLE
PHOTO VIDYA DEHEJIA
FIG. 1

A surprisingly large number of bronze images of Chandesha exist, and the reason for this lies not in the character of the original story, but in the new role that he acquired during the Chola period as guardian and supervisor of Shiva temples. As Chola monarchs began to convert into impressive stone temples the early simple shrines that consisted only of sanctified *lingas*, often placed in the open under trees or enclosed in brick structures, a supervising agent was needed to ensure the sanctity of the shrine.

33

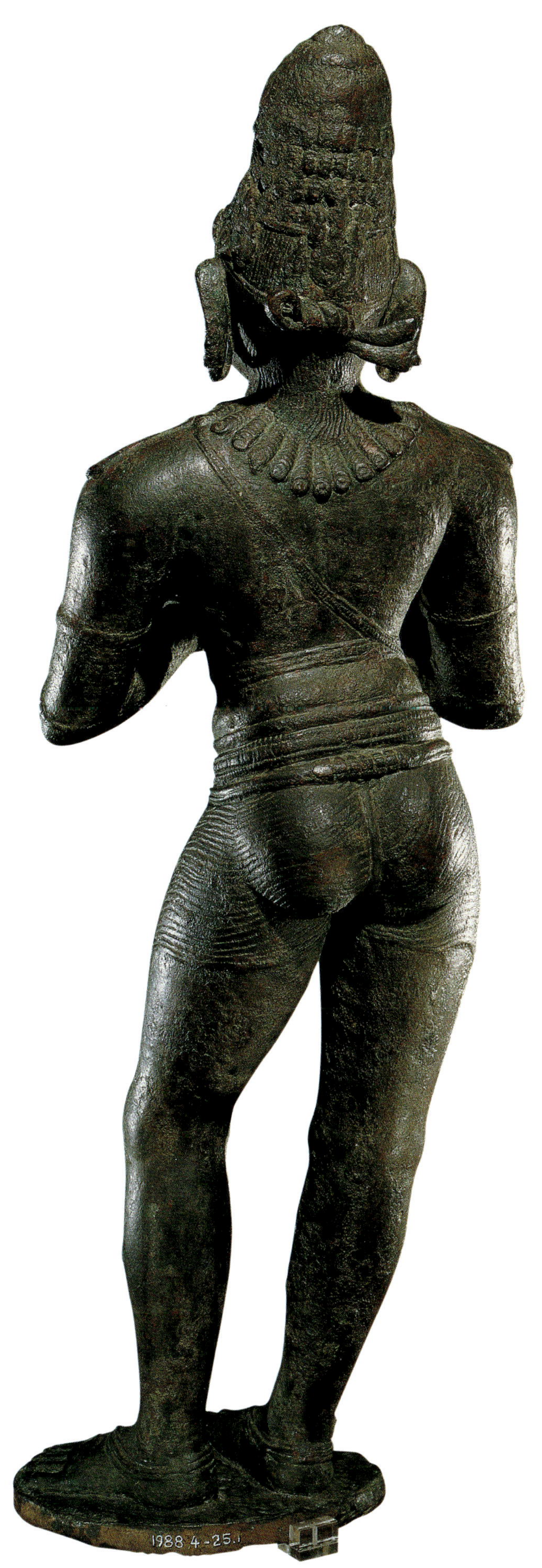

And who better than Chandesha, who had fiercely guarded the sanctity of a *linga* made of mud? A bronze image of Chandesha as divine supervisor was therefore placed in a shrine within the grounds of Shiva temples. To this day, Chandesha is regarded as the guardian of the temple and its possessions, and devotees stop by his shrine before leaving the temple grounds, clapping to show that their hands are empty and that they have not appropriated any temple property. Chandesha, also known as Chandeshvara, was further given the role of financial agent in whose name temple money was collected and dispensed. Several hundred temple inscriptions include references to this role, as does this one from the Tanjavur temple:

> We have received from Chandeshvara who is the first servant *(adi dasan)* of the Supreme Lord . . . 500 *kashu* out of the money that was deposited.[1]

Bronzes of Chandesha depict him standing with palms joined in adoration and carrying Shiva's battle-ax in the crook of his arm, with his hair piled high upon his head in imitation of Shiva's matted locks.

The Chandesha bronze from the British Museum (cat. no. 33) is a serene and elegant piece of the Sembiyan Mahadevi period that may be dated to around 970. The large knotted bow at the back of his head to secure the headband, and the concurrent omission of the *siraschakra* to conceal a utilitarian knot, recalls this feature seen in the Nataraja from Tiruvedikudi, now in the Asia Society collection (fig. 2), as also in a slender figure of Tripuravijaya from Velankanni.[2] In a manner that parallels the practice seen with images of Appar, in early images of Chandesha the battle-ax was cast separately and placed in the crook of the arm (missing in this instance), while later the ax was cast as an integral part of the sculptured figure.

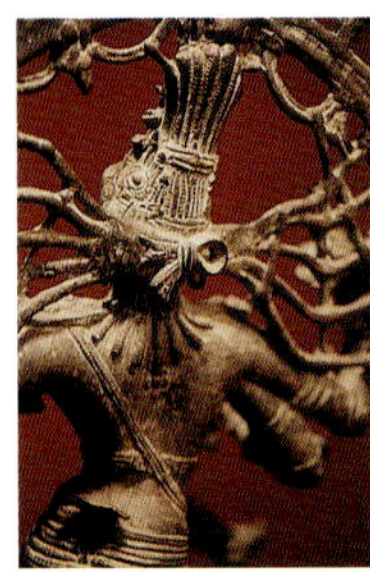

REAR VIEW OF SHIVA NATARAJA FROM TIRUVEDIKUDI, CA. 970. ASIA SOCIETY, NEW YORK; MR. AND MRS. JOHN D. ROCKEFELLER 3RD COLLECTION (1979.20)
PHOTO VIDYA DEHEJIA
FIG. 2

The exceedingly slender Nelson-Atkins Chandesha wears a patterned short waist-cloth held in place by a girdle with a large lion-head clasp and long pleated folds on both sides. Large circular earrings, elaborate armlets, bangles, anklets, two necklaces, a waistband, and a sacred thread complete his adornment. Prongs on the lotus pedestal indicate that the figure was enclosed by a *prabha*. The Nelson-Atkins Chandesha is a fine casting of around 1100.

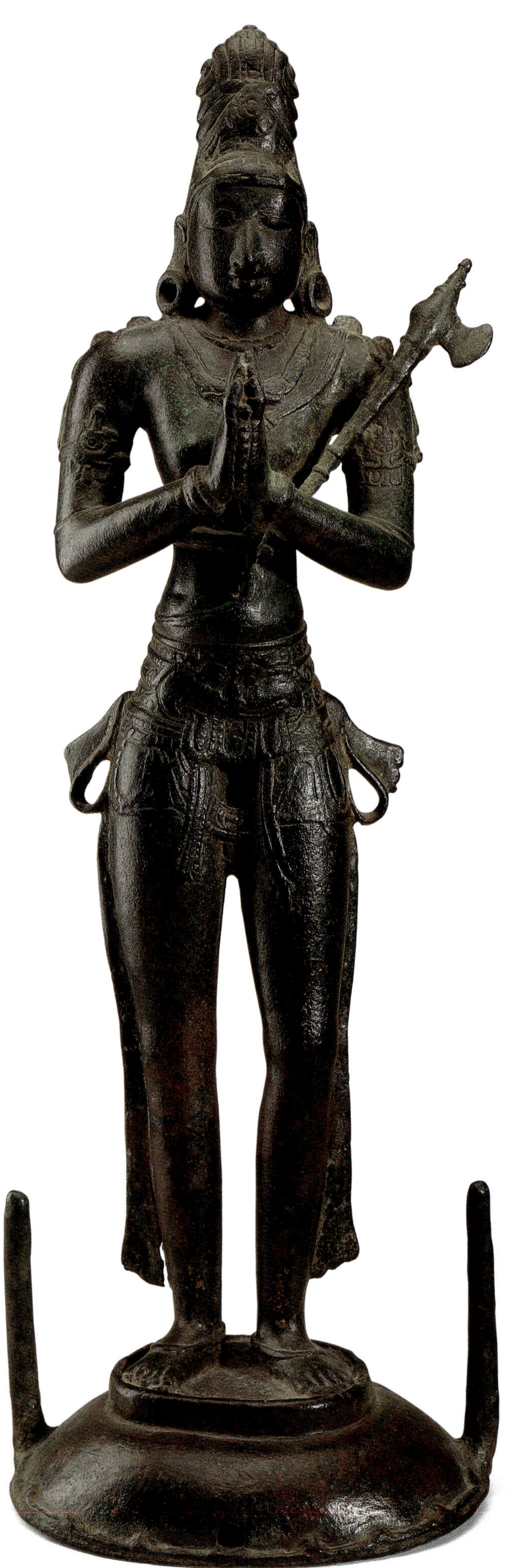

NOTES

1 E. Hultzsch, ed., *South Indian Inscriptions,* vol. 2 (New Delhi: Archaeological Survey of India, 1992 reprint), part 1, no. 19, p. 105.

2 Douglas Barrett, *Early Cola Bronzes* (Bombay: Bhulabhai Memorial Institute, 1965), pl. 68.

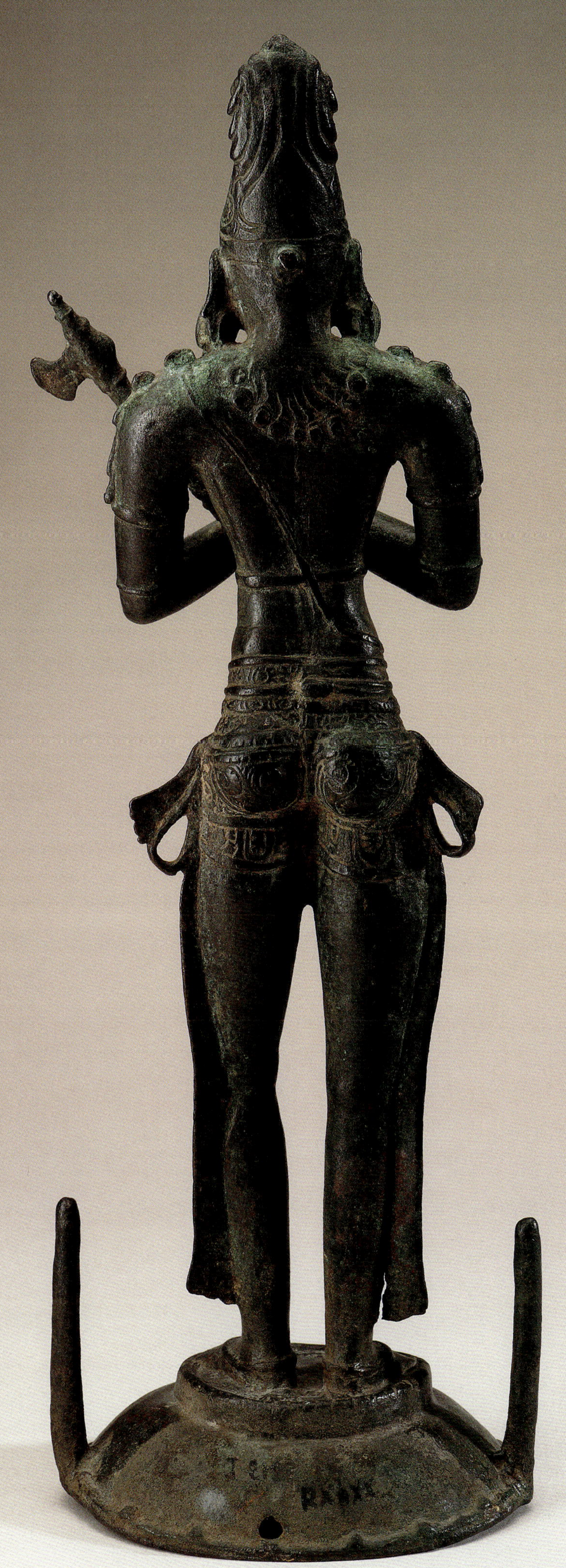

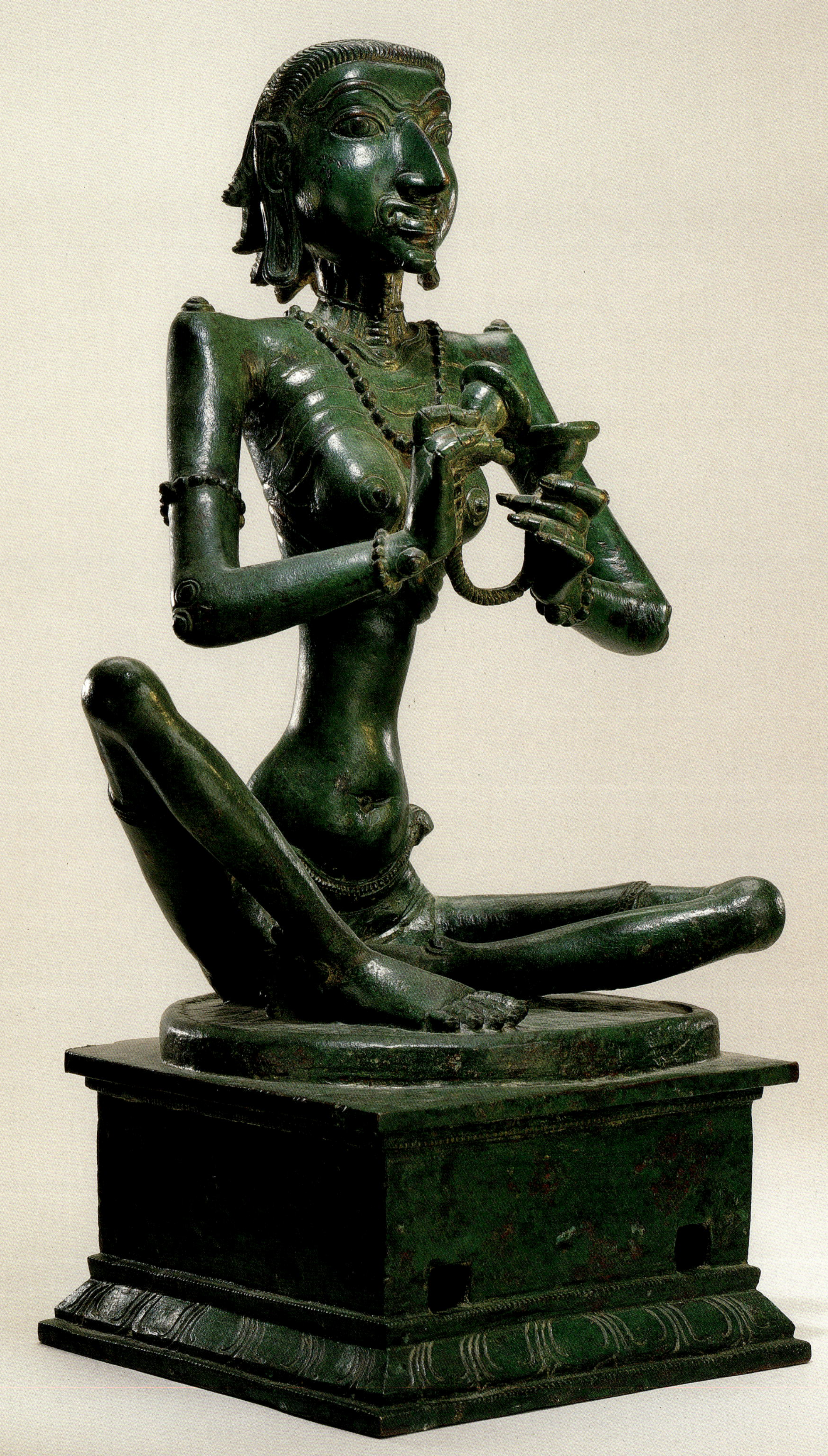

35 SAINT KARAIKKAL AMMAIYAR, MOTHER OF KARAIKKAL

CHOLA PERIOD, CA. 1050
BRONZE, 14 3/8 IN. (36.4 CM)
THE NELSON-ATKINS MUSEUM OF ART, KANSAS CITY, MISSOURI; PURCHASE: NELSON TRUST (33-533)

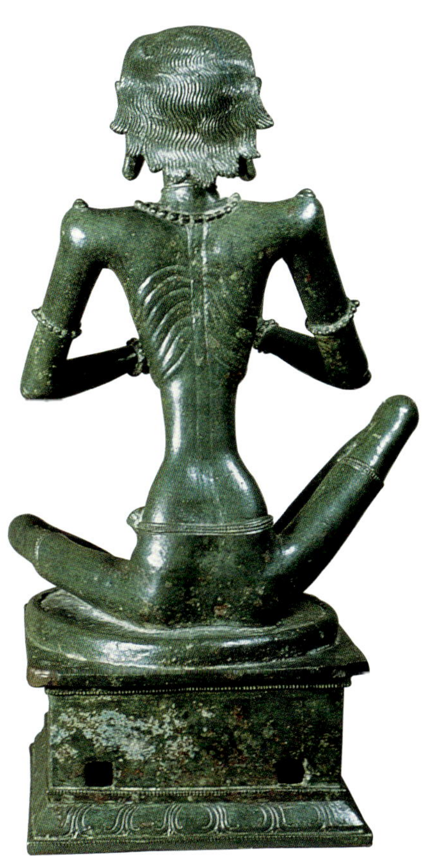

A woman named Punitavati was married to one Paramadatta, a trader in the coastal town of Karaikkal, and they lived a life of harmony, worshiping Shiva with devotion. One day Paramadatta sent home two mangoes, requesting that they be served with his lunch; his wife, however, gave one away to a sage who appeared on her doorstep asking for food. At lunchtime, Paramadatta ate the first mango, found it delicious and asked for the second. Instinctively Punitavati thought of Shiva and a mango appeared in her hand. Paramadatta realized it was not the one he had sent home and asked her where she got it. Disbelievingly, he reached out for the mango, but it disappeared. Much perturbed by this demonstration of her powers, Paramadatta left home. When tracked down several years later, he returned only to fall at Punitavati's feet and proclaim that all should worship her. Punitavati now appealed to Shiva to release her from the burden of her flesh and asked only that she be able to worship his dancing feet forever. A miracle occurred, and in place of the beautiful young Punitavati stood an emaciated ghoul who became known as Mother of Karaikkal.

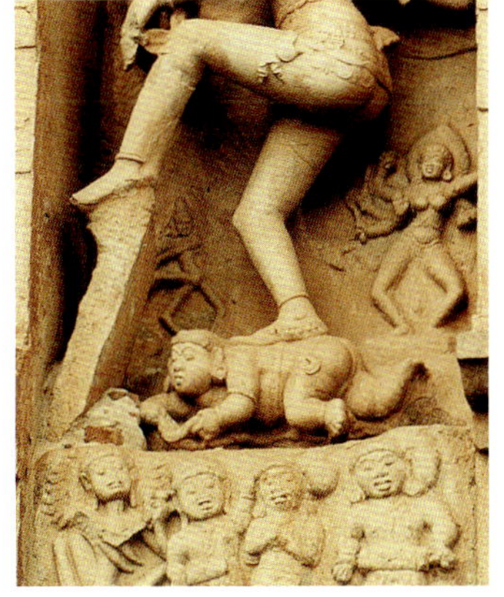

STONE RELIEF OF KARAIKKAL AMMAIYAR AT THE FOOT OF DANCING SHIVA, CA. 1030, GANGAIKONDACHOLAPURAM TEMPLE
PHOTO VIDYA DEHEJIA
FIG. 1

Karaikkal Ammaiyar sang about dancing Shiva, but she invariably visualized him dancing in fearsome surroundings inhabited by half-burnt corpses, jackals, vultures, owls, and emaciated female ghouls much like herself.

> ***Is the corpse really dead?***
> ***A ghoul creeps up***
> ***pointing with her finger***
> ***she shouts, she wails***
> ***she throws at it a burning ember—***
> ***In the grip of a terrible fright***
> ***she taps loudly her hollow stomach***
> ***Several other ghouls***
> ***disperse in fear—***
> ***There, in the garb of a madman***
> ***he dances, our Lord of dance.***[1]

Perhaps the bizarre nature of her poetry, revealing her fascination with the incongruous, fearsome, and grotesque, influenced the artist's portrayal of the emaciated saint in the Nelson-Atkins bronze. He has given her knobbly shoulders, chin, and elbows, fangs in the mouth, fearsomely curved eyebrows, wide-open eyes, and prominent vertebrae and ribs. It is almost as if he knew the signature verse of the song quoted above, and set out to reproduce the image she conjures of herself as:

> ***the ghoul of Karaikkal***
> ***who wanders in the forest***
> ***with incandescent teeth and mouth.***[2]

This powerful bronze of Karaikkal Ammaiyar appears to be the product of the eleventh century, dating perhaps to around 1050. She may be compared with the stone relief image on the exterior wall of the Gangaikondacholapuram temple, where, with stick-like limbs, pointed swinging breasts, and hair in disarray around her head, she squats at the feet of dancing Shiva, holding cymbals in her hands (fig. 1). The images are similar in their exaggerated treatment of bodily form, knobbly knees and shoulders, and in the fearsome face with fangs in the mouth.

NOTES

1 Vidya Dehejia, *Slaves of the Lord: The Path of the Tamil Saints* (Delhi: Munshiram Manoharlal, 1988), p. 131; Karaikkal Ammaiyar, "Tiruvalankadu Tirupadikam," v. 4.
2 Ibid., pp. 131–32; v. 11.

36 SAINT MANIKKAVACHAKAR

CHOLA PERIOD, CA. 1200
BRONZE, 28 IN. (71.1 CM)
COLLECTION DORIS WIENER, NEW YORK

Manikkavachakar, minister to Varaguna Pandya of Madurai, lived during the second half of the ninth century. En route to the west coast to purchase horses for the Pandyan cavalry, Manikkavachakar encountered Shiva in the guise of a teacher, and used the money instead to build a great temple to Shiva. Recalled by the king, Manikkavachakar returned to Madurai and was imprisoned twice; each time Shiva intervened and had him released. Finally the saint was permitted to leave and join his teacher and his many followers. Manikkavachakar wrote a large corpus of poems that comprise the eighth book of the Tamil sacred canon; some take up the mode of popular songs and adapt them to the glory of Shiva, while others reveal a philosophical bent. Here is a popular question-and-answer song adapted to the glory of Shiva.

Tell me friend
what strange man is this?
his form is smeared with ashes white
a serpent rears upon his hand
in cryptic speech he seems well versed
what manner of man is he?

Why look at his ashes
or fear his serpent
or heed his elusive Vedic talk?
he is the essence
the god of all
that lives and moves.[1]

Temples frequently possess two images of Manikkavachakar, one placed before the image of dancing Shiva, and the second taking its place in the grouping of the Revered Four. Wearing a brief loincloth tied in a simple knot that rests against his right thigh, this bronze of Manikkavachakar portrays him standing in simple elegance, with nothing more than a sacred thread as adornment. A single row of curls frames his forehead, and a double row is evident at the nape of his neck. In his hand he holds the manuscript that is his signature attribute, inscribed with the words *om nama Shivaya,* or praise be to Shiva. The bronze is a study in restraint and understatement, allowing the smooth lines of the form to speak for themselves; it is a masterpiece of late Chola art that belongs around the year 1200. Further confirmation of such a date comes from the paleography of the inscription's Grantha script, which may be assigned to the start of the thirteenth century.[2]

NOTES

1 Vidya Dehejia, *Slaves of the Lord: The Path of the Tamil Saints* (Delhi: Munishiram Manoharlal, 1988), p. 6: Tiruvachakam, "Tiru Calal," 12.1.
2 Personal communication from R. Nagaswamy.

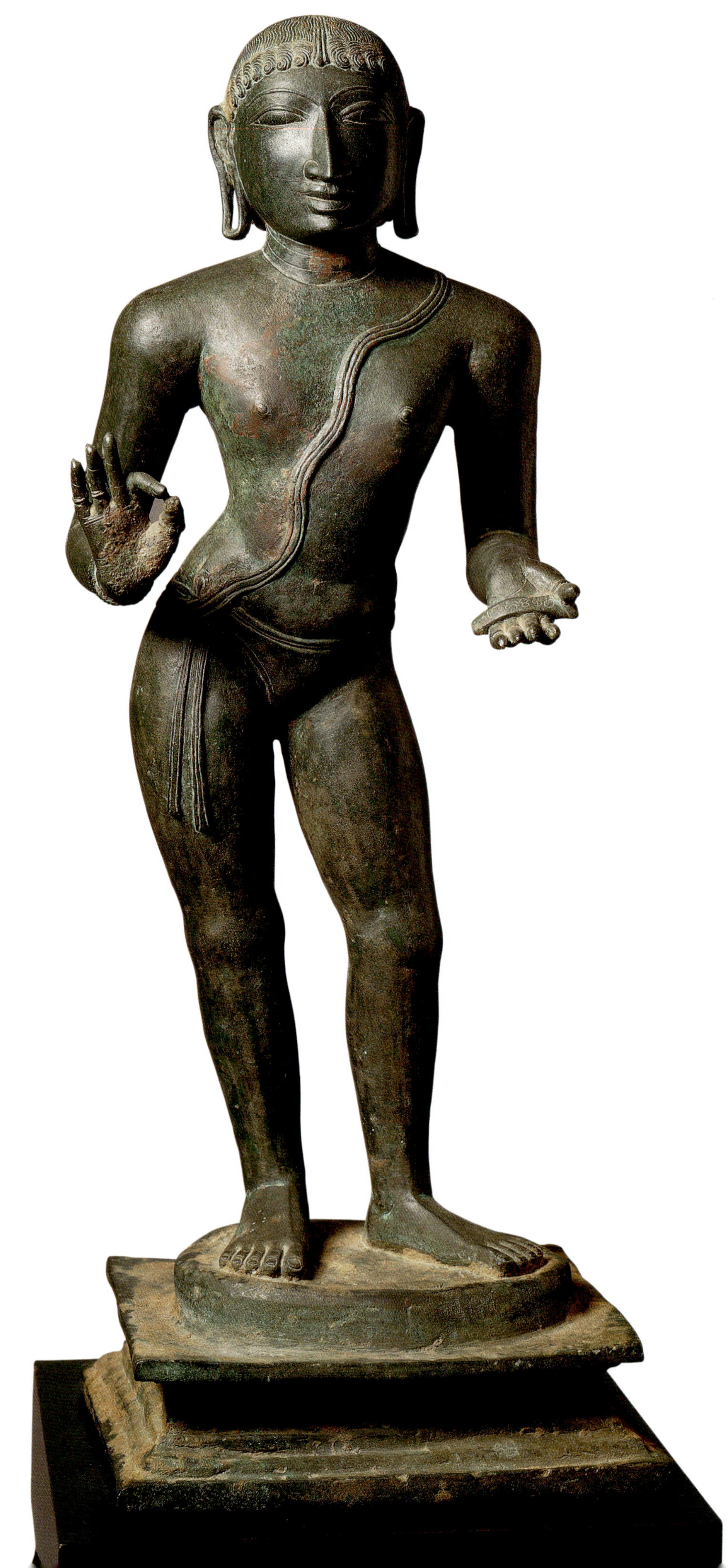

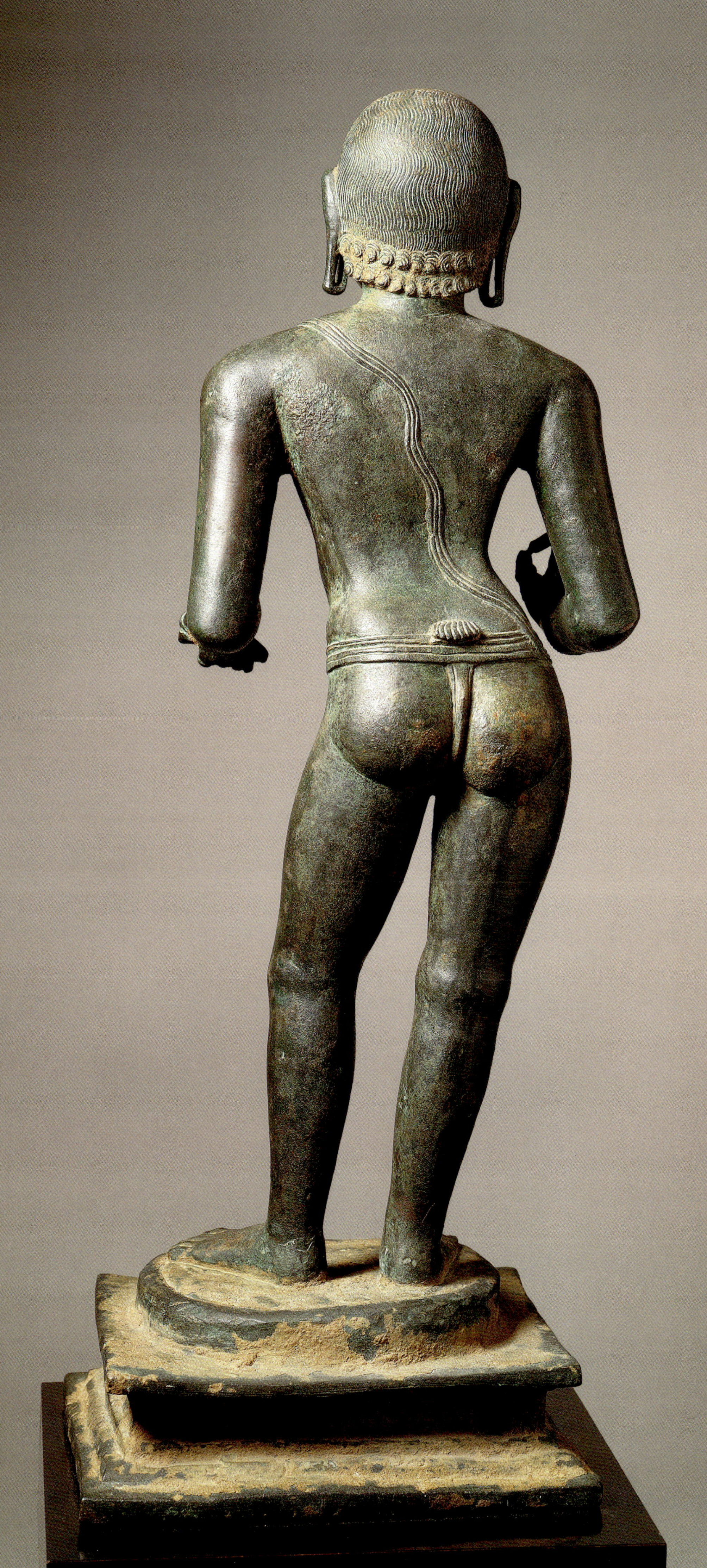

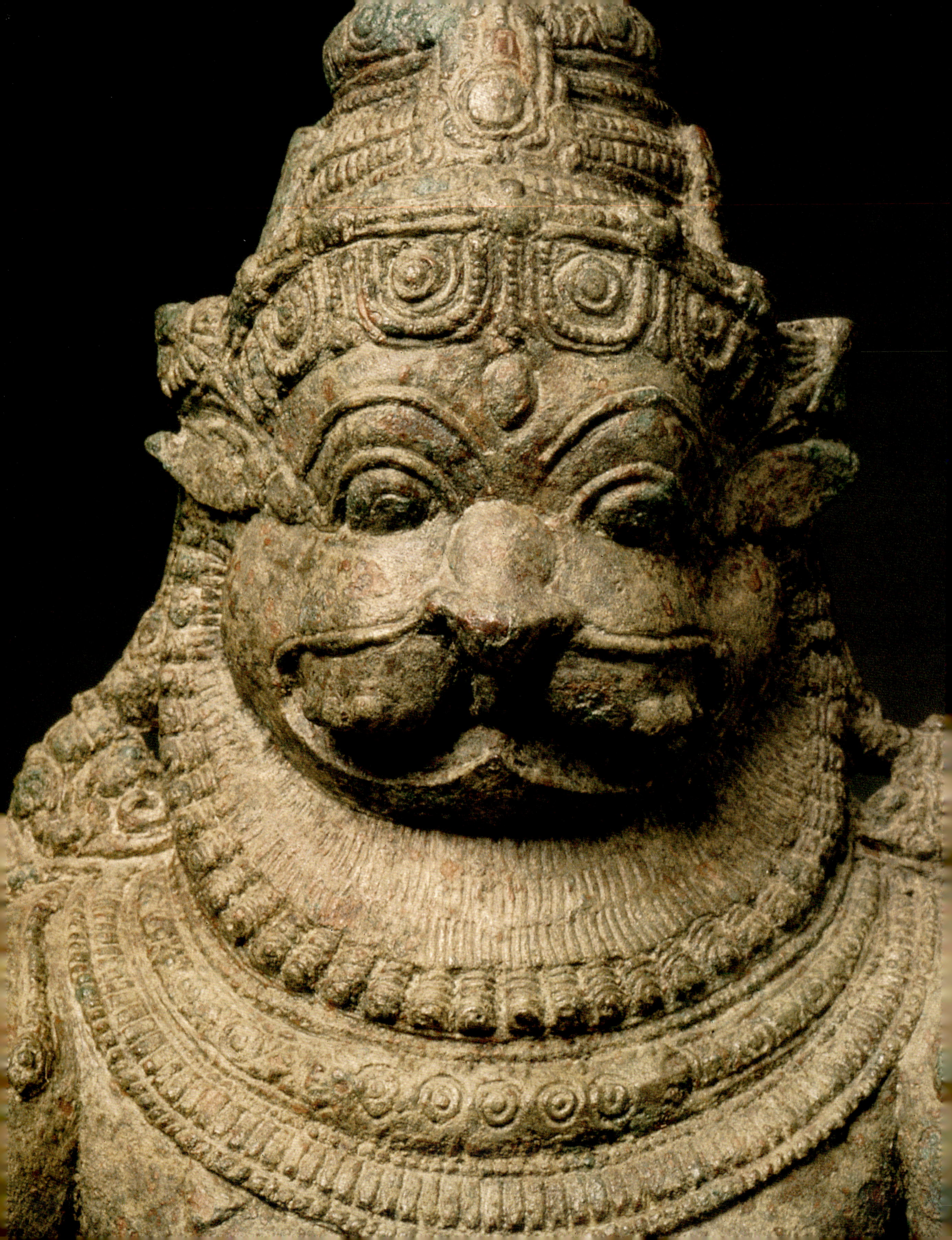

VISHNU—HIS TEMPLES, HIS IMAGES

The Shrivaishnavas of Tamil Nadu believe that Vishnu manifests in five different ways, of which the first, his supreme form *(para)*, is seen only in heaven. The second, represented in temples by the image of reclining Vishnu, comprises his emanations *(vyuha)* of Samkarshana, Pradyumna, and Aniruddha, which preside over the functions of creation, preservation, and dissolution. The third consists of his ten incarnations or avatars; the fourth is his subtle form that resides in the heart *(antaryamin)*; and last is the worshiped image *(archa)*.[1]

Although Shiva also occasionally manifested on earth, a doctrine of avatars is attached to the form of Vishnu alone. The accepted ten are Matsya (fish), Kurma (tortoise), Varaha (boar), Narasimha (man-lion), Vamana (dwarf), Parashurama, Rama, Krishna, the Buddha, and Kalki (the avatar yet to come). Certain versions omit the Buddha and include instead Krishna's half-brother Balarama. The earliest clear statement of the doctrine of avatar is contained in the *Bhagavad Gita*, a late addition to the *Mahabharata* epic that was composed between 400 B.C.E. and C.E. 400. Its fourth chapter contains two verses that admit the paradox that the lord is unborn and unchanging, yet enters into the world of becoming and is born through his own wondrous power. The reason for such a birth is the lessening of *dharma* (righteousness) and the increase of *adharma* (unrighteousness).

Whenever sacred duty decays
and chaos prevails,
then, I create
myself, Arjuna.

To protect men of virtue
and destroy men who do evil,
to set the standard of sacred duty
I appear in age after age.[2]

During the Chola period, it would appear that the avatars sculptured most often in bronze were those of Rama, Krishna, the man-lion Narasimha, and the giant boar Varaha.[3] It was only after Chola times that the entire series of incarnations, as bronze images, entered the ritual cycle.

Shrivaishnava theology assigns a very special position to Vishnu's fifth manifestation in the form of the image; it is considered to be Vishnu's "permanent descent into the world in the form of an image which can be worshipped."[4] The image, or *archa,* is viewed as "an actual and real manifestation of the deity," as "wholly and completely God, though it does not exhaust his essence."[5] Whether an *archa* is immovable, as is the sanctum image, or movable, as in the case of bronze festival images (and the *shalagrama* stone), it is the means by which Vishnu makes himself accessible to humanity. The image, in the context of Shrivaishnava worship in Tamil Nadu, "is a personal god, luminous, and complete with all auspicious qualities; it is transcendent and supreme, yet easily accessible—a bit of heaven on earth."[6]

It will be apparent that the Shrivaishnava view of the image as an actual manifestation of Vishnu is very different from the Shaiva Siddhanta view of the image as a mere physical support for Shiva's specially invoked, and temporary, presence. And yet, it may well be that those assembled to view a temple ritual will be struck by the similarities, and not differences, between the Vaishnava and Shaiva

YOGA NARASIMHA, VISHNU IN HIS MAN-LION AVATAR (DETAIL OF CAT. NO. 45)

approach to the image. After all, for the course of the ritual, Shiva takes up residence in the image which is therefore honored in like manner to the Vishnu image. Only those who view the treatment of the images of Shiva and Vishnu in their respective temples once worship is complete will realize that the philosophy behind the divinity or otherwise of the image is, in fact, different.

The sanctum of a Vishnu temple invariably enshrines an anthropomorphic image of the god, which is either reclining, standing, or seated. A certain number of temples of the Pallava (ca. 550–850) and Chola periods are constructed so as to have three sanctums, one above the other, in order to enshrine all three images and thereby harness their power.[7] Vishnu's two most important attributes are the conch shell *(shankha)* and the discus *(chakra)*, which he holds in two of his hands (cat. no. 38). A verse about a young girl intoxicated by her love of Vishnu unquestionably associates these attributes with him:

Night and day, her eyes know no sleep.
She splashes her tears with her hands.
O conch, O wheel, she cries and folds her hands
O Lotus Eyes, she cries
and grows faint.[8]

Woman saint Andal addressed an entire hymn to the shell that was fortunate enough to make its home in Vishnu's palm and to taste the nectar of his lips when he blew the conch.

O king of conches,
as the swan imbibes
the honey of the fresh pink lotus,
you climbed
into the beauteous hand of Vasudeva,
dark lord of glowing eyes,
you imbibe the nectar of his lips.
Great indeed is your glory[9]

Another attribute of Vishnu is a mark on the proper right side of his chest known as a *shrivatsa,* which is sometimes depicted as a rhomboidal anthropomorph, and at other times as a simple triangle. Specially associated with him is the sacred basil or *tulasi* leaf that is grown in all Vaishnava temples and always woven into the flower garlands offered to Vishnu.

Contrasting with the practice in Shiva temples, it is customary for the festival bronzes of a Vishnu temple to be placed within the sanctum itself, at the feet of the Vishnu image. Only rarely, as in the Vishnu temple at Tirucherai, do some of these bronze images reside in a separate chamber.

VISHNU (DETAIL OF CAT. NO. 38)

NOTES

1 For a detailed discussion of the views presented here all too briefly, see Vasudha Narayanan, "Arcavatara: On Earth as He Is in Heaven," in Joanne Punzo Waghorne and Norman Cutler, *Gods of Flesh, Gods of Stone: The Embodiment of Divinity in India* (Chambersburg, Pa.: Anima, 1985), p. 54.

2 Barbara Stoler Miller, trans., *The Bhagavad-Gita: Krishna's Counsel in Time of War* (New York: Bantam, 1986), p. 49.

3 A single stunning bronze of Trivikrama, part of the fifth incarnation as a dwarf, is enshrined in a temple at Singanallur. See R. Nagaswamy, "Trivikrama: Singanallur, Coimbatore District," *Lalit Kala* 25 (1990): 25, fig. 1.

4 Narayanan, "Arcavatara," p. 54.

5 Ibid.

6 Ibid., p. 62.

7 This is a simplistic way of stating a complex doctrine, explicated fully Dennis Hudson's forthcoming and eagerly awaited book on these temples *The Body of God: Text, Image, and Liturgy in the Vaikuntha Perumal Temple at Kancipuram* (Oxford University Press).

8 Vasudha Narayanan, *The Vernacular Veda: Revelation, Recitation, and Ritual* (Columbia: University of South Carolina Press, 1994), pp. 173–74: Nammalvar 7.2.1.

9 Vidya Dehejia, *Antal and Her Path of Love: Poems of a Woman Saint from South India* (Albany: State University of New York Press, 1990), p. 100: *Nachiyar Tirumoli* 7.7.

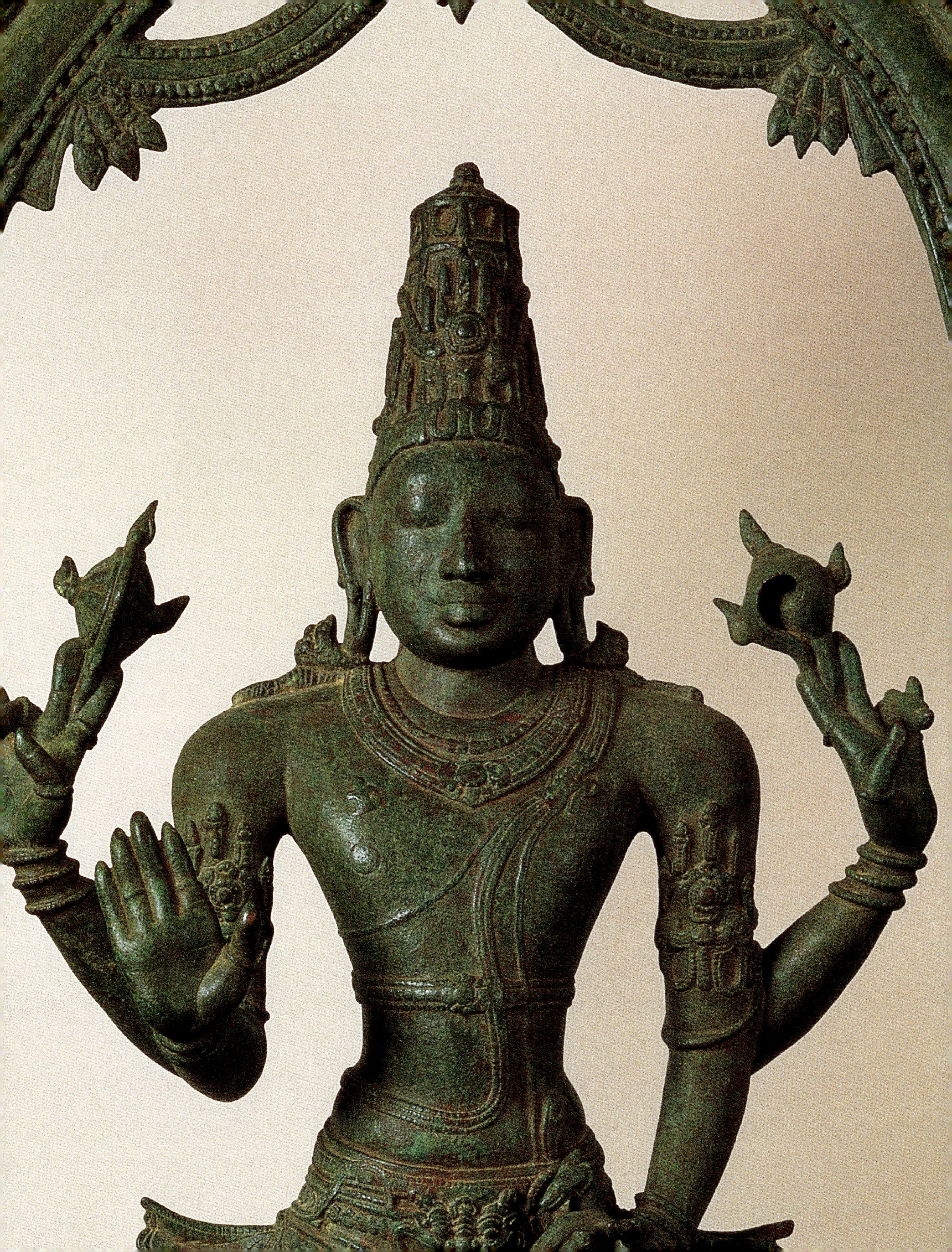

37 **VISHNU**
PALLAVA-CHOLA TRANSITION PERIOD, CA. 850
BRONZE, 14 3/8 IN. (36.5 CM)
PRIVATE COLLECTION

38 **VISHNU**
CHOLA PERIOD, CA. 925
BRONZE, 38 1/8 IN. (97 CM)
PRIVATE COLLECTION

39 **VISHNU**
CHOLA PERIOD, CA. 925; KONGU-NADU
BRONZE, 13 3/4 IN. (35 CM)
TRUSTEES OF THE BRITISH MUSEUM; BROOKE SEWELL PERMANENT FUND (1967.12-15.1)

40 **VISHNU**
CHOLA PERIOD, CA. 975; KONGU-NADU
BRONZE, 26 3/8 IN. (67 CM)
VICTORIA & ALBERT MUSEUM (IM 127-1927)

41 **VISHNU**
CHOLA PERIOD, CA. 990-1000
BRONZE, 25 1/2 IN. (64.7 CM)
VIRGINIA MUSEUM OF FINE ARTS, RICHMOND; THE ADOLPH D. AND WILKINS C. WILLIAMS FUND (98.37)

Eyes like the red lotus, lips like the luscious red fruit,
Lord with four shoulders, my ambrosia, my life!
Lord of Sacred Venkata where the glowing gems
negate darkness and make night seem day!
O my Lord, my Lord, I am your servant,
cannot for a second move away from your feet.[1]

Thus did the ninth-century Vaishnava saint Nammalvar sing of the beauty and glory of Vishnu at Venkata (modern Tirupati), to this day a sacred site of Vishnu.

A second ninth-century saint, Kulashekhara, sang that his desire to see Vishnu at Venkata was so great that he would chose to be any manner of inanimate object at that sacred site just as long as it gave him the chance to gaze at the magnificence of Vishnu.

Would that I could stand
as a champak tree
in holy Venkatam
where humming bees
sing their melodies
that I may forever see
the lotus feet of the Lord . . .

O Lord, O Venkata
Would that I were a step
at the entrance to your shrine
trodden upon by devotees
by gods and apsaras
who crowd to worship you—
. . .
ceaselessly I need to see
your lips of coral hue.
May I lie as a step
upon your threshold.[2]

Though bronze-casting had been known in south India since at least the third century, when images of the Buddha began to be cast in the Andhra region, it was only toward the end of the Pallava period, between around 750 and 850, that Hindu metal images began to be produced. The first bronze images to appear were those of god Vishnu, initially no more than seven to eight inches high, but progressively increasing in size. It is not entirely clear why bronze images of Vishnu alone, and not of Shiva, were created during this phase; presumably it reflects the greater popularity of Vishnu before Shiva became a more dominant deity during the Chola period. Bronze processional images of Vishnu are, by and large, standing images. While Shiva is often depicted in an exaggerated contrapposto position of *tribhanga* (triple-bend), Vishnu invariably stands straight upright with weight distributed evenly on both feet (*samabhanga*).

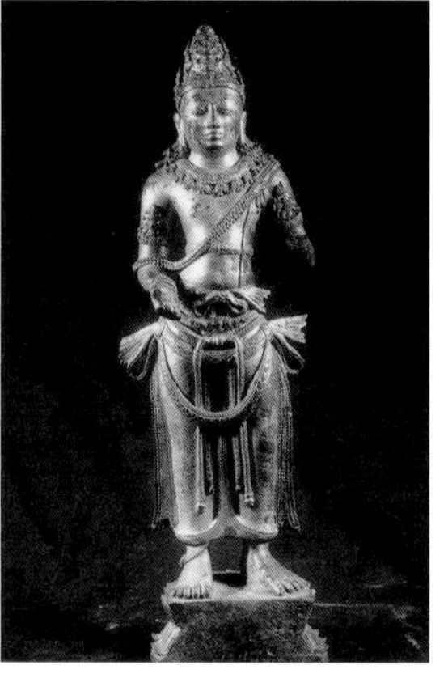
GILT BRONZE OF THE FUTURE BUDDHA MAITREYA, FROM MELAIYUR, CA. 840.
TANJAVUR ART GALLERY
PHOTO VIDYA DEHEJIA
FIG. 1

The earliest bronze on view here is a striking Vishnu from a private collection (cat. no. 37) that belongs to just around the year 850, a time that is often labeled the Pallava-Chola transition. Two rear hands hold the flame-tipped discus and the conch, one hand rests against his thigh in a gesture of ease *(katyavalambita)*, while the other, with thumb and index finger joined, reveals a raised blossom on the open palm. Vishnu's eyes are inlaid with beads. The image bears many similarities to earlier Pallava bronzes, including the Pallava "signature" traits of the sacred thread wrapping over the arm to circle the torso, and the discus presented edge-on to the viewer. The closest stylistic parallel to this Vishnu is the gilt-bronze Maitreya of around 840 from Melaiyur in Tanjavur district (fig. 1), with which it shares several features, including the second sacred thread that hangs below the lower garment all the way to Vishnu's right foot. Both images have heavy lower garments with tassels, loops, and securing strings arranged in elegant folds and knots, but Vishnu's girdle now has a lion-head clasp. Both figures have *makara* earrings, elaborate armlets with *makaras* at their bases, and a sacred thread made up of three strands of pearls. The arrangement of the ringlet curls in two rows along the nape of the neck and the *siraschakra* with a tassel suspended from its center show close similarity even in details. However, this Vishnu bronze lacks the attenuation of Pallava images and is larger in size, suggesting that it belongs to the days of the inception of the Chola period.

Also from a private collection comes an impressive image of Vishnu, framed by a *prabha* that fits in customary fashion over the vertical tangs on the base (cat. no. 38); the *prabha* is adorned with three-tipped flames and rises on each side from a *kirtimukha* or face of glory. The image is a sensational bronze of early Chola date, displaying a svelte elegance that places it roughly contemporaneous with an image of around 925 from Paruthiyur village in Tanjavur district.[3] The triple-strand sacred thread no longer encircles the arm but only the torso, and the front right hand is no longer in the lowered open gesture seen in Pallava images but in the typical Chola raised mode of *abhaya* or protection. The other front hand is poised against the hip in the gesture of ease, while the two rear hands hold discus and conch. The discus remains in the early edge-on view, whereas later it would be turned to face the viewer directly. The regularly ridged folds of the garment are now spaced out generously, but the curlicued ends of the extra folds of the waist-cloth on both sides, so sharply depicted in the Pallava-Chola transition image, are still apparent. Vishnu's identifying attribute, the *shrivatsa* emblem, is seen as a rhomboid against the right of his chest. The figure is elaborately adorned with *makara* earrings, a *katisutra* with a central floral medallion, large armlets, an

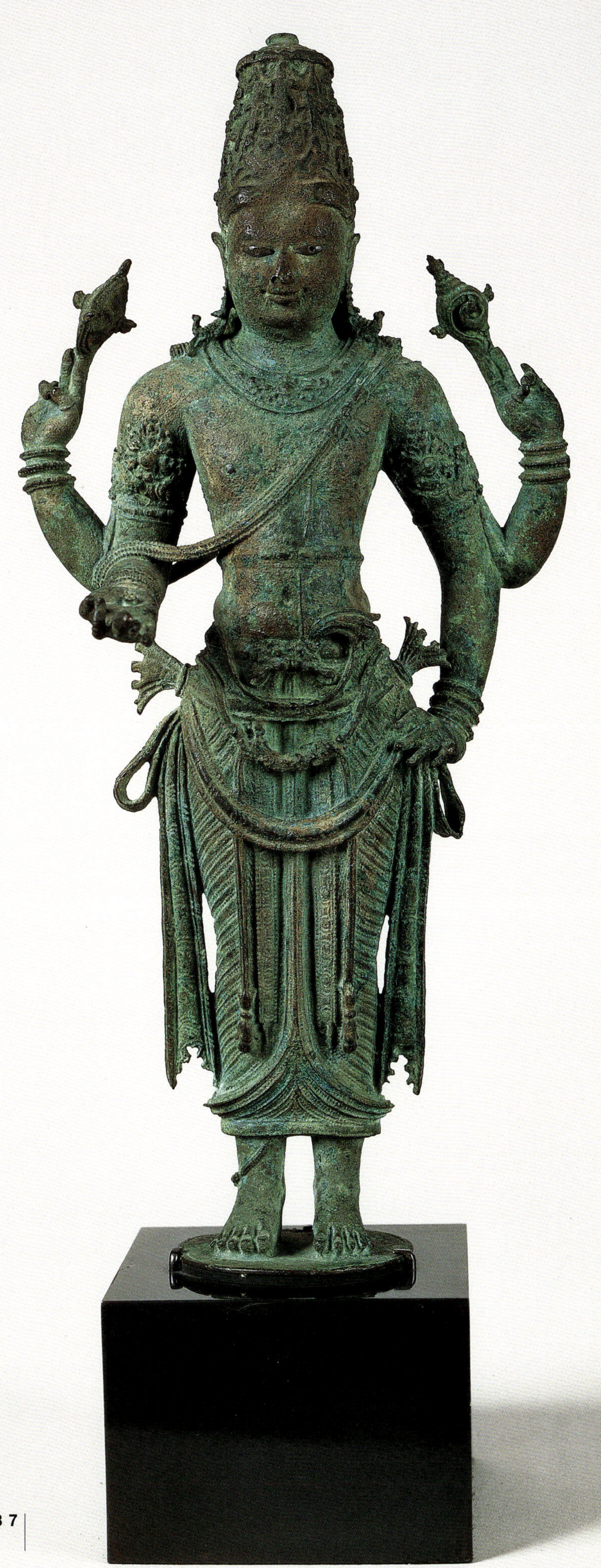

37

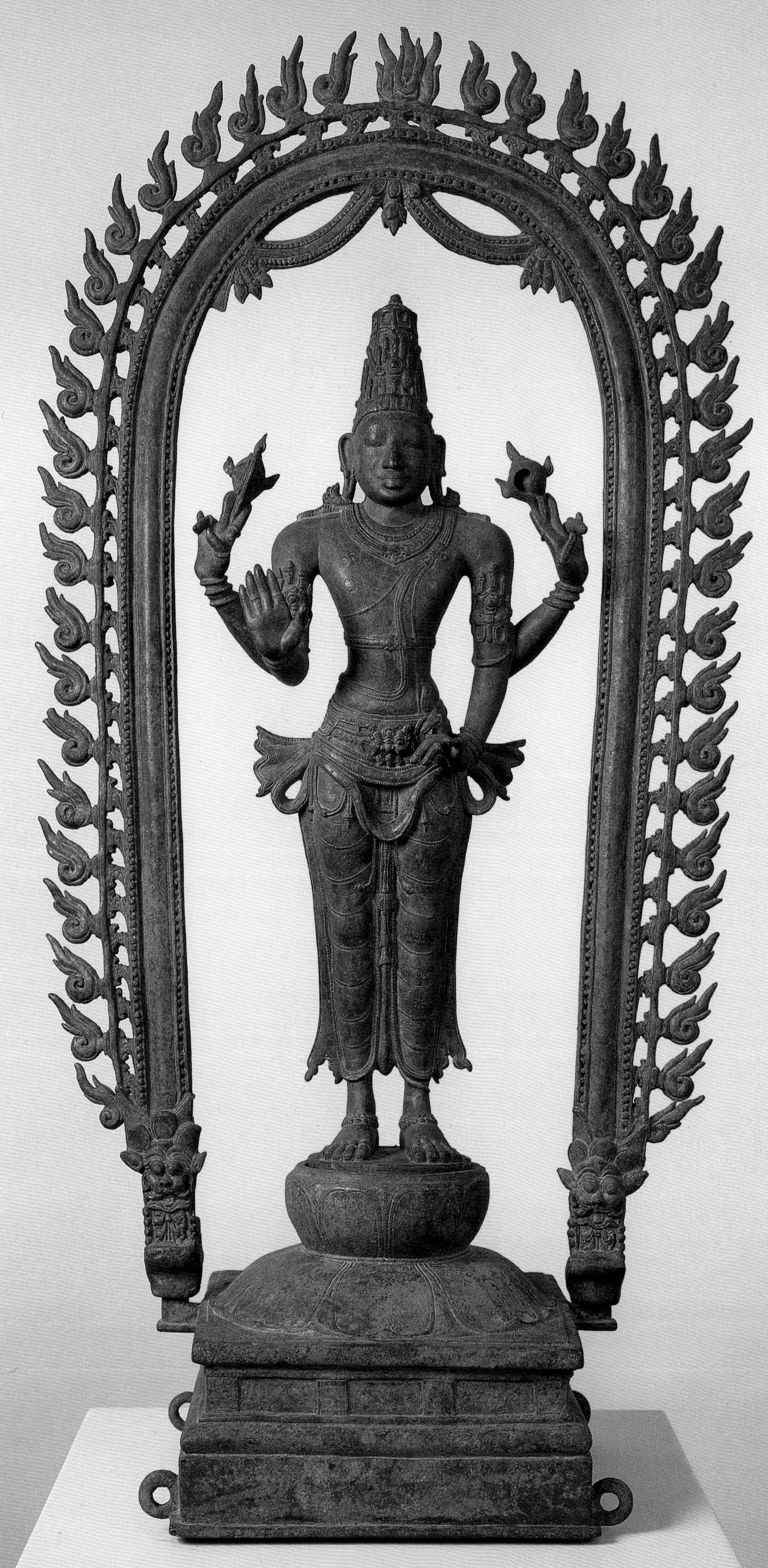

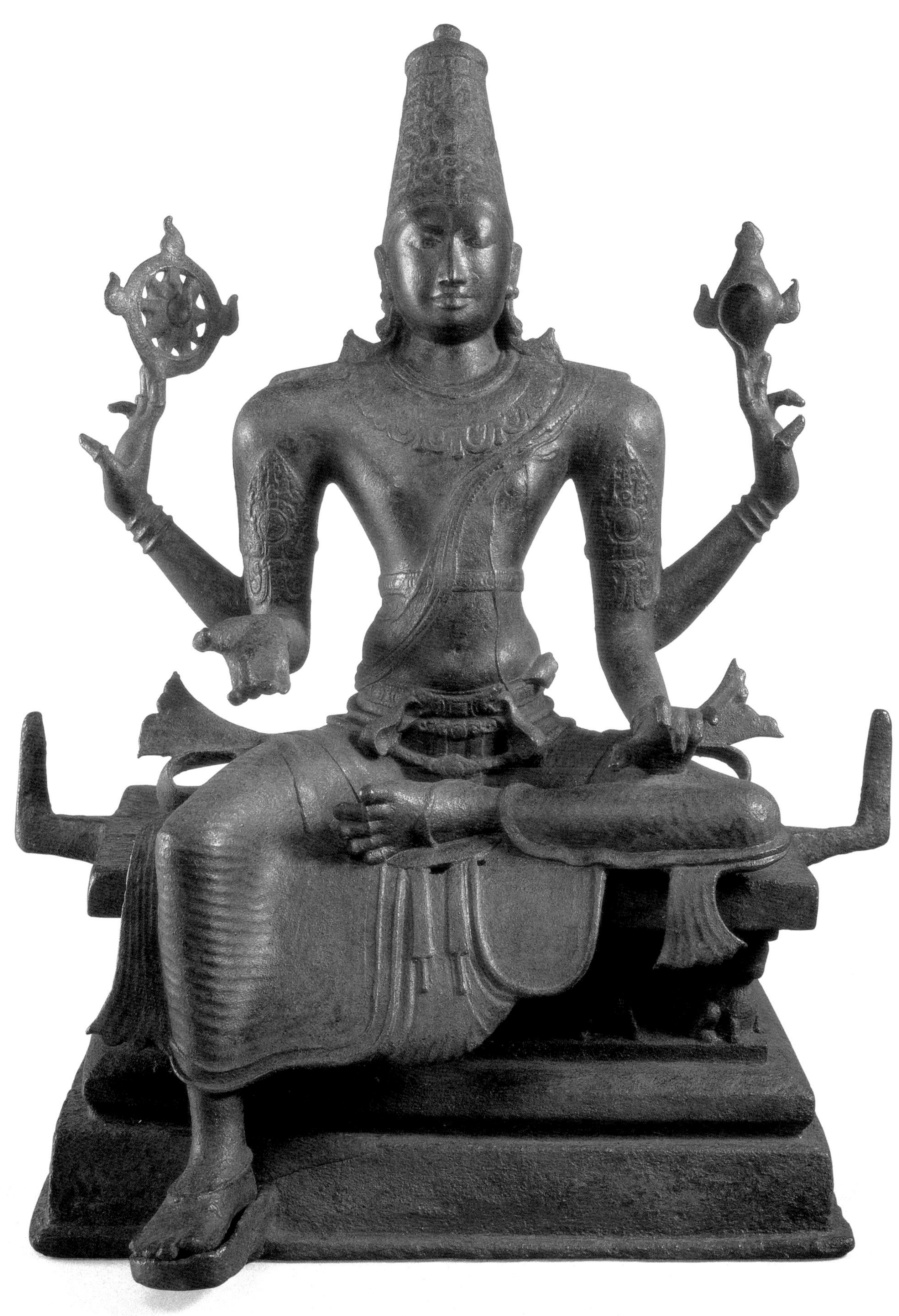

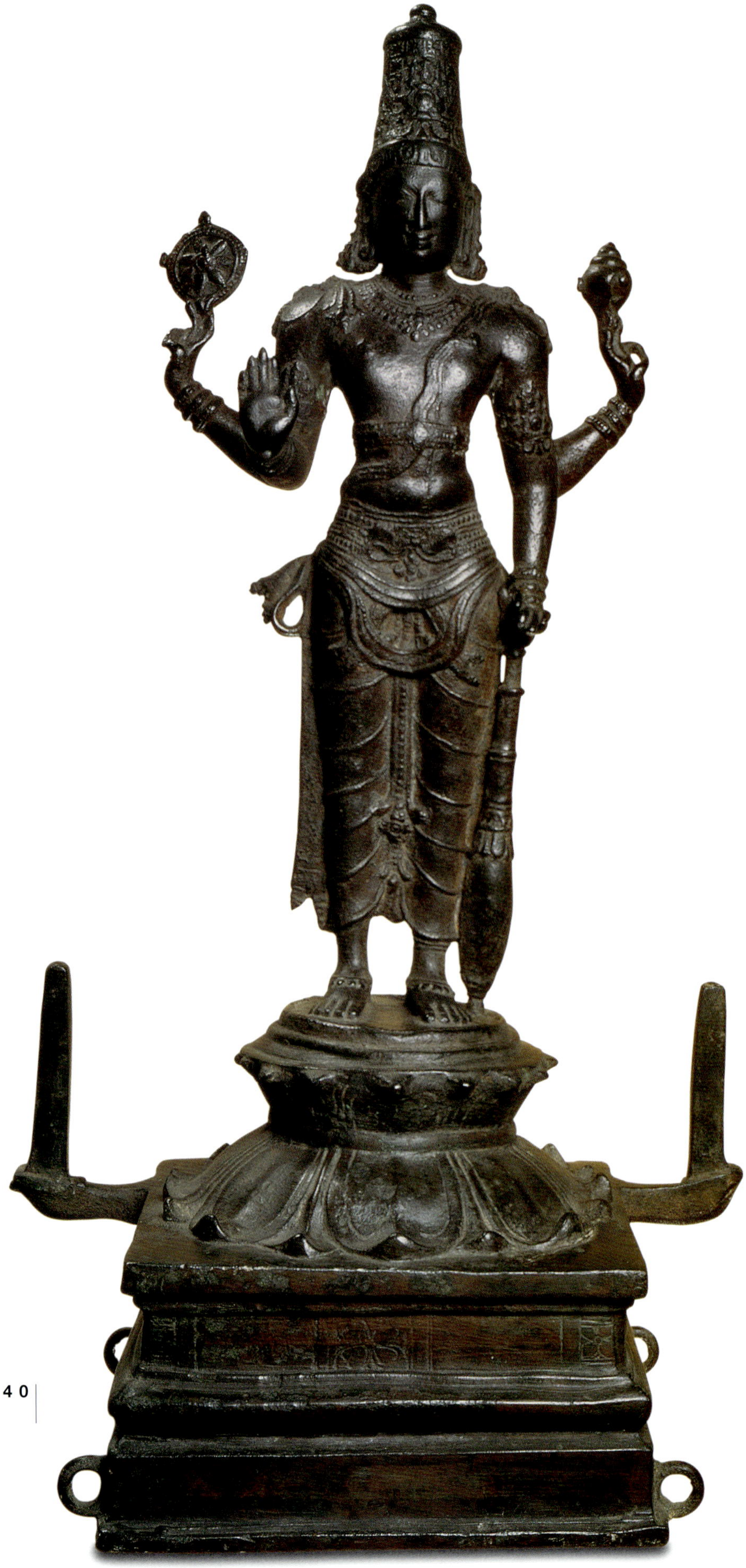

40

elaborate lion-head clasp to the girdle that culminates in elegant chainlike ornaments. The decorative *kunjalam* tassel of the necklace string, as it rests between the rear shoulder blades, has acquired the clasp shaped like a *pipal* leaf that was the standard throughout the tenth century. The full sensuous lips of the bronze are noteworthy, and the well-worn condition of the eyes testifies to centuries of ritual worship prior to its burial, probably around 1310. The rear of the bronze is exquisitely modeled, and the curve of the buttocks, glossed over in all Pallava bronzes, including the previous, transitional image, is here distinctly sensuous. The prominent fanlike fold of the waist-cloth that is pulled back to the rear and displayed at a 45-degree angle is also typical of the early tenth century, and not seen in Pallava or Pallava-transition images.

An impressive seated image of Vishnu from Kongu-nadu (cat. no. 39), with exaggeratedly wide shoulders and exceedingly narrow torso characteristic of the western region of Tamil Nadu, also dates to around 925. This bronze, now in the British Museum, depicts Vishnu with a tall crown shaped like a truncated cone, and seated on a lion throne in the position of royal ease known as *lalitasana*. While rear hands hold the discus and conch shell, one front hand is lowered in the *varada* gesture of wish-granting, while the other rests in an elegant gesture upon his folded knee. Unusual, almost unknown, is the manner in which the drapery of the *veshti* is arranged to hang over the throne; usually, the fabric is tucked away rather than displayed. His long ringlet curls are pleasingly arranged to reach below the nape of the neck, and an elegant *siraschakra* conceals the tie of the headband. The closely placed garment folds resemble those on the Pallava-Chola transition image, but the discus has already been turned toward the front. The magnificence and awesome dignity of the richly adorned image is striking.

Also from the Kongu region, but made a half century later,[4] is a richly adorned image of Vishnu (cat. no. 40) now in the Victoria & Albert Museum, with one front hand lowered to rest upon his club *(gada)*. Its similarities to a Kaveri Delta bronze (cat. no. 41) reinforce the difficulties of pinning down regional differences within the Chola empire, particularly in the early days of the dynasty. Vishnu wears *makara* earrings, and his *shrivatsa* emblem appears along the upper area of his right chest. The decorative string that secures his necklaces does not hang between his shoulders at the rear but instead is brought forward to rest along his right shoulder. The chain pendant of his girdle clasp rests between his legs, and his waist-cloth has elegant knots and folds on either side. The somewhat perfunctory and flattened treatment of the drapery folds in rear view is noteworthy. This Vishnu is an obviously well-worn image that has witnessed centuries of ritual worship.

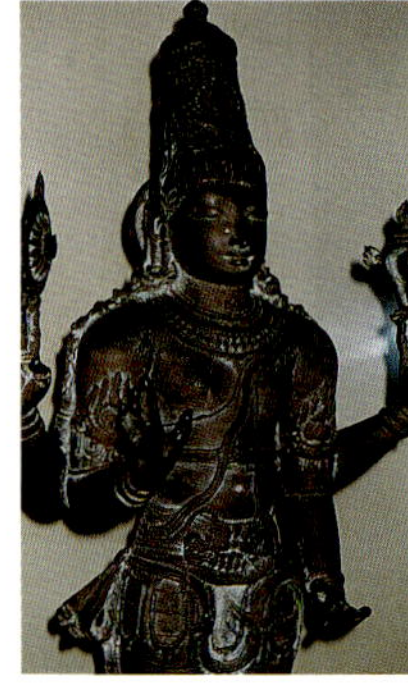

VISHNU, FROM PERUNTOTTAM,
CA. 1000. TANJAVUR ART GALLERY
PHOTO VIDYA DEHEJIA
FIG. 2

Displaying the grounded stability and assured maturity typical of Kaveri Delta bronzes of the Rajaraja period is the Vishnu from the Virginia Museum of Fine Arts (cat. no. 41). It compares well in treatment of form and decorative details with an early-eleventh-century Vishnu from Peruntottam, now in the Tanjavur Art Gallery (fig. 2), which it resembles. The treatment of the crown and headband, the *makara* earrings, the triangular *shrivatsa,* the flower-adorned strands of hair resting along the shoulders and upper arms, the high knot of the triple-strand sacred thread, the necklaces, the wide armlets, the lion-head girdle clasp, simple bangles, and the folds and loops of the waist-cloth are all closely parallel. However, the discus in the Tanjavur image remains in three-quarter view, while that in the image from the Virginia Museum has been swiveled around to face the viewer in an almost direct frontal view.

NOTES

1 John Braisted Carman and Vasudha Narayanan, *The Tamil Veda: Pillan's Interpretation of the Tiruvaymoli* (Chicago: University of Chicago Press, 1989), p. 232: Nammalvar 6.10.9.

2 Vidya Dehejia, *Slaves of the Lord: The Path of the Tamil Saints* (Delhi: Munshiram Manoharlal, 1988), p. 92: Kulashekhara, *Perumal Tirumoli* 4.4,9.

3 R. Nagaswamy, *Masterpieces of Early South Indian Bronzes* (New Delhi: National Museum, 1983), no. 58, pp. 155, 156.

4 Museum records indicate that it was a gift from the citizens of Coimbatore to Lord Curzon and is part of what is known as the Curzon bequest.

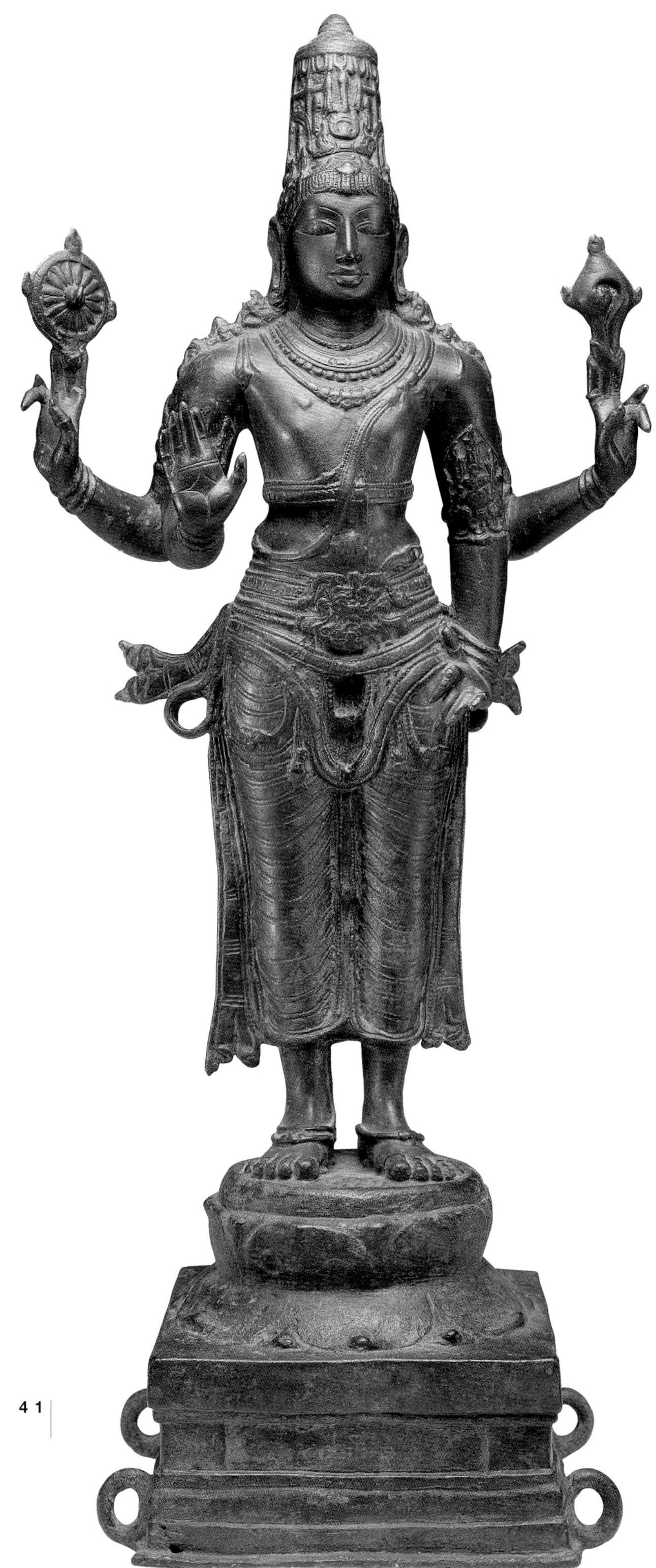

41

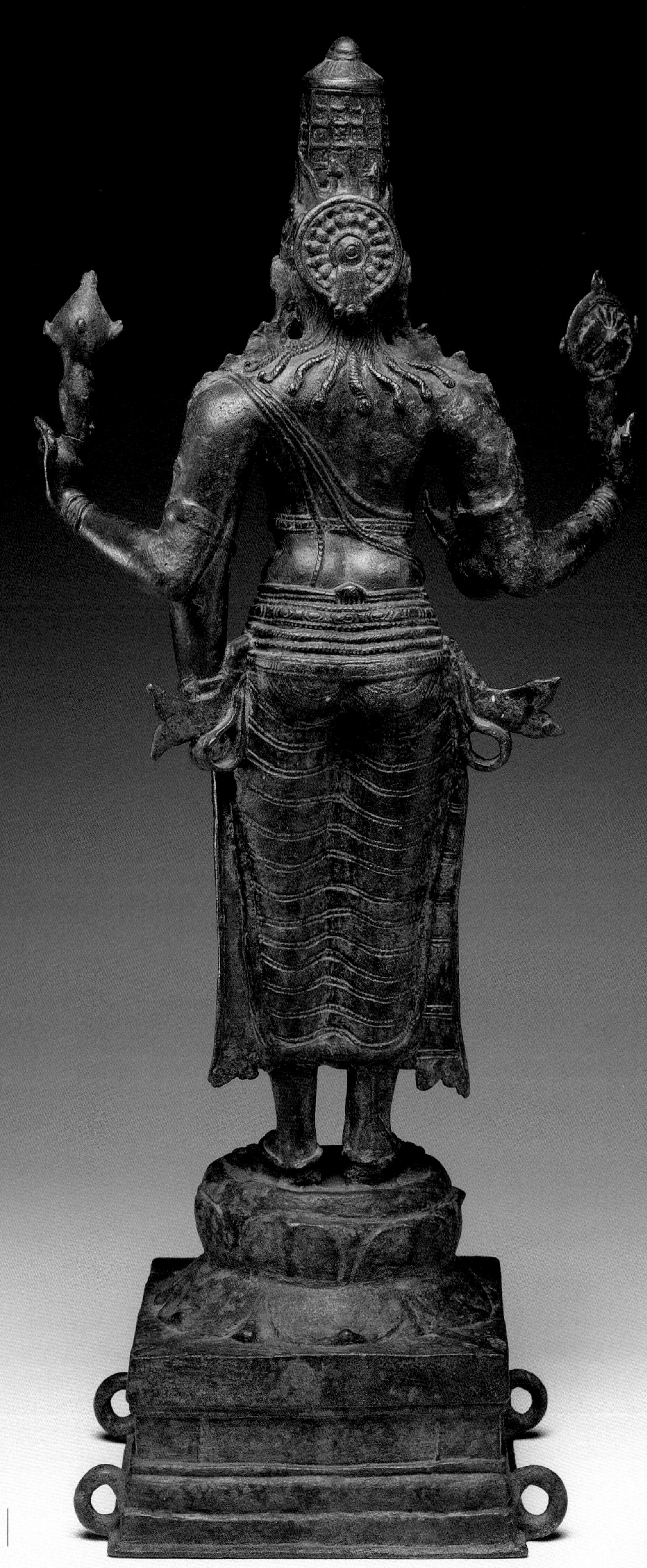

41

42 SHRI LAKSHMI, GODDESS OF WEALTH AND FORTUNE
CHOLA PERIOD, CA. 975; KONGU-NADU
BRONZE, 21 1/4 IN. (54 CM)
VICTORIA & ALBERT MUSEUM (IM149–1927)

43 BHU LAKSHMI
CHOLA PERIOD, CA. 990
BRONZE, 28 1/4 IN. (71.9 CM)
PRIVATE COLLECTION

Lakshmi, goddess of wealth and fortune, also known as Shri, and often addressed by poets as the lady of the lotus, is the prime consort of Vishnu. Just as Devi Uma is Shiva's constant companion, Shri is inseparable from her lord and often described as resting on Vishnu's chest. In fact, a popular name for Vishnu in Tamil Nadu is Shrinivasa or the abode of Shri. Here is how the much-revered ninth-century saint Nammalvar speaks of Shri as he addresses Vishnu:

> *O you on whose breast resides the lady of the flower*
> *Who says: "I cannot move away from him even for a second!"*[1]

Vishnu's second consort is Bhu devi or Goddess Earth, also known as Bhu Lakshmi, whom he rescued from the depths of the cosmic ocean in his incarnation as the great boar, Varaha. Nammalvar laments that he cannot get close to Vishnu because the lord is preoccupied with his two beloved wives.

> *He is the bridegroom of the lady of the flower*
> *and the lady of the earth.*
> *My dear one, the life of the world and the divine ones,*
> *reigns over heaven [but] desires to dwell*
> *in the sacred city of ships.*
> *When can I see him*
> *and drink him in with my eyes and rejoice*[2]

Images of Vishnu's two consorts are closely similar in iconography with the main distinction being that Shri Lakshmi is always given a breast-band, while Bhu Lakshmi is generally without one.

Belonging to the very end of the tenth century is the bronze image of Shri Lakshmi from the Victoria & Albert Museum (cat. no. 42); she holds a lotus in her right hand, wears a *channavira* with a central pendant, while a patterned breast-band encloses her breasts. A clue to her Kongu-nadu origin[3] comes from the somewhat exaggerated breadth of the shoulders and an exceedingly narrow waist. The figure is voluptuous and sensuous, and a comparison with an image of Uma still in worship in the Shiva temple at Avanashi, some thirty miles from the town of Coimbatore, makes the point of her Kongu origin (fig. 1). Other common features include the conical shape of the crown (much worn down in the case of the temple image), the manner in which the strands of hair flow down the shoulders, the pendant high around the throat, the simple tasseled elbow bands, and the fullness of the lips. Shri Lakshmi wears large stud earrings with a flower above and behind her ears, and, as with the Kongu standing Vishnu image (see cat. no. 40), the strings that secure her necklaces are not left to rest against her neck at the rear but are brought forward to adorn her right shoulder. The fabric of Shri Lakshmi's skirt has a light diamond pattern, and its ties and folds rest along both sides and down the center, where a chain pendant hangs from the girdle clasp. Although the image is fully three-dimensional, details of the drapery folds, as well as the curls that rest along her shoulders and upper arms, are fully modeled only along the front and treated in a flattened and cursory manner along the rear, as is the case with the Vishnu image from Kongu.

Belonging to the closing days of the Sembiyan workshop in the heart of Chola territory, and now in a private collection, is a richly adorned figure of the goddess Bhu Lakshmi, holding a lotus in her right hand (cat. no. 43). The image bears so striking a resemblance to a Bhu devi from Rasipuram now in the Pudukottai Museum, that it seems the two images were created in the same workshop (fig. 2). We see a similar treatment of bodily form, with slightly exaggerated width to the shoulders, exceedingly slender waist, and relatively narrow hips. A variety of telling details of adornment include the splayed tasseled elbow bands, the wide bracelet with a flanged clasp, the pendant on a string that rests snugly around her throat, and the manner in which the ringlet curls rest against the neck and shoulders. Closely similar too is the treatment of the skirt, its patterned fabric, the inner fold that rests against the sides, the pleated fold that hangs between the legs to enclose a dangling chain ornament with tassels swaying out in both directions, and the rear treatment of the drapery with a fan-shaped splayed end. Bhu Lakshmi wears a *channavira* that crosses her torso, and her girdle is composed of flat metal plaques. The main indication that this image is not Uma Parameshvari but Bhu Lakshmi is the fact that the Pudukottai image it so closely resembles was found together with an image of Vishnu.

NOTES

1 John Braisted Carman and Vasudha Narayanan, *The Tamil Veda: Pillan's Interpretation of the Tiruvaymoli* (Chicago: University of Chicago Press, 1989), p. 233: Nammalvar 6.10.10.

2 Ibid., p. 240: Nammalvar 9.8.5.

3 Like the Vishnu of cat. no. 40, this image is part of the Curzon bequest.

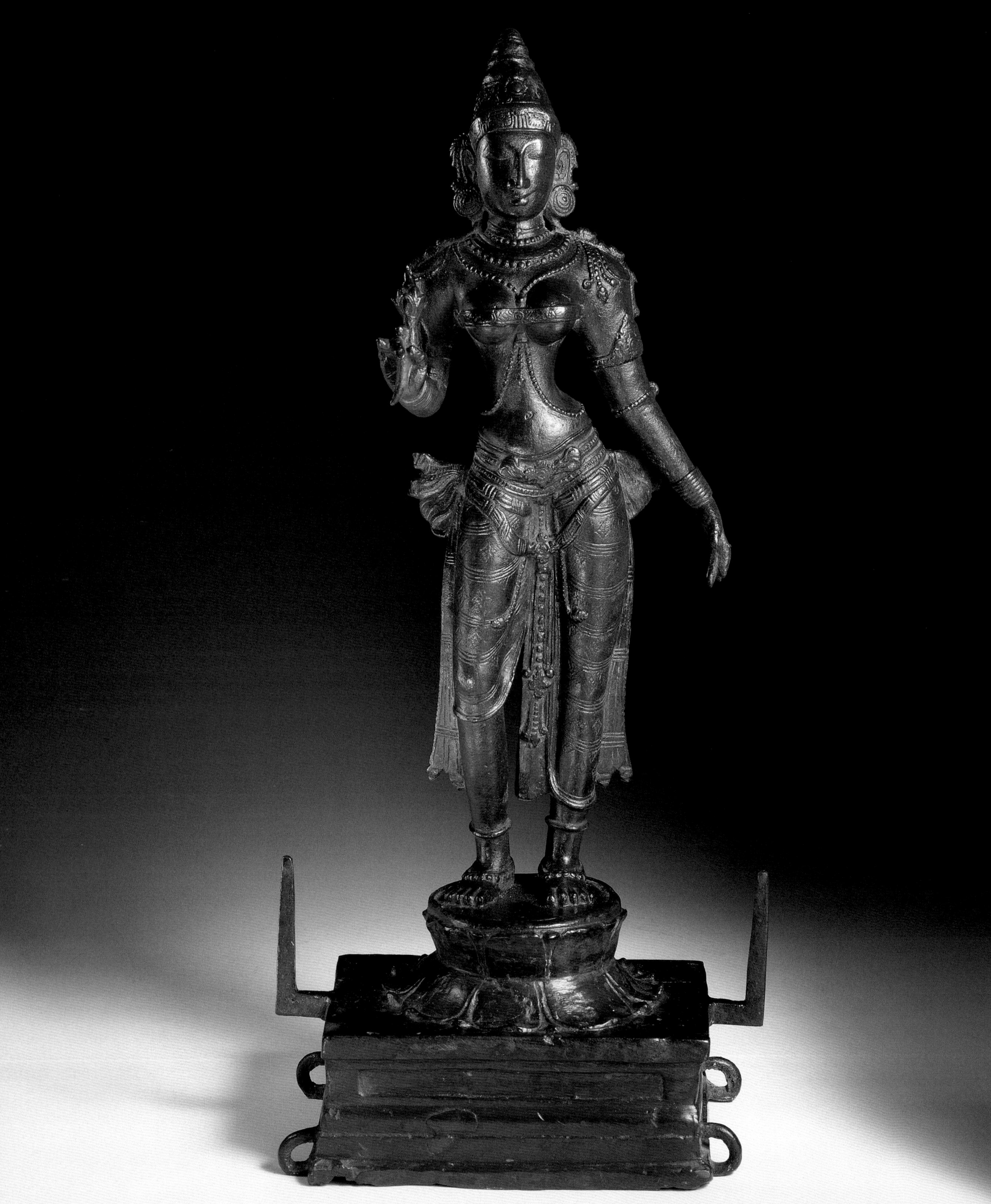

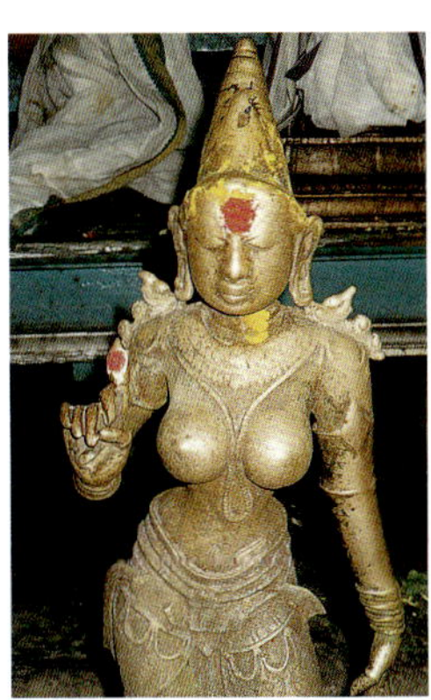

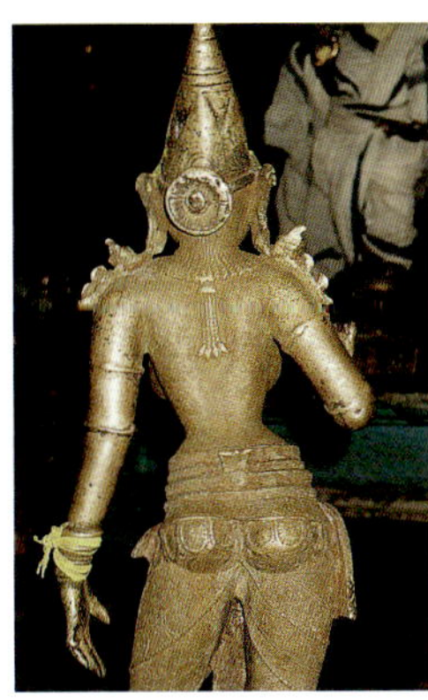

UMA (TWO VIEWS), CA. 1012,
AVANASHI TEMPLE
PHOTOS VIDYA DEHEJIA
FIG. 1

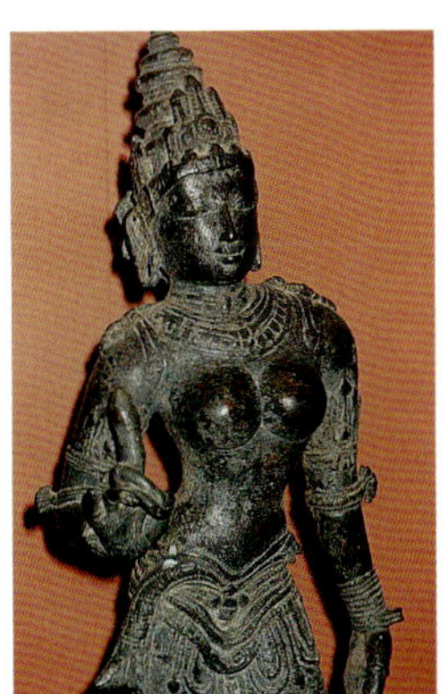

BHU DEVI, FROM RASIPURAM,
CA. 990. PUDUKOTTAI MUSEUM
PHOTO VIDYA DEHEJIA
FIG. 2

43

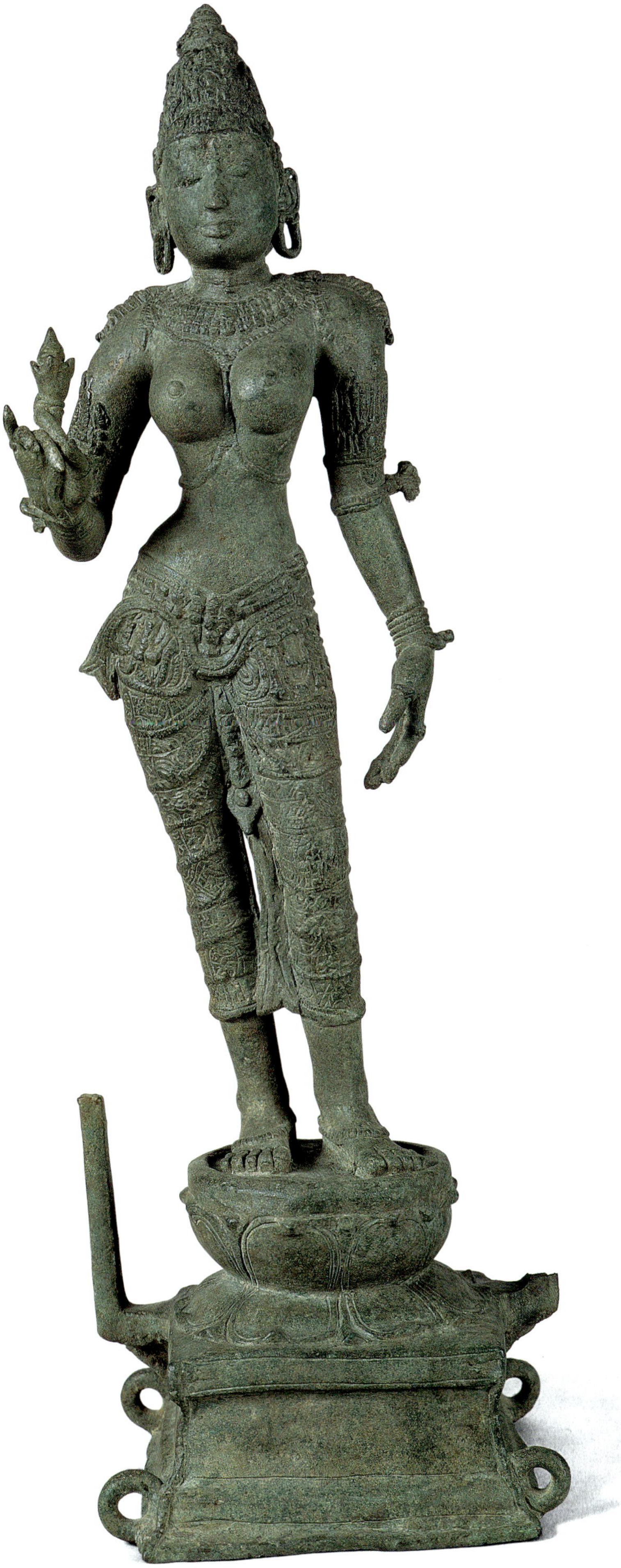

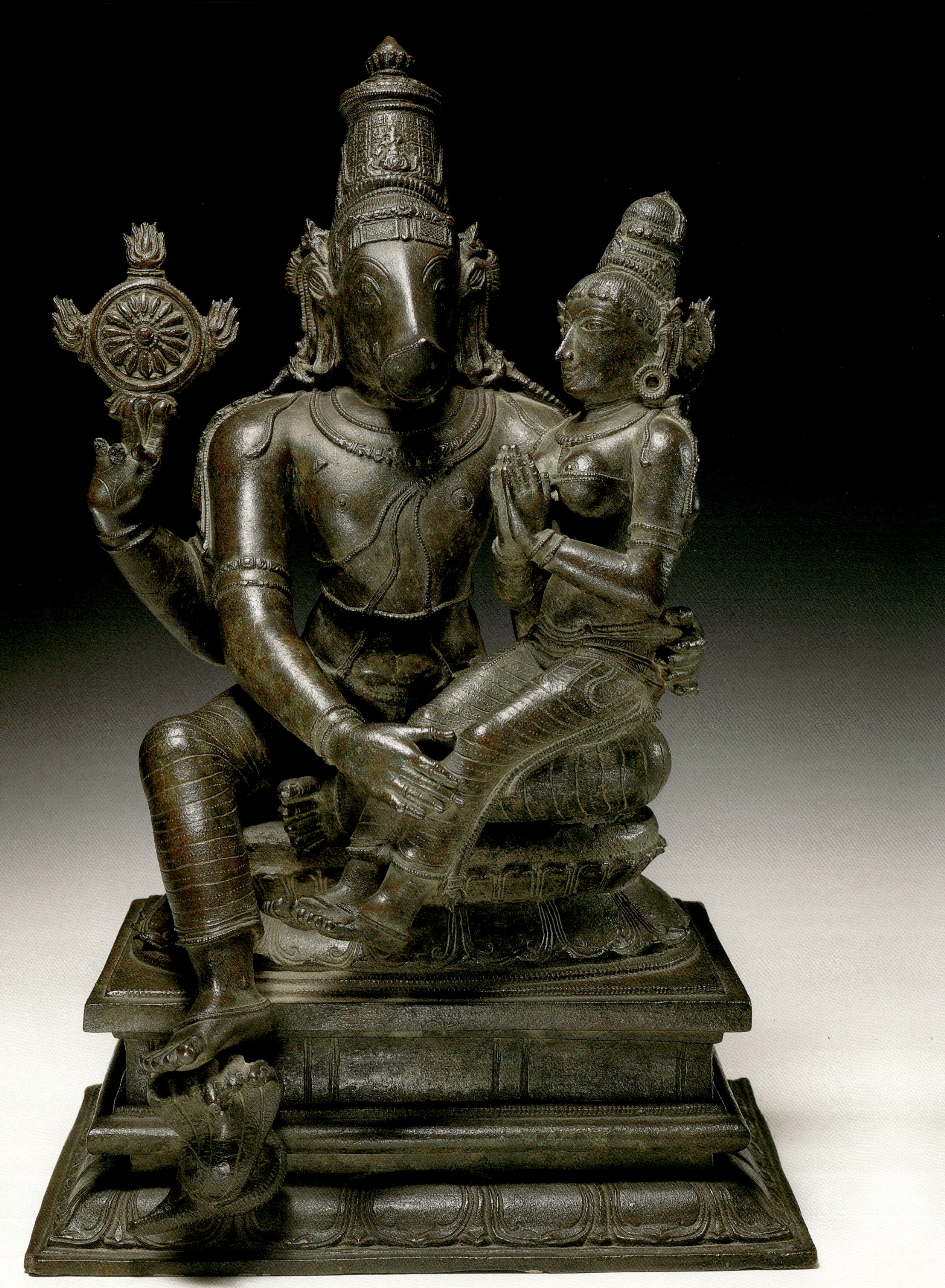

44 BHU-VARAHA, VISHNU'S AVATAR AS GIGANTIC BOAR, EMBRACING GODDESS EARTH

CHOLA PERIOD, 13TH CENTURY
BRONZE, 17 7/8 IN. (45.5 CM)
VICTORIA & ALBERT MUSEUM (IM6-1924)

Bronzes of Vishnu's third avatar—as the gigantic boar, who dived into the depths of the cosmic ocean to rescue the earth, personified as goddess Bhu devi, who was in danger of drowning—became popular in temple ritual somewhat late in the Chola period. However, the theme had caught the imagination of many of the early Vaishnava poet-saints. Nammalvar sang thus of the resplendent Varaha Vishnu:

Like a blue mountain that clutches
And lifts up two crescent moons,
My father, you, as a resplendent boar,
Raised your tusks, carrying Earth.
O you who churned the deep blue sea!
I have obtained you,
Would I now let you go?[1]

By contrast, the woman-saint Andal dwelt on the lowly form that Vishnu took for the love of Bhu devi:

Once long ago
for the sake of the maiden earth
forlorn in moss-ridden body,
he took the shameful form
of a filthy
water-dripping boar.[2]

This image of the late thirteenth century portrays the giant boar seated on a lotus seat in the *lalitasana* posture of royal ease, with one leg folded and the other pendant to rest upon the hood of a five-headed cobra. His consort Bhu devi, or Bhu Lakshmi, wearing a breast-band, sits somewhat formally on his folded knee, with her palms joined in adoration. Varaha holds the discus and conch in two rear hands, while his two front arms gently enfold the seated goddess. Crowned Varaha's *shrivatsa* attribute is rendered as a triangle against his upper right shoulder, and he wears a triple-strand sacred thread. The elaborate treatment of the hair above the ears and along the shoulders is noteworthy. The garments of both figures are decorated with a series of dots suggestive of the tie-and-dye *shungudi* fabric typical of the Madurai region. The bronze composition carries hints of the sharpness and precision that was to become standard in images after the Chola period.

NOTES

1 John Braisted Carman and Vasudha Narayanan, *The Tamil Veda: Pillan's Interpretation of the Tiruvaymoli* (Chicago: University of Chicago Press, 1989), p. 255: Nammalvar 10.10.7.

2 Vidya Dehejia, *Antal and the Path of Love* (New York: State University of New York Press, 1990), p. 117: *Nacchiyar Tirumoli* 11.8.

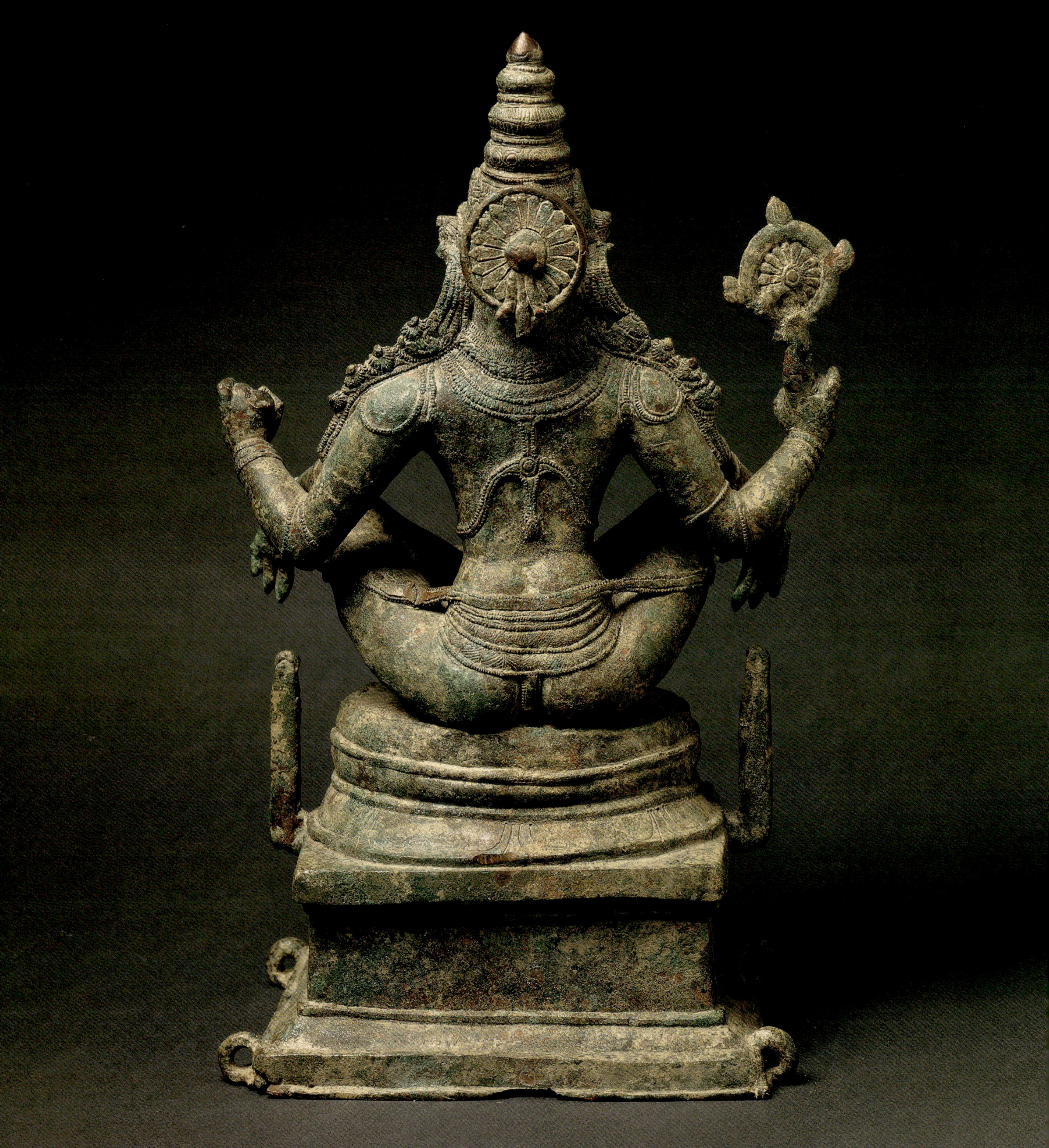

45 YOGA NARASIMHA, VISHNU IN HIS MAN-LION AVATAR
CHOLA PERIOD, CA. 1250
BRONZE, 21 3/4 IN. (55.3 CM)
THE CLEVELAND MUSEUM OF ART; GIFT OF DR. NORMAN ZAWORSKI (1973.187)

Vishnu's fourth incarnation, as man-lion Narasimha, revolves around King Hiranyakashipu, who had received a boon from Brahma by which he could be killed by neither man nor beast, neither on earth nor in the heavens, neither by day nor night, and not through the use of any known weapon. In this invincible position, his power rivaled and threatened that of the gods, who appealed to Vishnu for help. To destroy him while respecting the conditions of the boon, Vishnu took a form that was neither man nor beast, raised him up into the air (neither earth nor heaven) at the moment of dusk (neither night nor day), and tore him apart with his lion claws (not a conventional weapon). While temple relief carvings and painted murals may depict the actual destruction of Hiranyakashipu, bronze images generally portray Narasimha seated with a yoga band around his knees, two front hands in the position of quiet meditation, and two rear hands displaying Vishnu's attributes of discus and conch shell (here missing).

The image is a powerful one, and the avatar finds frequent mention in the poems of the saints. An unusual song composed by Nammalvar is placed on the lips of a mother who describes her love-stricken daughter and expresses wonder that the lovely young girl should have fallen in love with the fierce lion-headed Narasimha.

She danced and danced
with melting heart—
Sang song after song
eyes brimming with tears—
Searching everywhere
crying "Narasingha!"—
She wilts and fades
this maiden young.[1]

This powerful image of Yoga Narasimha belongs to the thirteenth century, perhaps around 1250, and may be compared with an image of similar date, now in the National Museum, New Delhi.[2]

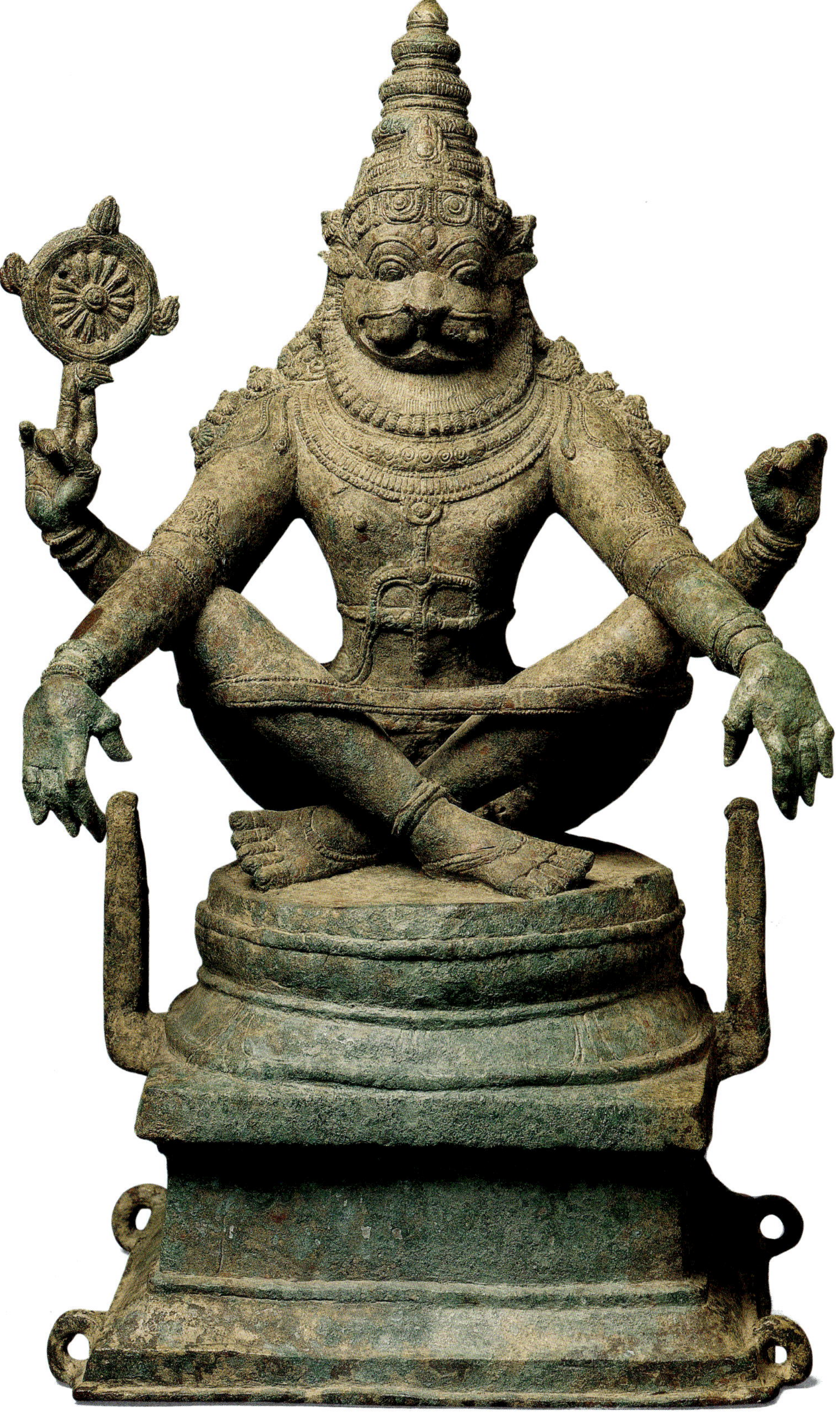

NOTES

1 Vidya Dehejia, *Slaves of the Lord: The Path of the Tamil Saints* (New Delhi: Munshiram Manoharlal, 1988), p. 114: Nammalvar 2.4.1.
2 R. Nagaswamy, *Masterpieces of Early South Indian Bronzes* (New Delhi: National Museum, 1983), p. 164.

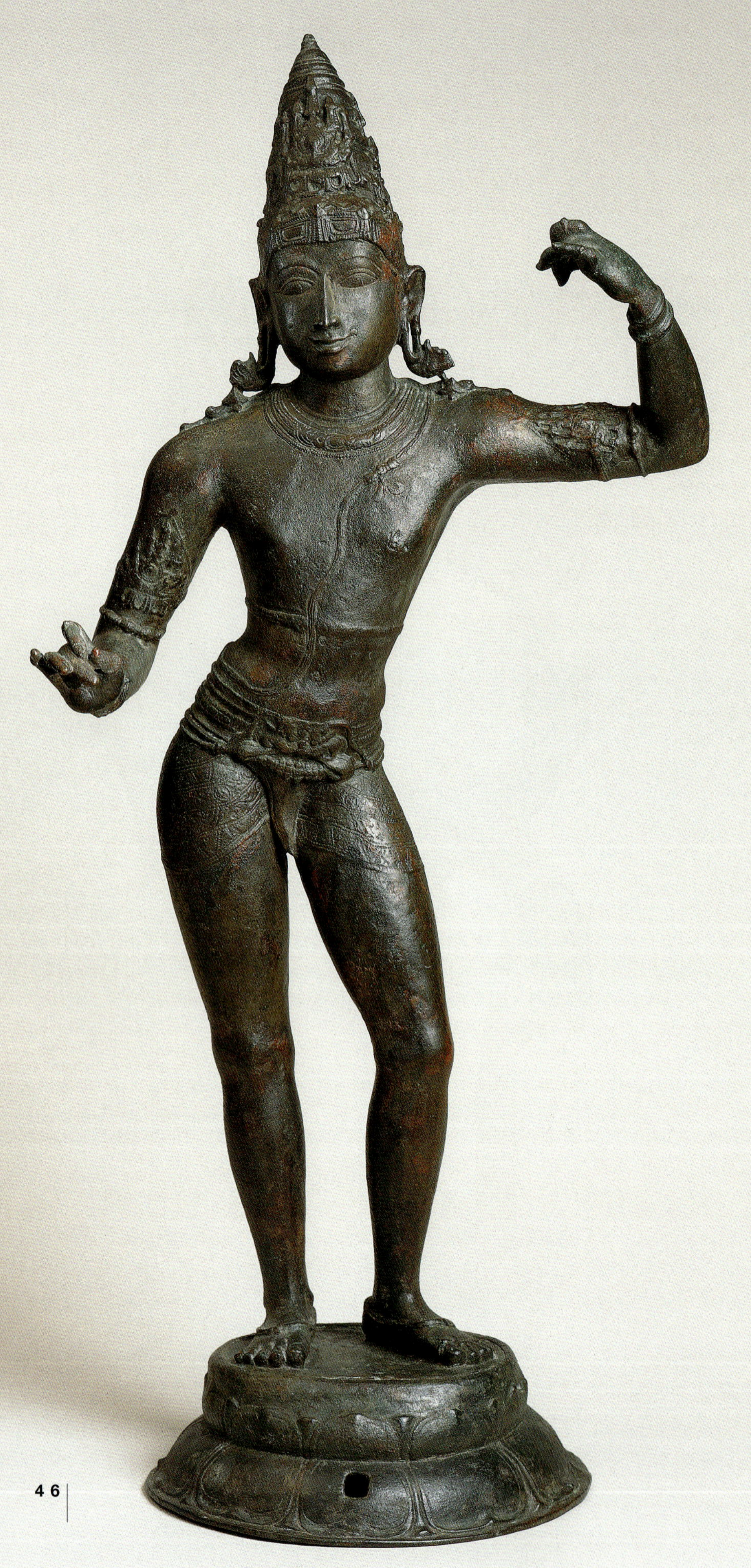

46

46 RAMA
CHOLA PERIOD, CA. 975
BRONZE, 31 7/8 IN. (81 CM)
PHILADELPHIA MUSEUM OF ART; W. P. WILSTACH, JOHN D. McILHENNY, AND WOMEN'S COMMITTEE FUND (W1982-106-1)

47 SITA, RAMA'S CONSORT
CHOLA PERIOD, CA. 980–90
BRONZE, 26 IN. (66 CM)
LINDEN-MUSEUM, STUTTGART (SA 33610L)

48 MONKEY GENERAL HANUMAN
CHOLA PERIOD, CA. 1000
BRONZE, 31 5/8 IN. (80.3 CM)
THE CLEVELAND MUSEUM OF ART; JOHN L. SEVERANCE FUND (1980.26)

49 MONKEY GENERAL HANUMAN
CHOLA PERIOD, CA. 1020; KONGU-NADU
BRONZE, 16 1/8 IN. (41 CM)
VICTORIA & ALBERT MUSEUM (IM135-1927)

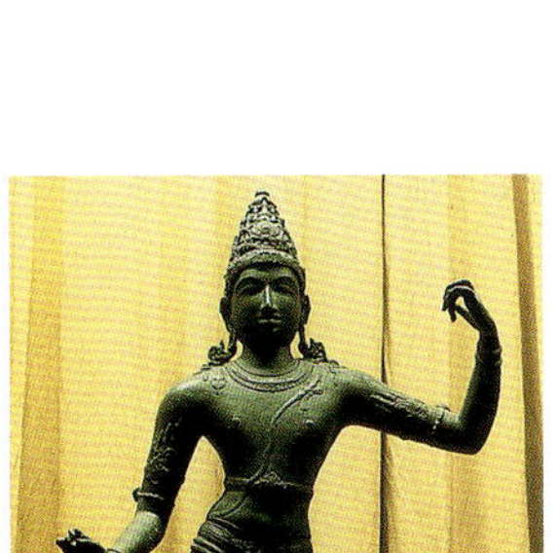

RAMA, FROM VADAKUPPANAIYAR, CA. 950.
GOVERNMENT MUSEUM, CHENNAI
PHOTO VIDYA DEHEJIA
FIG. 1

O child of Kausalya
of radiant eyes
your strong broad shoulders
carry the bow—
Used to sleep on a soft bed
your bed will now be one of stones
beneath the shade of forest trees—
How will you learn to do this?
O unfortunate that I am!
O Kakustha!
O dark youth![1]

So laments king Dasharatha, after sending his son Rama, born of his senior queen, Kausalya, into forest exile in order to honor a pledge he had once made to his youngest queen.

For more than two thousand years, the exhilarating and poignant story of Rama has appealed to the most diverse range of persons, from the simple villager to the erudite scholar. It has served as an enthralling bedtime story for generations of Indian children who have lamented Ravana's violent abduction of Sita, extolled the virtues of the monkeys who built a causeway to Lanka, and exulted over the defeat of Ravana and his demons. At the other end of the spectrum, learned commentators through the ages have studied the subtleties of the story and have searched each line for hidden theological significance. Rama is loved precisely because he is a human hero who is also a god. Here is a man who suffered the pangs of love and reproached himself bitterly for having left his wife alone in the forest. The story line itself requires an emphasis on Rama's humanity since Ravana had won from Brahma a boon that he could not be slain by gods or demons but, in his arrogance, he had not asked for protection from man. So while Rama is an avatar of god Vishnu, he was a man while on earth.

Vishnu temples normally house a group of four to represent the legend, commissioning images of Rama, his wife Sita, his brother Lakshmana who accompanied them into exile, and the devoted monkey general Hanuman. The pieces brought together in the exhibition, while fairly close in date, are not part of a single commission; however, their juxtaposition will give an idea of such groupings.

The Rama from the collection of the Philadelphia Museum of Art (cat. no. 46), who once held his *kodanda* bow with his upraised arm and an arrow in the lowered hand (both missing today), is an exquisite bronze dating from the end of the tenth century. A comparison with the group from Paruthiyar,[2] or from Vadakuppanaiyar (fig. 1), both belonging to around 950, is instructive. The Philadelphia Rama bears strong resemblances to both images in the modeling of bodily form, as well as in a number of details. These include the design of a variety of ornaments—necklace, jeweled armlets, *makara* earrings, the tall, conical jeweled crown, the petaled *siraschakra,* and the lion-head girdle clasp—as well as in the treatment of the short, patterned waist-cloth with a triangular fold in front. A double row of curls rests along the nape of Rama's neck, and below them is the dangling chain clasp of the necklace. The image clearly came from the Kaveri Delta region, and its assured handling suggests a date around the year 975.

The Sita from the Linden-Museum (cat. no. 47) is an image of astounding beauty and sophistication that, in many ways, resembles the Sita image from Vadakuppanaiyar (fig. 2), as also that from Paruthiyar. Ringlet curls frame her forehead, and her elegant chignon, with its decorative blossoms and curls, is a masterpiece that any contemporary hair stylist would be proud to emulate. The images share the treatment of the pendant high around the throat, the broad beaded necklace, the *channavira* that falls between the breasts and then separates to encircle the torso, the armlet, the tasseled elbow band, and the wide beaded bracelet encircling the wrist. The fabric of Sita's skirt is patterned with rows of alternating rosettes, scrolls, and triangles, and a series of beaded loops hang down from the girdle. The inner fold of the skirt that rests against her thigh and the patterned garment are suggestive of Sembiyan workmanship. The Stuttgart image appears to come from the Sembiyan workshop in around 980–90.

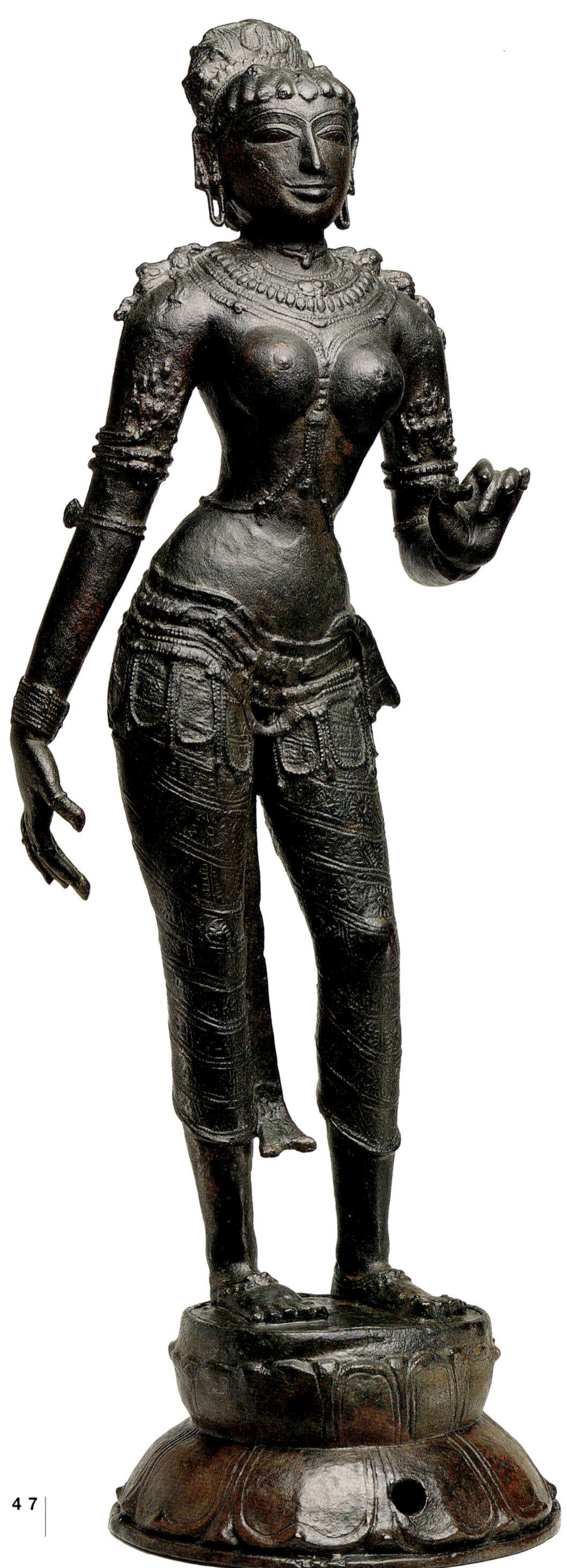

47

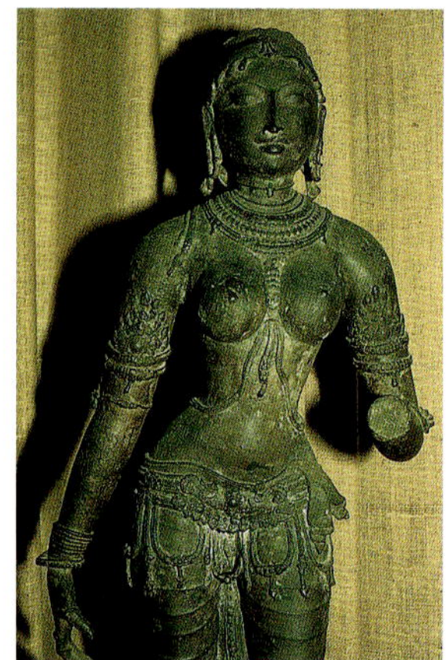

SITA, FROM VADAKUPPANAIYAR,
CA. 950. GOVERNMENT MUSEUM, CHENNAI
PHOTO VIDYA DEHEJIA
FIG. 2

The Hanuman from the Cleveland Museum of Art (cat. no. 48) is a most appealing figure. Standing bent forward in a typical manner that suggests his humility, the part-simian, part-human figure has one hand before his mouth in a gesture of wondrous adoration and the other hanging down in front of him. Wearing a short, patterned waist-cloth, this richly adorned, whimsical figure epitomizes the character at his very best—humble, yet powerful. Here is the monkey general adored by countless devotees for the impossible feat he performed—locating Sita by jumping across the ocean to Lanka, giving her a message from Rama, and returning to fight the final battle. He is the one whom devotees beseech for help when confronting difficulties:

> ***Lord who achieved the impossible***
> ***before you how can one speak of the impossible?***
> ***O messenger of Rama, O ocean of mercy***
> ***make my task achievable, O Lord.***[3]

The Hanuman now in the Victoria & Albert Museum (cat. no. 49), with his tail resting gracefully on the ground behind him, is a bronze from Kongu-nadu.[4] It is an exquisite image that is even less simian and more human than the one from Cleveland. Hanuman wears a sacred thread of pearls, and large stud earrings similar to those worn by the Shri Lakshmi from Kongu-nadu (cat. no. 42). His patterned waist-cloth is tied in elaborate, large knots on both sides, and a floral clasp holds the girdle in place. He sports an enchanting hairdo of ringlet curls neatly arranged in tiers around his head. Two strands of curls rest along his shoulders, and their flat, summary treatment in rear view is noteworthy. This piece, a fanciful bronze of early-eleventh-century date, shows Hanuman standing bent forward with his hand before his mouth in a gesture typical of him.

NOTES

1 Vidya Dehejia, *Slaves of the Lord: The Path of the Tamil Saints* (New Delhi: Munshiram Manoharlal, 1988), p. 95. This is a poem written by saint Kulashekhara (*Perumal Tirumoli* 7.8) in which King Dasaratha laments the banishment of his son Rama and grieves for the hardships Rama would have to undergo in the forest.

2 R. Nagaswamy, *Masterpieces of Early South Indian Bronzes* (New Delhi: National Museum, 1983), pp. 154–57.

3 A popular Sanskrit prayer to Hanuman, known in both north and south India.

4 Like the Vishnu (cat. no. 40) and Lakshmi (cat. no. 42), this image is part of the Curzon bequest.

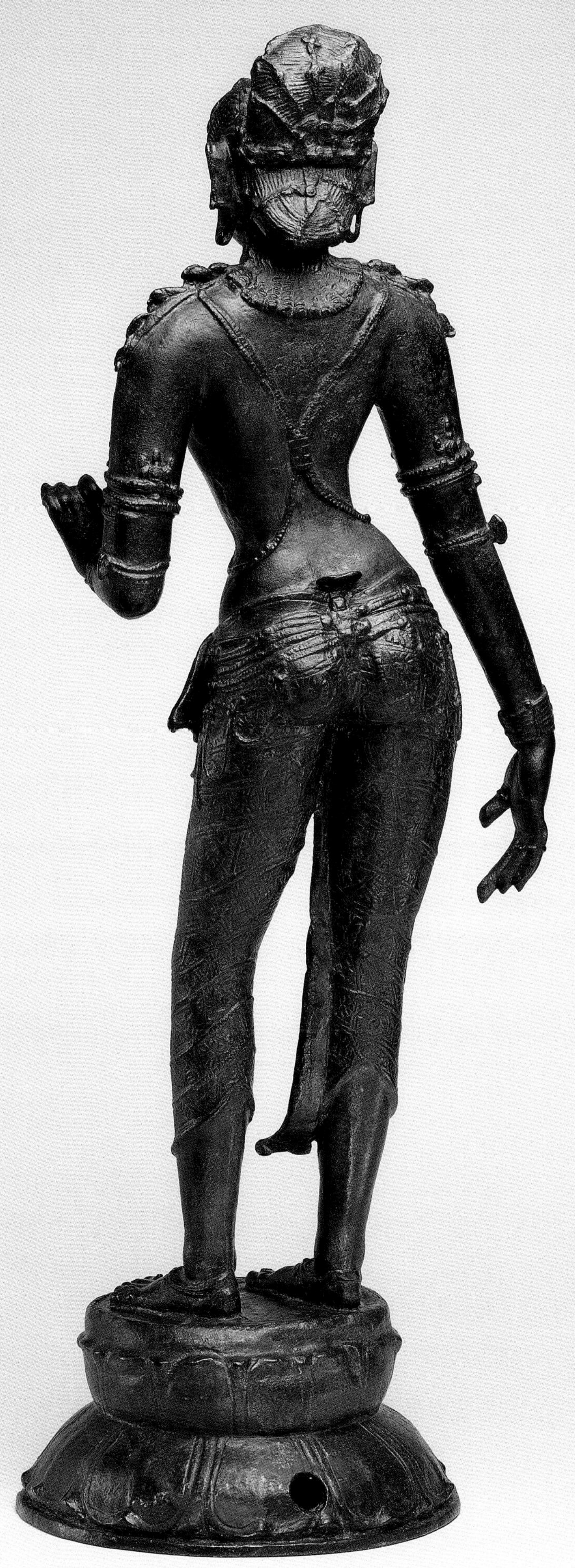

47

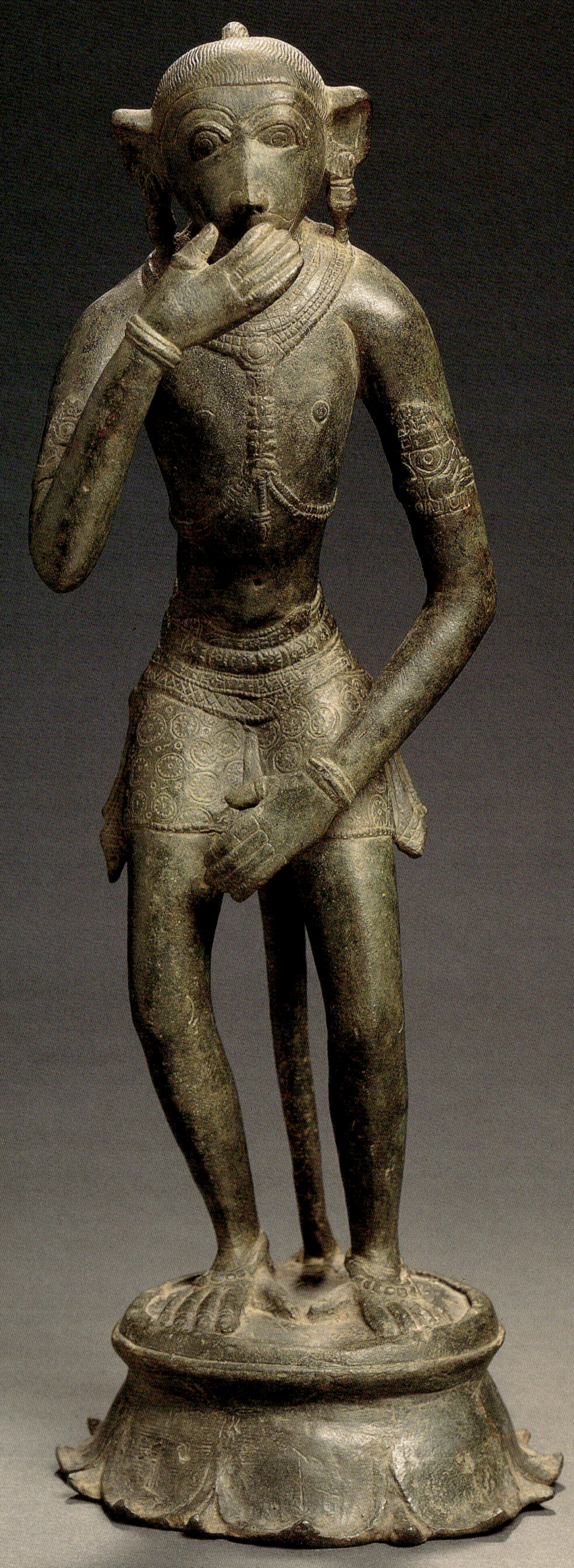

48

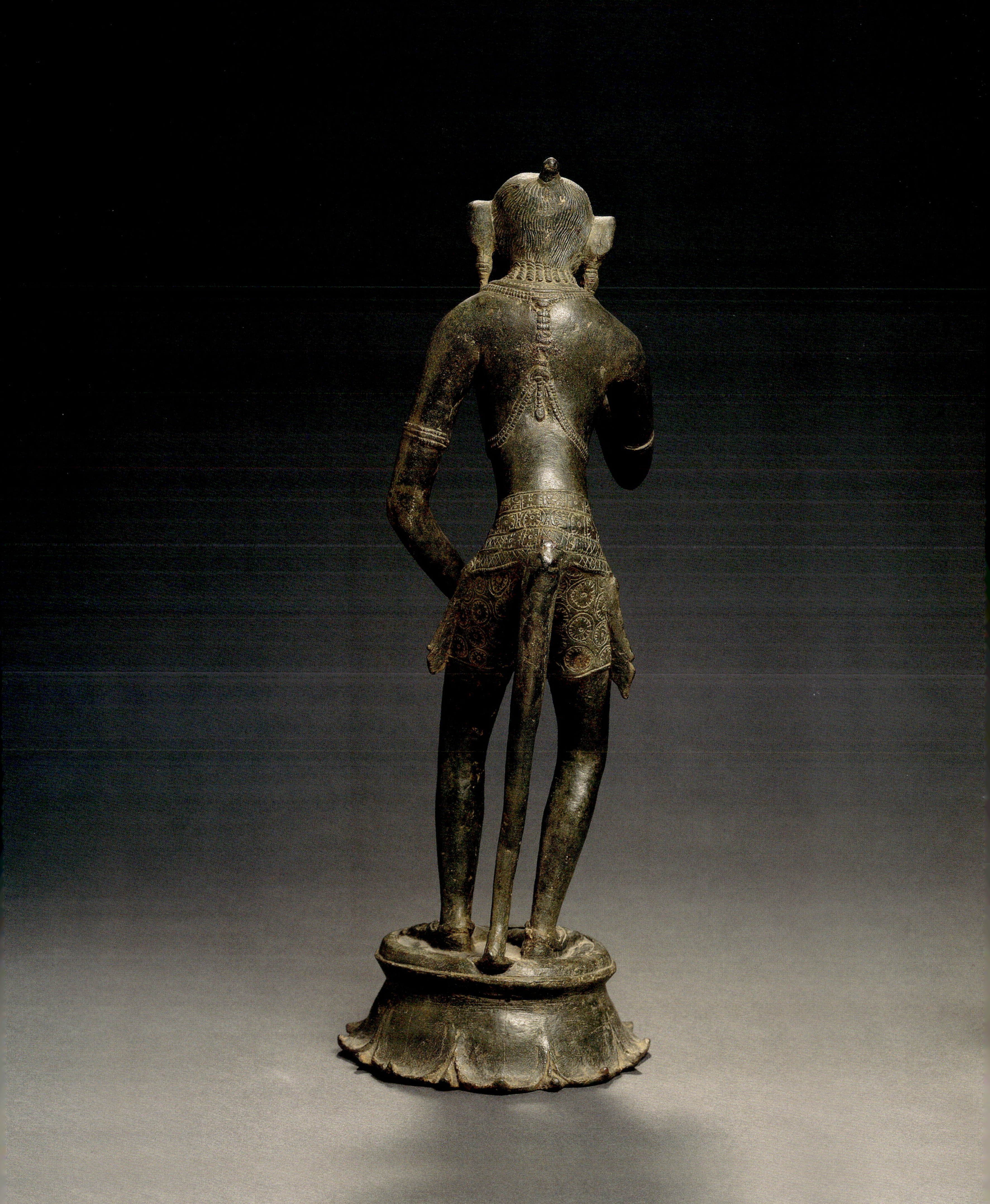

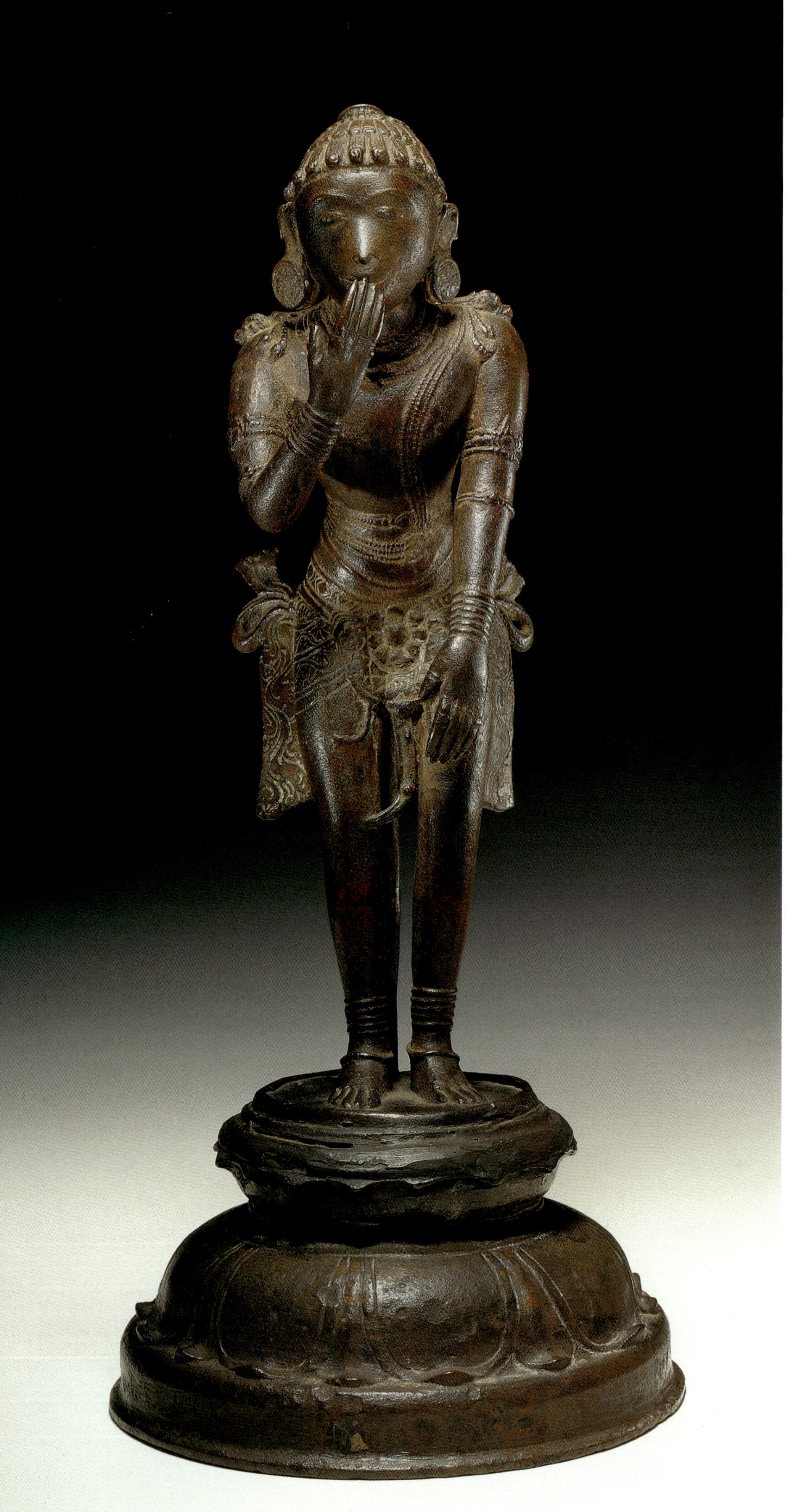

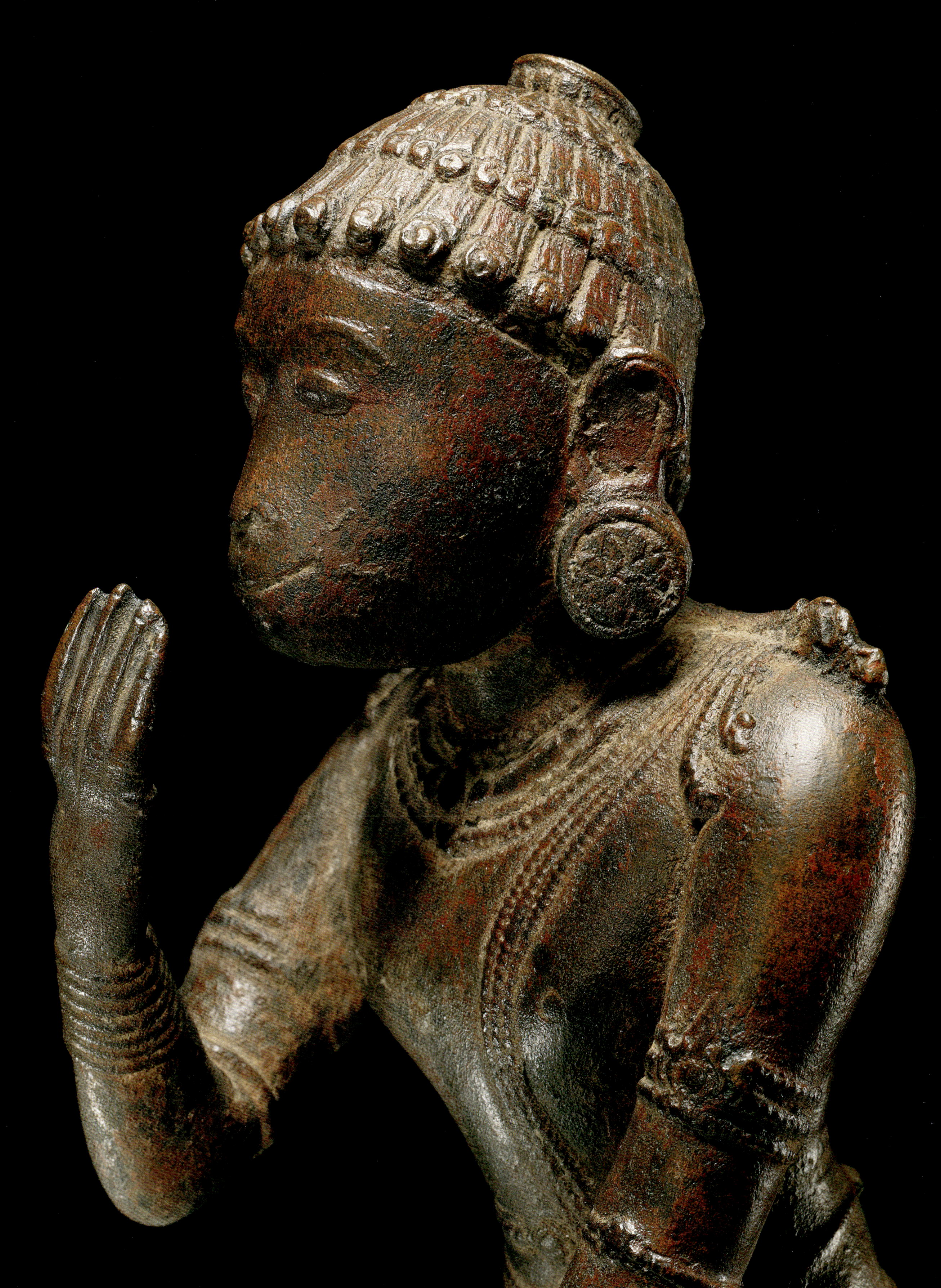

50 YASHODA NURSING BABY KRISHNA
CHOLA PERIOD, 13TH CENTURY
BRONZE, 13 1/8 IN. (33.3 CM)
THE METROPOLITAN MUSEUM OF ART;
PURCHASE, LITA ANNENBERG HAZEN
CHARITABLE TRUST GIFT, IN HONOR OF
CYNTHIA HAZEN AND LEON BERNARD
POLSKY, 1982 (1982.220.8)

51 DANCING CHILD KRISHNA
CHOLA PERIOD, CA. 1100–1150
BRONZE, 23 3/4 IN. (60.2 CM)
PRIVATE COLLECTION

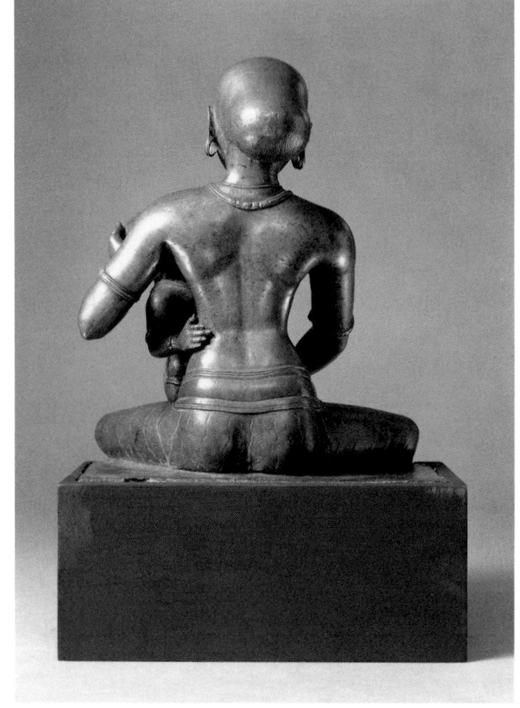

Perhaps the most appealing of Vishnu's avatars is his incarnation as Krishna, and within that life on earth the legend of infant Krishna captivates the hearts of all devotees. He was born to Devaki and Vasudeva in the palace at Mathura, yet grew up in the cowherd village of Ayarpadi (Tamil for Gokula) with foster parents named Yashoda and Nandagopal. Kamsa, the evil king of Mathura, had been told that a child born to his sister Devaki would kill him, and accordingly he arranged for all her offspring to be slain. But the newborn Krishna was secretly taken to Ayarpadi, where he was reared as a cowherd. As a toddler Krishna won the hearts of all around him. Saint Kulashekhara (ca. 800) composed verses that approached Krishna from an unusual angle. He portrayed Krishna's birth mother Devaki lamenting the fact that the joys of motherhood, so apparent in this sensitive rendering of Yashoda nursing Krishna, were denied to her and had fallen instead to the lot of his foster mother Yashoda.

> ***These joys I have not known—***
> ***to see the** cutti **swing on forehead bright***
> ***to get a kiss from his sweet lips***
> ***to feel my heart rise with joy***
> ***seeing his likeness to his father***
> ***to see him with little finger raised to mouth***
> ***to hear his innocent prattle.***
> ***None of these joys have I known—***
> ***they belong to the fortunate Yashoda!***[1]

The bronze from the Metropolitan Museum (cat. no. 50) is a sensitive rendering of a mother nursing her child, with not the slightest emphasis on divinity. Infant Krishna does not look at the viewer but is absorbed in his mother as he plays with one nipple while suckling from the other. The mother, in turn, sits in serene comfort with one hand supporting the infant's head and the other cradling his thigh. Yashoda, portrayed as the simple village woman that she was, wears a plain skirt wrapped around her hips and the most basic of jewelry. While the theme of Yashoda suckling Krishna is known from a number of small bronzes, from both Tamil Nadu and Karnataka, it is indeed rare to find it portrayed as a sizeable bronze.

Child Krishna was a favorite with several of the Vaishnava Tamil saints. Periyalvar (ca. 800), for instance, conjures up a vision of the enchanting infant, placing his verses in the lips of foster mother Yashoda.

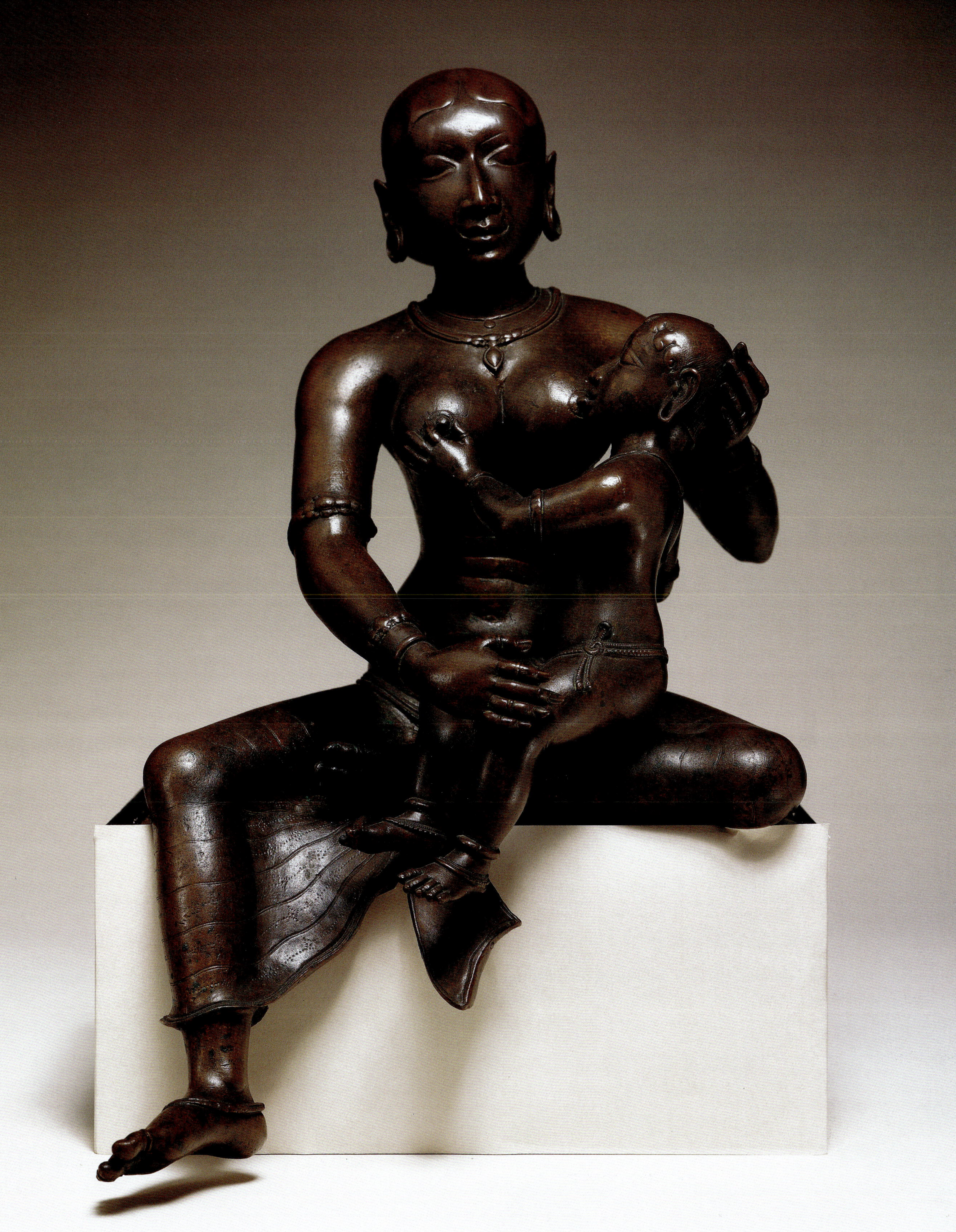

He smiles his charming smile
little white teeth in pink mouth
like silvery crescent moon
in a coral sunset sky—
The lord who reclines on Ananta
the great precious gem
Vasudeva from whose conch-strung girdle
hangs the tortoise pendant—
will he not walk his toddling walk!

With chuckling laughter he comes
dripping water from his mouth
like sugarcane from an open pot—
I am drowned in waves of joy
as he trips forward
to kiss me with that honeyed mouth.
That cloud-colored One
Lord of the sacred form—
over the heads of those who oppose him
will he not walk his toddling walk![2]

It is difficult to remember that these enchanting verses celebrating a mother's joy in her infant were written by a man, and a bachelor at that.

The most popular imagery for child Krishna is as a dancing infant, with one hand in the divine gesture of protection *(abhaya)* and the other stretched out in the movement of dance. Clothing is absent and child Krishna is clad only in ornaments that include the traditional *kinkini* girdle of bells and a range of necklaces, armlets, and anklets. In this bronze from a private collection (cat. no. 51), a series of ringlet curls are piled high upon his head and topped by a single large flower, while blossoms further adorn the strand of curls that rest along each shoulder. A comparison with the image of dancing child-saint Sambandar (cat. no. 28) reveals the close formal and iconographic similarities. As remarked upon earlier, it would appear that the Chola-period sculptors borrowed, almost in its entirety, the popular, well-established form of dancing Krishna and adapted it to portray the Shaiva child-saint. The rechiseling of the eyes of this Krishna image reveals that it remained in active worship for centuries until excessive wear resulted in temple authorities taking steps necessary to assure its potency for the *darshan* of devotees.

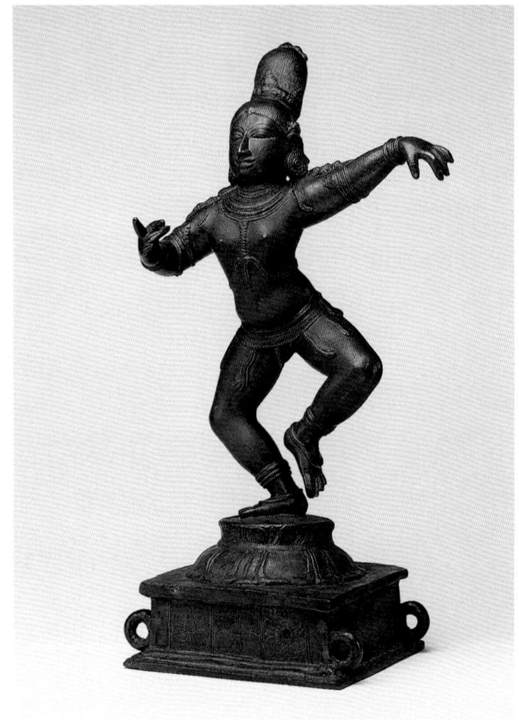

DANCING CHILD-SAINT SAMANDAR
(CAT. NO. 28)

NOTES

1 Vidya Dehejia, *Slaves of the Lord: The Path of the Tamil Saints* (New Delhi: Munshiram Manoharlal, 1988), p. 96: Kulashekhara, *Perumal Tirumoli* 7.5.

2 Ibid., p. 101: Periyalvar, *Periyalvar Tirumoli* 1.7.2.

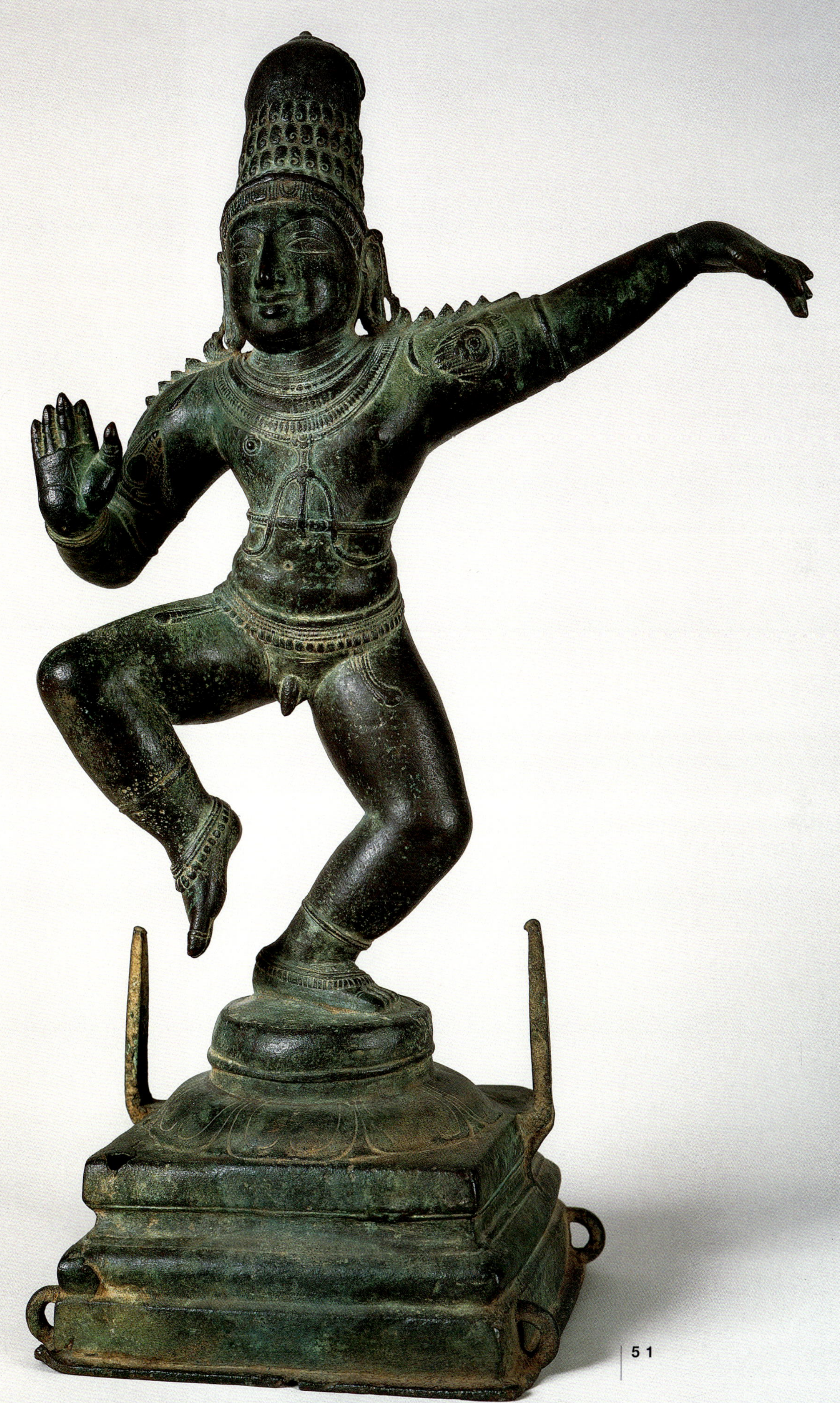

52 A–D KRISHNA WITH CONSORTS RUKMINI AND SATYABHAMA AND DIVINE EAGLE GARUDA

CHOLA PERIOD, 13TH CENTURY
BRONZE, 34 IN., 27 IN., 28 IN., AND 19¼ IN.
(86.4 CM, 68.6 CM, 71.1 CM, AND 48.9 CM)
LOS ANGELES COUNTY MUSEUM OF ART;
GIFT OF MR. AND MRS. HAL B. WALLIS
(M.70.69.1–4)

All was set for the wedding—
Sisupala was resolved
to take her hand in marriage.
All of a sudden
his glow vanished,
he stood petrified.
The divine bridegroom
stepped in,
took her hand in marriage.
Arankam
is the name of his
chosen abode.[1]

After the young cowherd Krishna grew up and killed wicked Kamsa, he left his cowherd village and reigned as king of Dvarka in western India. Rukmini, daughter of the king of Kundinapura, fell deeply in love with him, but her father insisted upon her betrothal and marriage to the Chedi prince Sisupala. She sent a desperate message to Krishna, who arrived just in time to appear before the guests assembled for the wedding ceremony and boldly abduct her in sight of all. Pursuing armies were kept at bay by Krishna's half-brother Balarama, and at Dvarka Krishna wedded Rukmini. Krishna's second wife, Satyabhama, was daughter of Shatrajit, a devout worshiper of Surya, the sun god, who had given him a miraculous gem named Shyamantaka that, like the sun, dispelled darkness. When the gem was stolen, Krishna recovered it for him and the delighted Shatrajit offered him his daughter's hand in marriage. Since Krishna was viewed as an incarnation of god Vishnu, theologians emphasized that in like manner Rukmini was to be viewed as Sri Lakshmi, and Satyabhama as Bhu Lakshmi. Such a concept is evident in this four-piece grouping.

Krishna stands in an elegant contrapposto posture with his left hand raised to rest upon the shoulder of his favorite consort, Satyabhama, and the other hand lowered to hold a staff. It seems likely that the iconography for this image type originated with the visualization of Shiva as Rider of the Bull, in which Shiva stands with his arm similarly poised to rest on the back of his bull Nandi. The image type was also adopted to portray Shaiva saint Sundarar who, in a closely parallel manner, stands resting his bent elbow upon the shoulder of his wife Paravai.[2] Here Krishna's curly locks are arranged high upon his head to appear like a crown, and he is richly adorned with elaborate *makara* earrings, necklaces, a triple-strand sacred thread, waist-band, armlets, bangles, and anklets. His short, patterned waist-cloth is held in place by a girdle with a large lion-head clasp. The bronze appears to date to the start of the thirteenth century, perhaps around the year 1200.

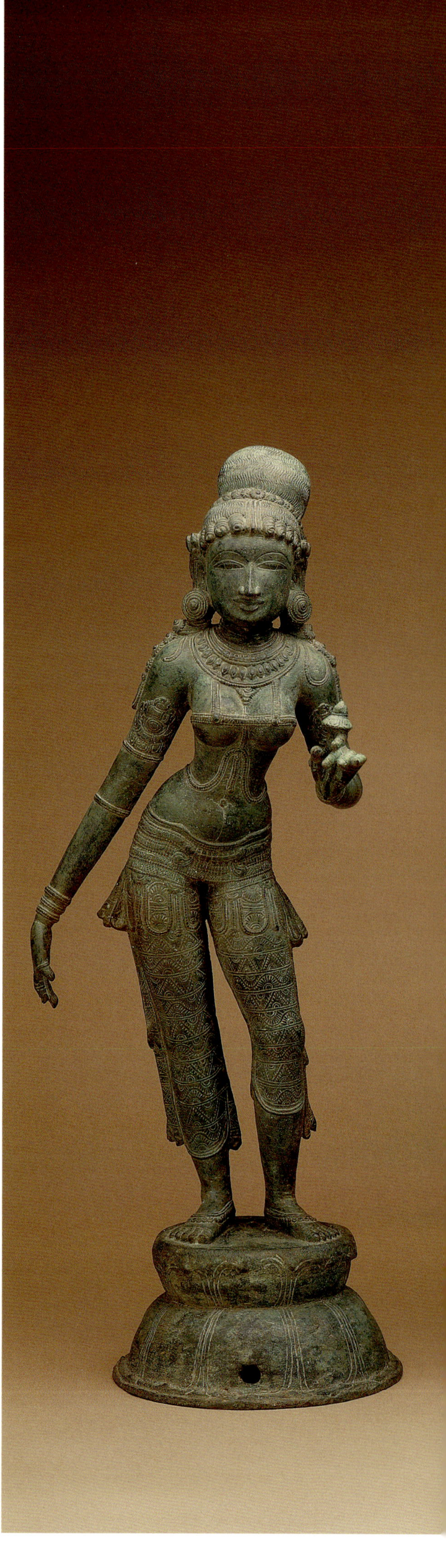

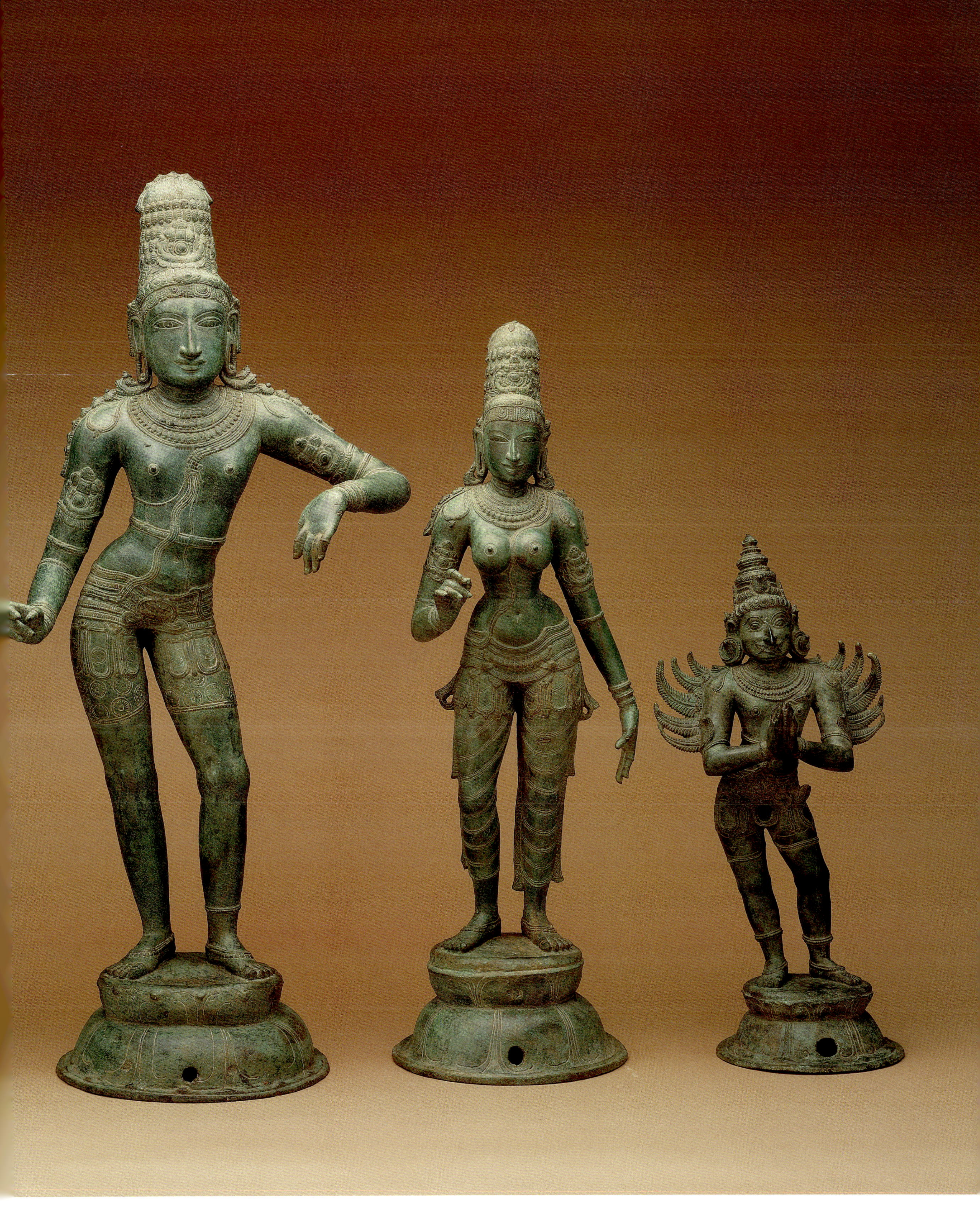

Satyabhama, who stands beside Krishna with a lotus in her right hand, has her hair arranged in a manner similar to that of Krishna. Her long skirt with simple striations is slung low on her hips and held in place by a jeweled girdle with decorative beaded and tasseled loops. She too is elaborately adorned. Her rounded breasts, placed high up and close together, and the circles around her nipples speak of a date in the thirteenth century, and if found on its own this figure might have been placed as late as 1270. Rukmini, Krishna's senior queen, holds a lotus in her left hand. Her hair is arranged quite differently, with curls framing her face and then drawn up into an elegant chignon. She wears large stud earrings and is adorned much as Satyabhama except that she wears a breast-band (which speaks of her identification with goddess Shri), and her skirt is created from patterned fabric. Her figure is less heavily stylized, and the artist whose hand created this bronze, and that of Krishna, was clearly more accomplished and sensitive than the one who carved the fine but somewhat stiff image of Satyabhama.

Garuda, the divine eagle mount of Vishnu, who puts the wind to shame with the speed of his flight, is a striking image with a beaked nose, fangs, and wings to indicate his avian nature. He stands with palms joined in adoration, with a lion-head-clasped girdle securing a short waist-cloth that reveals muscular legs. Garuda is known for his hatred of serpents, which he uses here to serve as his armlets and earrings, and a central serpent adorns his conical crown. In rear view, it can be seen that his wings emerge from the nape of his neck and appear almost like extensions of his ringlet curls. With the rest of this strikingly refined group, he too belongs to the thirteenth century.

NOTES

1 Vidya Dehejia, *Antal and Her Path of Love: Poems of a Woman Saint from South India* (Albany: State University of New York Press, 1990), p. 117: *Nacchiyar Tirumoli* 11.9.

2 See Pratapaditya Pal, *Krishna: The Cowherd King* (Los Angeles: Los Angeles County Museum of Art, 1972); and Vidya Dehejia, "Iconographic Transference between Krsna and Three Saiva Saints," in *Indian Art and Connoisseurship: Essays in Honour of Douglas Barrett*, ed. John Guy (Ahmedabad: Mapin Publishing, 1995), pp. 140–49.

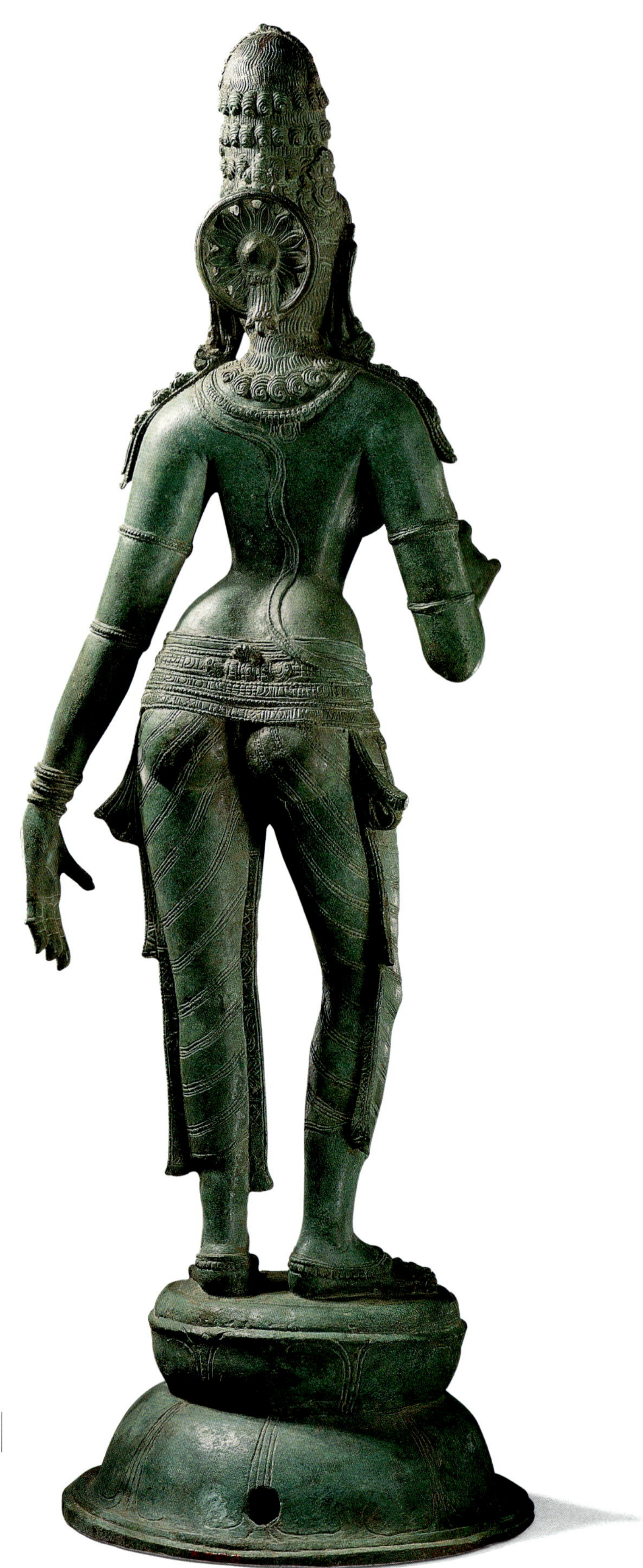

52C

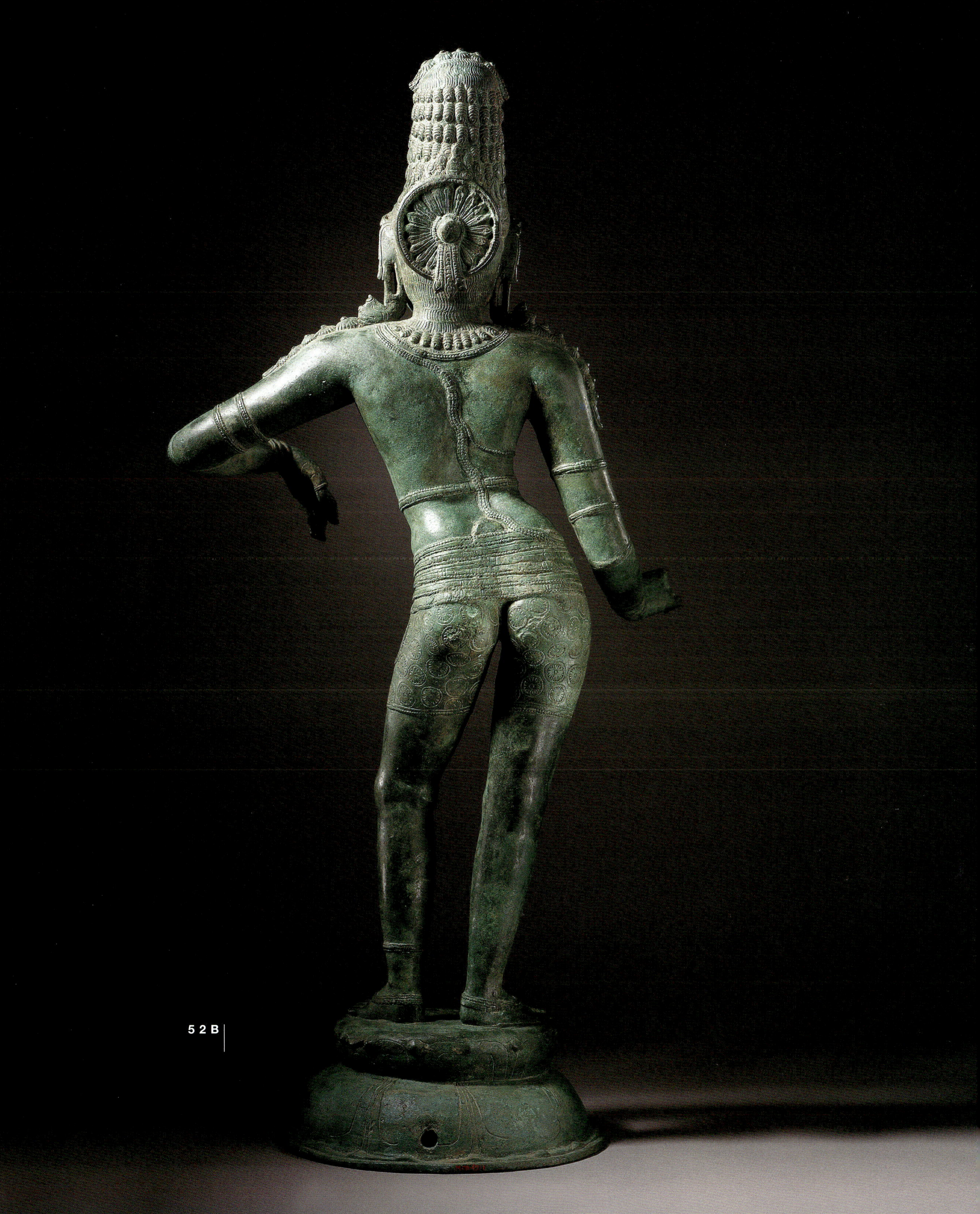

52B

53 SURYA, THE SUN GOD

CHOLA PERIOD, CA. 1070–1100
BRONZE, $19\frac{1}{4}$ IN. (48.8 CM)
THE METROPOLITAN MUSEUM OF ART;
SAMUEL EILENBERG COLLECTION, BEQUEST
OF SAMUEL EILENBERG, 1998 (2000.284.1)

Surya, the god of the celestial orb, the sun, has only one temple dedicated to him in all of Tamil Nadu, and it is located at Suryanarkoil in Tanjavur district. But images of Surya had a role to play in temples dedicated to other deities, as is evidenced, for instance, by the twelve stone images of the twelve Adityas (forms of Surya) found at Rajendra Chola's Shiva temple at Gangaikondacholapuram.[1] Inscriptions confirm that Surya images were equally at home in Vishnu and Shiva temples. For example, an ancient inscription in the Vishnu temple at Jambai speaks of the gift of gold for offerings to the shrine of Surya, and of ninety sheep to maintain a perpetual lamp at the shrine.[2] At the same time, among the more than sixty bronzes commissioned for Rajaraja's monumental Shiva temple at Tanjavur was an image of Surya, the gift of a highly ranked treasury official.[3]

Surya stands erect on a lotus pedestal, holding a lotus in both hands, with an orblike halo setting off his crowned head. His lower garment is secured with a girdle, and the waist scarf forms a distinct U-shaped loop in front. He wears a sacred thread, and is adorned with earrings, necklaces, waist-band, armlets, bangles, and anklets. In the imagery of northern India, Surya regularly wears boots; in Tamil Nadu, however, footwear of any form is unknown for Surya, who is invariably barefoot, as are all other deities.

NOTES

1 Pierre Pichard, ed., *Vingt ans apres Tanjavur, Gangaikondacholapuram* (Paris: Ecole française d'Extreme-Orient, 1994), pls. 288–96.
2 S. R. Balasubrahmanyam, *Early Chola Temples: Parantaka I to Rajaraja I, A.D. 907–985* (Bombay: Orient Longman, 1971), p. 251.
3 E. Hultzsch, ed., *South Indian Inscriptions*, vol. 2 (New Delhi: Archaeological Survey of India, 1992 reprint), part 2, no. 56, p. 226.

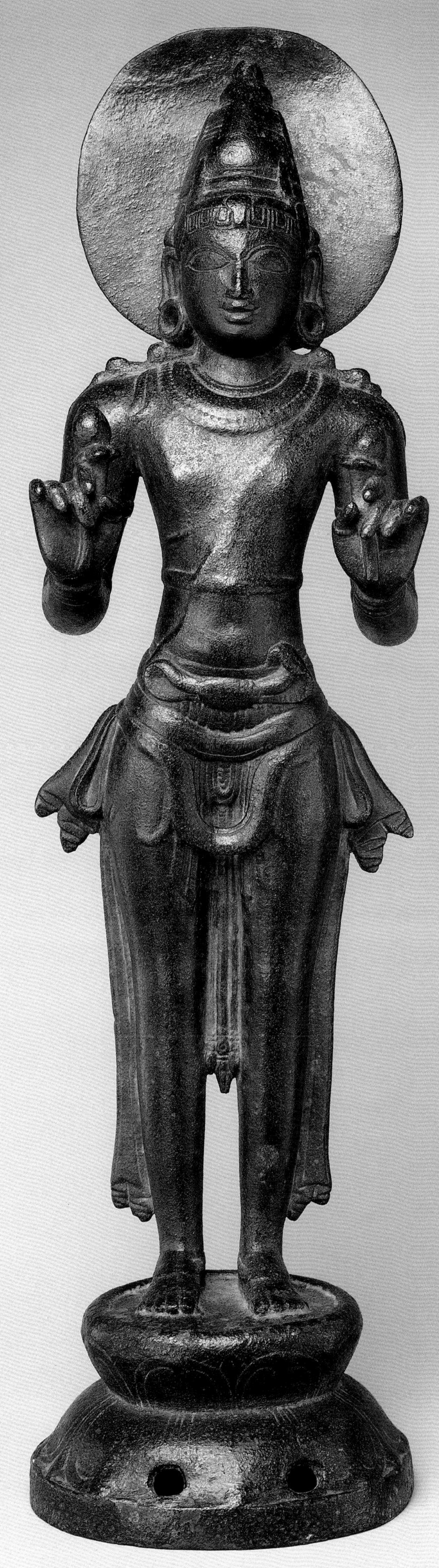

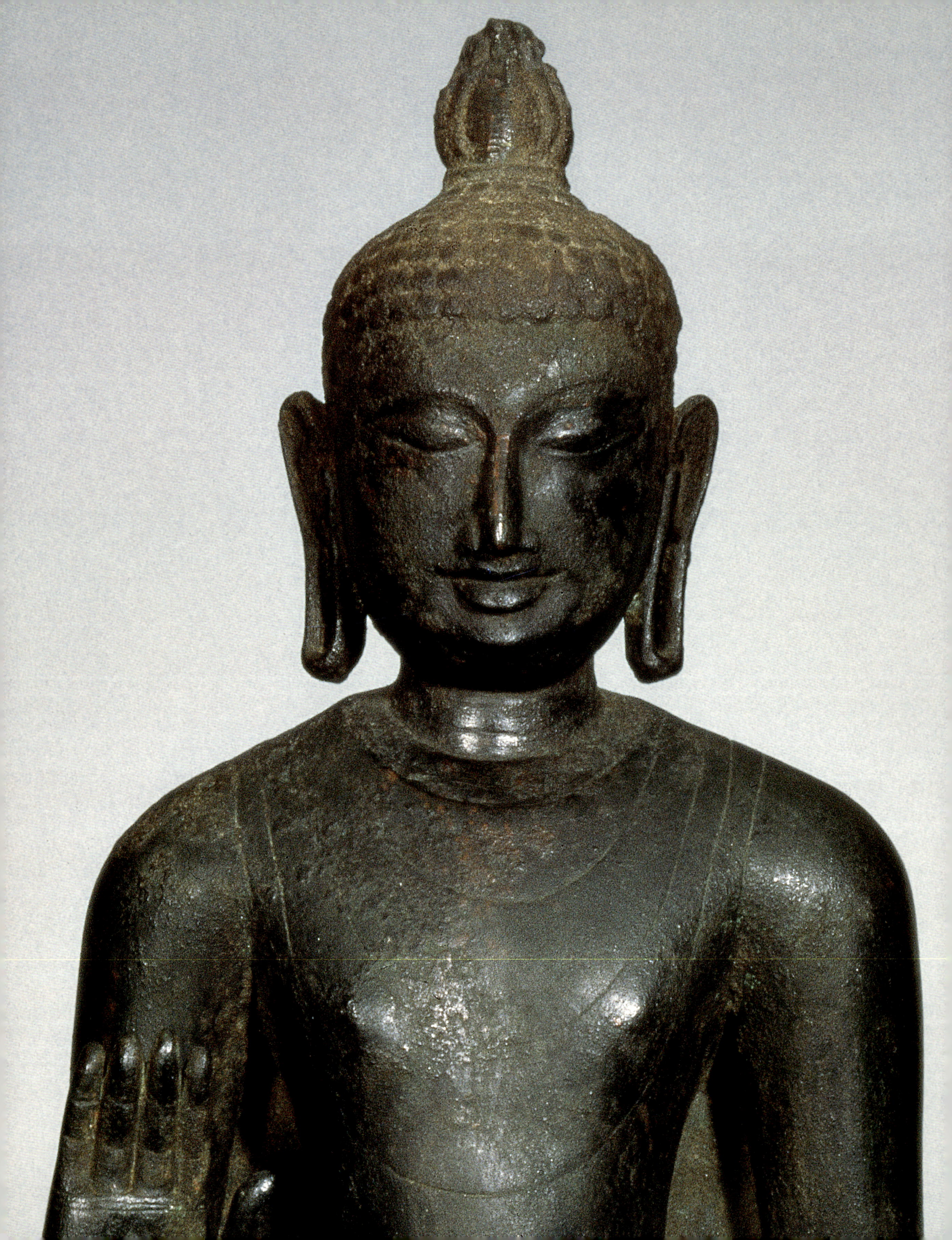

BUDDHIST AND JAIN SHRINES

The term "Chola bronzes" generally evokes a vision of sensuous images of Hindu deities. In south India, however, both the Buddhist and Jain faiths were quite vital in the Chola period, and the followers of these faiths too commissioned processional bronze images for their shrines. Buddhist monasteries attracted donations of individual images of the Buddha, as well as of a range of Buddhist deities that bear striking similarities to their Hindu counterparts. Indeed, a casual viewer might well mistake an image, such as a Nagapattinam bronze of Maitreya, the Buddha of the Future (fig. 1), for Shiva as Tripuravijaya. Since the figure holds a rosary and a bunch of flowers that are not characteristic of Shiva, one might examine the image closer and then discover Maitreya's attribute, a Buddhist stupa, in the headdress. Clearly, Chola craftsmen producing bronze images of Hindu deities made images for Buddhist temples as well, and stylistically one may distinguish both Hindu and Buddhist bronzes of the Chola dynasty from those of the following Vijayanagar dynasty (1336–1565). The Jain faith attracted royal sponsorship throughout the Chola period; for instance, Rajaraja's chief queen, Lokamahadevi, erected a shrine for the Jina Mahavira, while his sister Kundavai built two Jain shrines. Like bronzes of the Buddha himself, images of the Jina, with their emphasis on ascetic simplicity, are easily distinguished.

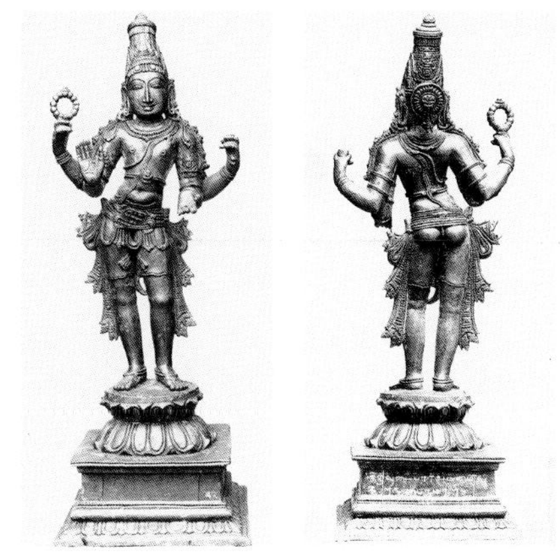

THE FUTURE BUDDHA MAITREYA (TWO VIEWS), FROM NAGAPATTINAM, 13TH CENTURY. GOVERNMENT MUSEUM, CHENNAI
PHOTOS VIDYA DEHEJIA
FIG. 1

BUDDHISM

The early arrival of Buddhism in south India is evident from the numerous ancient Buddhist monastic sites that dot the Godaveri and Krishna river basins of the Andhra region, several of which date back to the first century before the common era, the largest and most prominent being Amaravati and Nagarjunakonda. Literary sources too suggest that Buddhism became entrenched early in the far south. In the Buddhist text the *Gandavyuha,* written in the first or second century and translated into Chinese by 420, its hero Sudhana is advised to travel further south from Amaravati to acquire Buddhist teachings from a range of holy men.[1] The Tamil epic *Manimekhalai*, written around the year 550, speaks of the prosperous condition of the Buddhist establishments at Kanchipuram, mentioning in particular a chapel erected in the city center to house a golden *bodhi* tree with emerald leaves, and another to house an image of the Buddha.[2] A farcical play written by the Pallava king Mahendravarman around the year 600 indicates a prominent Buddhist presence in Kanchipuram.[3] When the Chinese pilgrim Xuanzang visited south India around 630, he found that Kanchipuram housed some one hundred monasteries and ten thousand Buddhist monks of the Sthavira school.[4]

Within a hundred years, the dynamic upsurge of a series of Hindu saints, the Shaiva *nayanmars* and the Vaishnava *alvars*, greatly reduced the power of the Buddhists. The Hindu saints wandered the countryside singing songs in praise of their own gods, but also belittling the Buddhists and the Jains. In fact, Vaishnava texts report in undisturbed fashion that the eighth-century Vaishnava saint Tirumangai, a robber-chieftain prior to his conversion by Vishnu, stole a golden Buddha from a *vihara* at Nagapattinam and melted it down, then used the gold to decorate the Vishnu temple at Srirangam.

During the ninth century there was a vibrant renewal of artistic activity in the coastal town of Nagapattinam. A Buddhist presence was evident there as early as the seventh century, when Chinese pilgrim Yijing noted that a monk named Wuhing stopped at Nagapatana on his journey to Sri Lanka.[5] Buddhism in south India seems to have received new impetus during the eleventh century, partly due

BUDDHA, ENLIGHTENED ONE
(DETAIL OF CAT. NO. 54)

to the arrival of a colony of Buddhists from the kingdom of Shrivijaya in Indonesia. In the year 1006, Emperor Rajaraja Chola granted permission to an embassy from the Shailendra king of Java, Chula-mani-varman, to build a Buddhist monastery "of such high loftiness as belittled Kanakagiri (mount Meru) . . . at Nagapattana, delightful on account of many a temple, rest-house, water-shed, and pleasure-garden and brilliant with arrays of various kinds of mansions."[6] Within this monastery named after the Javanese monarch was built a chapel called the Rajaraja-perum-palli (Great Chapel of Rajaraja), and the Chola monarch granted the village of Anaimangalam to the Buddha of this chapel.[7]

In the year 1090, during the rule of the Chola Kulottunga I, we hear of the arrival of two ambassadors from the Shailendra kingdom and the grant of further privileges to the Chula-mani-varma monastery. A new chapel was added and named Rajendra-perum-palli, taking its name from Kulottunga's given name Rajendra, as he provided further support for the shrine.[8] Some three hundred and fifty Buddhist images in stone and bronze were produced in Nagapattinam between the ninth and seventeenth centuries, and speak unequivocally of the persisting vitality of the Buddhist faith in south India. Several of these images were undoubtedly intended for the royal Javanese shrine, parts of which seem to have been intact until 1867, when it was pulled down by French Jesuits to erect their own buildings on the site.[9]

JAINISM

Early Tamil inscriptions reveal that the Jains were a major presence in south India as early as the Buddhists. Scattered over Tamil Nadu, but particularly in the district of Tiruchirapalli, as also in the more southern districts of Madurai and Tirunelveli, are a number of small natural caverns occupied at one time by Jain ascetics. Engraved on the brow of one such cave on the Mankulam hill is a set of six Tamil inscriptions in the Brahmi script of the second or first century B.C.E. One dedicatory inscription reads thus:

> ***Hail to Kaniyananta, the monk living yonder.***
> ***This monastic abode was given by Katalan Valuttiyar, officer under Neduncalaiyan.***[10]

A corpus of Tamil inscriptions reveals at least fifty such records in caves at various sites dating from the centuries before the common era. When we move on to the first centuries of the common era, the number of such cave inscriptions reaches several hundred. A record from the third century at Pugalur seems to indicate the increasing strength of Jainism since a cave was donated by a local chieftain, who had perhaps adopted the faith:

> ***This abode of Cenkayappan, a Jain monk of Yarur.***
> ***This stone abode was cut by Ilankutunko . . .***
> ***when he became heir apparent.***[11]

The records are all written in Tamil, indicating that the Jains adopted the local language early on.

The Jain epic *Shilappadikaram* of about the year 450 (its story of Kannaki and Kovalan is known to all in south India) reflects the cordial relationship that existed early on between the Jains and Hindus. The Jain nun Kavundi Adigal, a prominent character in the story, listens patiently to a discourse from a brahmin about the gods to be worshiped and the benefits to be gained from so doing. She then replied courteously:

> O brahmin of good conduct who is learned in the Vedas! I have no desire to go on your route for realising the ends you have described . . . You go ahead to worship the gods you love. We shall also go on our way.[12]

Toward the end of the fifth century, however, a degree of discord and rivalry developed between the Jains and Hindus, who had thus far lived in comparative harmony. From time to time, the Jains secured royal patronage which came from monarchs of the Kalabhra dynasty, the Pandyas, Pallavas, and the western Gangas.[13] The legends of several Hindu saints indicate open conflict between Shaivas and Jains, and saint Appar was himself a Jain before he converted to the worship of Shiva. Saint Sambandar referred scornfully to the Jains as "unclad monkeys."[14] The hagiographic stories of Appar and Sambandar, clearly intended to position the Jains as a dangerous "other,"[15] whether true or not in their details, testify to the distrust and antagonism that arose between the sects in the seventh century. The Jain Pallava king is said to have thrown Appar into a lime kiln, forced him to drink poison, set an enraged elephant on him, and cast him into the waters bound with a rock. But Appar emerged unharmed. Sambandar is said to have healed a kind of incurable fever (the Jains failed), and his Shaiva document was unharmed by both fire and water, while the Jain document was destroyed by both. These events are said to have converted the Pandya king from the Jain faith to Shaivism.

While Hinduism certainly prevailed in Tamil Nadu, the Jain faith by no means disappeared but continued instead to attract a devout group of worshipers. Throughout the Chola period, royalty continued to support the Jains. For instance, Kundavai, the sister of Rajaraja Chola, who built one Shiva temple and one Vishnu temple, also built two Jain temples, both named Kundavai Jinalaya, one at the town of Dadapuram and the other at Tirumalai.[16] And just as the artists who constructed the Hindu temples also built those dedicated to the Jain faith, the same sculpture workshops produced both Hindu and Jain bronze images.

NOTES

1 For a summary of this text, see A. J. Barnet Kempers, *Ageless Borobudur* (Wassenar: Servire, 1976), chapter 10, "Gandavyuha and Bhadracari: Inventory of Reliefs," pp. 121–41.

2 See Alain Danielou, trans., *Manimekhalai (The Dancer with the Magic Bowl) By Merchant-Prince Shattan* (New York: New Directions, 1989): canto 28, pp. 141–49.

3 Michael Lockwood and Vishnu Bhatt, *Mattavilasa Prahasana* (Madras: The Christian Literature Society, 1981), pp. 43–45.

4 Xuanzang, *Si-Yu-Ki: Buddhist Records of the Western World,* trans. Samuel Beal, reprint (Delhi: Oriental Reprint, 1969): 2:229.

5 J. Takakasu, *A Record of the Buddhist Religion,* reprint (Delhi: Munshiram Manoharlal, 1966), p. xlvi.

6 K. V. Subrahmanya Aiyer, "The Larger Leiden Plates of Rajaraja I," *Epigraphia Indica* 22 (1933–34): 257.

7 Ibid.

8 K. V. Subrahmanya Aiyer, "The Smaller Leiden Plates of Kulottunga I," *Epigraphia Indica* 22 (1933–34): 279.

9 Vidya Dehejia, "The Persistence of Buddhism in Tamil Nadu," in *A Pot-Pourri of Indian Art*, ed. Pratapaditya Pal (Bombay: Marg Publications, 1988), pp. 53–74.

10 Iravatham Mahadevan, "Corpus of the Tamil-Brahmi Inscriptions," in *Seminar on Inscriptions,* ed. R. Nagaswamy (Madras: Books [India] Private Ltd., 1968), p. 60.

11 Ibid., p. 65.

12 Translated by C. V. Narayana Ayyar, *Origin and Early History of Saivism in South India* (Madras: University of Madras, 1939), p. 286; canto 11.

13 See Vidya Dehejia, *Slaves of the Lord: The Path of the Tamil Saints* (Delhi: Munshiram Manoharlal, 1988), pp. 26ff.

14 Sambandar 3.39.4.

15 Indira V. Peterson, "Sramanas Against the Tamil Way: Jains as Others in Tamil Saiva Literature," in *Open Boundaries. Jain Communities and Cultures in Indian History*, ed. John E. Cort, pp. 163–85 (Albany: State University of New York Press, 1998). See also Richard H. Davis, "The Story of the Disappearing Jains: Retelling the Saiva-Jain Encounter in Medieval South India," in *Open Boundaries,* pp. 213–24.

16 B. Venkataraman, *Temple Art Under the Chola Queens* (Faridabad: Thomson Press, 1976), pp. 72–84.

54 BUDDHA, ENLIGHTENED ONE

CHOLA PERIOD, EARLY 11TH CENTURY
BRONZE, 27 1/4 IN. (69.2 CM)
ASIA SOCIETY, NEW YORK; THE MR. AND MRS. JOHN D. ROCKEFELLER 3RD COLLECTION (1979.15)

This impressive Buddha, with a serenely elegant face and elongated ear lobes, stands erect with his right hand raised in the *abhaya* gesture of protection and his left lowered in the *varada* gesture of wish-granting. His head is covered with tiny curls, and rising from the top of the head is a stylized flame, characteristic of south Indian images of the Buddha, that represents the true knowledge said to hover like a flame above the enlightened one's head. His monastic robe, draped so as to cover both shoulders, with lightly incised lines to suggest folds, fully reveals the sinuous form beneath; the scalloped folds along its lower outer edges is a feature that becomes highly pronounced from the twelfth century onwards.

The large caches of Buddhist bronzes discovered at Nagapattinam suggest the existence of a local workshop that catered to the requirements of its Buddhist shrines. However, the close stylistic similarity of images of Hindu and Buddhist deities (aside from those of the Buddha himself) indicates that the same artists sculpted images for the differing faiths. Like their Hindu counterparts, Chola Buddhist bronzes are portable images intended for processional festivities, as is evident from the holes in this Buddha's circular lotus pedestal intended to receive bamboo poles with which to hoist the image onto the shoulders of monks and devotees. But in contrast to Hindu practice—in which bronzes rarely carry inscriptions on their pedestals, as patrons preferred to engrave such records on the temple walls—the majority of the Nagapattinam Buddhist bronzes have inscriptions engraved along their bases.

Buddhist festivals—focusing on an image provided with ornaments, placed on a palanquin or wagon decorated with banners and flags, and carried in procession through the town by monks, to the accompaniment of music—were apparently known since early times. Gregory Schopen has recently brought to light a neglected text, the *Uttaragrantha* of the influential *Mulasarvastivadin Vinaya,* that belongs to the early centuries of the common era.[1] It specifies that a festival should be advertised in the town seven or eight days prior to its occurrence and announced in prominent locations including the marketplace and crossroads. The original purpose of such a Buddhist portable image—to provide a substitute for the absent Buddha and to attract donations from the townsfolk—may have differed from the motivation for making Hindu festival images. However, it is likely that by Chola times the clear-cut distinctions that lay behind the creation of Buddhist and Hindu processional images had blurred, and there is little doubt that their ceremonial aspects overlapped considerably.

The record inscribed on this Buddha bronze from the Asia Society collection carries invaluable information. It tells us that the image, a processional bronze, was commissioned by a guild of metal-workers for the Rajendra-perum-palli chapel, presumably within the Chula-mani-varman monastery at Nagapattinam. The festival itself seems to have been sponsored by a devotee from the town of Sirutavur. The epigraph reads:

> Well-being and prosperity. The *nayakar* [Buddha] of all of the eighteen countries, of the metal-workers. The procession image, for the sacred festival of the *alvar* temple, which was caused to be taken in procession by the respected one *(utaiyar)* from Sirutavur, endowed with the four *gunas*; in the perum-palli of the metal-workers, in the perum-palli of Rajendra-Chola.[2]

Paleographically, the inscription is early, and R. Nagaswamy confirms emphatically that the Tamil letters belong to the time of Rajendra I (r. 1012–44), and not to the reign of Kulottunga, also known as Rajendra, who a century later built another Buddhist chapel at Nagapattinam.[3] This bronze thus becomes a benchmark for the style of Buddhist images during the first half of the eleventh century.

NOTES

1 Gregory Schopen, "On Sending the Monks Back to Their Books: Cult and Conservatism in Early Mahayana Buddhism," paper given at the conference "Investigating the Early Mahayana," Stanford University, May 2001. Schopen analyzes more than one reference to a processional image, and quotes in its entirety a lengthy passage, translated from the Tibetan version of the text (Derge, Pa 175b.1–177b.7). He points out that a summary of this text is preserved in Sanskrit in R. Sankrityayana, ed., *Vinayasutra of Bhadanta Gunaprabha* (Bombay: n.p., 1981), pp. 120–21.

2 Translation is mine. See Denise Patry Leidy, *Treasures of Asian Art: The Asia Society's Mr. and Mrs. John D. Rockefeller 3rd Collection* (New York: Asia Society Galleries, 1994), p. 58.

3 R. Nagaswamy, personal communication.

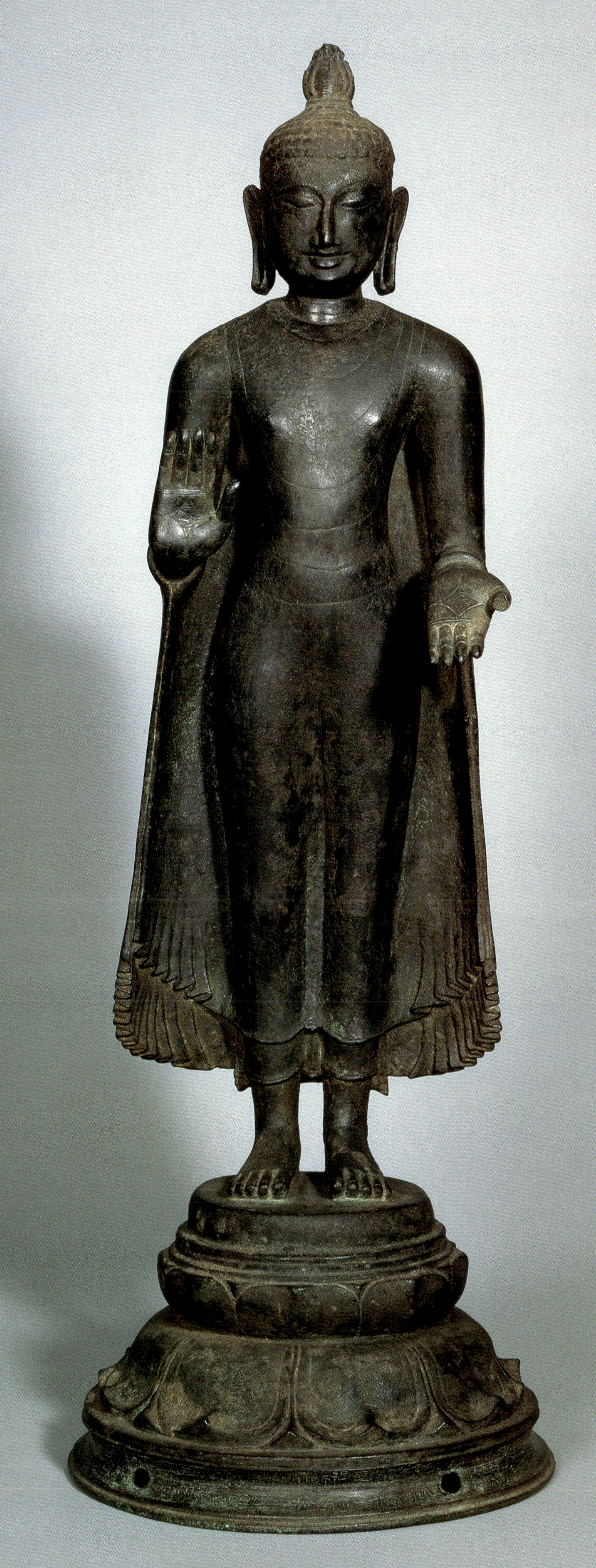

55 JINA (VICTOR)
CHOLA PERIOD, CA. 900
BRONZE, 8¼ IN. (21 CM)
COLLECTION DR. SIDDHARTH BHANSALI, NEW ORLEANS

56 JINA (VICTOR)
CHOLA PERIOD, 10TH CENTURY
BRONZE, 13½ IN. (34.3 CM)
COLLECTION ROSEMARY AND GEORGE LOIS

Mahavira, propagator of the Jain faith and chieftain of the republic of Vaishali in eastern India, appears to have been an elder contemporary of the Buddha. Like the Buddha, he left home at around the age of thirty, and upon achieving enlightenment Mahavira became known as the Jina or Victor. The path he propagated laid great emphasis upon penance and austerity. As the faith developed, it proposed the existence of twenty-three Jinas prior to Mahavira, who was considered the last of the line. An early schism within the monastic order resulted in the formation of two sects, the Shvetambara or white-clad monks and the Digambara or sky-clad, that is, naked, monks.

Although each of the twenty-four Jinas has his own attribute, these are frequently not depicted, as is the case with these two images, both of which may, in fact, represent Mahavira. As is customary, both images stand with hands stretched downward at the sides, in the stiff upright position known as *kayotsarga* that represents the detached posture of penance. As is evident from their nakedness, both images represent a Jina belonging to the Digambara (sky-clad) sect of Jains.

The image from the collection of Dr. Siddharth Bhansali (cat. no. 55), standing on a double lotus pedestal with prongs (only one remains) to receive a *prabha*, appears to belong to an early date, perhaps around 900. Such a date is reinforced by the three-line Tamil inscription along the front of its pedestal, of which the Tamil characters belong, paleographically, to the very end of the ninth century. The inscription informs us that the portrait *(pratima)* was consecrated at the sacred temple of Cinnamulur by the lady Ara-manavatti, wife of the chieftain Iladai-araiyan of Elummur in the subdivision of Amur Velanadu.[1] A few characters are indistinct but the general meaning of the epigraph is clear enough. This inscribed and roughly dated piece is significant in providing us with evidence for stylistic comparison and hence for dating other Jain bronzes.

The Jina from the Lois collection (cat. no. 56), which belongs roughly a hundred years later, displays a sensitive modeling of the smooth outlines of the body that, despite portraying an ascetic figure, retains the touch of sensuous form typical of Chola workmanship. Broad shoulders narrow to a slender torso placed on firm strong legs, while the arms taper to elegant hands with elongated fingers. The bronze is a highly accomplished work of an early Chola artist. It would have been set into a lotus pedestal and, like its Buddhist and Hindu counterparts, may have been a portable festival image.

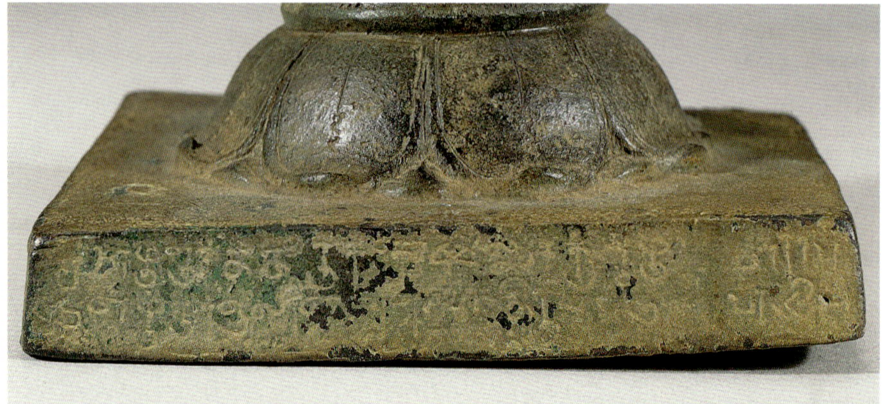

NOTE

1 I am grateful to R. Nagaswamy for this translation and his palaeographic dating of the three-line inscription:

1. *Cinarmulur tiruk-koyilukku Amur velana*
2. *ttu elummur iladai araiyan thiru aramanavatti*
3. *ceyvitta patimam*

55

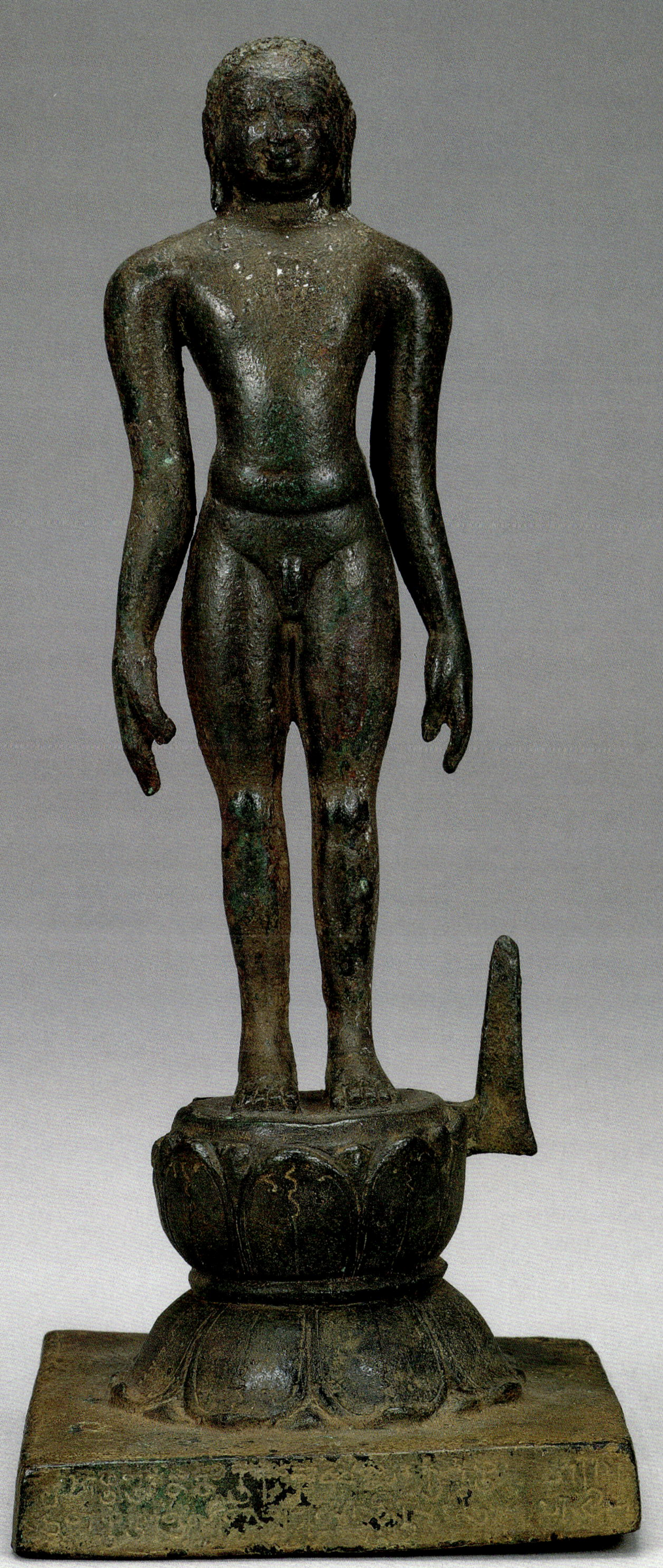

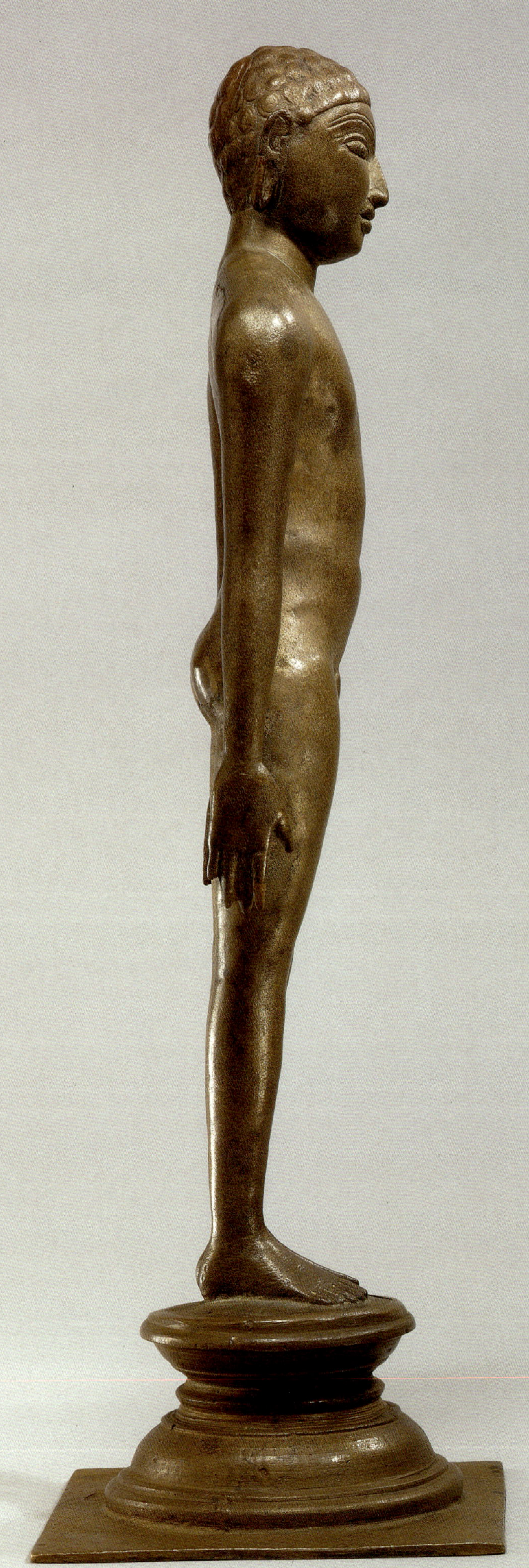

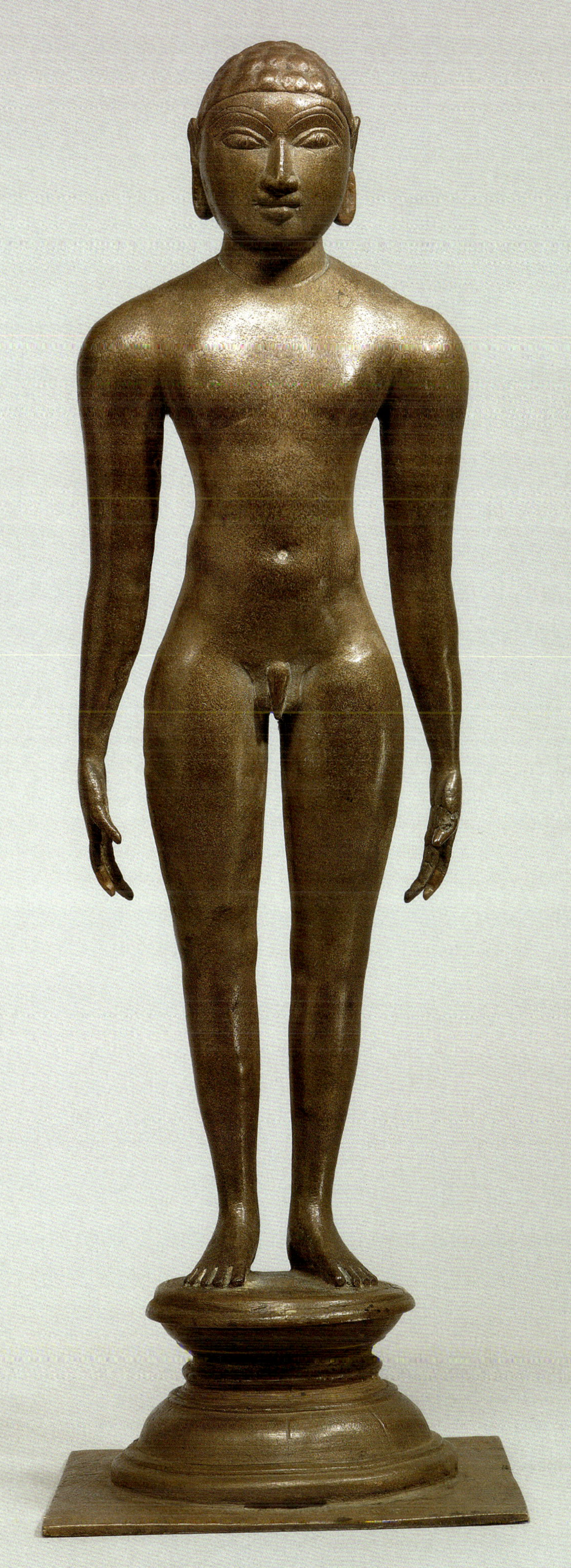

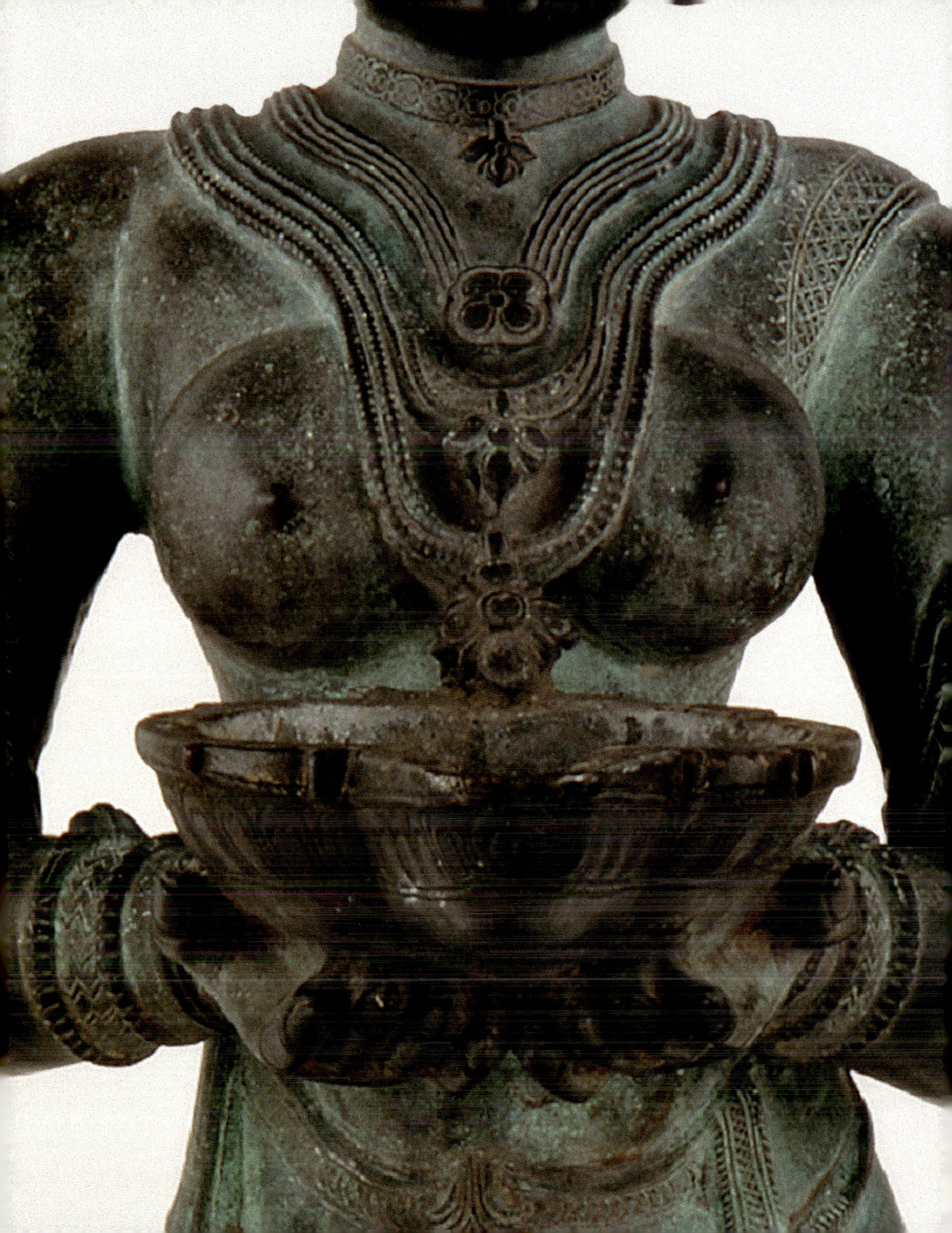

RITUAL LAMPS

57 A,B PORTRAIT LAMPS OF A DONOR AND WIFE
NAYAK PERIOD, 17TH CENTURY
BRONZE, 34 IN. (86.4 CM)
ARTHUR M. SACKLER GALLERY, SMITHSONIAN INSTITUTION, WASHINGTON, D.C.; PURCHASE (S2000.9)

58 GAJALAKSHMI LAMP
CA. 1850
BRONZE, 11 5/8 IN. (29.5 CM)
KAPOOR GALLERIES, INC., NEW YORK

Priests conducting temple worship require a wide range of ritual paraphernalia that, since at least the early Chola period, were gifts from devotees. At Rajaraja's royal temple, such items were occasionally of gold, and one donation of gold utensils from his sister Kundavai speaks of the gift of one plate, two bowls, four waterpots, one cup, one container for sacred ashes together with a stand, and one box for lime paste.[1] Most ritual objects gifted to the temple were of silver. Another inscription tells us that by the twenty-ninth year of his reign (1014), Rajaraja had presented the temple with eleven trumpets, thirty dishes, twenty-five bowls, nine water-pots, twelve censers, six spouted baskets, two small baskets, twenty-four cups, four receptacles for sacred ashes, three spoons, five pots, and twelve salvers.[2] These items, all of silver, were required to carry out daily *puja* to the main deity and also to honor the festival bronzes.

From early Chola times, oil lamps, among the most important ritual objects in a temple, were gifts primarily from members of the merchant and trading community. They came in all shapes and sizes, and an inscription in the Shiva temple at Tiruvaiyaru speaks of several varieties that included hanging lamps *(toongu vilakku)*, zinc lamps, snake-hood lamps, Kerala lamps, Sri Lankan lamps, and Chola lamps.[3] In a twelfth-century Arabic letter from Aden, a Jewish trader writes thus to his supplier in the Chola kingdom, describing what resembles a popular Tamil Nadu model, the *kutti vilakku*, that continues to be made in two or three parts with a spiral column:

> Make me a nice lamp from the rest of all the copper. Its column should be octagonal and stout, its base should be in the form of a lamp stand with strong feet. On its head should be a copper lamp with two wicks, which should be set on the end of the column so that it could move up or down. The three parts, the column, the stand and the lamp, should be separate from one another. If they could make the feet in spirals, then let it be so; for this is more beautiful.[4]

An eleventh-century inscription from the coastal town of Nagapattinam speaks of local craftsmen who specialized in producing temple lamps, and of one in particular, named Cadaiyan alias Devarakanda acariyan, who received a commission from the Shrivijaya king; these lamps were then presented to a local temple in honor of the Chola emperor Kulottunga I.[5]

Certain types of lamps were intended largely to provide an auspicious light whereby devotees could gaze at the images, and one such popular mode was the portrait lamp. By making such a gift to the temple, a donor and his/her family gained a permanent place in the temple where, with hands holding the bowl in which were placed oil and a wick, they obtained the privilege of eternally worshiping the deity. An inscription in the temple at Tiruvaduturai, examined in the context of the assemblage of bronzes in a small Shiva temple, testifies to the donation, prior to the year 1000, of two copper-alloy portrait lamps. One was a self-portrait lamp presented by a donor, and the second was a portrait of a second donor's mother. To this day, most temple shrines contain several such portrait lamps. Their appeal is immediate and, in the context of human nature, totally understandable.

The two bronze portrait lamps in the exhibition are handsome examples of seventeenth-century workmanship in the Pandyan region, which was at this time under the control of the Nayak rulers of Madurai; they had started out as viceroys of the Vijayanagar rulers but soon declared themselves independent monarchs. Stylistically the lamp figures parallel the portraits of Nayak royalty sculpted against the stone pillars in the main halls of Nayak-period temples (fig. 1). Standing in a dignified posture, yet displaying deferential surrender to the deity, both figures have their palms cupped to hold a large lipped oil lamp. The male donor wears a long *veshti* held around his waist with a decorated cloth band, and a turban of the type favored by Nayak nobility and royalty. The female is more richly adorned: she wears four necklaces of different lengths, armlets, bracelets, anklets, and large rounded earrings. Her rich array of hair ornaments includes a rounded gem-studded *rakodi* on the back of her head, an elaborate plait ornament commencing with a serpent hood and ending with a tassel, a chain down the central parting of her hair arranged so as to frame her face, and a sun-and-moon ornament on either side of the parting. A twisted metal-belt-cum-ornamental-girdle holds in place her long skirt, which ends in a billowing fold around her ankles. It is possible that the bronzes were commissioned for a temple in the vicinity of the town of Karaikudi, south of Madurai.

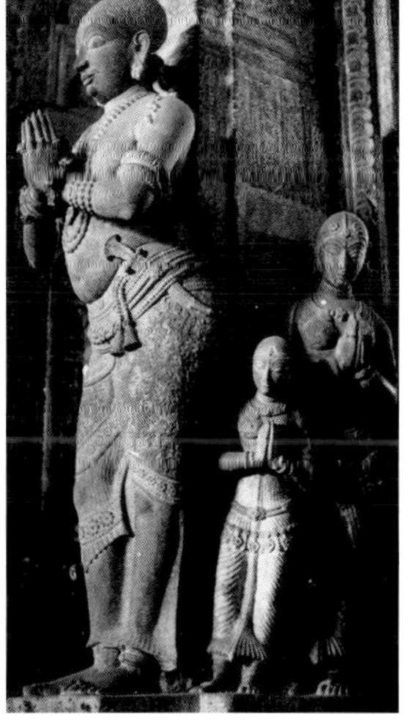

PORTRAIT OF NAYAK RULER AND WIVES SCULPTED AGAINST STONE PILLAR, PUDUMANDAPAM, MINAKSHI TEMPLE, MADURAI
PHOTO VIDYA DEHEJIA
FIG. 1

PORTRAIT LAMP (DETAIL OF CAT NO. 57B)

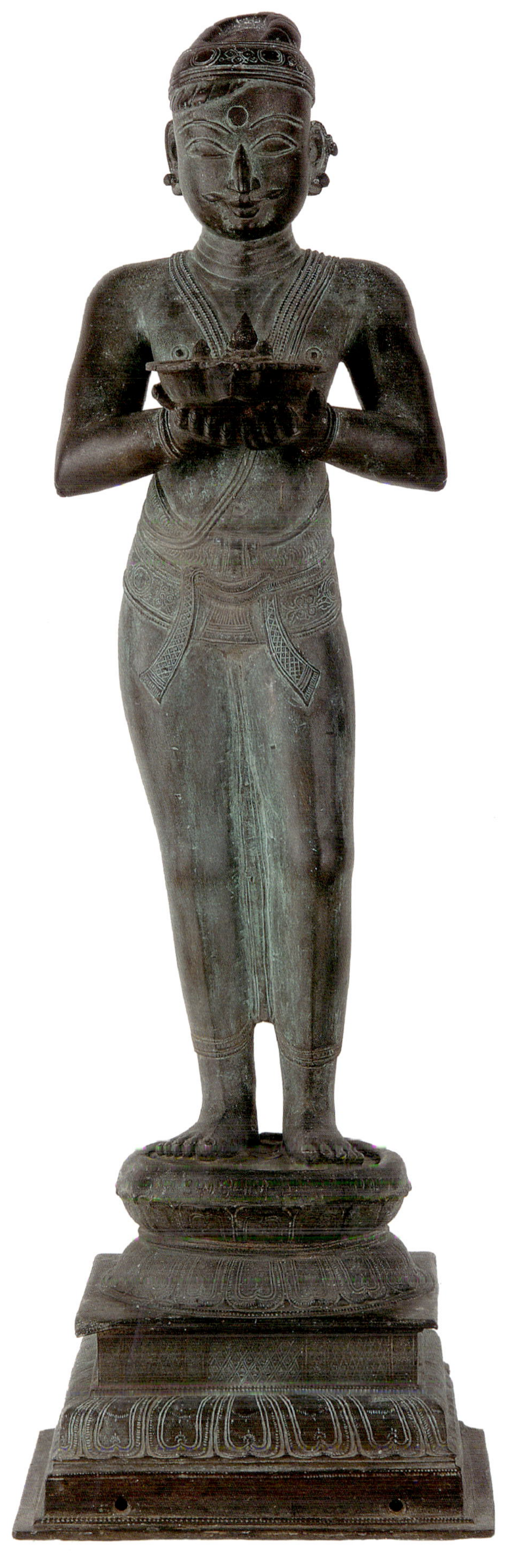

57A

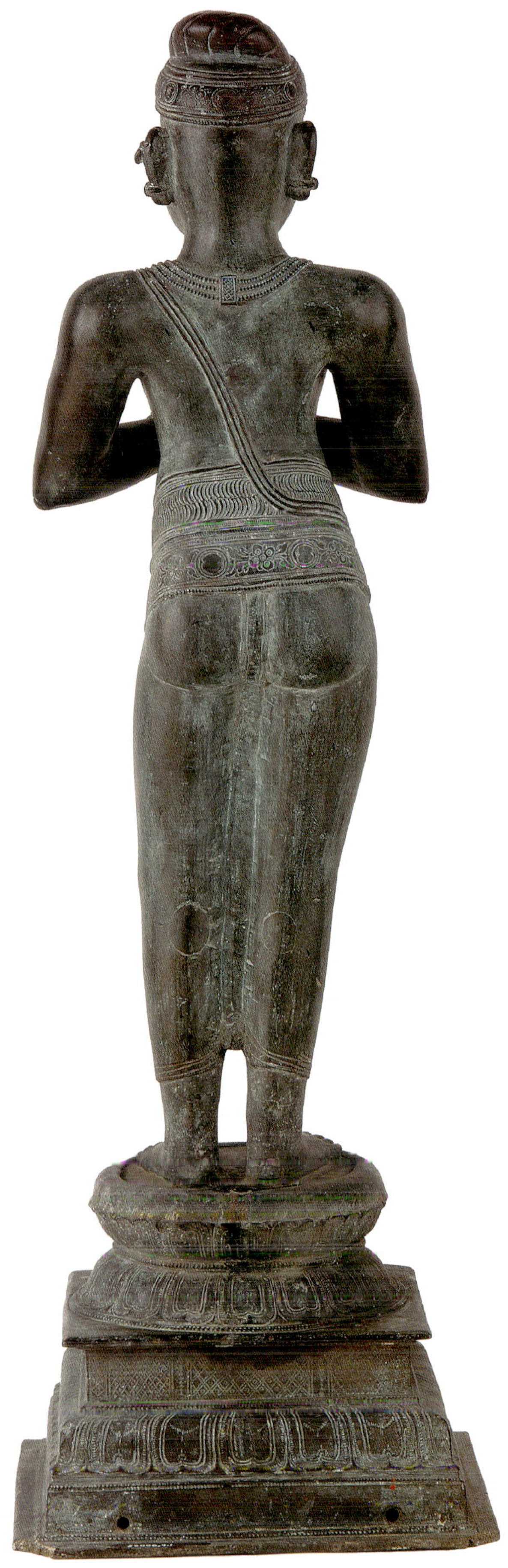

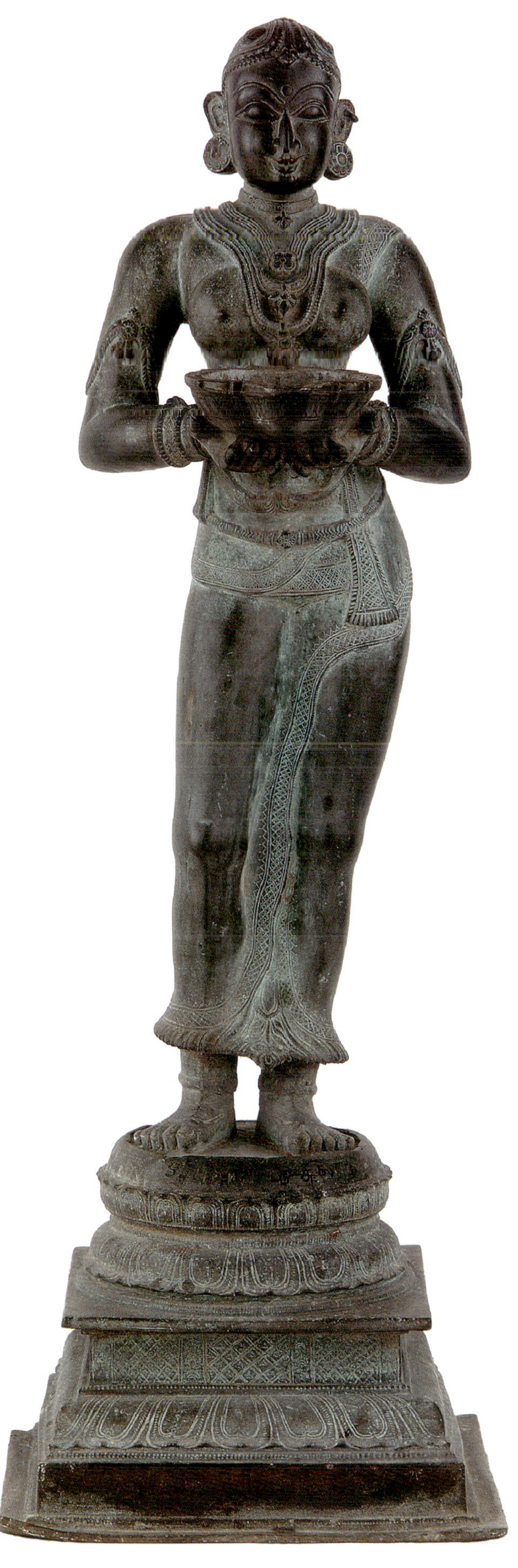

57B

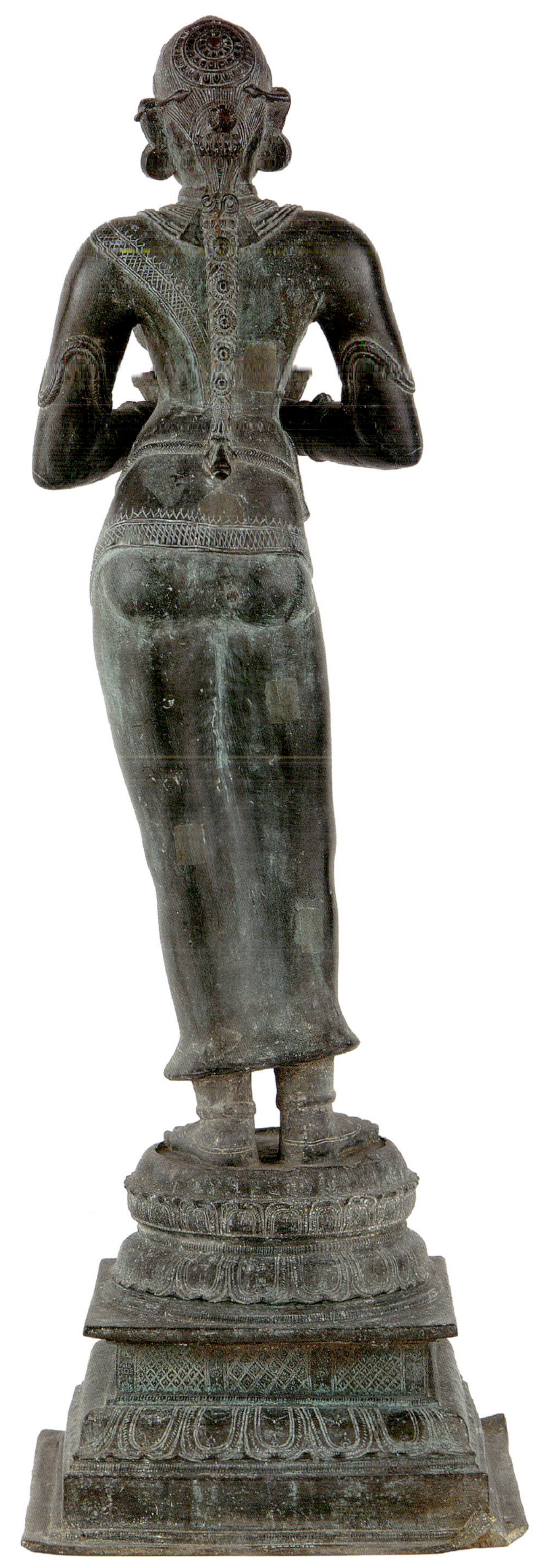

Each figure lamp has a brief inscription, of relatively modern date, along the upper portion of its lotus base. R. Nagaswamy confirms that the letter *nii* that follows the first numeral (340 on the male and 341 on the female) stands for "number," but he doubts that the numerals in the inscriptions are either revenue records or weights. Perhaps the numbers were added at a time when temples no longer functioned as autonomous units but, during British rule, were grouped together for management purposes under a single authority.[6] With images gathered for safe keeping in common spaces, it became necessary to add inscribed (later painted) labels to indicate the temple that owned each bronze.

Also intended primarily to provide light for viewing the image, and often suspended as a hanging lamp, is the handsome Gajalakshmi, or Lakshmi with Elephants, lamp. This form, typical to Tamil Nadu, continues to be produced to this day; here a galloping horse-and-rider adorn both sides of its bowl. Its rear ornamental section commences with a row of *hamsas* (geese) topped by an image of Lakshmi being lustrated by two elephants. The arched frame terminates in a *kirtimukha* (face of glory) motif; miniature oil lamps adorn the juncture between lamp and frame, and more *hamsas* are placed on both lamp and frame.

Lamps are also a vital part of the daily *puja*. The rite of *diparadhana* or honoring with light consists of waving lamps before the god and goddess once they have been fully dressed and adorned. For this rite, a small tower-like lamp, in several tiers, attached to a stable handle are placed on a tray that the priest waves ceremonially before the images. *Diparadhana* is a climactic moment of temple ritual that is accompanied by the ringing of bells and indicates that the deity is now ready to receive homage from those gathered at the shrine.

NOTES

1 E. Hultzsch, ed., *South Indian Inscriptions,* vol. 2 (New Delhi: Archaeological Survey of India, 1992 reprint), part 1, no. 1, pp. 9–10; no. 2, p. 17.

2 Ibid., no. 19, pp. 419–24.

3 *Madras Epigraphy Report,* 1894, no. 222.

4 S. D. Goitein, *Letters of Medieval Jewish Traders* (Princeton: Princeton University Press, 1973), p. 195.

5 *Madras Epigraphy Report,* 1956–57, no. 161.

6 R. Nagaswamy, personal communication.

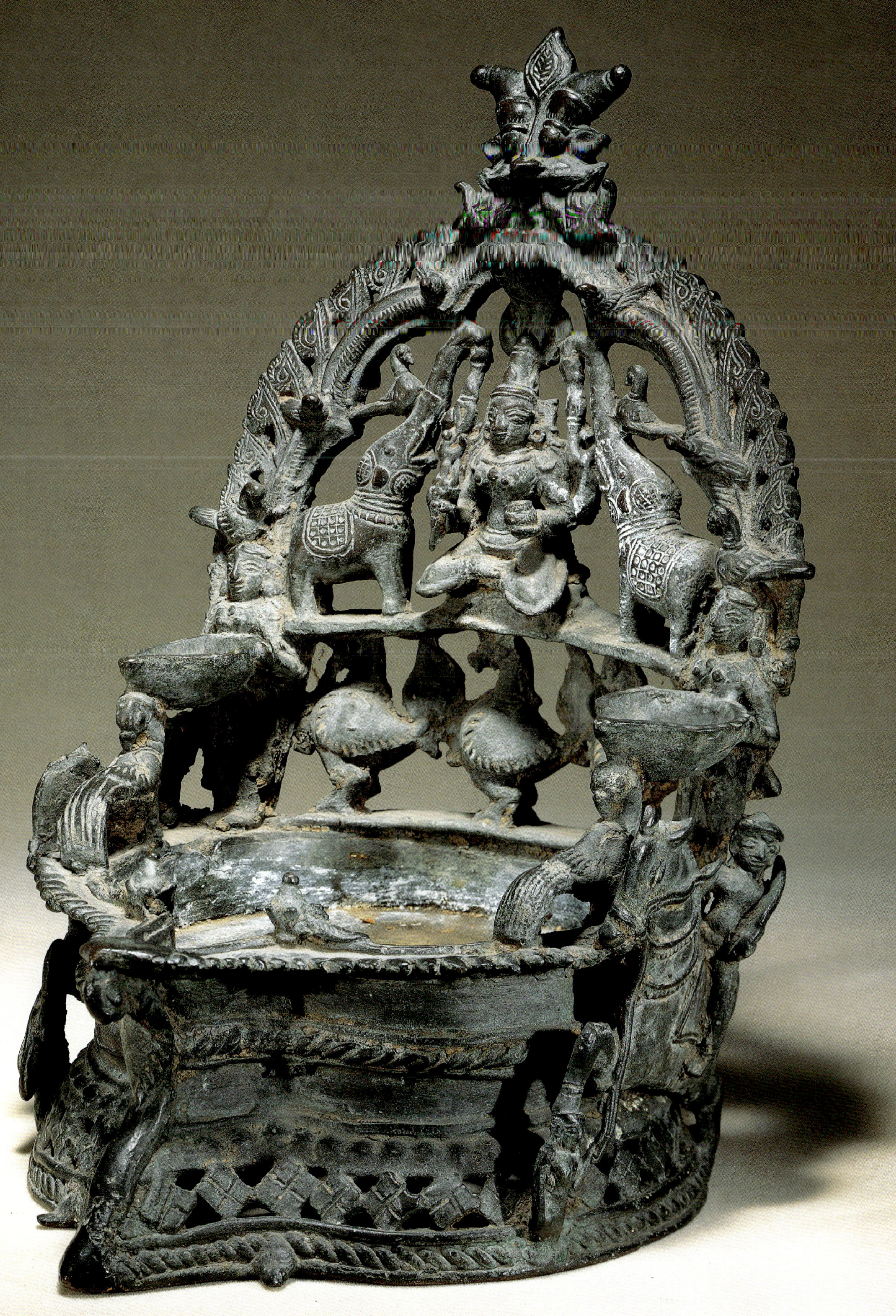

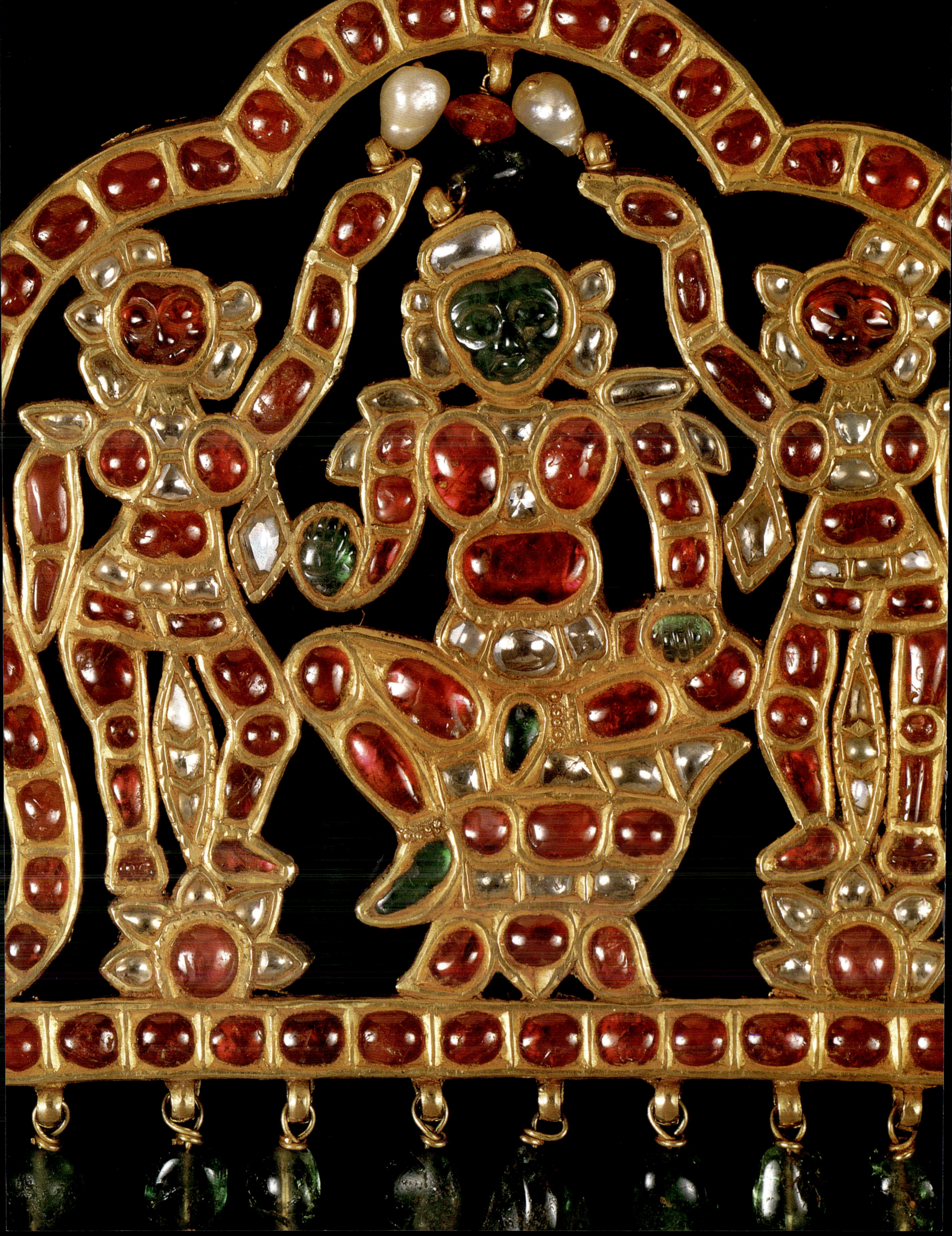

JEWELS FOR TEMPLE BRONZES

For centuries, gold has been the material of choice for jewelry in India, and gold ornaments have routinely been melted down and refashioned for the following generation, so very few pieces of ancient jewelry survive in their original form. However, elaborate descriptions in literary texts down the ages apprise us of their richness, and of the centrality of jeweled ornamentation to the ancient concept of beauty. Gemstones too were of great importance, and the gem market, as well as the goldsmiths' quarters, of the town of Madurai are described thus in the fifth-century poem *Shilappadikaram*, or Tale of an Anklet:

ORNAMENTAL GIRDLE OF RUKMINI
(DETAIL OF CAT. NO. 52C)

In the wealthy neighbourhoods . . .
were shops glittering with diamonds
emeralds of brilliant green . . .
. . . rubies called the red lotus,
sapphire, pearl, and flawless crystal;
the pushparaga stones covered in gold
and resembling a cat's eye; the pure sardonyx,
the color of honey and sunlight; the onyx
like clear darkness; two-colored opals . . .
pearls of the finest quality that sparkled
. . . lay in heaps,
as also branches of red coral
. . .
Kovalan passed through the renowned goldsmiths' streets
flying tiny pennants to help dealers
identify the four kinds of gold:
natural gold, gold the color
of parrots' wings, atakam, and campunatam.[1]

Jewelry continued to hold a position of prime importance during the Chola period. While Chola jewelry has not survived as corroborative evidence, even a cursory examination of a temple bronze reveals both the character and the importance accorded to jeweled ornamentation. In his wax image, the sculptor painstakingly delineated elaborate jeweled crowns, headbands, earrings, necklaces, armlets, bracelets, girdles, anklets, and rings for both fingers and toes. By its very nature, the lost-wax process reproduced these details exactly in the resulting bronze image; the presence of such ornamentation has been noted in individual catalogue entries.

Ignoring the existence of such adornment in the sacred bronzes, donors vied with one another to gift to these very images complete ensembles of gold ornaments, set with diamonds, rubies, crystals, corals, pearls, and lapis lazuli.

> One sacred girdle adorning the hips *(tiru-pattigai)*, containing gold weighing 521.9 grams [1.1 lbs.]. Six hundred and sixty-seven large and small diamonds with smooth edges set into it, including such as had spots, cracks, red dots, black dots, and marks as of burning, weighing 12.5 grams. Eighty-three large and small rubies—twenty-two *halahalam* [a type of ruby] of superior quality, twenty *halahalam*, twenty smooth rubies, nine bluish rubies, two *sattam*, ten unpolished

GOLD PENDANT WITH RUBIES,
DIAMONDS, EMERALDS, AND PEARLS
(DETAIL OF CAT. NO. 65)

rubies . . . —weighed 60.3 grams. Two hundred and twelve pearls including round pearls, roundish pearls, polished pearls, small pearls, *nimbolam, ambumudu*, pearls of brilliant water and of red water, weighed 97.5 grams. Altogether the girdle weighed 684.4 grams [1.5 lbs.], and was valued at 4,500 gold coins.[2]

This inscription, reading almost like a jeweler's manual, is engraved on the wall of the great royal temple at the capital of Tanjavur by Emperor Rajaraja's sister Kundavai. The details relate to a piece of jewelry gifted to the bronze image of Uma-Parameshvari as consort of dancing Shiva, known as Adavallar Dakshina Meru Vitankar. The inscription specifies:

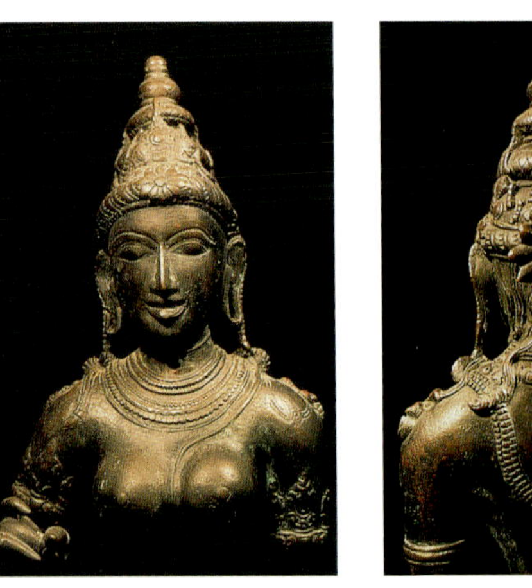

UMA'S CROWN (DETAILS OF CAT. NO. 7)

Gold was weighed by the stone used in the city and called Adavallan, and jewels were weighed by the jewel weight called Dakshina Meru Vitankar. Those gems that could be weighed separately were weighed without the threads, frames, copper tacks, lac and *pinju*. Those gems of which the net weight could not be ascertained as they were united with the lac and *pinju* were weighed together with these.[3]

These are extraordinary details but by no means unique; indeed, there are nearly a hundred records that read in like manner. Here is one more just to convey the meticulous flavor of these records:

One sacred crown with gold weighing 1844.8 grams [4 lbs.]. Eight hundred and fifty-nine diamonds set into it, of which six hundred and thirty-six had smooth edges, one hundred and sixty-nine square diamonds with smooth edges, thirty-two flat diamonds with smooth edges . . . including those with spots, cracks, red dots, black dots, and marks as of burning, weighed 45.7 grams. Three hundred and nine large and small rubies, namely one hundred and twenty-five *halahalam* of superior quality, one hundred and twenty-two *halahalam*, forty-one smooth rubies, eleven bluish rubies, ten unpolished rubies—including those with cavities, cuts, holes, specks . . . and such as still adhered to the ore—weighed 81.1 grams. Six hundred and sixty-nine large and small pearls set into it including round pearls, roundish pearls, polished pearls, small pearls . . . old pearls, such as had been polished while still adhering to the shell, pearls of red water and brilliant water, pearls with lines, stains, red dots, and white specks, weighed 192.3 grams . . . Altogether the crown weighed 2166.6 grams [4.7 lbs.], and was valued at 5,000 gold coins.[4]

A crown weighing over four and a half pounds is doubtless a significant piece of adornment.

Another inscription lists thirty-three sets of gold ornaments, each accompanied by minutia worthy of a jewelers' log-book, that were given to the bronze image of Uma Parameshvari. In her role of consort of dancing Shiva, this bronze received one crown (detailed above); one garland; one pendant; seven pairs of earrings (so she could have variety from day to day); a string of beads for her marriage *tali* necklace (the Tamil Nadu equivalent of the wedding ring); five different necklaces; six pairs of armlets; three sets of bracelets; two ornamental hip girdles (one detailed above); four sets of anklets; and two complete sets of ten toe rings.[5] The varied ornaments gifted to a second bronze image of Uma Parameshvari as consort of Shiva as Tanjai Vitankar (perhaps Tripuravijaya) confirms the fact that lavish adornment was an accepted practice. This bronze Uma received two crowns, a garland, a pendant, three sets of earrings, a beaded string for her marriage *tali*, three necklaces, a pair of armlets, two sets of bracelets, two sets of anklets, and a set of toe rings.[6]

The concept of jewelry as an enhancement of the beauty and grandeur of temple bronzes is further established by the fact that the male figure was equally if not more richly adorned than the female. The Tanjavur bronze figure of Shiva as Tripuravijaya, or Victor of the Three Cities, standing 97.9 cm high, was richly endowed with multifarious gold jewels; the gifts were listed as one long garland strung with *talis* and weighing 482.3 grams (1.06 lbs.); four single-strand necklaces, each set with pearls, coral, and lapis; a *shrichanda* ornament set with two thousand, five hundred and twenty-four pearls and weighing 563 grams [1.2 lbs.]; a pair of earrings of dangling pearls; two armlets; eight bracelets; an elaborate girdle strung with two thousand, three hundred and thirty nine pearls with diamonds and crystals on its clasps that weighed 430.5 grams [0.94 lb.]; four anklets; and a gold scimitar.[7]

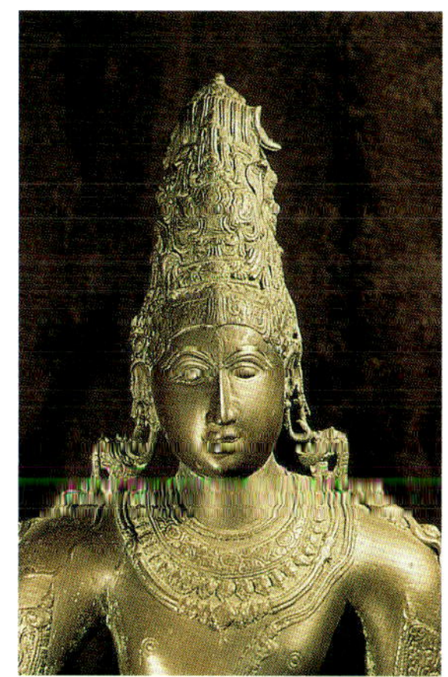

SHIVA AS TRIPURAVIJAYA (DETAIL OF CAT. NO. 6)

SHIVA AS TRIPURAVIJAYA (DETAIL OF CAT. NO. 7)

The process of adornment, or *abharana*, is an integral part of temple worship commencing with the lustration of the images, followed by clothing them in silks and cottons. The next rite which decorates the clothed images with jewelry is often spoken of as *padadikesham*, or from foot to head, indicating the order in which ornaments are placed on the image, starting with the toe rings and ending with the crown. Prior to commencing this systematic adornment, it is customary to first place on the god his jeweled sacred thread, and on the goddess her marriage necklace strung with a *tali* and known as *tiru-mangalyam.* In fact, several temples report that these ornaments are never removed even during the process of lustration and clothing. It is only after these two symbolically significant jeweled ornaments are placed (or retained) on the deities that the rest of the adornment proceeds. When the jewelry ritual is complete, puja continues with the offering of aromatics *(gandham)*, usually sandal paste, flowers or garlands *(pushpam)*, burning of incense or camphor *(dupam)*, and concluding with the final rite of oil lamps *(deepam)* that illuminate the deities and enable devotees to admire and honor them.

Glowing testimony to the quality of the gemstones that adorned the temple images of south India is contained in a work titled *Khazainul Futuh* or Treasures of Victory, composed by the poet Amir Khusrau for Sultan Alauddin Khilji of Delhi (r. 1296–1316), describing the glowing wealth of the temple coffers.

> The diamonds were of such a colour that the sun will have to stare hard for ages before the like of them is made in the factories of the rocks. The pearls glistened so brilliantly that the brow of the clouds will have to perspire for years before such pearls again reach the treasury of the sea. For generations the mines will have to drink blood in the stream of the sun before rubies such as these are produced. The emeralds were of water so fine that if the blue sky broke itself into fragments, none of its fragments would equal them. Every diamond sparkled brightly, it seemed as if it was a drop fallen from the sun. As to the other stones, their luster eludes description just as water escapes out of a small vessel.[8]

In the context of such literally rich statistics, it is useful to remember that it was the fabled wealth of the temple jewelry of the Tamil country that was the driving force behind the Muslim invasions of south

India. Desperately in need of funds to sustain his armies in readiness against the ever-present threats presented by the northwest frontier region, Alauddin Khilji, ruler of the Delhi sultanate, sent his general Malik Kafur, followed by general Khushru Khan, on foraging raids into Tamil Nadu. Inscriptions such as those in Rajaraja's great temple at Tanjavur affirm that the sultan was correct in his expectations; the Tamil temples were indeed the equivalent of Fort Knox. And these treasures were guarded only by temple priests, and the unseen, invisible authority of lord Shiva or lord Vishnu that the Muslim generals could happily ignore as irrelevant. Both expeditions were highly successful, and the Muslim generals seized vast amounts of gold ornaments and gem-encrusted gold jewelry with which to swell their coffers. Rubies, associated in mythology with Surya, god of the sun, came from Burma; diamonds from the Deccan mines of Golconda; and pearls, associated with Chandra, god of the moon, from fisheries in the gulf of Mannar between south India and Sri Lanka.

Though the pieces of jewelry described below, and on view in the exhibition, do not belong to the Chola period, jewels of a similar nature were abundantly evident in the Chola and following periods. Indeed, even today, goldsmiths and jewelers in the Tamil country receive regular commissions for ornaments intended solely for gifting to temple images.

TALIS AND PENDANTS (PADAKKAMS)

Today the south Indian *tali* is exclusively a marriage ornament. But in pre-Chola times, it referred to any ornamental pendant that formed part of a necklace, the word *tali* being derived from *taludal* or that which is suspended. Women, as well as boys and girls, are described as wearing different types of *talis*, many of which seem to have been talismans worn to ward off evil.[9] The *Shilappadikaram* (ca. 450), in describing the marriage of its hero Kovalan to Kannagi, makes no reference to a *tali* being tied around the neck of the bride to seal the bond of marriage. So too, woman saint Andal's poem (ca. 800) that describes in detail her dream wedding to god Vishnu makes no reference at all to the *tali* rite. The omission of this all-important wedding rite has a simple explanation. It was only during the eleventh century that the *tali*, as a symbol of the sacred state of being a married woman became a part of the marriage ritual, and then too, not always or invariably. The *tali* worn by a married woman, is mentioned first in the *Kanda Purana* of the eleventh century, which refers to the auspicious thread with the golden *tali* strung on it, worn by the wives of the celestials.[10] Kamban's *Ramavataram* of the twelfth century does not specify the *tali* rite as part of the marriage ceremonies of Rama and Sita; it speaks, however, of a dream narrated to Sita exiled in Lanka's Ashoka garden, and mentions how the *talis* of the demonesses break loose and fall from their necks, foreboding the death of the demons. These literary references suggest that the *tali* rite first became a part of the south Indian marriage ceremony only from the eleventh century onwards.

A reference to the *tali* occurs in several early eleventh century inscriptions of Rajaraja and his queens on the great temple at Tanjavur. While we cannot be certain of the form they took, it is possible that some resembled the later classic M-shaped gold ornament, with a gold bead on either side, usually strung on a gold chain. A *tali*, given to Uma as consort of dancing Shiva, was set with diamonds[11]; a second intended for a bronze portrait of the queen mother, Vanavan Mahadevi, is unspecific in its details[12]; while a third, for goddess Durga, was set with rubies and diamonds.[13] More intriguing is a reference to a garland for sun god Surya that apparently had no less than seventeen *talis* strung on it.[14]

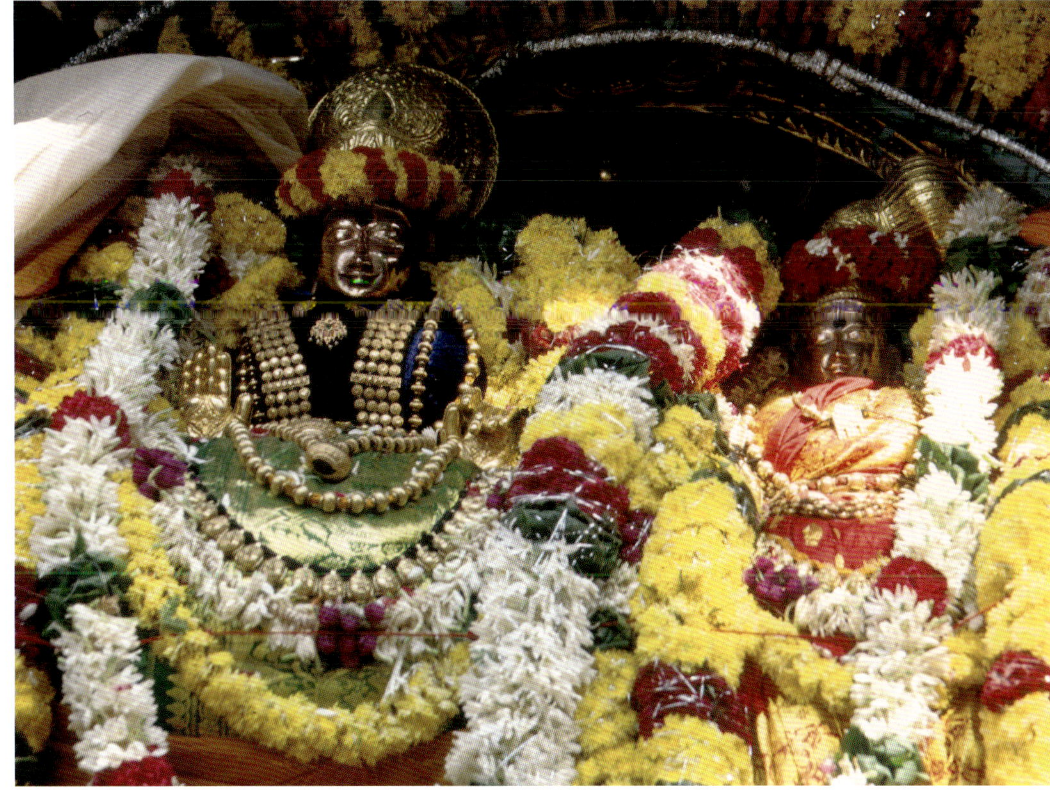

LAVISHLY ADORNED BRONZES OF SHIVA AND UMA IN PROCESSION, TIRUVANNAMALAI

PHOTO NEIL GREENTREE, 2000

FIG. 1

NOTES

1 R. Parthasarathy, *The Tale of an Anklet, An Epic of South India: The Cilappatikaram of Ilanko Atikal* (New York: Columbia University Press, 1993), p. 148, Canto 14, "The Sights of the City."

2 Adapted from E. Hultzsch, ed., *South Indian Inscriptions*, vol. 2 (New Delhi: Archaeological Survey of India, 1992 reprint), part 1, inscription no. 8, pp. 87–88. The following system has been followed for the conversion of the ancient measures which are red, and black-and-red seeds: 1 *kalanju* = 5.3 grams; 1 *manjadi* = 1.06 grams; 1 *kunri* = 0.5 gram. The grams to pounds conversion uses 453.6 grams = 1 lb.

3 Ibid., p. 87.

4 Adapted from Hultzsch, no. 7, p. 81.

5 Four different inscriptions, two of Rajaraja and two of his son Rajendra, record donations to the same image: see Hultzsch, pp. 18–20, no. 6, p. 73; no. 7, p. 81; no. 8, pp. 87–88.

6 Hultzsch, no. 8, p. 89.

7 Hultzsch, no. 51, pp. 213–16.

8 Habib Muhammad (trans.), *The Campaigns of Alauddin Khilji, being the Khazainul Futuh (Treasures of Victory) of Hazrat Amir Khusrau of Delhi* (Madras: D. B. Taraporewala Sons & Co., 1931), pp. 106–7.

9 C. J. Jayadev, "Literary and Ethnographic References to the Tali and the Tali Rite," in *Transactions of the Archaeological Society of South India 1959–60* (Madras, 1960), pp. 43–46.

10 Ibid., p. 51ff. Of the three weddings mentioned in this text, those of Uma with Shiva, and of Valli with Skanda contain no mention of the *tali*, while the marriage of Devayani with Skanda speaks of the tying of a sacred thread. It is only when describing Shiva swallowing poison that there is reference to Shiva protecting the golden talis of the wives of the celestials.

11 Hultzsch, no. 2, pp. 10–20.

12 Hultzsch, no. 6, p. 73.

13 Hultzsch , no. 79, pp. 398–400.

14 Hultzsch , no. 56, p. 227.

TALIS

59 **(LEFT) GOLD *TALI* WITH RUBY, FLANKED BY GOLD BEADS**
TAMIL NADU, 18TH–19TH CENTURY
2 IN. (5 CM)
COLLECTION SUSAN L. BENINGSON

60 **(CENTER) GOLD *TALI* STUDDED WITH RUBIES, AND CARRYING AN EMBOSSED DESIGN OF BIRDS AND LOTUS PETALS ON ITS REVERSE**
TAMIL NADU, 19TH CENTURY
5 1/4 IN. (13.4 CM)
COLLECTION SUSAN L. BENINGSON

61 **(RIGHT) GOLD *TALI*, FLANKED BY GOLD BEADS**
TAMIL NADU OR KERALA, 19TH CENTURY
1 1/2 IN. (3.9 CM)
COLLECTION SUSAN L. BENINGSON

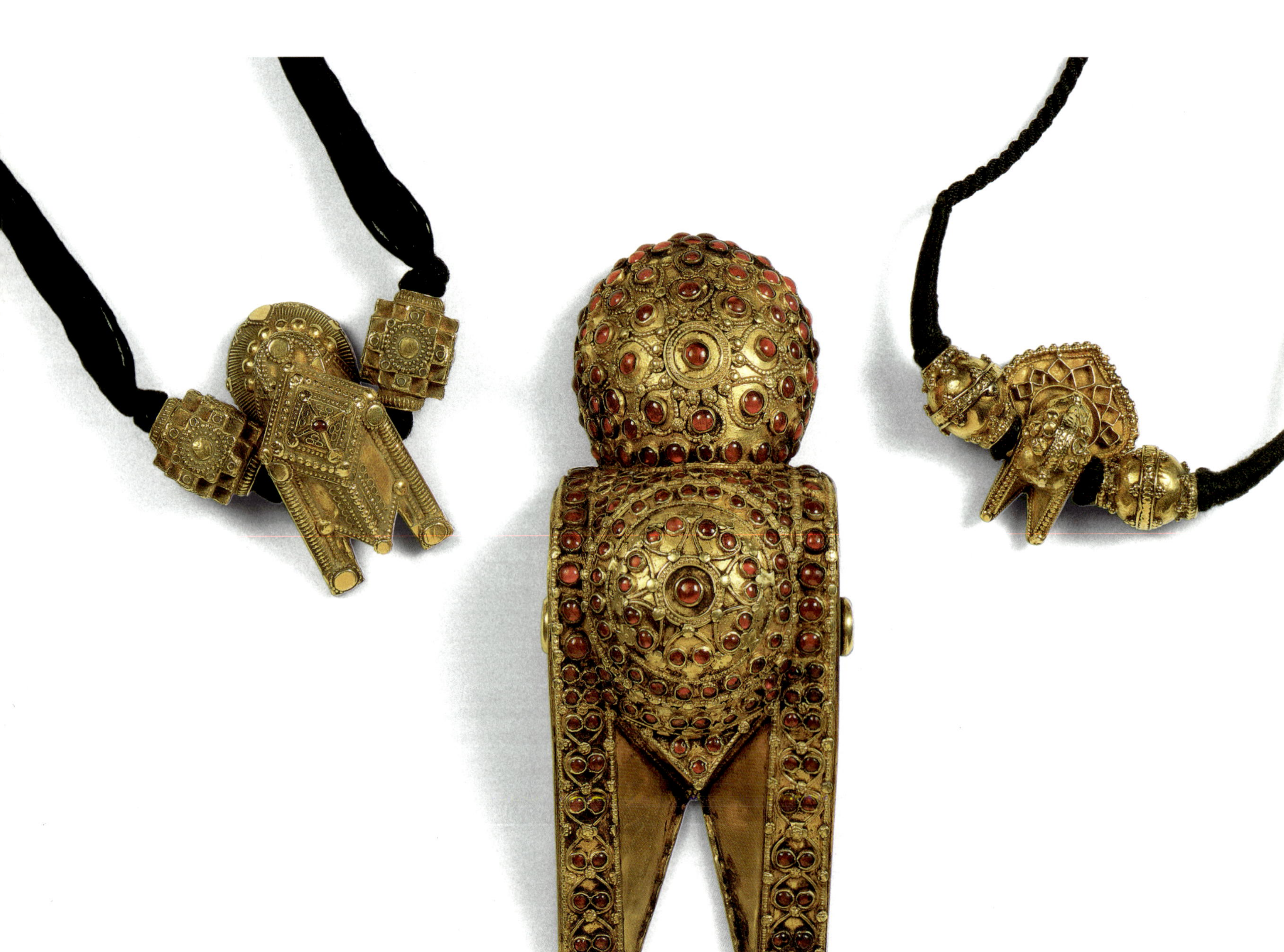

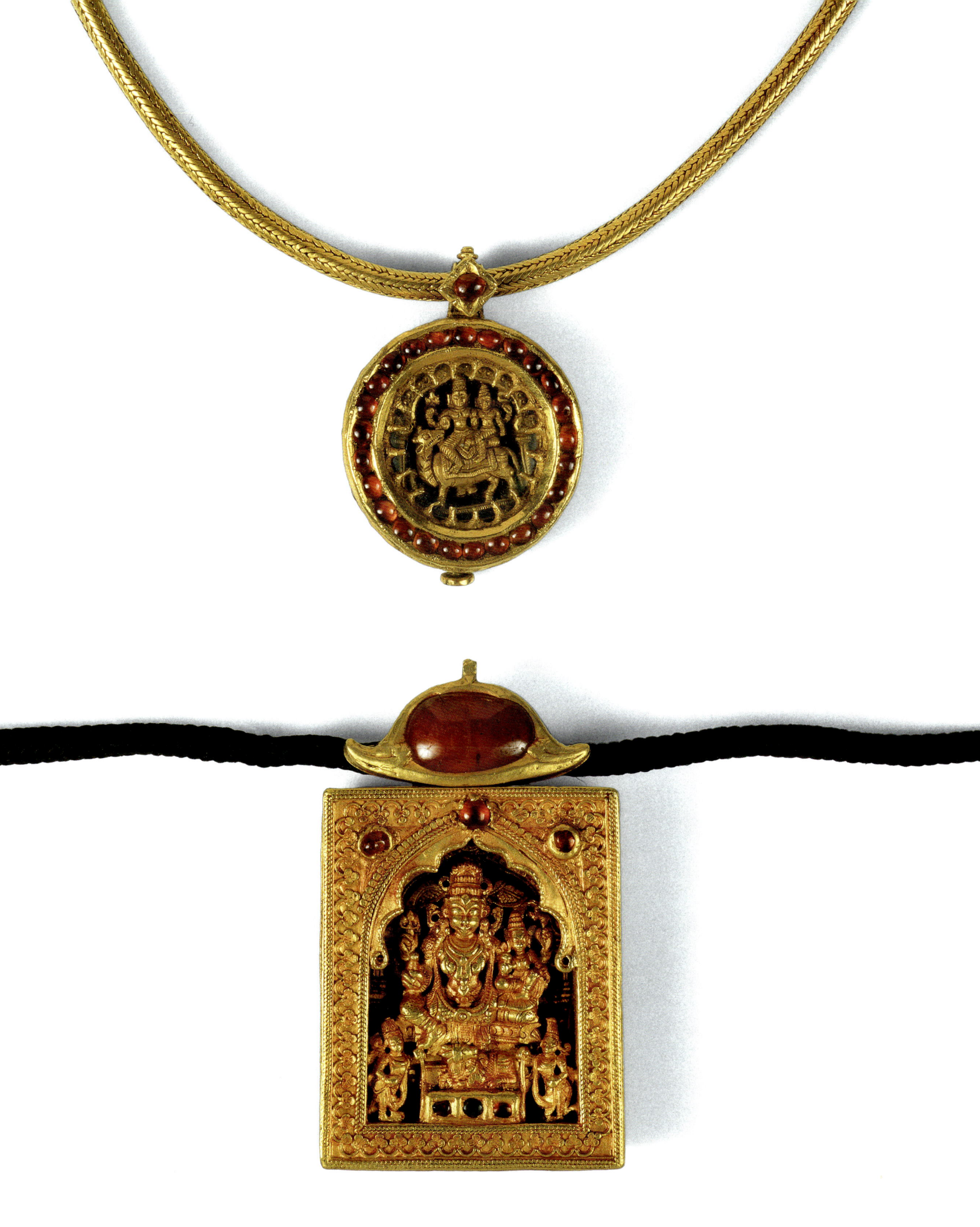

68 GOLD ROPE CHAIN
TAMIL NADU, 19TH CENTURY
COLLECTION SUSAN L. BENINGSON

69 GOLD NECKLACE, SET WITH DIAMONDS AND BORDERED WITH PEARLS
TAMIL NADU, 19TH CENTURY
COLLECTION SUSAN L. BENINGSON

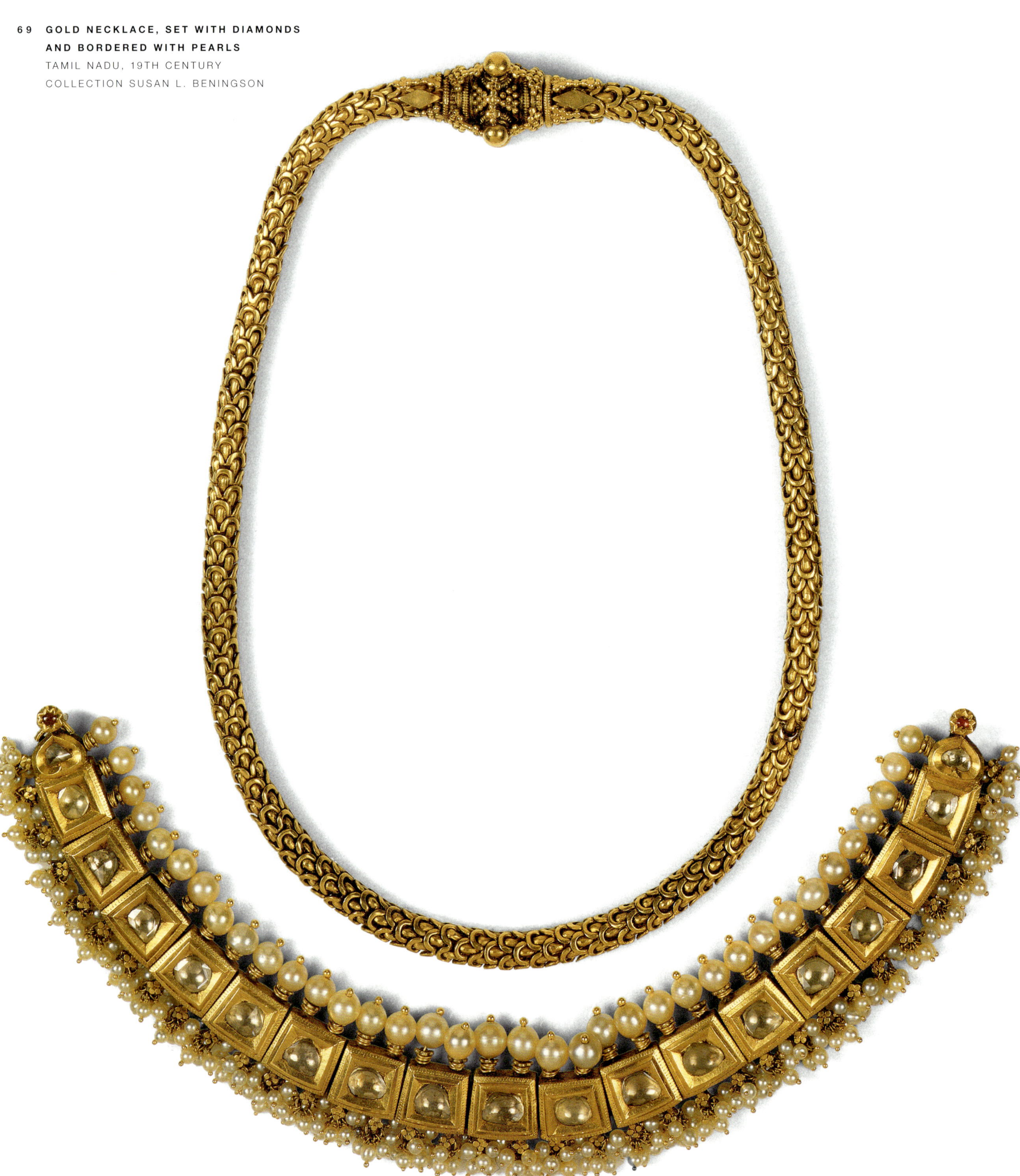

70 **NECKLACE OF GOLD AND RUBIES WITH A DEER-SHAPED CLASP**
TAMIL NADU, 19TH CENTURY
COLLECTION SUSAN L. BENINGSON

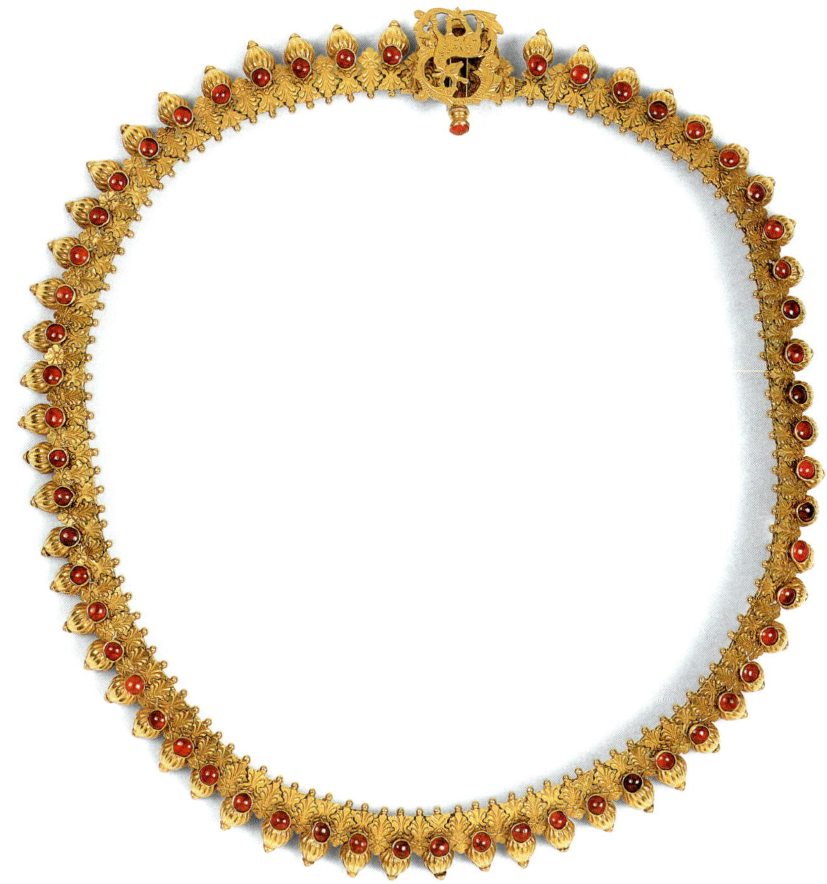

71 **GOLD NECKLACE WITH BEADS IN THE SHAPES OF SEEDS AND BERRIES**
TAMIL NADU, 19TH CENTURY
COLLECTION SUSAN L. BENINGSON

72 **GOLD BEAD NECKLACE STUDDED WITH RUBIES**
TAMIL NADU, 19TH CENTURY
COLLECTION SUSAN L. BENINGSON

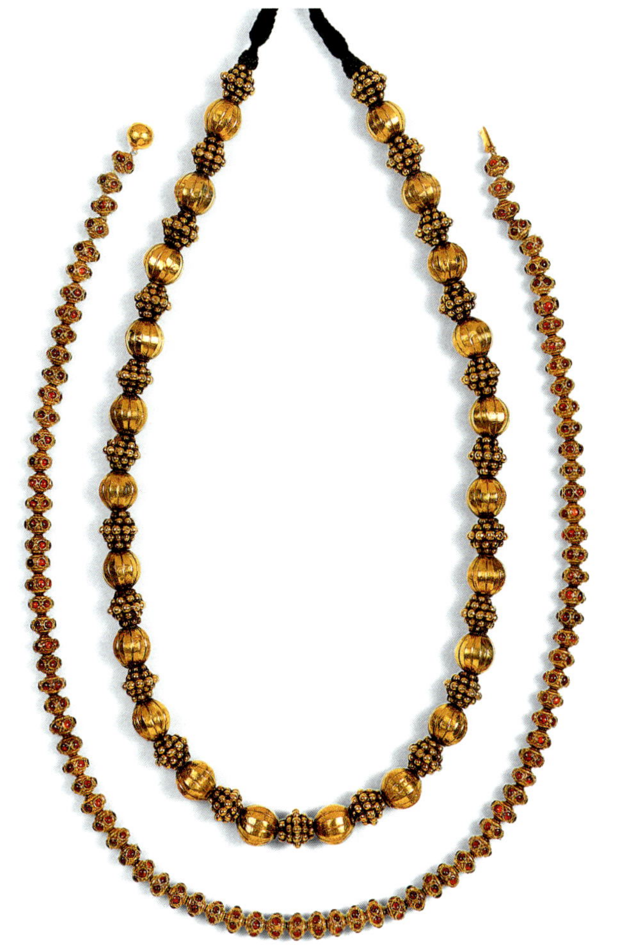

73 **GOLD RUBY-STUDDED CHOKER WITH CENTRAL FLORAL MOTIF, GOLD BEAD TERMINATIONS, AND GOLD BEAD EDGING**
TAMIL NADU, 19TH CENTURY
COLLECTION SUSAN L. BENINGSON

74 **GOLD NECKLACE WITH PENDANT, SET WITH RUBIES, EMERALDS, DIAMONDS, AND PEARLS**
TAMIL NADU, 19TH CENTURY
COLLECTION SUSAN L. BENINGSON

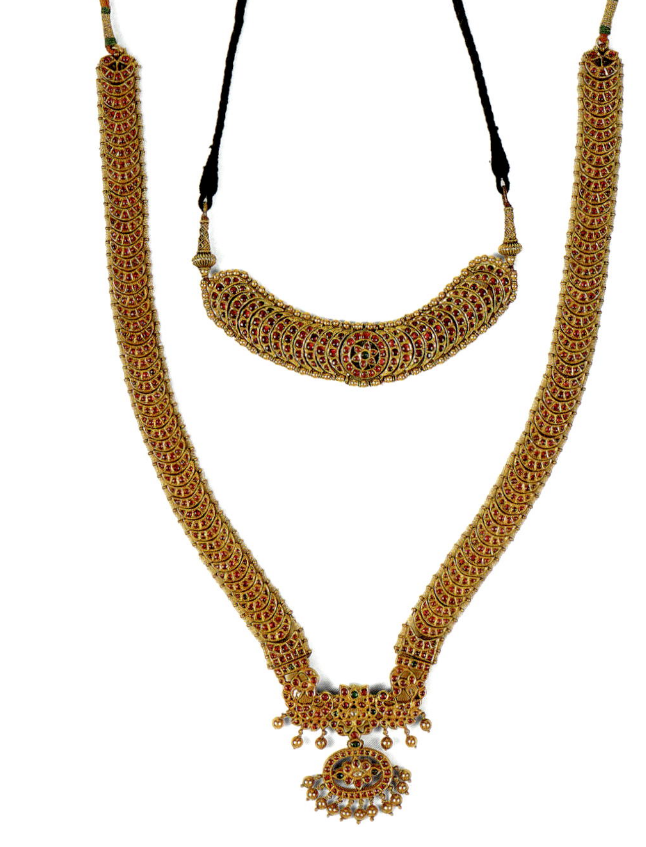

75 **PAIR OF BRACELETS, EACH WITH EIGHT "MOUNTAINS" OF NESTED PEARLS WITH CENTRAL FLORAL ORNAMENTS MADE OF GOLD WITH RUBIES OR EMERALDS AND DIAMONDS, SEPARATED BY BANDS OF GOLD SET WITH RUBIES AND DIAMONDS, ALL SEWN ONTO HEAVY FABRIC BACKING**
TAMIL NADU, 19TH CENTURY
COLLECTION SUSAN L. BENINGSON

76 **PAIR OF GOLD BRACELETS IN A CHAIN-CUM-ROPE DESIGN**
TAMIL NADU, 19TH CENTURY.
COLLECTION SUSAN L. BENINGSON

77 **PAIR OF GOLD BRACELETS, SET WITH DIAMONDS**
TAMIL NADU, 18TH CENTURY
COLLECTION SUSAN L. BENINGSON

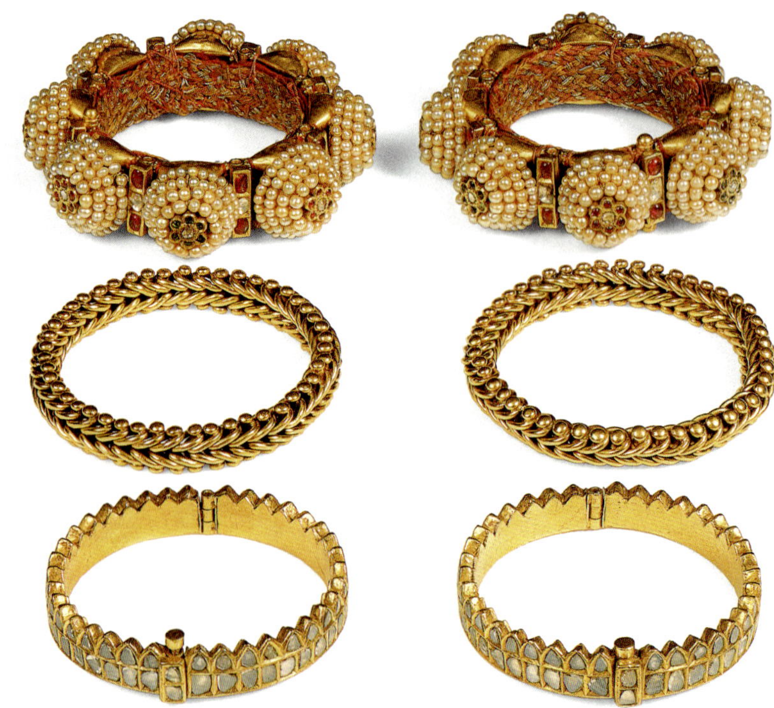

EAR ORNAMENTS

(CLOCKWISE FROM TOP)

78 **GOLD EARPLUGS, STUDDED WITH RUBIES**
TAMIL NADU, 18TH–19TH CENTURY
COLLECTION SUSAN L. BENINGSON

79 **GOLD *URUKKUMANI* (MOLTEN BEADS) EARRINGS**
TAMIL NADU, 18TH–19TH CENTURY
COLLECTION SUSAN L. BENINGSON

80 **GEOMETRIC *TANDATTI* (SANDALWOOD STEM) EAR ORNAMENT, OF GOLD SHEET METAL OVER A LAC CORE**
TAMIL NADU, 18TH–19TH CENTURY
COLLECTION SUSAN L. BENINGSON

81 **GOLD *MUDICCHU* (KNOT) EARRINGS**
TAMIL NADU, 18TH–19TH CENTURY
COLLECTION SUSAN L. BENINGSON

82 **GOLD *THODUS* (EAR STUDS) SET WITH PEARLS**
TAMIL NADU, 18TH–19TH CENTURY
COLLECTION SUSAN L. BENINGSON

83 **GOLD *PUCHIKUDU* (INSECT NEST) TUBULAR EARRINGS**
TAMIL NADU, 18TH–19TH CENTURY
COLLECTION SUSAN L. BENINGSON

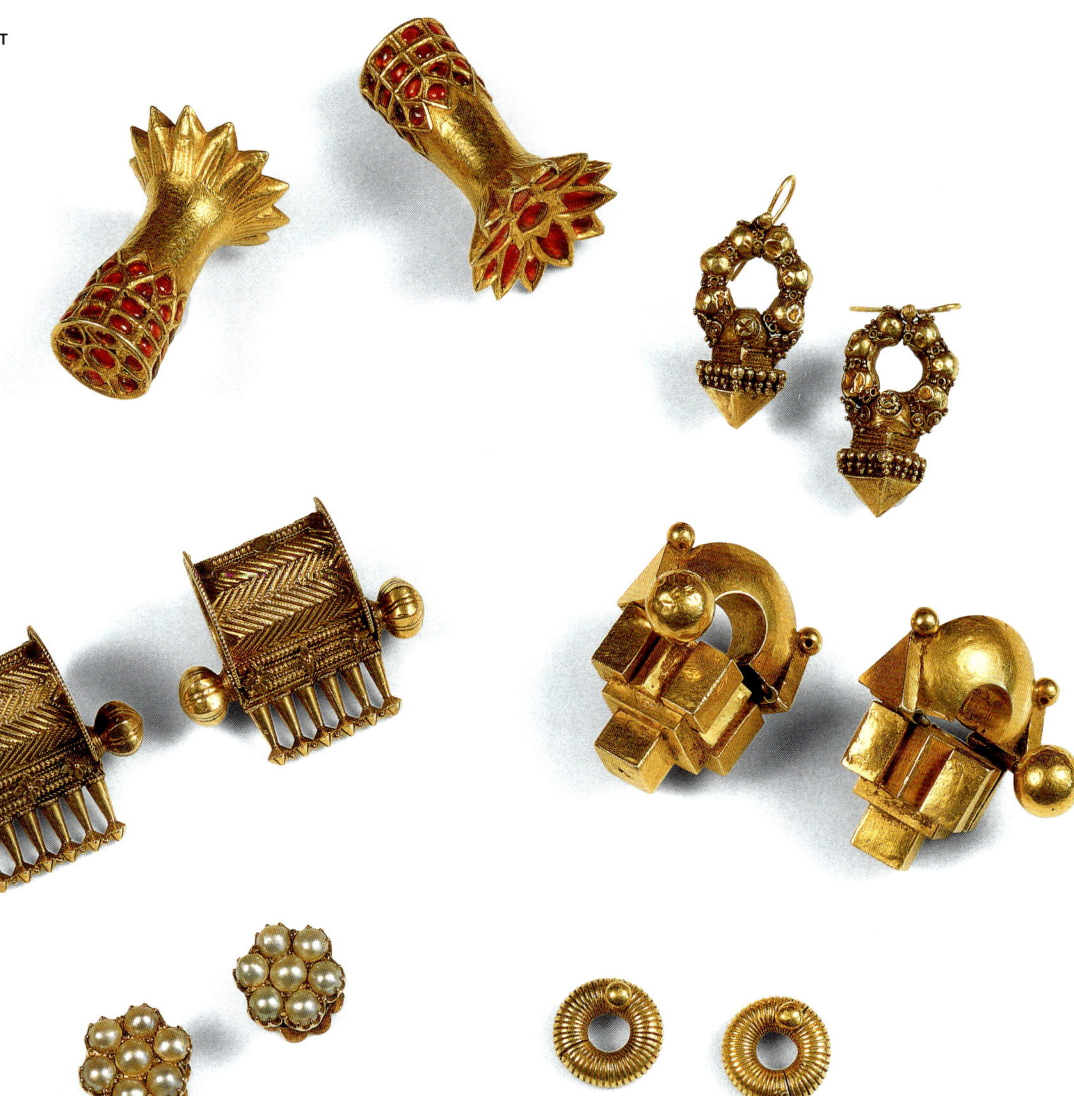

EAR ORNAMENTS
(CLOCKWISE FROM TOP RIGHT)

84 **GOLD ROPE/PENDANT EARRINGS**
TAMIL NADU, 18TH–19TH CENTURY
COLLECTION SUSAN L. BENINGSON

85 **DOUBLE-SIDED GOLD EARRINGS WITH GODDESS LAKSHMI FLANKED BY ATTENDANTS**
TAMIL NADU, 18TH–19TH CENTURY
COLLECTION SUSAN L. BENINGSON

86 **STYLIZED COBRA EAR ORNAMENTS OF GOLD WITH APPLIED STAMPED MOTIFS, WIRES, AND GRANULATION**
TAMIL NADU, 18TH–19TH CENTURY
COLLECTION SUSAN L. BENINGSON

87 ***KOPPU* CLOVE-SHAPED EAR STUDS OF SHEET GOLD, WORN ON HELIX OF EAR**
TAMIL NADU, 18TH–19TH CENTURY
COLLECTION SUSAN L. BENINGSON

88 **GOLD EAR ORNAMENT OF *RUDRAKHSA*-LIKE BEADS**
TAMIL NADU, 18TH–19TH CENTURY
COLLECTION SUSAN L. BENINGSON

89 **GOLD *JIMKIS* (SWINGING DROPS) WITH RED STONES**
TAMIL NADU, 18TH–19TH CENTURY
COLLECTION SUSAN L. BENINGSON

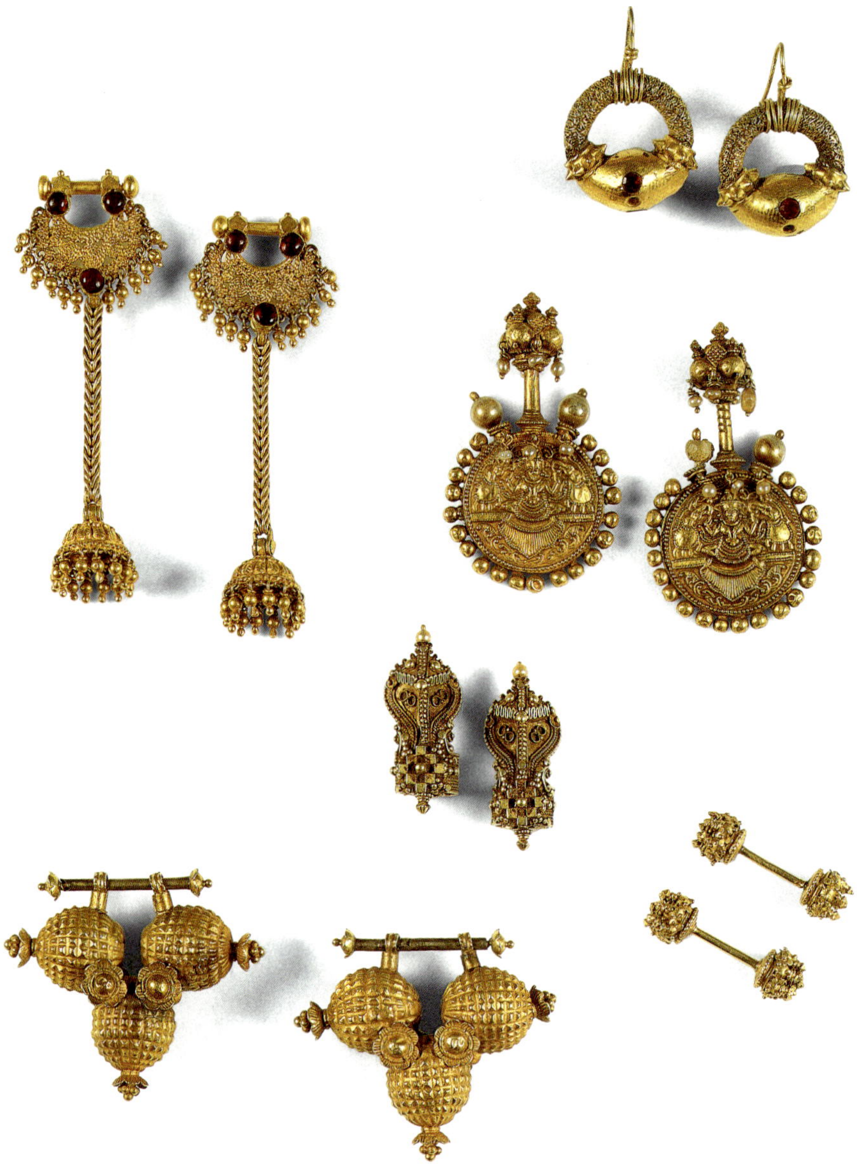

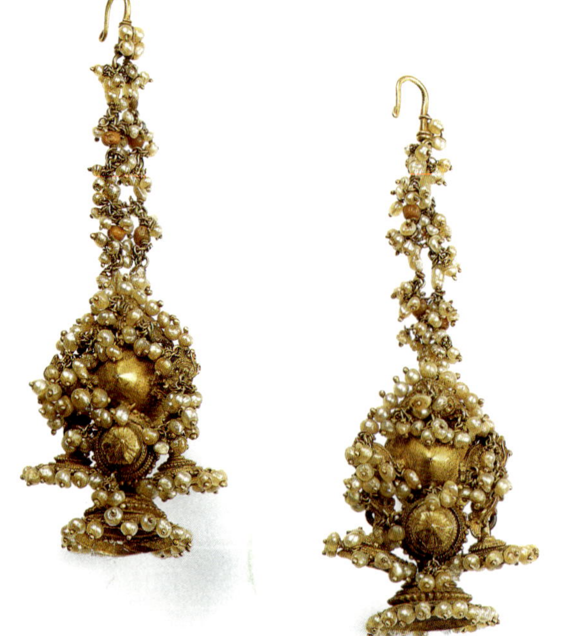

90 **LARGE *JIMKI* EARRINGS OF GOLD, PEARL, AND CORAL**
TAMIL NADU, 18TH–19TH CENTURY
COLLECTION SUSAN L. BENINGSON

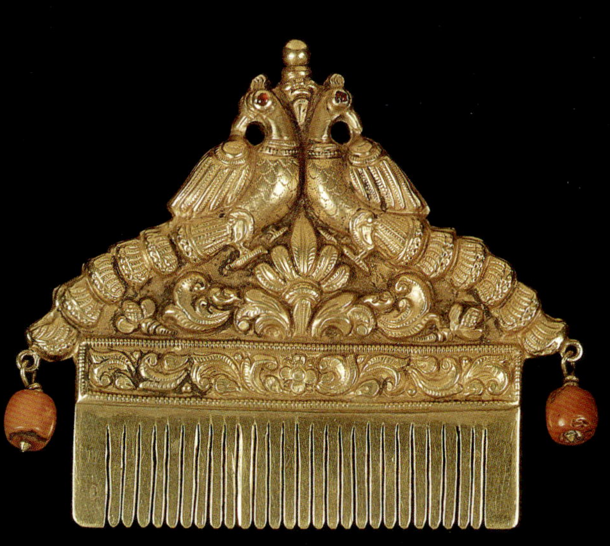

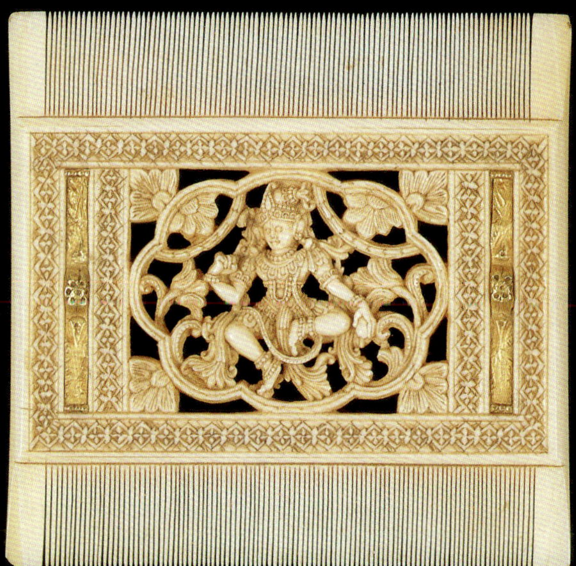

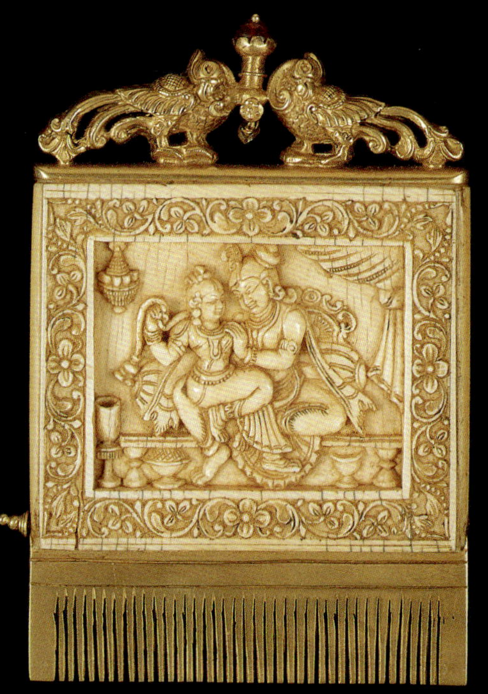

COMBS

91 **GOLD COMB WITH RUBIES AND CORAL, WITH ITS HANDLE ADORNED WITH PEACOCKS AND FLORAL MOTIFS**
TAMIL NADU, 19TH CENTURY
COLLECTION SUSAN L. BENINGSON

92 **IVORY AND GOLD DOUBLE-SIDED COMB, WITH A DANCING MALE FIGURE CARVED INTO THE IVORY**
TAMIL NADU, 19TH CENTURY
COLLECTION SUSAN L. BENINGSON

93 **IVORY AND GOLD COMB TOPPED WITH GOLD PEACOCKS**
TAMIL NADU, 17TH CENTURY
COLLECTION SUSAN L. BENINGSON

The ivory panel is carved with lovers on a couch within decorative floral borders. The reverse is incised with a floral panel within similar decorative borders.

94 **GOLD *PADUKA* OR SANDALS, SET WITH RUBIES, DIAMONDS, EMERALDS, AND PEARLS**
TAMIL NADU, 17TH OR EARLY 18TH CENTURY
COLLECTION SUSAN L. BENINGSON

95 **SILVER GILDED SWING FOR IMAGE OF A DEITY, WITH TWO RODS TO PUSH THE SWING**
TAMIL NADU, 18TH CENTURY
COLLECTION SUSAN L. BENINGSON

This piece is for use in the context of a home shrine rather than a temple.

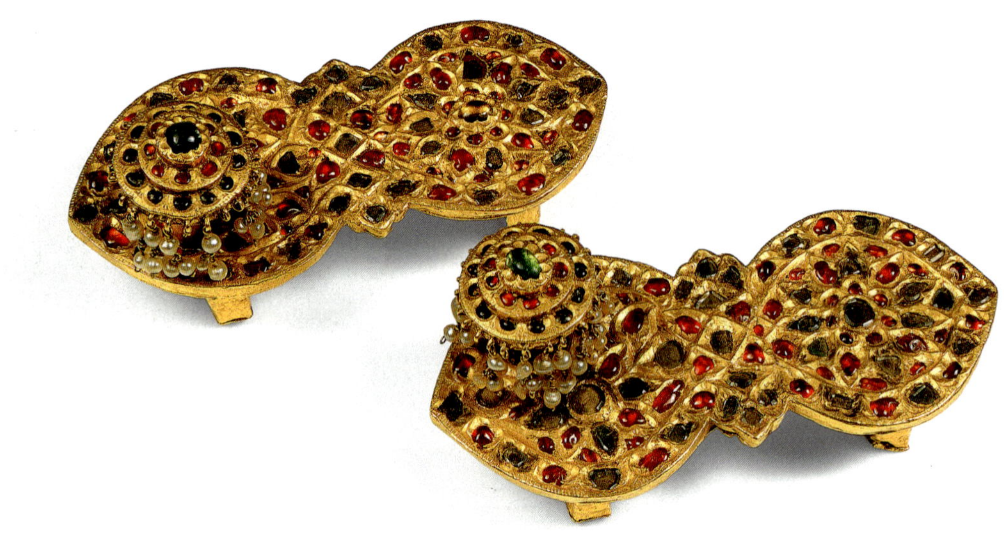

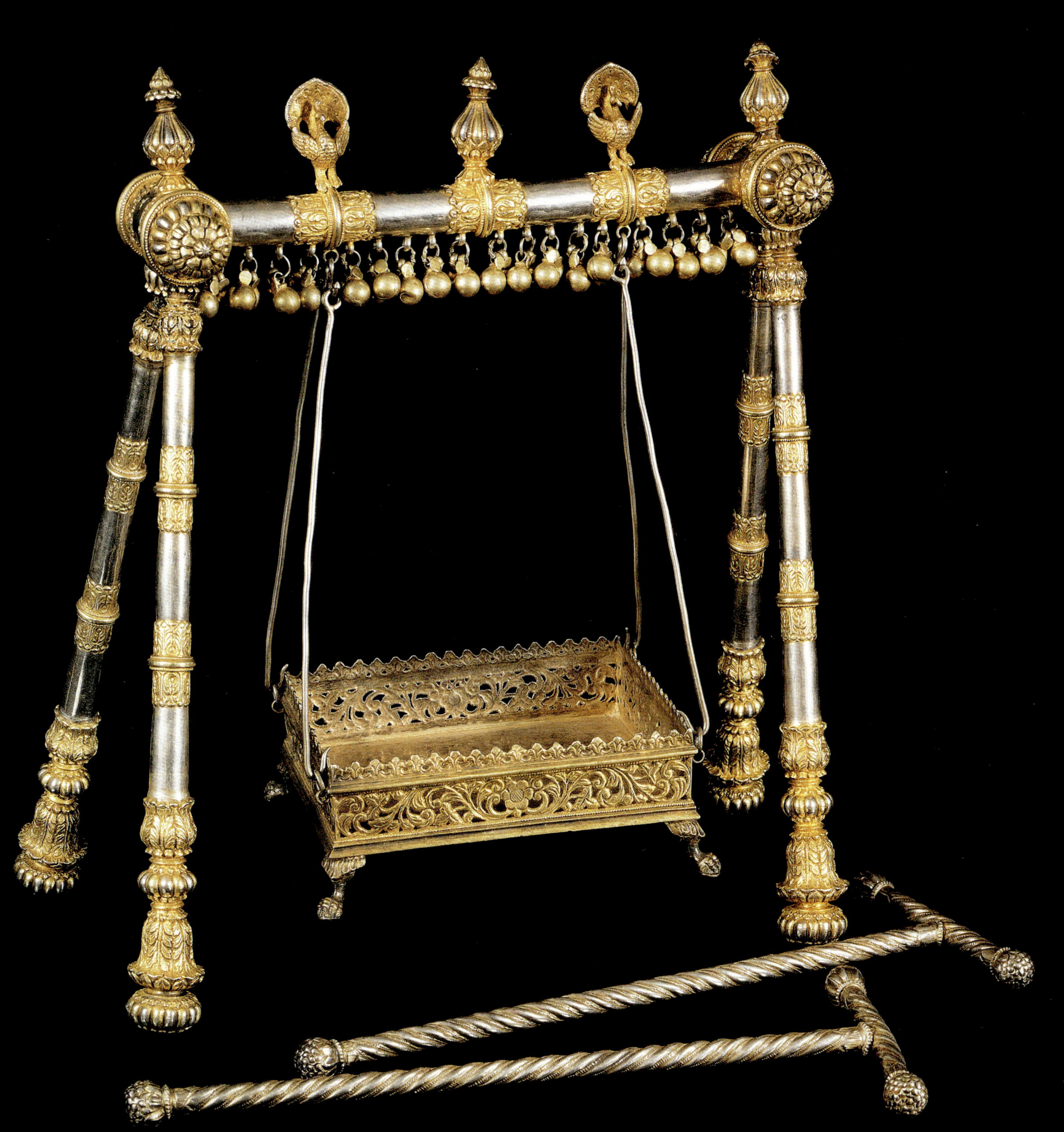

APPENDIX 1

Saint Sambandar's hymn celebrating the festival cycle at the Kapalishvara Shiva temple in Mylapur[1]

Pumpavai, O beautiful girl! *verse 1*
Would you go without having seen the feasts
in which our Lord who loves the temple
in beautiful Mayilai,
whose beach is lined with fragrant punnai *trees,*
the Lord who dwells in Kapaliccaram shrine,
feeds his many devotees who love him?

Pumpavai, O beautiful girl! *verse 2*
Would you go without having seen the feast
enjoyed by holy men
at Aippaci's [October–November] Onam festival
held at the Kapaliccaram shrine
of our Lord whose sacred ash is our blessing,
in great Mayilai,
town of beautiful women
with sparkling, kohl-darkened eyes?

Pumpavai, O beautiful girl! *verse 3*
Would you go without having seen
on the rich streets of Mayilai,
town of beautiful young women with bracelets,
and town of our Lord in the Kapaliccaram temple,
the flawless celebration of the ancient Karttikai
[November–December] feast
at which young girls
with sandal paste on their breasts
light many lamps?

Pumpavai, O beautiful girl! *verse 4*
Would you go without having seen
the Atirai [December–January] festival day
in great Mayilai town with wave-washed shores,
in whose settlements live strong heroes
who win battles with their sharp spears,
town of our Lord who dwells in Kapaliccaram
shrine
surrounded by dark woods?

Pumpavai, O beautiful girl! *verse 5*
Would you go without having seen
The Taipuccam [January–February] festival
celebrated by women who feed guests
with good boiled rice and ghee,
in the great town of Mayilai,
home of many beautiful women
with sparkling kohl-darkened eyes,
town of our Lord with the sacred ash,
who dwells in the Kapaliccaram shrine?

Pumpavai, O beautiful girl! *verse 6*
Would you go without having seen
in Mayilai,
fringed with coconut palms with broad fronds,
and town of our Lord who dwells in Kapaliccaram
shrine,
the festival of bathing in the sea
in the month of Maci [February–March],
at which women dance, singing the praise
of the feet of the Lord
who rides the mighty bull?

Pumpavai, O beautiful girl! *verse 7*
Would you go without having seen
on the streets of great Mayilai,
always busy with festive crowds,
the festival of Pankuni Uttiram [March–April]
with its great sound of celebration,
at which beautiful women
sing and distribute alms,
at the Lord's Kapaliccaram shrine,
center of many festivals?

Pumpavai, O beautiful girl! *verse 8*
Would you go without having seen
to your heart's content
the festival of the Eighth Day,
in honor of Siva's eighteen ganas,
resounding with melodious hymns,
in glorious Mayilai, at the Kapaliccaram shrine
of the Lord who blessed the furious demon
by crushing his arms?

Pumpavai, O beautiful girl! *verse 9*
Would you go without having seen
the ceremony of the golden swing
held for him who dwells in Kapaliccaram shrine,
where devotees praise the feet of the Lord
whom the four-headed god on the lotus seat
and Narayana himself
could not fully comprehend?

Pumpavai, O beautiful girl! *verse 10*
Would you go without having seen
at the Lord's Kapaliccaram temple
surrounded by green groves,
the festival of the Great Purification
slandered by the naked Jains
and the base Buddhists in voluminous robes?

As Sambandar sang the final verse, Pumpavai is said to have been brought back to life. As a postscript to this poem, it may be noted that hagiography records that the delighted father offered the resurrected girl as bride to Sambandar, who countered that since he had given Pumpavai life, he was more in the role of father than bridegroom!

NOTE

1 Sambandar II:47, vs. 1–10; translated by Indira Viswanathan Peterson, in *Poems to Siva: The Hymns of the Tamil Saints* (Princeton: Princeton University Press, 1989), pp. 186–89.

APPENDIX 2

Preambles to Chola Royal Inscriptions

Chola monarchs, who alternately took the title of Rajakesari (King-lion) or Parakesari (Supreme lion), commence their inscriptions with an instantly recognizable preamble; those familiar with historical epigraphy need but encounter the first phrase to identify the monarch who issued the grant or copper-plate charter. For instance, the starting phrase *tirumanni valara,* or "to increase prosperity," is all that is needed to identify the inscription as belonging to Rajendra I. Sometimes a monarch used alternative preambles, but none were reused by others, so each phrase remains unique to a single Chola ruler. The sampling given below of the most frequently used preambles of selected Chola monarchs gives a flavor of the inscriptional style of the period and of the increasing grandeur of phraseology that persists all the way through to the end of Chola rule in 1279, when dynastic power was weak.

Vijayalaya Chola r. 850–71	*tanjaikonda koparakesari* King Parakesari who captured Tanjavur
Aditya Chola r. 871–907	*tondainadu paviya korajakesari* King Rajakesari who extended his rule in Tondai-nadu
Parantaka r. 907–55	*maduraiyum ilamum konda koparakesari* King Parakesari who captured Madurai and Lanka
Rajaraja r. 985–1014	*tirumakalpola perunilashelviyum tanakke urimai* one who took as his wife the goddess of earth, just as he had already taken the goddess of wealth
Rajendra r. 1012–44	*tirumanni valara irunila madantaiyum porsheya pavaiyum shirtani shelviyum tan perundeviyaraki inpura* to increase prosperity, one who took as his gratified wives the goddesses of the two worlds (earth and heaven), the goddess of victory in battle, and the goddess of wealth
Kulottunga I r. 1070–1125	*pukalshulnda punari* one surrounded by the ocean of fame
Vikrama Chola r. 1118–35	*pumalai midainda* one who took [the earth] as a garland of tender flowers for himself
Kulottunga II r. 1133–50	*pumevi valara* one who extended the spread of the earth
Kulottunga III r. 1178–1218	*maduraiyum ilamum karuvurum pandiyan mupadatalaiyum konda* one who captured Madurai, Lanka, Karur, and the head of the Pandya

GLOSSARY

abharana adornment

abhaya mudra hand gesture of protection

abhisheka ritual anointing of sacred image; also of human monarch

achala immoveable

Adavallan Master of dance, Tamil term for Shiva as Nataraja

Aditya another name for Surya, the sun god

adiyar slave/servant of the lord

adu to dance

agama ritual text

Agni fire; god of (the sacrificial) fire

Alingana Chandrashekhara Shiva as Chandrashekhara Embracing Uma

alvar saint of Vishnu

amruta ambrosia

ananda tandava Shiva's dance of bliss

anjali mudra hand gesture with palms joined, indicating reverence or salutation

apsara celestial nymph

Aran Shiva

aravatti-muvar-ula festival of the sixty-three saints *(nayanmars)*

Ardhanari Shiva as Half-Woman, Half-Man

archa image of worship

avahana ritual invitation to a deity to temporarily take up residence in an image of worship

avatar descent; divine incarnation, especially of Vishnu

Ayan Vishnu

ayudha puja weapon worship

Bhairava fierce *(ugra)* or destructive (samhara) form of Shiva

bhakta one who practices bhakti or devotion

bhakti deep devotion to a personal godhead

Bhikshatana Enchanting Mendicant form of Shiva

Bhu "Earth," the goddess Earth

Bhu Lakshmi Earth Lakshmi, consort of Vishnu

chakra discus; attribute of Vishnu

Chandrashekhara Shiva with the Moon in his Crown

channavira chain ornament that encircles the female torso

Dakshinameru World Mountain of the South

Dakshinamurti Shiva as Great Teacher

damaru small double drum shaped like an hourglass

darshan ritual "seeing" of the enshrined temple deity that involves a dynamic act of awareness

deepam oil lamp

Durga "Impassable One"; the great goddess

dvarapala door guardian

gada club; attribute of Vishnu

ganas dwarflike members of Shiva's entourage

Ganesha elephant-headed god, elder son of Shiva and Uma, remover of obstacles

Ganga the river Ganga (Ganges) personified as a goddess

garbhagrha womb house, temple sanctum

gopuram pyramidal entrance gateway to a south Indian temple

gunas qualities

halahalam a type of ruby

Kali power of time, the black one, name of the great goddess in her fearsome aspect

kamandalu ritual water jug; attribute of Brahma

kapala skull cup; attribute of Bhairava and Kali

kati sutra decorative waist-band on male torso worn high above the waist

katyavalambita elegant gesture in which hand rests against hip

kayotsarga upright standing position with both hands flat against the sides; the detached posture of penance

kinkini sara belt of bells

kirtimukha face of glory

kodanda name of bow held by Rama

konrai wild cassia flowers worn by Shiva

koshuvam pleated folds of lower garment wrapped around waist

koyil temple, palace; literally "abode of the lord/king"

Kshetrapala Shiva as Guardian of the Sacred Site

Kumara a name meaning "young one," used also for Skanda, younger son of Shiva and Uma

kunjalam tassel

kusha sacred grass

kuttu dance

kuttadavallan master who dances the dance

kuttu-perumal lord of dance

Lakshmi goddess of wealth and good fortune; consort of Vishnu

lalitasana seated position of royal ease with one leg pendant and other bent at the knee

linga literally sign; aniconic, pillarlike form of Shiva; phallic emblem, often placed in a yoni-shaped base

makara mythical crocodile-like creature

mandapa hall, place of assembly

Manmatha god of love

mariyatai temple honors bestowed upon dignitaries and generous donors

modaka rounded sweet adored by Ganesha

mudra a hand position with specific meaning

mulamurti deity enshrined in the sanctum

murti anthropomorphic form of a deity in sculpture or painting

muvar Revered Three (saints of Shiva)

naga serpent, a snake deity

nagaram merchant township

nagasvaram south Indian temple trumpet

nalvar Revered Four (saints of Shiva)

Nandi bull vehicle of Shiva

Nataraja Shiva as Lord of Dance

nayanmar saint of Shiva

nityotsava daily festivals

palliyarai devi *devi* of the bedroom

panchaloha alloy of five metals

paraiyan untouchable

patra-kundala large circular earring

pipal Ficus religiosa or bodhi-tree, with a heart-shaped leaf

prabha aureole

Pradoshamurti "twilight image"; term applied to Alingana Chandrashekhara

pratima portrait

pratistha establishment

prayaschitta abhishekha repentance ritual bath

puja ritual worship of a deity

puram town

rakodi round hair ornament

ratna kundala round ear stud set with gems

samabhanga standing position with weight evenly distributed on both feet

Sangam Bardic poetry of the literary academies of 100 B.C.E.–C.E. 250

shankha conch; attribute of Vishnu

shikhara temple tower

Shiva major Hindu god

Shivananda-kuttu Shiva's dance of bliss; in Sanskrit *ananda-tandava*

Shrikantha Shiva as drinker of poison

shrivatsa attribute of Vishnu; a triangular or rhomboid mark on the right side of his chest

siraschakra literally head-wheel; circular ornamentation at rear of head that covers the knot of the forehead band

Skanda younger son of Shiva and Uma; also known by various other names, including Kumara and Subrahmanya

Somaskanda Shiva with Uma and infant Skanda

shrichhanda ancient heavy ornament mentioned in inscriptions

Surya sun; the sun god

tali pendant that is sign of a married woman

tani amman Uma as Lone Goddess

tirumangalyam marriage necklace

tiru-palli-arai sacred bedroom

tribhanga "three bends"; exaggerated contrapposto

Tripurantaka Shiva as Destroyer of the Three Cities

Tripurasundari Uma as Beauty of the Three Cities

Tripuravija Shiva as Victor of the Three Cities

Tripuravijayi Consort of Tripuravijaya

trishula trident, attribute of Shiva

tulasi sacred basil associated with Vishnu

ukkatu "choker" necklace

Uma consort of Shiva

Uma-sahita Shiva and Uma together

udaiyar respected one

utsava-murti portable festival image

vahana vehicle, mount on which deity rides

varada mudra hand gesture of wish-granting

Varaha incarnation of Vishnu as a giant boar who saved earth from drowning in the cosmic waters

veshti *dhoti*; male lower garment wrapped around waist

Vighneshvara one who wards off obstacles, epithet of Ganesha

vilaiyadal play, sport

vina stringed lutelike musical instrument

Vinadhara "player of the lute"; epithet of Shiva as Lord of Music

visarjana ritual bidding farewell to the deity temporarily resident in an image

Vishnu major Hindu god

Vrishabhavahana Rider of the Bull, epithet of Shiva

SELECTED BIBLIOGRAPHY

Aiyar, Ramakrishna. *The Economy of a South Indian Temple*. Annamalainagar: Annamalai University, 1946.

Ali, Daud. "Royal Eulogy as World History: Rethinking Copper-Plate Inscriptions in Cola India." In Ronald Inden, Jonathan Walters, and Daud Ali, *Querying the Medieval: Texts and the History of Practices in South Asia*, pp. 165–229. New York: Oxford University Press, 2000.

Appadurai, Arjun, and Carol Breckenridge. "The South Indian Temple: Authority, Honour, and Redistribution." *Contributions to Indian Sociology*, n.s. 10, no. 2 (1976): 187–211.

Arokiaswami, M. *The Kongu Country: Being the History of the Modern Districts of Coimbatore and Salem from the Earliest Times to the Coming of the British*. Madras: University of Madras, 1956.

Auboyer, Jeannine. *Rarities of the Musée Guimet*. New York: Asia House Gallery, distributed by New York Graphic Society, 1975.

Ayyar, P. V. Jagadisa. *South Indian Shrines*. Revised and enlarged edition. New Delhi: Asian Educational Services, 1982.

Balasubrahmanyam, S. R. *Four Chola Temples*. Heritage of Indian Art Series. Bombay: N. M. Tripathi, 1963.

———. *Early Chola Art*. Poona: Asia Publishing House, 1966.

———. *Early Chola Temples: Parantaka I to Rajaraja I, A.D. 907–985*. Bombay: Orient Longman, 1971.

———. *Middle Chola Temples: Rajaraja I to Kulottunga I, A.D. 985–1070*. Faridabad: Oriental Press, 1975.

———. *Later Chola Temples: Kulottunga I to Rajendra III, A.D. 1070–1280*. Madras: Mudgala Trust, 1979.

———. "A Dated Bronze of Appar." *Lalit Kala* 17 (1974): 42–43.

Barrett, Douglas. *Early Cola Bronzes*. Bombay: Bhulabhai Memorial Institute, 1965.

———. *Early Cola Architecture and Sculpture, 866–1014 A.D.* London: Faber, 1974.

Bhatt, N. R. *Ajitagama*. Publications de l'institut français d'indologie, 24. Pondicherry: Institut français d'indologie, 1964–67.

Brinker, Helmut, and Eberhard Fischer. *Treasures from the Rietberg Museum*. New York: Asia Society in association with J. Weatherhill, 1980.

Carman, John Braisted. *The Theology of Ramanuja: An Essay in Interreligious Understanding*. Yale Publications in Religion 18. New Haven and London: Yale University Press, 1974.

Carman, John Braisted, and Vasudha Narayanan. *The Tamil Veda: Pillan's Interpretation of the Tiruvaymoli*. Chicago: University of Chicago Press, 1989.

Champakalakshmi, R. *Trade, Ideology, and Urbanization: South India 300 B.C. to A.D. 1300*. Delhi: Oxford University Press, 1996.

Coomaraswamy, Ananda K. *The Dance of Shiva: Fourteen Indian Essays*. 2d ed. New Delhi: Munshiram Manoharlal, 1970.

Cutler, Norman. *Songs of Experience: The Poetics of Tamil Devotion*. Religion in Asia and Africa Series. Bloomington: Indiana University Press, 1987.

Dagens, Bruno, ed. and trans. *Mayamatam: Treatise of Housing, Architecture, and Iconography*. Kalamulasastra Granthamala Series 14–15. New Delhi: Indira Gandhi National Centre for the Arts and Motilal Banarsidass Publishers, 1994.

Damodaran, K., ed. *Tolliyal Nokkiya Tamilaham*. Chennai: Tamil State Historical Society, 1999.

Davis, Richard H. *Ritual in an Oscillating Universe: Worshiping Siva in Medieval India*. Princeton: Princeton University Press, 1991.

———. "The Origin of Linga Worship." In *Religions of India in Practice*, edited by Donald S. Lopez, Jr., pp. 637–48. Princeton: Princeton University Press, 1995.

———. *Lives of Indian Images*. Princeton: Princeton University Press, 1997.

Dehejia, Vidya. *Slaves of the Lord: The Path of the Tamil Saints*. New Delhi: Munshiram Manoharlal, 1988.

———. "Southern Indian Art." In South and Southeast Asian Art in the Norton Simon Museum, Pasadena. *Orientations*, July 1988, pp. 34–47.

———. *Art of the Imperial Cholas*. The Polsky Lectures in Indian and Southeast Asian Art and Archaeology. New York: Columbia University Press, 1990.

———. *Antal and Her Path of Love: Poems of a Woman Saint from South India*. SUNY Series in Indian Studies. Albany: State University of New York Press, 1990.

———. "Sculptures from Southern India." In The Florence and Herbert Irving Galleries at the Metropolitan Museum of Art. *Orientations*, March 1994, pp. 44–53.

———. "Iconographic Transference Between Krsna and Three Saiva Saints." In *Indian Art and Connoisseurship: Essays in Honour of Douglas Barrett*, edited by John Guy, pp. 141–49. Ahmedabad: Indira Gandhi National Centre for the Arts in association with Mapin Publishing, 1995.

Dieux de bronze en pays tamoul. Paris: Le bronze industriel Rene Loiseau et cie., 1974.

Dirks, Nicholas B. "Political Authority and Structural Change in Early South Indian History." *Indian Economic and Social History Review* 13, no. 2 (1976): 125–57.

———. *The Hollow Crown: Ethnohistory of an Indian Kingdom*. Cambridge: Cambridge University Press, 1987.

Eck, Diana L. *Darsan: Seeing the Divine Image in India.* New York: Columbia University Press, 1998.

Filliozat, Pierre-Sylvain. "Le droit d'entrer dans les temples de Siva au XIe siècle." *Journal asiatique* 263 (1975): 103–17.

Goitien, S. D. *Letters of Medieval Jewish Traders.* Princeton: Princeton University Press, 1973.

Gopal Iyer, T. V., and François Gros. *Tevaram: Hymnes Sivaïtes du pays tamoul*. 2 volumes. Publications de l'institut français d'indologie 68. Pondicherry: Institut français d'indologie, 1984 and 1985.

Goudriaan, Teun, trans. *Kasyapa's Book of Wisdom (Kasyapa-jnanakandah): A Ritual Handbook of the Vaikhanasas.* Disputationes Rheno-Trajectinae 10. The Hague: Mouton & Co, 1965.

Govindacarya, Sri U. V. *Sri Paramesvara Samhita*. Srirangam: Sri Vilasam Press, 1953.

Graefe, W. "Legends as Mile-Stones in the History of Tamil Literature." In *Professor P K Gode Commemoration Volume*, edited by H. L. Hariyappa and M. M. Patkar, pp. 129–46. Poona Oriental Series 93. Poona: Oriental Book Agency, 1960.

Hardy, Friedhelm. *Viraha-Bhakti: The Early History of Krsna Devotion in South India*. Delhi: Oxford University Press, 1983.

———. "Tiruppan-Alvar: The Untouchable Who Rode Piggy-Back on the Brahmin." In *Devotion Divine: Bhakti Traditions from the Regions of India; Studies in Honour of Charlotte Vaudeville*, edited by Diana L. Eck and Françoise Mallison, pp. 129–54. Groningen Oriental Studies 8. Groningen: Egbert Forsten, 1991.

Harman, William P. *The Sacred Marriage of a Hindu Goddess*. Religion in Asia and Africa Series. Bloomington: Indiana University Press, 1989.

Heitzman, James. "State Formation in South India, 850–1280." *The Indian Economic and Social History Review* 24, no. 1 (1987): 35–61.

Hirth, Friedrich, and W. W. Rockhill. *Chau Ju Kua: His Work on the Chinese and Arab Trade in the Twelfth and Thirteenth Centuries, Entitled Chu-fan-chi.* Taipei: Ch'eng-Wen, 1970.

Hopkins, Steven P. "In Love with the Body of God: Eros and the Praise of Icons in South Indian Devotion." *Journal of Vaisnava Studies* 2 (1993): 17–54.

Hudson, Dennis. "Siva, Minakshi, Visnu—Reflections on a Popular Myth in Madurai." In *South Indian Temples—An Analytical Reconsideration*, edited by Burton Stein, pp. 107–18. New Delhi: Vikas Publishing House, 1978.

Janaki, S. S. *Dhvaja-Stambha: Critical Account of Its Structural and Ritualistic Details.* Madras: Kuppuswami Sastri Research Institute, 1988.

Kaimal, Padma. "Early Cola Kings and 'Early Cola Temples': Art and the Evolution of Kingship." *Artibus Asiae* 56, no. 1/2 (1966): 33–66.

______. "Shiva Nataraja: Shifting Meanings of an Icon." *Art Bulletin* 81, no. 3 (1999): 390–419.

______. "The Problem of Portraiture in South India, circa 870-970 A.D." *Artibus Asiae* 59, no. 1/2 (1999): 59–133.

______. "The Problem of Portraiture in South India, circa 970-1000 A.D." *Artibus Asiae* 60, no. 1 (2000): 139–79.

Karashima, Noboru. *South Indian History and Society: Studies from Inscriptions A.D. 850–1800*. Delhi: Oxford University Press, 1984

Khandalavala, Karl J., ed. *Indian Bronze Masterpieces*. New Delhi: Festival of India, 1988.

Kramrisch, Stella. *Manifestations of Shiva*. Philadelphia: Philadelphia Museum of Art, 1981.

Krishnaswami Aiyangar, S, ed. and trans. *Paramasamhita, of the Pancharatra*. Gaekwad's Oriental Series 86. Baroda: Oriental Institute, 1940.

Leidy, Denise Patry. *Treasures of Asian Art: The Asia Society's Mr. and Mrs. John D. Rockefeller 3rd Collection*. New York: Asia Society Galleries and Abbeville Press, 1994.

L'Hernault, Françoise. *Darasuram: Epigraphical study; étude architecturale; étude iconographique*. 2 volumes. Publications de l'Ecole française d'Extrême-Orient: Mémoires archéologiques 16. Paris: Ecole française d'Extrême-Orient, 1987.

Lorenzen, David N. *The Kapalikas and Kalamukhas: Two Lost Saivite Sects.* Australian National University Centre of Oriental Studies Oriental Monograph Series 12. New Delhi: Thomson Press (India), 1972.

Maloney, Clarence. "The Beginning of Civilization in South India." *Journal of Asian Studies* 29, no. 3 (1970): 603–16.

Master Bronzes of India. Chicago: Art Institute of Chicago, 1965.

Mukund, Kanakalatha. *The Trading World of the Tamil Merchant: Evolution of Merchant Capitalism in the Coromandel*. Chennai: Orient Longman, 1999.

Nagaswamy, R. "Rare Bronzes from Kongu Country." *Lalit Kala* 9 (1961): 7–10.

———. "Some Adavallan and Other Bronzes of the Early Chola Period." *Lalit Kala* 10 (1961): 34–40.

———. "Adavallan and Dakshinameruvitankar of the Tanjore Temple." *Lalit Kala* 12 (1962): 36–38.

———. "Kongu Bronzes in the Victoria and Albert Museum." *Lalit Kala* 13 (1963): 41–42.

———. "Some Contributions of the Pandya to South Indian Art." *Artibus Asiae* 27, no. 3 (1964–65): 265–74.

———. "Pallava Bronzes from Vadakkalathur." *Oriental Art* 17, no. 1 (1971): 55–59.

———. "Dancing Kali and Other Early Chola Bronzes." *Lalit Kala* 18 (1977): 9–13.

———. "A Note on Nisumbhasudani Installed by Vijayalaya Chola in Tanjore." *Lalit Kala* 18 (1977): 39–40.

———. *Studies in Ancient Tamil Law and Society*. Madras: Institute of Epigraphy, State Department of Archaeology, Government of Tamilnadu, 1978.

———. "Chidambaram Bronzes." *Lalit Kala* 19 (1979): 9–17.

———. "A Nataraja Bronze and an Inscribed Uma from Karaiviram Village." *Lalit Kala* 19 (1979): 17–19.

———. "Nallur Bronzes." *Lalit Kala* 20 (1982): 9–11.

———. *Masterpieces of Early South Indian Bronzes*. New Delhi: National Museum, 1983.

———. "Iconography and Significance of the Brhadisvara Temple, Tanjavur." In *Discourses on Siva: Proceedings of a Symposium on the Nature of Religious Imagery*, edited by Michael W. Meister, pp. 170–81. Philadelphia: University of Pennsylvania Press, 1984.

———. "Archaeological Finds in South India: Esalam Bronzes and Copper-Plates." *Bulletin de l'Ecole française d'Extrême-Orient* 76 (1987): 1–51.

———. *Siva-Bhakti*. New Delhi: Navrang, 1989.

———. "On Dating South Indian Bronzes." In *Indian Art and Connoisseurship: Essays in Honour of Douglas Barrett*, edited by John Guy, pp. 101–29. Ahmedabad: Mapin Publishing, 1995.

———. "Bengal and Chidambaram." *Journal of Bengal Art* 4 (1999): 33–47.

Nagaswamy, R., ed. *South Indian Studies II*. Madras: Society for Archaeological, Historical, and Epigraphical Research, 1979.

Nalayira Divya Prabandham. Madras: Virodikirudur Vaikashi Vishakam, 1971.

Nandagopal, Choodamani, and Vatsala Iyengar. *Temple Treasures*. Vol. 1, *Ritual Utensils*. Bangalore: Crafts Council of Karnataka, 1995.

———. *Temple Treasures*. Vol. 2, *Temple Jewellery*. Bangalore: Crafts Council of Karnataka, 1997.

Natarajan, B, trans. *Tirumantiram: A Tamil Scriptural Classic—By Tirumular.* Madras: Sri Ramakrishna Math, 1991.

Nilakantha Sastri, K. A. *The Colas*. Revised edition. Madras University Historical Series 9. Madras: University of Madras, 1955.

O'Flaherty, Wendy Doniger. *Hindu Myths: A Sourcebook*. New York: Viking Press, 1975.

Orr, Leslie C. *Donors, Devotees, and Daughters of God: Temple Women in Medieval Tamilnadu*. New York: Oxford University Press, 2000.

Pal, Pratapaditya. *Krishna: The Cowherd King.* Los Angeles: Los Angeles County Museum of Art, 1972.

———. *The Sensuous Immortals: A Selection of Sculptures from the Pan-Asian Collection*. Los Angeles: Los Angeles County Museum of Art, 1978.

———. *Indian Sculpture: A Catalogue of the Los Angeles County Museum of Art Collection*. Vol. 2, *700–1800*. Los Angeles and Berkeley: Los Angeles County Museum of Art and University of California Press, 1988.

———. *A Collecting Odyssey: Indian, Himalayan, and Southeast Asian Art from the James and Marilynn Alsdorf Collection*. Chicago and New York: Art Institute of Chicago and Thames and Hudson, 1997.

Peterson, Indira Viswanathan. "Lives of the Wandering Singers: Pilgrimage and Poetry in Tamil Saivite Hagiography." *History of Religions* 22 (1983): 338–60.

———. *Poems to Siva: The Hymns of the Tamil Saints*. Princeton Library of Asian Translations. Princeton: Princeton University Press, 1989.

Pichard, Pierre, ed. *Vingt ans après Tanjavur, Gangaikondacholapuram*. 2 volumes. Publications de l'Ecole française d'Extrême-Orient: Mémoires archéologiques 20. Paris: Ecole française d'Extrême-Orient, 1994.

———. *Tanjavur Brhadisvara: An Architectural Study.* New Delhi: Indira Gandhi National Centre for the Arts, 1995.

Pollock, Sheldon. "The Sanskrit Cosmopolis, 300–1300: Transculturation, Vernacularization, and the Question of Ideology." In *Ideology and the Status of Sanskrit: Contributions to the History of the Sanskrit Language*, edited by Jan E. M. Houben, pp. 197–247. Leiden: E. J. Brill, 1996.

Pope, Rev. G. U. *The Tiruvacagam, or Sacred Utterances of the Tamil Poet, Saint, and Sage Manikka-vachakar*. Oxford: Clarendon Press, 1900.

Prentiss, Karen Pechilis. *The Embodiment of Bhakti.* New York: Oxford University Press, 1999.

Ramachandran, K. S., and C. Krishnamurthy. "A Unique Bronze Nataraja from Tranquebar," *Lalit Kala* 8 (1960): 73–74.

Ramachandran, T. N. "Bronze Images from Tiruvenkadu-Svetaranya (Tanjore District)." *Lalit Kala* 3–4 (1957): 55–60.

———. *The Nagapattinam and Other Buddhist Bronzes in the Madras Museum*. Bulletin of the Madras Government Museum. Reprint edition. Madras: the Museum, 1992.

Ramachandran, T. N., trans. *St. Sekkizhar's Periya Puranam*. Thanjavur: Tamil University, 1990.

Ramanujan, A. K. *Speaking of Siva*. Harmondsworth: Penguin Books, 1973.

———. *Hymns for the Drowning: Poems for Visnu by Nammalvar*. Princeton Library of Asian Translations. Princeton: Princeton University Press, 1981.

Rangachari, K. *The Sri Vaisnava Brahmans*. Bulletin of the Madras Government Museum. Madras: Government Press, 1931.

Schwindler, Gary J. "Speculations on the Theme of Siva as Tripurantaka as It Appears during the Reign of Rajaraja I in the Tanjore Area ca. A.D. 1000," *Ars Orientalis* 17 (1987): 163–74.

Sewell, Robert. *The Historical Inscriptions of Southern India and Outlines of Political History*. Madras: Diocesan Press, 1932.

Shulman, David Dean, trans. *Songs of the Harsh Devotee: The Tevaram of Cuntaramurttinayanar*. University of Pennsylvania Studies on South Asia 6. Philadelphia: Department of South Asia Regional Studies, University of Pennsylvania, 1990.

Sivaramamurti, C. *South Indian Bronzes*. New Delhi and Bombay: Lalit Kala Akademi, 1963.

Smith, David. *The Dance of Siva: Religion, Art, and Poetry in South India*. Cambridge: Cambridge University Press, 1996.

Spencer, George W. "Religious Networks and Royal Influence in Eleventh-Century South India," *Journal of the Economic and Social History of the Orient* 12 (1969): 42–56.

———. "Royal Initiative under Rajaraja I." *The Indian Economic and Social History Review* 7, no. 3 (1970): 431–42.

———. "The Sacred Geography of the Tamil Shaivite Hymns." *Numen* 17 (1970): 232–44.

———. "The Politics of Plunder: The Cholas in Eleventh-Century Ceylon." *Journal of Asian Studies* 35, no. 3 (1976): 405–19.

Spencer, George W., and Kenneth Hall. "Towards an Analysis of Dynastic Hinterlands: The Imperial Cholas of Eleventh-Century South India." *Asian Profile* 2, no. 1 (1974): 51–62.

Splendours of Tamil Nadu. Bombay: Marg Publications, 1980.

Srinivasan, P. R. "Rare Sculptures of the Early Chola Period." *Lalit Kala* 5 (1959): 59–67.

———. *Bronzes of South India*. Bulletin of the Madras Government Museum. Madras: Controller of Stationery and Printing, 1963.

Stein, Burton, ed. *Essays on South India*. Asian Studies at Hawai'i 15. Honolulu: University of Hawai'i Press, 1975.

———. *All the Kings' Mana: Papers on Medieval South Indian History*. Madras: New Era Publications, 1984.

Svaminatha Sivacarya, C. *Kamikagama, Purvabhaga*. Madras: South Indian Archaka's Association, 1975.

Swaminathan, K. D. *Early South Indian Temple Architecture: Study of Tiruvalisvaram Inscriptions*. Trivandrum: CBH Publications, 1990.

Thomas, Job. *Tiruvengadu Bronzes*. Madras: Cre-A, 1986.

Tirumalai, R. *Rajendra Vinnagar*. Madras: Institute of Epigraphy, Tamilnadu State Department of Archaeology, 1980.

Veluthat, Kesavan. *The Political Structure of Early Medieval South India*. New Delhi: Orient Longman, 1993.

Venkataraman, B. *Rajarajesvaram: The Pinnacle of Chola Art*. Madras: Mudgala Trust, 1985.

———. *Temple Art Under the Chola Queens*. Faridabad: Thomson Press, 1976.

Waghorne, Joanne Punzo. "Dressing the Body of God: South Indian Bronze Sculpture in Its Temple Setting." *Asian Art* (Summer 1992): 9–33.

Waghorne, Joanne Punzo, and Norman Cutler. *Gods of Flesh, Gods of Stone: The Embodiment of Divinity in India.* Chambersburg, Pa.: Anima, 1985.

Yocum, Glenn. *Hymns to the Dancing Siva: A Study of Manikkavacakar's Tiruvacakam*. New Delhi: Heritage Publishers, 1982.

———. "Brahmin, King, Sannyasi, and the Goddess in a Cage: Reflections on the 'Conceptual Order of Hinduism' at a Tamil Saiva Temple." *Contributions to Indian Sociology,* n.s. 20, no. 1 (1986): 15–39.

Younger, Paul. "Ten Days of Wandering and Romance with Lord Ranganathan: The Pankuni Festival in Srirankam Temple, South India." *Modern Asian Studies* 16, no. 4 (1982): 623–56.

———. *The Home of Dancing Sivan: The Traditions of the Hindu Temple in Citamparam.* New York: Oxford University Press, 1995.

Zvelebil, Kamil V. *Ananda-Tandava of Siva-Sadanrttamurti*. Madras: Institute of Asian Studies, 1985.

PHOTO CREDITS

Photographs of the works in the exhibition were in most cases provided by the institution or individual owning the works and are reproduced with permission. Additional information on photograph sources follows.

ED BERNIK Plate 31

BOB HASHIMOTO Plate 29

ROBERT LORENZSON Plates 59–95

JAMISON MILLER Plate 34

MAGGIE NIMKIN Plates 6, 30, and 56

COPYRIGHT RÉUNION DES MUSÉES NATIONAUX/ART RESOURCE, NY; PHOTO HERVÉ LEWANDOWSKI Plate 10

E.G. SCHEMPF Plate 35

MIKI SLINGSBY Plates 13, 17, 18, 20, 23, 37, 38, 43, and 51

RICHARD A. STONER Plate 32

VICTORIA & ALBERT PICTURE LIBRARY
Plates 27, 40, 42, 44, and 49

WETTSTEIN & KAUF Plate 21

KATHERINE WETZEL Plate 41

INDEX

Page numbers in *italics* refer to illustration captions.

L

M

N

P

R

S

T

U

V

W

Y

Z

AMERICAN FEDERATION OF ARTS

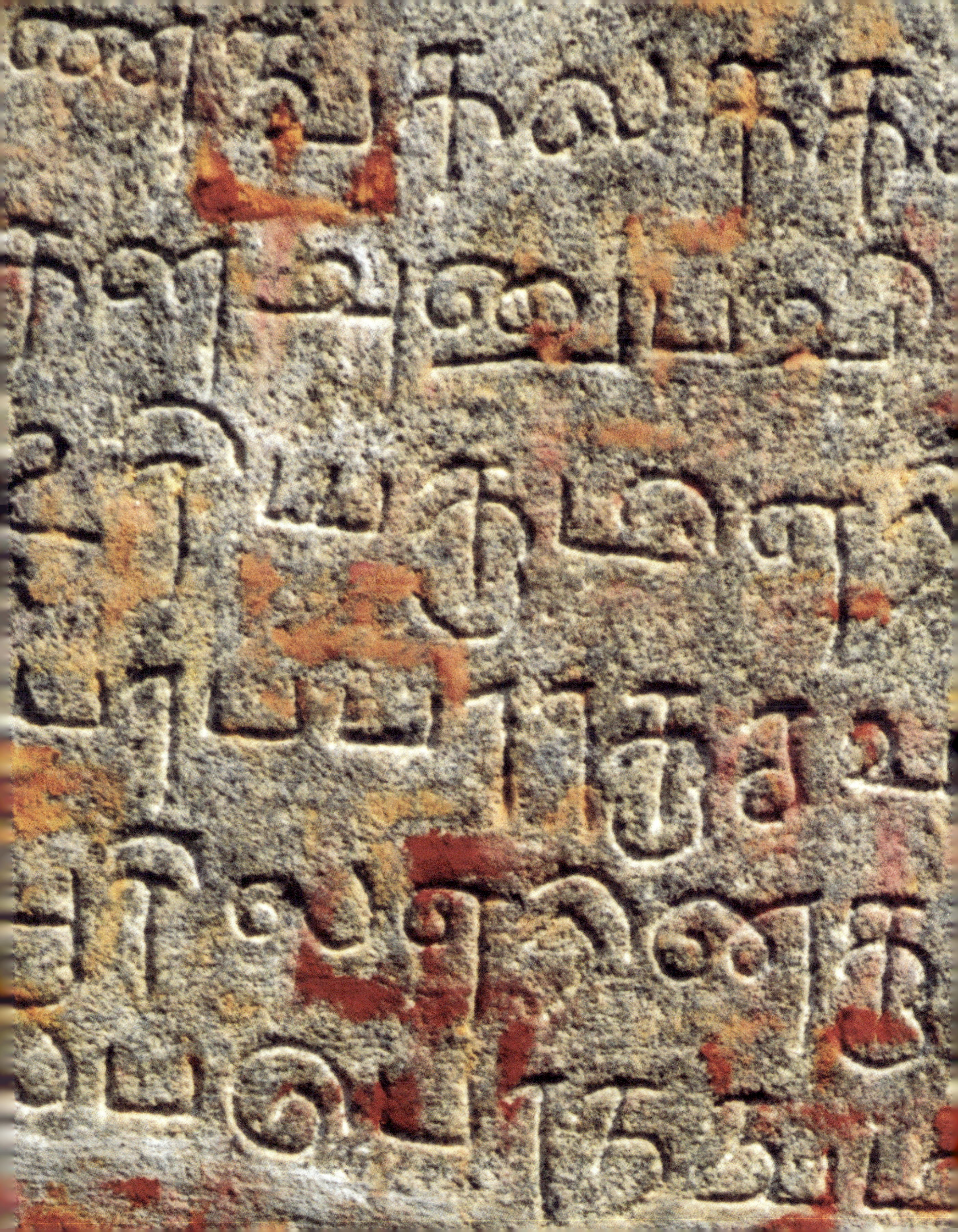

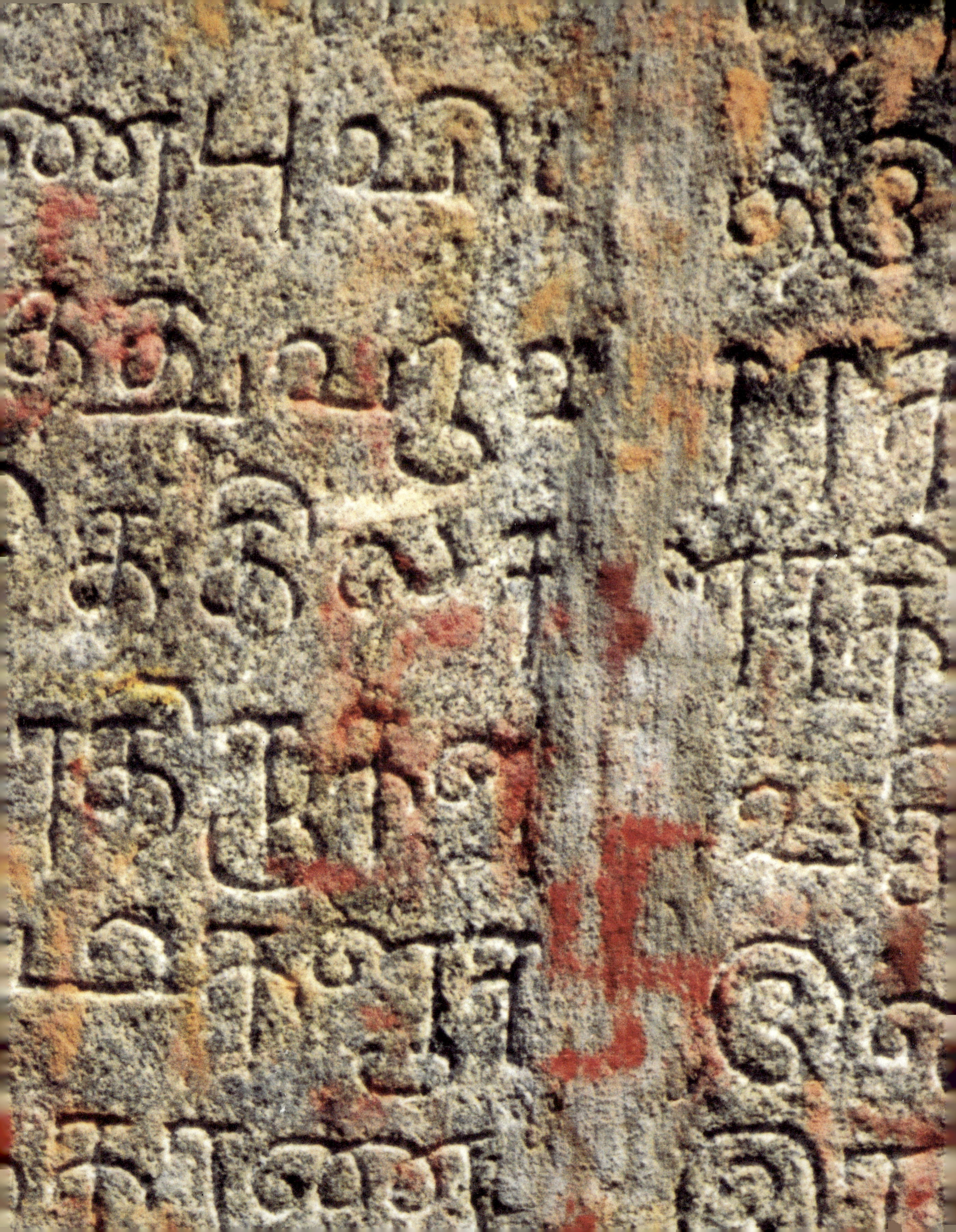